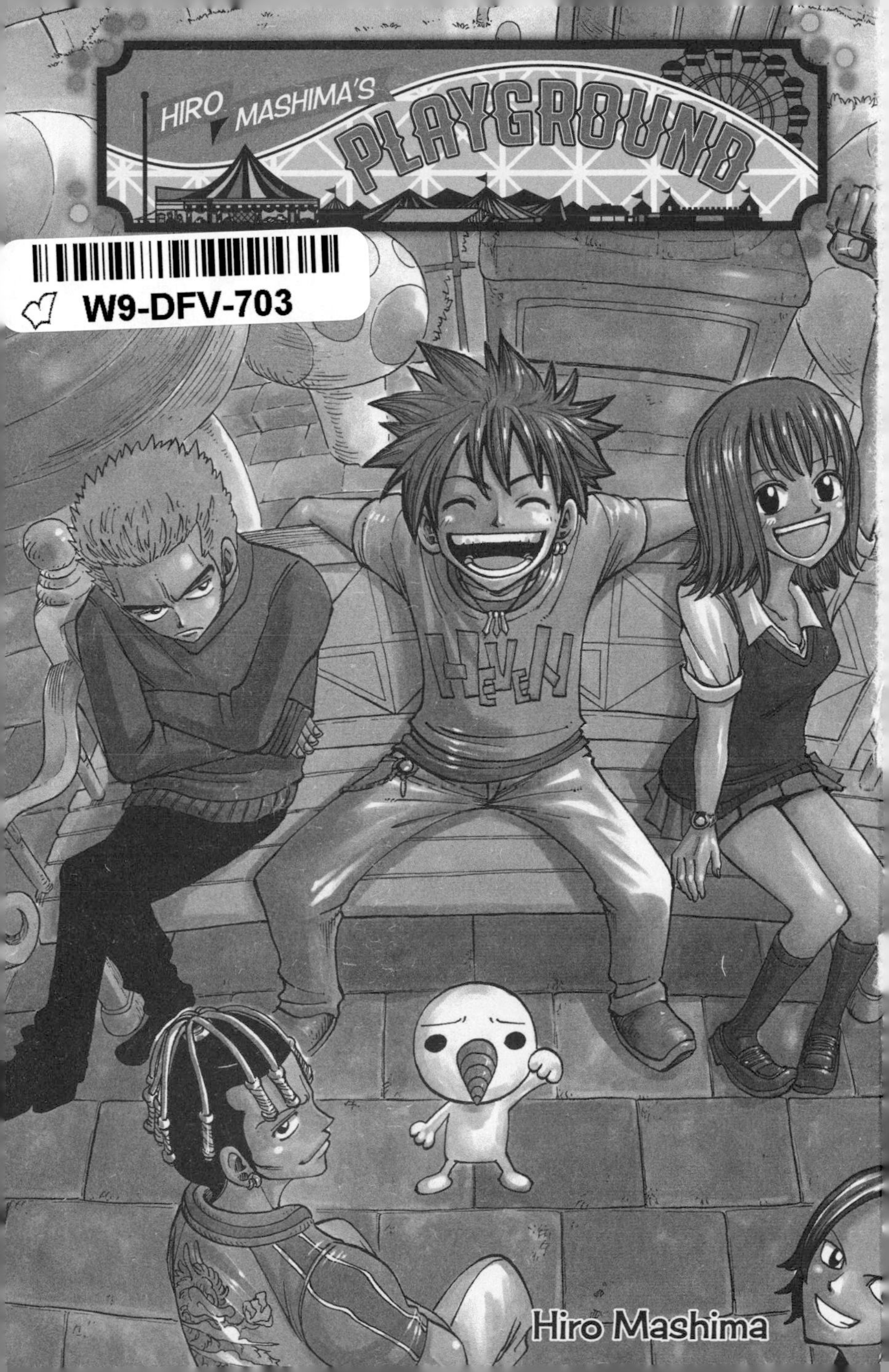
HIRO MASHIMA'S
PLAYGROUND
HEVEN
Hiro Mashima

HIRO MASHIMA'S PLAYGROUND PART 1

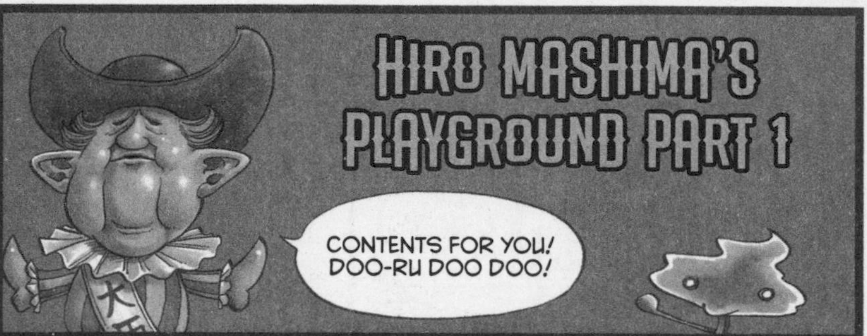
CONTENTS FOR YOU! DOO-RU DOO DOO!

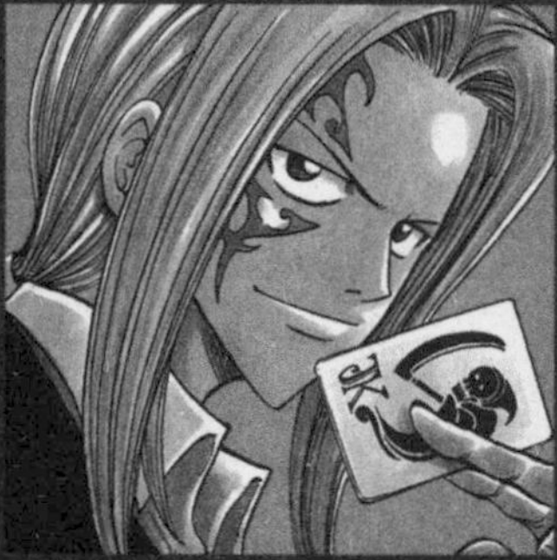

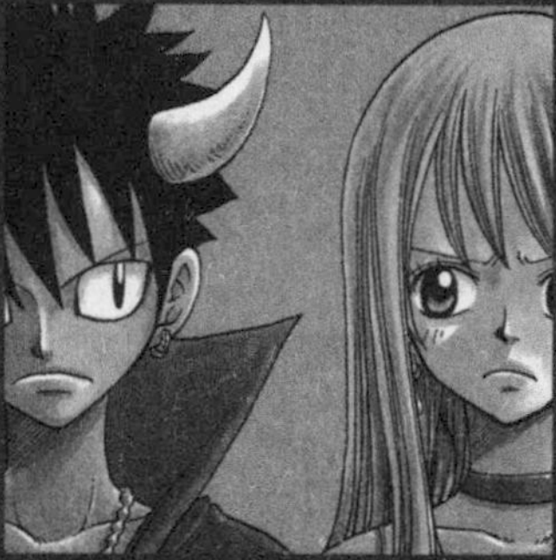

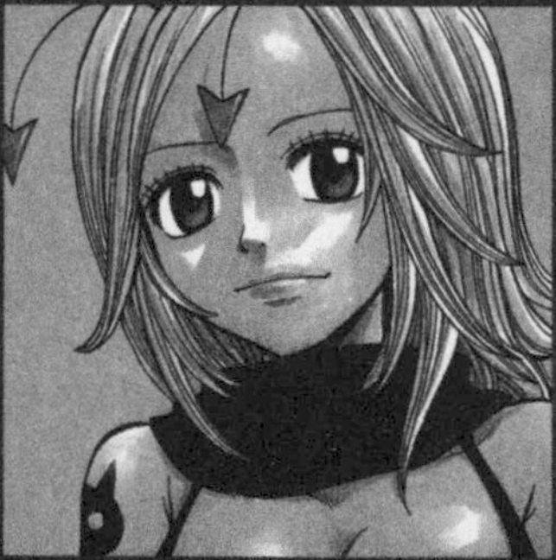

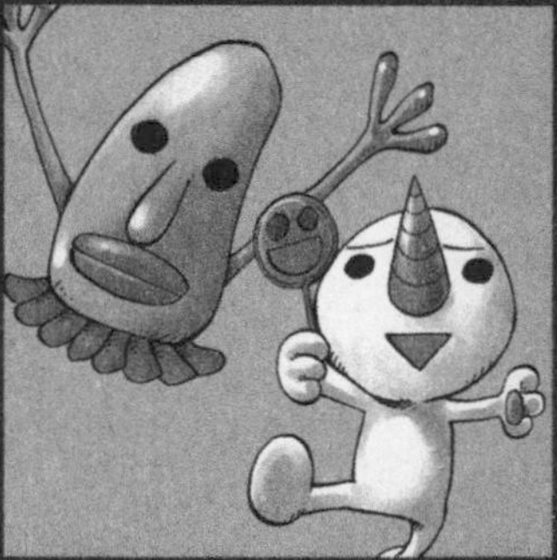

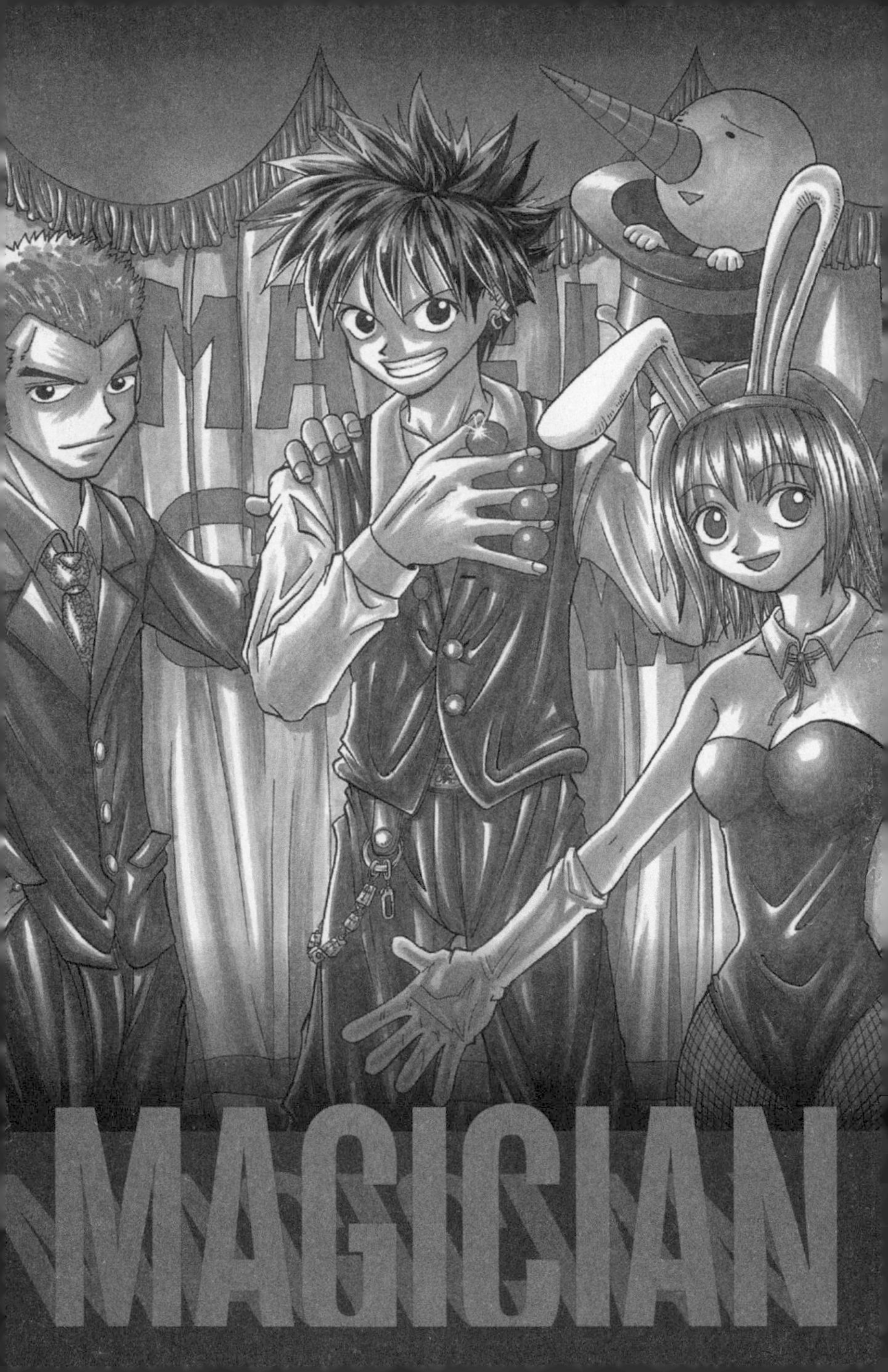
MAGICIAN

MAGICIAN

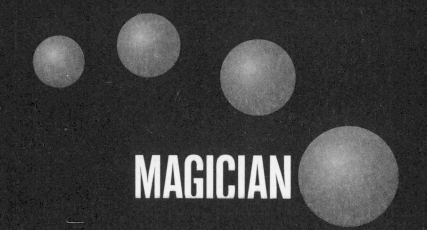

MAGICIAN

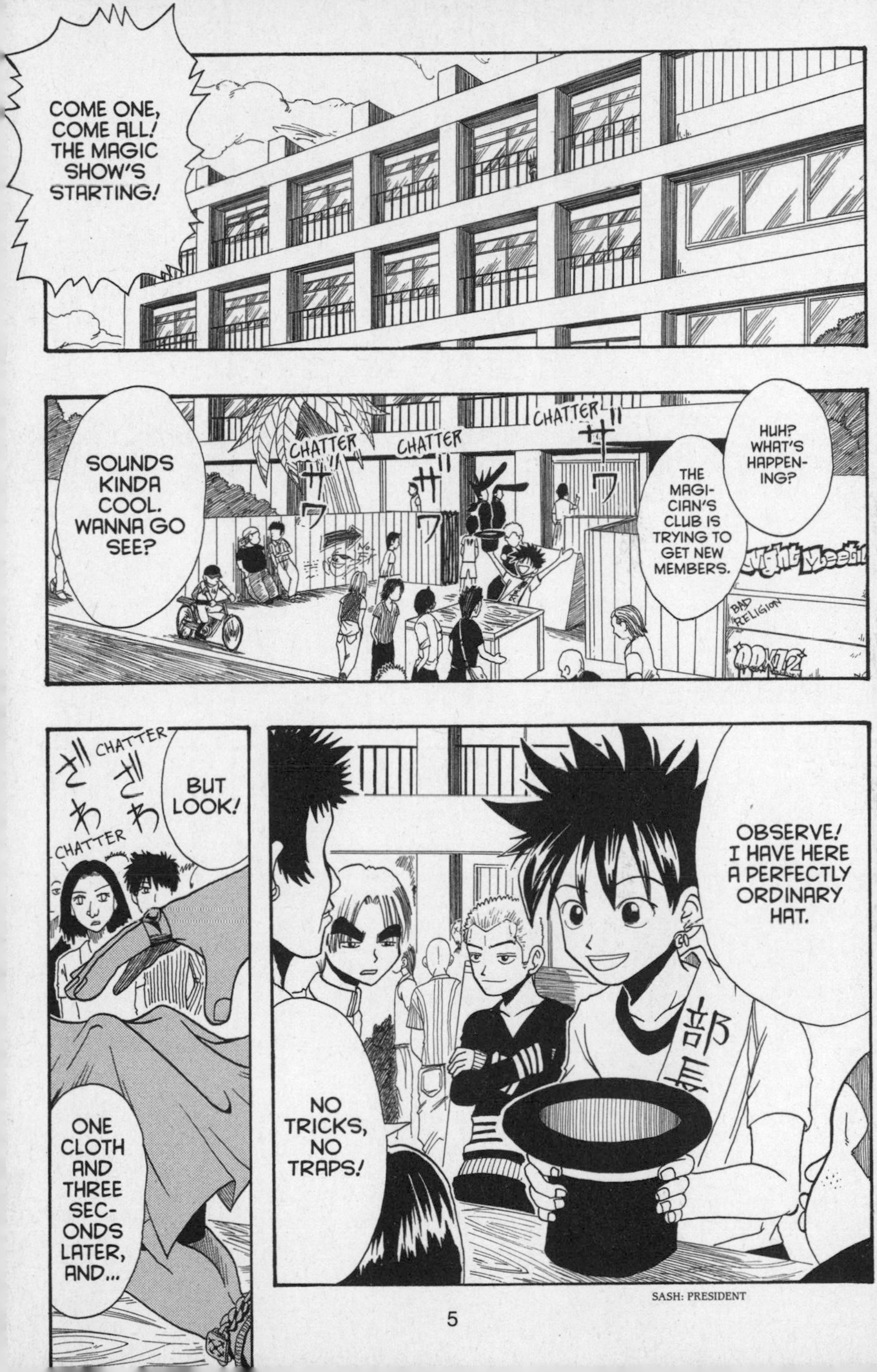
COME ONE, COME ALL! THE MAGIC SHOW'S STARTING!
HUH? WHAT'S HAPPEN-ING?
THE MAGI-CIAN'S CLUB IS TRYING TO GET NEW MEMBERS.
CHATTER
ザワ
CHATTER
ザワ
CHATTER
ザワ
BAD RELIGION
SOUNDS KINDA COOL. WANNA GO SEE?
OBSERVE! I HAVE HERE A PERFECTLY ORDINARY HAT.
部長
NO TRICKS, NO TRAPS!
BUT LOOK!
ざわ
CHATTER
ざわ
CHATTER
ONE CLOTH AND THREE SEC-ONDS LATER, AND...

SASH: PRESIDENT

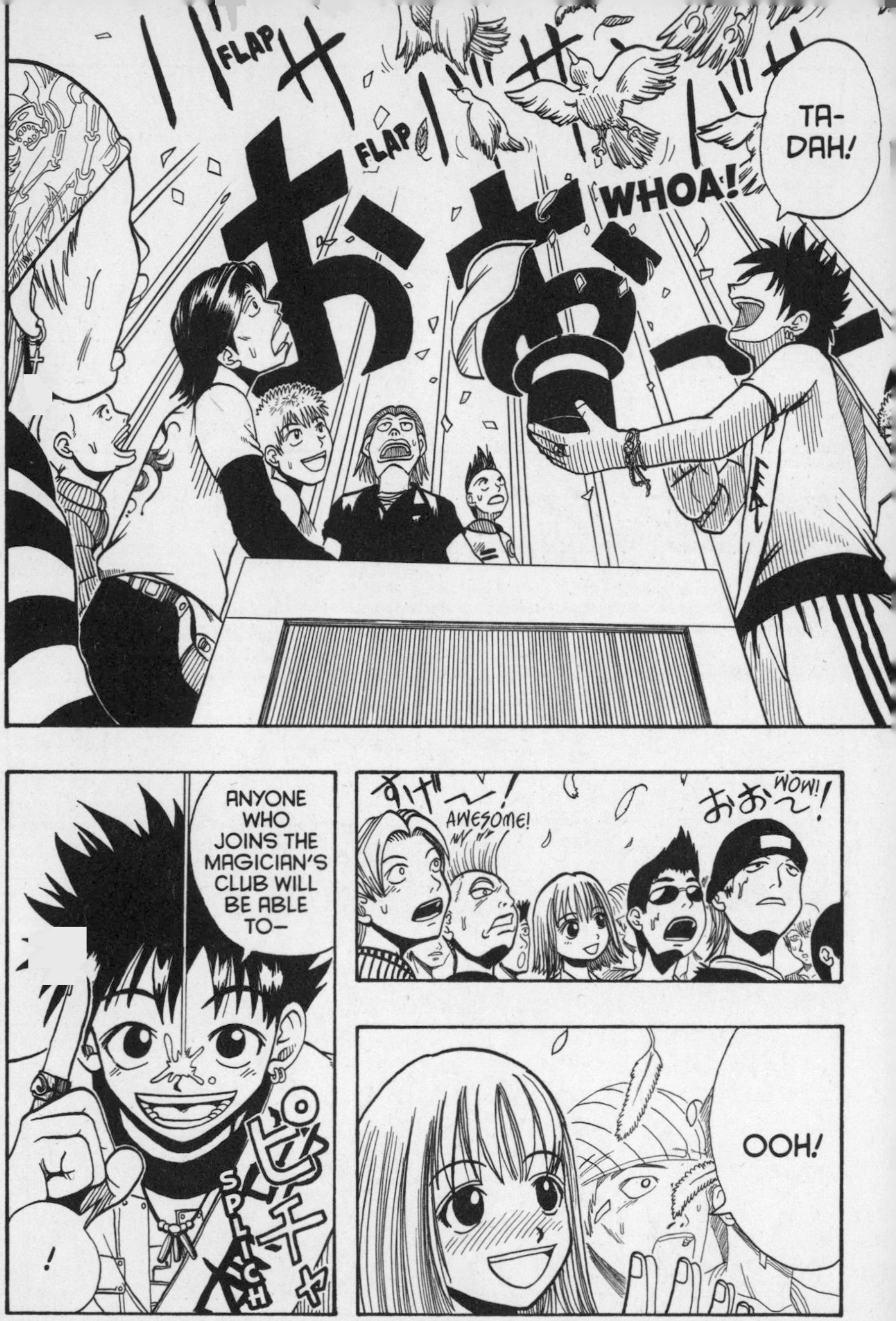

TA-DAH!
WHOA!
FLAP
FLAP
すげ〜!
AWESOME!
おお〜!
WOW!
OOH!
ANYONE WHO JOINS THE MAGICIAN'S CLUB WILL BE ABLE TO—
ピチャ
SPLITCH
!

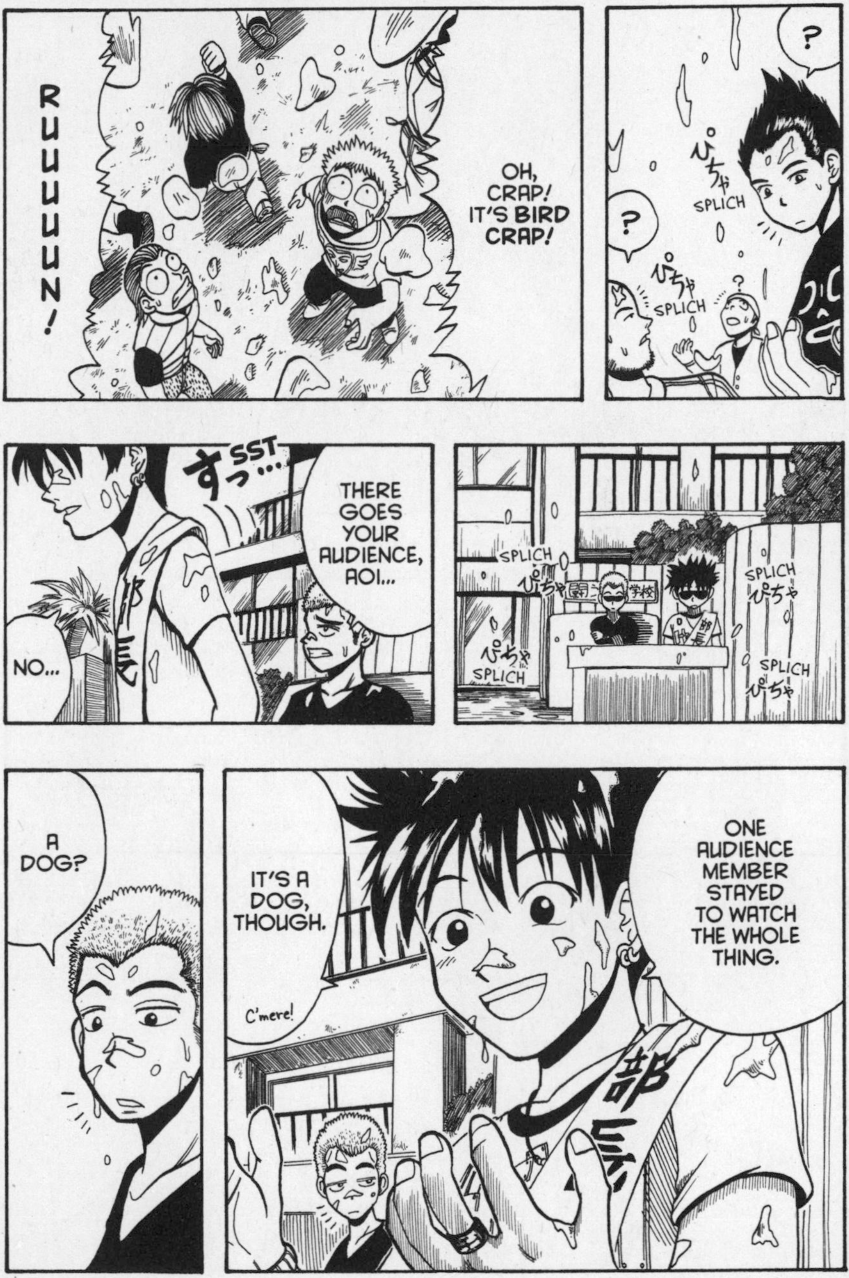
?
ぴちゃ SPLICH
?
ぴちゃ SPLICH
?
OH, CRAP! IT'S BIRD CRAP!
RUUUUUUN!
SPLICH ぴちゃ
SPLICH ぴちゃ
SPLICH ぴちゃ
ぴちゃ SPLICH
すっ… SST…
THERE GOES YOUR AUDIENCE, AOI…
NO…
ONE AUDIENCE MEMBER STAYED TO WATCH THE WHOLE THING.
IT'S A DOG, THOUGH.
C'mere!
A DOG?

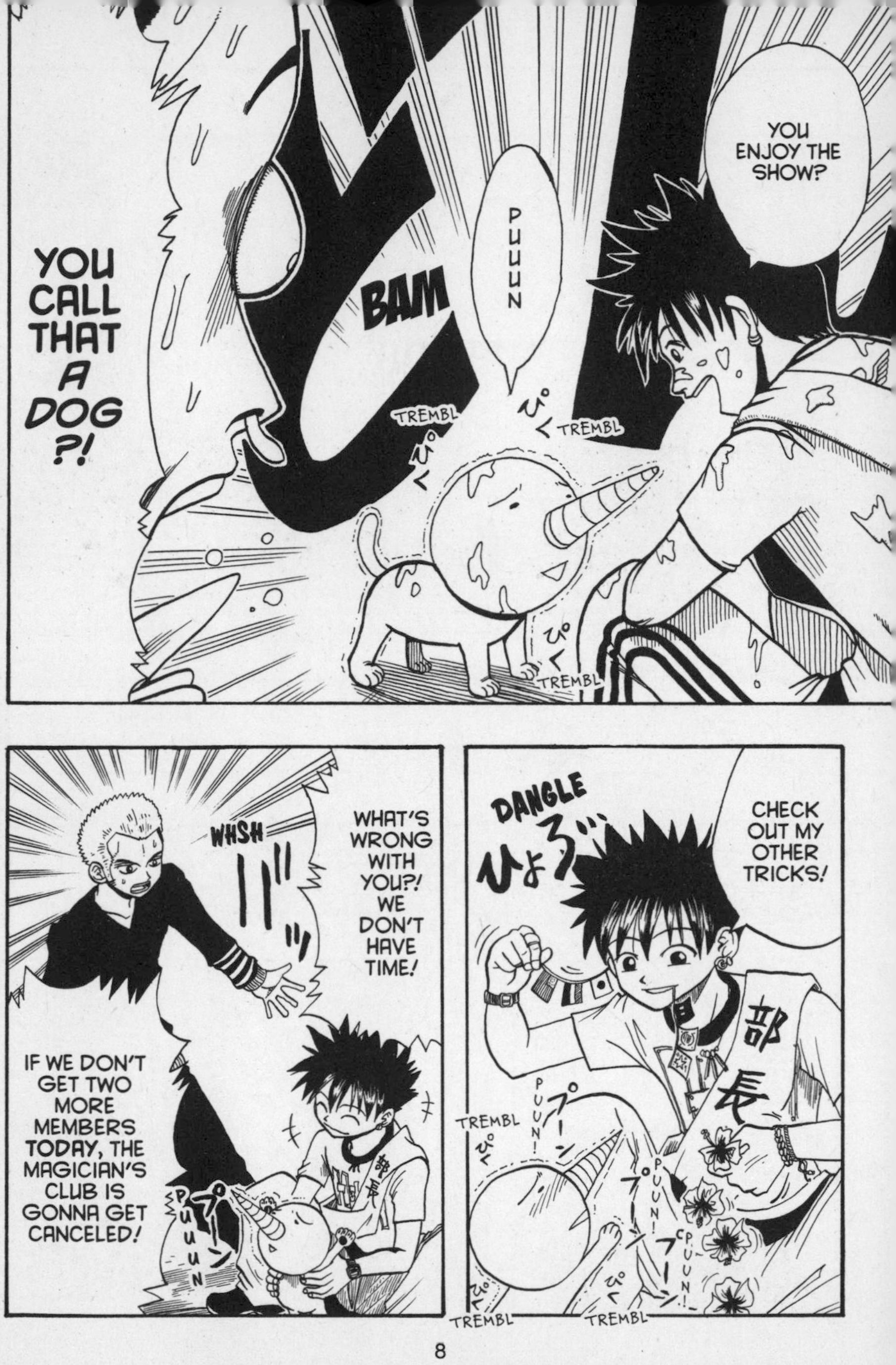
YOU ENJOY THE SHOW?
PUUUN
BAM
TREMBL
TREMBL
TREMBL
YOU CALL THAT A DOG?!
CHECK OUT MY OTHER TRICKS!
DANGLE
PUUN!
PUUN!
PUUN!
TREMBL
TREMBL
WHAT'S WRONG WITH YOU?! WE DON'T HAVE TIME!
WHSH
IF WE DON'T GET TWO MORE MEMBERS TODAY, THE MAGICIAN'S CLUB IS GONNA GET CANCELED!
PUUUN

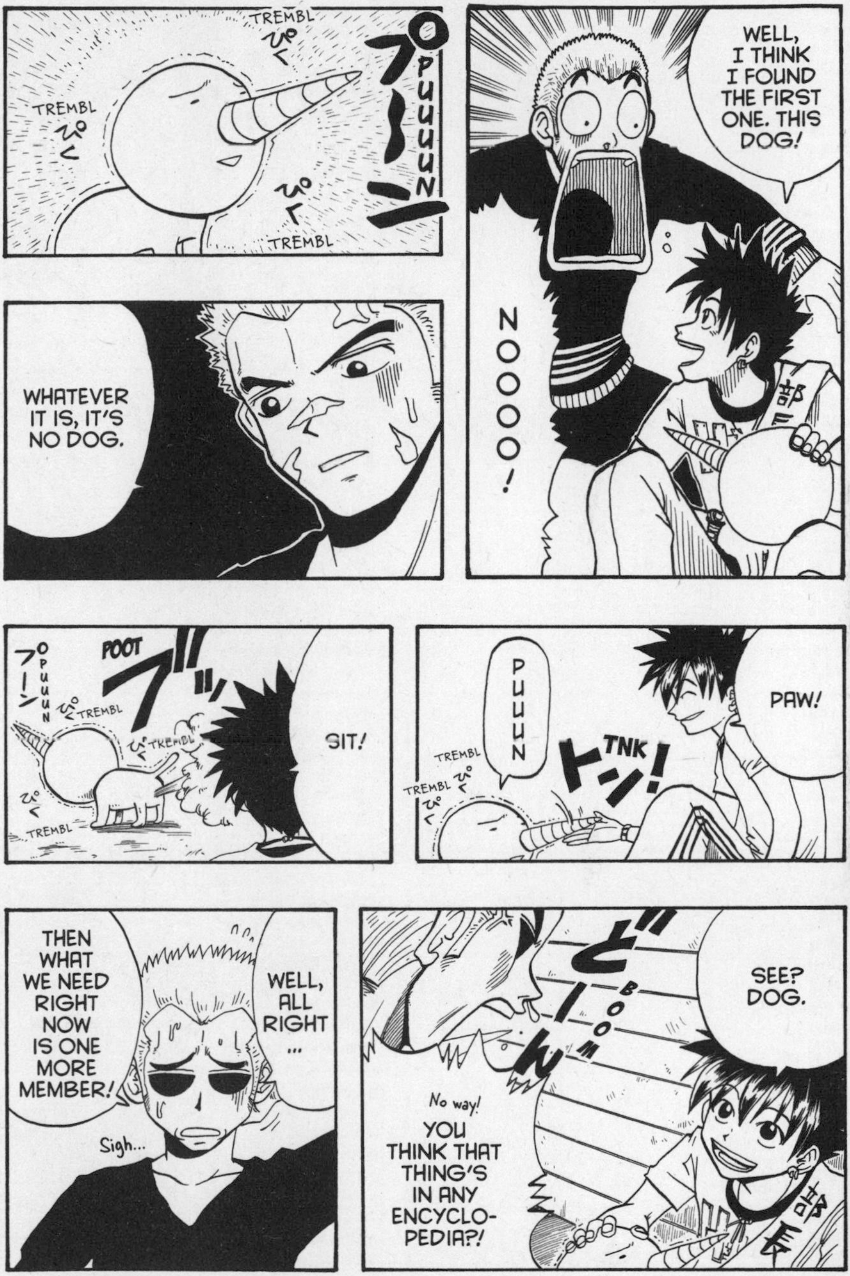
WELL, I THINK I FOUND THE FIRST ONE. THIS DOG!
NOOOOO!
TREMBL
PUUUUN
TREMBL
TREMBL
WHATEVER IT IS, IT'S NO DOG.
PAW!
PUUUN
TNK
TREMBL
TREMBL
SIT!
POOT
PUUUUN
TREMBL
TREMBL
TREMBL
SEE? DOG.
BOOM
No way!
YOU THINK THAT THING'S IN ANY ENCYCLOPEDIA?!
WELL, ALL RIGHT...
THEN WHAT WE NEED RIGHT NOW IS ONE MORE MEMBER!
Sigh...

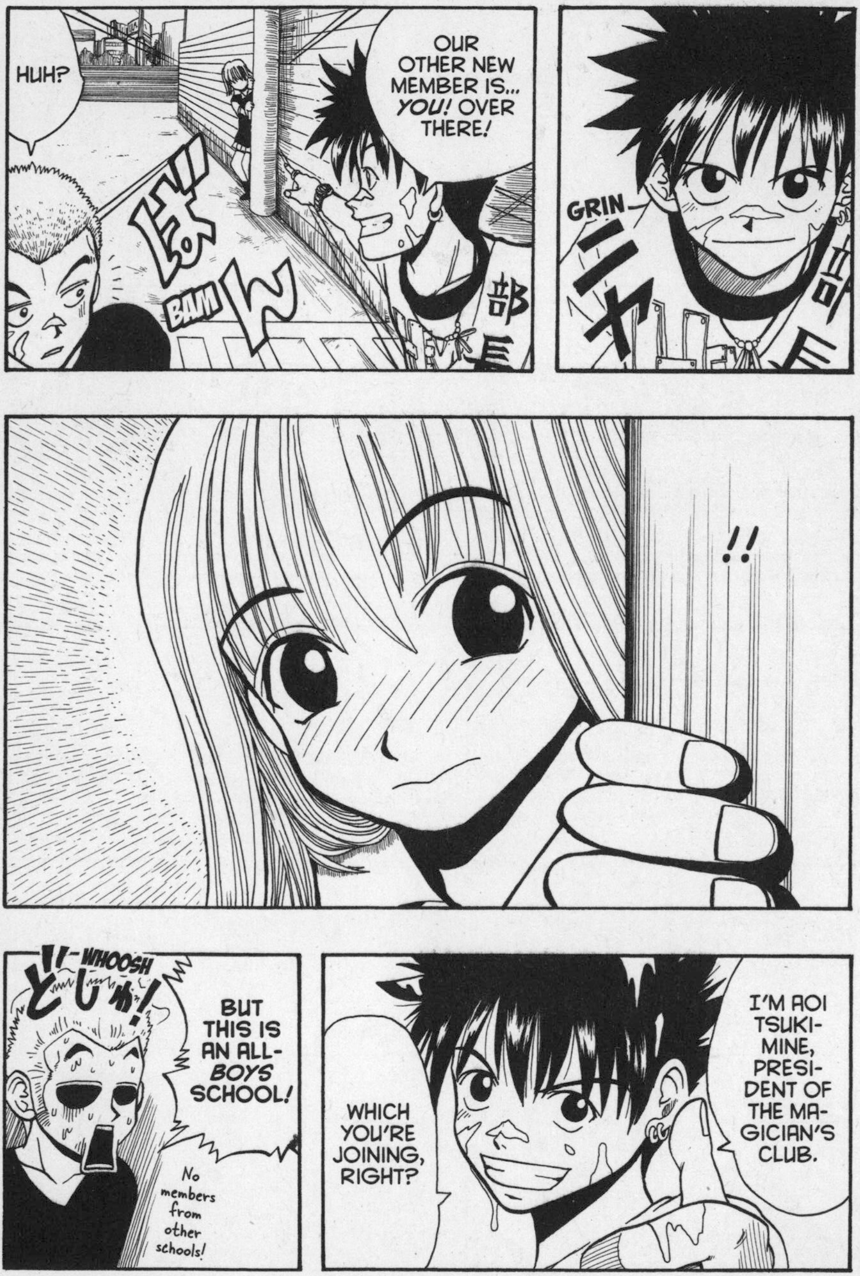
GRIN
OUR OTHER NEW MEMBER IS... *YOU!* OVER THERE!
HUH?
BAM
!!
I'M AOI TSUKI-MINE, PRESI-DENT OF THE MA-GICIAN'S CLUB.
WHICH YOU'RE JOINING, RIGHT?
WHOOSH
BUT THIS IS AN ALL-*BOYS* SCHOOL!
No members from other schools!

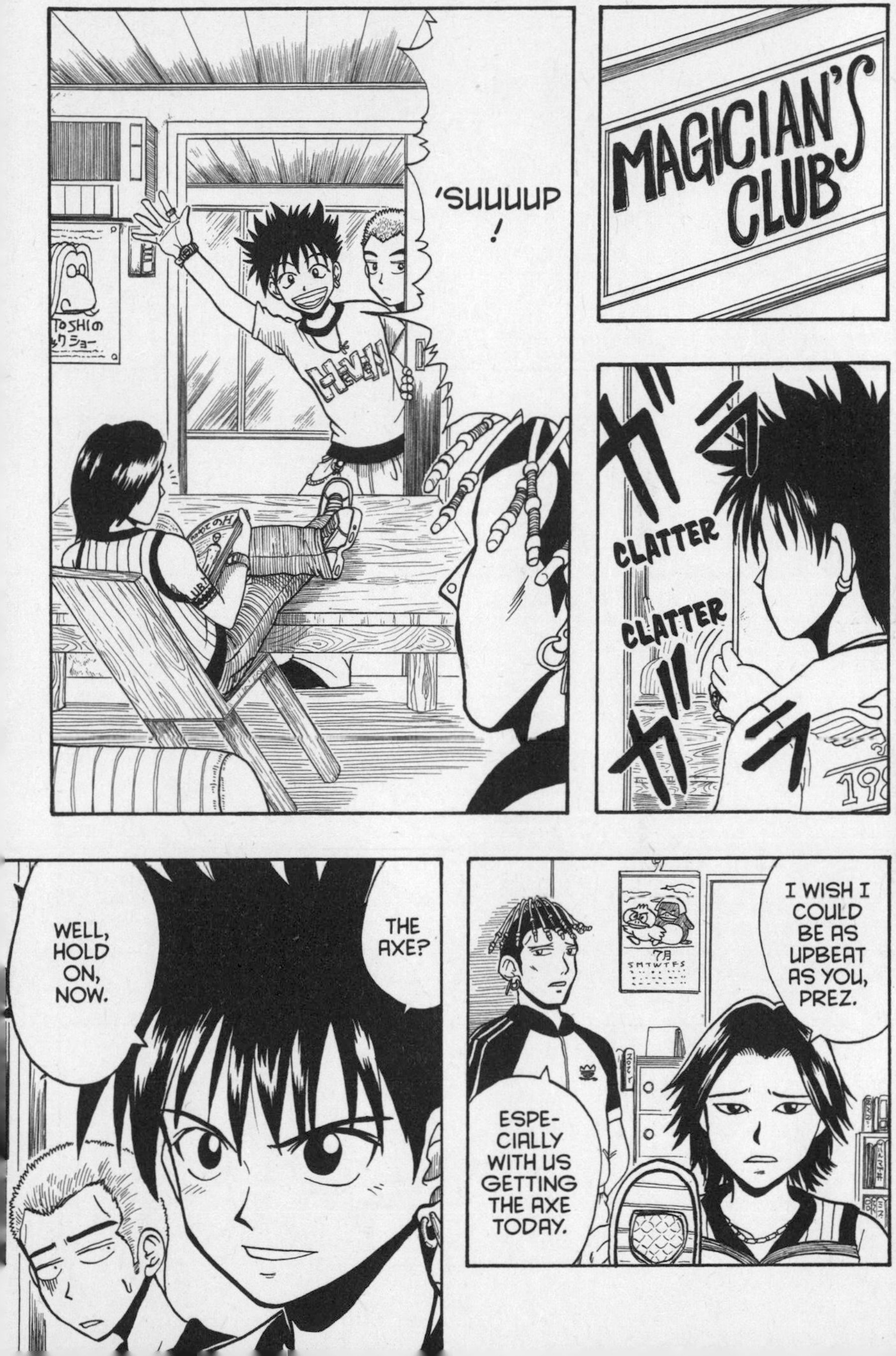
MAGICIAN'S CLUB
ガラ
CLATTER
CLATTER
ガラ
'SUUUUP!
I WISH I COULD BE AS UPBEAT AS YOU, PREZ.
ESPECIALLY WITH US GETTING THE AXE TODAY.
THE AXE?
WELL, HOLD ON, NOW.

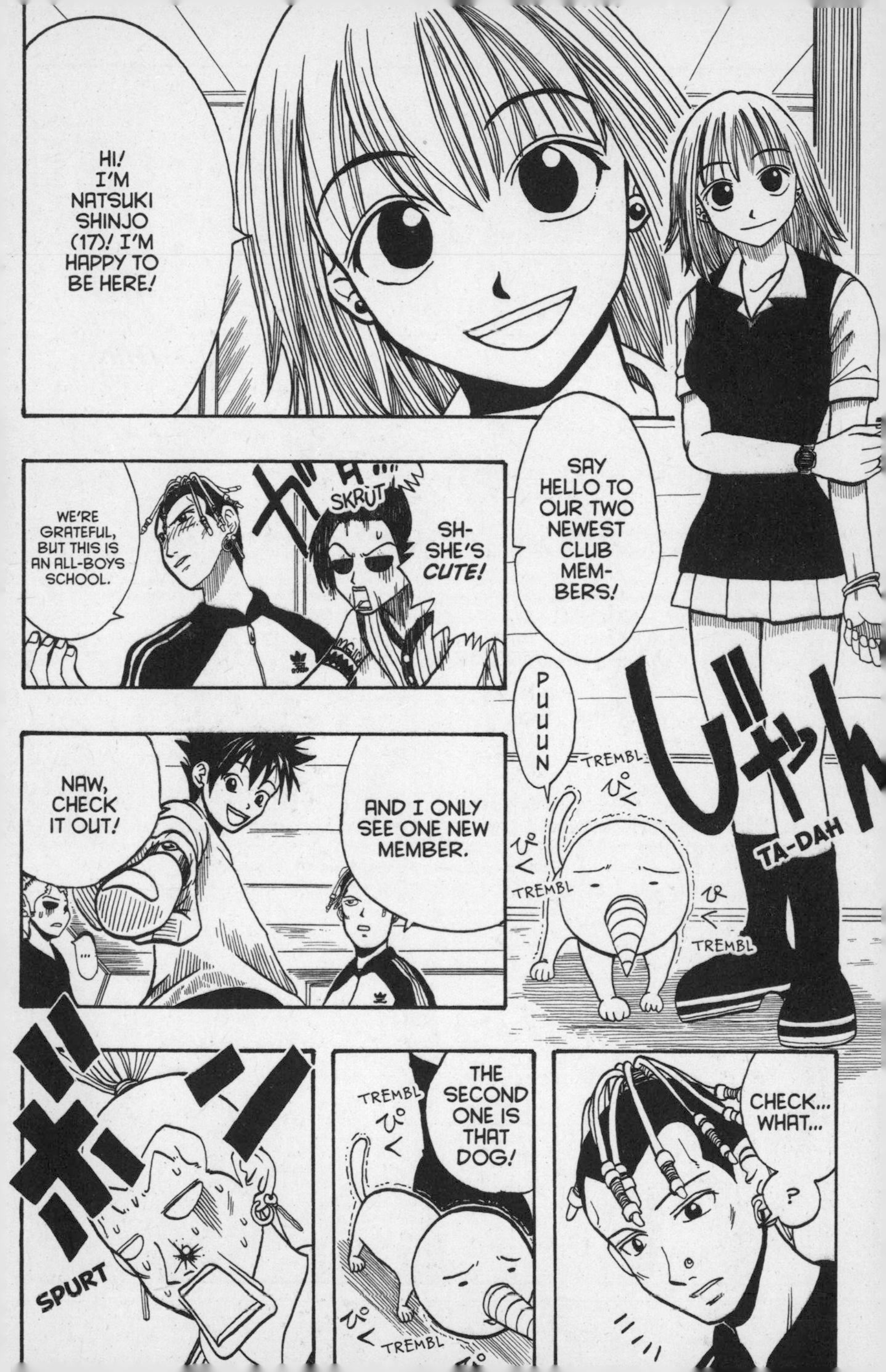
SAY HELLO TO OUR TWO NEWEST CLUB MEM-BERS!
PUUUUN
TREMBL
TREMBL
TREMBL
TA-DAH
HI! I'M NATSUKI SHINJO (17)! I'M HAPPY TO BE HERE!
SKRUT
SH-SHE'S *CUTE!*
WE'RE GRATEFUL, BUT THIS IS AN ALL-BOYS SCHOOL.
AND I ONLY SEE ONE NEW MEMBER.
NAW, CHECK IT OUT!
...
CHECK... WHAT...
?
THE SECOND ONE IS THAT DOG!
TREMBL
TREMBL
SPURT

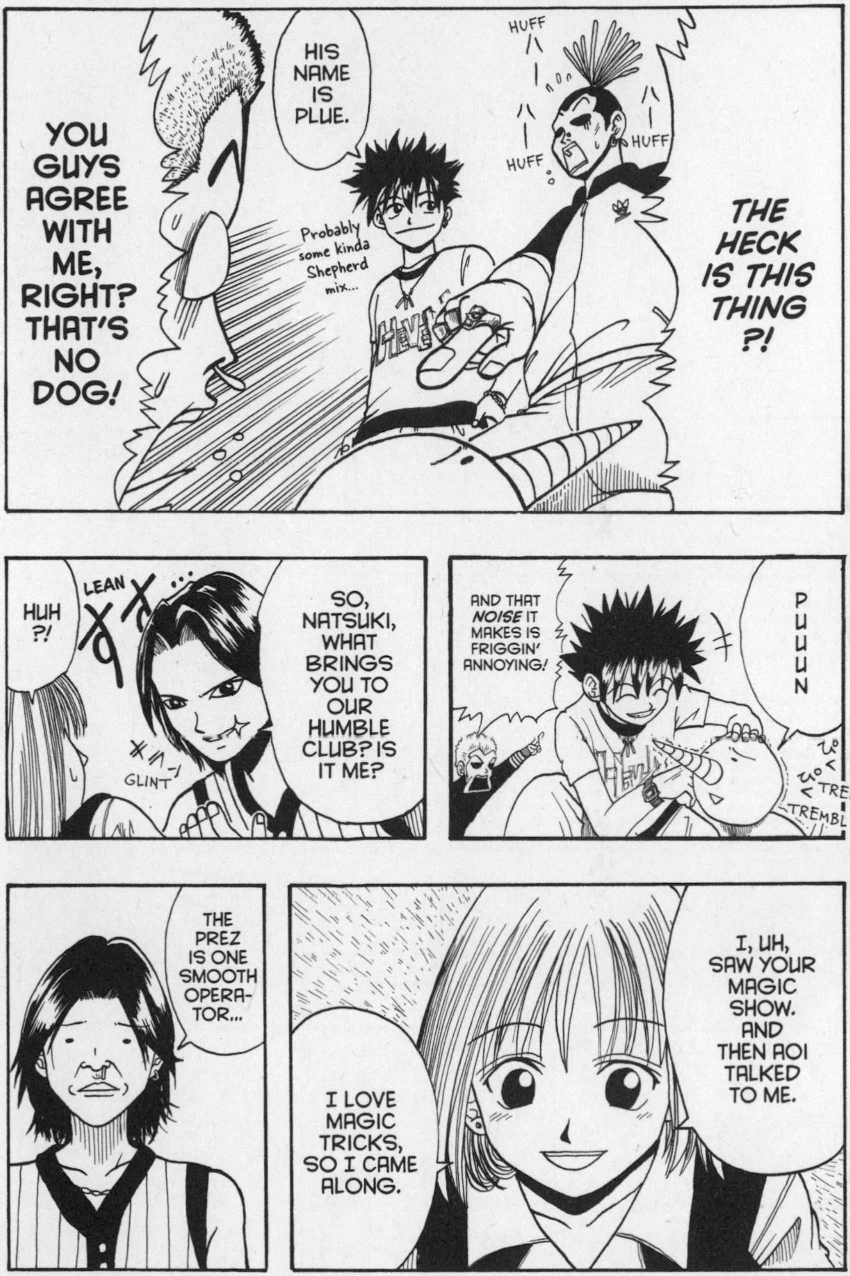
THE HECK IS THIS THING?!
HUFF
HUFF
HUFF
HIS NAME IS PLUE.
Probably some kinda Shepherd mix...
YOU GUYS AGREE WITH ME, RIGHT? THAT'S NO DOG!
PUUUN
TREMB
TREMBL
AND THAT NOISE IT MAKES IS FRIGGIN' ANNOYING!
SO, NATSUKI, WHAT BRINGS YOU TO OUR HUMBLE CLUB? IS IT ME?
LEAN
HUH?!
GLINT
I, UH, SAW YOUR MAGIC SHOW. AND THEN AOI TALKED TO ME.
I LOVE MAGIC TRICKS, SO I CAME ALONG.
THE PREZ IS ONE SMOOTH OPERA-TOR...

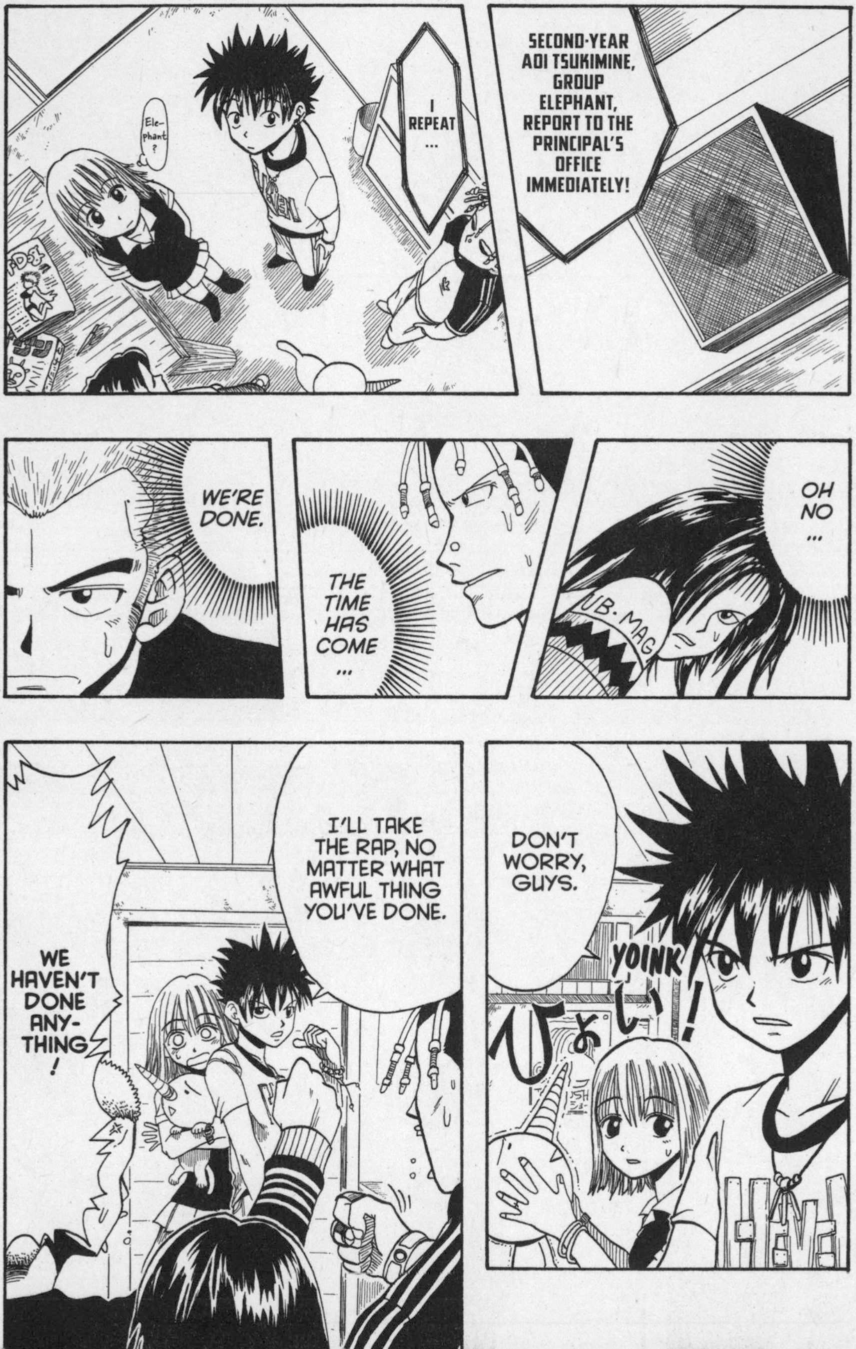
SECOND-YEAR AOI TSUKIMINE, GROUP ELEPHANT, REPORT TO THE PRINCIPAL'S OFFICE IMMEDIATELY!
I REPEAT ...
Ele-phant?
OH NO ...
THE TIME HAS COME ...
WE'RE DONE.
DON'T WORRY, GUYS.
YOINK
ひょい!
I'LL TAKE THE RAP, NO MATTER WHAT AWFUL THING YOU'VE DONE.
WE HAVEN'T DONE ANYTHING!

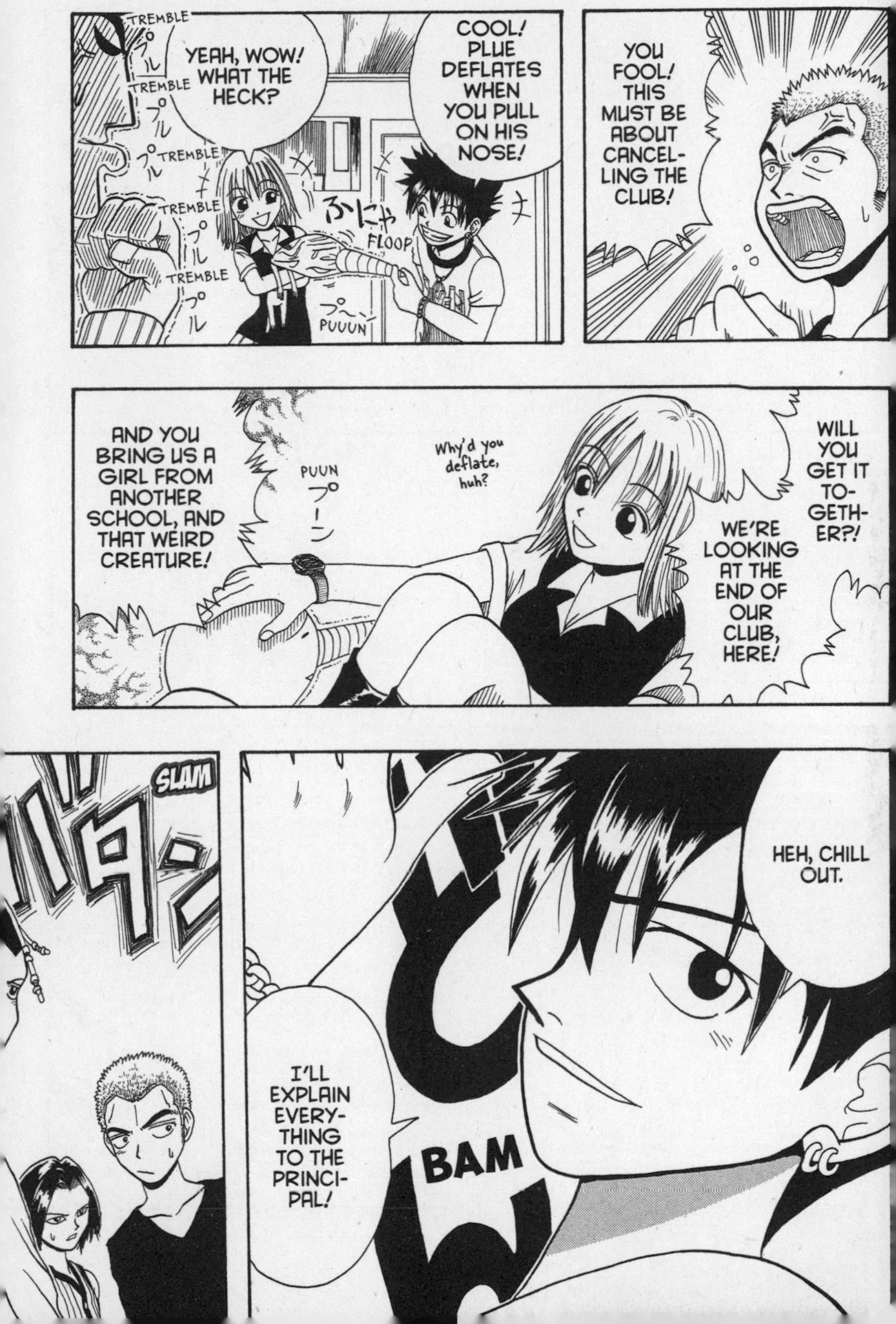
YOU FOOL! THIS MUST BE ABOUT CANCEL-LING THE CLUB!
COOL! PLUE DEFLATES WHEN YOU PULL ON HIS NOSE!
YEAH, WOW! WHAT THE HECK?
TREMBLE
TREMBLE
TREMBLE
TREMBLE
TREMBLE
FLOOP
PUUUN
WILL YOU GET IT TO-GETH-ER?!
WE'RE LOOKING AT THE END OF OUR CLUB, HERE!
Why'd you deflate, huh?
PUUN
AND YOU BRING US A GIRL FROM ANOTHER SCHOOL, AND THAT WEIRD CREATURE!
HEH, CHILL OUT.
I'LL EXPLAIN EVERY-THING TO THE PRINCI-PAL!
BAM
SLAM

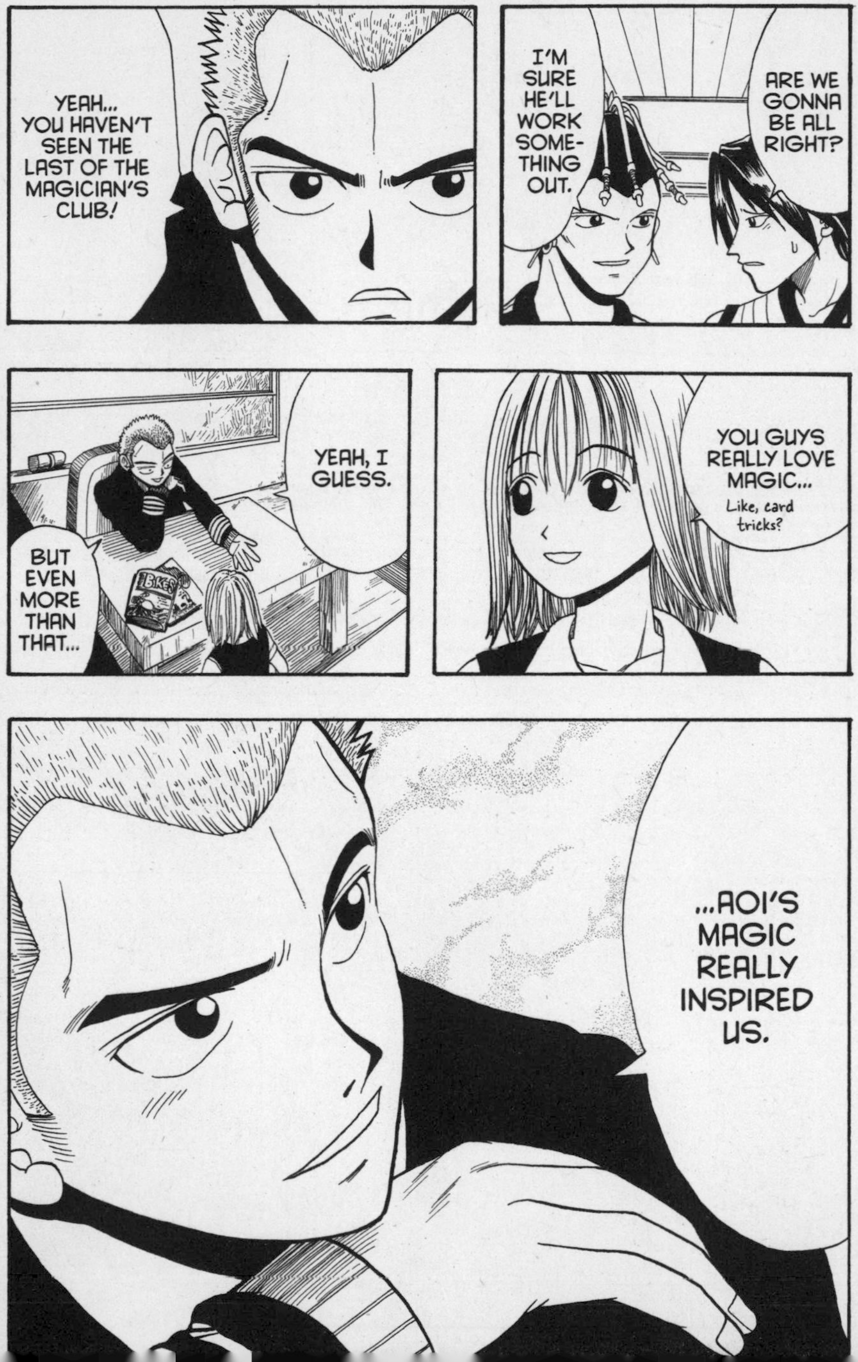
ARE WE GONNA BE ALL RIGHT?
I'M SURE HE'LL WORK SOME-THING OUT.
YEAH... YOU HAVEN'T SEEN THE LAST OF THE MAGICIAN'S CLUB!
YOU GUYS REALLY LOVE MAGIC...
Like, card tricks?
YEAH, I GUESS.
BUT EVEN MORE THAN THAT...
...AOI'S MAGIC REALLY INSPIRED US.

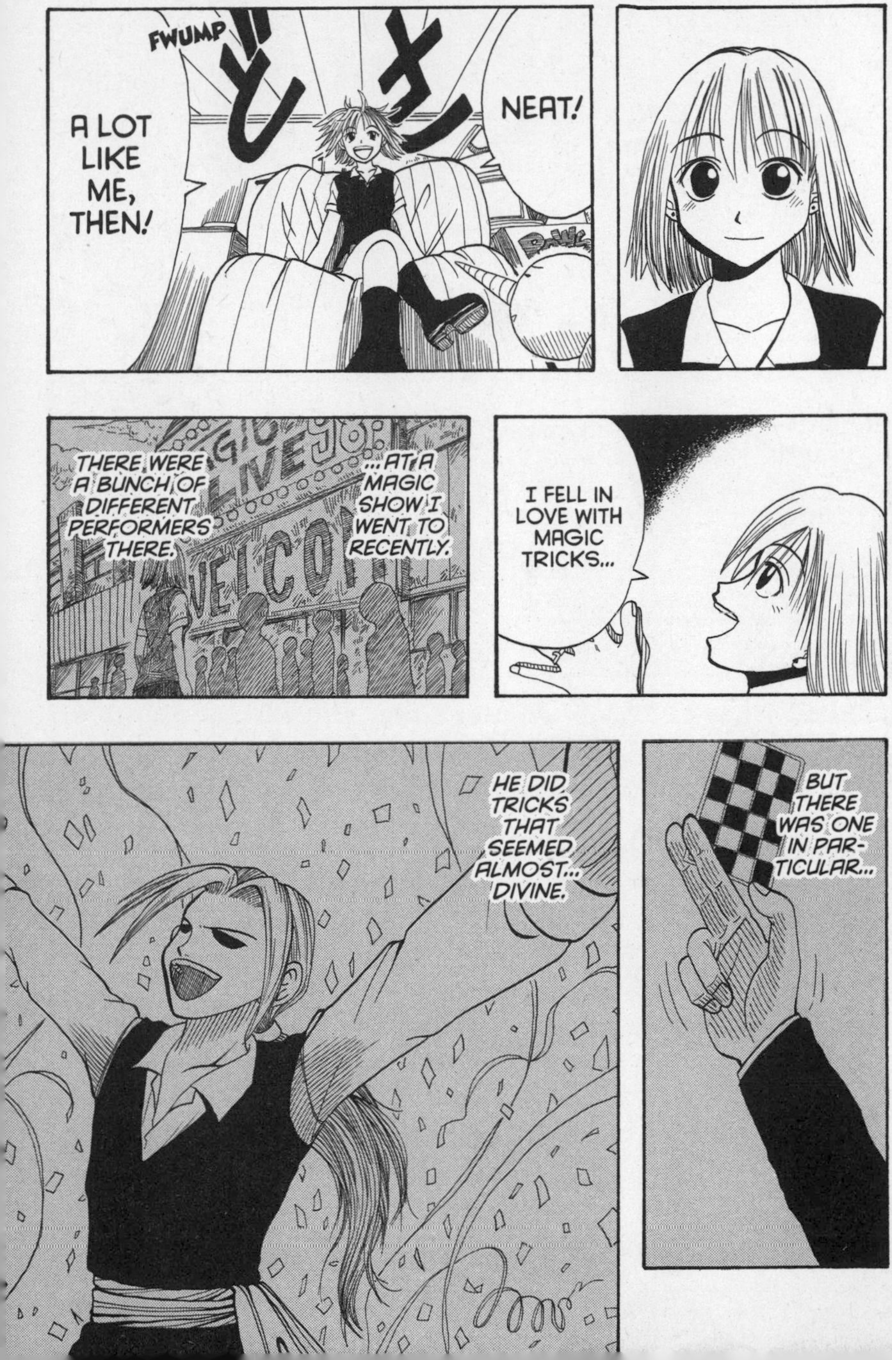
NEAT!
FWUMP
A LOT LIKE ME, THEN!
I FELL IN LOVE WITH MAGIC TRICKS...
...AT A MAGIC SHOW I WENT TO RECENTLY.
THERE WERE A BUNCH OF DIFFERENT PERFORMERS THERE.
BUT THERE WAS ONE IN PAR-TICULAR...
HE DID TRICKS THAT SEEMED ALMOST... DIVINE.

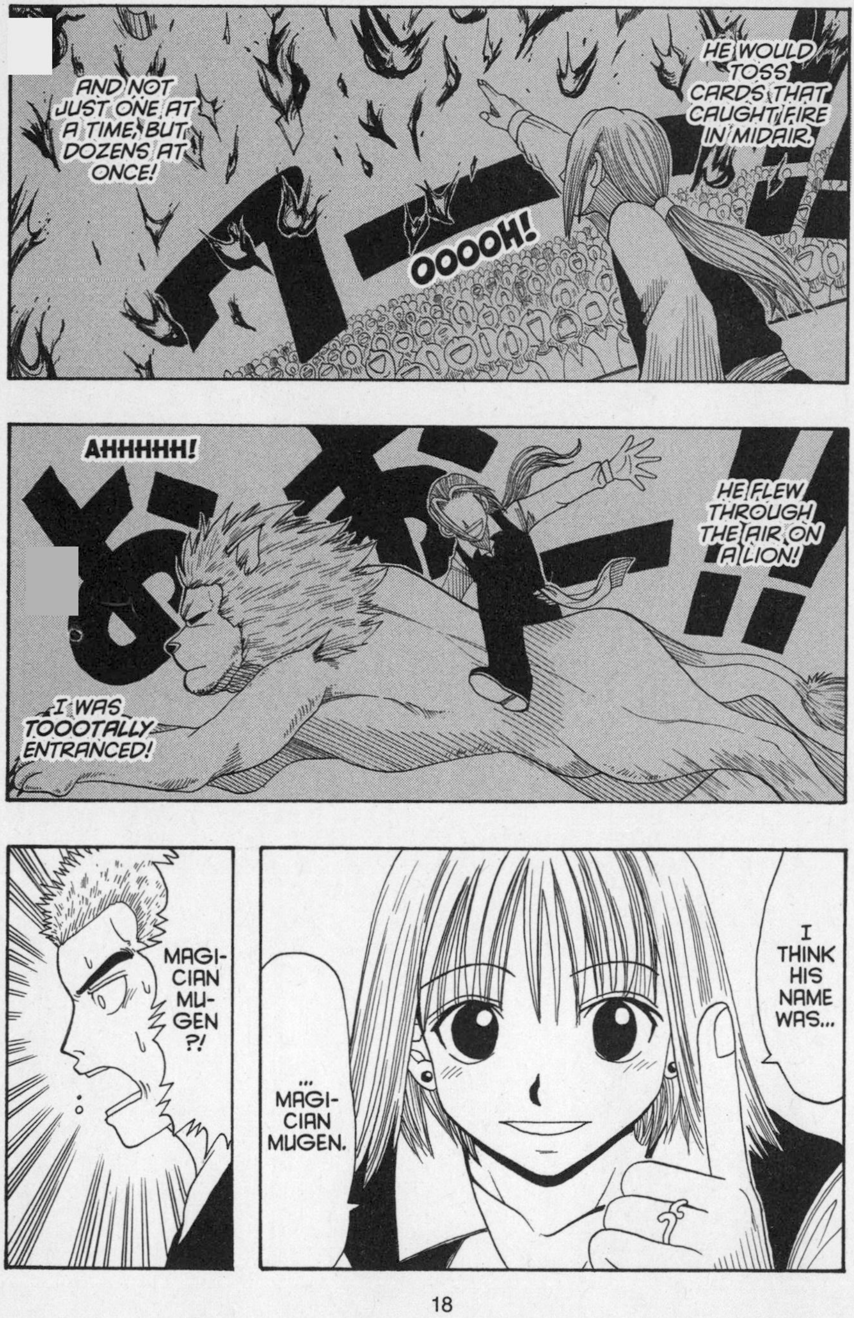
HE WOULD TOSS CARDS THAT CAUGHT FIRE IN MIDAIR.
OOOOH!
AND NOT JUST ONE AT A TIME, BUT DOZENS AT ONCE!
HE FLEW THROUGH THE AIR ON A LION!
AHHHHHH!
I WAS TOOOTALLY ENTRANCED!
I THINK HIS NAME WAS...
...MAGICIAN MUGEN.
MAGICIAN MUGEN?!

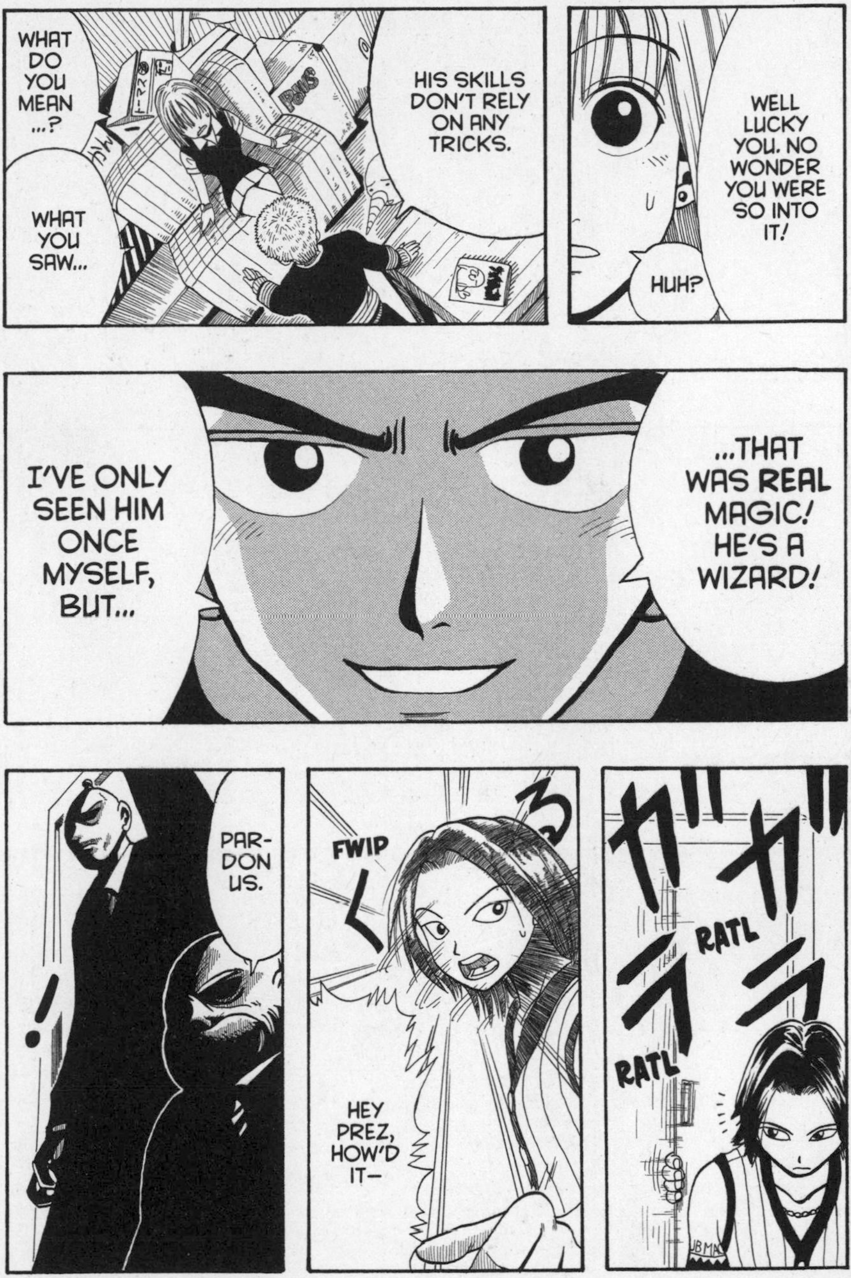
WELL LUCKY YOU. NO WONDER YOU WERE SO INTO IT!
HUH?
HIS SKILLS DON'T RELY ON ANY TRICKS.
WHAT DO YOU MEAN...?
WHAT YOU SAW...
I'VE ONLY SEEN HIM ONCE MYSELF, BUT...
...THAT WAS REAL MAGIC! HE'S A WIZARD!
RATL
RATL
FWIP
HEY PREZ, HOW'D IT—
PAR-DON US.

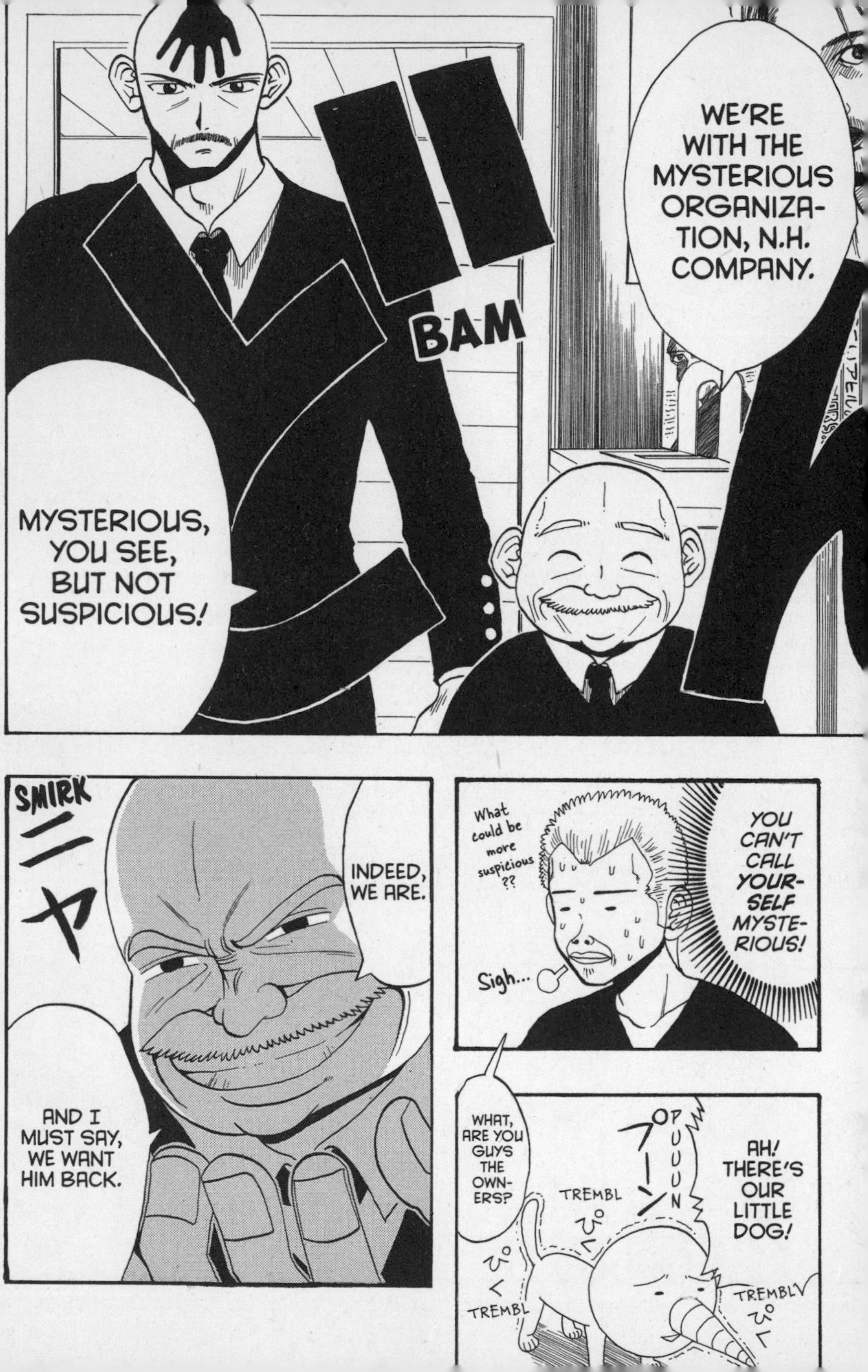
WE'RE WITH THE MYSTERIOUS ORGANIZATION, N.H. COMPANY.
BAM
MYSTERIOUS, YOU SEE, BUT NOT SUSPICIOUS!
YOU CAN'T CALL YOURSELF MYSTERIOUS!
What could be more suspicious??
Sigh...
AH! THERE'S OUR LITTLE DOG!
POUUUN
TREMBL
TREMBL
TREMBL
WHAT, ARE YOU GUYS THE OWNERS?
SMIRK
INDEED, WE ARE.
AND I MUST SAY, WE WANT HIM BACK.

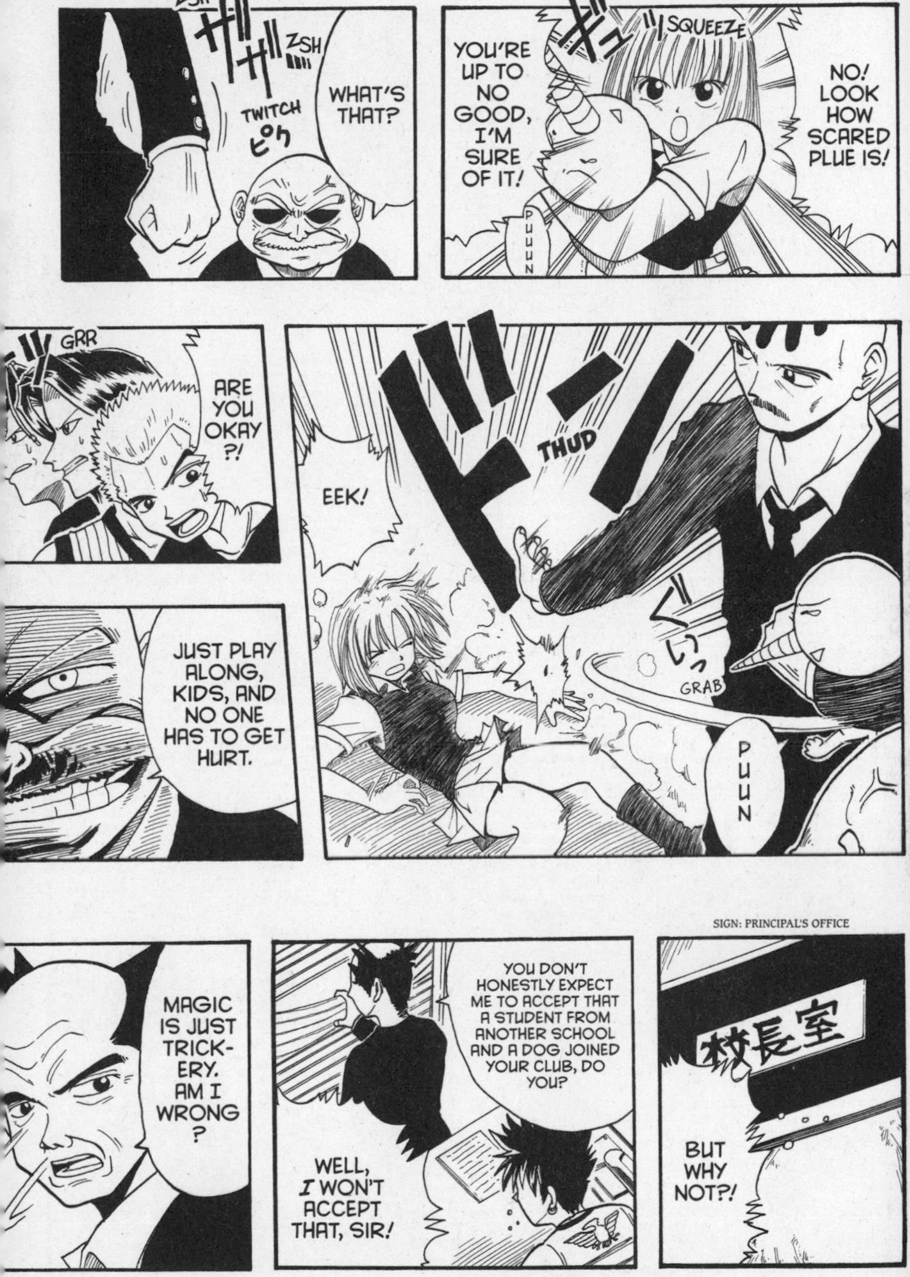
SQUEEZE
NO! LOOK HOW SCARED PLUE IS!
YOU'RE UP TO NO GOOD, I'M SURE OF IT!
PUUUN
ZSH
ZSH
TWITCH
WHAT'S THAT?
THUD
EEK!
GRAB
PUUN
GRR
ARE YOU OKAY?!
JUST PLAY ALONG, KIDS, AND NO ONE HAS TO GET HURT.
校長室
BUT WHY NOT?!
YOU DON'T HONESTLY EXPECT ME TO ACCEPT THAT A STUDENT FROM ANOTHER SCHOOL AND A DOG JOINED YOUR CLUB, DO YOU?
WELL, *I* WON'T ACCEPT THAT, SIR!
MAGIC IS JUST TRICKERY. AM I WRONG?
SIGN: PRINCIPAL'S OFFICE

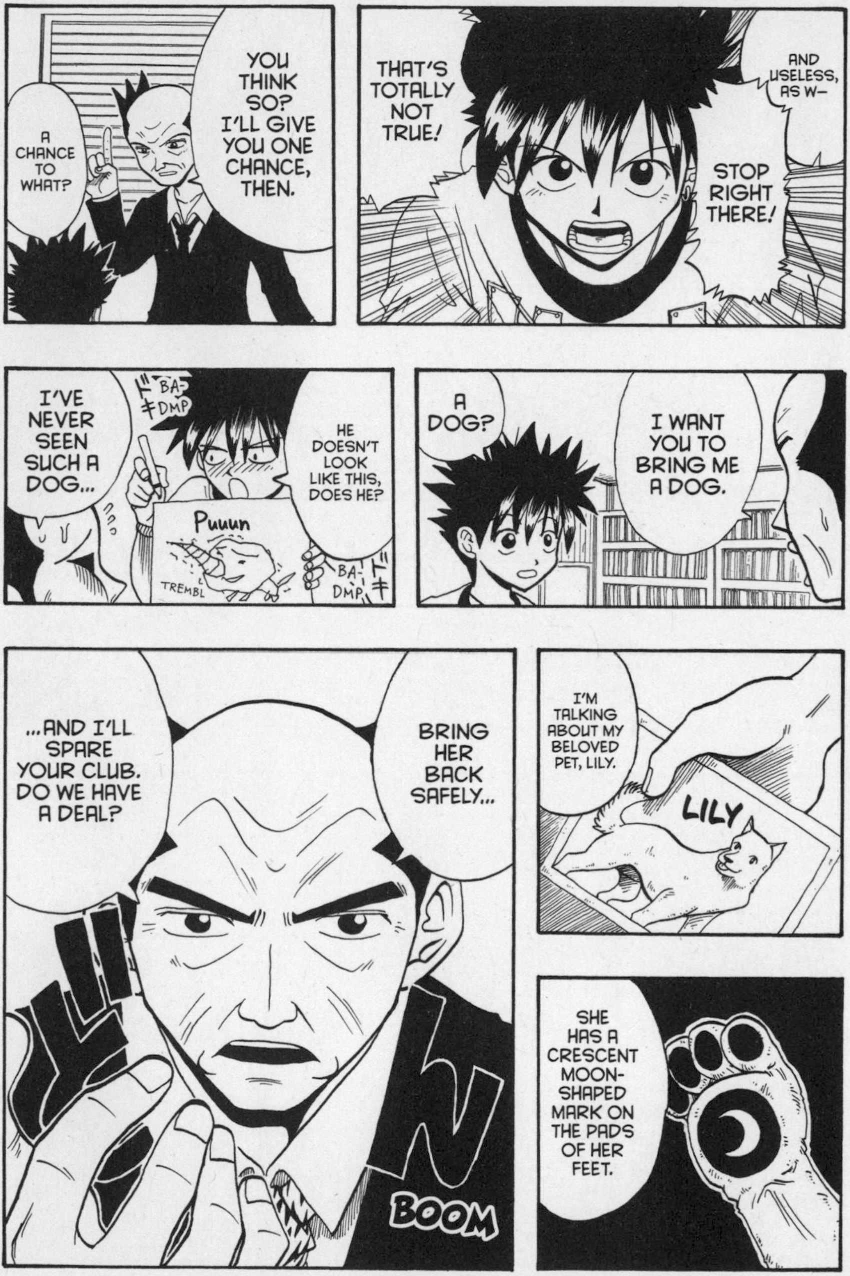
AND USELESS, AS W—
STOP RIGHT THERE!
THAT'S TOTALLY NOT TRUE!
YOU THINK SO? I'LL GIVE YOU ONE CHANCE, THEN.
A CHANCE TO WHAT?
I WANT YOU TO BRING ME A DOG.
A DOG?
BA-DMP
HE DOESN'T LOOK LIKE THIS, DOES HE?
BA-DMP
Puuun
TREMBL
I'VE NEVER SEEN SUCH A DOG...
I'M TALKING ABOUT MY BELOVED PET, LILY.
LILY
SHE HAS A CRESCENT MOON-SHAPED MARK ON THE PADS OF HER FEET.
BRING HER BACK SAFELY...
...AND I'LL SPARE YOUR CLUB. DO WE HAVE A DEAL?
BOOM

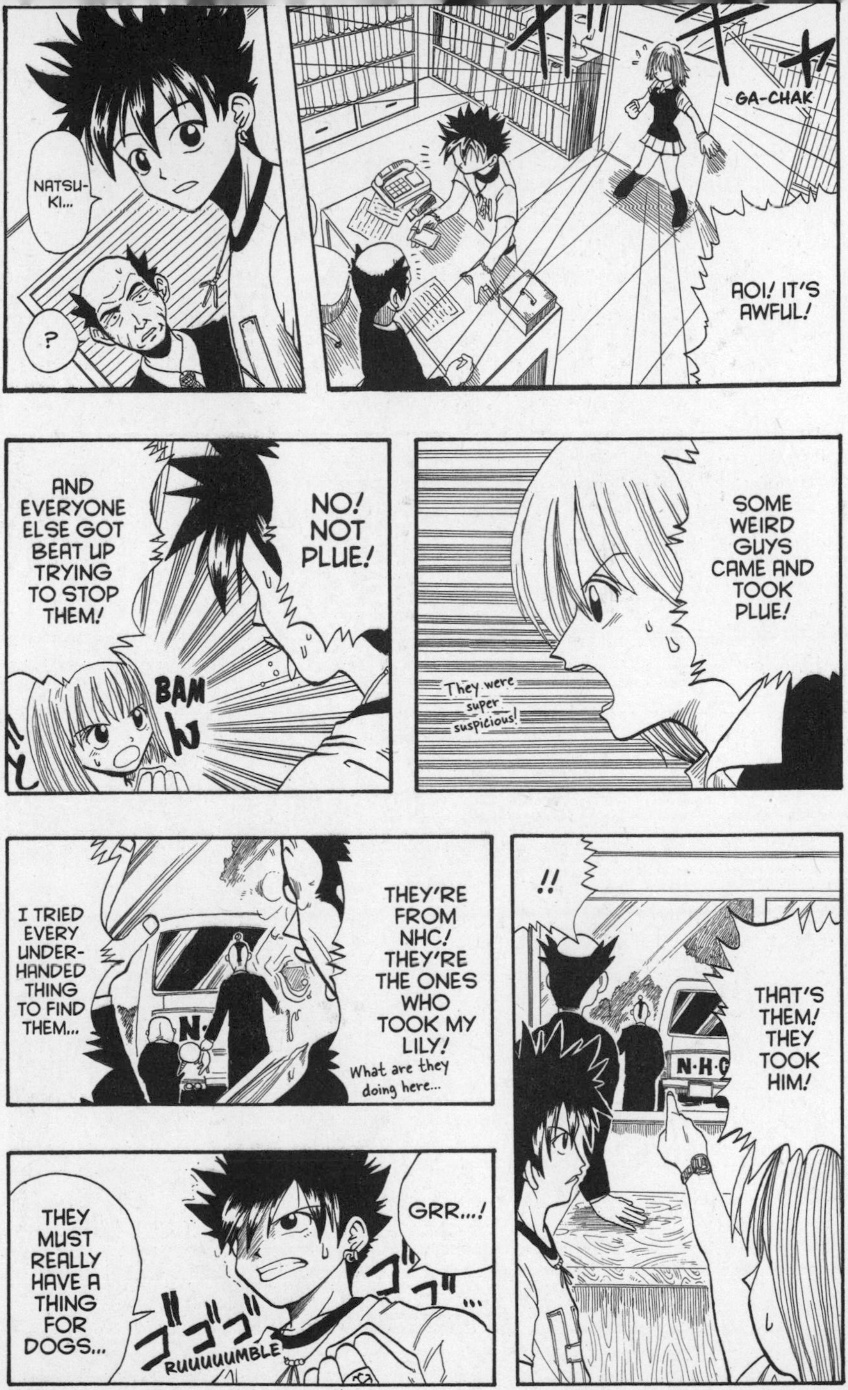
GA-CHAK
AOI! IT'S AWFUL!
NATSU-KI...
?
SOME WEIRD GUYS CAME AND TOOK PLUE!
They were super suspicious!
NO! NOT PLUE!
AND EVERYONE ELSE GOT BEAT UP TRYING TO STOP THEM!
BAM
!!
THAT'S THEM! THEY TOOK HIM!
N·H·C
THEY'RE FROM NHC! THEY'RE THE ONES WHO TOOK MY LILY!
What are they doing here...
I TRIED EVERY UNDER-HANDED THING TO FIND THEM...
GRR...!
THEY MUST REALLY HAVE A THING FOR DOGS...
RUUUUUMBLE

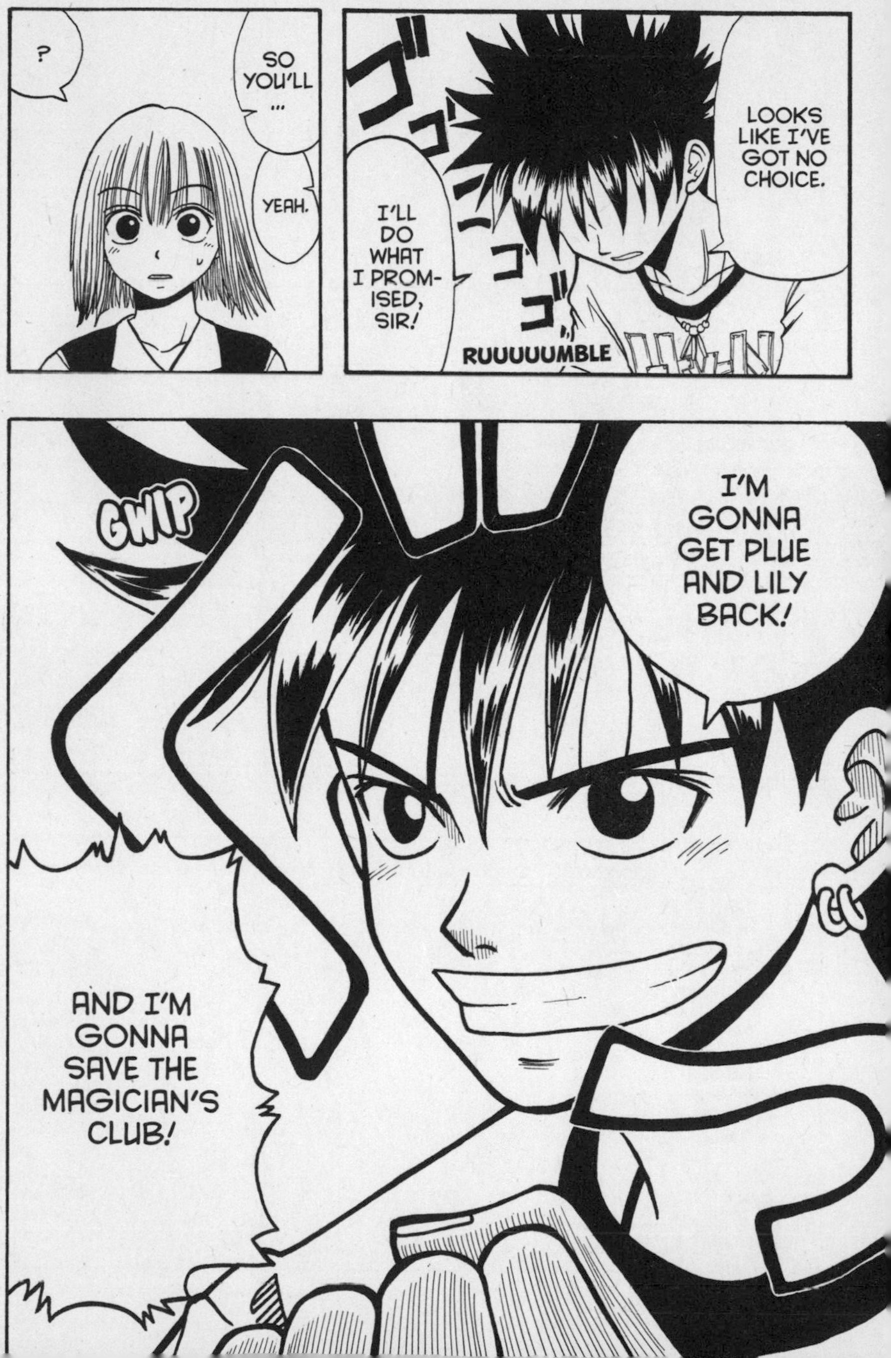
LOOKS LIKE I'VE GOT NO CHOICE.
I'LL DO WHAT I PROMISED, SIR!
RUUUUUMBLE
SO YOU'LL ....
?
YEAH.
I'M GONNA GET PLUE AND LILY BACK!
GWIP
AND I'M GONNA SAVE THE MAGICIAN'S CLUB!

SIGN: KARAOKE BIG NOSE

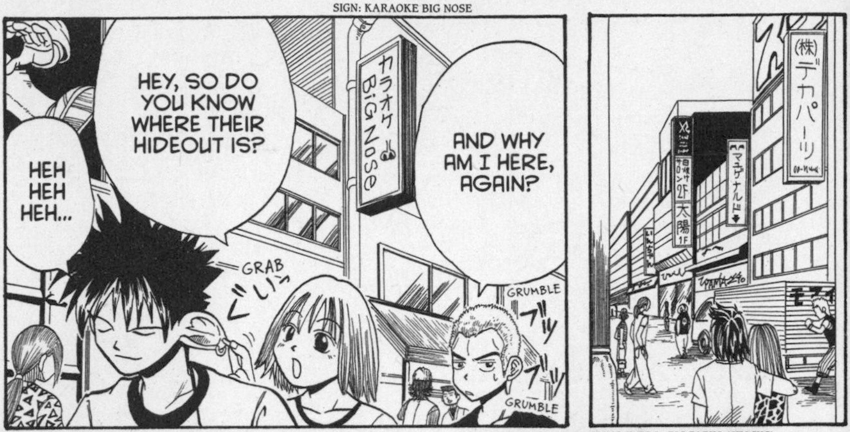
(株)デカパーツ
AND WHY AM I HERE, AGAIN?
GRUMBLE
GRUMBLE
カラオケ BiG Nose
HEY, SO DO YOU KNOW WHERE THEIR HIDEOUT IS?
GRAB
HEH HEH HEH...

SIGNS, R TO L: BIG PARTS (STOCKS), MCBROWNALD'S, TANNING SALON 2F, SUN 1F, INCHAN.

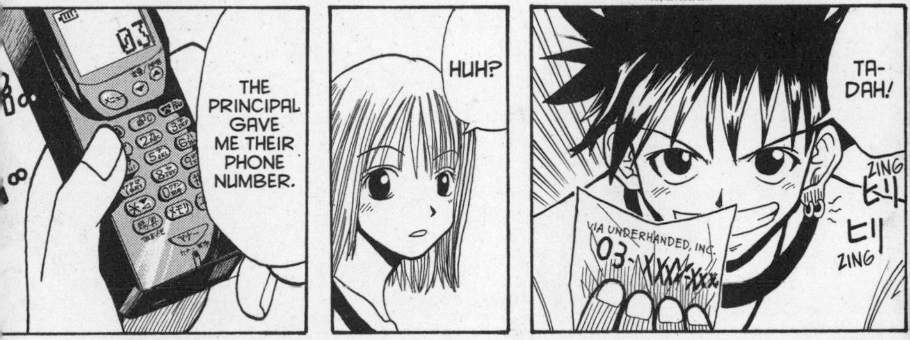
TA-DAH!
ZING
ZING
VIA UNDERHANDED, INC.
03-XXXX-XXX
HUH?
THE PRINCIPAL GAVE ME THEIR PHONE NUMBER.

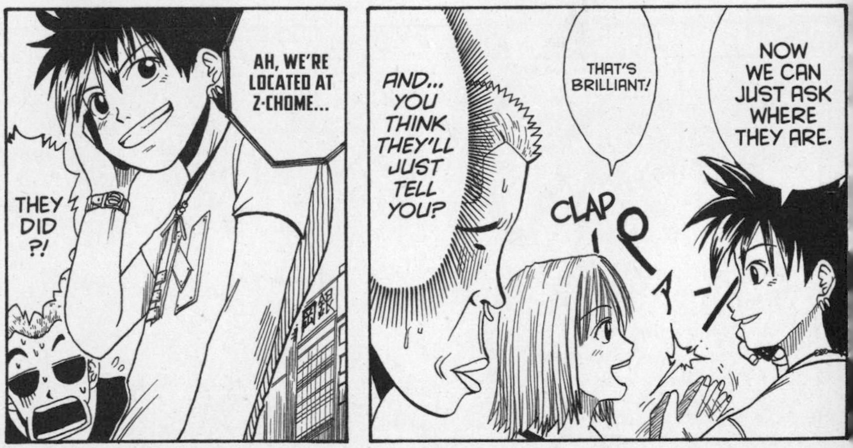
NOW WE CAN JUST ASK WHERE THEY ARE.
THAT'S BRILLIANT!
CLAP
AND... YOU THINK THEY'LL JUST TELL YOU?
AH, WE'RE LOCATED AT Z-CHOME...
THEY DID ?!

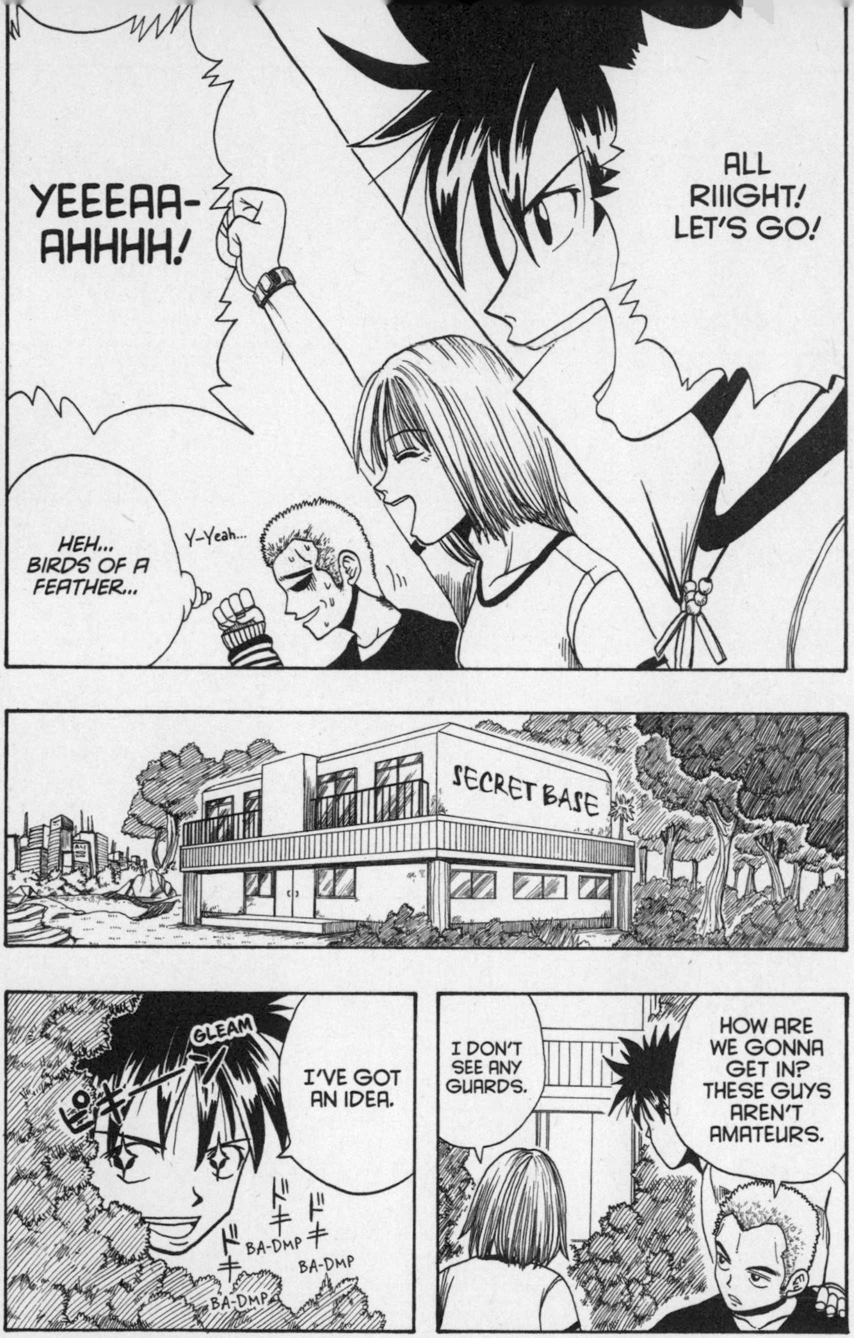
ALL RIIIGHT! LET'S GO!
YEEEAA-AHHHH!
Y-Yeah...
HEH... BIRDS OF A FEATHER...
SECRET BASE
HOW ARE WE GONNA GET IN? THESE GUYS AREN'T AMATEURS.
I DON'T SEE ANY GUARDS.
GLEAM
I'VE GOT AN IDEA.
ドキ
BA-DMP
ドキ
BA-DMP
ドキ
BA-DMP

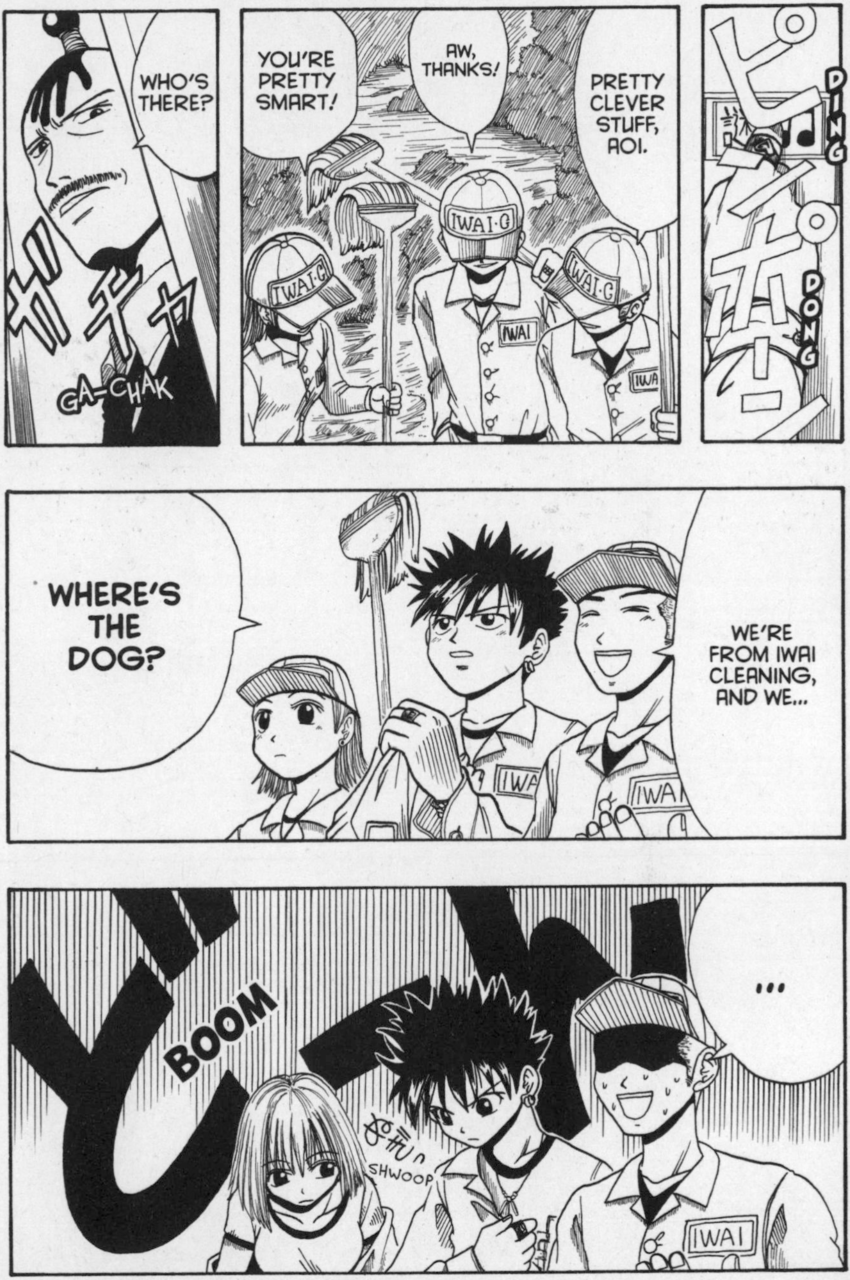
DING
DONG
PRETTY CLEVER STUFF, AOI.
AW, THANKS!
YOU'RE PRETTY SMART!
WHO'S THERE?
GA-CHAK
WE'RE FROM IWAI CLEANING, AND WE...
WHERE'S THE DOG?
...
BOOM
SHWOOP

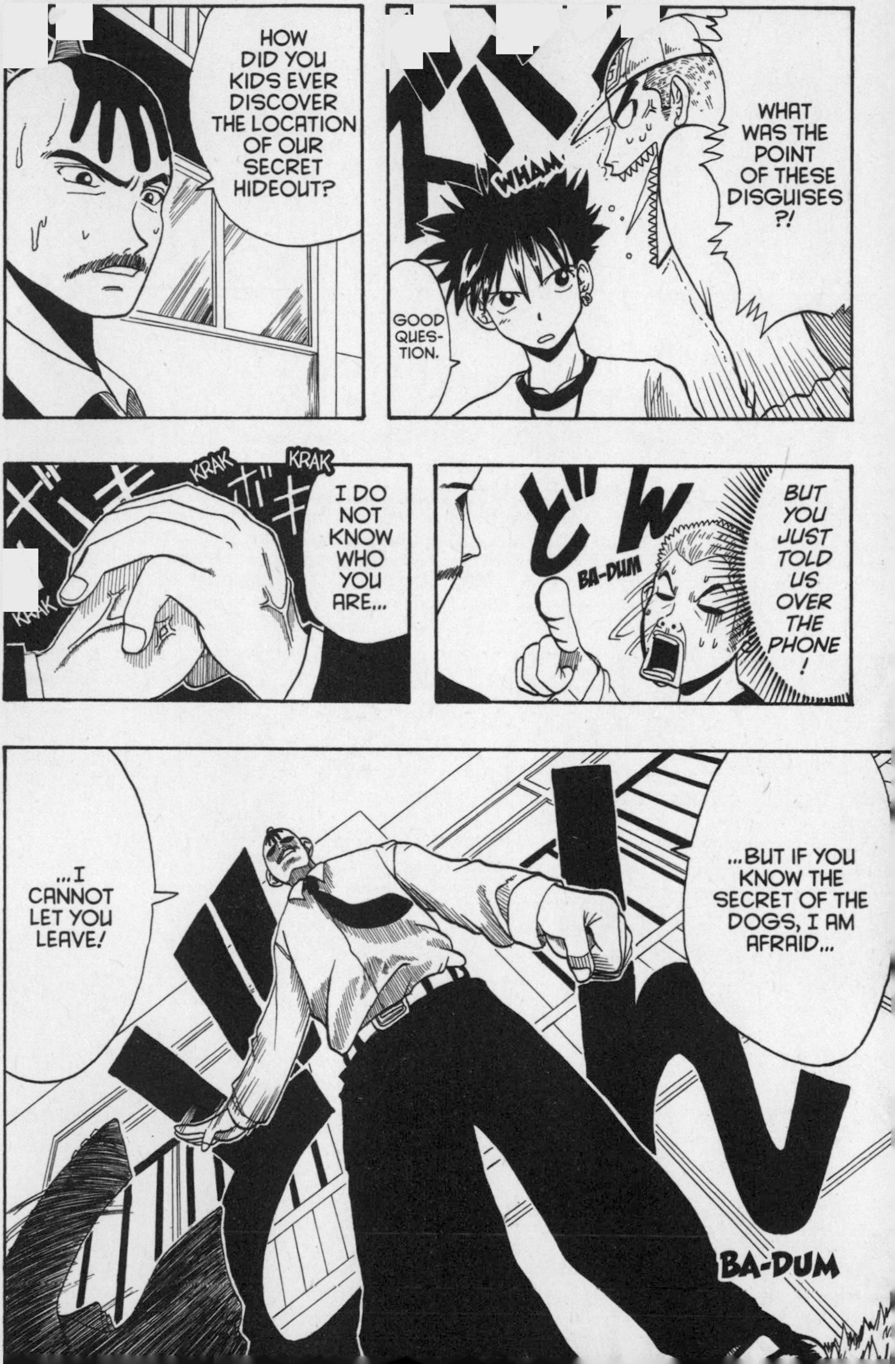
WHAT WAS THE POINT OF THESE DISGUISES ?!
WHAM
GOOD QUES-TION.
HOW DID YOU KIDS EVER DISCOVER THE LOCATION OF OUR SECRET HIDEOUT?
BUT YOU JUST TOLD US OVER THE PHONE !
BA-DUM
KRAK
KRAK
I DO NOT KNOW WHO YOU ARE...
KRAK
...BUT IF YOU KNOW THE SECRET OF THE DOGS, I AM AFRAID...
...I CANNOT LET YOU LEAVE!
BA-DUM

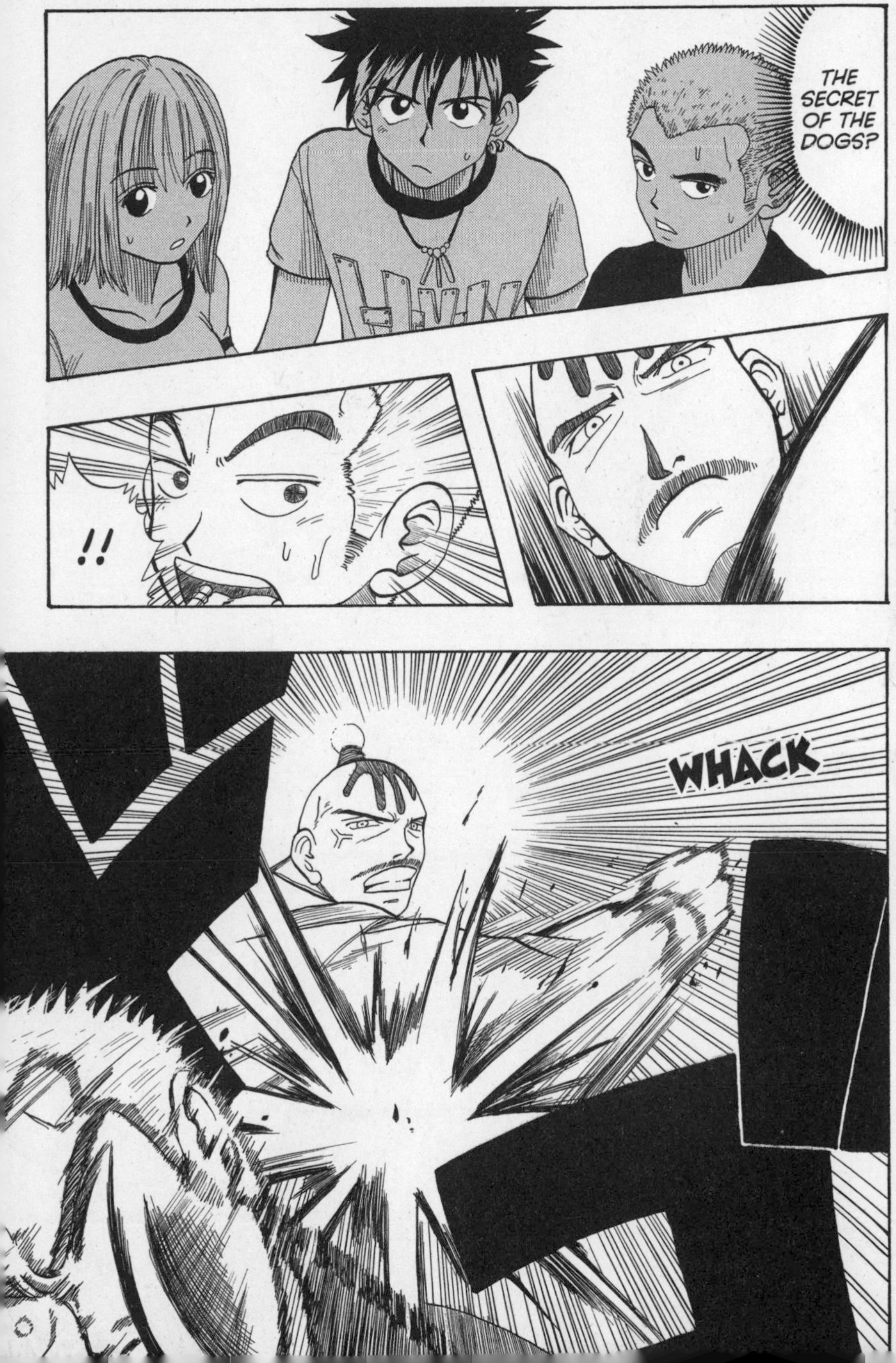
THE SECRET OF THE DOGS?
!!
WHACK

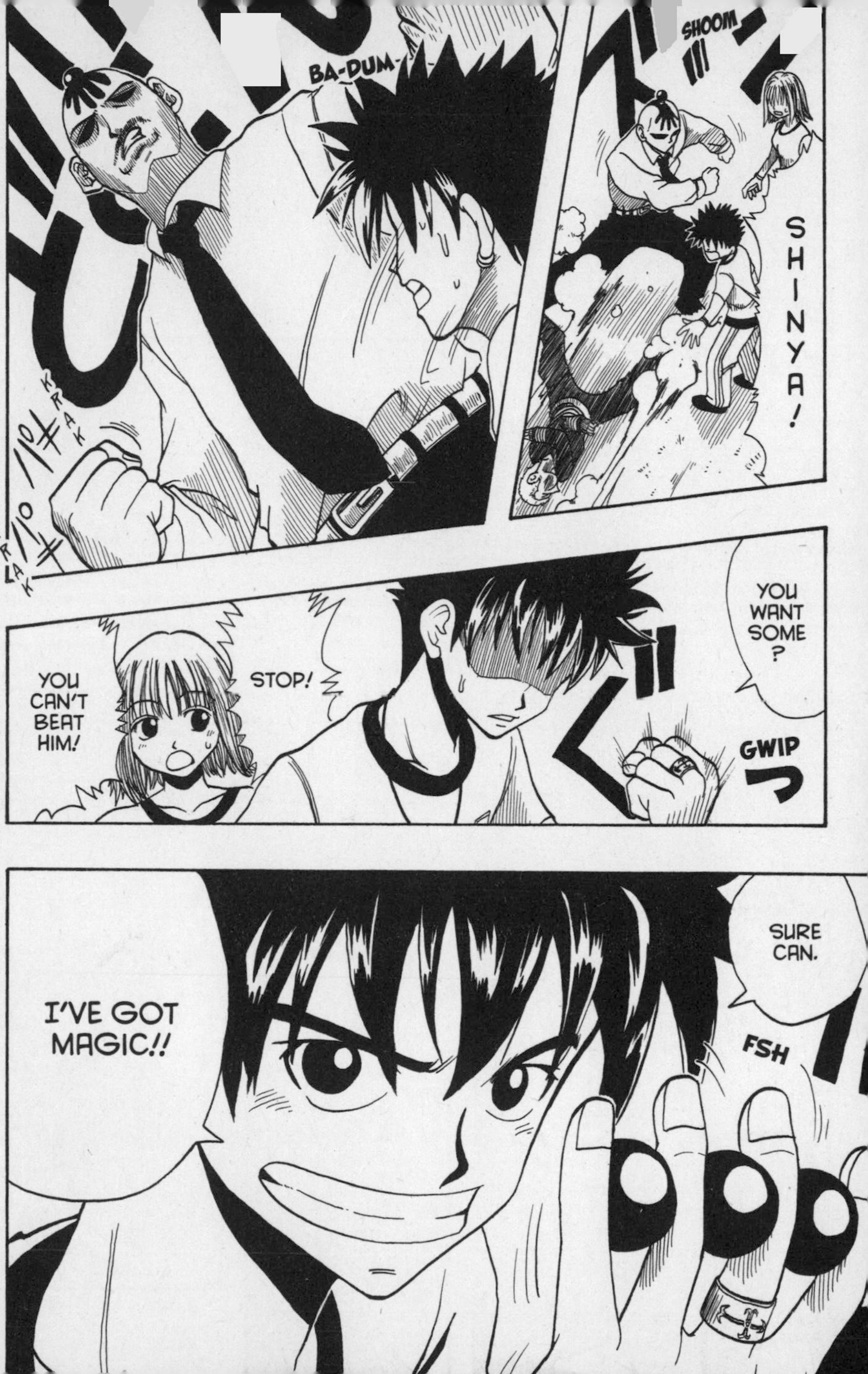
SHOOM
SHINYA!
BA-DUM
KRAK
KRAK
YOU WANT SOME?
GWIP
STOP!
YOU CAN'T BEAT HIM!
SURE CAN.
FSH
I'VE GOT MAGIC!!

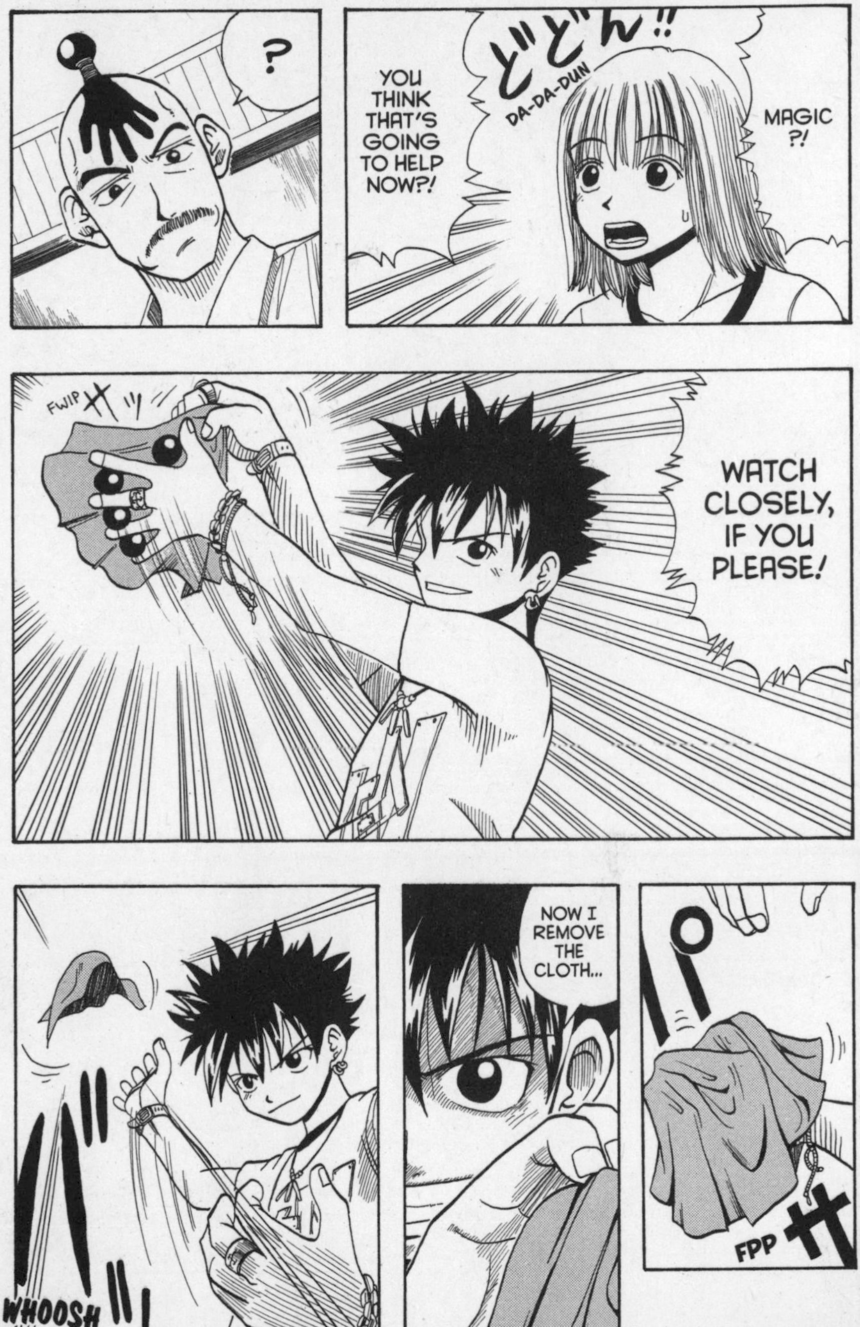
どどん!!
DA-DA-DUN
MAGIC ?!
YOU THINK THAT'S GOING TO HELP NOW?!
?
WATCH CLOSELY, IF YOU PLEASE!
FWIP
FPP
NOW I REMOVE THE CLOTH...
WHOOSH

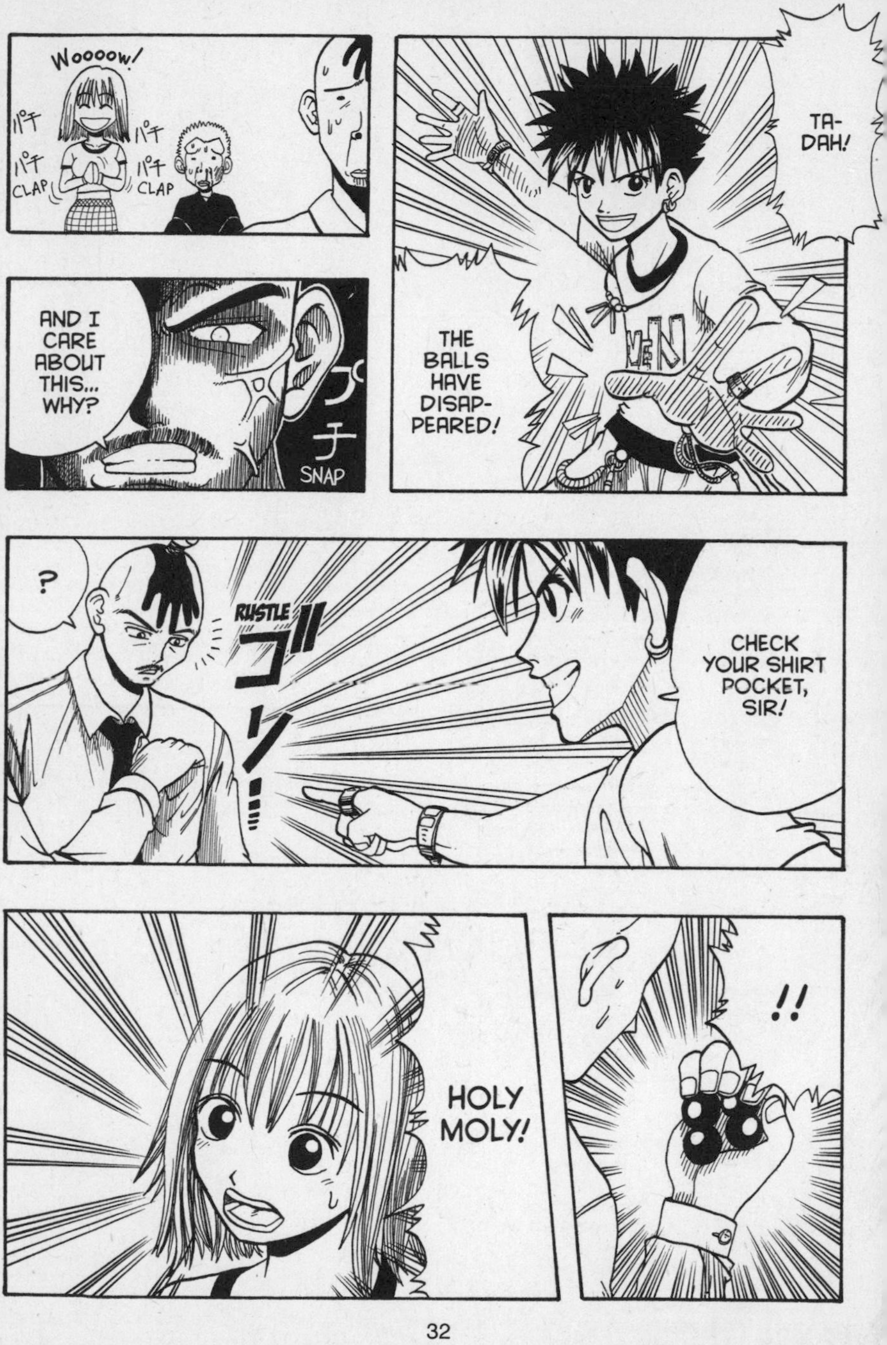
TA-DAH!
THE BALLS HAVE DISAPPEARED!
WOOOOW!
パチ パチ CLAP
パチ パチ CLAP
AND I CARE ABOUT THIS... WHY?
プチ SNAP
CHECK YOUR SHIRT POCKET, SIR!
RUSTLE ゴソ
?
!!
HOLY MOLY!

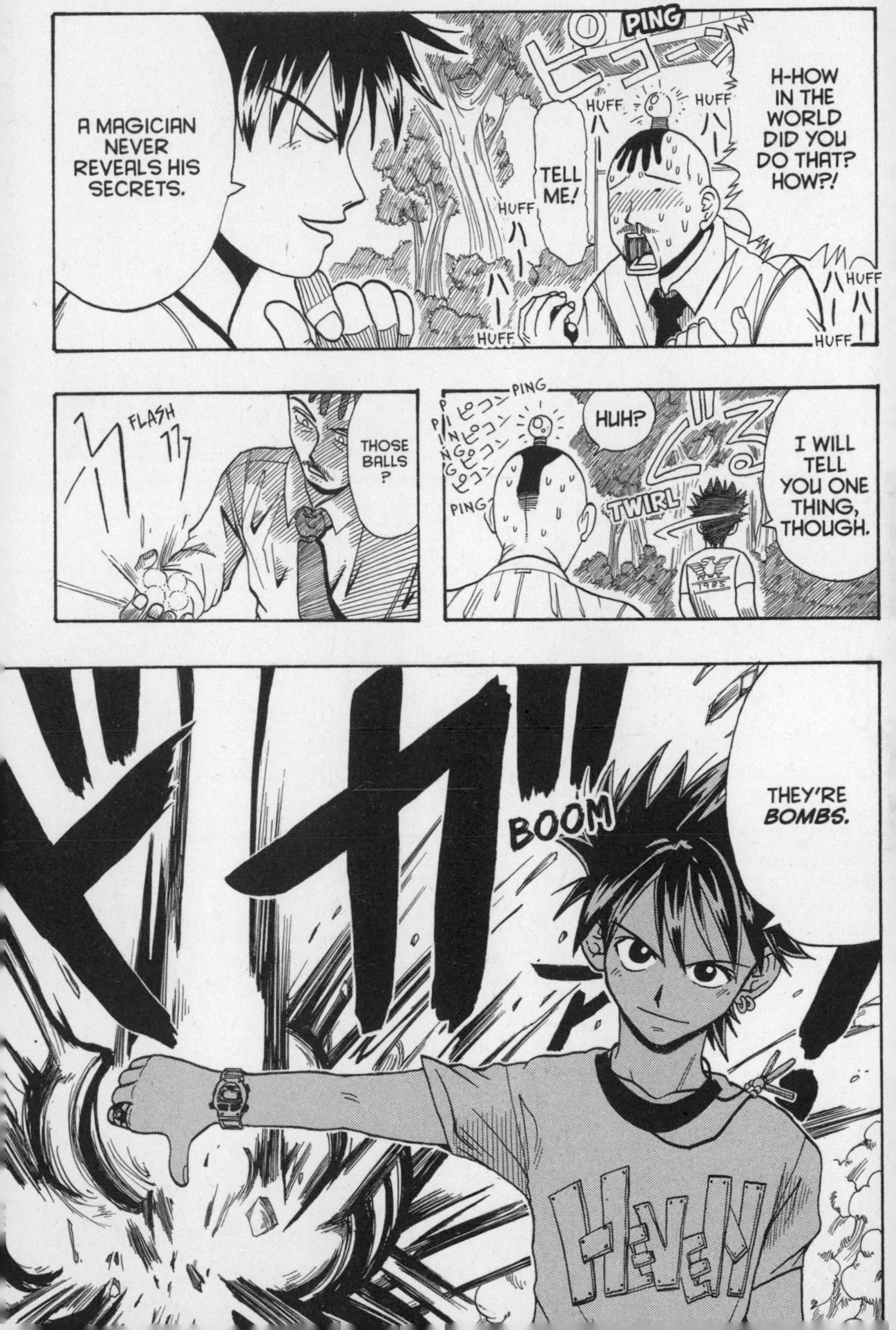
PING
H-HOW IN THE WORLD DID YOU DO THAT? HOW?!
HUFF HUFF
HUFF HUFF
TELL ME!
HUFF HUFF
A MAGICIAN NEVER REVEALS HIS SECRETS.
I WILL TELL YOU ONE THING, THOUGH.
TWIRL
HUH?
PING
ピコン
ピコン
ピコン
ピコン
PING
THOSE BALLS?
FLASH
THEY'RE *BOMBS.*
BOOM

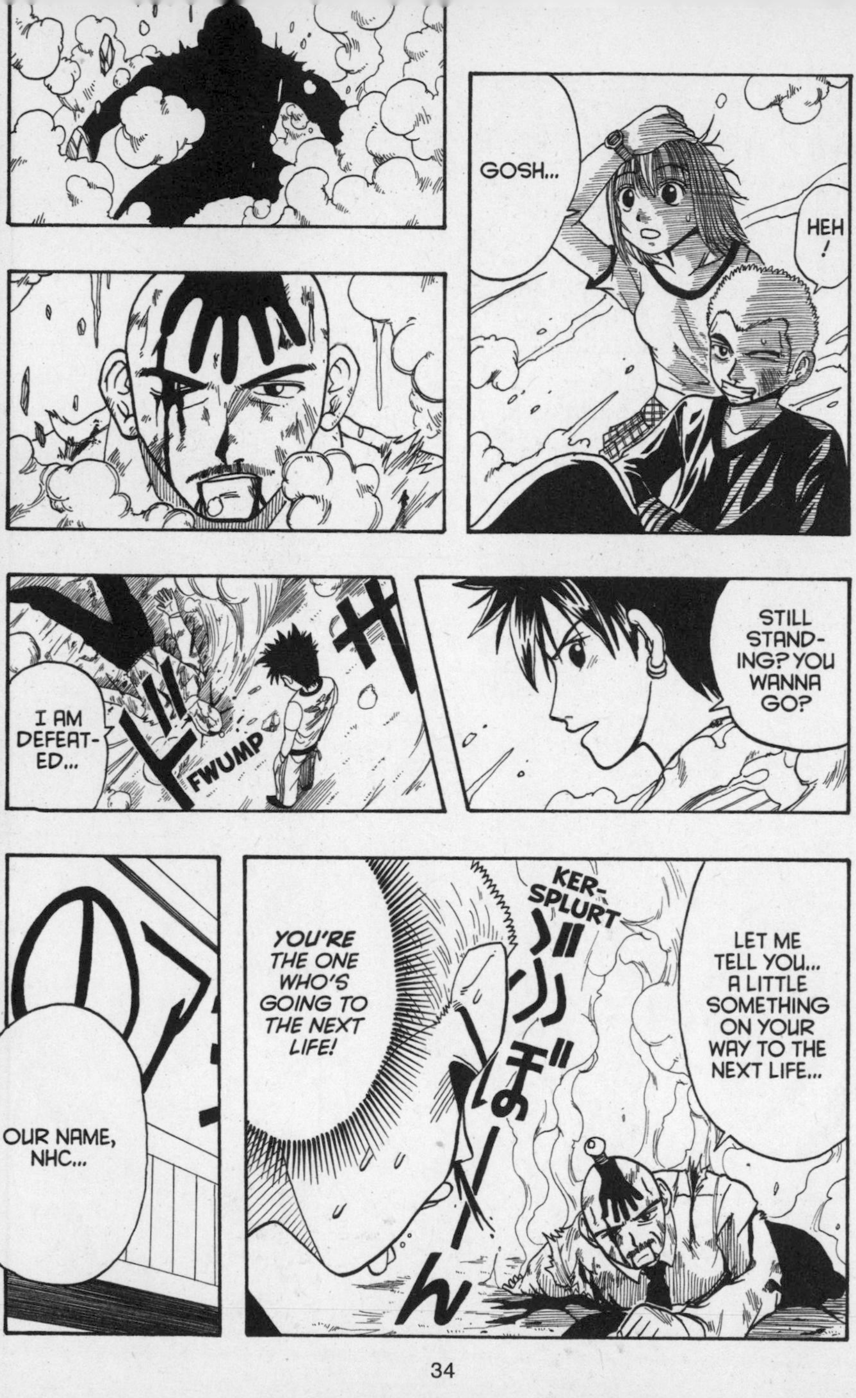
GOSH...
HEH!
STILL STAND-ING? YOU WANNA GO?
I AM DEFEAT-ED...
FWUMP
LET ME TELL YOU... A LITTLE SOMETHING ON YOUR WAY TO THE NEXT LIFE...
KER-SPLURT
YOU'RE THE ONE WHO'S GOING TO THE NEXT LIFE!
OUR NAME, NHC...

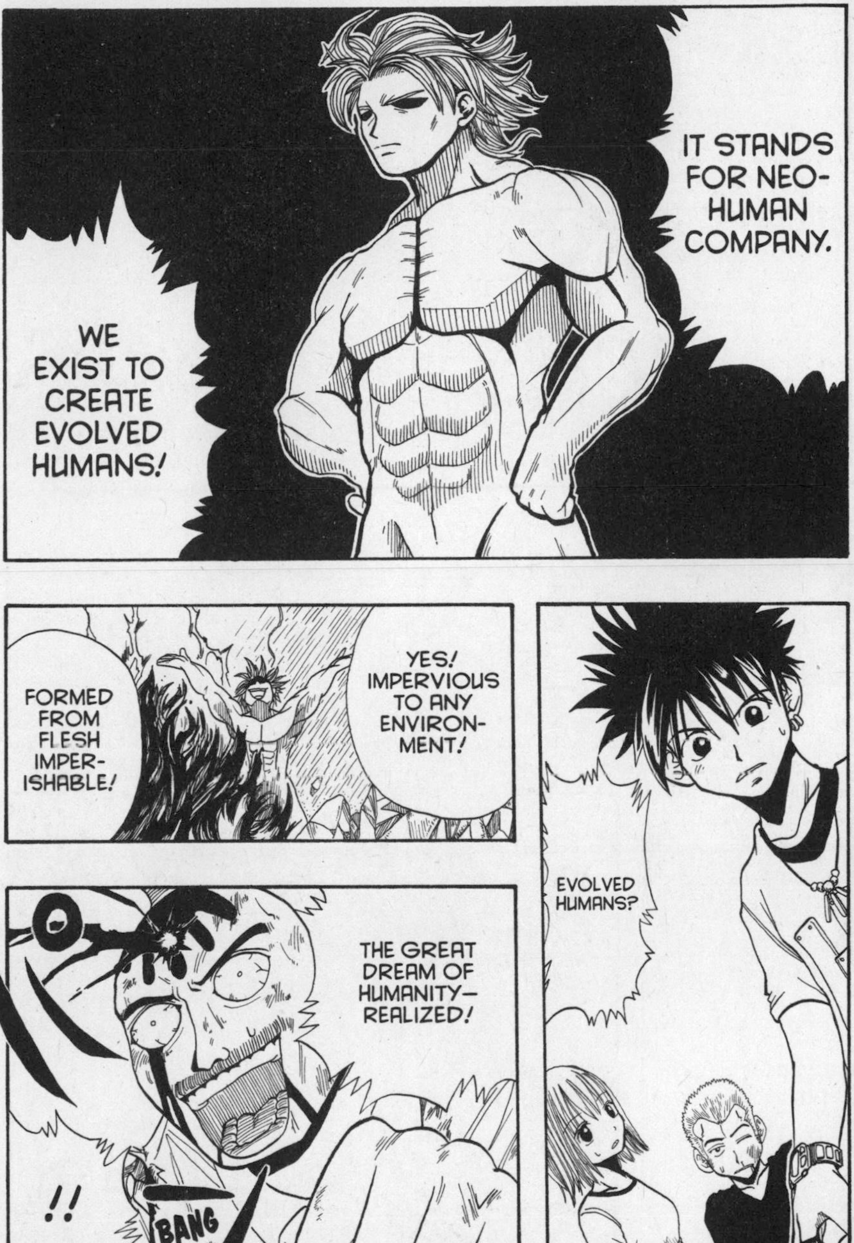
IT STANDS FOR NEO-HUMAN COMPANY.
WE EXIST TO CREATE EVOLVED HUMANS!
EVOLVED HUMANS?
YES! IMPERVIOUS TO ANY ENVIRON-MENT!
FORMED FROM FLESH IMPER-ISHABLE!
THE GREAT DREAM OF HUMANITY—REALIZED!
!!
BANG

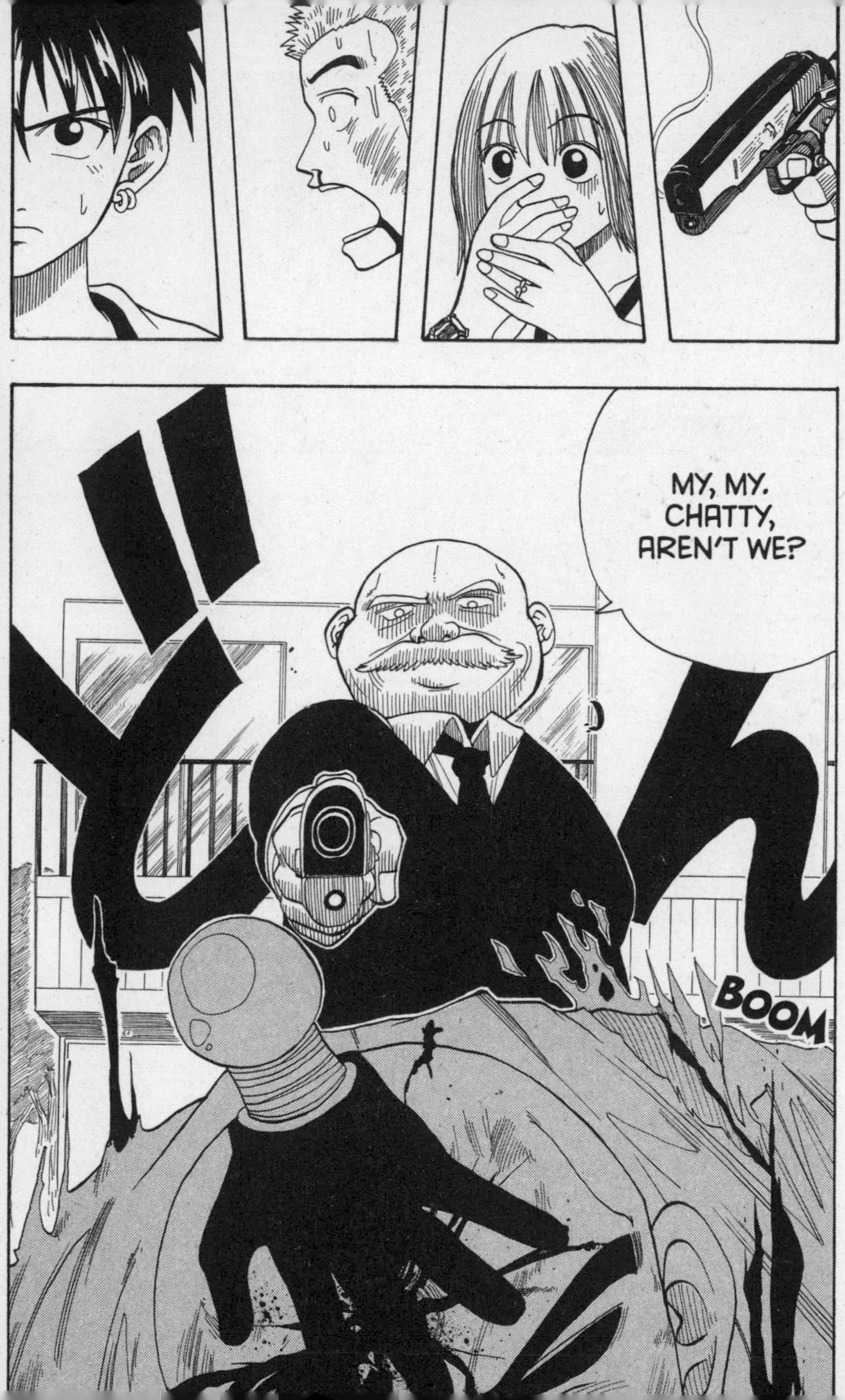
MY, MY. CHATTY, AREN'T WE?
BOOM

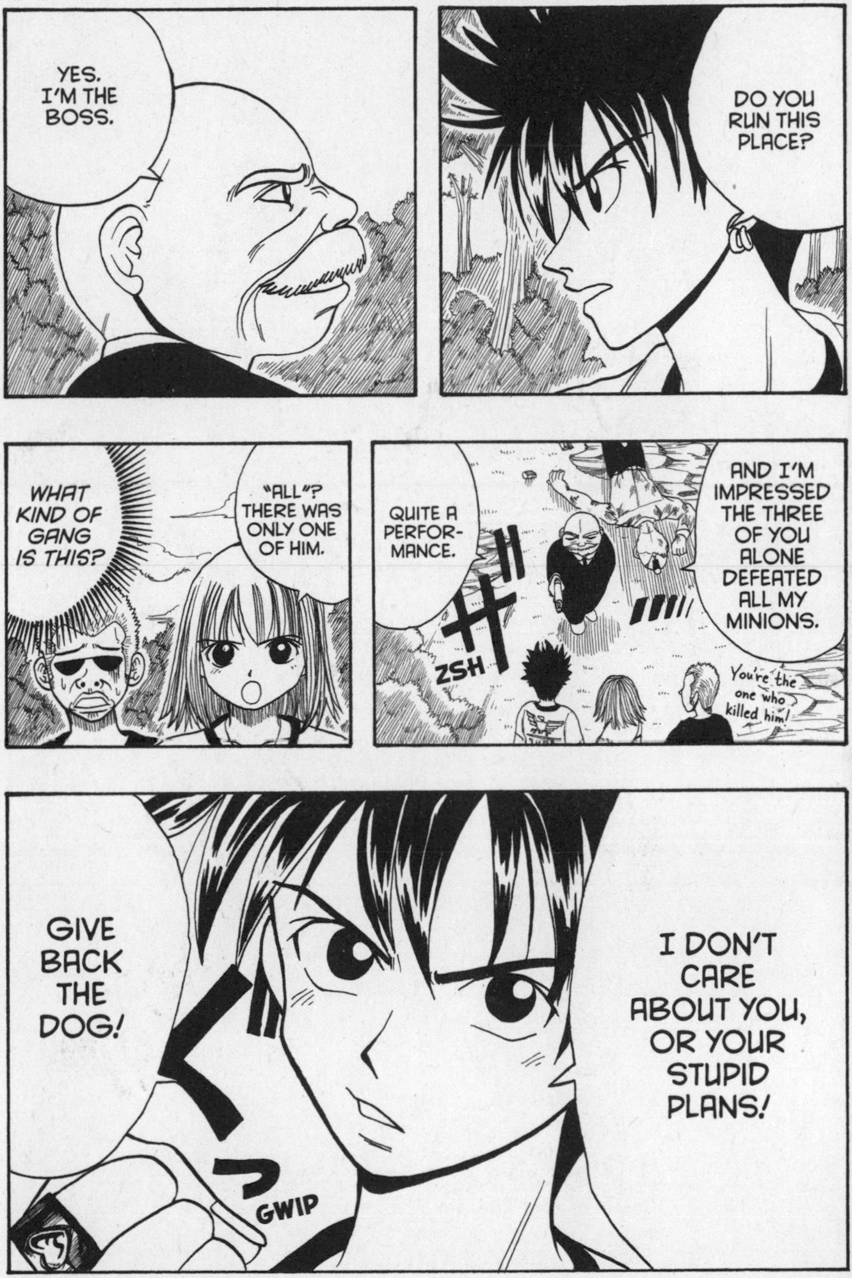
DO YOU RUN THIS PLACE?
YES. I'M THE BOSS.
AND I'M IMPRESSED THE THREE OF YOU ALONE DEFEATED ALL MY MINIONS.
QUITE A PERFORMANCE.
ZSH
You're the one who killed him!
"ALL"? THERE WAS ONLY ONE OF HIM.
WHAT KIND OF GANG IS THIS?
I DON'T CARE ABOUT YOU, OR YOUR STUPID PLANS!
GIVE BACK THE DOG!
GWIP

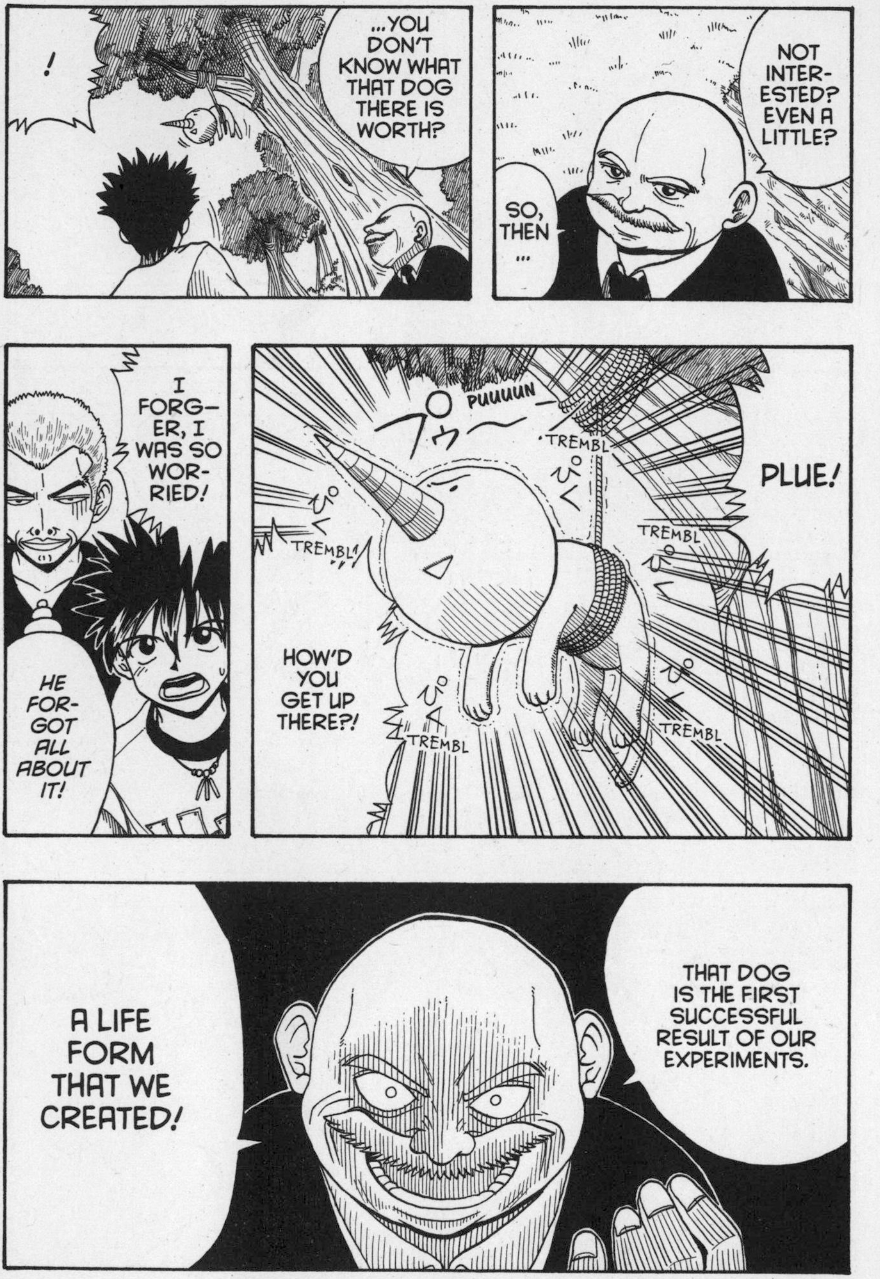
NOT INTERESTED? EVEN A LITTLE?
SO, THEN ...
...YOU DON'T KNOW WHAT THAT DOG THERE IS WORTH?
!
プゥ〜
PUUUUN
ぴく
TREMBL
PLUE!
ぴく
TREMBL
ぴく
TREMBL
ぴく
TREMBL
HOW'D YOU GET UP THERE?!
ぴく
TREMBL
I FORGER, I WAS SO WORRIED!
HE FORGOT ALL ABOUT IT!
THAT DOG IS THE FIRST SUCCESSFUL RESULT OF OUR EXPERIMENTS.
A LIFE FORM THAT WE CREATED!

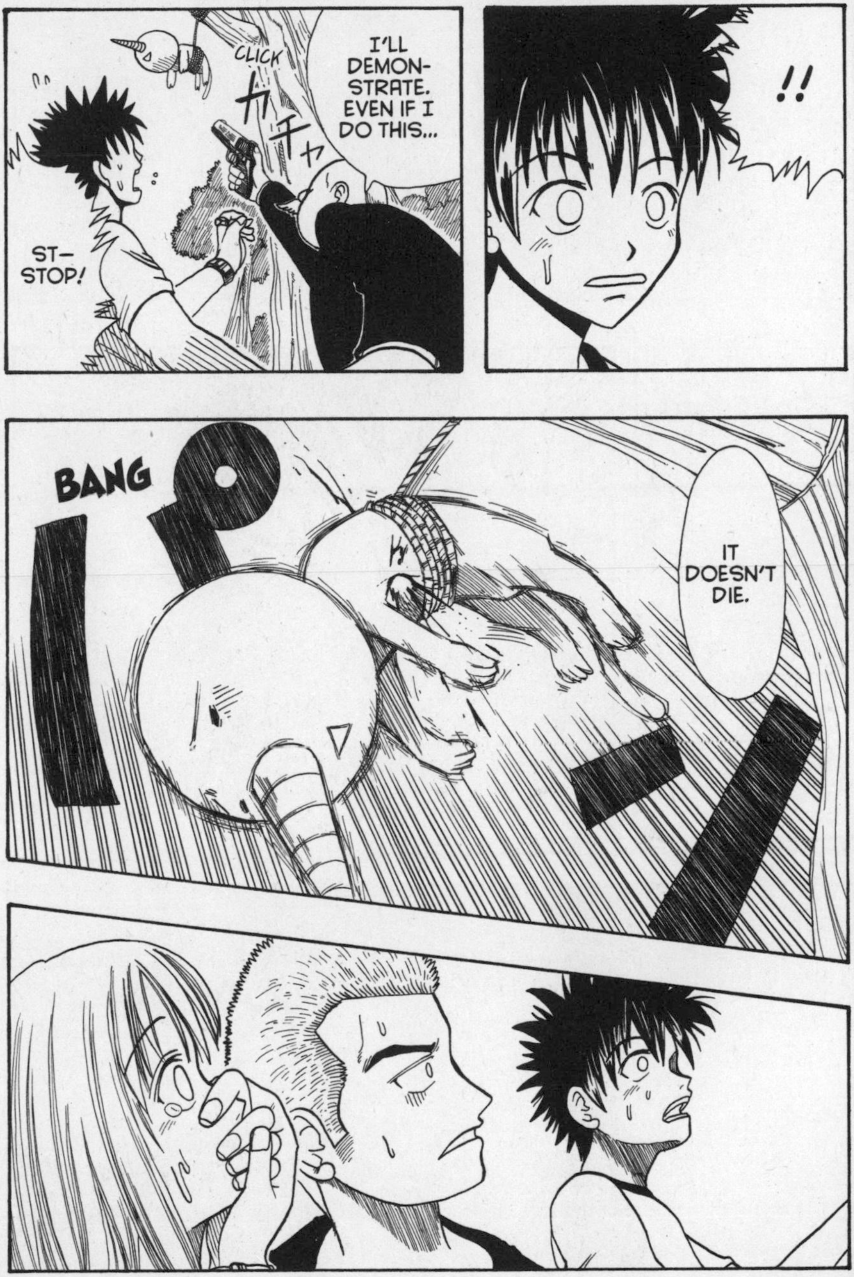
!!
I'LL DEMONSTRATE. EVEN IF I DO THIS...
CLICK
カチャ
ST— STOP!
IT DOESN'T DIE.
BANG

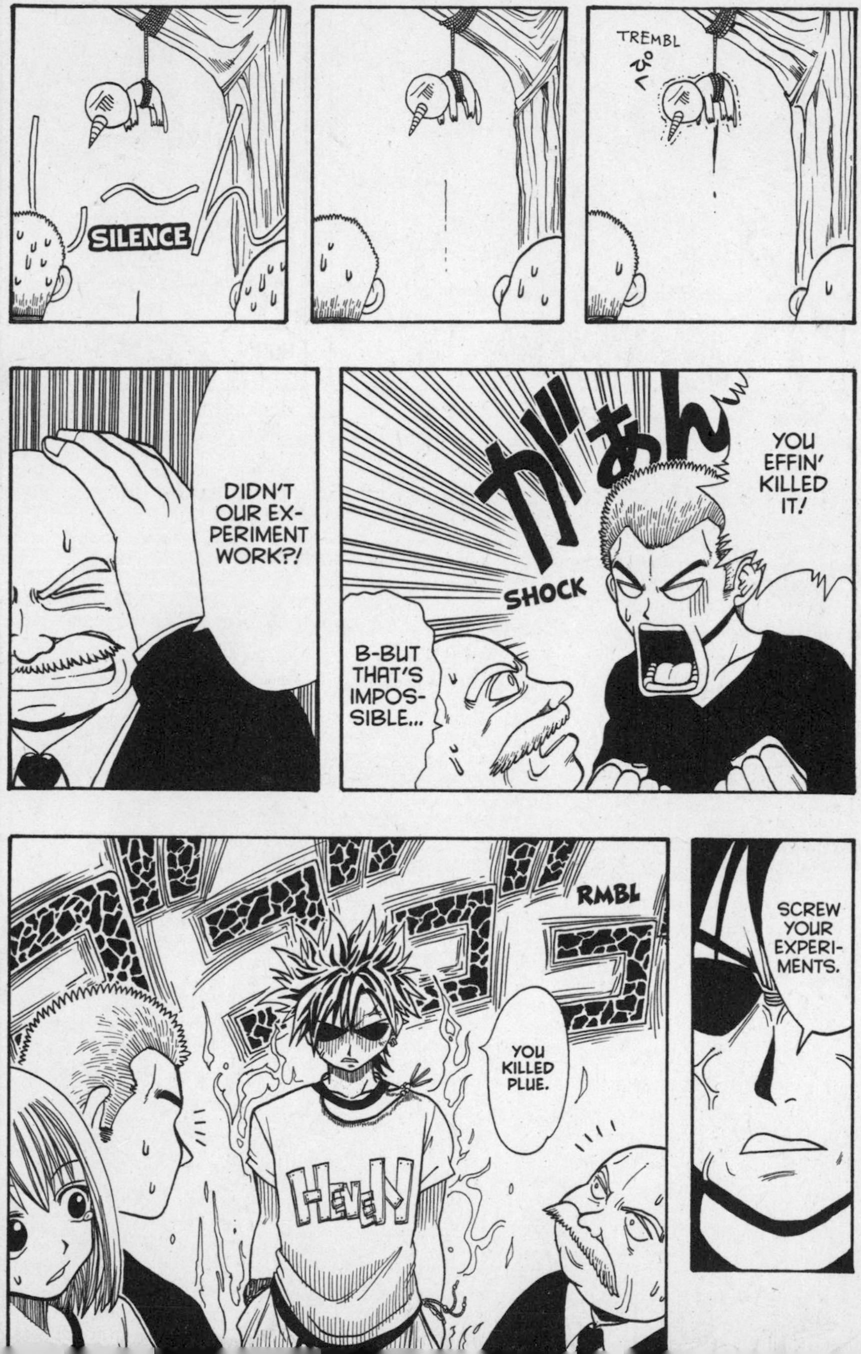
TREMBL
ぴく
SILENCE
があん
YOU EFFIN' KILLED IT!
SHOCK
B-BUT THAT'S IMPOSSIBLE...
DIDN'T OUR EXPERIMENT WORK?!
SCREW YOUR EXPERIMENTS.
RMBL
YOU KILLED PLUE.

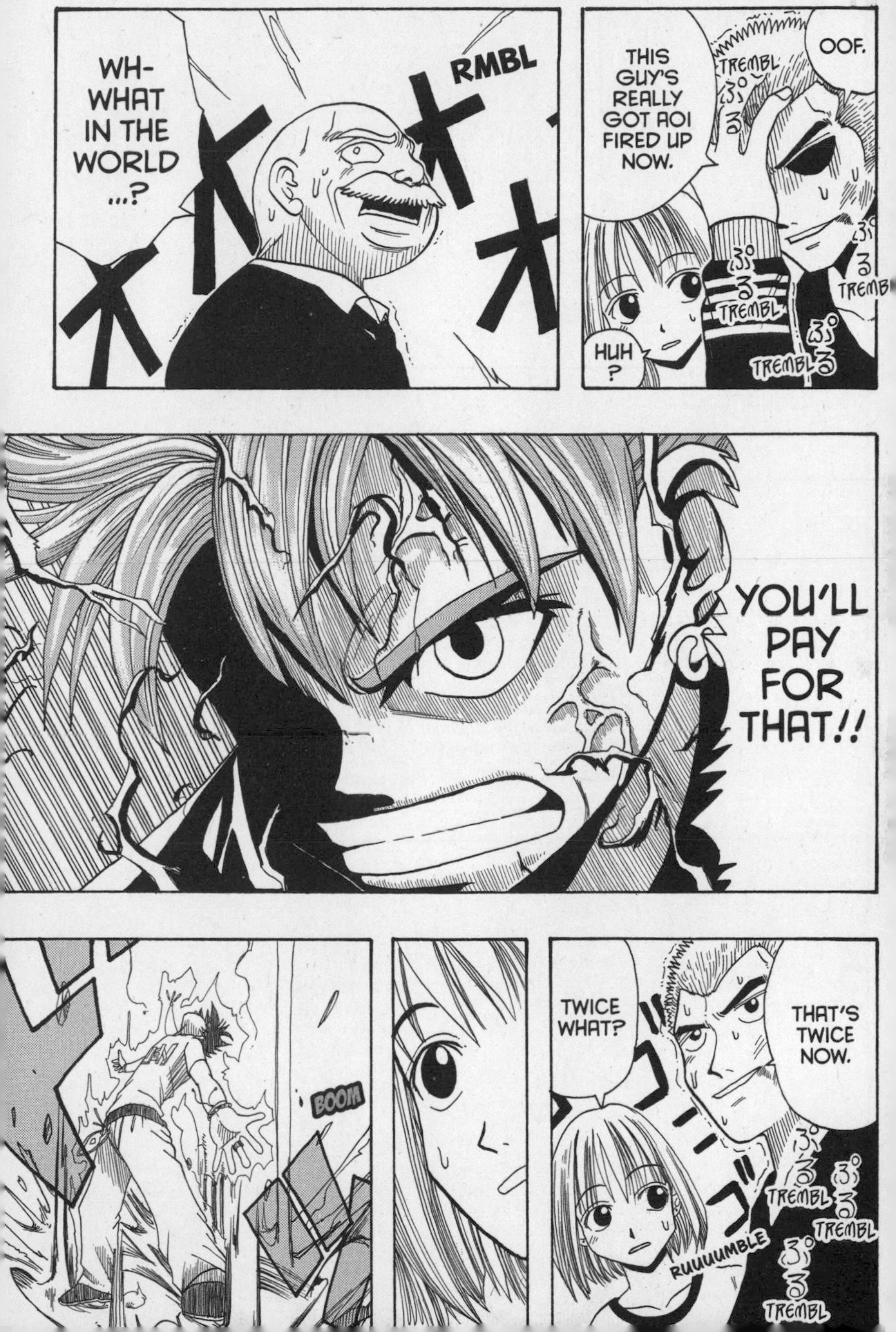
OOF.
THIS GUY'S REALLY GOT AOI FIRED UP NOW.
TREMBL ぷる
TREMBL ぷる
TREMBL ぷる
TREMBL ぷる
HUH?
RMBL
WH- WHAT IN THE WORLD ...?
YOU'LL PAY FOR THAT!!
THAT'S TWICE NOW.
TWICE WHAT?
TREMBL ぷる
TREMBL ぷる
TREMBL ぷる
RUUUUMBLE
BOOM

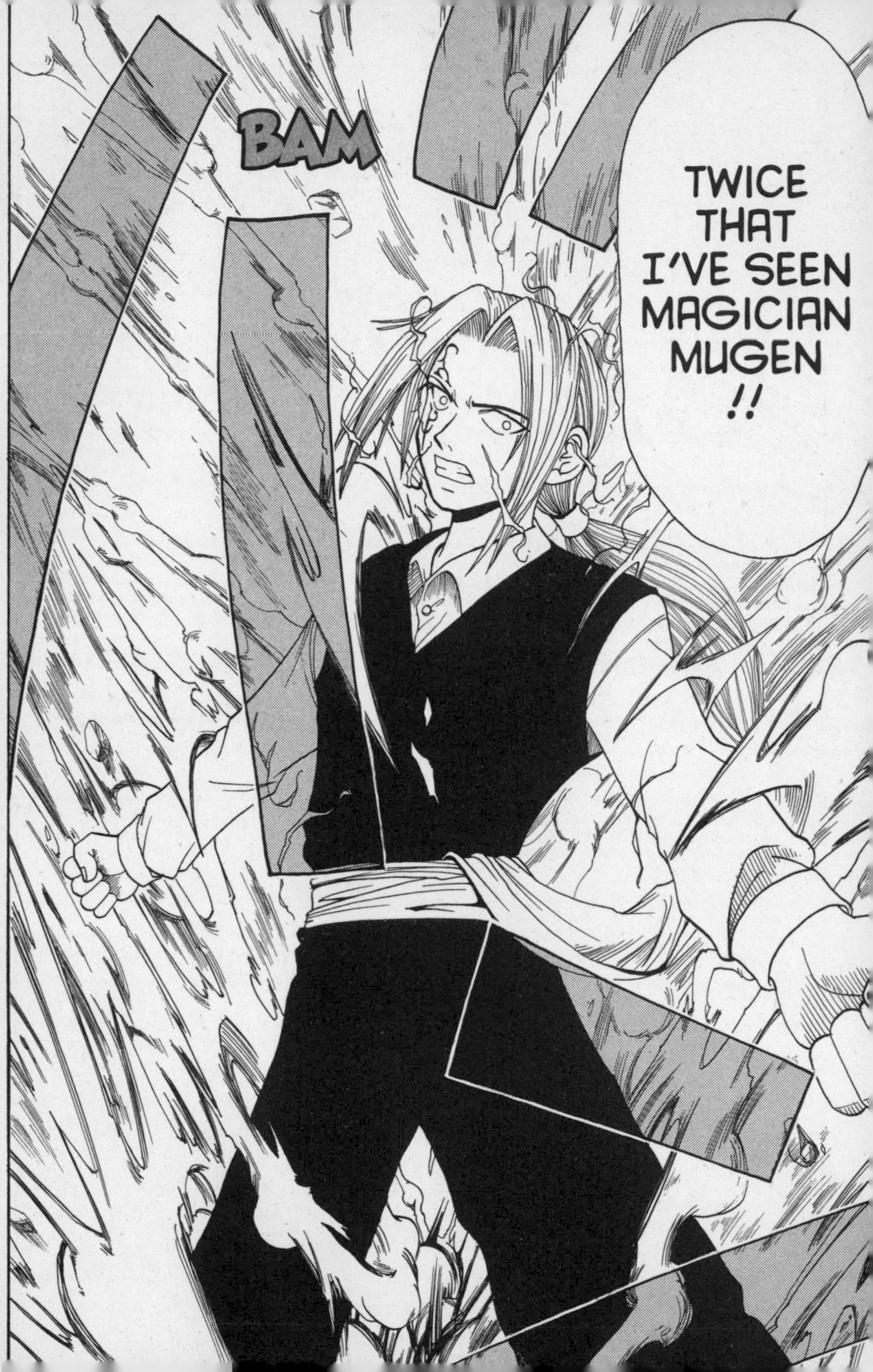
TWICE THAT I'VE SEEN MAGICIAN MUGEN !!
BAM

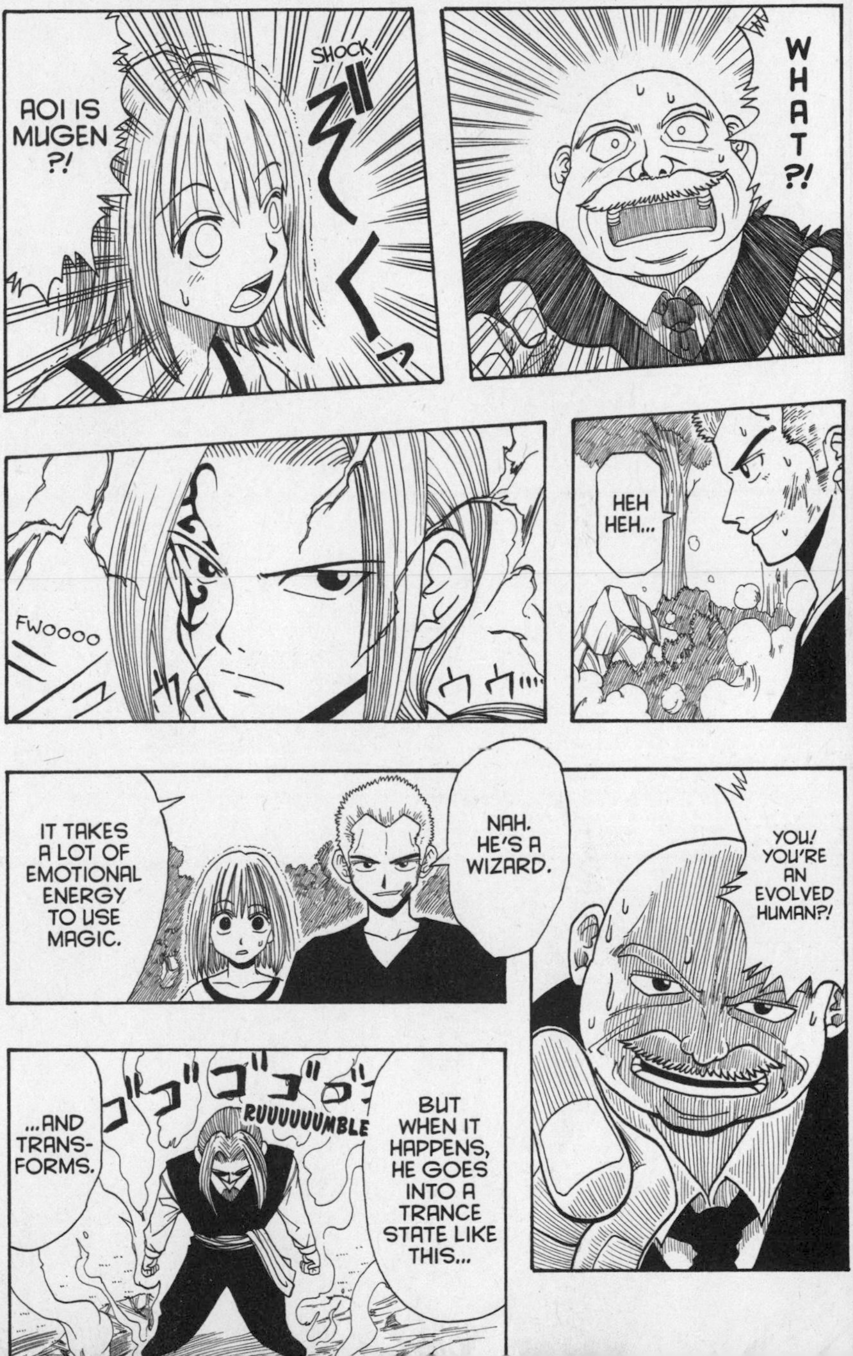
WHAT?!
AOI IS MUGEN?!
SHOCK
HEH HEH...
FWOOOO
YOU! YOU'RE AN EVOLVED HUMAN?!
NAH. HE'S A WIZARD.
IT TAKES A LOT OF EMOTIONAL ENERGY TO USE MAGIC.
BUT WHEN IT HAPPENS, HE GOES INTO A TRANCE STATE LIKE THIS...
RUUUUUUMBLE
...AND TRANS-FORMS.

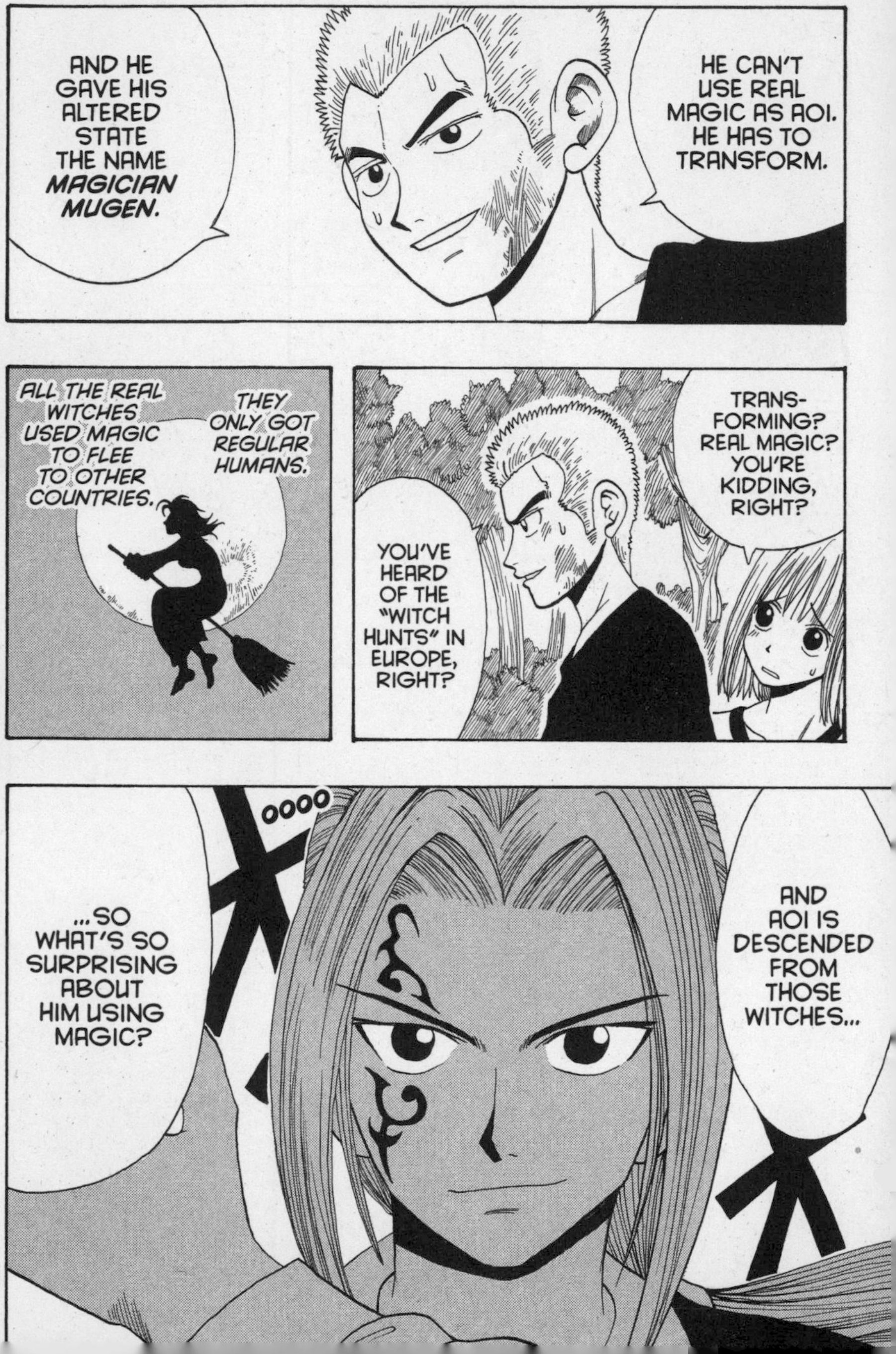
HE CAN'T USE REAL MAGIC AS AOI. HE HAS TO TRANSFORM.
AND HE GAVE HIS ALTERED STATE THE NAME *MAGICIAN MUGEN.*
TRANS-FORMING? REAL MAGIC? YOU'RE KIDDING, RIGHT?
YOU'VE HEARD OF THE "WITCH HUNTS" IN EUROPE, RIGHT?
THEY ONLY GOT REGULAR HUMANS.
ALL THE REAL WITCHES USED MAGIC TO FLEE TO OTHER COUNTRIES.
AND AOI IS DESCENDED FROM THOSE WITCHES...
OOOO
...SO WHAT'S SO SURPRISING ABOUT HIM USING MAGIC?

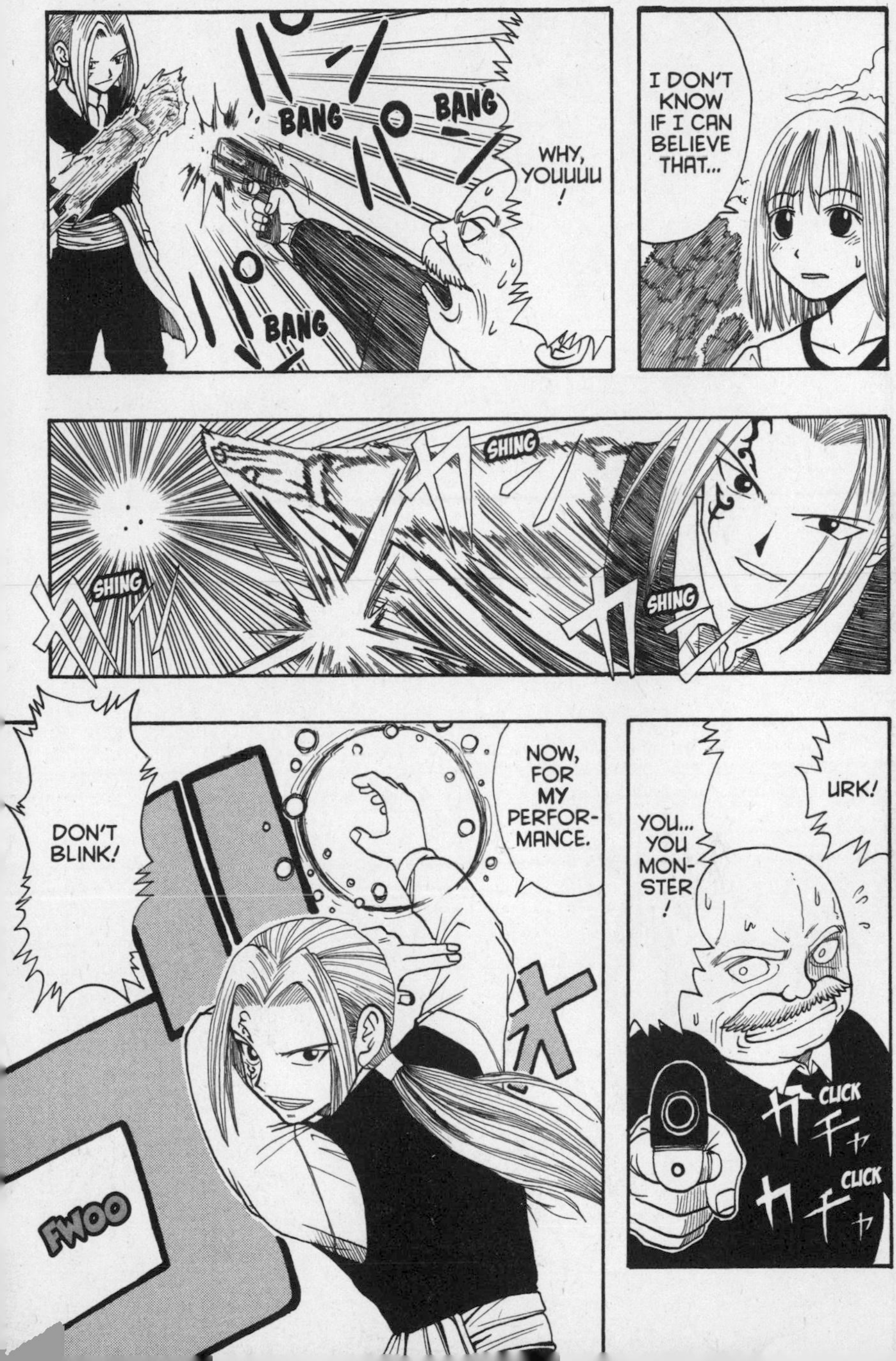

I DON'T KNOW IF I CAN BELIEVE THAT...
BANG
WHY, YOUUUU!
BANG
BANG
SHING
SHING
SHING
URK!
YOU... YOU MONSTER!
CLICK
CLICK
NOW, FOR MY PERFORMANCE.
DON'T BLINK!
FWOO

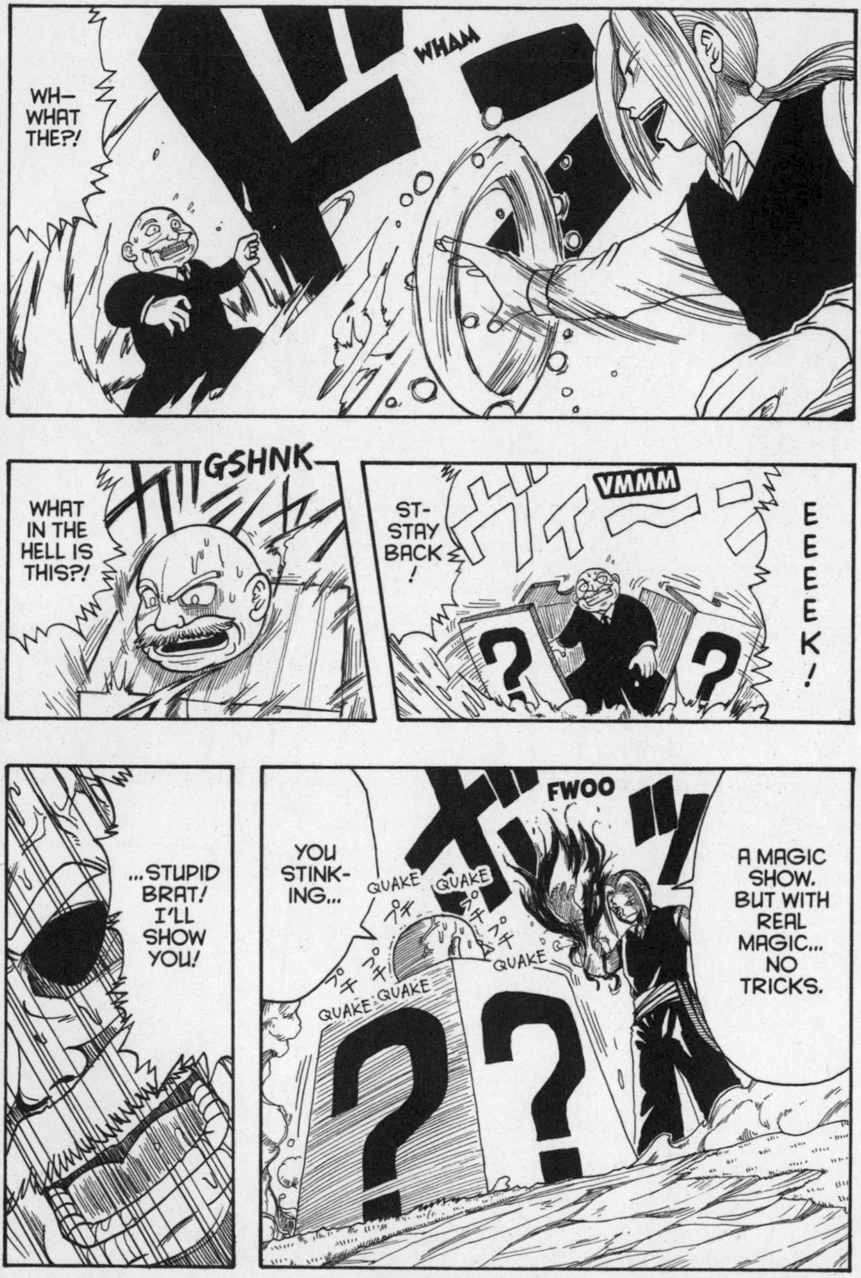

WHAM
WH— WHAT THE?!
VMMM
EEEEEK!
ST- STAY BACK!
GSHNK
WHAT IN THE HELL IS THIS?!
FWOO
A MAGIC SHOW. BUT WITH REAL MAGIC... NO TRICKS.
QUAKE
QUAKE
QUAKE
YOU STINKING...
QUAKE QUAKE
...STUPID BRAT! I'LL SHOW YOU!

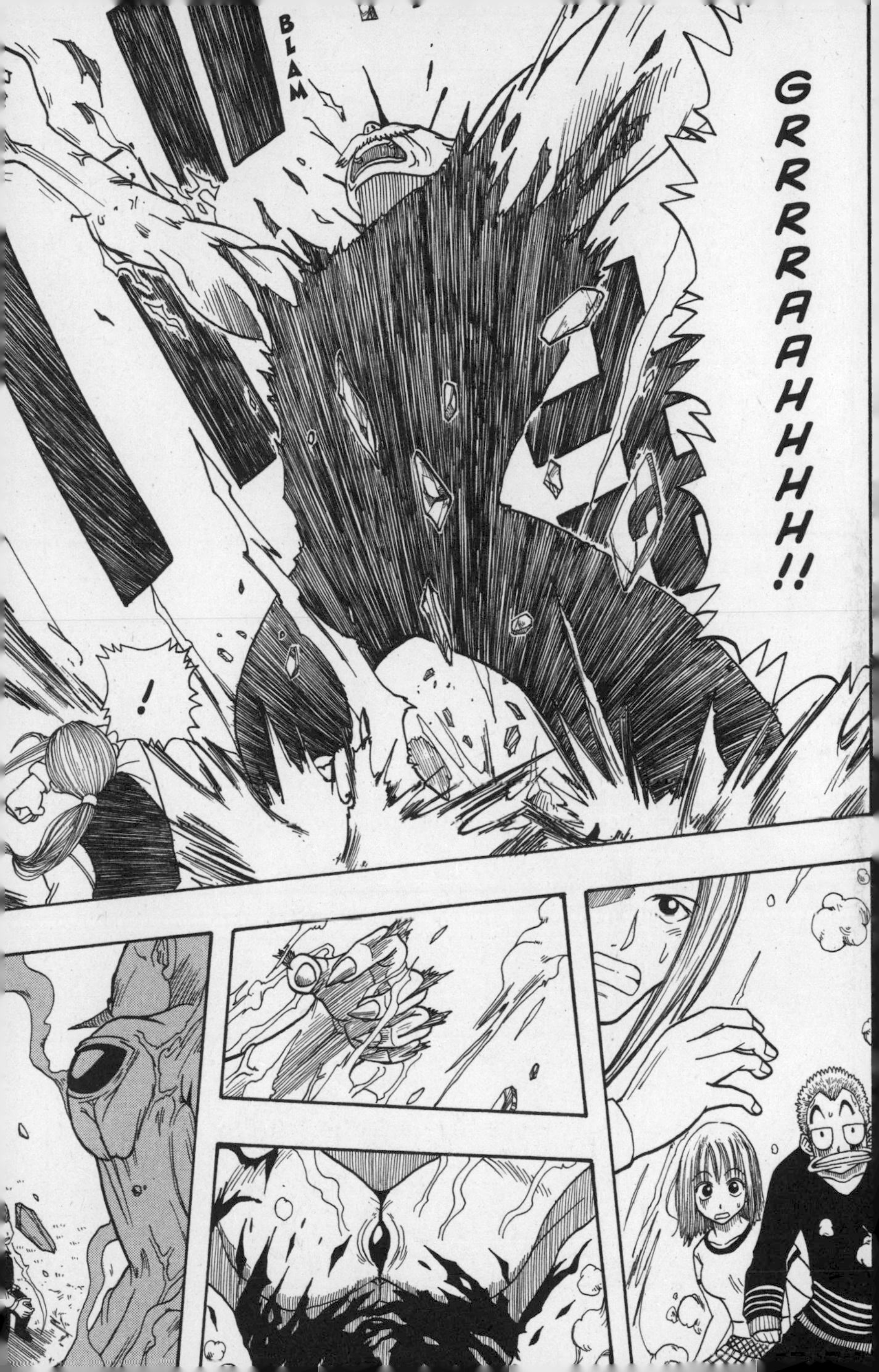
GRRRRAAHHHHH!!
BLAM
!

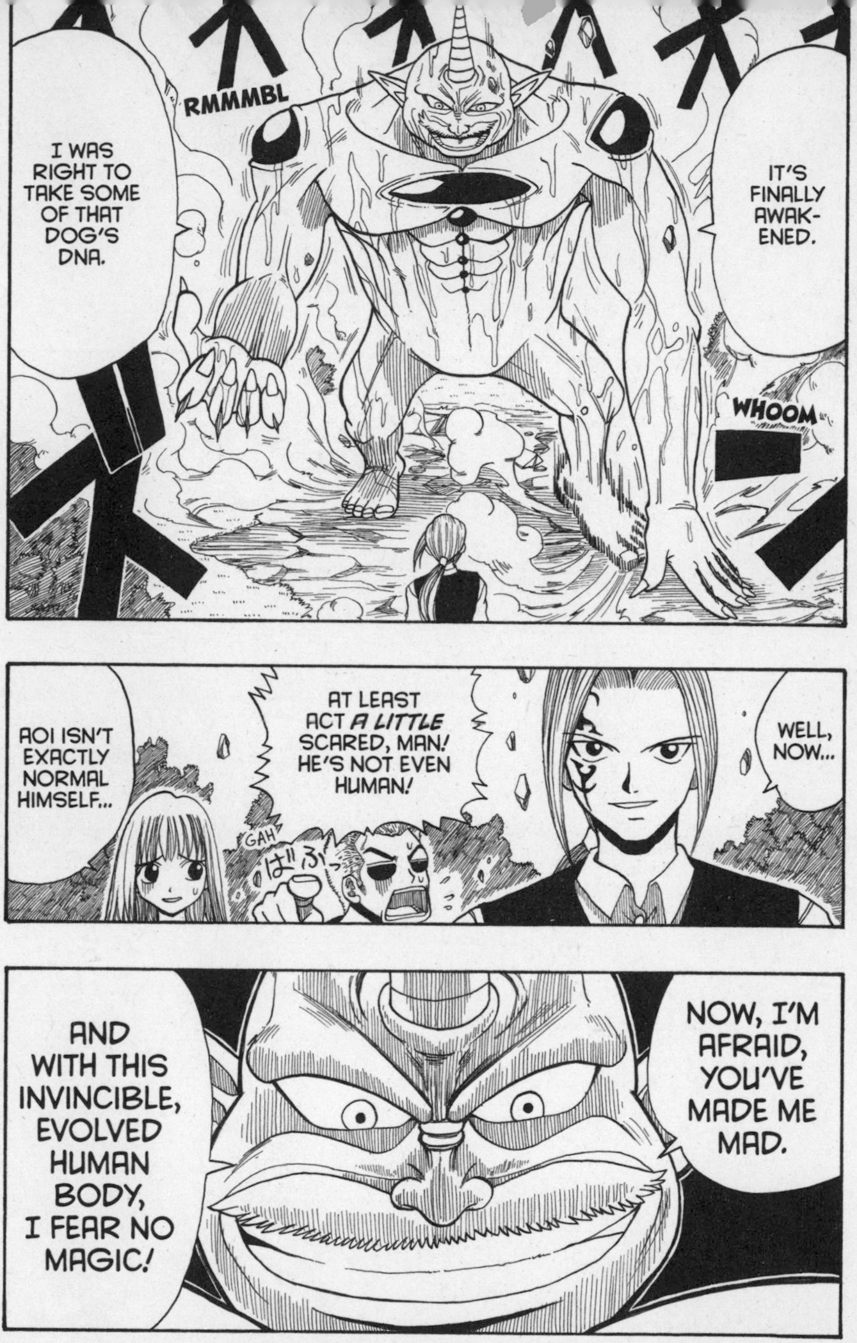

WHOOM
IT'S FINALLY AWAKENED.
RMMMBL
I WAS RIGHT TO TAKE SOME OF THAT DOG'S DNA.
WELL, NOW...
AT LEAST ACT *A LITTLE* SCARED, MAN! HE'S NOT EVEN HUMAN!
GAH
ばふっ
AOI ISN'T EXACTLY NORMAL HIMSELF...
NOW, I'M AFRAID, YOU'VE MADE ME MAD.
AND WITH THIS INVINCIBLE, EVOLVED HUMAN BODY, I FEAR NO MAGIC!

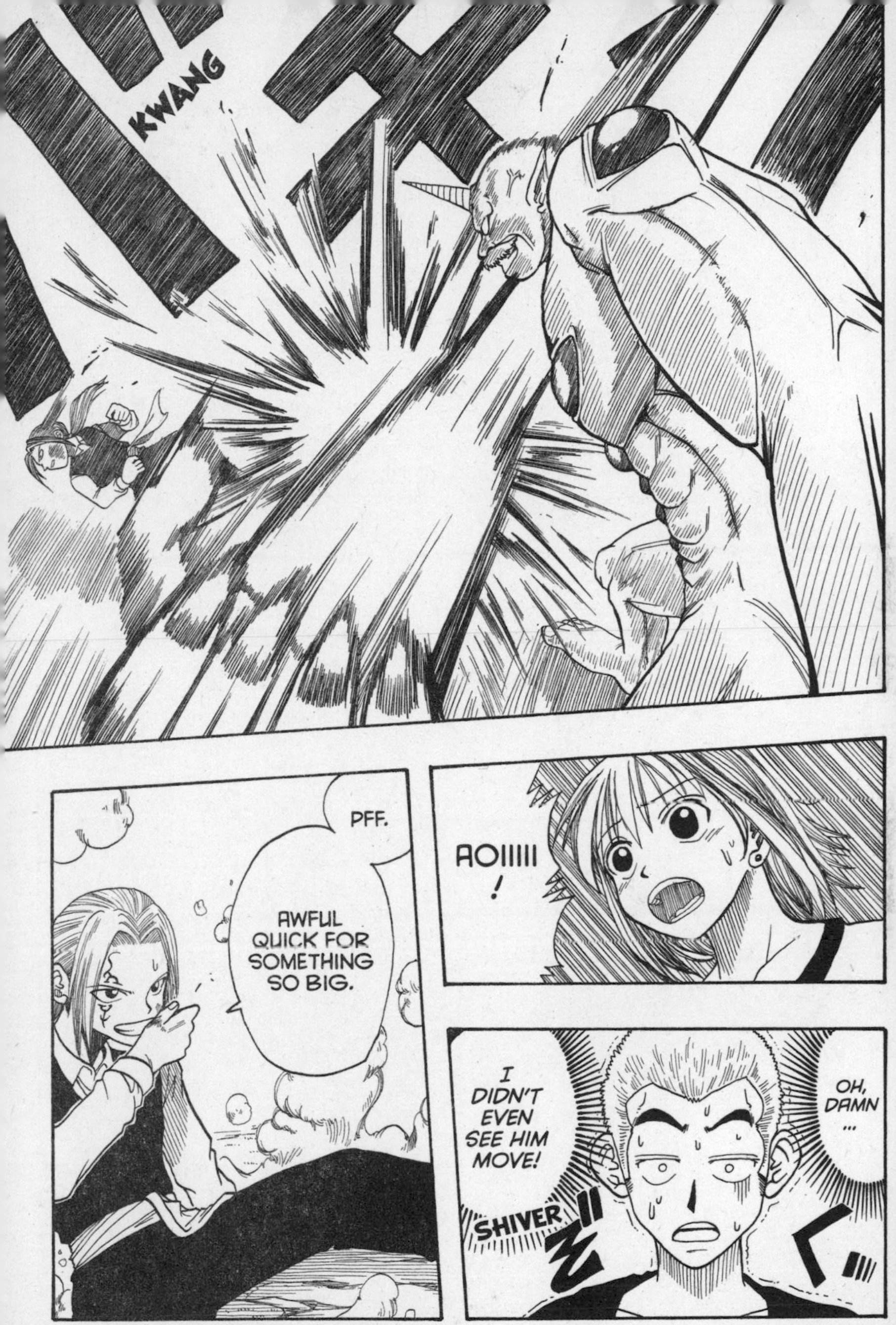
KWANG
AOIIIII !
OH, DAMN ...
I DIDN'T EVEN SEE HIM MOVE!
SHIVER
PFF.
AWFUL QUICK FOR SOMETHING SO BIG.

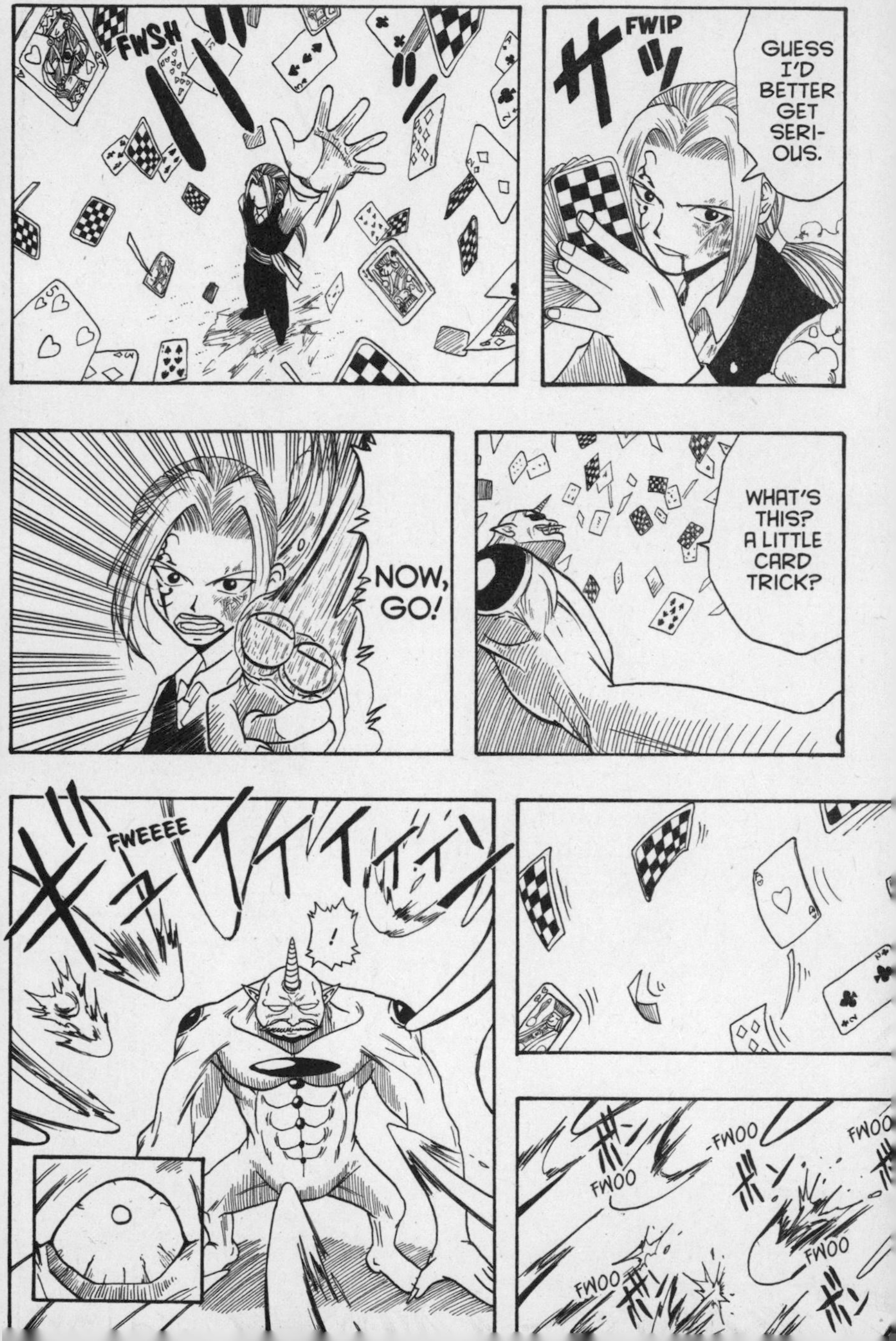
FWIP
GUESS I'D BETTER GET SERIOUS.
FWSH
WHAT'S THIS? A LITTLE CARD TRICK?
NOW, GO!
FWOO
-FWOO
FWOO
FWOO
FWOO
FWOO
FWEEEE
!

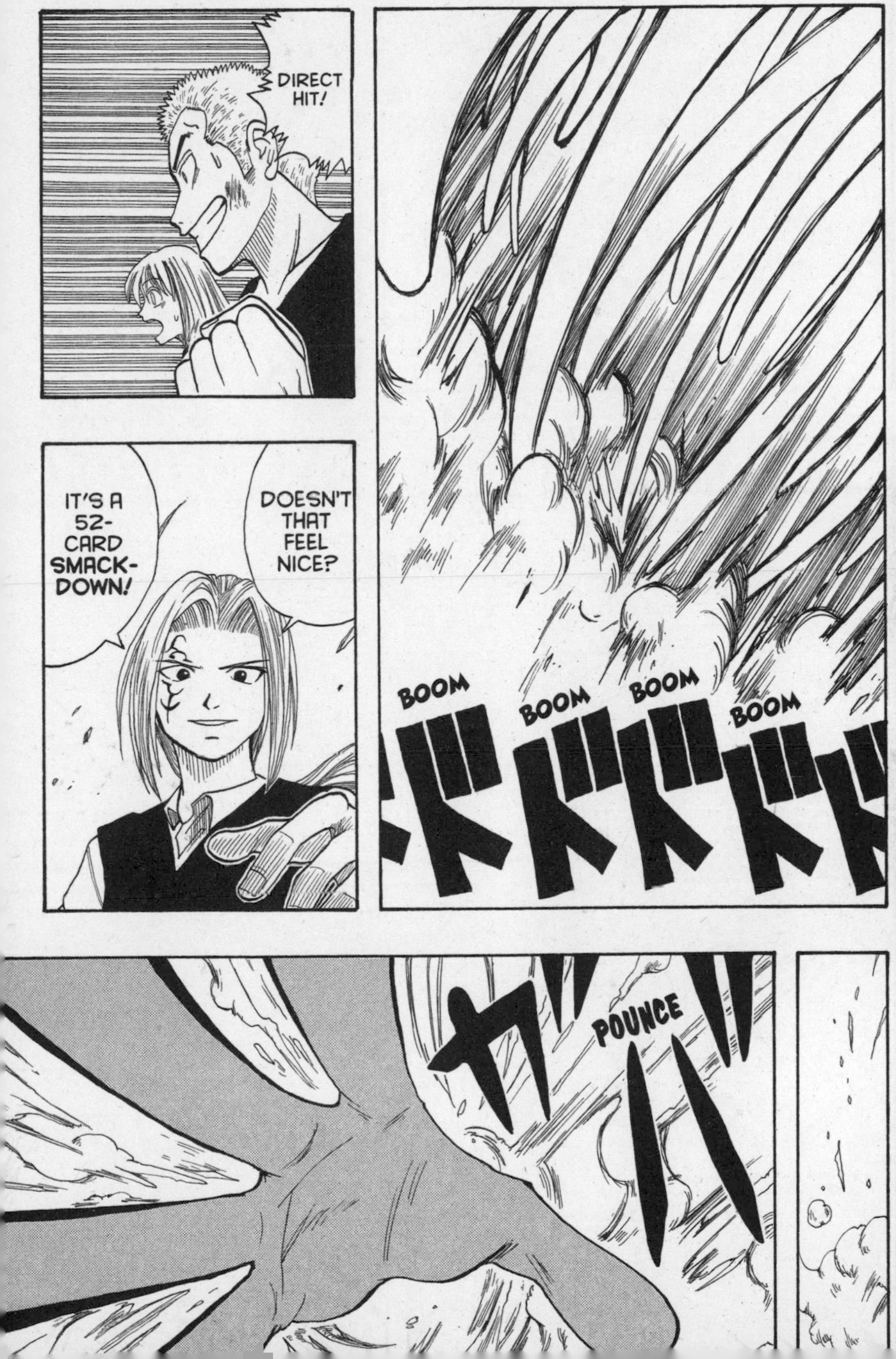
BOOM
BOOM
BOOM
BOOM
DIRECT HIT!
DOESN'T THAT FEEL NICE?
IT'S A 52-CARD SMACKDOWN!
POUNCE

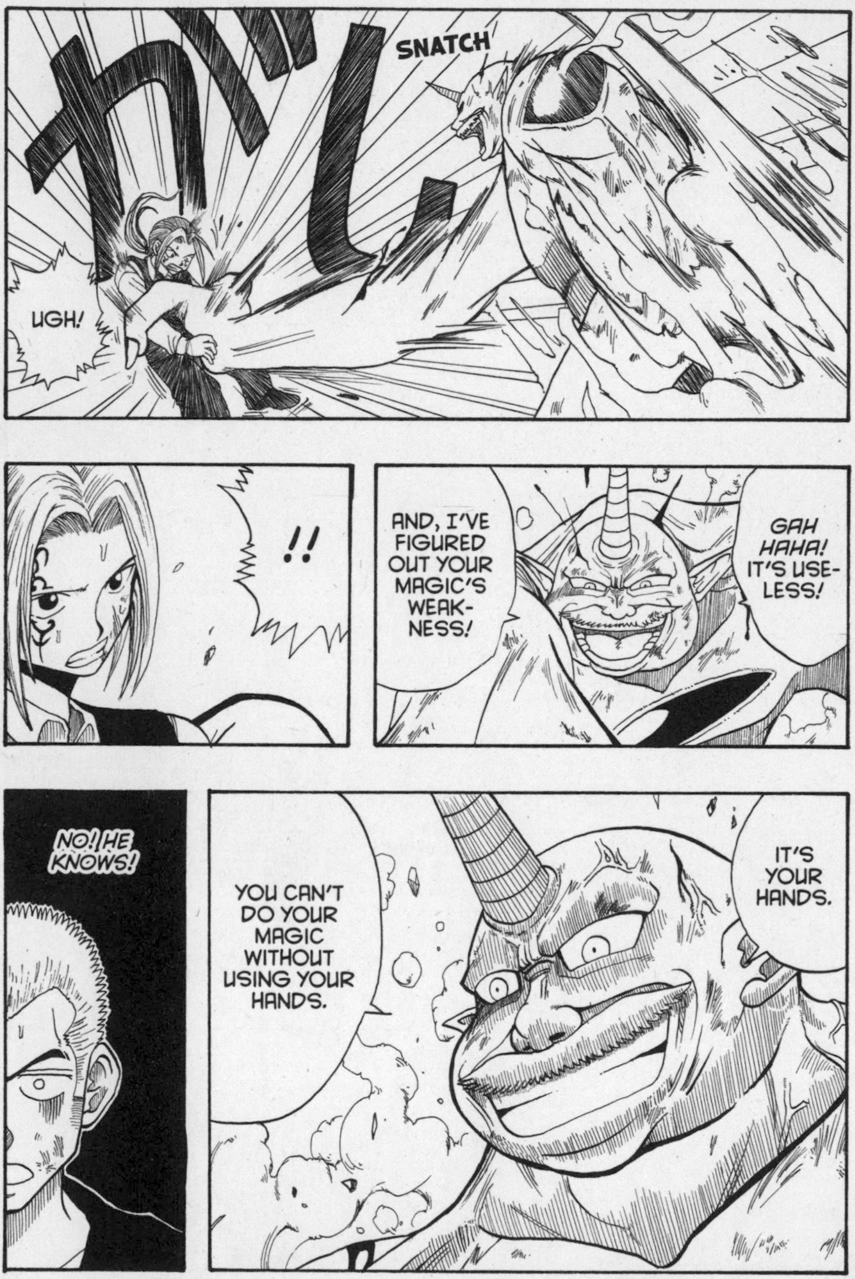
SNATCH
UGH!
GAH HAHA! IT'S USELESS!
AND, I'VE FIGURED OUT YOUR MAGIC'S WEAKNESS!
!!
IT'S YOUR HANDS.
YOU CAN'T DO YOUR MAGIC WITHOUT USING YOUR HANDS.
NO! HE KNOWS!

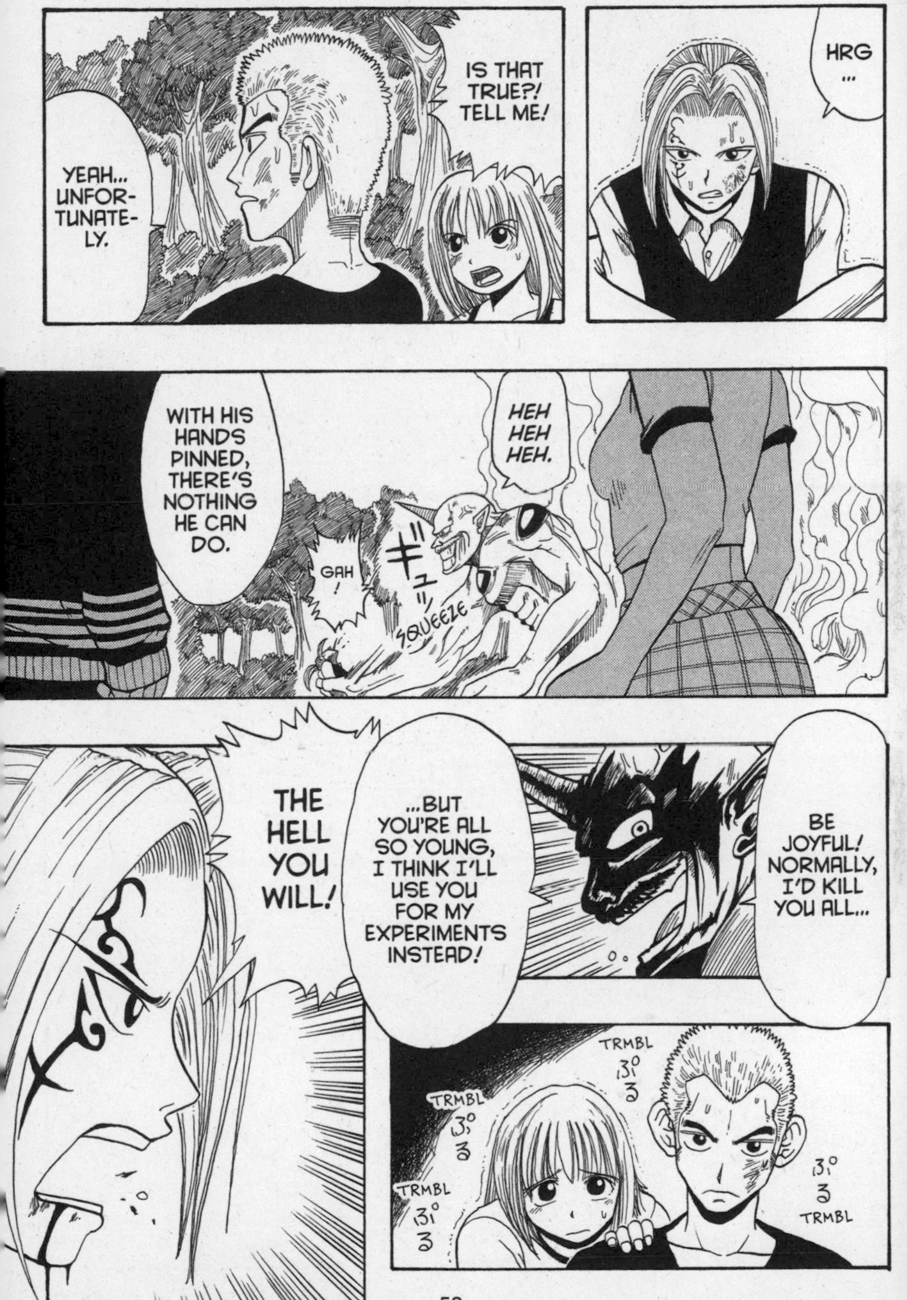
HRG ...
IS THAT TRUE?! TELL ME!
YEAH... UNFORTUNATELY.
HEH HEH HEH.
WITH HIS HANDS PINNED, THERE'S NOTHING HE CAN DO.
GAH!
ギュッ
SQUEEZE
BE JOYFUL! NORMALLY, I'D KILL YOU ALL...
...BUT YOU'RE ALL SO YOUNG, I THINK I'LL USE YOU FOR MY EXPERIMENTS INSTEAD!
ぶる TRMBL
ぶる TRMBL
ぶる TRMBL
ぶる TRMBL
THE HELL YOU WILL!

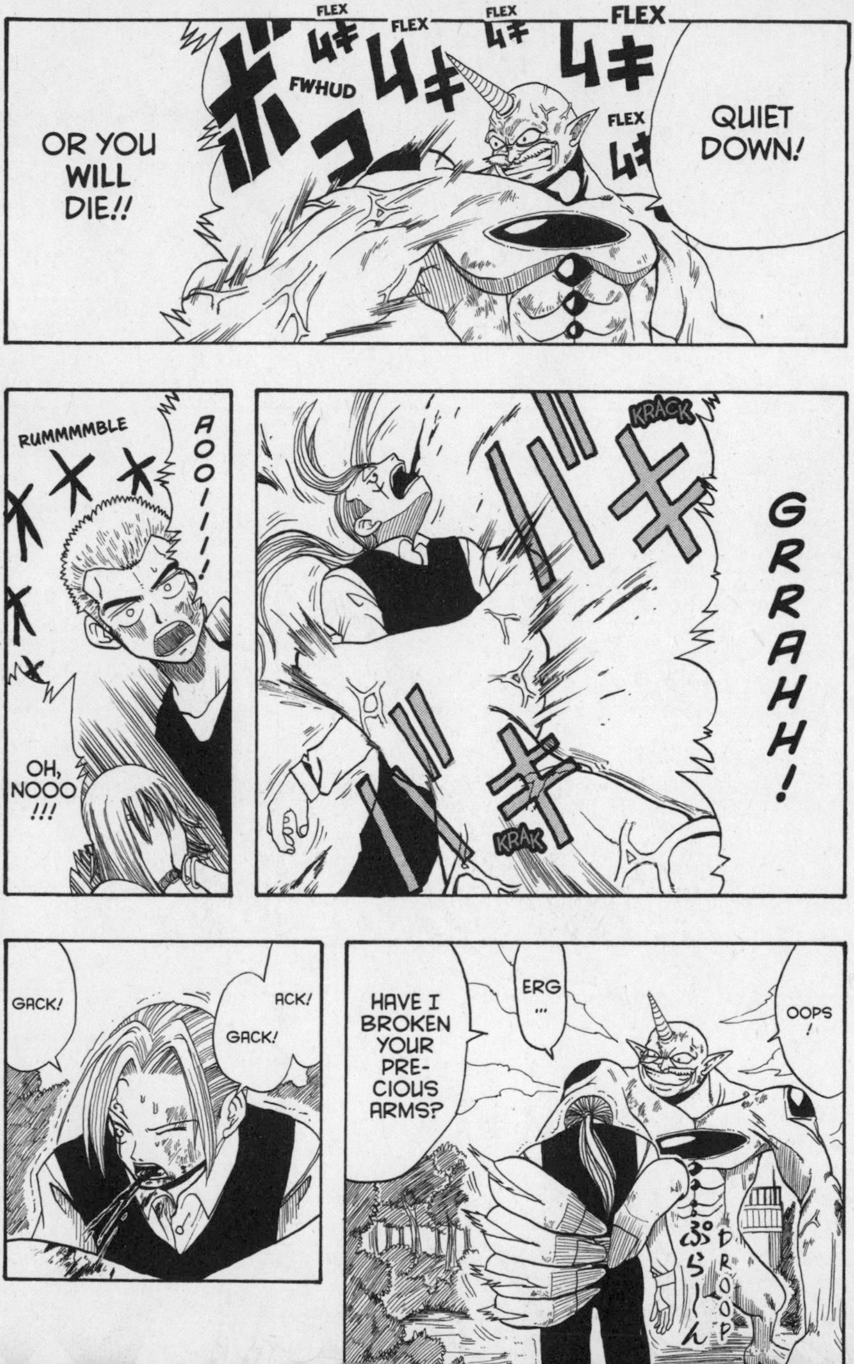
FLEX
QUIET DOWN!
FLEX
FLEX
FLEX
FLEX
FWHUD
OR YOU WILL DIE!!
KRACK
GRRAHH!
KRAK
AOO!!!!!
RUMMMMBLE
OH, NOOO!!!
OOPS!
ERG...
HAVE I BROKEN YOUR PRE-CIOUS ARMS?
DROOP
ACK!
GACK!
GACK!

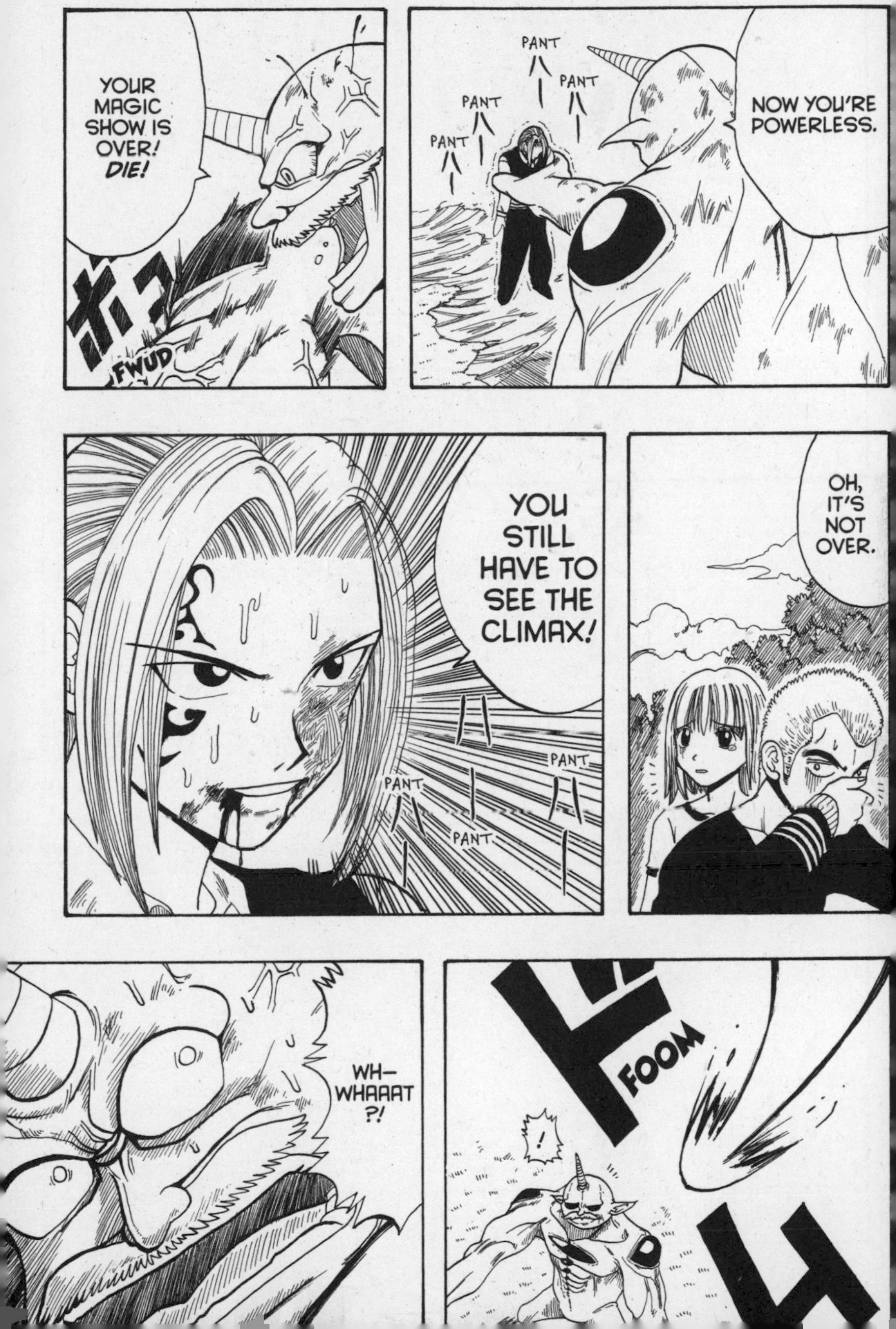
NOW YOU'RE POWERLESS.
PANT
PANT
PANT
PANT
YOUR MAGIC SHOW IS OVER! DIE!
FWUD
OH, IT'S NOT OVER.
YOU STILL HAVE TO SEE THE CLIMAX!
PANT
PANT
PANT
FOOM
!
WH-WHAAAT?!

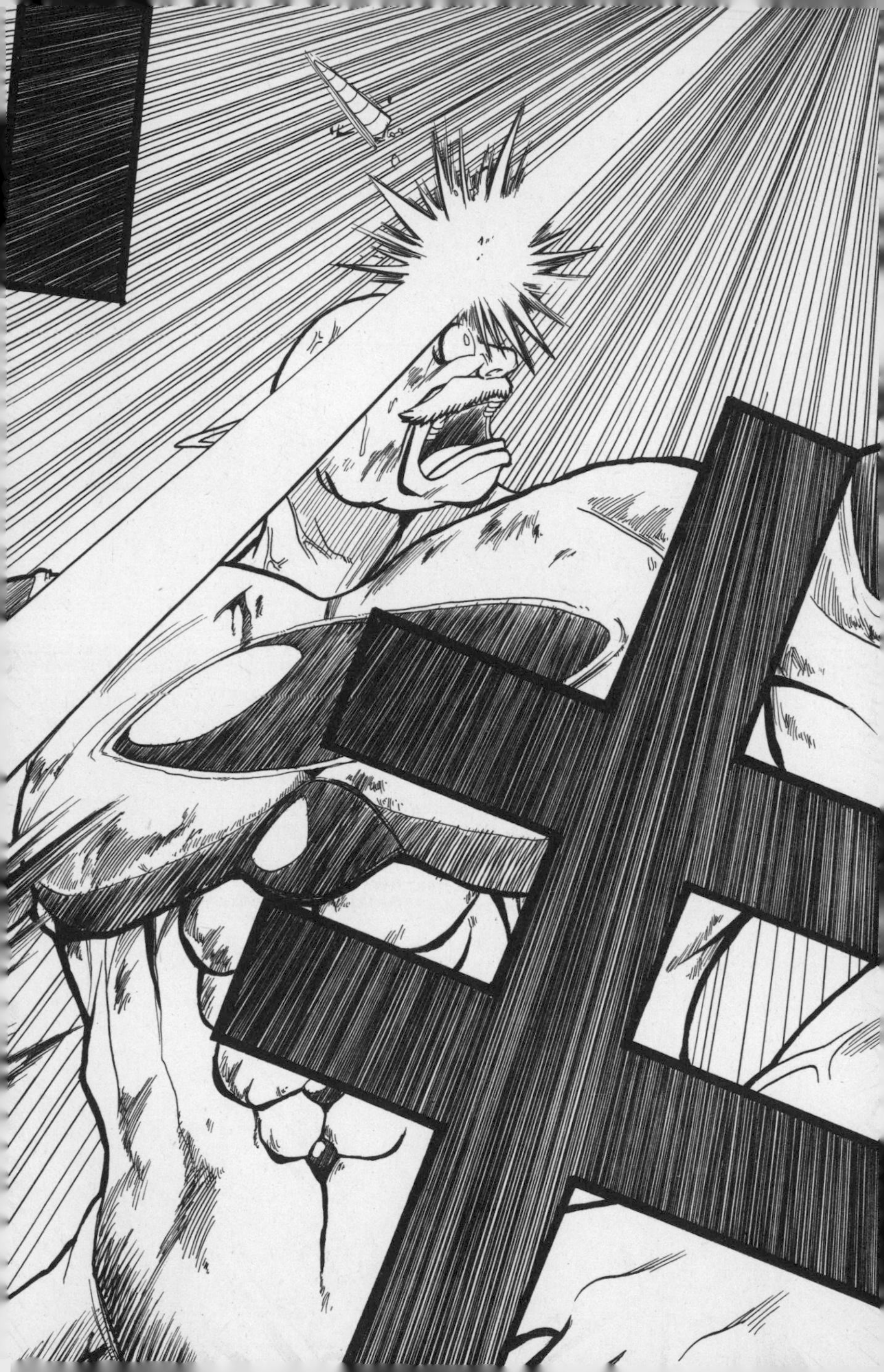

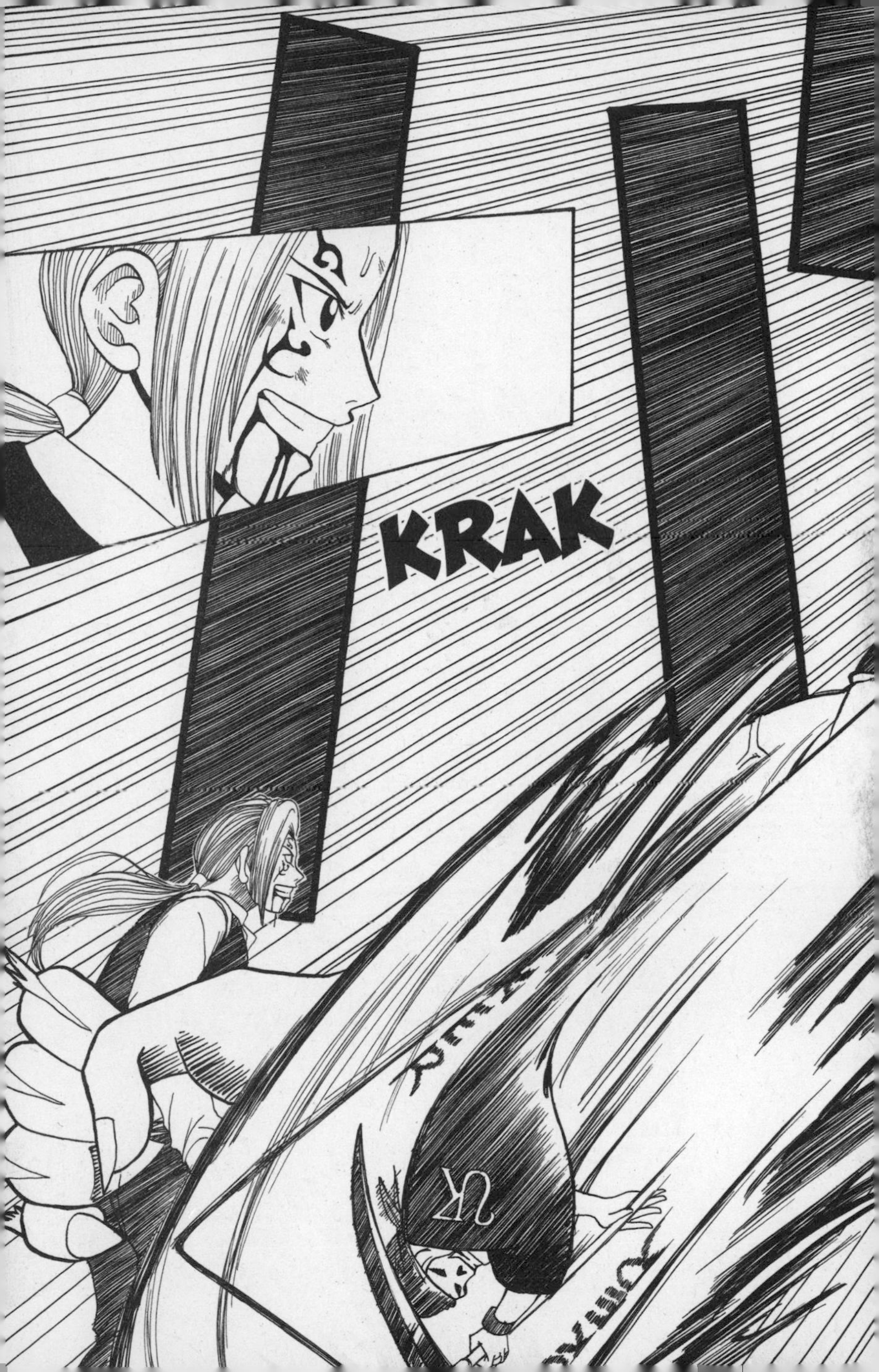
KRAK

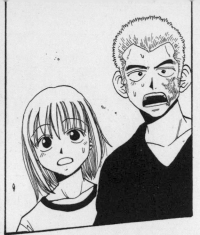

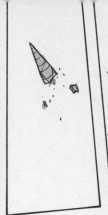

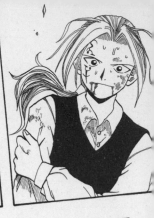

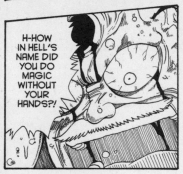

GRAAAAAHHH!
SPLURT ブチ
SPLURT ブチ
SPLURT ブチ
SPLURT ブチ
SPLURT ブチ
WHY?! HOW?!
H-HOW IN HELL'S NAME DID YOU DO MAGIC WITHOUT YOUR HANDS?!
A TRUMP DECK HAS FIFTY-THREE CARDS.
DOESN'T THAT FEEL NICE?
IT'S A 52-CARD SMACK-DOWN!
GET IT? I PUT ONE CARD ON A TIME DELAY.

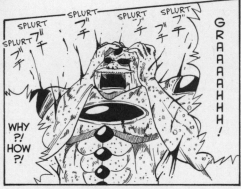

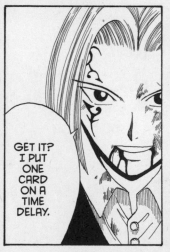

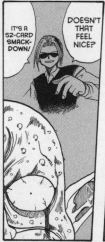

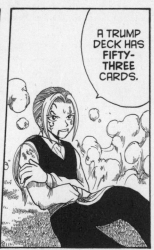

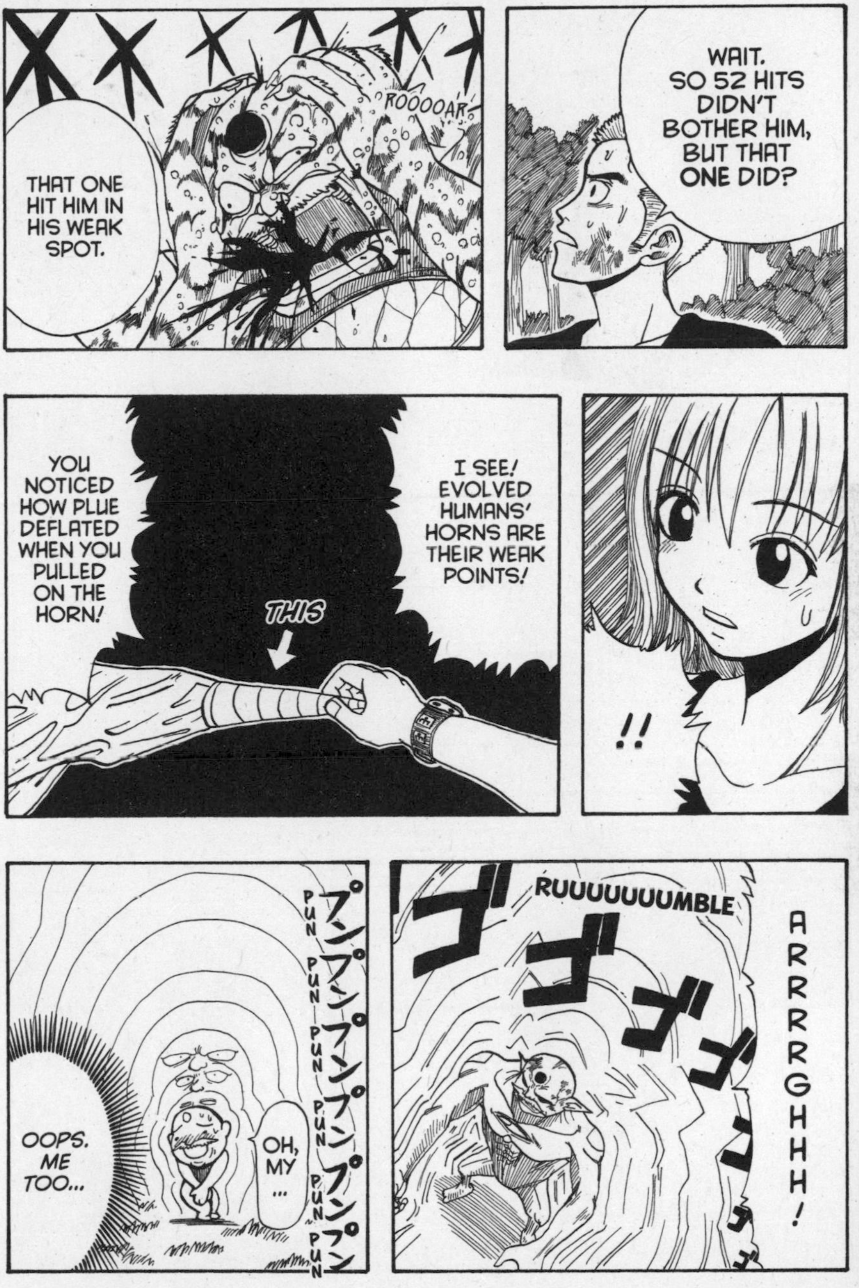
WAIT. SO 52 HITS DIDN'T BOTHER HIM, BUT THAT ONE DID?
ROOOOAR
THAT ONE HIT HIM IN HIS WEAK SPOT.
!!
I SEE! EVOLVED HUMANS' HORNS ARE THEIR WEAK POINTS!
YOU NOTICED HOW PLUE DEFLATED WHEN YOU PULLED ON THE HORN!
THIS
RUUUUUUUMBLE
ARRRRGHHH!
PUN PUN PUN PUN PUN PUN
OH, MY ...
OOPS. ME TOO...

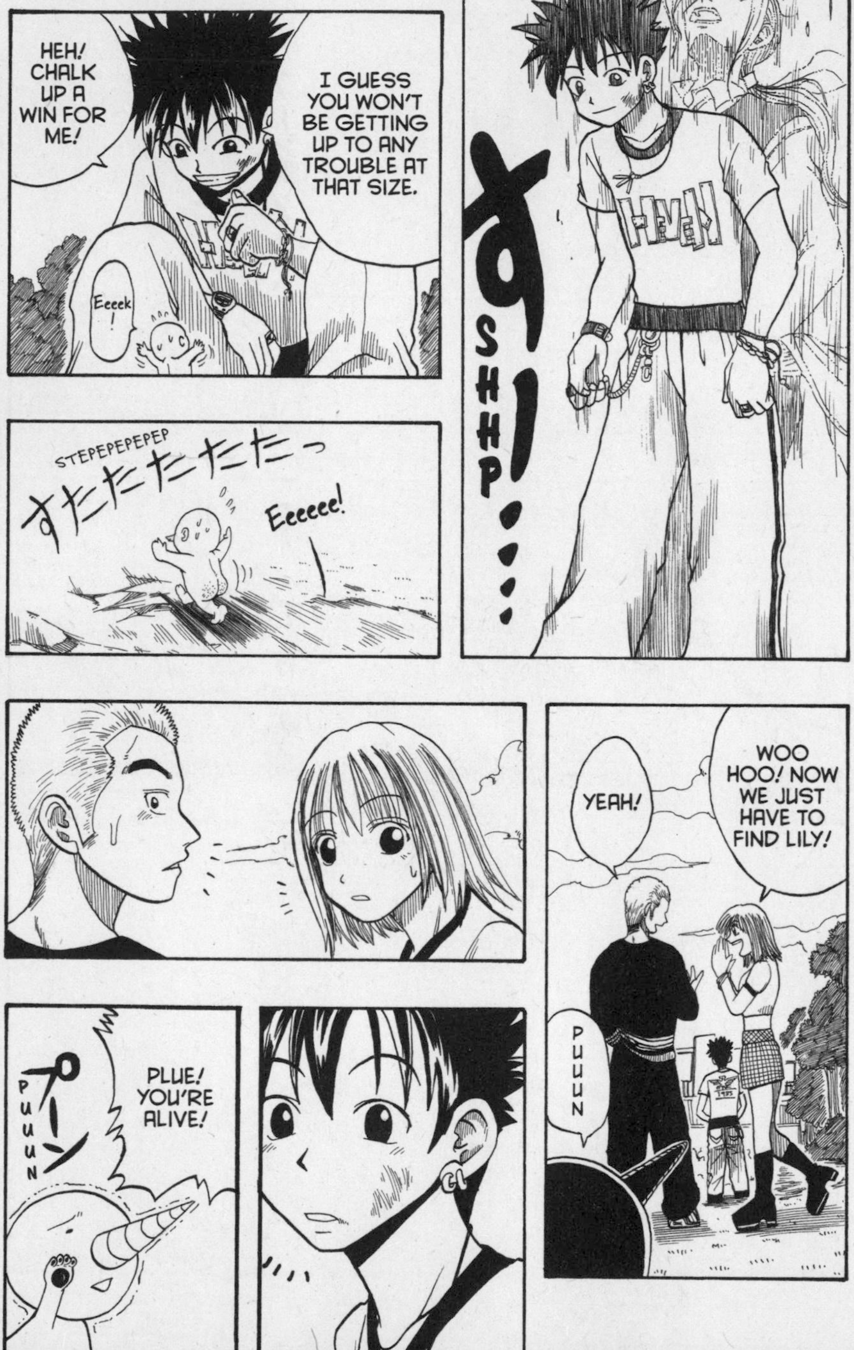
すっ
SHHP...
I GUESS YOU WON'T BE GETTING UP TO ANY TROUBLE AT THAT SIZE.
HEH! CHALK UP A WIN FOR ME!
Eeeek!
すたたたたたっ
STEPEPEPEPEP
Eeeeee!
WOO HOO! NOW WE JUST HAVE TO FIND LILY!
YEAH!
PUUUN
PLUE! YOU'RE ALIVE!
プーン
PUUUN

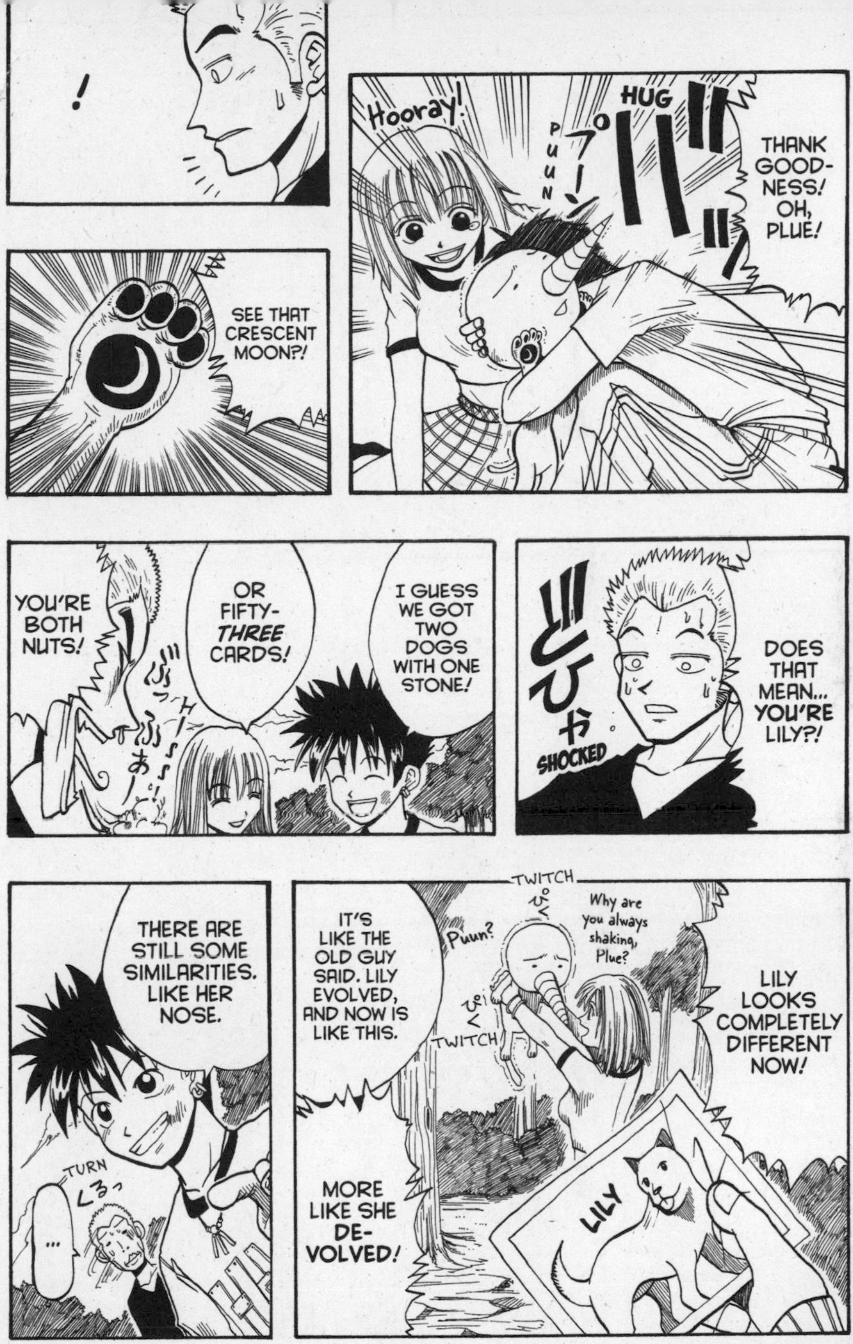

THANK GOODNESS! OH, PLUE!
HUG
PUUN
Hooray!
!
SEE THAT CRESCENT MOON?!
DOES THAT MEAN... YOU'RE LILY?!
SHOCKED
I GUESS WE GOT TWO DOGS WITH ONE STONE!
OR FIFTY-THREE CARDS!
YOU'RE BOTH NUTS!
LILY LOOKS COMPLETELY DIFFERENT NOW!
TWITCH
Why are you always shaking, Plue?
Puun?
IT'S LIKE THE OLD GUY SAID. LILY EVOLVED, AND NOW IS LIKE THIS.
TWITCH
LILY
MORE LIKE SHE DE-VOLVED!
THERE ARE STILL SOME SIMILARITIES. LIKE HER NOSE.
TURN
...

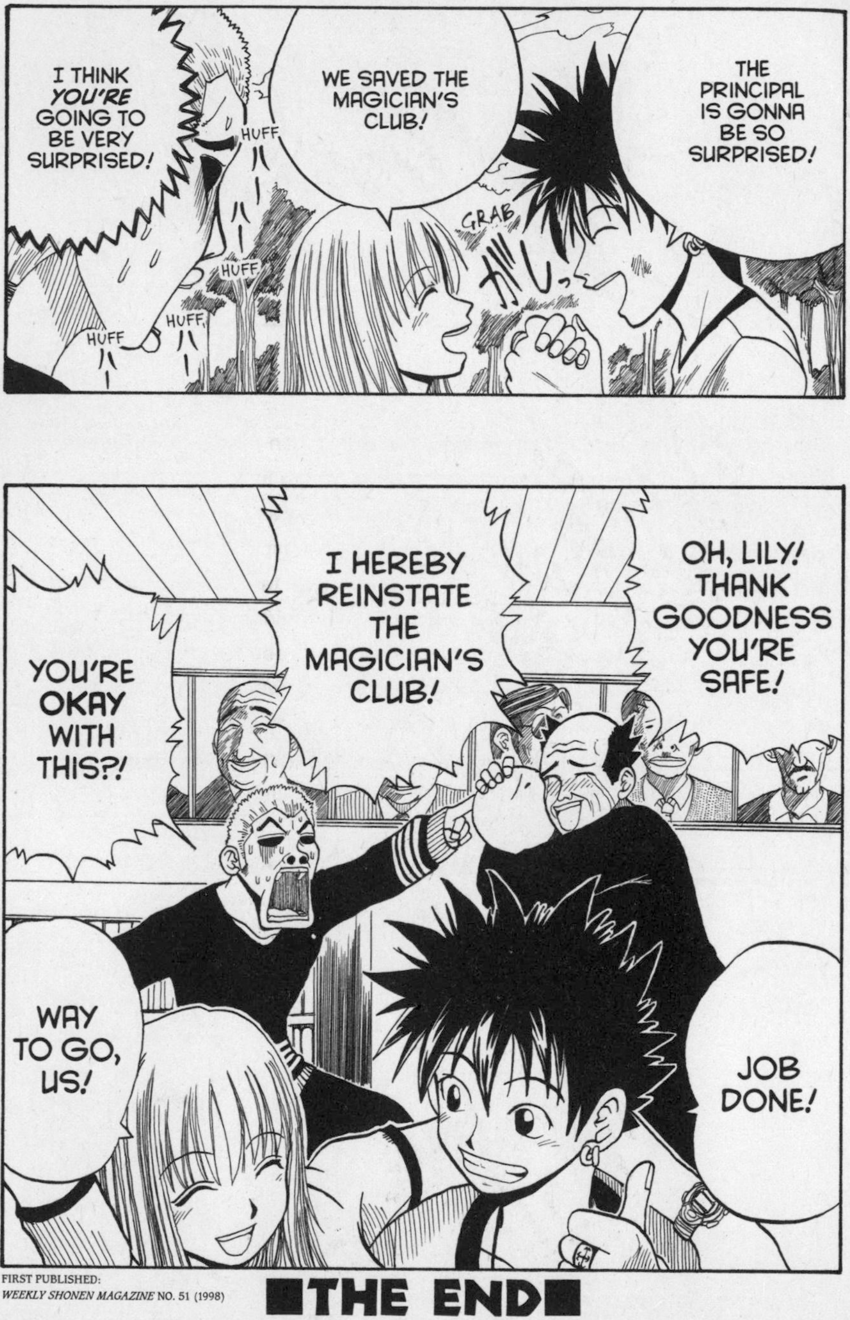

THE PRINCIPAL IS GONNA BE SO SURPRISED!
GRAB
WE SAVED THE MAGICIAN'S CLUB!
I THINK *YOU'RE* GOING TO BE VERY SURPRISED!
HUFF
HUFF
HUFF
HUFF
OH, LILY! THANK GOODNESS YOU'RE SAFE!
I HEREBY REINSTATE THE MAGICIAN'S CLUB!
YOU'RE OKAY WITH THIS?!
JOB DONE!
WAY TO GO, US!

FIRST PUBLISHED:
WEEKLY SHONEN MAGAZINE NO. 51 (1998)

THE END

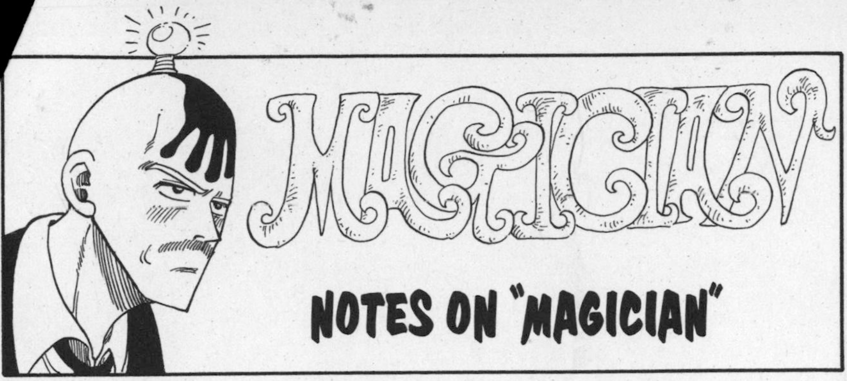
MAGICIAN

NOTES ON "MAGICIAN"

Wooh! This is the piece that won me *Weekly Shonen Magazine's* Rookie Prize. May it be remembered as the day Plue came into the world (and I debuted in an actual magazine). Oooh! How embarrassing! At the time I drew this, I was in Tokyo working part-time at an arcade. The job didn't exactly keep me busy, so any time the boss wasn't looking, I'd doodle. That, or sleep. Right there on the counter in the middle of my shift. (Bad boy!) But it turned out that even if the boss didn't see me sketching and napping, the security camera did, and I was fired. (What did I think was gonna happen?!) But with the prize money this story brought me (a cool 700,000 yen*!), I managed to keep eating... Without a job, though, my savings swiftly dwindled. I was convinced that I would go straight from point A (Rookie Prize) to point B (pro manga artist), but it wasn't that easy. Things were touch and go for a while there... At one point, I think I was eating Yoshinoya beef bowls eight times a week.

Whoops, looks like I've wasted the entire page babbling. Anyway, the seed for this story was "wouldn't it be really silly if the main character saved himself with sleight-of-hand when he was cornered?" That scene sort of wound up as the centerpiece. It's still silly, though.

*About $7,000

Hiro Mashima's Road to Becoming a Manga Artist: B

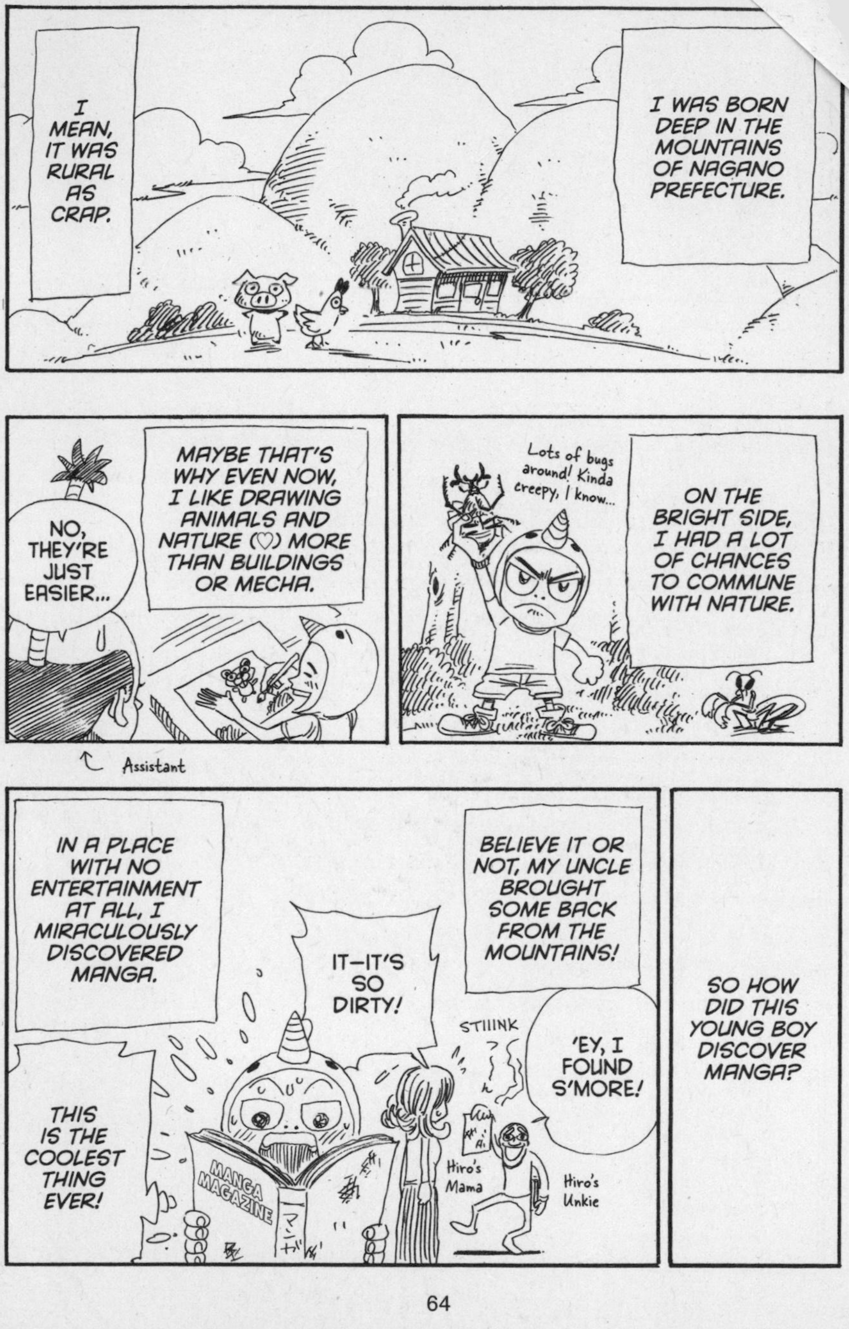

I WAS BORN DEEP IN THE MOUNTAINS OF NAGANO PREFECTURE.
I MEAN, IT WAS RURAL AS CRAP.
ON THE BRIGHT SIDE, I HAD A LOT OF CHANCES TO COMMUNE WITH NATURE.
Lots of bugs around! Kinda creepy, I know...
MAYBE THAT'S WHY EVEN NOW, I LIKE DRAWING ANIMALS AND NATURE (♡) MORE THAN BUILDINGS OR MECHA.
NO, THEY'RE JUST EASIER...
Assistant
SO HOW DID THIS YOUNG BOY DISCOVER MANGA?
BELIEVE IT OR NOT, MY UNCLE BROUGHT SOME BACK FROM THE MOUNTAINS!
'EY, I FOUND S'MORE!
STIIINK
Hiro's Unkie
Hiro's Mama
IN A PLACE WITH NO ENTERTAINMENT AT ALL, I MIRACULOUSLY DISCOVERED MANGA.
IT—IT'S SO DIRTY!
MANGA MAGAZINE
THIS IS THE COOLEST THING EVER!

My Father's Words

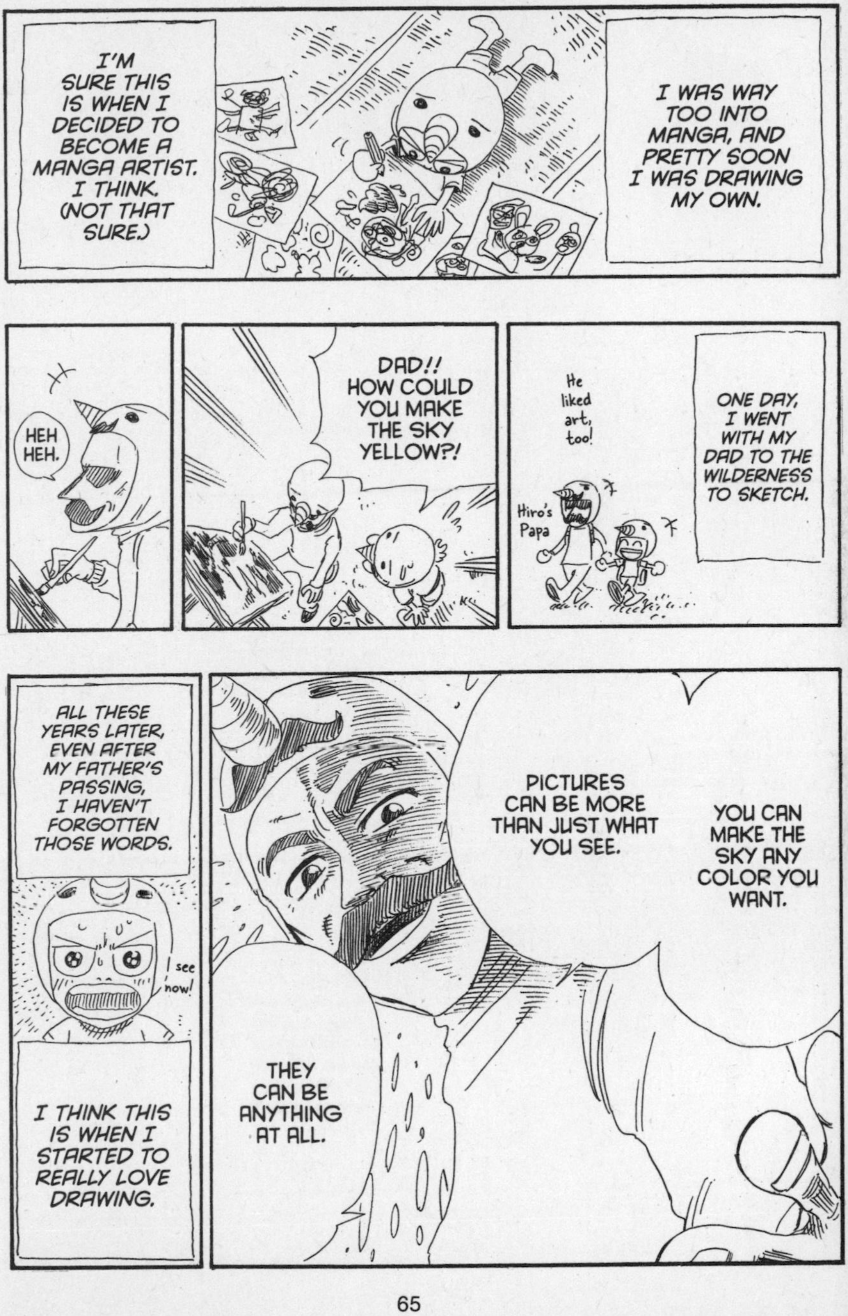
I WAS WAY TOO INTO MANGA, AND PRETTY SOON I WAS DRAWING MY OWN.
I'M SURE THIS IS WHEN I DECIDED TO BECOME A MANGA ARTIST. I THINK. (NOT THAT SURE.)
ONE DAY, I WENT WITH MY DAD TO THE WILDERNESS TO SKETCH.
He liked art, too!
Hiro's Papa
DAD!! HOW COULD YOU MAKE THE SKY YELLOW?!
HEH HEH.
YOU CAN MAKE THE SKY ANY COLOR YOU WANT.
PICTURES CAN BE MORE THAN JUST WHAT YOU SEE.
THEY CAN BE ANYTHING AT ALL.
ALL THESE YEARS LATER, EVEN AFTER MY FATHER'S PASSING, I HAVEN'T FORGOTTEN THOSE WORDS.
I see now!
I THINK THIS IS WHEN I STARTED TO REALLY LOVE DRAWING.

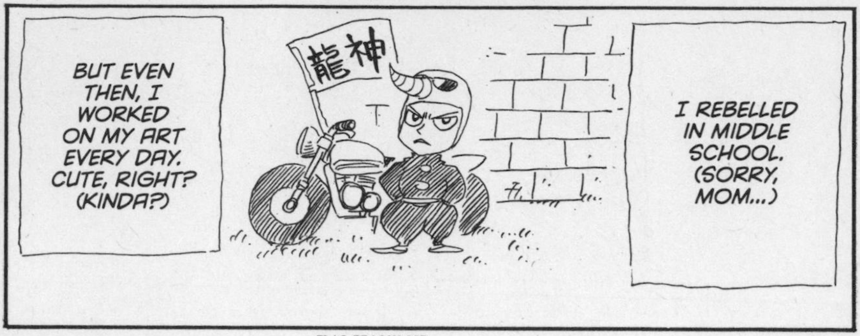
I REBELLED IN MIDDLE SCHOOL. (SORRY, MOM...)
龍神
BUT EVEN THEN, I WORKED ON MY ART EVERY DAY. CUTE, RIGHT? (KINDA?)

FLAG: DRAGON GOD

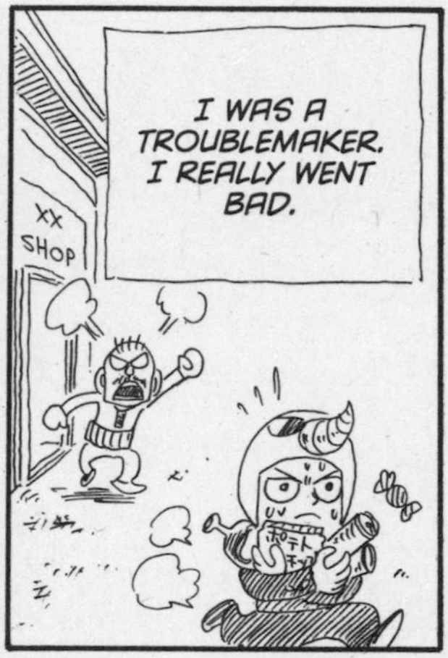
I WAS A TROUBLEMAKER. I REALLY WENT BAD.
XX SHOP

BAG: POTATO CHIPS

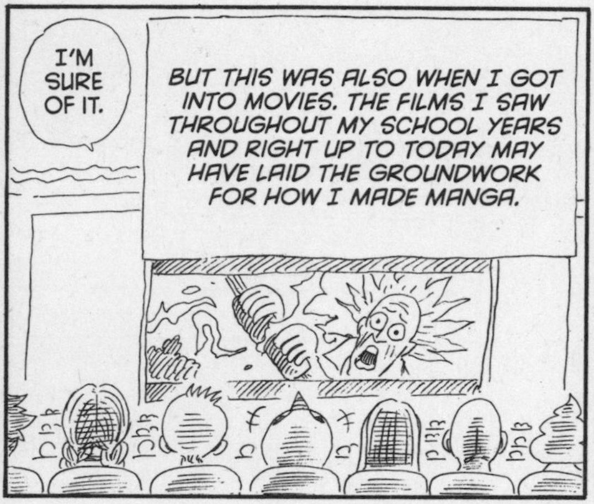
BUT THIS WAS ALSO WHEN I GOT INTO MOVIES. THE FILMS I SAW THROUGHOUT MY SCHOOL YEARS AND RIGHT UP TO TODAY MAY HAVE LAID THE GROUNDWORK FOR HOW I MADE MANGA.
I'M SURE OF IT.

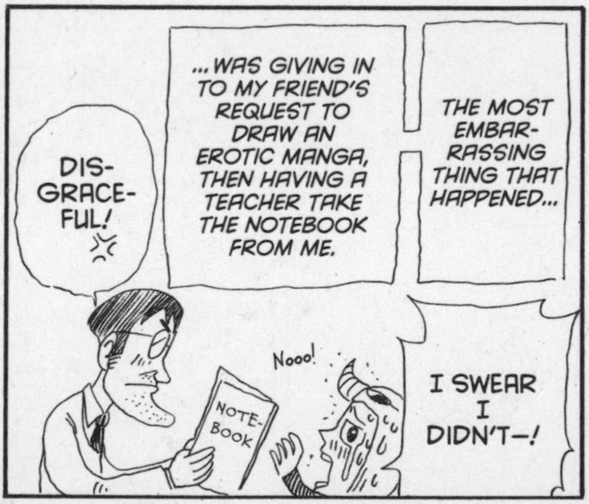
THE MOST EMBARRASSING THING THAT HAPPENED...
...WAS GIVING IN TO MY FRIEND'S REQUEST TO DRAW AN EROTIC MANGA, THEN HAVING A TEACHER TAKE THE NOTEBOOK FROM ME.
DISGRACEFUL!
I SWEAR I DIDN'T—!
Nooo!
NOTEBOOK

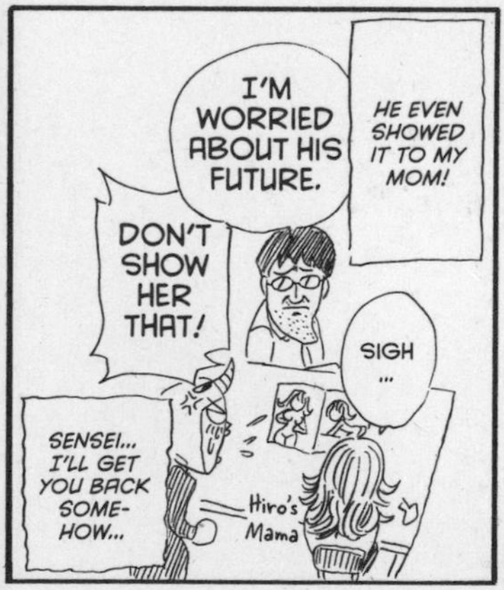
HE EVEN SHOWED IT TO MY MOM!
I'M WORRIED ABOUT HIS FUTURE.
DON'T SHOW HER THAT!
SIGH...
SENSEI... I'LL GET YOU BACK SOMEHOW...
Hiro's Mama

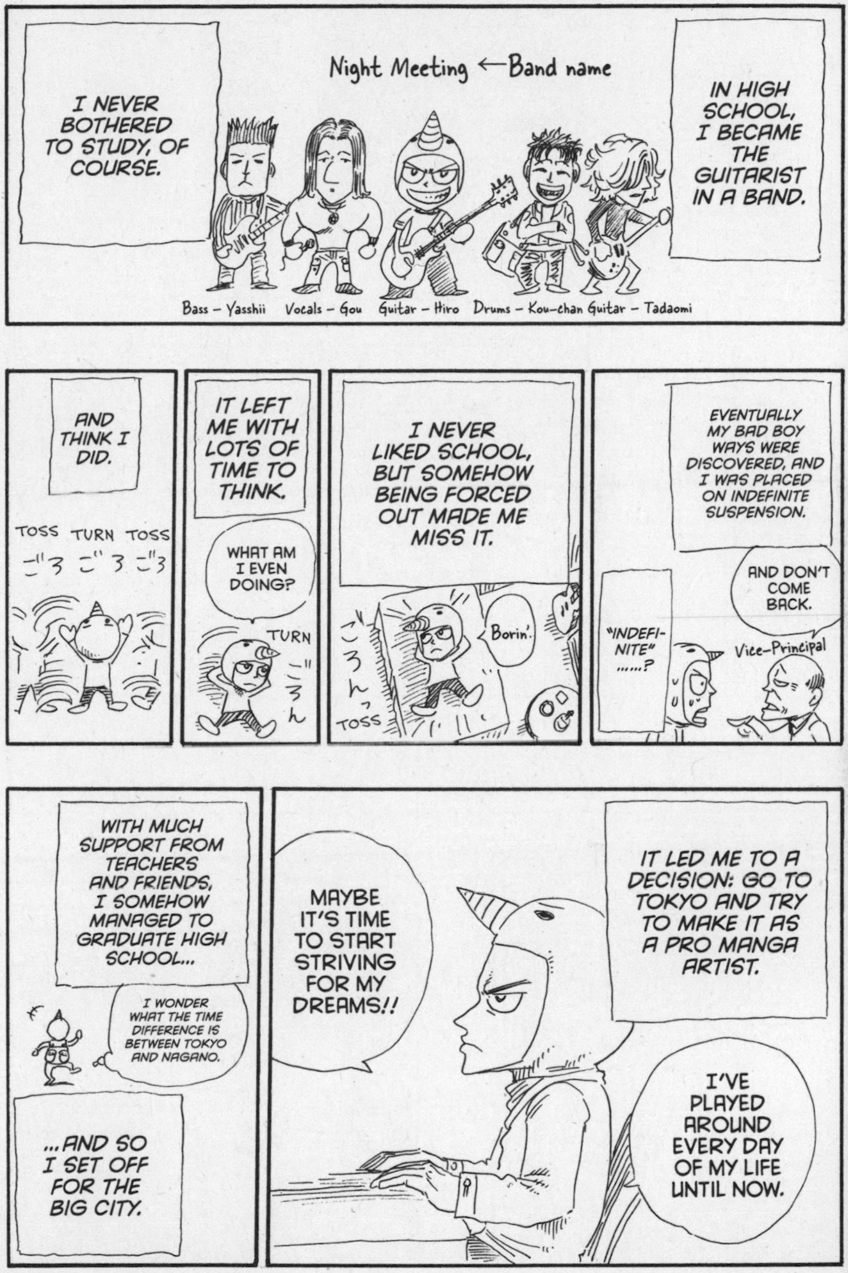
IN HIGH SCHOOL, I BECAME THE GUITARIST IN A BAND.
Night Meeting ←Band name
I NEVER BOTHERED TO STUDY, OF COURSE.
Bass – Yasshii Vocals – Gou Guitar – Hiro Drums – Kou-chan Guitar – Tadaomi
EVENTUALLY MY BAD BOY WAYS WERE DISCOVERED, AND I WAS PLACED ON INDEFINITE SUSPENSION.
AND DON'T COME BACK.
Vice-Principal
"INDEFINITE" ......?
I NEVER LIKED SCHOOL, BUT SOMEHOW BEING FORCED OUT MADE ME MISS IT.
Borin'.
ごろんっ
TOSS
IT LEFT ME WITH LOTS OF TIME TO THINK.
WHAT AM I EVEN DOING?
TURN
ごろん
AND THINK I DID.
TOSS TURN TOSS
ごろごろごろ
IT LED ME TO A DECISION: GO TO TOKYO AND TRY TO MAKE IT AS A PRO MANGA ARTIST.
I'VE PLAYED AROUND EVERY DAY OF MY LIFE UNTIL NOW.
MAYBE IT'S TIME TO START STRIVING FOR MY DREAMS!!
WITH MUCH SUPPORT FROM TEACHERS AND FRIENDS, I SOMEHOW MANAGED TO GRADUATE HIGH SCHOOL...
I WONDER WHAT THE TIME DIFFERENCE IS BETWEEN TOKYO AND NAGANO.
...AND SO I SET OFF FOR THE BIG CITY.

Life in Tokyo

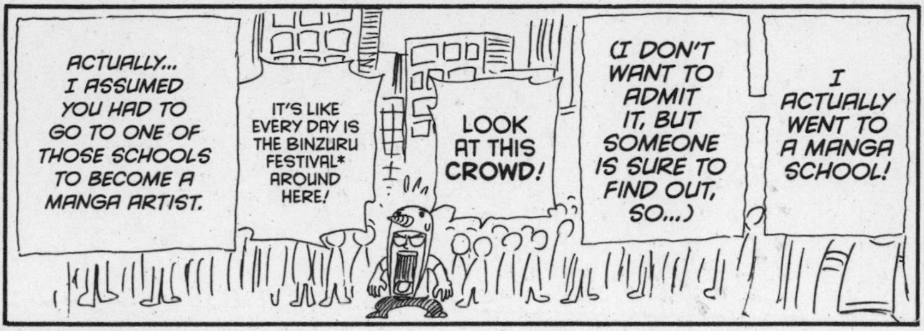
I ACTUALLY WENT TO A MANGA SCHOOL!
(I DON'T WANT TO ADMIT IT, BUT SOMEONE IS SURE TO FIND OUT, SO...)
LOOK AT THIS CROWD!
IT'S LIKE EVERY DAY IS THE BINZURU FESTIVAL* AROUND HERE!
ACTUALLY... I ASSUMED YOU HAD TO GO TO ONE OF THOSE SCHOOLS TO BECOME A MANGA ARTIST.

*A BUDDHIST SUMMER DANCE FESTIVAL IN NAGANO

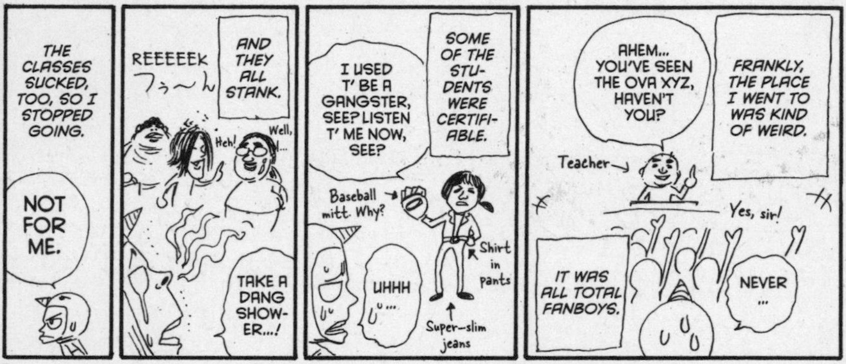
FRANKLY, THE PLACE I WENT TO WAS KIND OF WEIRD.
AHEM... YOU'VE SEEN THE OVA XYZ, HAVEN'T YOU?
Teacher
Yes, sir!
NEVER ...
IT WAS ALL TOTAL FANBOYS.
SOME OF THE STU-DENTS WERE CERTIFI-ABLE.
I USED T' BE A GANGSTER, SEE? LISTEN T' ME NOW, SEE?
Baseball mitt. Why?
Shirt in pants
Super-slim jeans
UHHH ...
AND THEY ALL STANK.
REEEEEK
フぅ～ん
Well, I...
Heh!
TAKE A DANG SHOW-ER...!
THE CLASSES SUCKED, TOO, SO I STOPPED GOING.
NOT FOR ME.

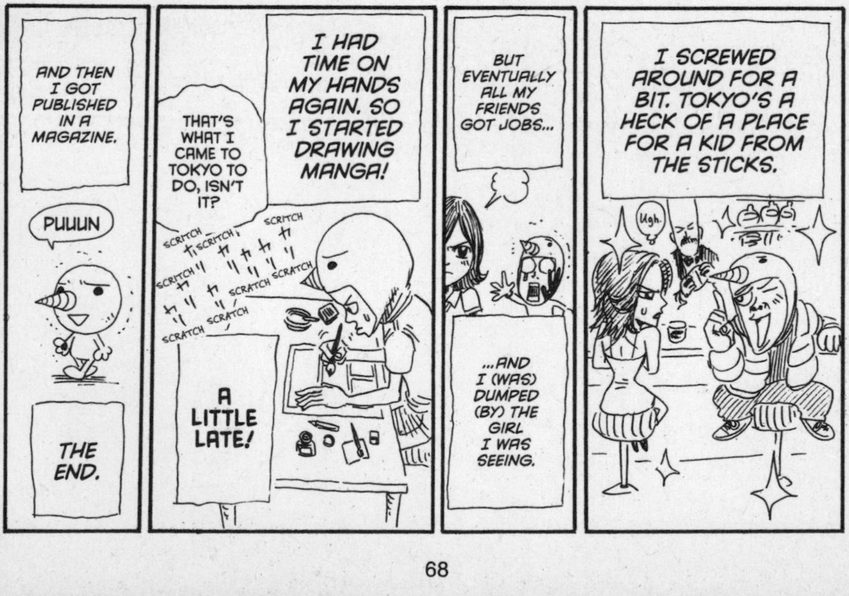
I SCREWED AROUND FOR A BIT. TOKYO'S A HECK OF A PLACE FOR A KID FROM THE STICKS.
Ugh.
BUT EVENTUALLY ALL MY FRIENDS GOT JOBS...
...AND I (WAS) DUMPED (BY) THE GIRL I WAS SEEING.
I HAD TIME ON MY HANDS AGAIN. SO I STARTED DRAWING MANGA!
THAT'S WHAT I CAME TO TOKYO TO DO, ISN'T IT?
SCRITCH SCRITCH SCRITCH SCRITCH SCRATCH SCRATCH SCRATCH SCRATCH
A LITTLE LATE!
AND THEN I GOT PUBLISHED IN A MAGAZINE.
PUUUN
THE END.

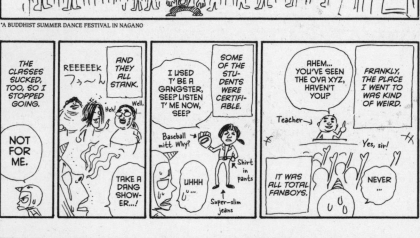

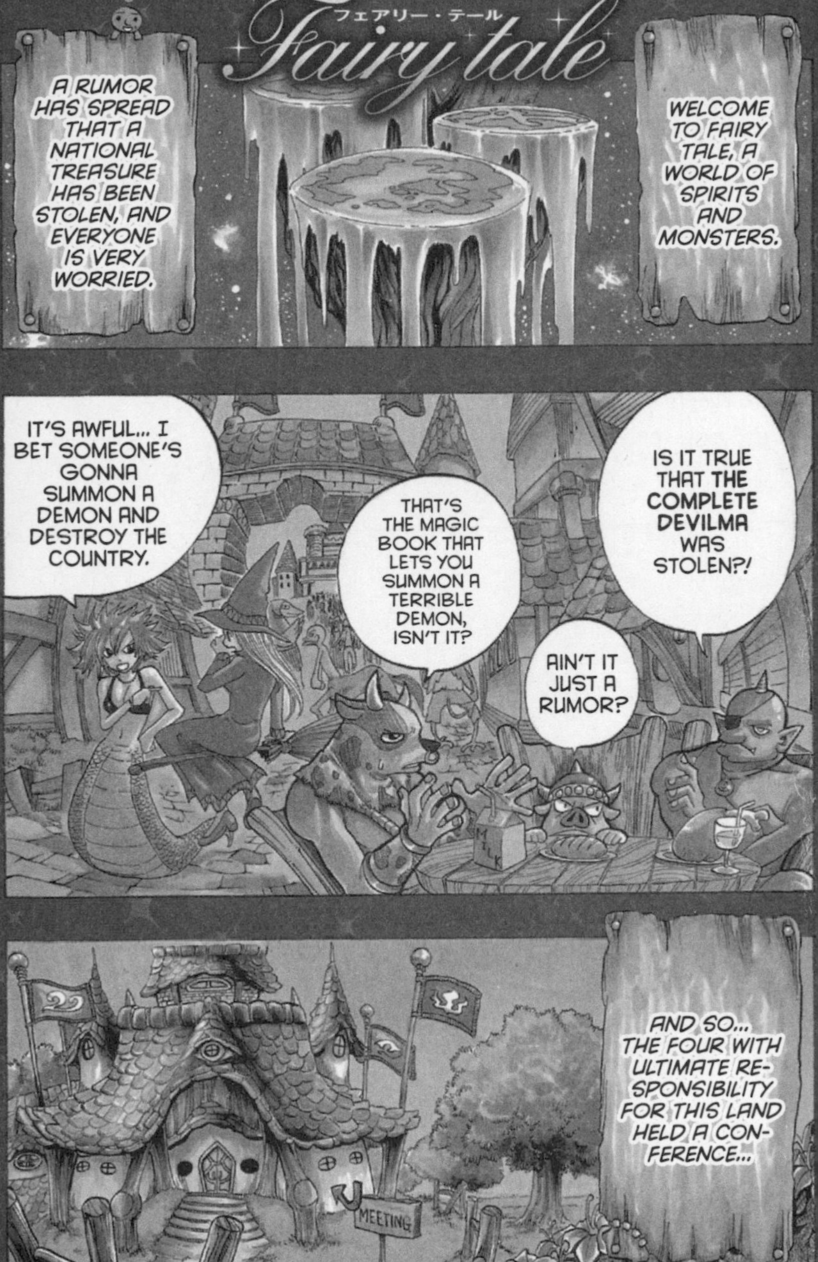
Fairy tale
フェアリー・テール
WELCOME TO FAIRY TALE, A WORLD OF SPIRITS AND MONSTERS.
A RUMOR HAS SPREAD THAT A NATIONAL TREASURE HAS BEEN STOLEN, AND EVERYONE IS VERY WORRIED.
IS IT TRUE THAT THE COMPLETE DEVILMA WAS STOLEN?!
AIN'T IT JUST A RUMOR?
THAT'S THE MAGIC BOOK THAT LETS YOU SUMMON A TERRIBLE DEMON, ISN'T IT?
IT'S AWFUL... I BET SOMEONE'S GONNA SUMMON A DEMON AND DESTROY THE COUNTRY.
MILK
AND SO... THE FOUR WITH ULTIMATE RE-SPONSIBILITY FOR THIS LAND HELD A CON-FERENCE...
MEETING

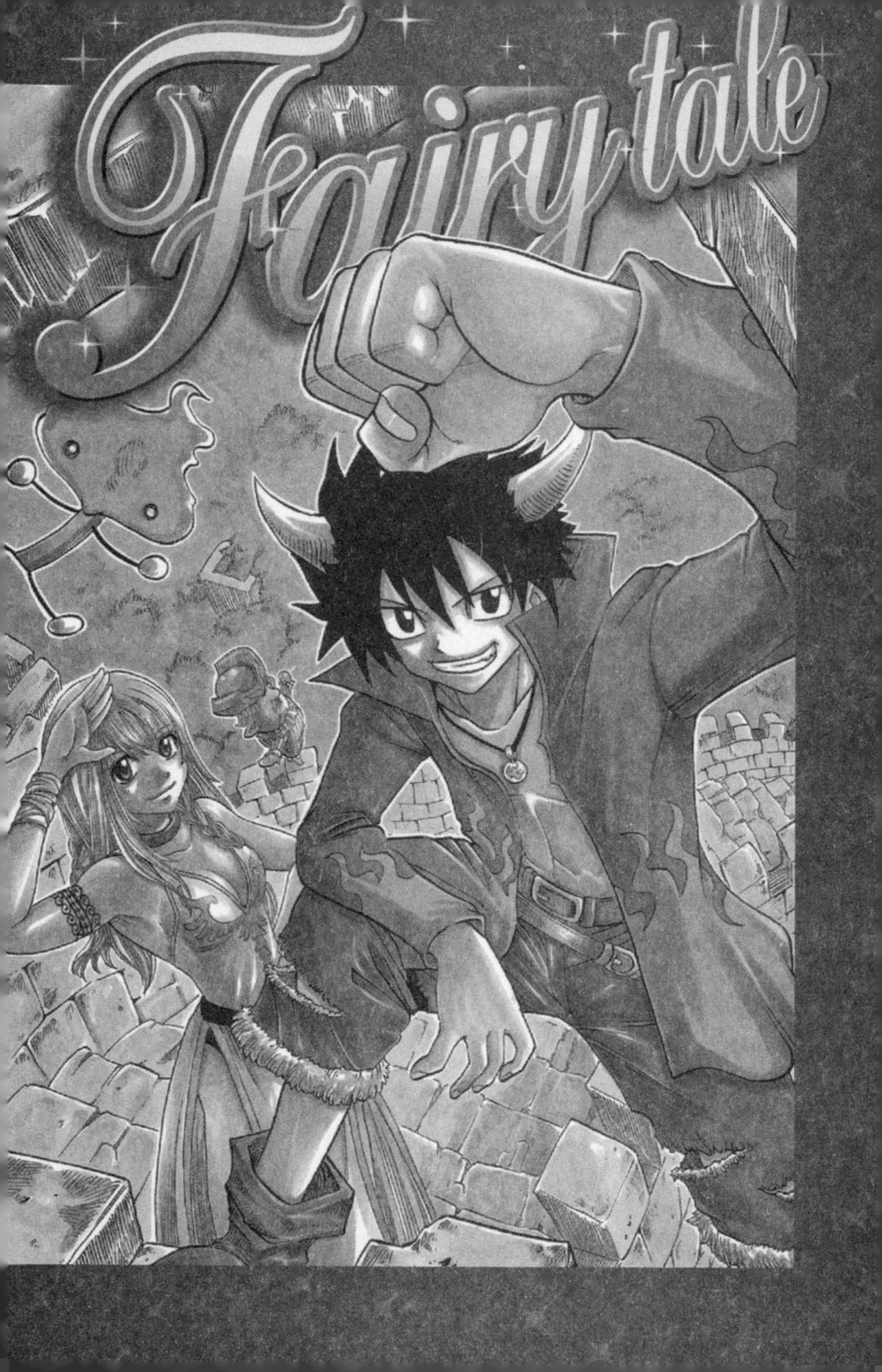
Fairy tale

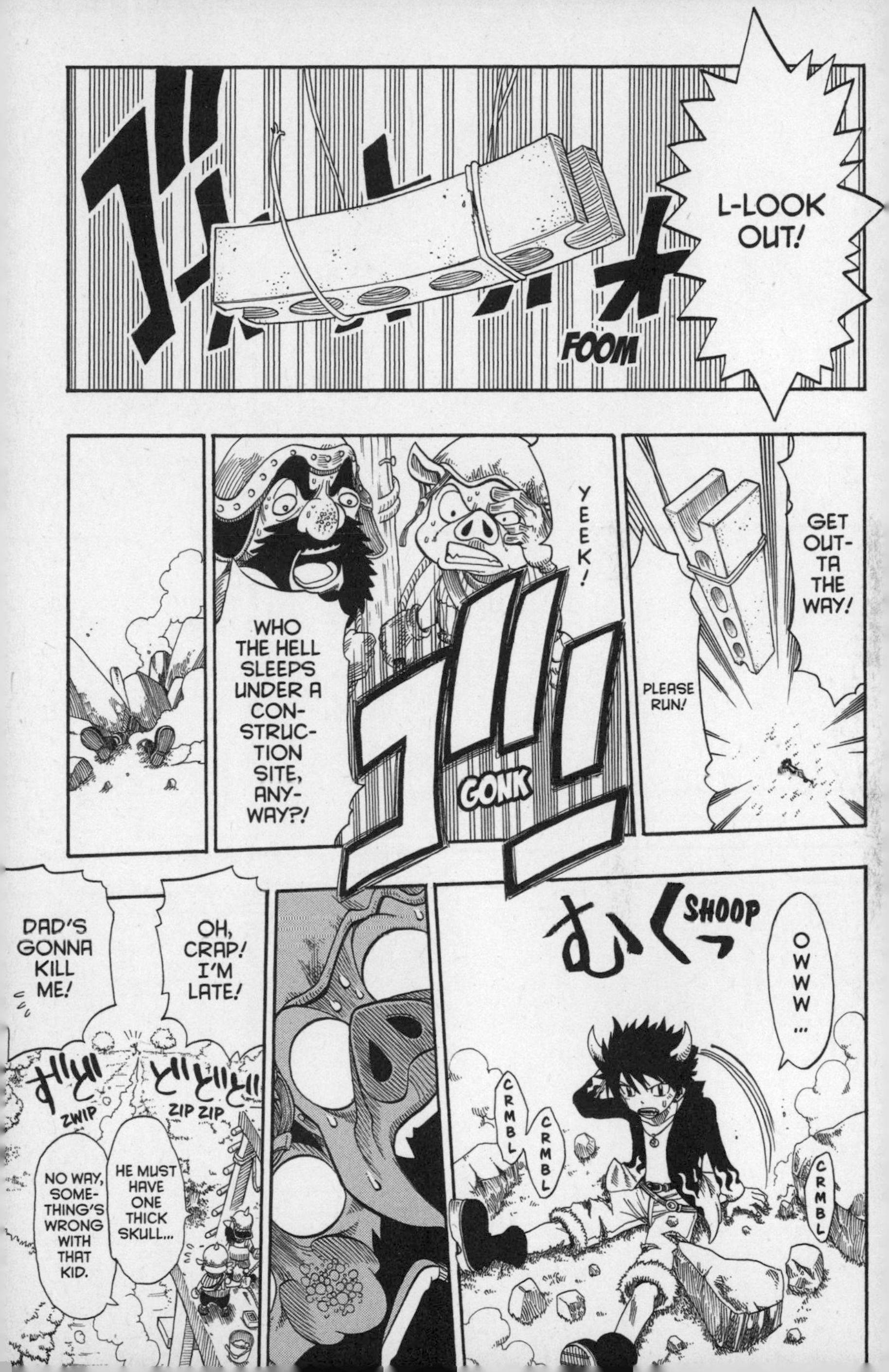
L-LOOK OUT!
FOOM
GET OUT-TA THE WAY!
PLEASE RUN!
YEEK!
WHO THE HELL SLEEPS UNDER A CON-STRUC-TION SITE, ANY-WAY?!
GONK
むくっ
SHOOP
OWWW...
CRMBL
CRMBL
CRMBL
OH, CRAP! I'M LATE!
DAD'S GONNA KILL ME!
ZIP ZIP
ZWIP
HE MUST HAVE ONE THICK SKULL...
NO WAY, SOME-THING'S WRONG WITH THAT KID.

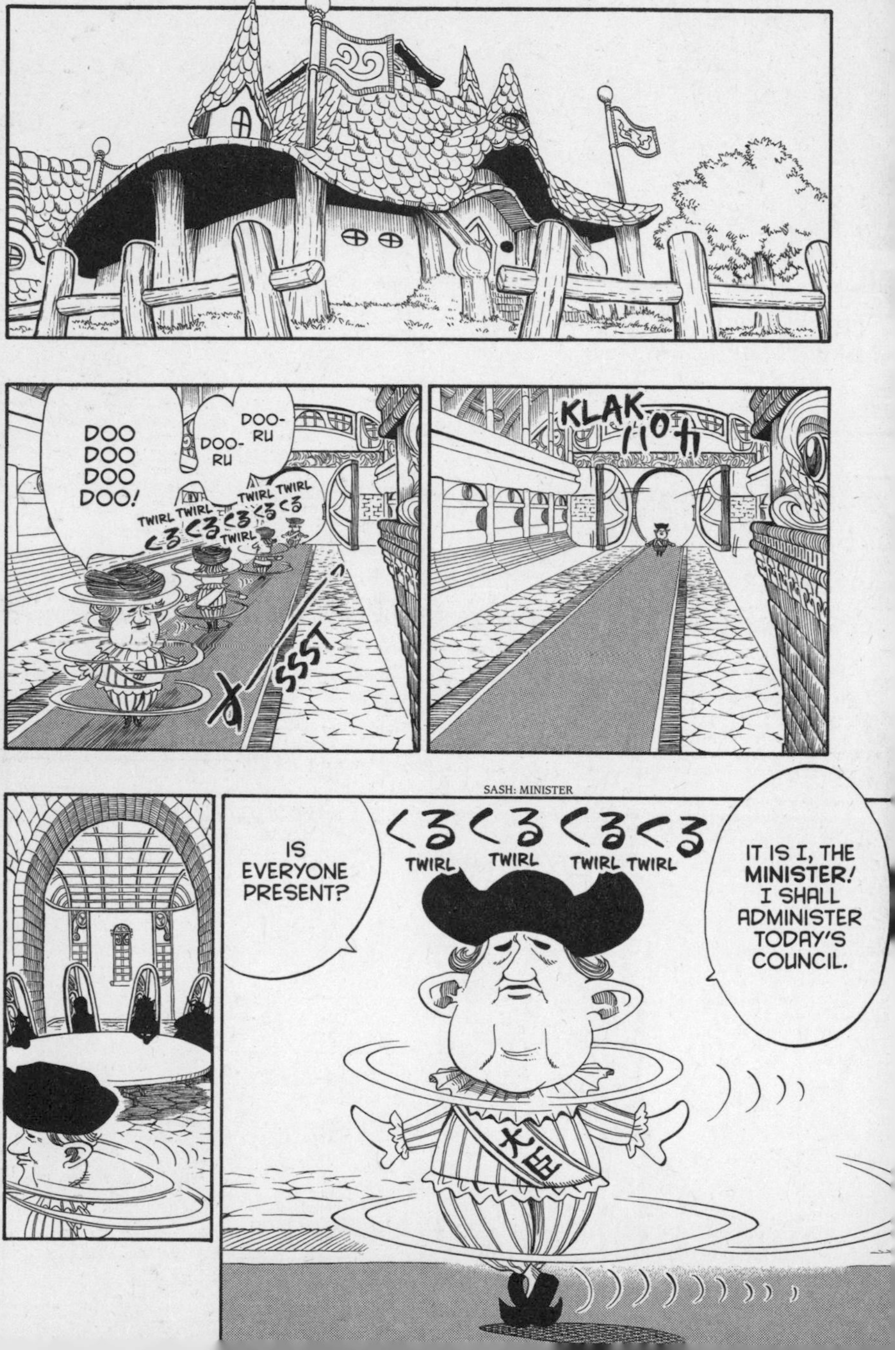
KLAK
DOO-RU
DOO-RU
DOO DOO DOO DOO!
TWIRL TWIRL くるくる
TWIRL TWIRL くるくる
TWIRL
SSST
SASH: MINISTER
IT IS I, THE MINISTER! I SHALL ADMINISTER TODAY'S COUNCIL.
くるくるくるくる
TWIRL TWIRL TWIRL TWIRL
IS EVERYONE PRESENT?

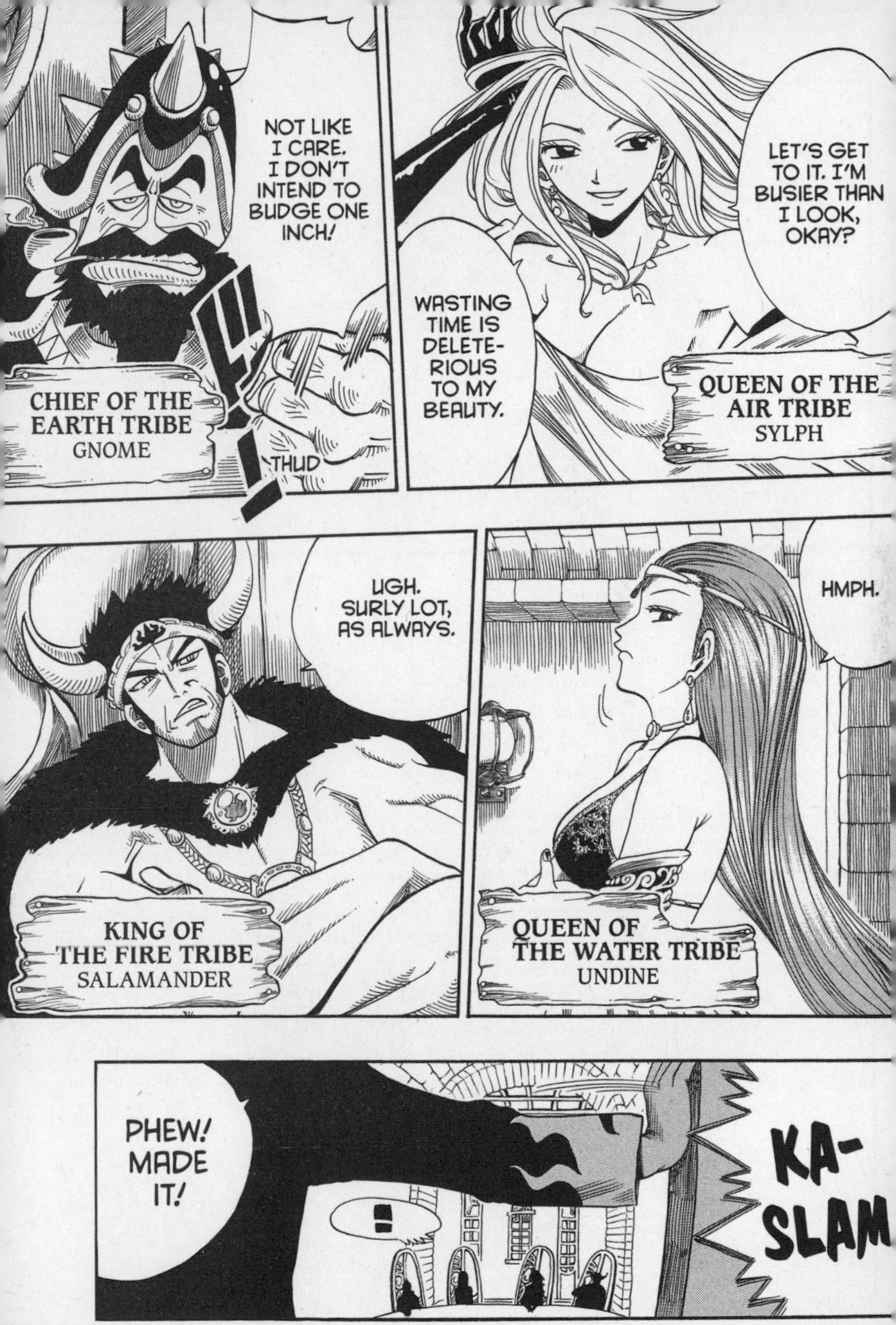
LET'S GET TO IT. I'M BUSIER THAN I LOOK, OKAY?
WASTING TIME IS DELETE-RIOUS TO MY BEAUTY.
QUEEN OF THE AIR TRIBE SYLPH
NOT LIKE I CARE. I DON'T INTEND TO BUDGE ONE INCH!
THUD
CHIEF OF THE EARTH TRIBE GNOME
HMPH.
QUEEN OF THE WATER TRIBE UNDINE
UGH. SURLY LOT, AS ALWAYS.
KING OF THE FIRE TRIBE SALAMANDER
KA-SLAM
PHEW! MADE IT!
!

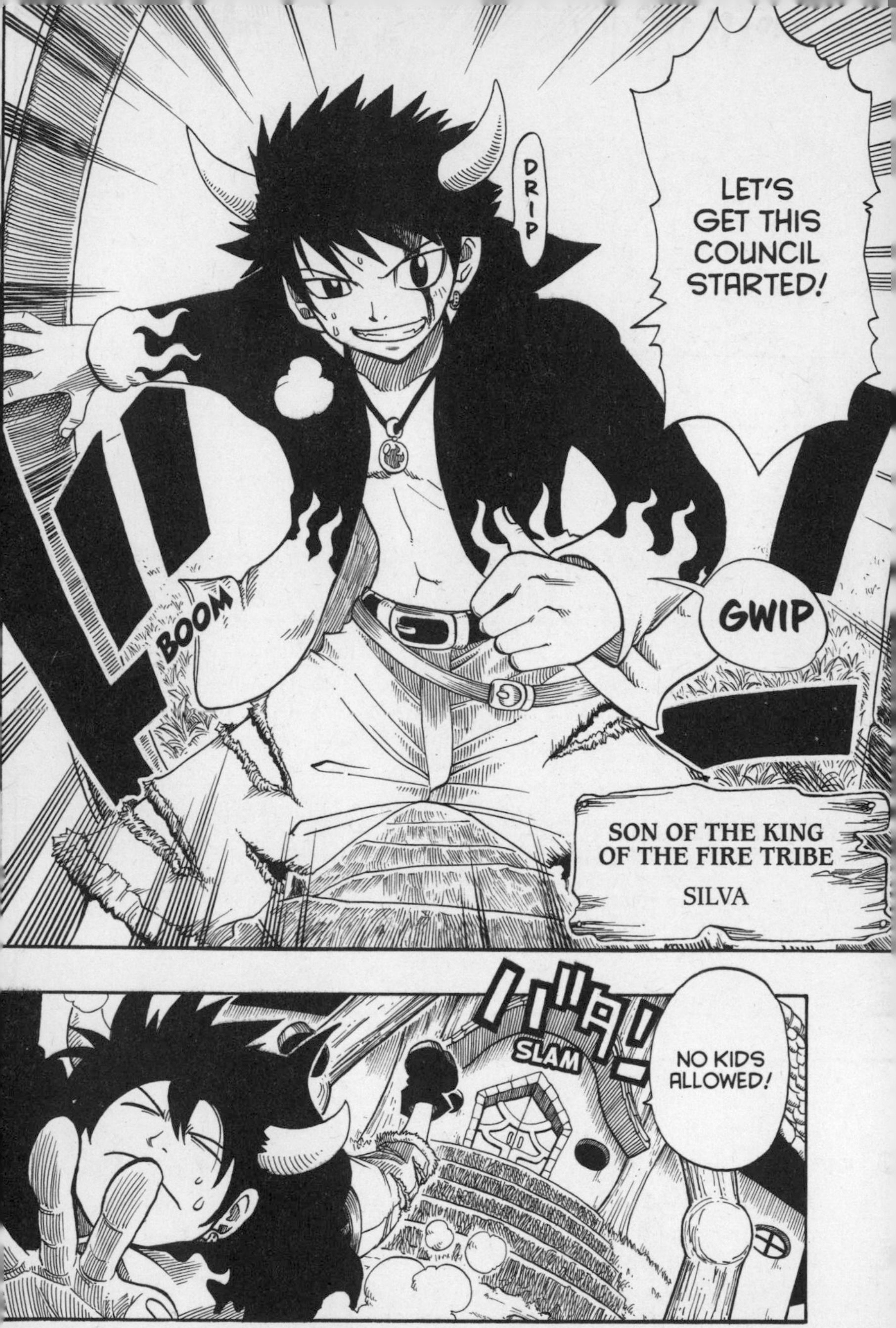
LET'S GET THIS COUNCIL STARTED!
DRIP
GWIP
BOOM
SON OF THE KING OF THE FIRE TRIBE
SILVA
NO KIDS ALLOWED!
SLAM

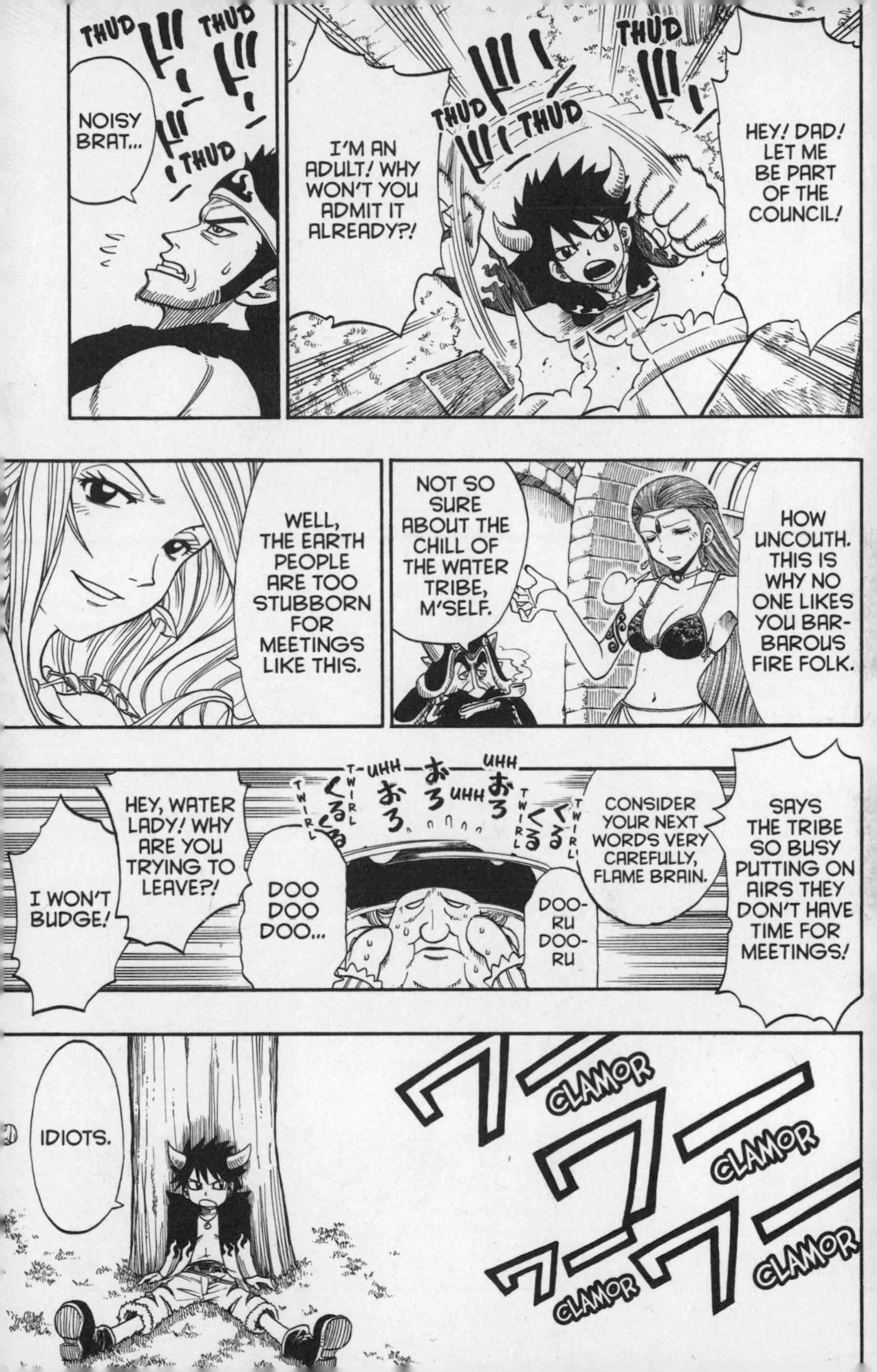
THUD
THUD
THUD
THUD
HEY! DAD! LET ME BE PART OF THE COUNCIL!
I'M AN ADULT! WHY WON'T YOU ADMIT IT ALREADY?!
THUD
THUD
THUD
NOISY BRAT...
HOW UNCOUTH. THIS IS WHY NO ONE LIKES YOU BAR-BAROUS FIRE FOLK.
NOT SO SURE ABOUT THE CHILL OF THE WATER TRIBE, M'SELF.
WELL, THE EARTH PEOPLE ARE TOO STUBBORN FOR MEETINGS LIKE THIS.
SAYS THE TRIBE SO BUSY PUTTING ON AIRS THEY DON'T HAVE TIME FOR MEETINGS!
CONSIDER YOUR NEXT WORDS VERY CAREFULLY, FLAME BRAIN.
TWIRL くるくる
TWIRL くるくる
UHH おろ
UHH おろ
UHH おろ
DOO-RU DOO-RU
DOO DOO DOO...
TWIRL くるくる
HEY, WATER LADY! WHY ARE YOU TRYING TO LEAVE?!
I WON'T BUDGE!
CLAMOR
CLAMOR
CLAMOR
CLAMOR
IDIOTS.

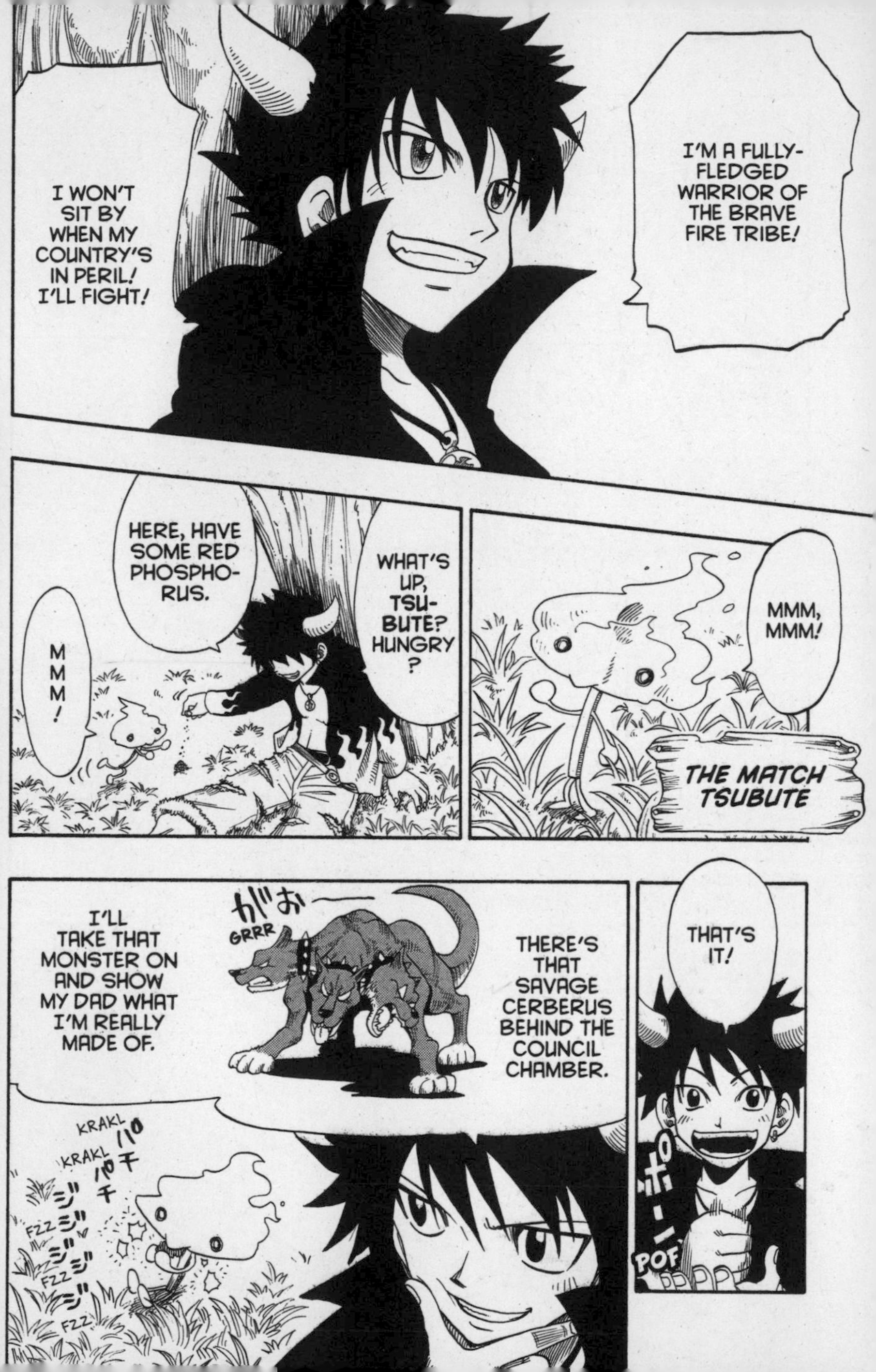
I'M A FULLY-FLEDGED WARRIOR OF THE BRAVE FIRE TRIBE!
I WON'T SIT BY WHEN MY COUNTRY'S IN PERIL! I'LL FIGHT!
MMM, MMM!
THE MATCH TSUBUTE
WHAT'S UP, TSUBUTE? HUNGRY?
HERE, HAVE SOME RED PHOSPHORUS.
MMM!
THAT'S IT!
ポー
POF
がお—
GRRR
THERE'S THAT SAVAGE CERBERUS BEHIND THE COUNCIL CHAMBER.
I'LL TAKE THAT MONSTER ON AND SHOW MY DAD WHAT I'M REALLY MADE OF.
パチパチ
KRAKL KRAKL
ジジジジジジ
FZZ FZZ FZZ

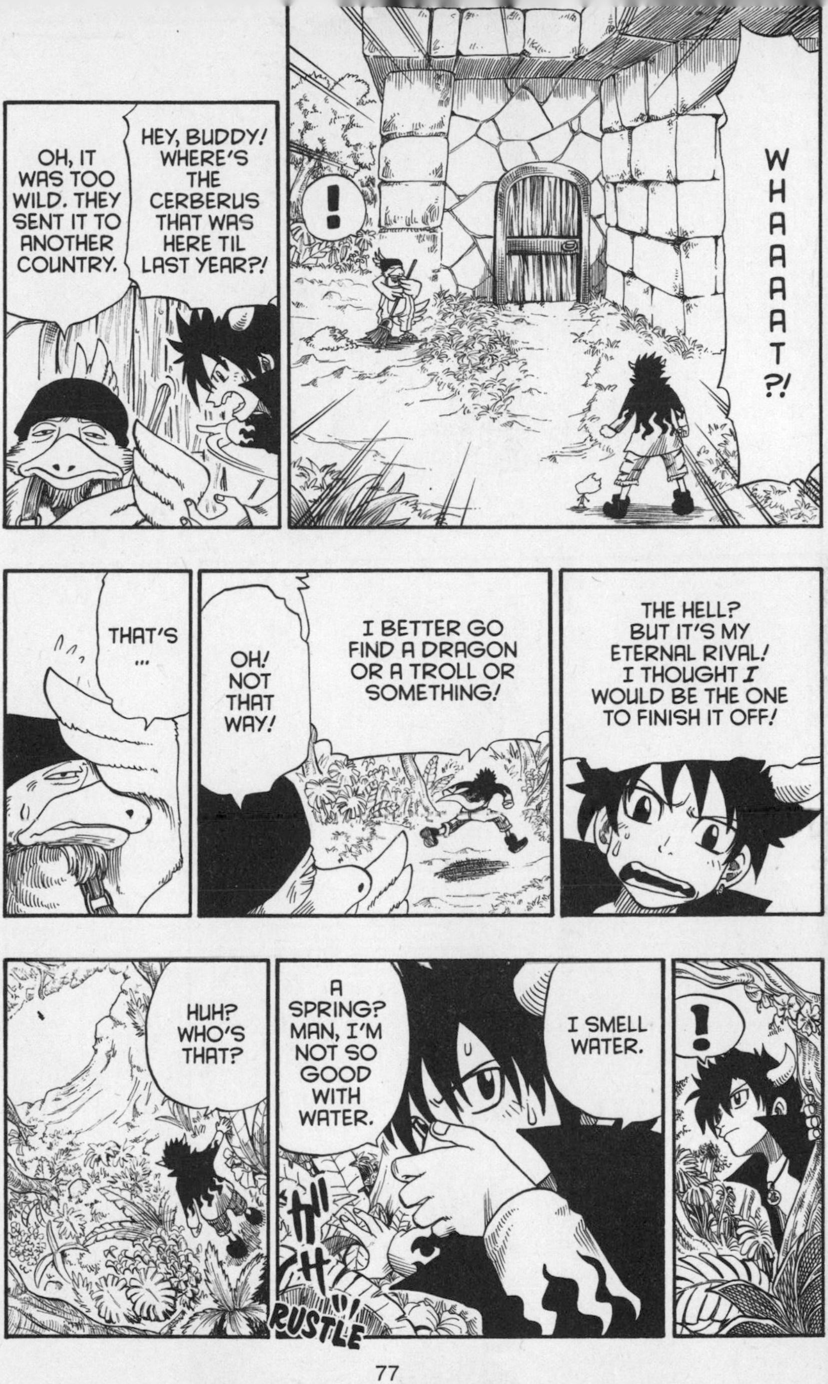

WHAAAAAT?!
!
HEY, BUDDY! WHERE'S THE CERBERUS THAT WAS HERE TIL LAST YEAR?!
OH, IT WAS TOO WILD. THEY SENT IT TO ANOTHER COUNTRY.
THE HELL? BUT IT'S MY ETERNAL RIVAL! I THOUGHT *I* WOULD BE THE ONE TO FINISH IT OFF!
I BETTER GO FIND A DRAGON OR A TROLL OR SOMETHING!
OH! NOT THAT WAY!
THAT'S ...
!
I SMELL WATER.
A SPRING? MAN, I'M NOT SO GOOD WITH WATER.
RUSTLE
HUH? WHO'S THAT?

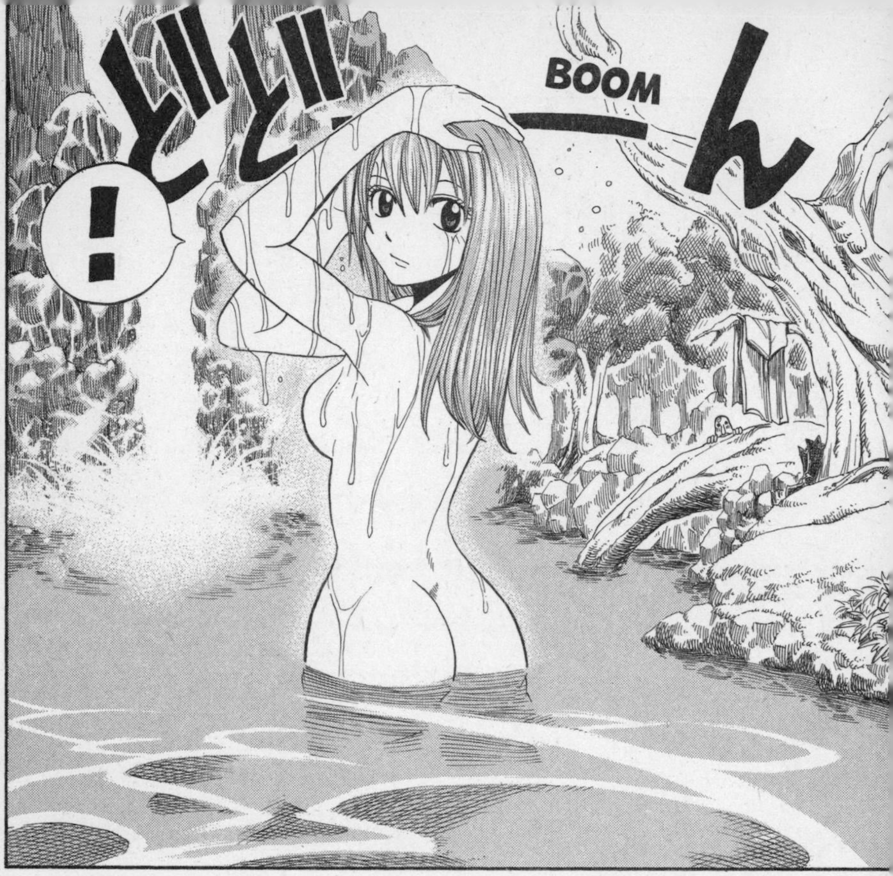
BOOM
!
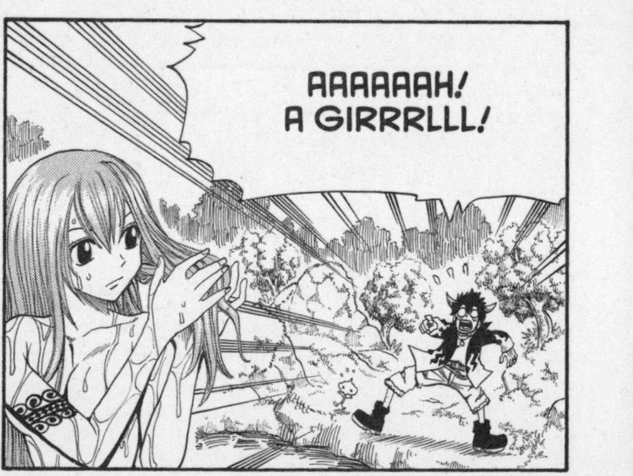
AAAAAAH! A GIRRRLLL!
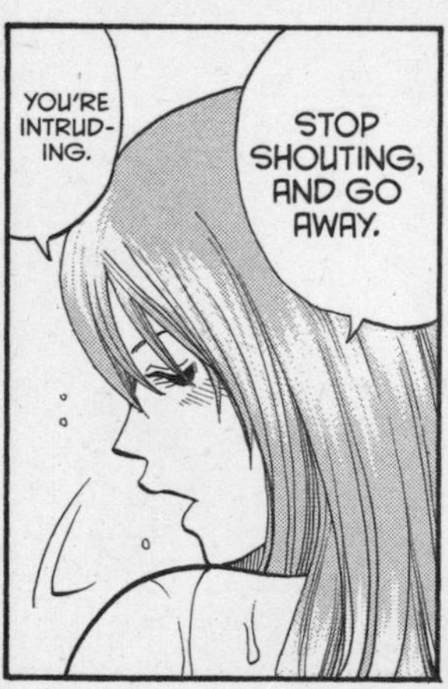
STOP SHOUTING, AND GO AWAY.
YOU'RE INTRUD-ING.

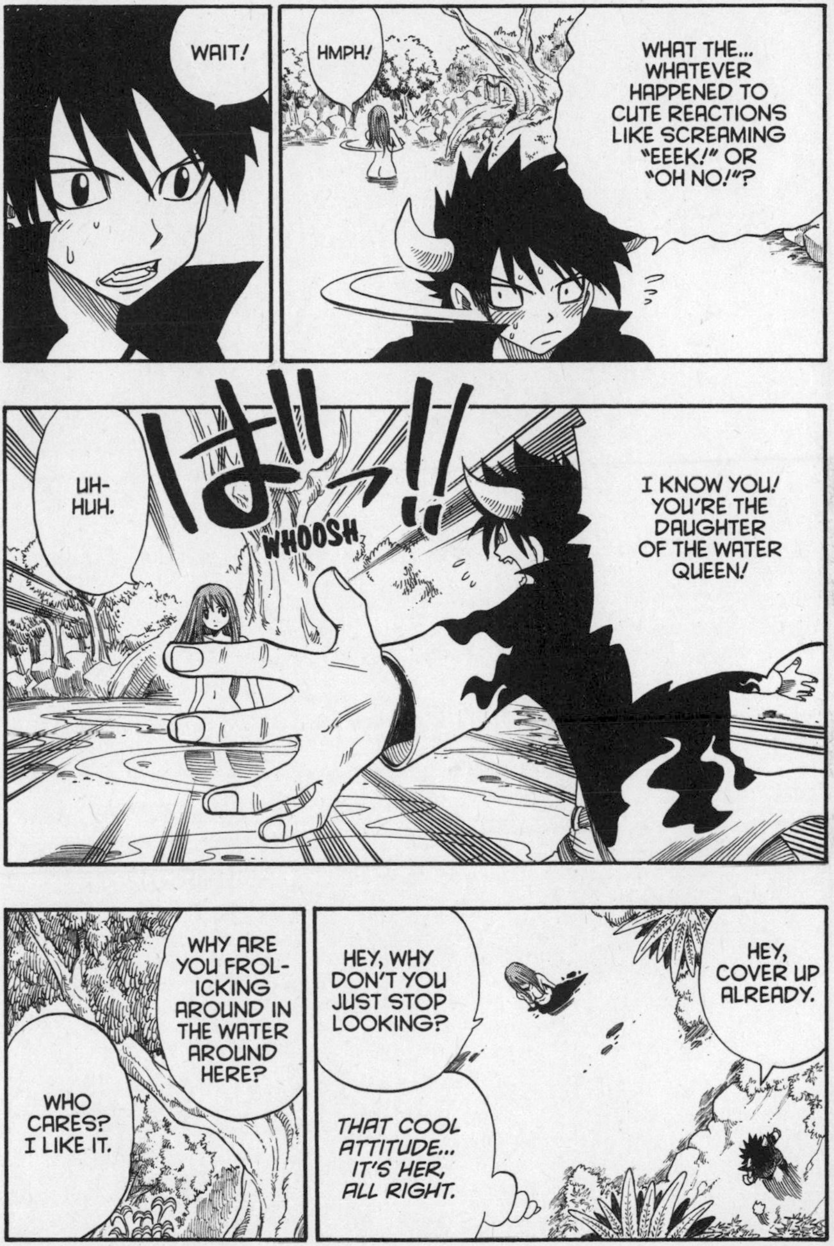
WHAT THE... WHATEVER HAPPENED TO CUTE REACTIONS LIKE SCREAMING "EEEK!" OR "OH NO!"?
HMPH!
WAIT!
I KNOW YOU! YOU'RE THE DAUGHTER OF THE WATER QUEEN!
ばっ!!
WHOOSH
UH-HUH.
HEY, COVER UP ALREADY.
HEY, WHY DON'T YOU JUST STOP LOOKING?
THAT COOL ATTITUDE... IT'S HER, ALL RIGHT.
WHY ARE YOU FROLICKING AROUND IN THE WATER AROUND HERE?
WHO CARES? I LIKE IT.

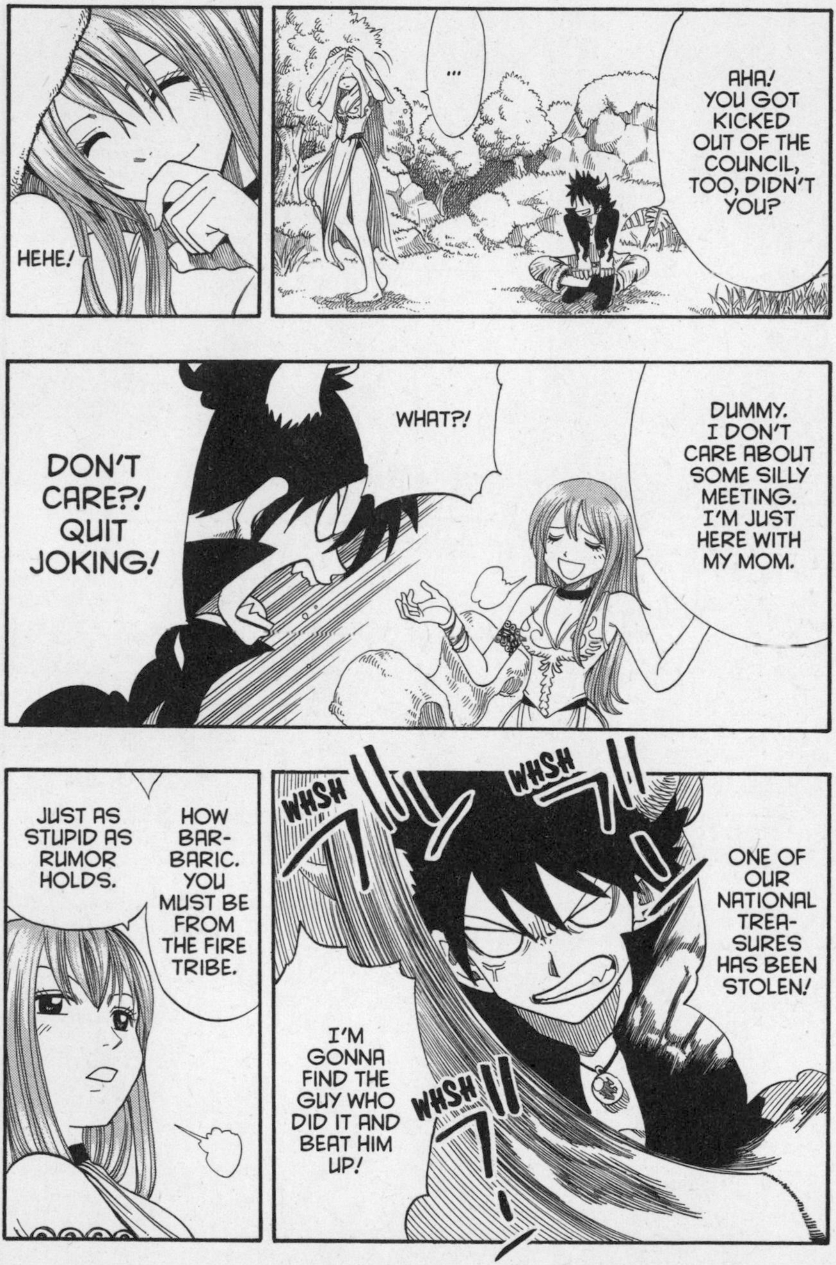
AHA! YOU GOT KICKED OUT OF THE COUNCIL, TOO, DIDN'T YOU?
...
HEHE!
DUMMY. I DON'T CARE ABOUT SOME SILLY MEETING. I'M JUST HERE WITH MY MOM.
WHAT?!
DON'T CARE?! QUIT JOKING!
WHSH
WHSH
ONE OF OUR NATIONAL TREA-SURES HAS BEEN STOLEN!
I'M GONNA FIND THE GUY WHO DID IT AND BEAT HIM UP!
WHSH
HOW BAR-BARIC. YOU MUST BE FROM THE FIRE TRIBE.
JUST AS STUPID AS RUMOR HOLDS.

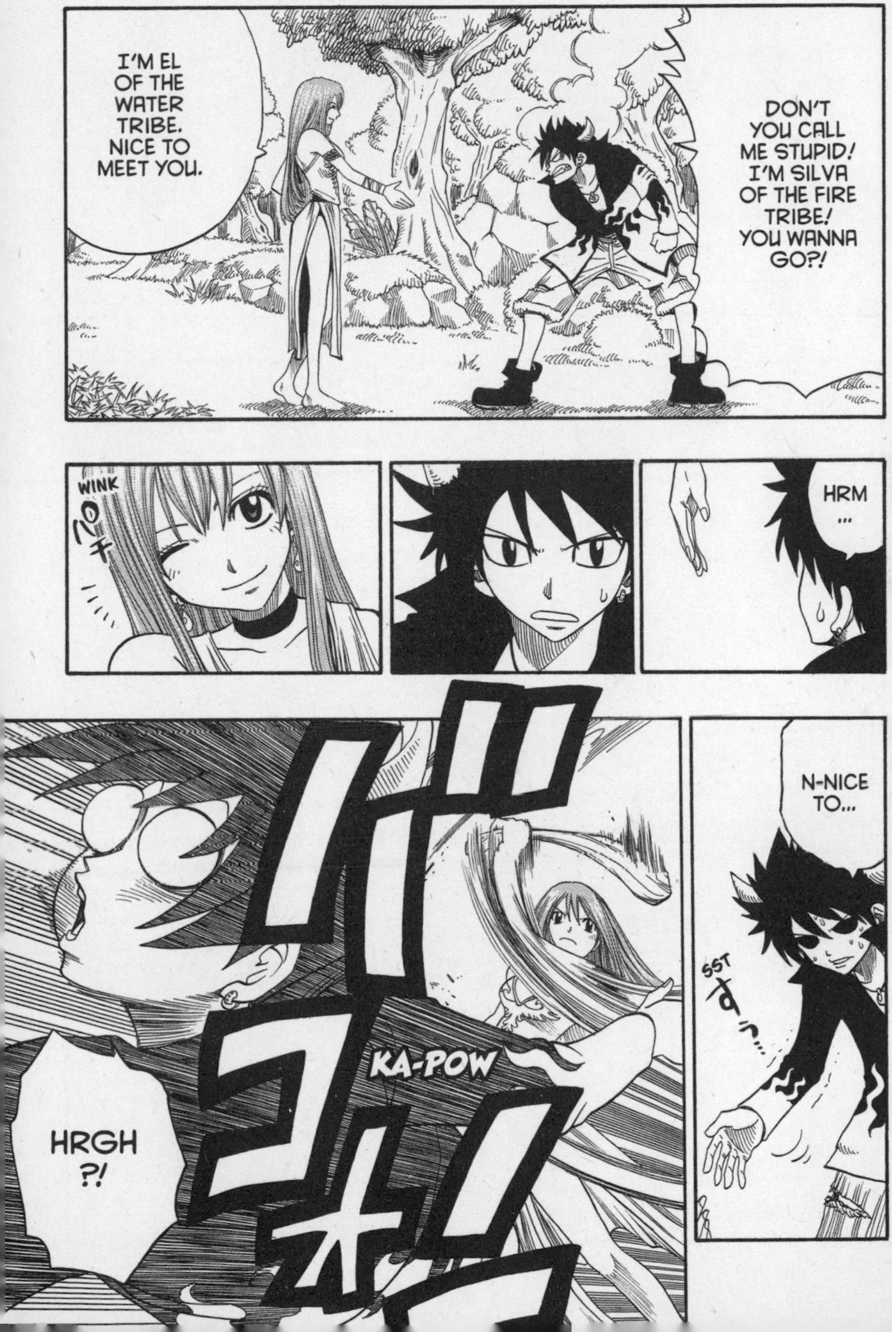
DON'T YOU CALL ME STUPID! I'M SILVA OF THE FIRE TRIBE! YOU WANNA GO?!
I'M EL OF THE WATER TRIBE. NICE TO MEET YOU.
HRM ...
WINK
N-NICE TO...
SST
KA-POW
HRGH ?!

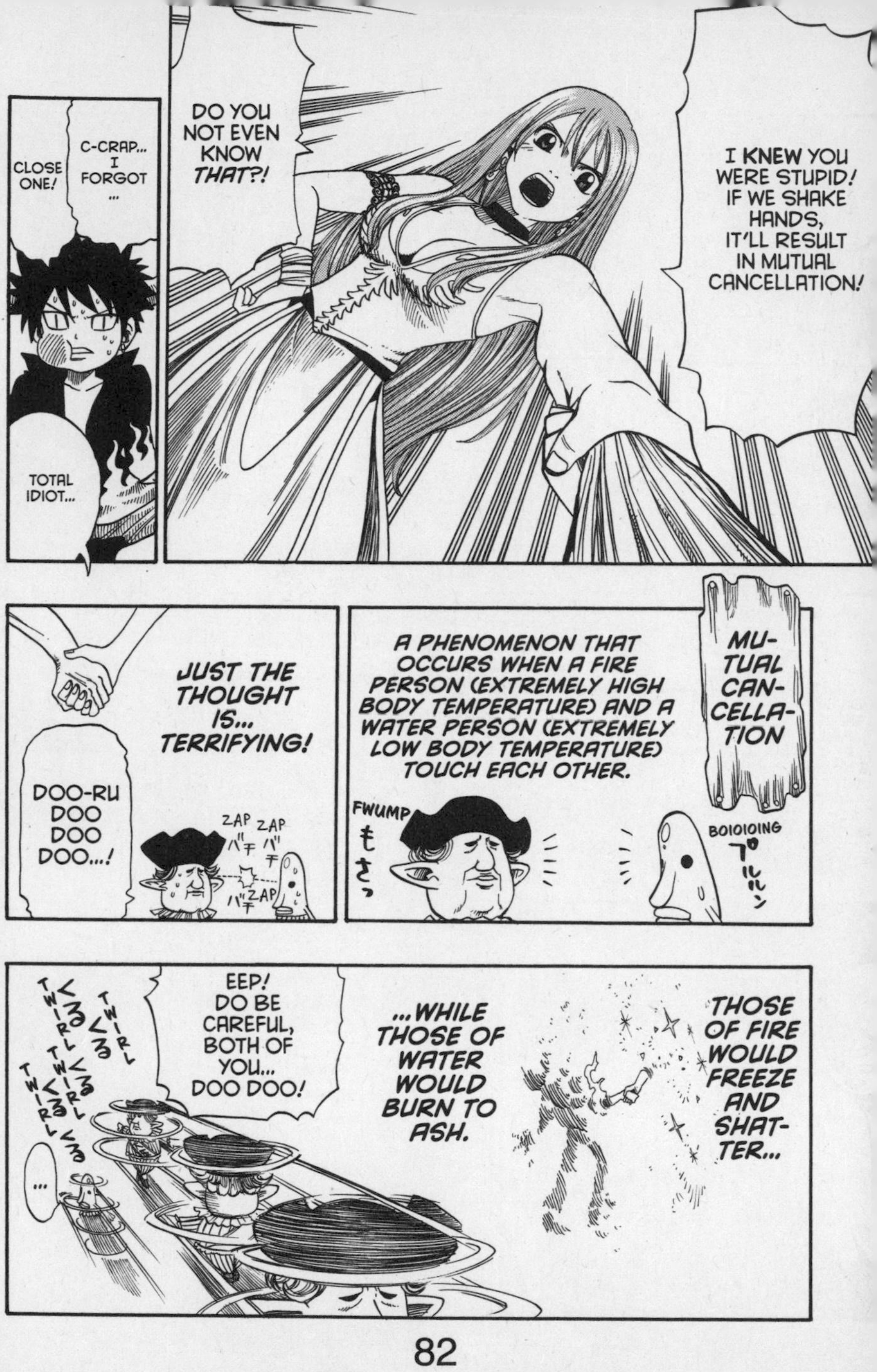
I KNEW YOU WERE STUPID! IF WE SHAKE HANDS, IT'LL RESULT IN MUTUAL CANCELLATION!
DO YOU NOT EVEN KNOW THAT?!
C-CRAP... I FORGOT ...
CLOSE ONE!
TOTAL IDIOT...
MU-TUAL CAN-CELLA-TION
A PHENOMENON THAT OCCURS WHEN A FIRE PERSON (EXTREMELY HIGH BODY TEMPERATURE) AND A WATER PERSON (EXTREMELY LOW BODY TEMPERATURE) TOUCH EACH OTHER.
BOIOIOING
プルルン
FWUMP
もさっ
JUST THE THOUGHT IS... TERRIFYING!
DOO-RU DOO DOO DOO...!
ZAP ZAP
バチ バチ
ZAP
バチ
THOSE OF FIRE WOULD FREEZE AND SHAT-TER...
...WHILE THOSE OF WATER WOULD BURN TO ASH.
EEP! DO BE CAREFUL, BOTH OF YOU... DOO DOO!
TWIRL くるくる
TWIRL くるくる
TWIRL くるくる
TWIRL くるくる
...

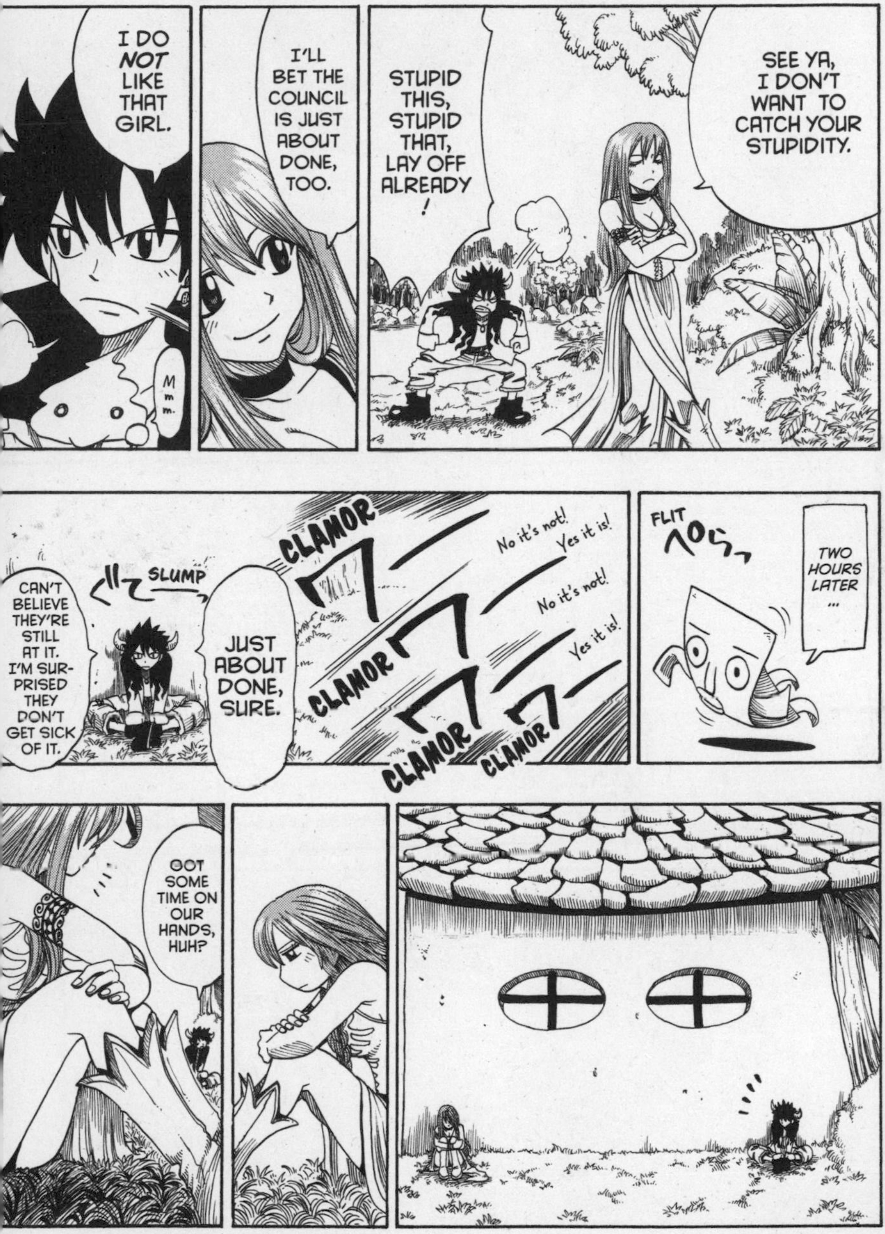
SEE YA, I DON'T WANT TO CATCH YOUR STUPIDITY.
STUPID THIS, STUPID THAT, LAY OFF ALREADY!
I'LL BET THE COUNCIL IS JUST ABOUT DONE, TOO.
I DO NOT LIKE THAT GIRL.
Mmm.
TWO HOURS LATER ...
FLIT
Yes it is!
No it's not!
Yes it is!
No it's not!
CLAMOR
CLAMOR
CLAMOR
CLAMOR
JUST ABOUT DONE, SURE.
SLUMP
CAN'T BELIEVE THEY'RE STILL AT IT. I'M SURPRISED THEY DON'T GET SICK OF IT.
GOT SOME TIME ON OUR HANDS, HUH?

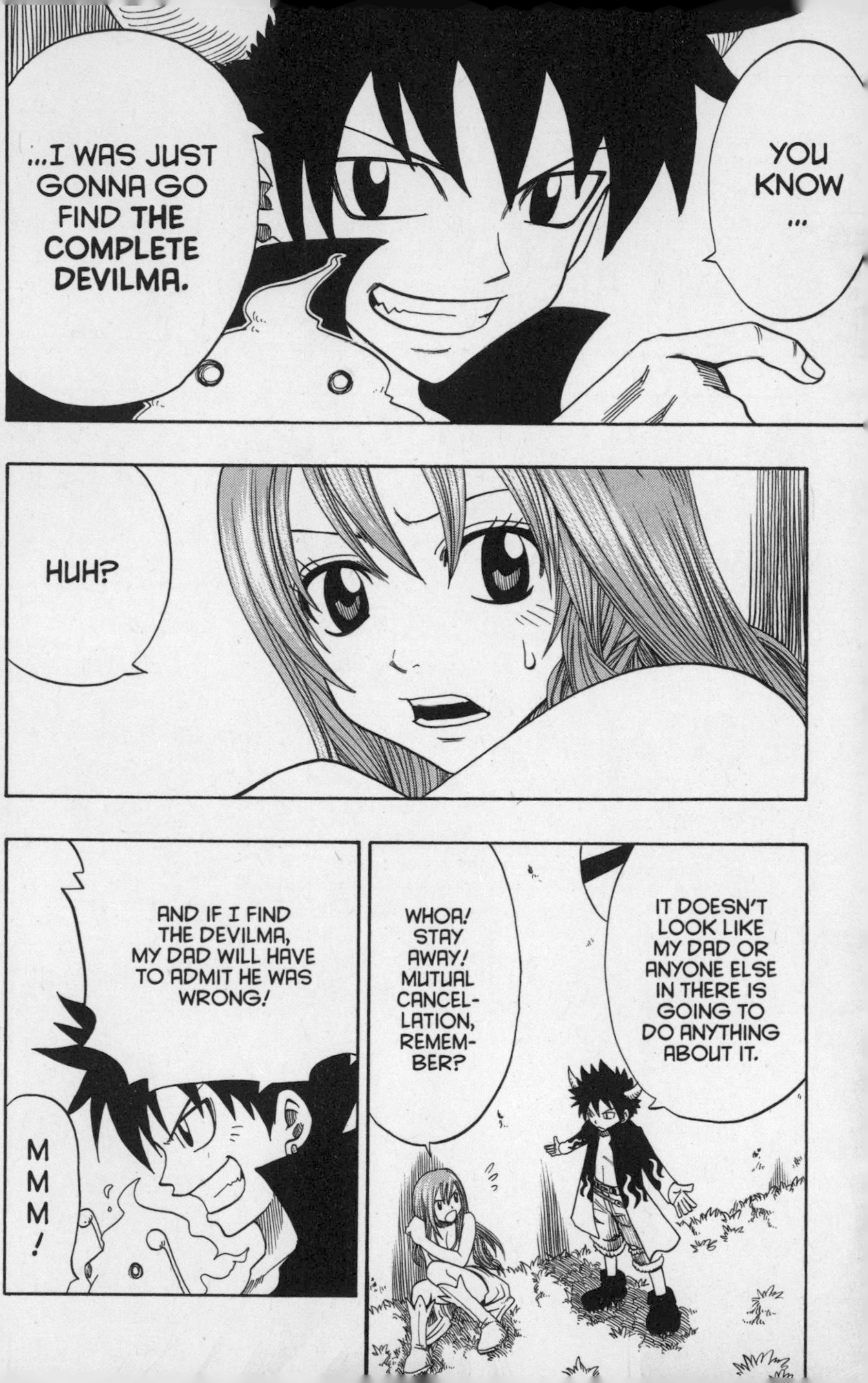
YOU KNOW ...
...I WAS JUST GONNA GO FIND THE COMPLETE DEVILMA.
HUH?
IT DOESN'T LOOK LIKE MY DAD OR ANYONE ELSE IN THERE IS GOING TO DO ANYTHING ABOUT IT.
WHOA! STAY AWAY! MUTUAL CANCEL-LATION, REMEM-BER?
AND IF I FIND THE DEVILMA, MY DAD WILL HAVE TO ADMIT HE WAS WRONG!
MMM!

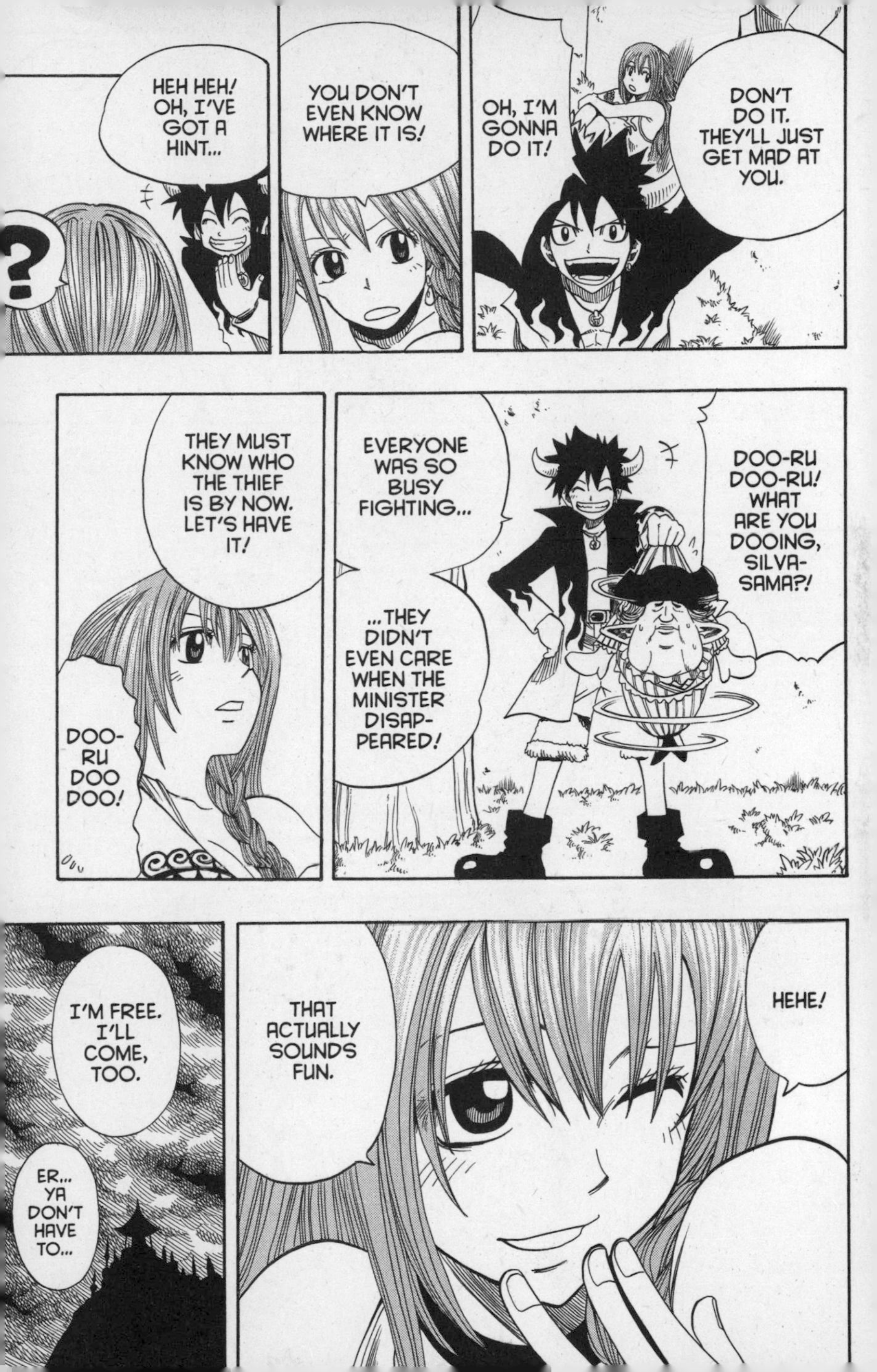
DON'T DO IT. THEY'LL JUST GET MAD AT YOU.
OH, I'M GONNA DO IT!
YOU DON'T EVEN KNOW WHERE IT IS!
HEH HEH! OH, I'VE GOT A HINT...
?
DOO-RU DOO-RU! WHAT ARE YOU DOOING, SILVA-SAMA?!
EVERYONE WAS SO BUSY FIGHTING...
...THEY DIDN'T EVEN CARE WHEN THE MINISTER DISAP-PEARED!
THEY MUST KNOW WHO THE THIEF IS BY NOW. LET'S HAVE IT!
DOO-RU DOO DOO!
HEHE!
THAT ACTUALLY SOUNDS FUN.
I'M FREE. I'LL COME, TOO.
ER... YA DON'T HAVE TO...

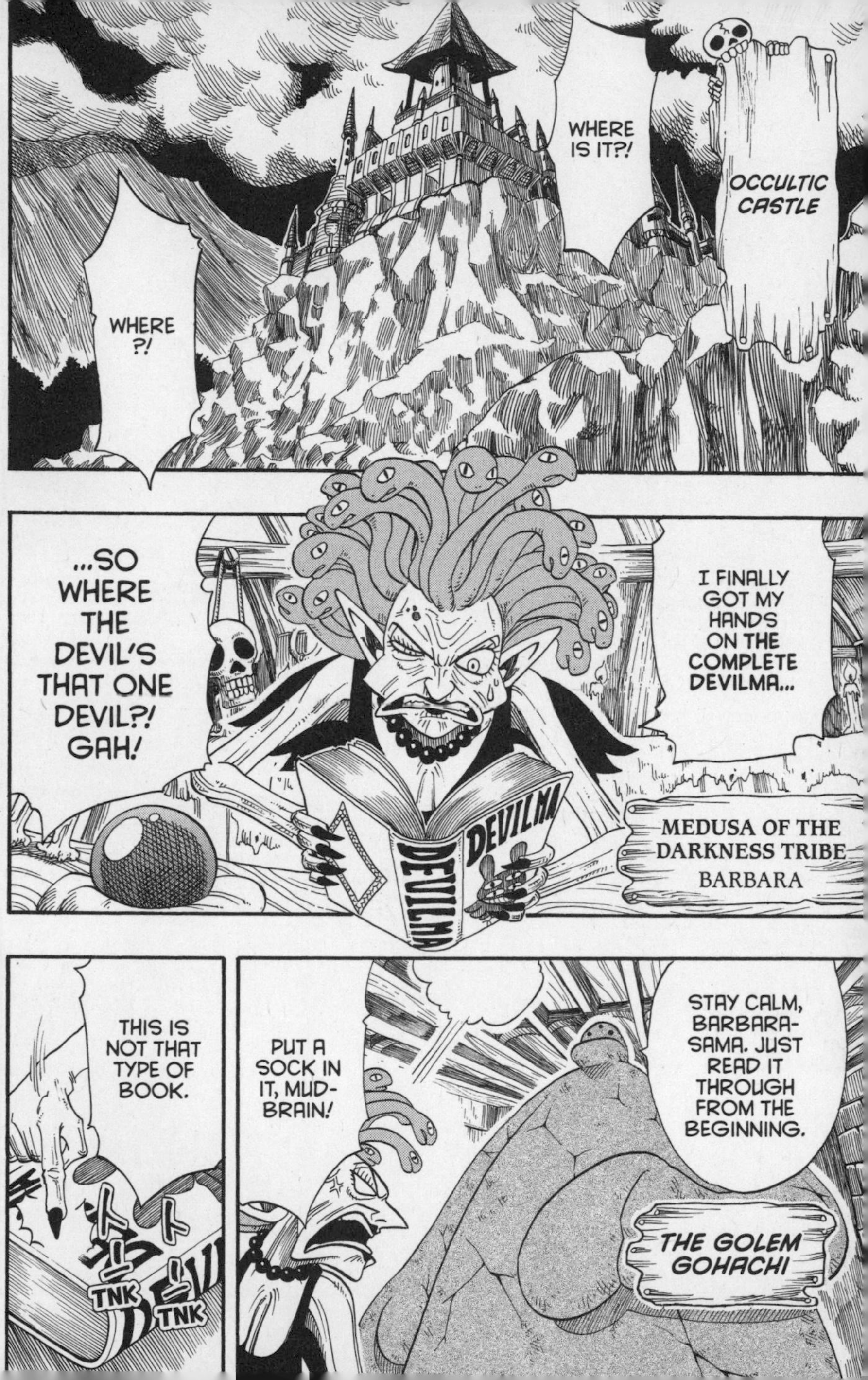
OCCULTIC CASTLE
WHERE IS IT?!
WHERE ?!
I FINALLY GOT MY HANDS ON THE COMPLETE DEVILMA...
MEDUSA OF THE DARKNESS TRIBE
BARBARA
...SO WHERE THE DEVIL'S THAT ONE DEVIL?! GAH!
DEVILMA
DEVILMA
STAY CALM, BARBARA-SAMA. JUST READ IT THROUGH FROM THE BEGINNING.
THE GOLEM GOHACHI
PUT A SOCK IN IT, MUD-BRAIN!
THIS IS NOT THAT TYPE OF BOOK.
TNK
TNK

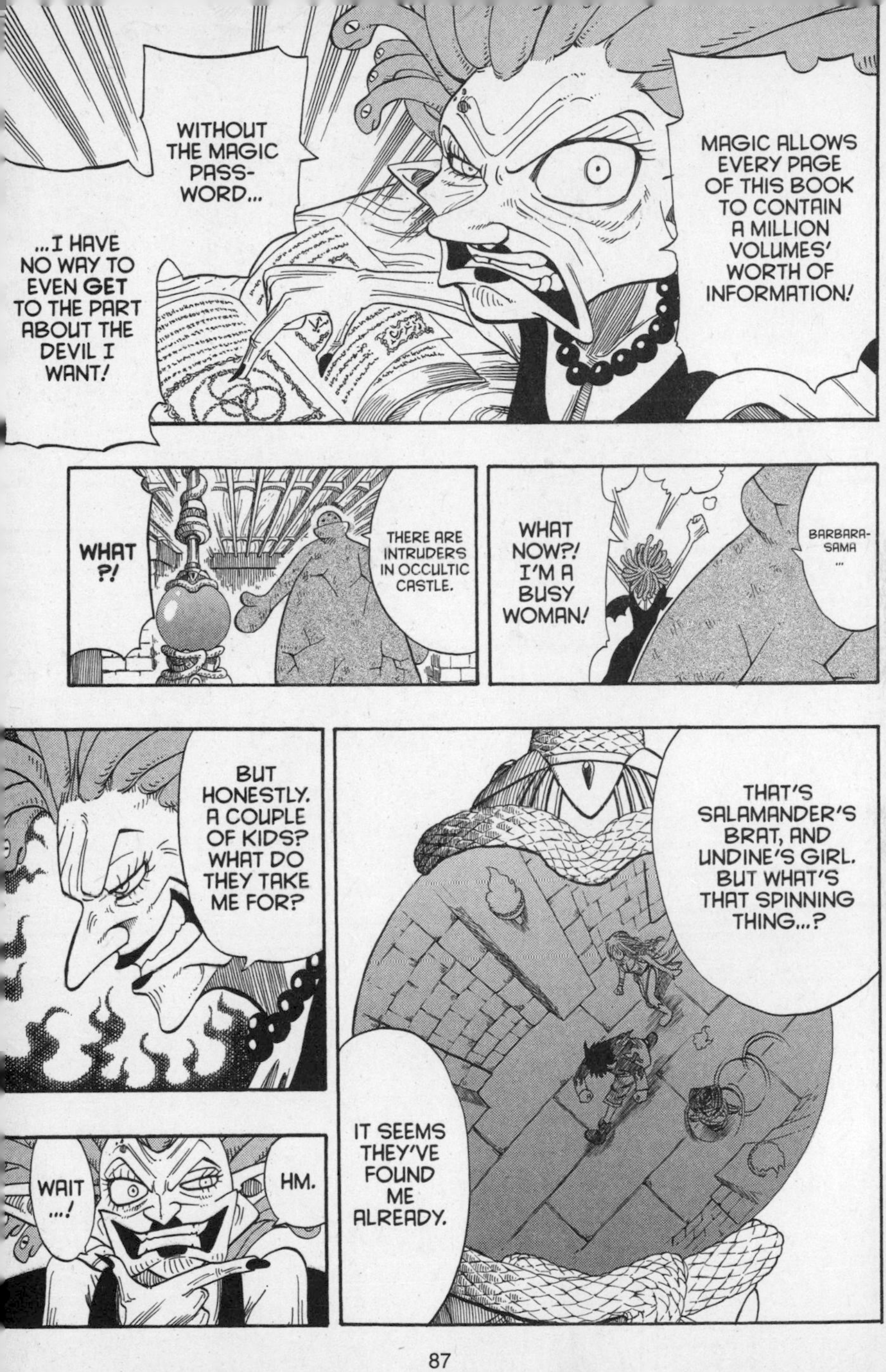
MAGIC ALLOWS EVERY PAGE OF THIS BOOK TO CONTAIN A MILLION VOLUMES' WORTH OF INFORMATION!
WITHOUT THE MAGIC PASS-WORD...
...I HAVE NO WAY TO EVEN GET TO THE PART ABOUT THE DEVIL I WANT!
BARBARA-SAMA ...
WHAT NOW?! I'M A BUSY WOMAN!
THERE ARE INTRUDERS IN OCCULTIC CASTLE.
WHAT ?!
THAT'S SALAMANDER'S BRAT, AND UNDINE'S GIRL. BUT WHAT'S THAT SPINNING THING...?
IT SEEMS THEY'VE FOUND ME ALREADY.
BUT HONESTLY. A COUPLE OF KIDS? WHAT DO THEY TAKE ME FOR?
HM.
WAIT ...!

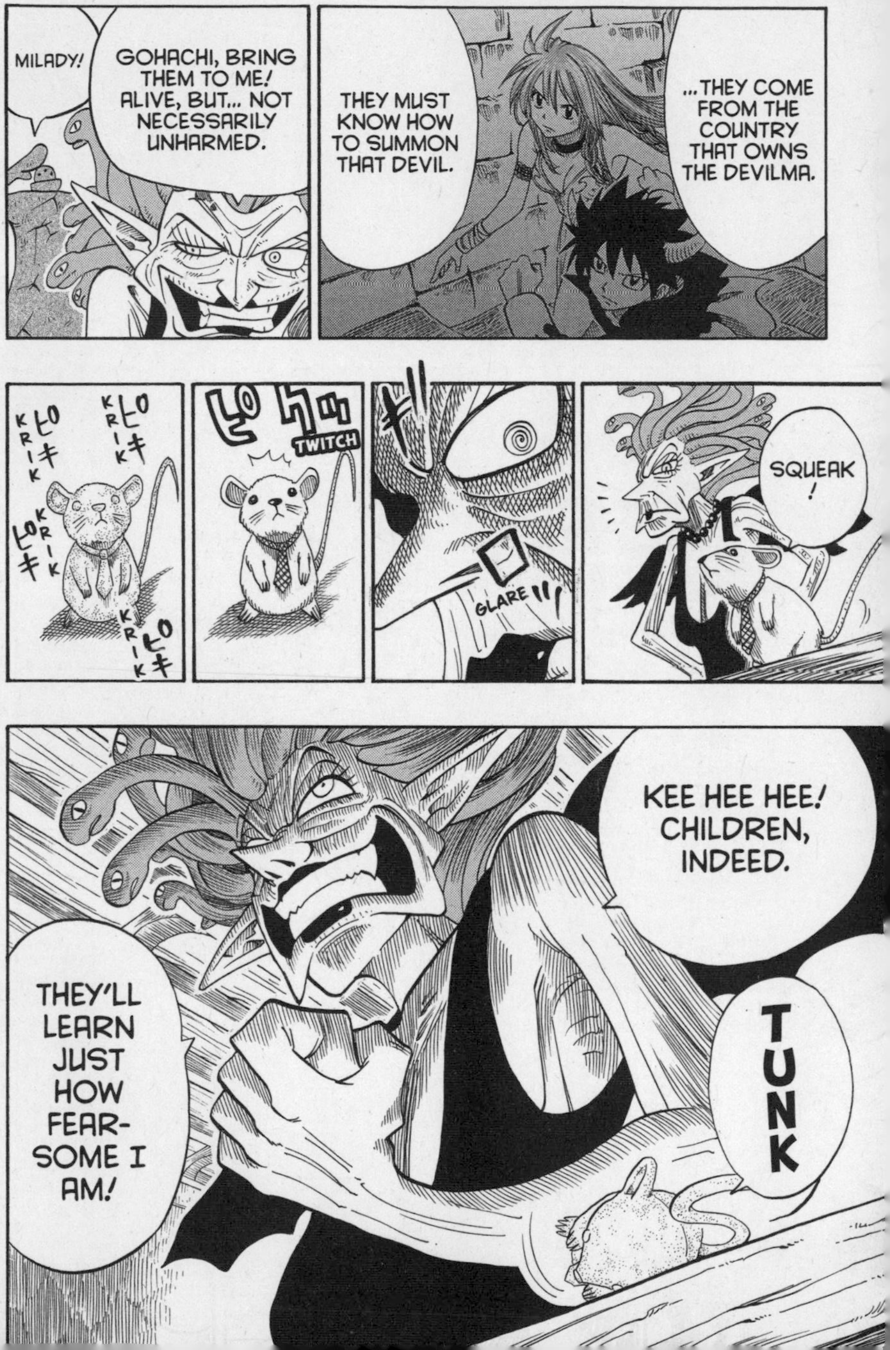
...THEY COME FROM THE COUNTRY THAT OWNS THE DEVILMA.
THEY MUST KNOW HOW TO SUMMON THAT DEVIL.
GOHACHI, BRING THEM TO ME! ALIVE, BUT... NOT NECESSARILY UNHARMED.
MILADY!
SQUEAK!
GLARE
TWITCH
KRIK
KRIK
KRIK
KRIK
KEE HEE HEE! CHILDREN, INDEED.
TUNK
THEY'LL LEARN JUST HOW FEAR-SOME I AM!

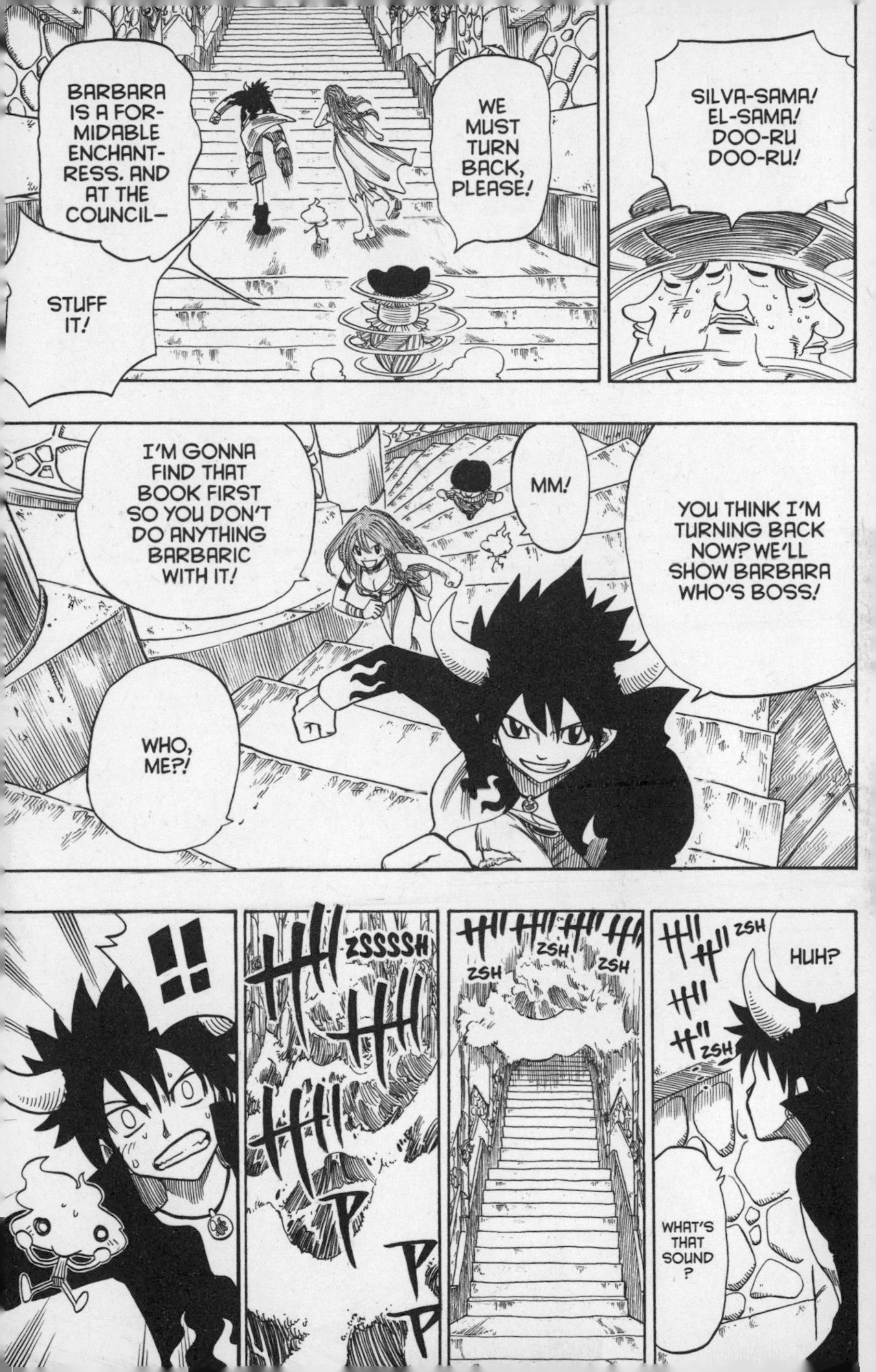
SILVA-SAMA! EL-SAMA! DOO-RU DOO-RU!
WE MUST TURN BACK, PLEASE!
BARBARA IS A FORMIDABLE ENCHANTRESS. AND AT THE COUNCIL—
STUFF IT!
YOU THINK I'M TURNING BACK NOW? WE'LL SHOW BARBARA WHO'S BOSS!
MM!
I'M GONNA FIND THAT BOOK FIRST SO YOU DON'T DO ANYTHING BARBARIC WITH IT!
WHO, ME?!
ZSH
HUH?
ZSH
WHAT'S THAT SOUND?
ZSH
ZSH
ZSH
ZSSSSH
!!

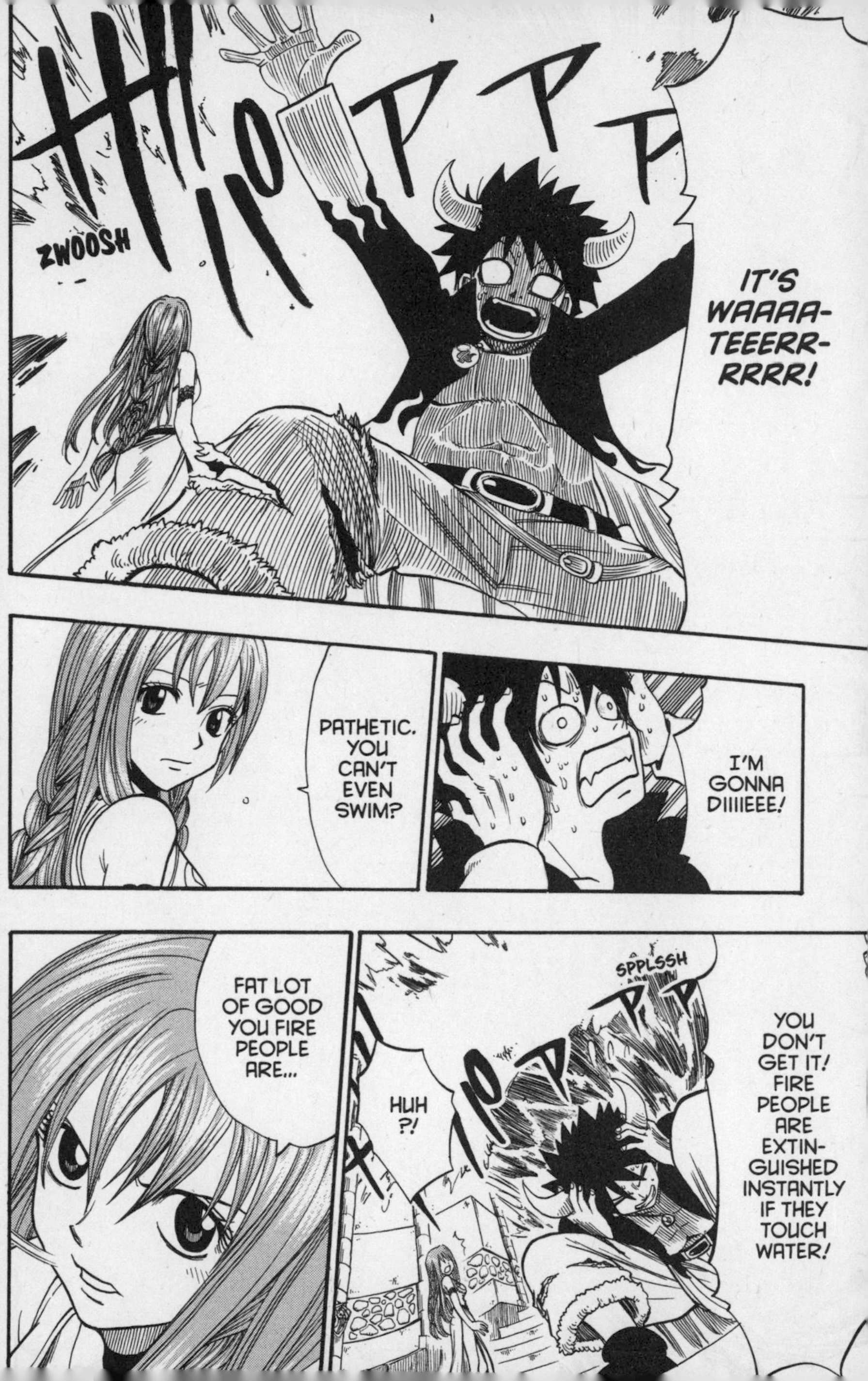
ZWOOSH
IT'S WAAAA-TEEERR-RRRR!
I'M GONNA DIIIIEEE!
PATHETIC. YOU CAN'T EVEN SWIM?
SPPLSSH
YOU DON'T GET IT! FIRE PEOPLE ARE EXTIN-GUISHED INSTANTLY IF THEY TOUCH WATER!
HUH ?!
FAT LOT OF GOOD YOU FIRE PEOPLE ARE...

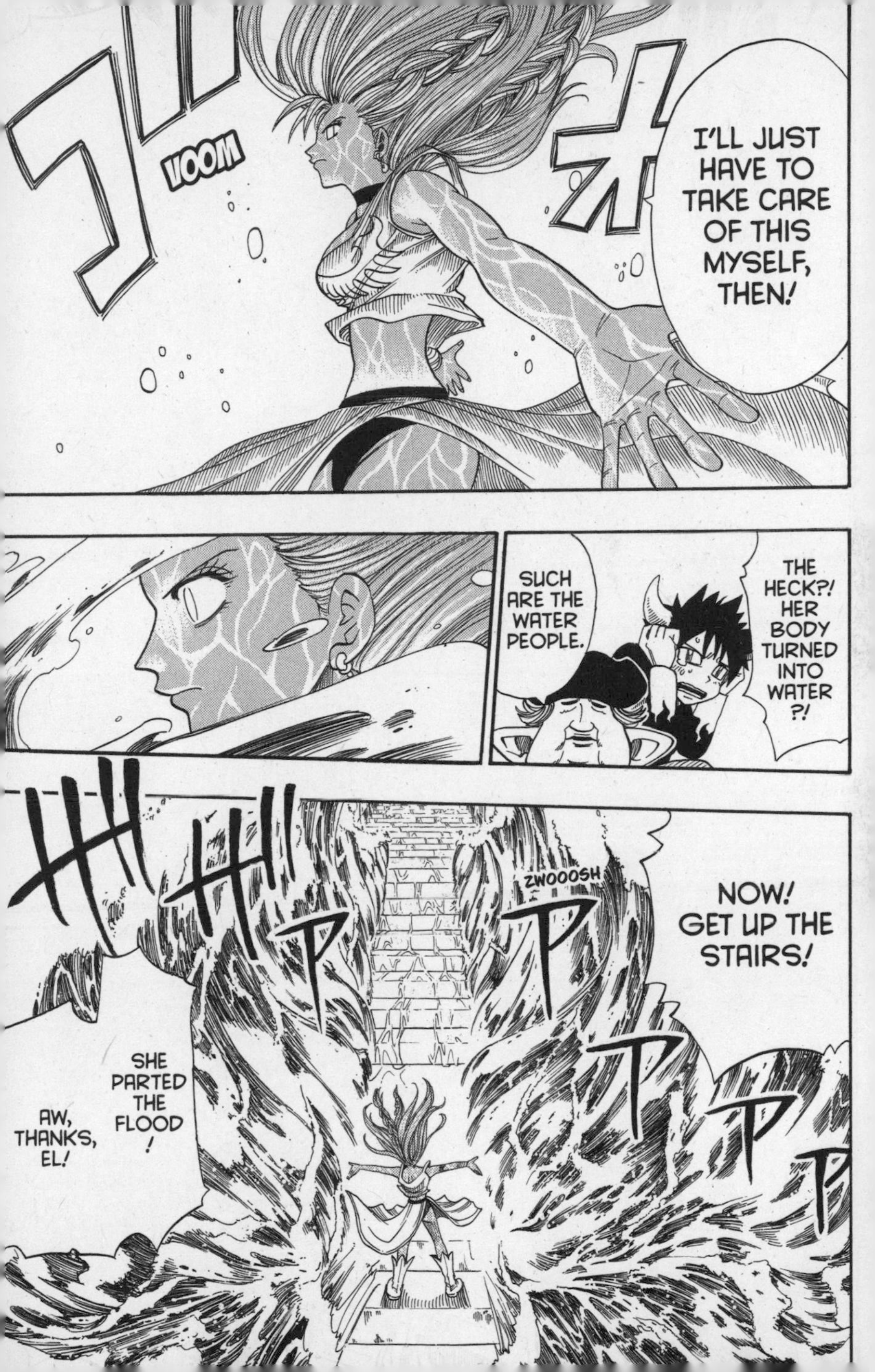
I'LL JUST HAVE TO TAKE CARE OF THIS MYSELF, THEN!
VOOM
THE HECK?! HER BODY TURNED INTO WATER?!
SUCH ARE THE WATER PEOPLE.
NOW! GET UP THE STAIRS!
ZWOOOSH
SHE PARTED THE FLOOD!
AW, THANKS, EL!

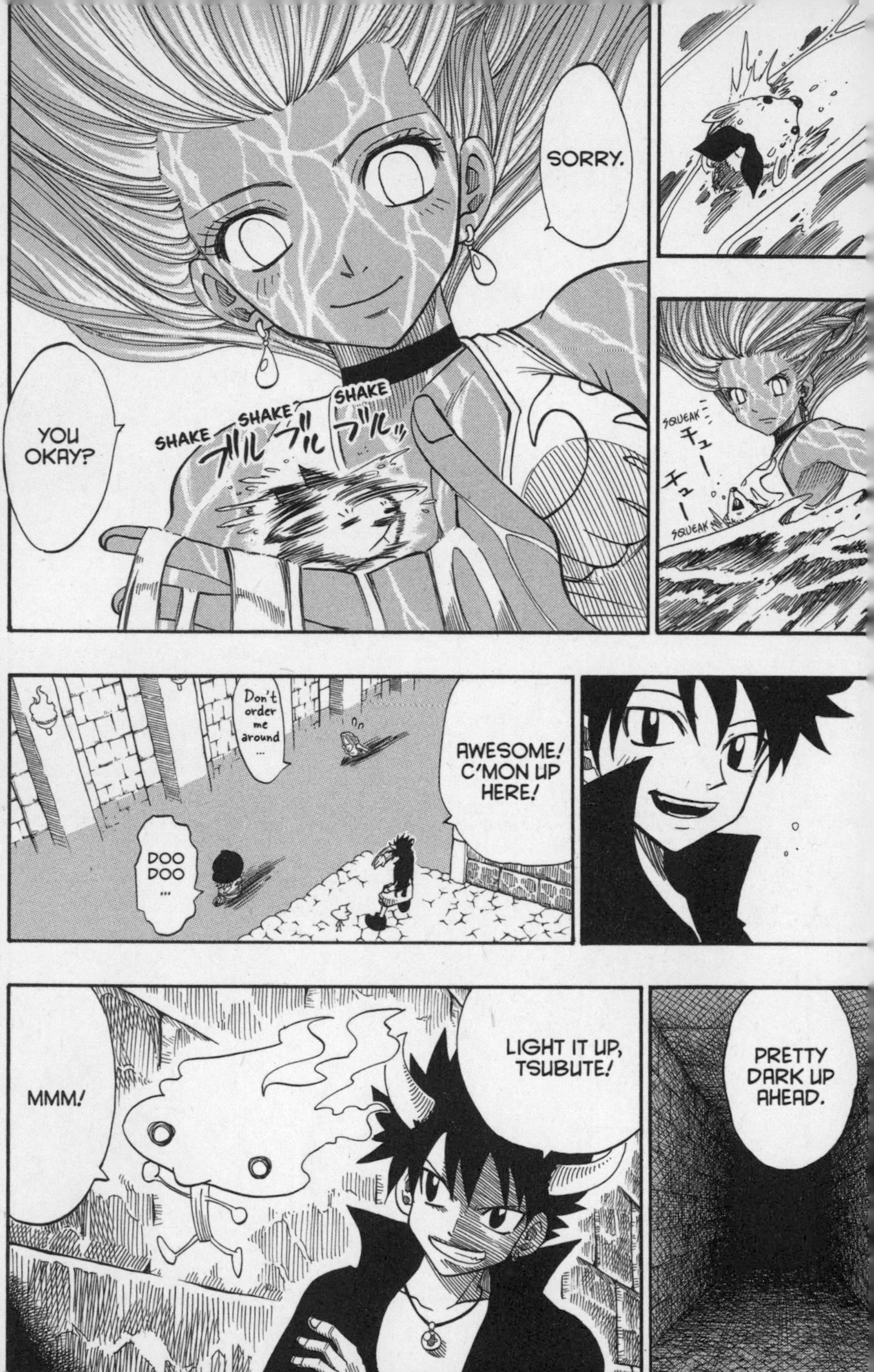
SQUEAK
チュー
チュー
SQUEAK
SORRY.
SHAKE SHAKE SHAKE
ブルブルブルッ
YOU OKAY?
AWESOME! C'MON UP HERE!
Don't order me around ...
DOO DOO ...
PRETTY DARK UP AHEAD.
LIGHT IT UP, TSUBUTE!
MMM!

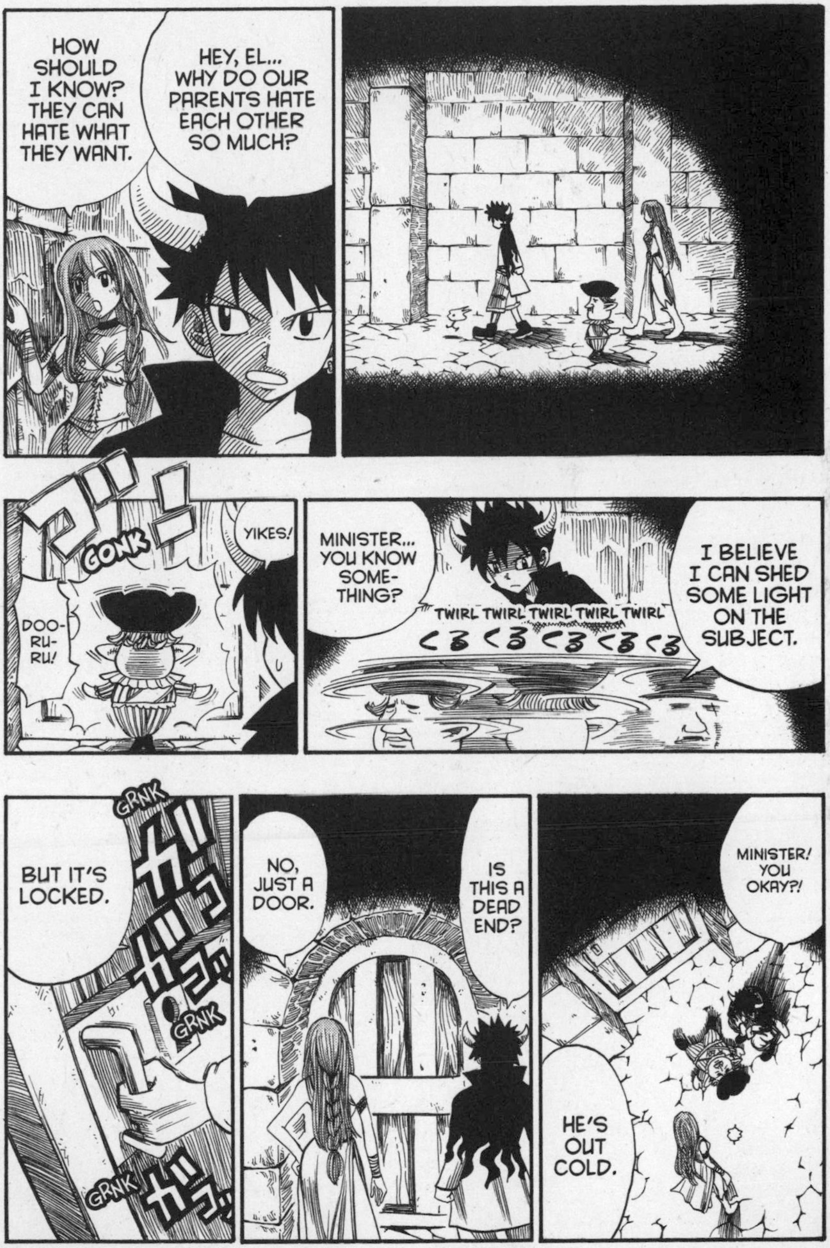
HEY, EL... WHY DO OUR PARENTS HATE EACH OTHER SO MUCH?
HOW SHOULD I KNOW? THEY CAN HATE WHAT THEY WANT.
I BELIEVE I CAN SHED SOME LIGHT ON THE SUBJECT.
MINISTER... YOU KNOW SOME-THING?
TWIRL TWIRL TWIRL TWIRL TWIRL
くるくるくるくるくる
YIKES!
GONK
DOO-RU-RU!
MINISTER! YOU OKAY?!
HE'S OUT COLD.
IS THIS A DEAD END?
NO, JUST A DOOR.
GRNK
BUT IT'S LOCKED.
GRNK
GRNK

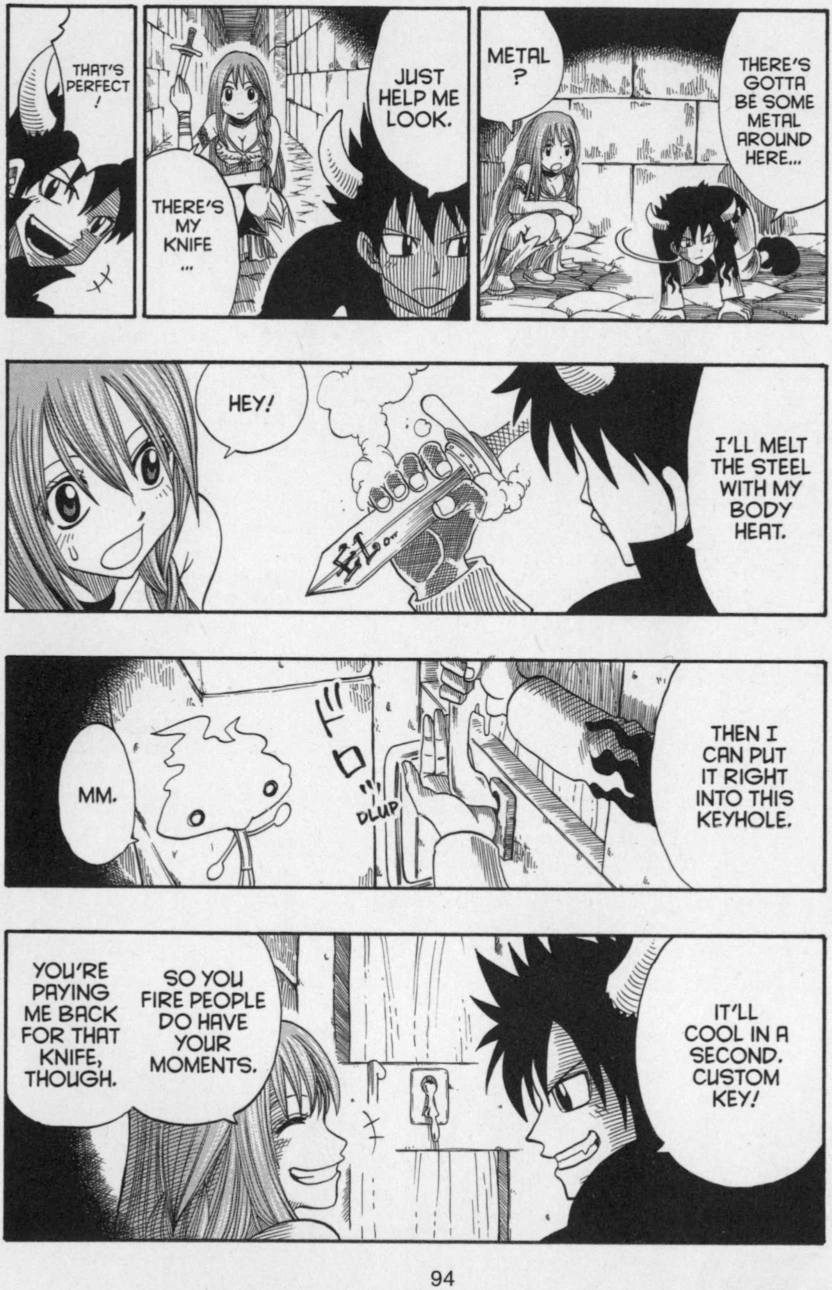
THERE'S GOTTA BE SOME METAL AROUND HERE...
METAL ?
JUST HELP ME LOOK.
THERE'S MY KNIFE ...
THAT'S PERFECT !
I'LL MELT THE STEEL WITH MY BODY HEAT.
HEY!
THEN I CAN PUT IT RIGHT INTO THIS KEYHOLE.
ドロッ
DLUP
MM.
IT'LL COOL IN A SECOND. CUSTOM KEY!
SO YOU FIRE PEOPLE DO HAVE YOUR MOMENTS.
YOU'RE PAYING ME BACK FOR THAT KNIFE, THOUGH.

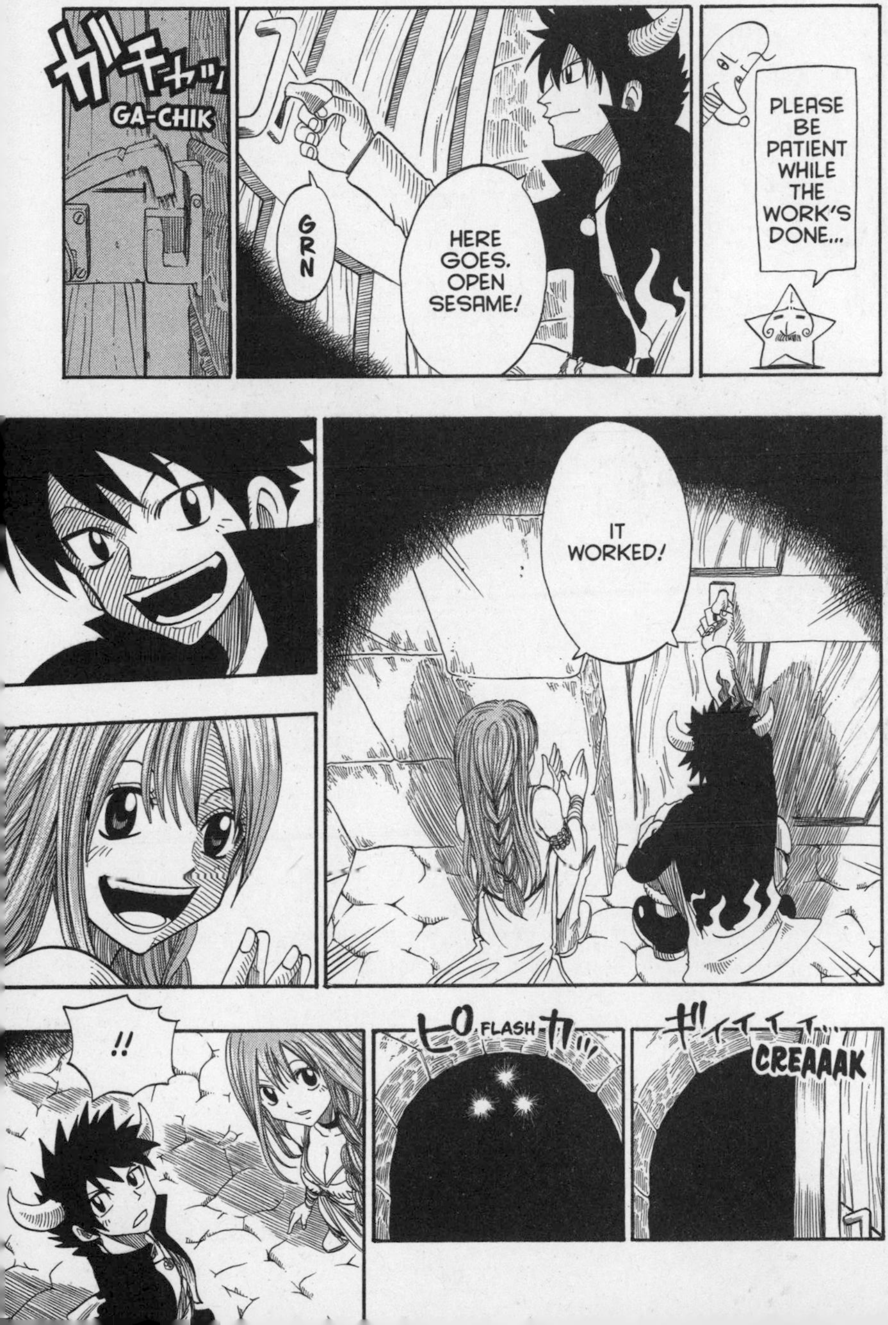
PLEASE BE PATIENT WHILE THE WORK'S DONE...
HERE GOES. OPEN SESAME!
GRN
GA-CHIK
IT WORKED!
CREAAAK
FLASH
!!

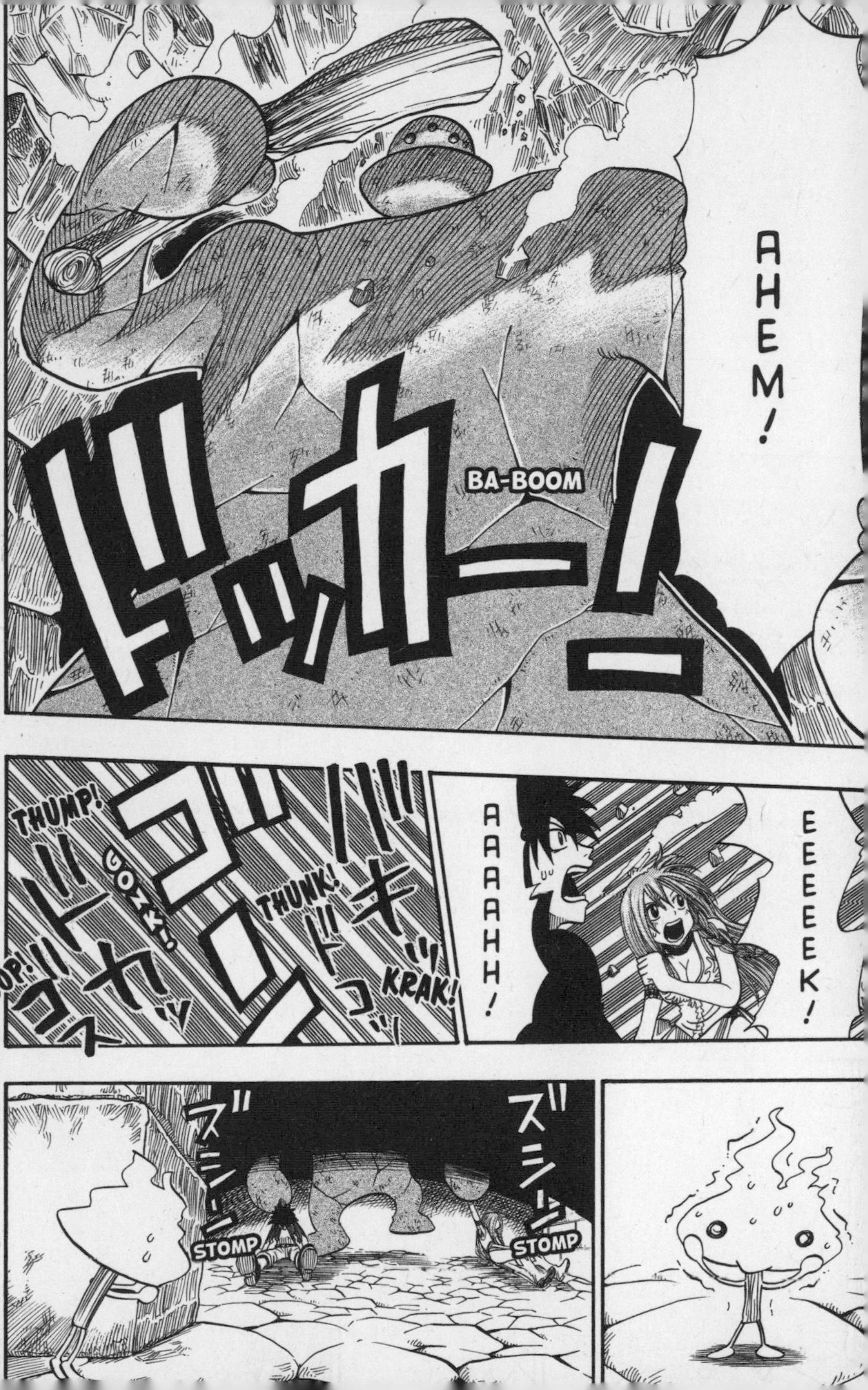
AHEM!
BA-BOOM
EEEEEK!
AAAAAHH!
KRAK!
THUNK!
GONK!
THUMP!
OOP!
STOMP
STOMP

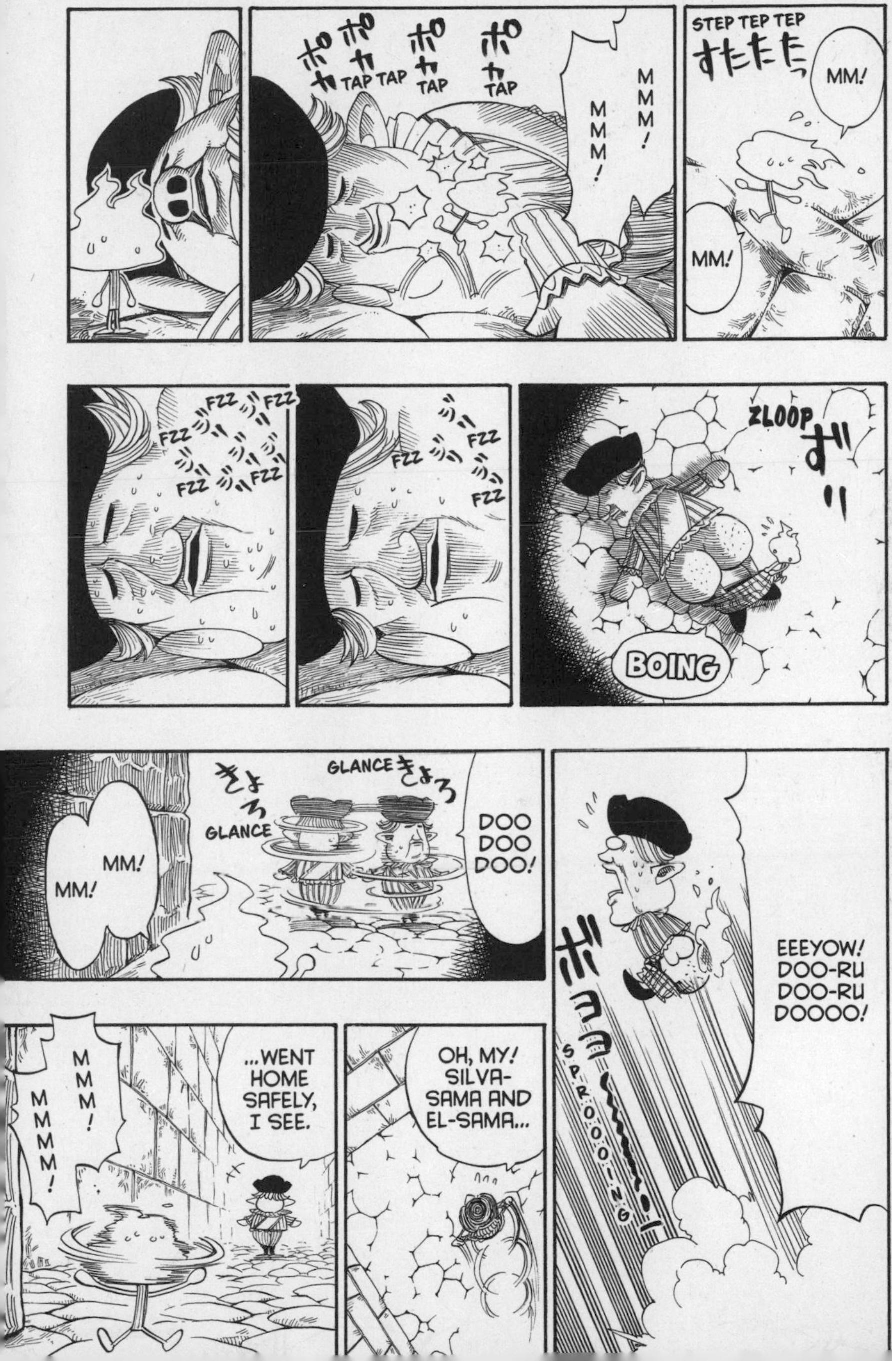
STEP TEP TEP
すたたたっ
MM!
MM!
ポカ
TAP
ポカ
TAP
ポカ
TAP TAP
ポカ
MMM!
MMM!
ZLOOP
ずり
BOING
FZZ
FZZ
FZZ
FZZ
FZZ
FZZ
FZZ
FZZ
ボヨヨ
SPROOOOING
EEEYOW! DOO-RU DOO-RU DOOOO!
DOO DOO DOO!
GLANCE きょろ
きょろ GLANCE
MM!
MM!
OH, MY! SILVA-SAMA AND EL-SAMA...
...WENT HOME SAFELY, I SEE.
MMM!
MMMM!

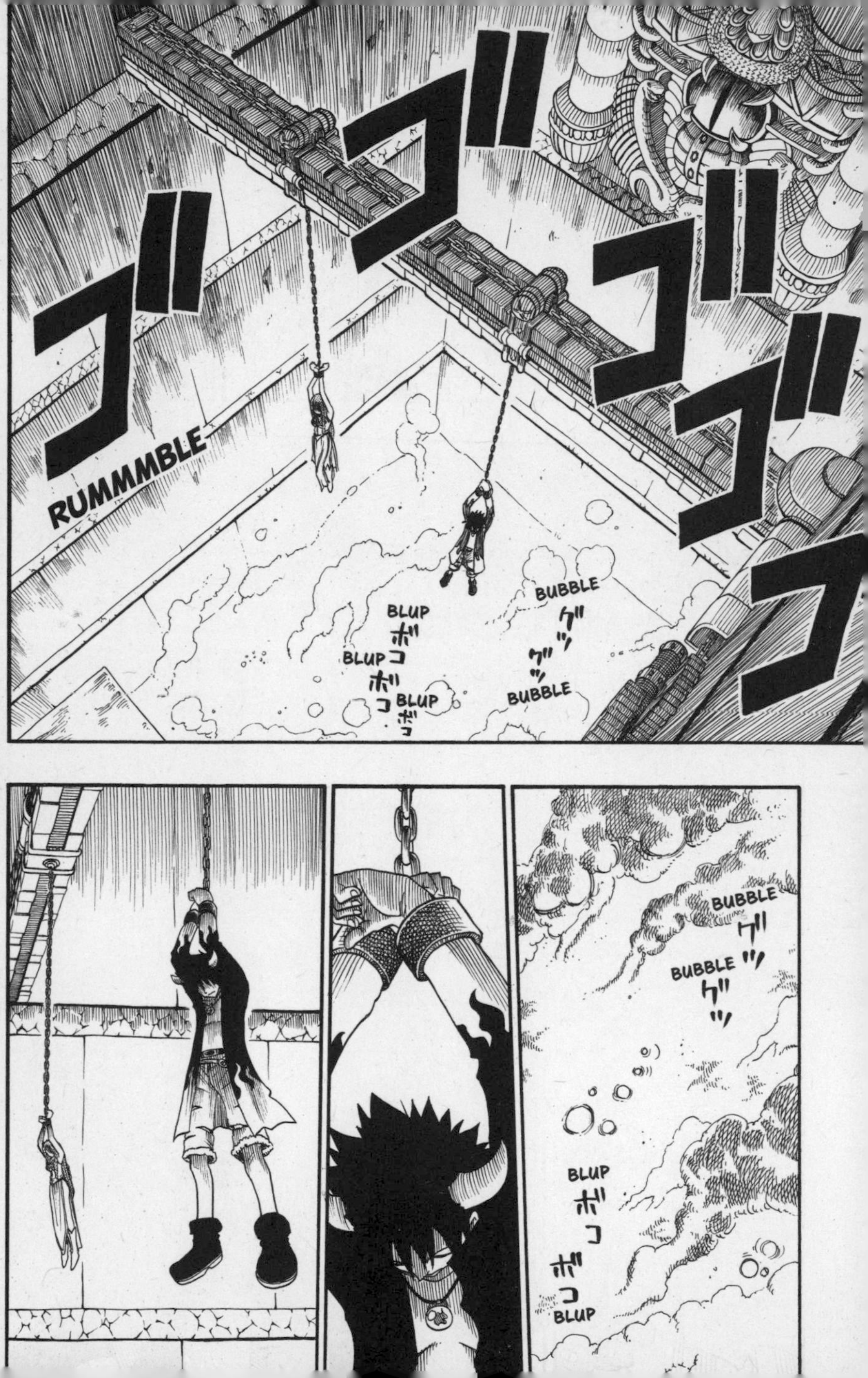
ゴゴゴゴ
ゴゴ
RUMMMBLE
BUBBLE
グツ
グツ
BUBBLE
BLUP
ボコ
BLUP
ボコ
BLUP
ボコ
BUBBLE
グツ
BUBBLE
グツ
BLUP
ボコ
ボコ
BLUP

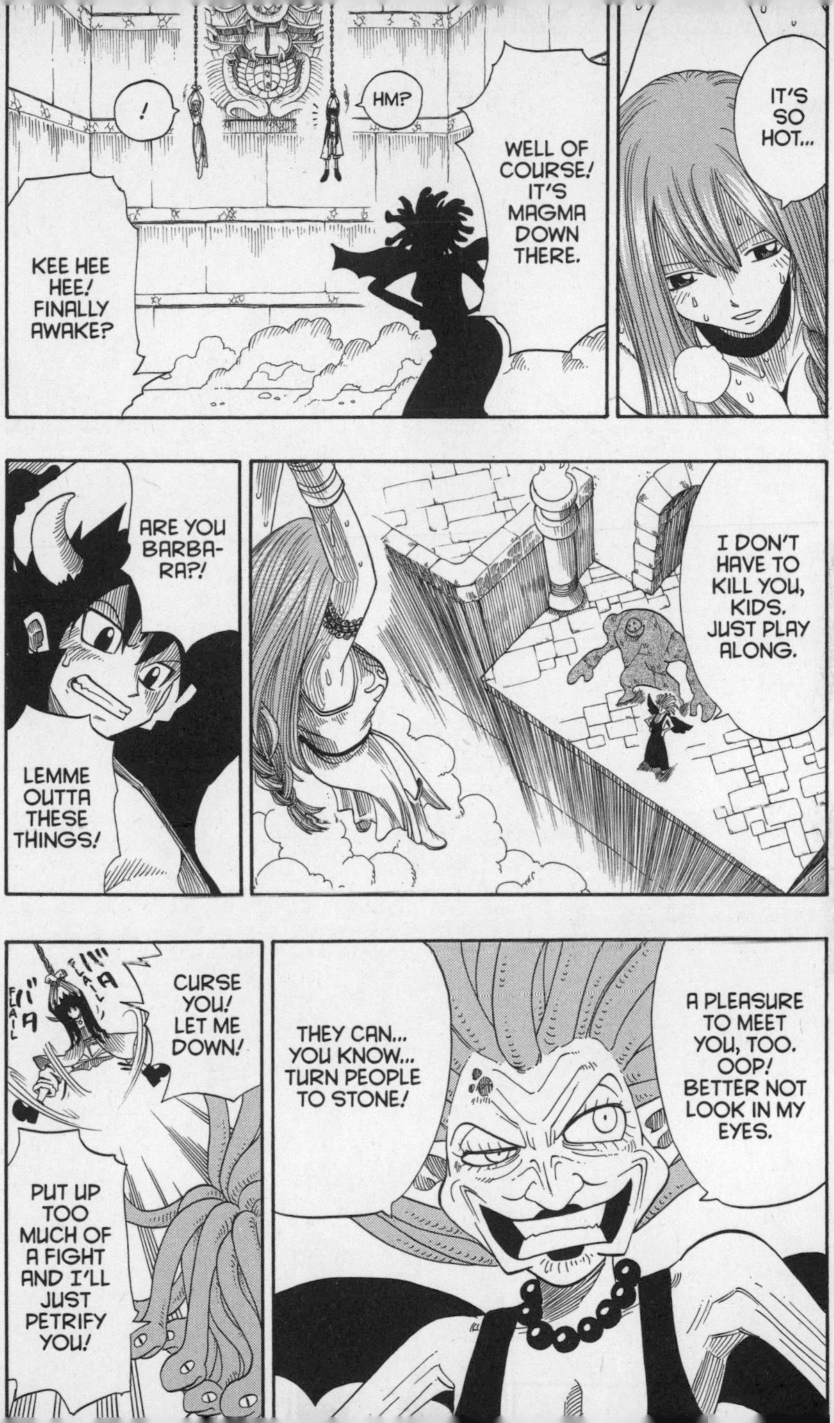

IT'S SO HOT...
WELL OF COURSE! IT'S MAGMA DOWN THERE.
HM?
!
KEE HEE HEE! FINALLY AWAKE?
I DON'T HAVE TO KILL YOU, KIDS. JUST PLAY ALONG.
ARE YOU BARBARA?!
LEMME OUTTA THESE THINGS!
A PLEASURE TO MEET YOU, TOO. OOP! BETTER NOT LOOK IN MY EYES.
THEY CAN... YOU KNOW... TURN PEOPLE TO STONE!
バ A
FLAIL
バ A
FLAIL
CURSE YOU! LET ME DOWN!
PUT UP TOO MUCH OF A FIGHT AND I'LL JUST PETRIFY YOU!

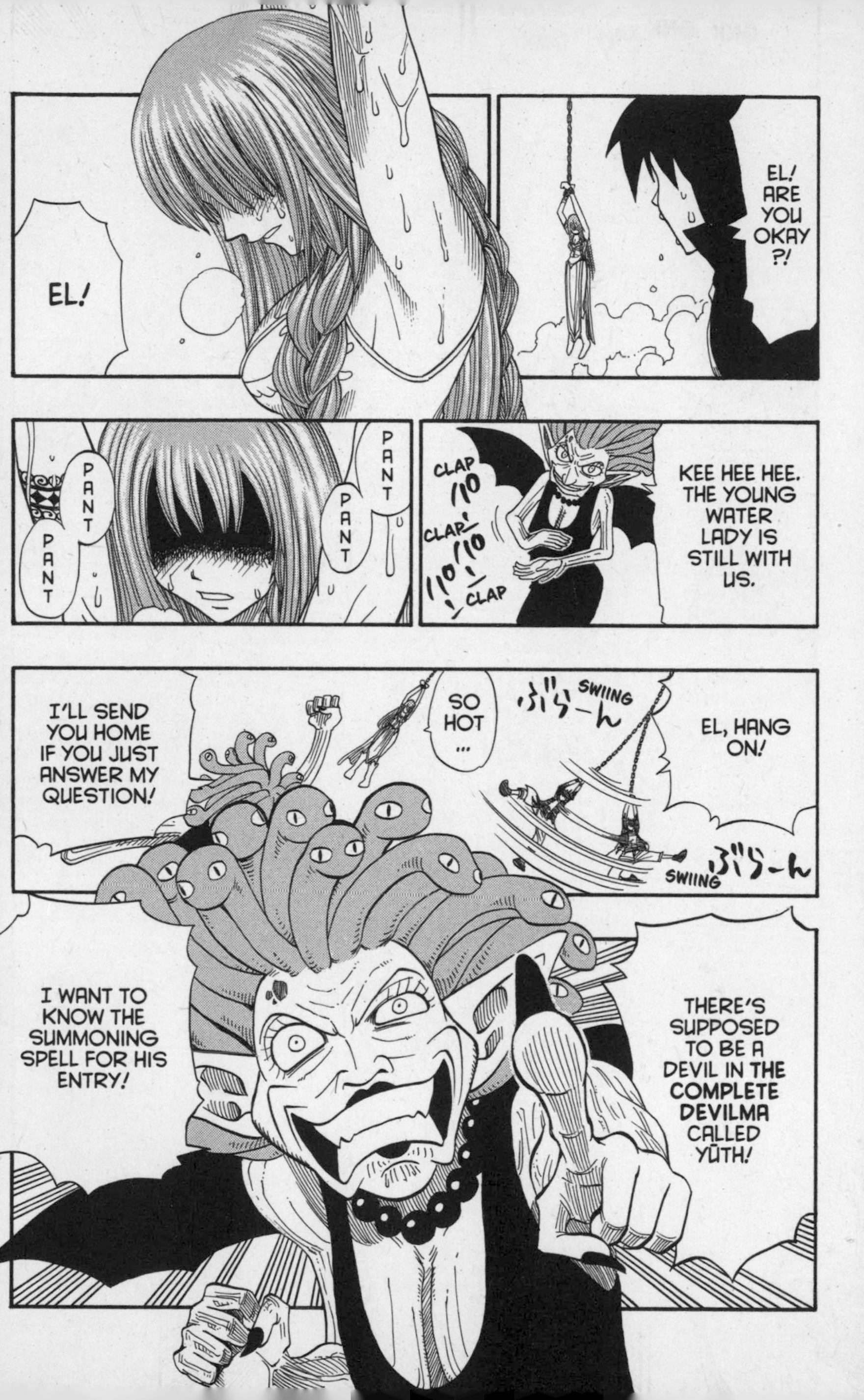
EL! ARE YOU OKAY?!
EL!
KEE HEE HEE. THE YOUNG WATER LADY IS STILL WITH US.
CLAP
CLAP
CLAP
PANT
PANT
PANT
PANT
EL, HANG ON!
SWIING
ぶらーん
SWIING
ぶらーん
SO HOT ...
I'LL SEND YOU HOME IF YOU JUST ANSWER MY QUESTION!
THERE'S SUPPOSED TO BE A DEVIL IN THE COMPLETE DEVILMA CALLED YŪTH!
I WANT TO KNOW THE SUMMONING SPELL FOR HIS ENTRY!

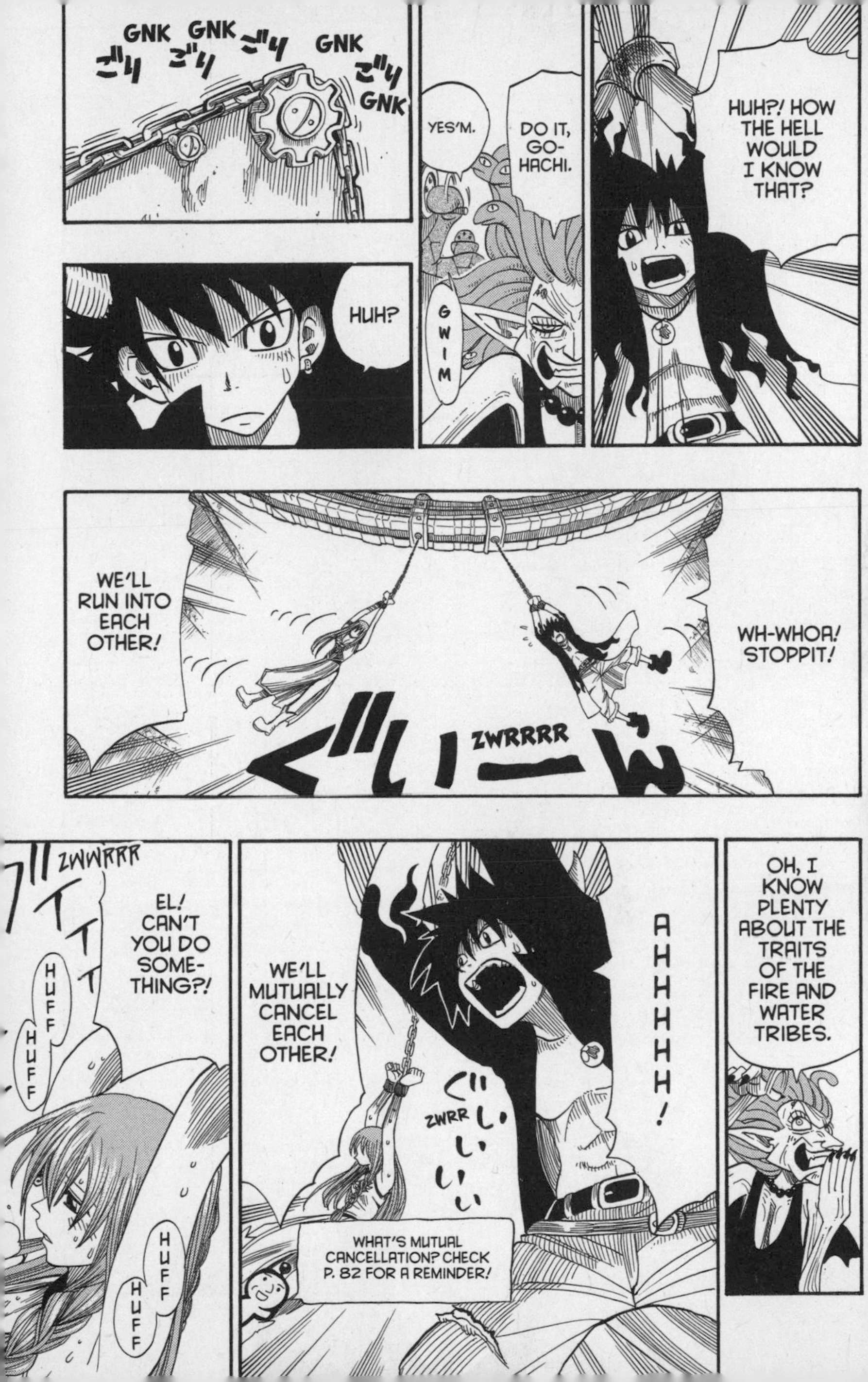
HUH?! HOW THE HELL WOULD I KNOW THAT?
DO IT, GO-HACHI.
YES'M.
GWIM
GNK GNK GNK GNK
ごり ごり ごり ごり
HUH?
WH-WHOA! STOPPIT!
WE'LL RUN INTO EACH OTHER!
ZWRRRR
OH, I KNOW PLENTY ABOUT THE TRAITS OF THE FIRE AND WATER TRIBES.
AHHHHHH!
WE'LL MUTUALLY CANCEL EACH OTHER!
ZWRR
WHAT'S MUTUAL CANCELLATION? CHECK P. 82 FOR A REMINDER!
ZWWRRR
EL! CAN'T YOU DO SOMETHING?!
HUFF HUFF
HUFF HUFF

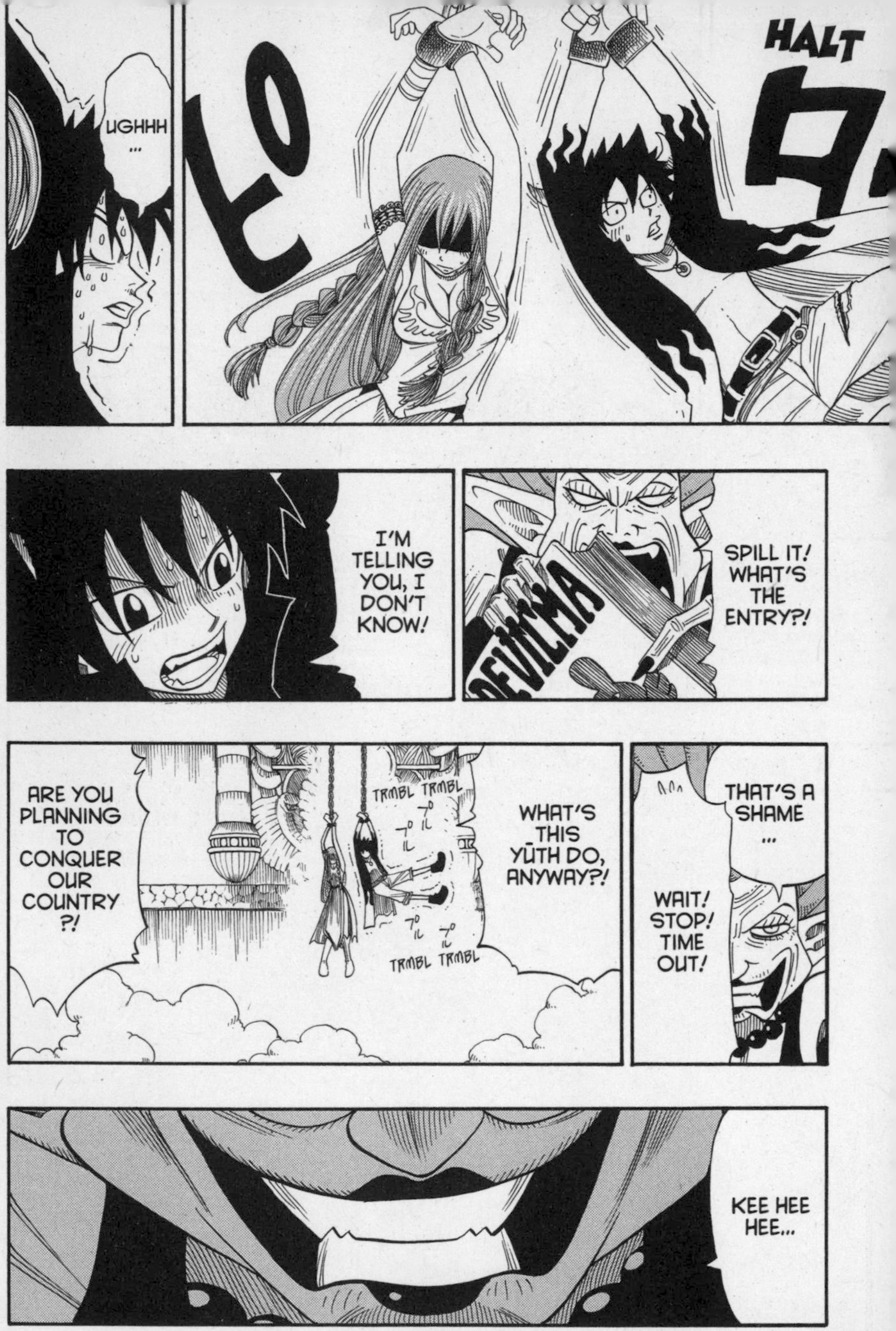
HALT
UGHHH ...
SPILL IT! WHAT'S THE ENTRY?!
I'M TELLING YOU, I DON'T KNOW!
THAT'S A SHAME ...
WAIT! STOP! TIME OUT!
WHAT'S THIS YŪTH DO, ANYWAY?!
TRMBL TRMBL
プル プル
プル プル
TRMBL TRMBL
ARE YOU PLANNING TO CONQUER OUR COUNTRY ?!
KEE HEE HEE...

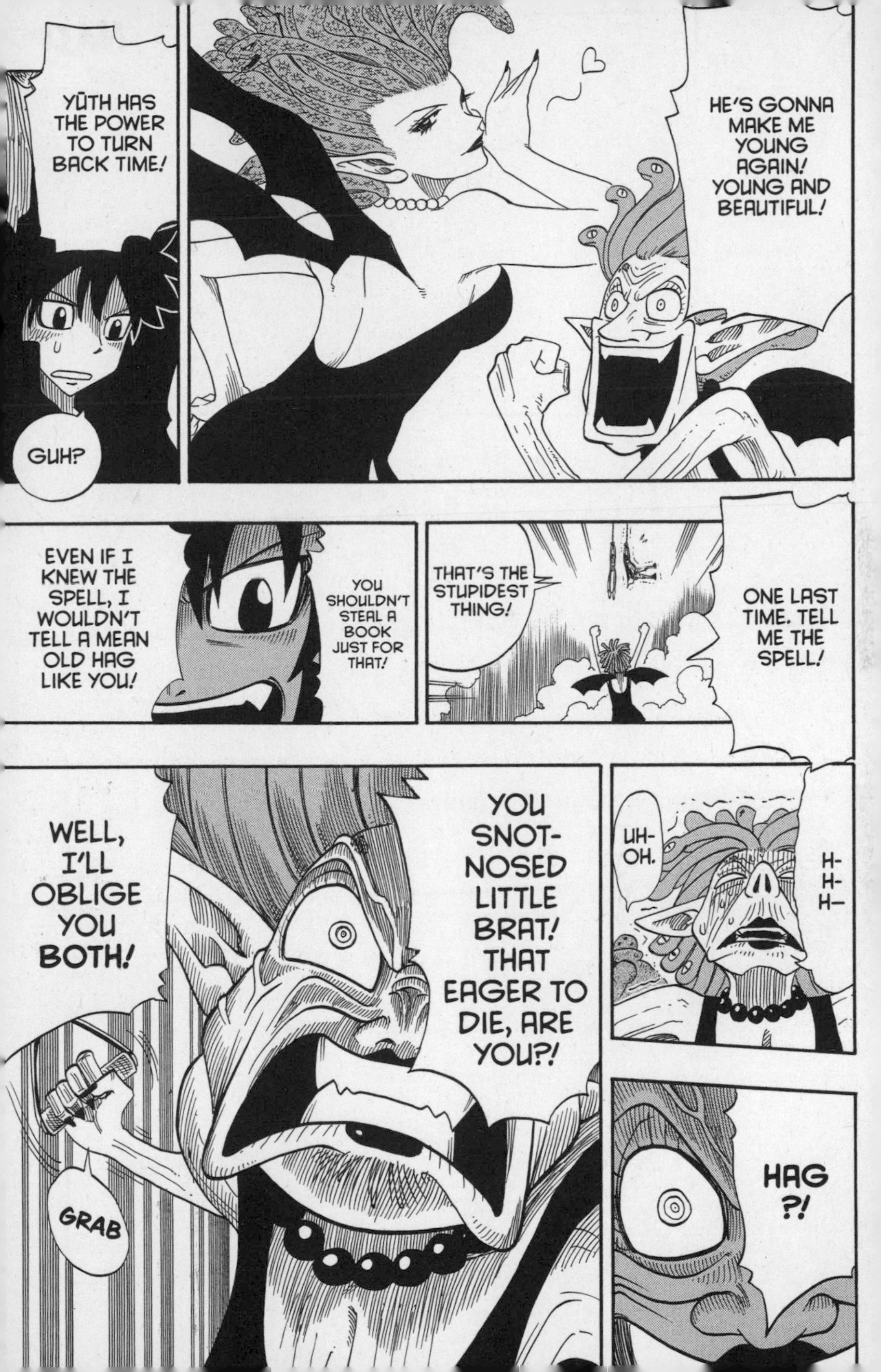
HE'S GONNA MAKE ME YOUNG AGAIN! YOUNG AND BEAUTIFUL!
YŪTH HAS THE POWER TO TURN BACK TIME!
GUH?
ONE LAST TIME. TELL ME THE SPELL!
THAT'S THE STUPIDEST THING!
YOU SHOULDN'T STEAL A BOOK JUST FOR THAT!
EVEN IF I KNEW THE SPELL, I WOULDN'T TELL A MEAN OLD HAG LIKE YOU!
H-H-H—
UH-OH.
HAG?!
YOU SNOT-NOSED LITTLE BRAT! THAT EAGER TO DIE, ARE YOU?!
WELL, I'LL OBLIGE YOU BOTH!
GRAB

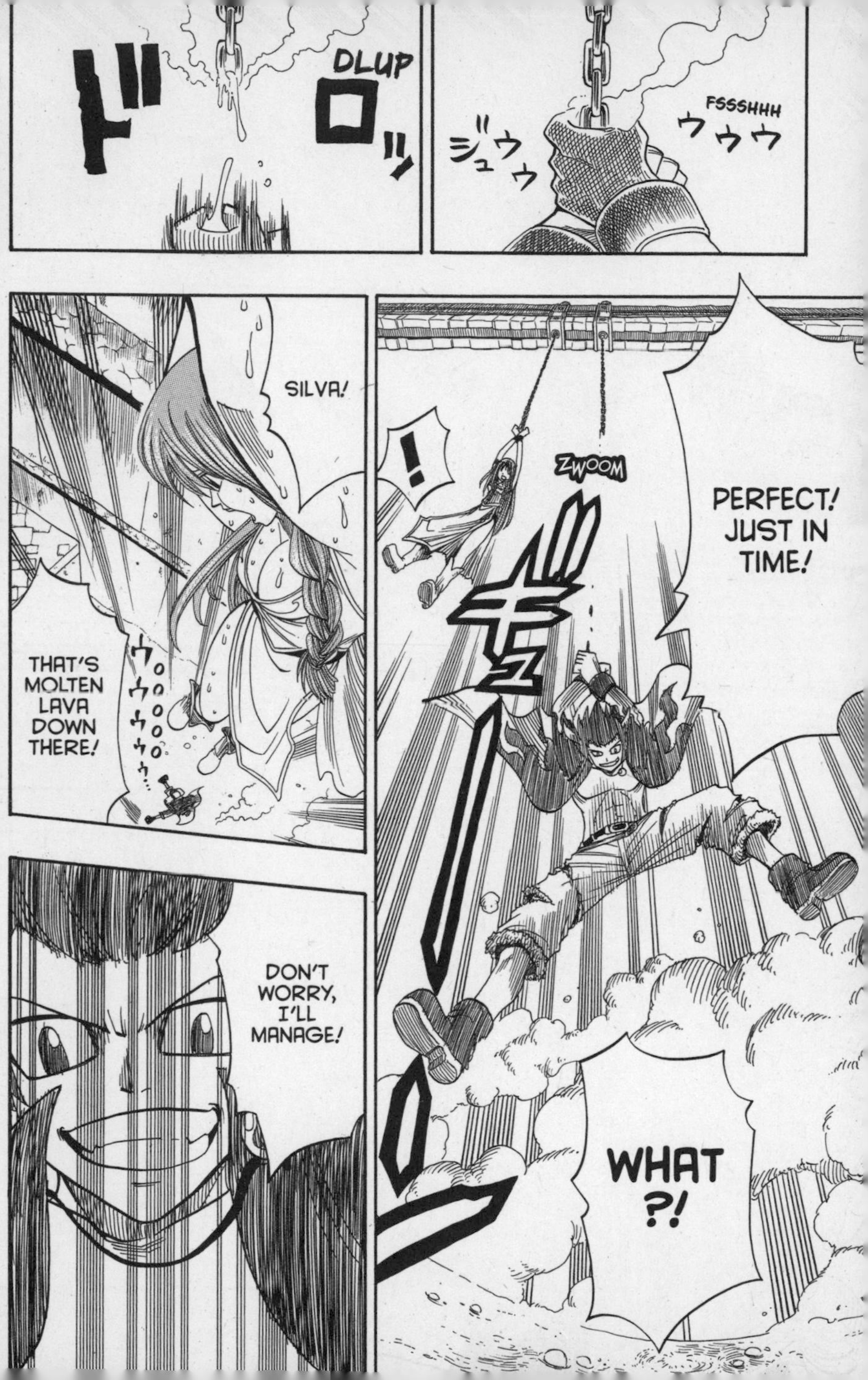
FSSSHHH
ジュウウ
ウウウ
DLUP
ドロッ
PERFECT! JUST IN TIME!
!
ZWOOM
ギュン
WHAT?!
SILVA!
THAT'S MOLTEN LAVA DOWN THERE!
DON'T WORRY, I'LL MANAGE!

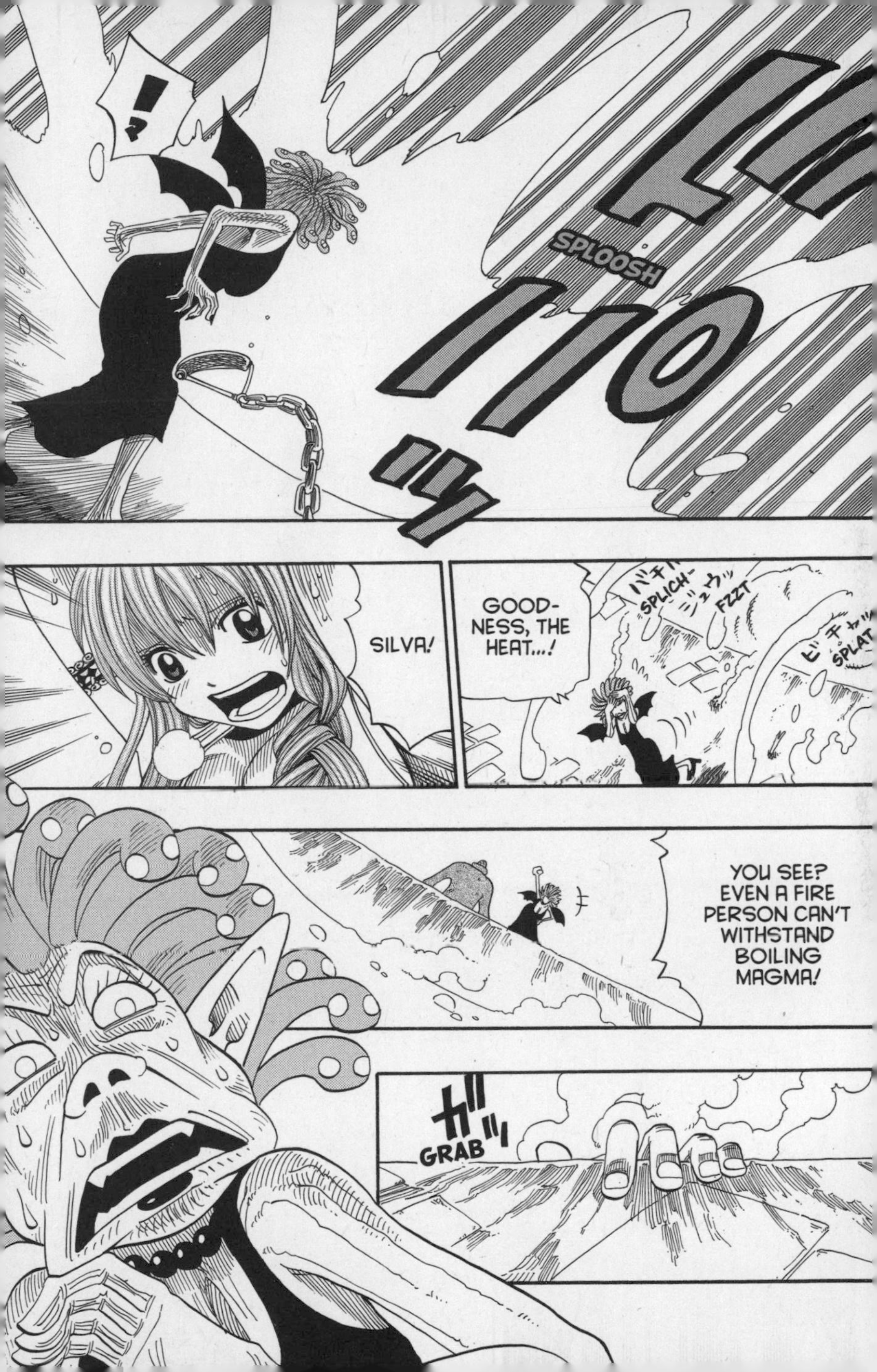
!
SPLOOSH
GOODNESS, THE HEAT...!
SPLICH
FZZT
SPLAT
SILVA!
YOU SEE? EVEN A FIRE PERSON CAN'T WITHSTAND BOILING MAGMA!
GRAB

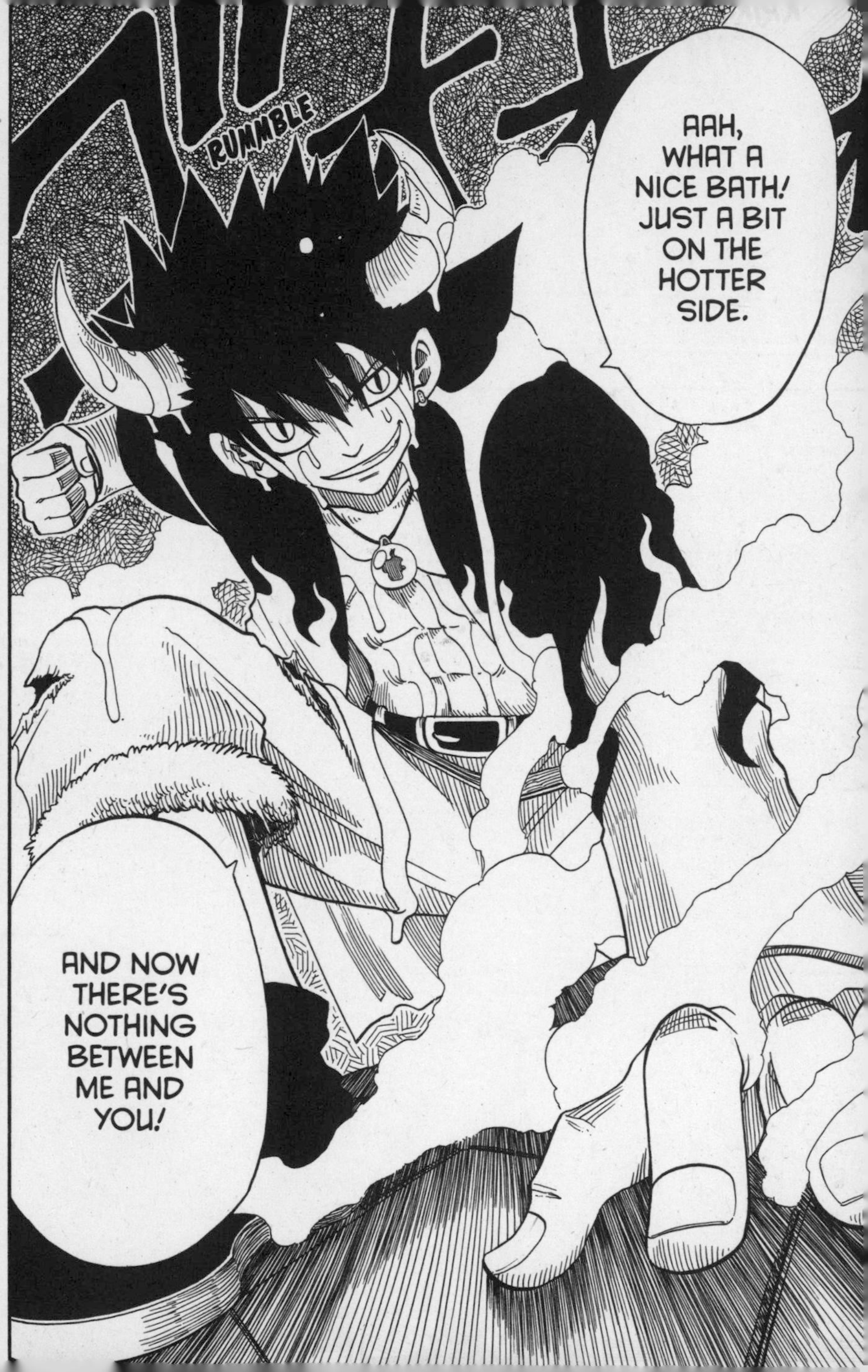
RUMMBLE
AAH, WHAT A NICE BATH! JUST A BIT ON THE HOTTER SIDE.
AND NOW THERE'S NOTHING BETWEEN ME AND YOU!

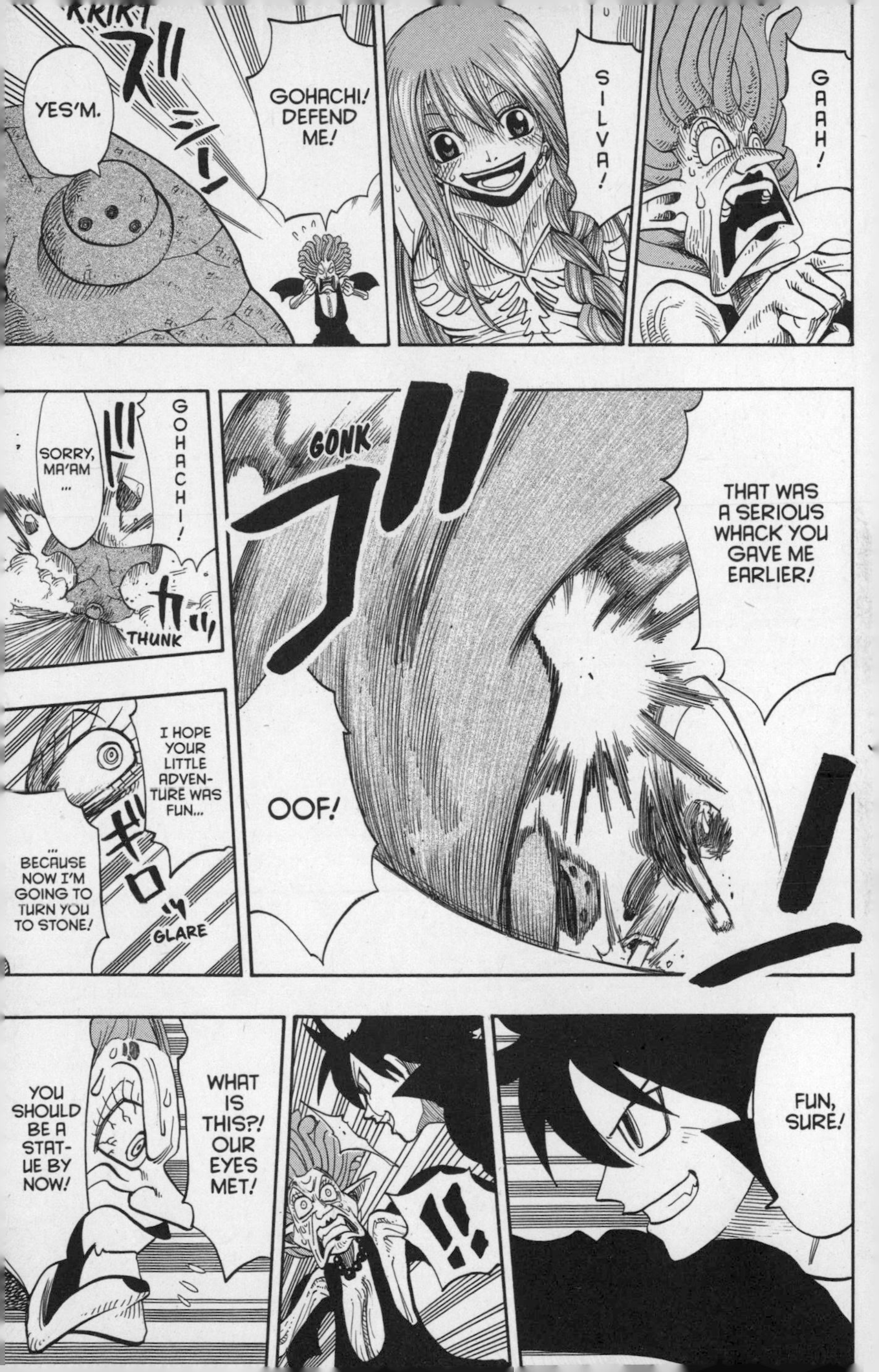
GAAAH!
SILVA!
GOHACHI! DEFEND ME!
KRIKT
YES'M.
THAT WAS A SERIOUS WHACK YOU GAVE ME EARLIER!
GONK
OOF!
GOHACHI!
SORRY, MA'AM ...
THUNK
I HOPE YOUR LITTLE ADVENTURE WAS FUN...
... BECAUSE NOW I'M GOING TO TURN YOU TO STONE!
GLARE
FUN, SURE!
!!
WHAT IS THIS?! OUR EYES MET!
YOU SHOULD BE A STATUE BY NOW!

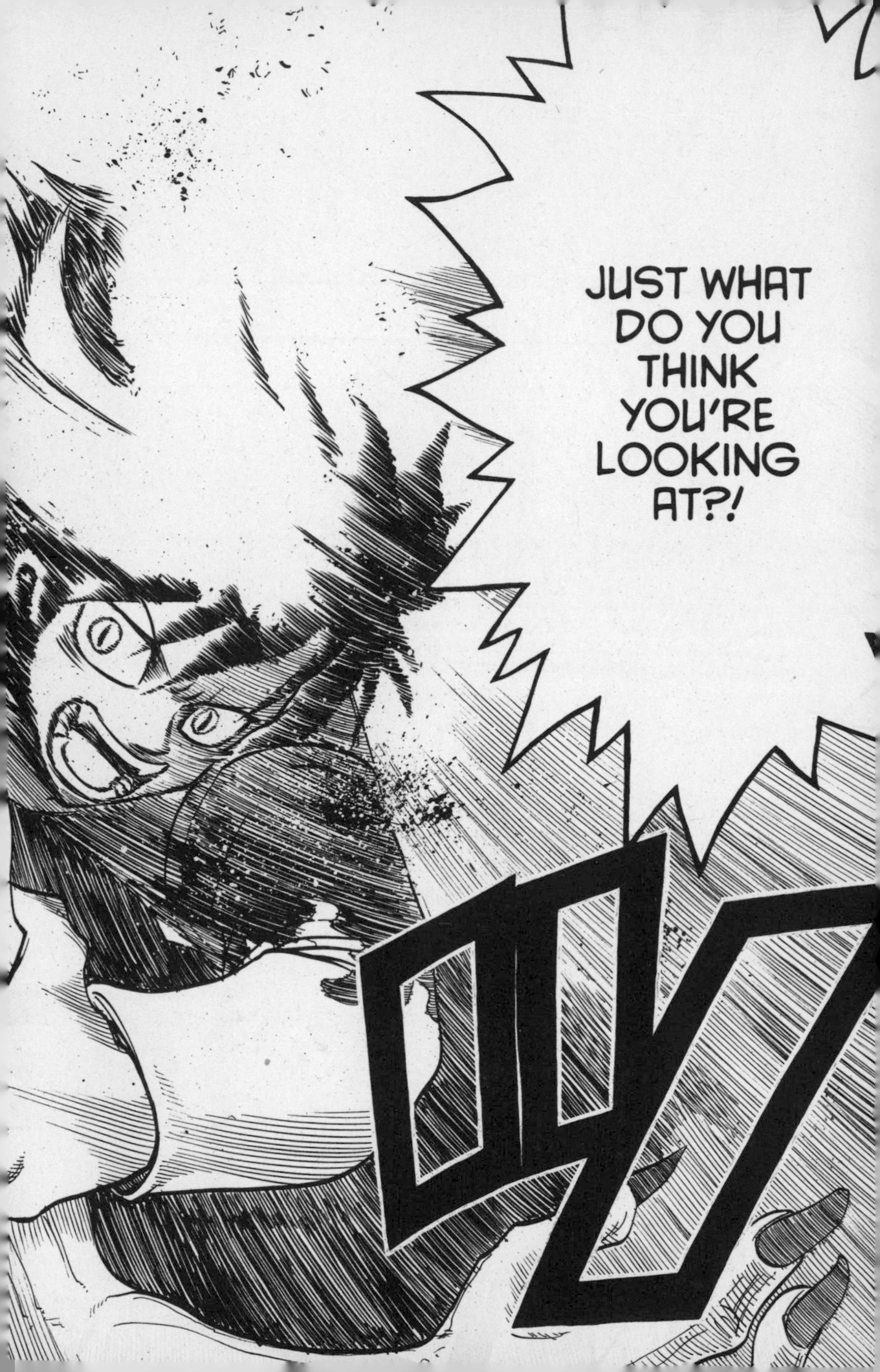
JUST WHAT DO YOU THINK YOU'RE LOOKING AT?!

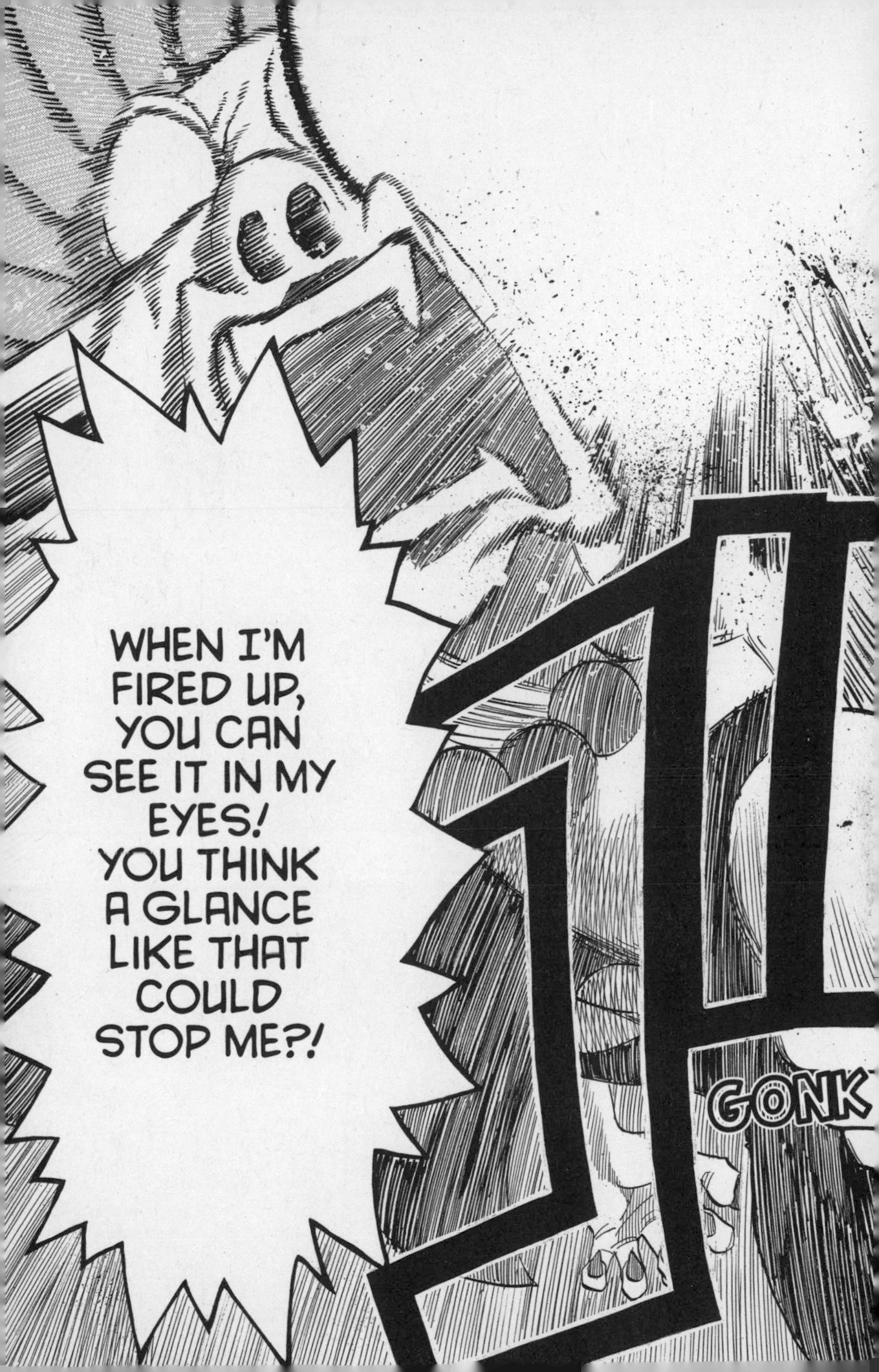
WHEN I'M FIRED UP, YOU CAN SEE IT IN MY EYES! YOU THINK A GLANCE LIKE THAT COULD STOP ME?!
GONK

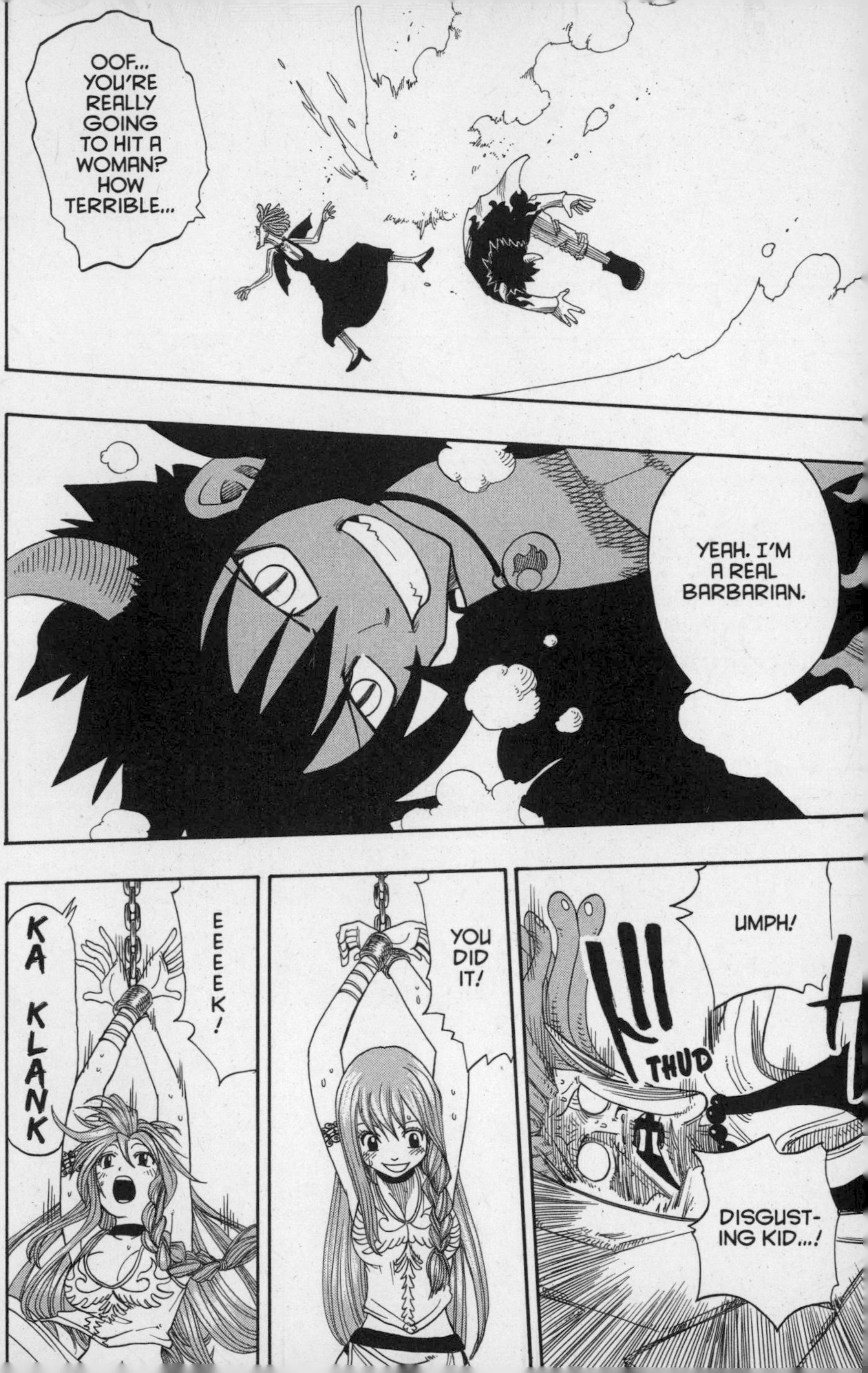
OOF... YOU'RE REALLY GOING TO HIT A WOMAN? HOW TERRIBLE...
YEAH. I'M A REAL BARBARIAN.
UMPH!
THUD
DISGUST-ING KID...!
YOU DID IT!
EEEEEK!
KA KLANK

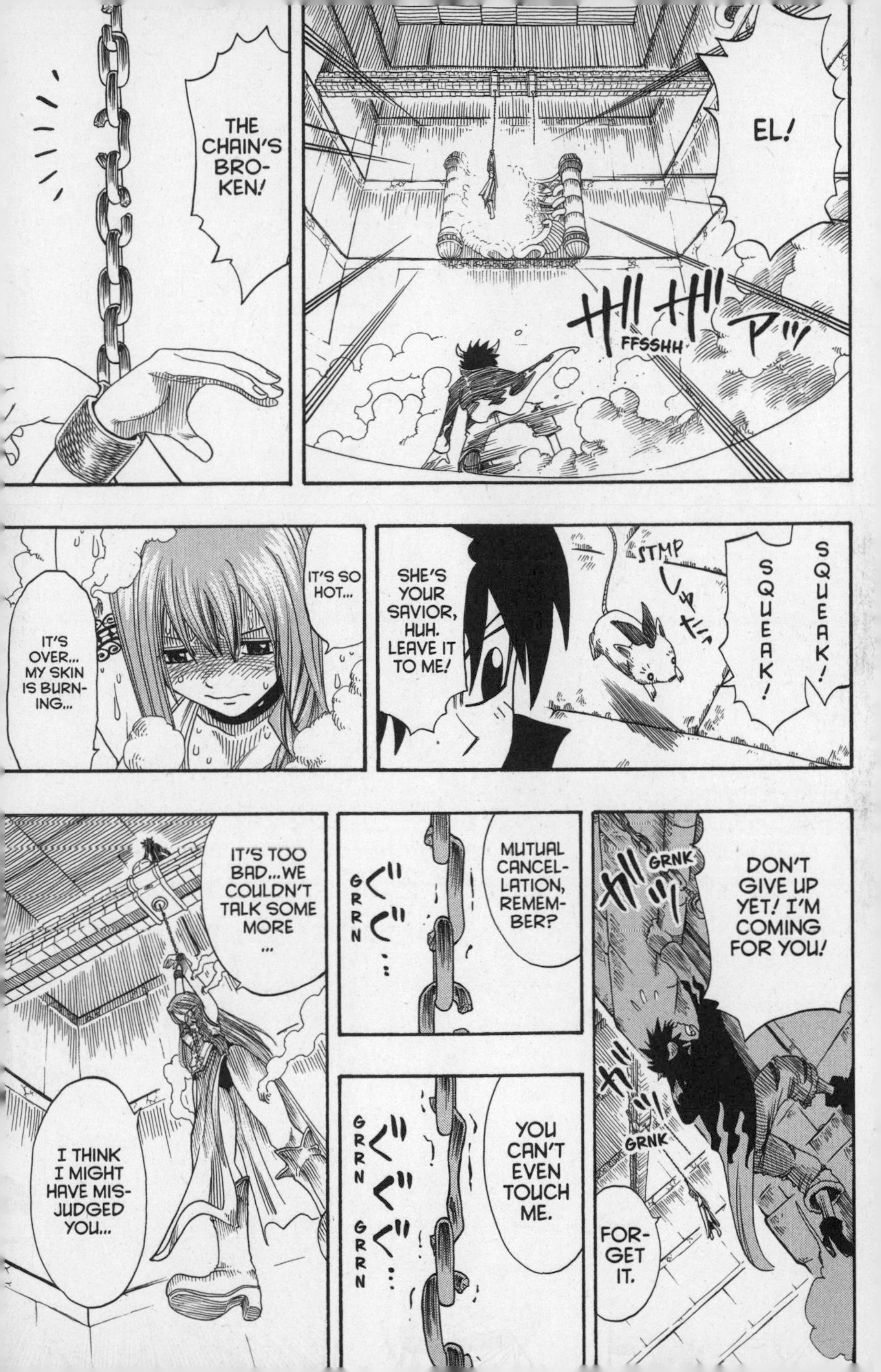
EL!
FFSSHH
THE CHAIN'S BRO-KEN!
SQUEAK! SQUEAK!
STMP
SHE'S YOUR SAVIOR, HUH. LEAVE IT TO ME!
IT'S SO HOT...
IT'S OVER... MY SKIN IS BURN-ING...
DON'T GIVE UP YET! I'M COMING FOR YOU!
GRNK
GRNK
FOR-GET IT.
MUTUAL CANCEL-LATION, REMEM-BER?
GRRN
YOU CAN'T EVEN TOUCH ME.
GRRN
GRRN
IT'S TOO BAD...WE COULDN'T TALK SOME MORE ...
I THINK I MIGHT HAVE MIS-JUDGED YOU...

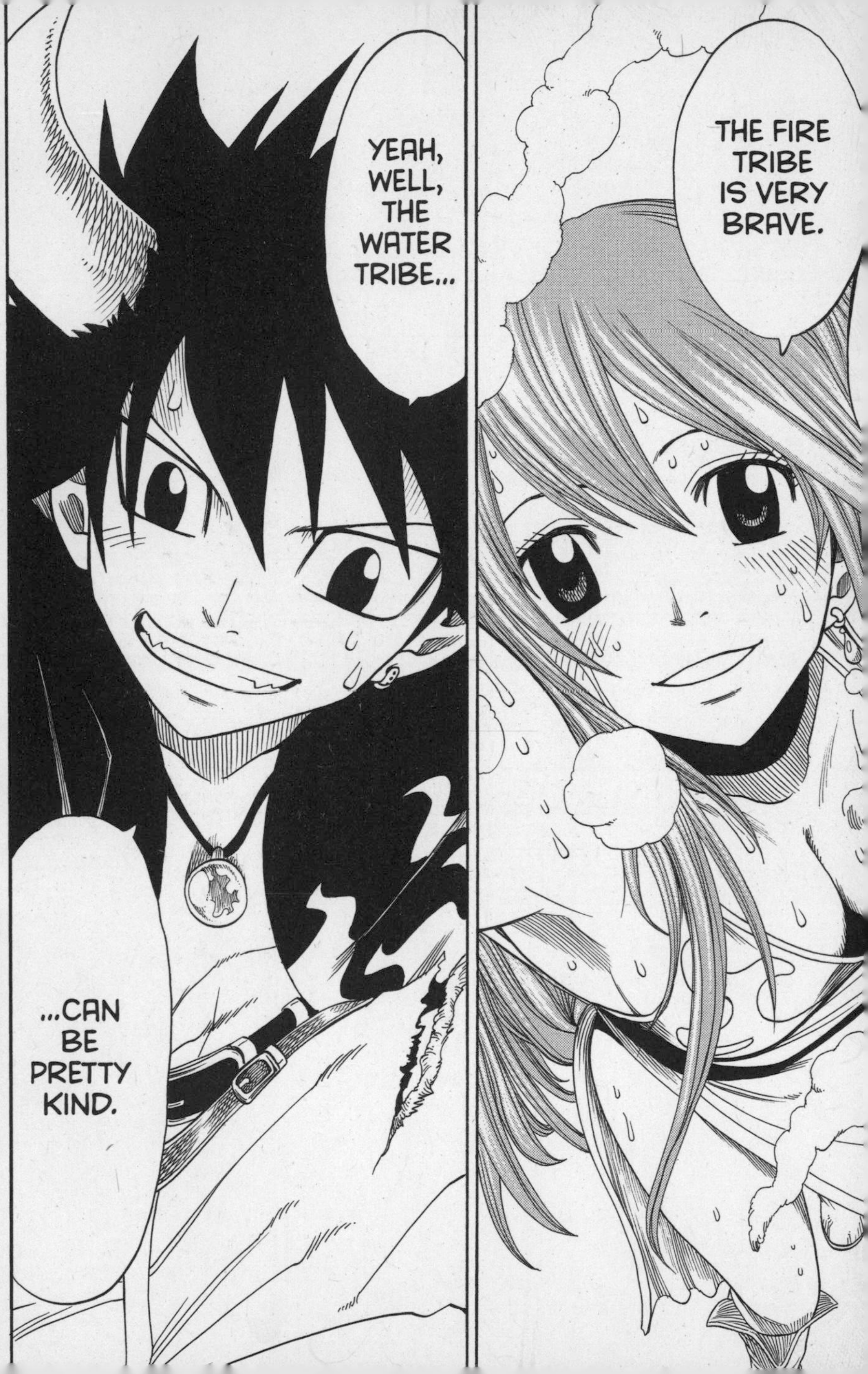
THE FIRE TRIBE IS VERY BRAVE.
YEAH, WELL, THE WATER TRIBE...
...CAN BE PRETTY KIND.

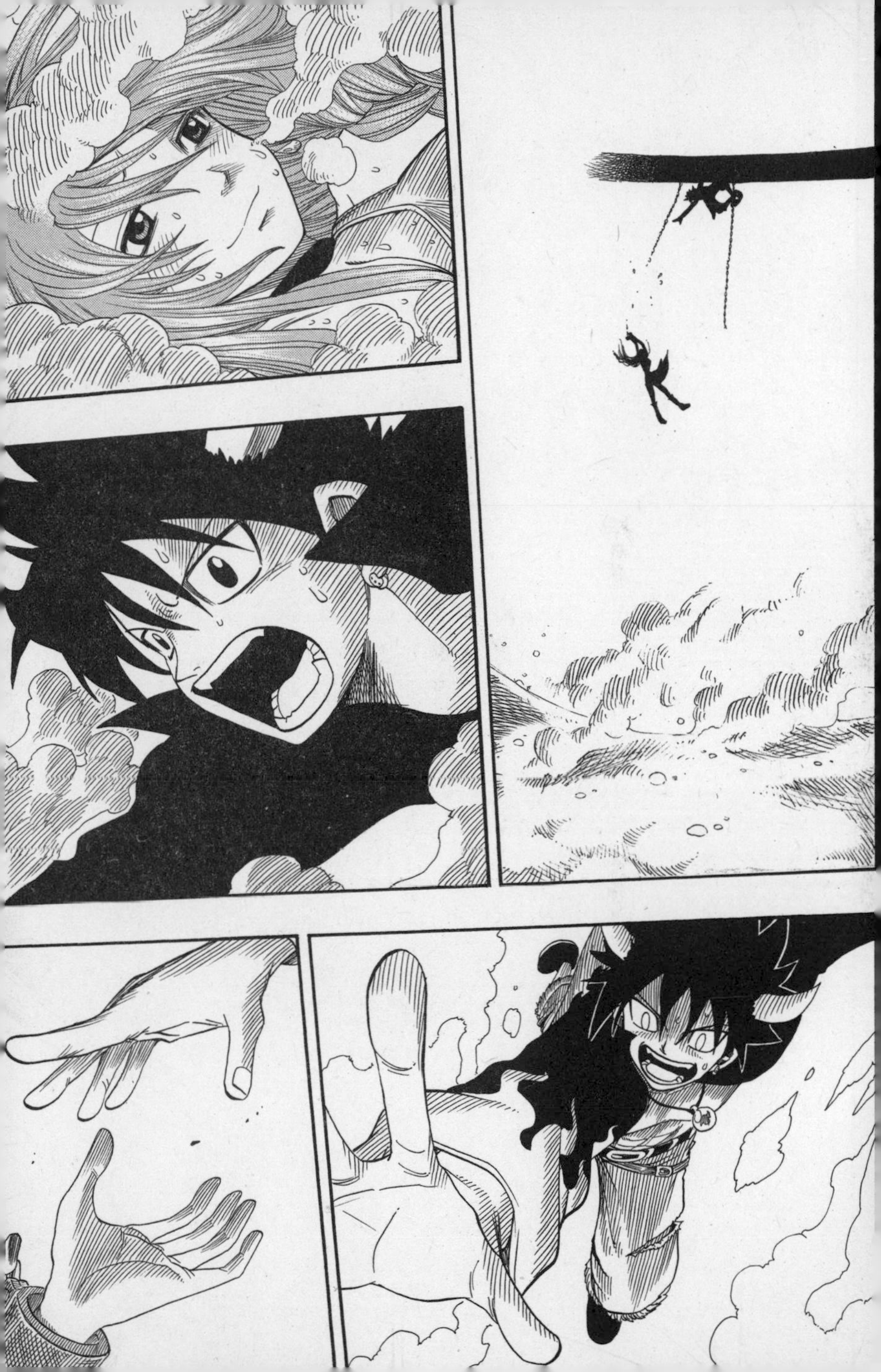

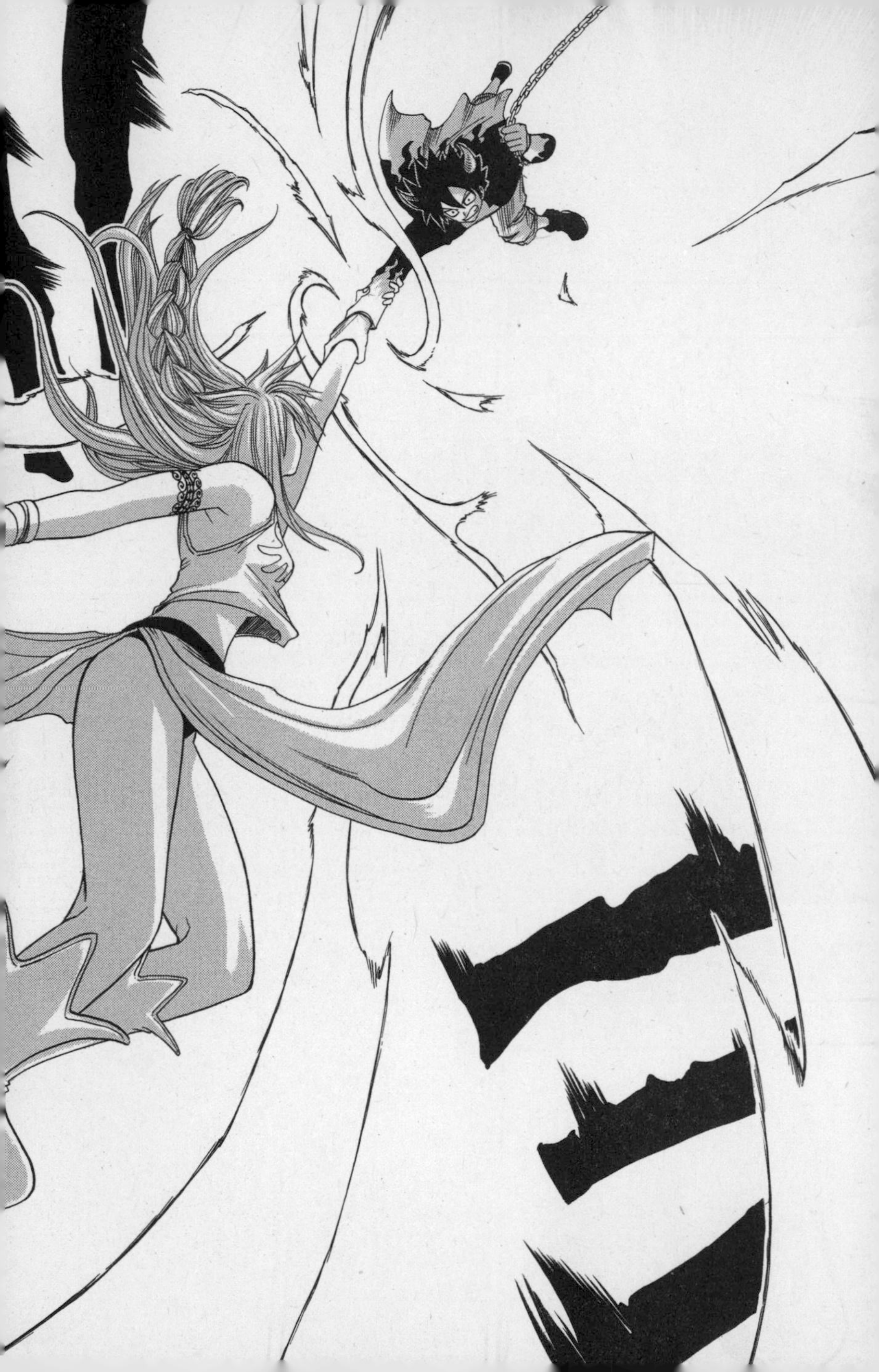

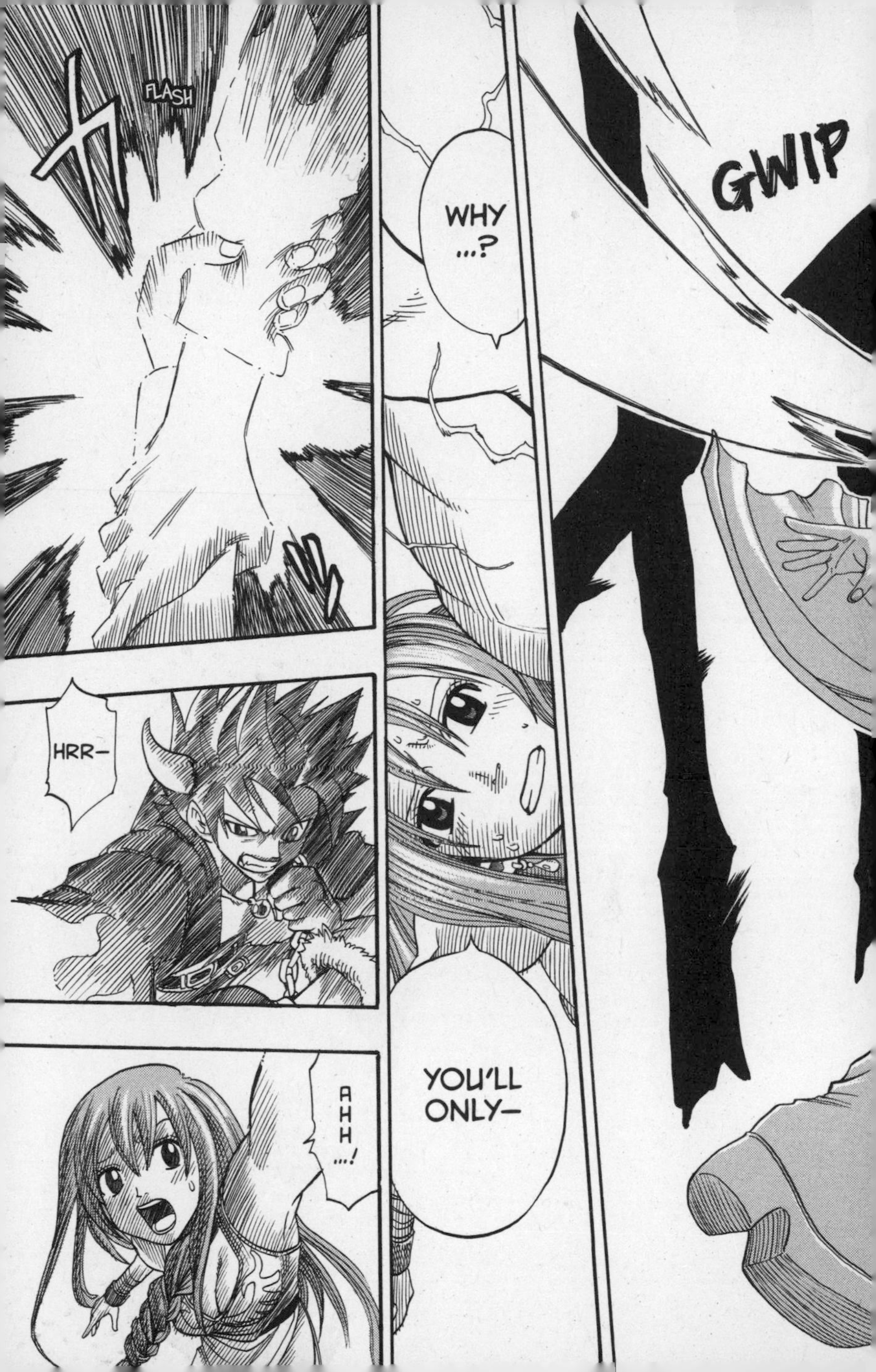
GWIP
WHY ...?
YOU'LL ONLY—
FLASH
HRR—
AHH ...!

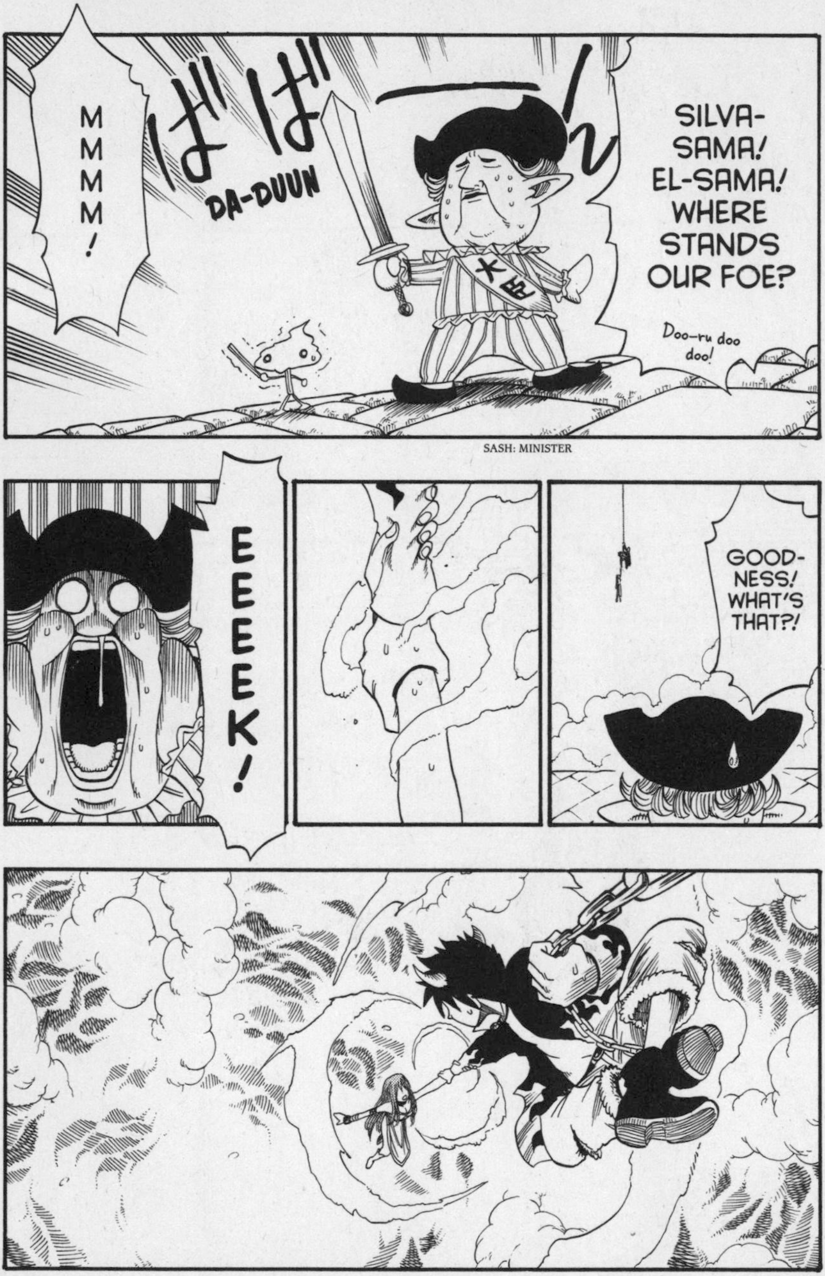
SILVA-SAMA! EL-SAMA! WHERE STANDS OUR FOE?
ばばーん
DA-DUUN
MMMM!
Doo-ru doo doo!
GOOD-NESS! WHAT'S THAT?!
EEEEEK!

SASH: MINISTER

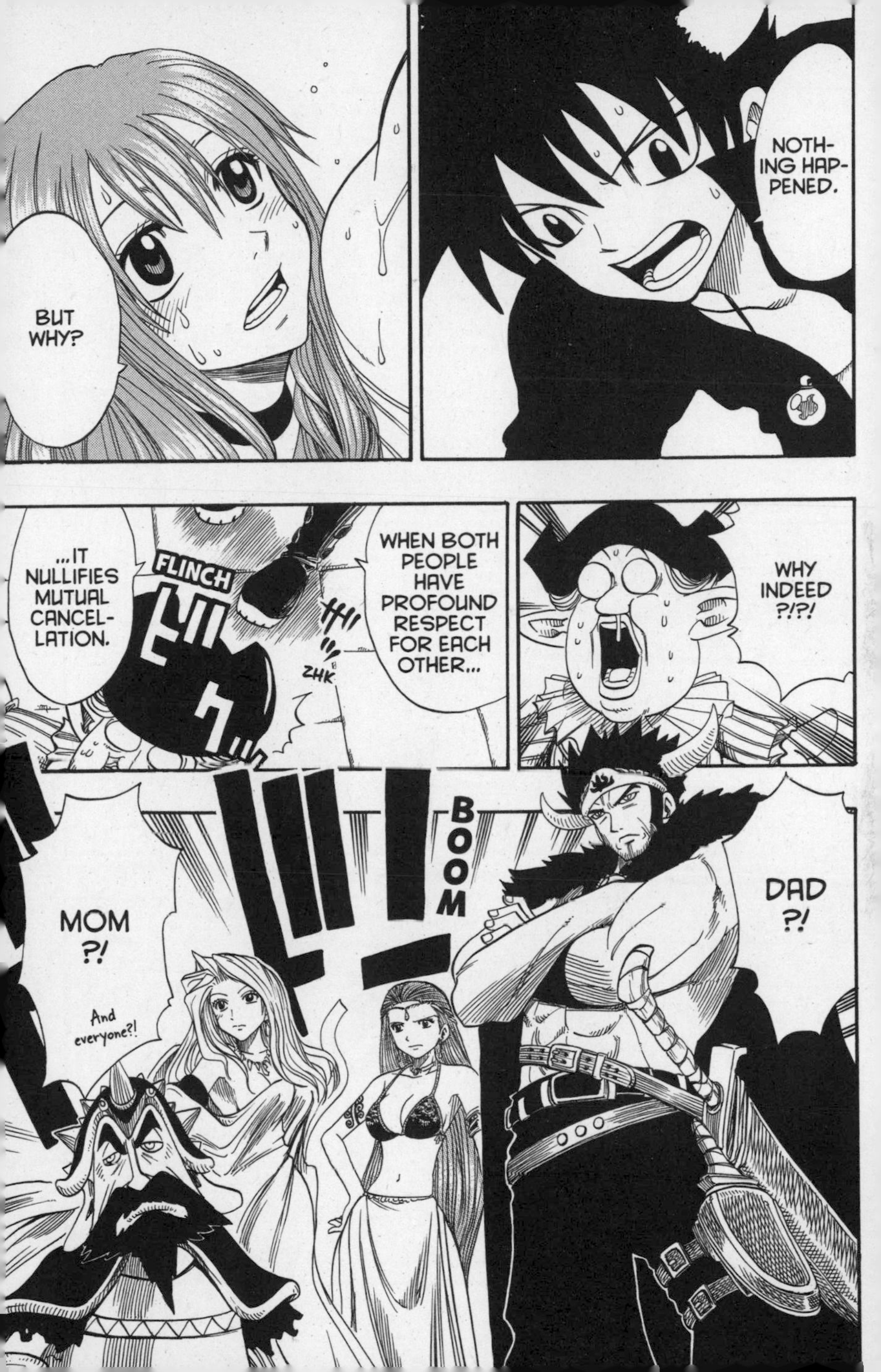
NOTH-ING HAP-PENED.
BUT WHY?
WHY INDEED?!?!
WHEN BOTH PEOPLE HAVE PROFOUND RESPECT FOR EACH OTHER...
ZHK
...IT NULLIFIES MUTUAL CANCEL-LATION.
FLINCH
DAD?!
BOOM
MOM?!
And everyone?!

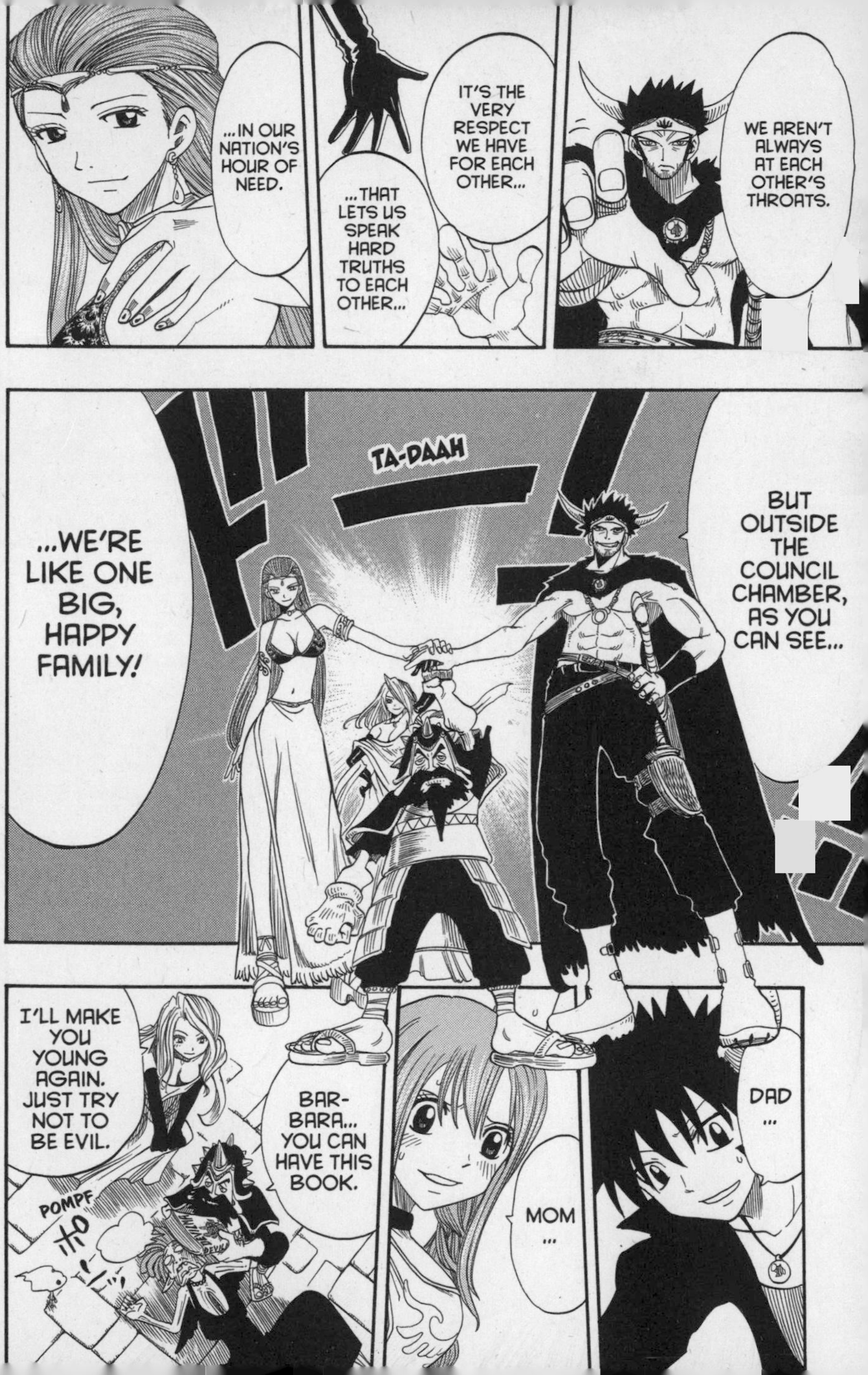
WE AREN'T ALWAYS AT EACH OTHER'S THROATS.
IT'S THE VERY RESPECT WE HAVE FOR EACH OTHER...
...THAT LETS US SPEAK HARD TRUTHS TO EACH OTHER...
...IN OUR NATION'S HOUR OF NEED.
BUT OUTSIDE THE COUNCIL CHAMBER, AS YOU CAN SEE...
TA-DAAH
...WE'RE LIKE ONE BIG, HAPPY FAMILY!
DAD ...
MOM ...
BAR-BARA... YOU CAN HAVE THIS BOOK.
I'LL MAKE YOU YOUNG AGAIN. JUST TRY NOT TO BE EVIL.
POMPF

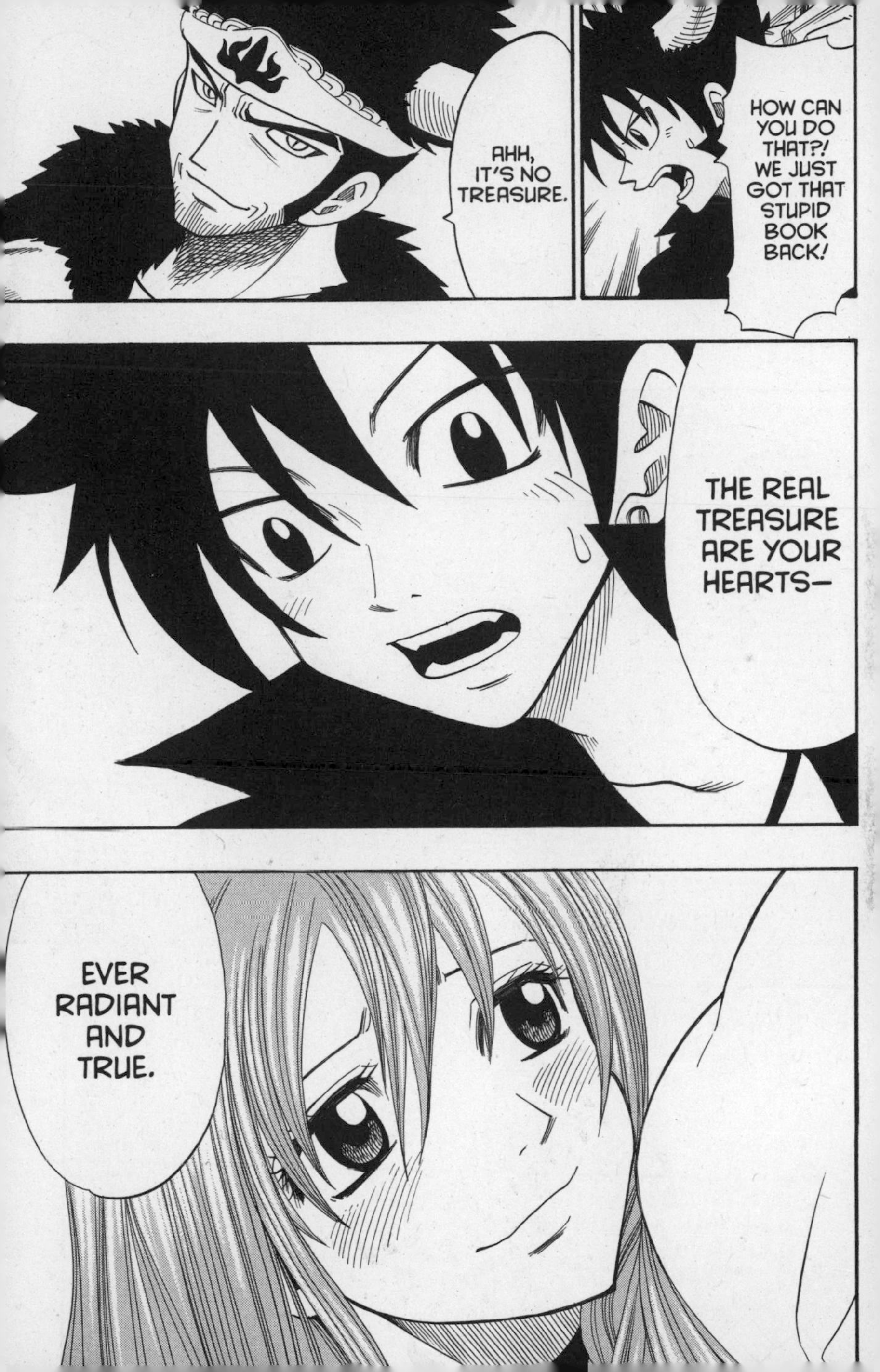
HOW CAN YOU DO THAT?! WE JUST GOT THAT STUPID BOOK BACK!
AHH, IT'S NO TREASURE.
THE REAL TREASURE ARE YOUR HEARTS—
EVER RADIANT AND TRUE.

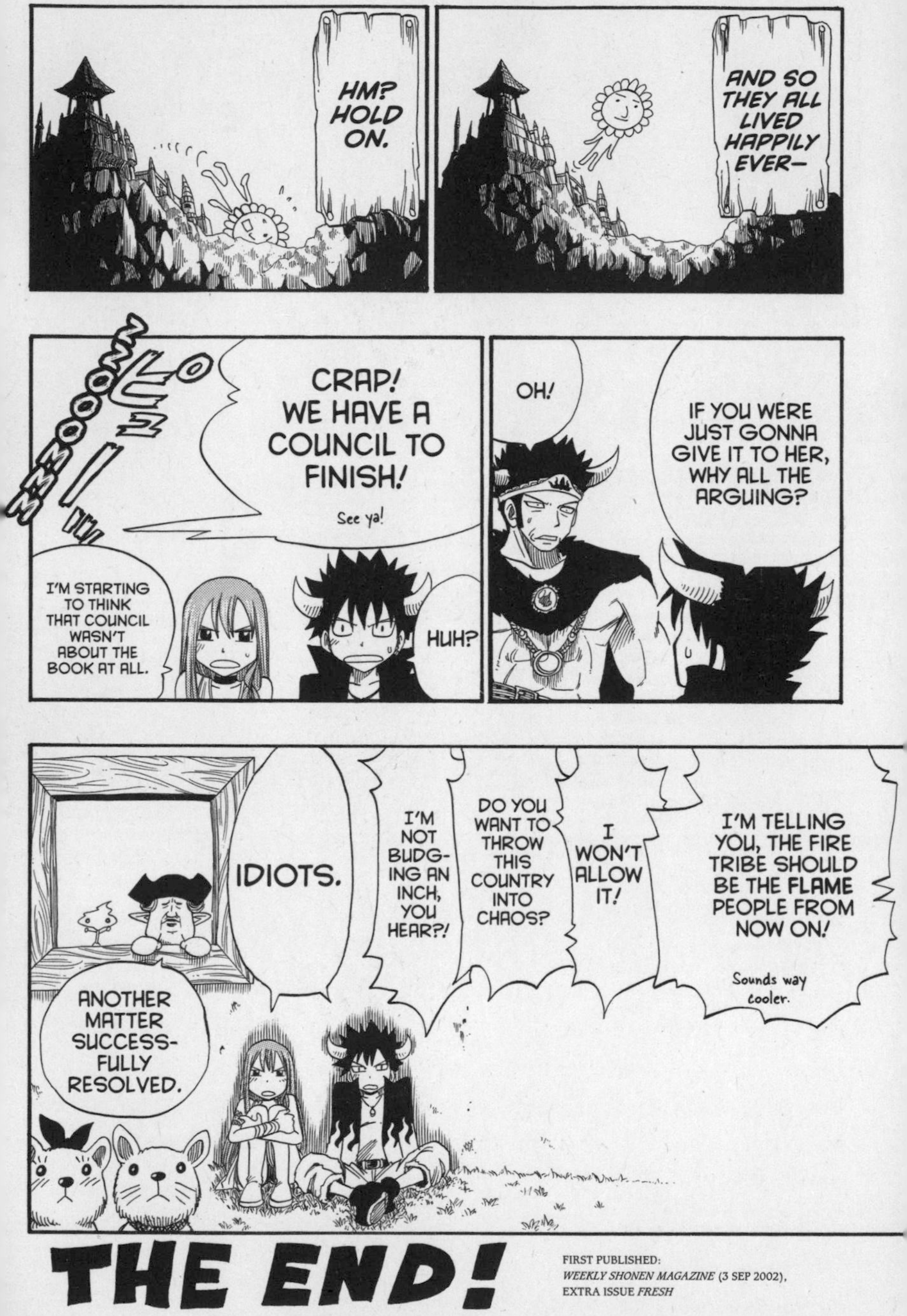
AND SO THEY ALL LIVED HAPPILY EVER—
HM? HOLD ON.
IF YOU WERE JUST GONNA GIVE IT TO HER, WHY ALL THE ARGUING?
OH!
CRAP! WE HAVE A COUNCIL TO FINISH!
See ya!
ZOOOOMMM
HUH?
I'M STARTING TO THINK THAT COUNCIL WASN'T ABOUT THE BOOK AT ALL.
I'M TELLING YOU, THE FIRE TRIBE SHOULD BE THE FLAME PEOPLE FROM NOW ON!
Sounds way cooler.
I WON'T ALLOW IT!
DO YOU WANT TO THROW THIS COUNTRY INTO CHAOS?
I'M NOT BUDGING AN INCH, YOU HEAR?!
IDIOTS.
ANOTHER MATTER SUCCESSFULLY RESOLVED.

THE END!

FIRST PUBLISHED:
WEEKLY SHONEN MAGAZINE (3 SEP 2002),
EXTRA ISSUE *FRESH*

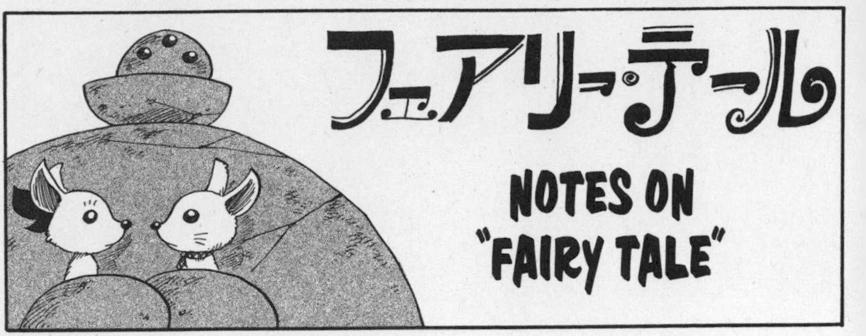

フェアリーテール

NOTES ON "FAIRY TALE"

This may be my favorite piece... Yeah, sure (laughs). I do think it's a pretty well-done story, if I may say so myself. I did conceive *Fairy tale* as a potential franchise (to run after the currently-serializing *Rave Master*), so it's relatively polished. For example, in addition to the characters who appear in this story, I came up with a lot of other ideas (some of which appear on the next page): Gnome's son, Sylph's daughter, and a prince of darkness, along with a young werewolf. So why did I ultimately make it a short story? Well, let me tell you! For starters, there's the fact that my editors asked me to do a short story. Factors of time meant that if I didn't get the rough pages in by such-and-such date, the inking wouldn't be done on schedule. That was the first deadline, if you will. (Incidentally, the second is the deadline for the final draft.) So anyway, immediately before this first deadline, I found out that the story I had drawn before *Fairy tale* had been **rejected**. Sheesh! I had two days and zero ideas. Ugh! So it was kind of like, bah, better just turn *Fairy tale* into a short story! And that's what I did. Heh heh... I've got plenty of other ideas for new series, so...it's all good.

From the *Fairy tale* Files

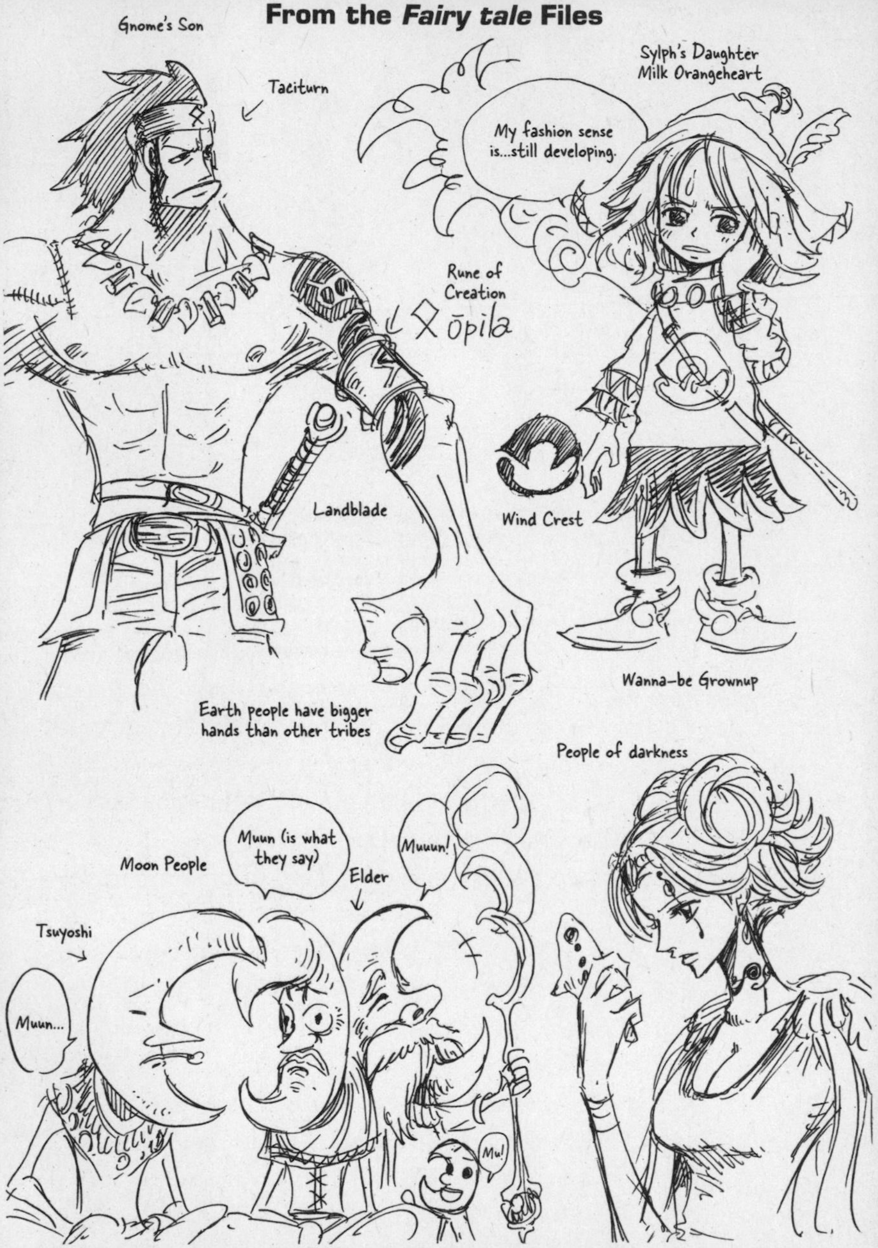
Gnome's Son
Taciturn
My fashion sense is...still developing.
Sylph's Daughter
Milk Orangeheart
Rune of Creation
ōpila
Landblade
Wind Crest
Wanna-be Grownup
Earth people have bigger hands than other tribes
People of darkness
Moon People
Muun (is what they say)
Muuun!
Elder
Tsuyoshi
Muun...
Mu!

THE IDEA OF "MUTUAL CANCELLATION" IS SOMETHING I CAME UP WITH FOR THE SHORT STORY; IN THE SERIES, ALL THE TRIBES WERE GOING TO HATE EACH OTHER, AND IT WOULD BE THE TASK OF THE PROTAGONIST FROM THE FIRE PEOPLE TO BRING EVERYONE TOGETHER IN THE FACE OF AN IMPENDING APOCALYPSE (NAMELY, THE END OF HUMANITY). "THE END OF HUMANITY," HUH? ...THESE PEOPLE AREN'T EVEN HUMAN!

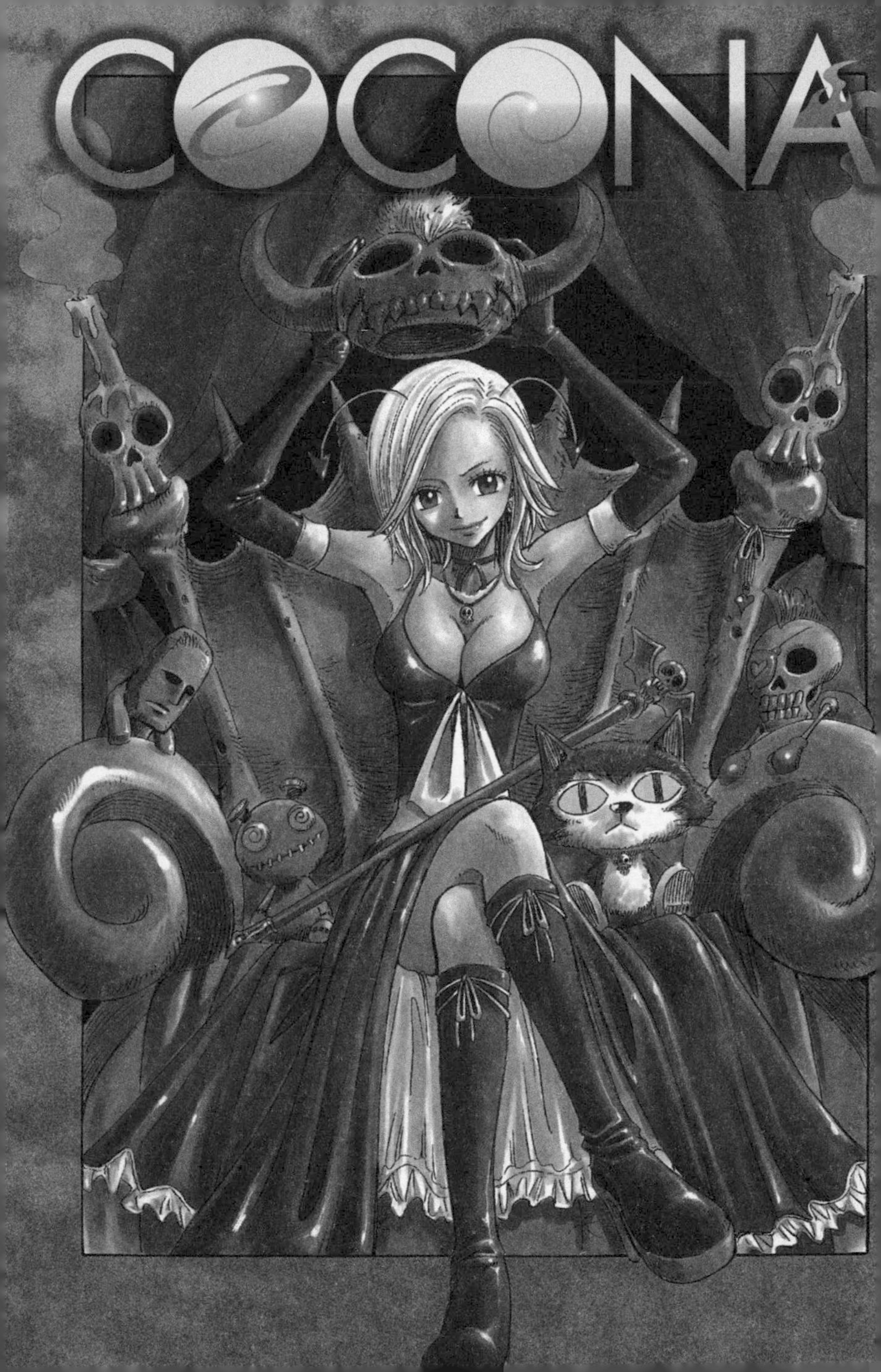
COCONA

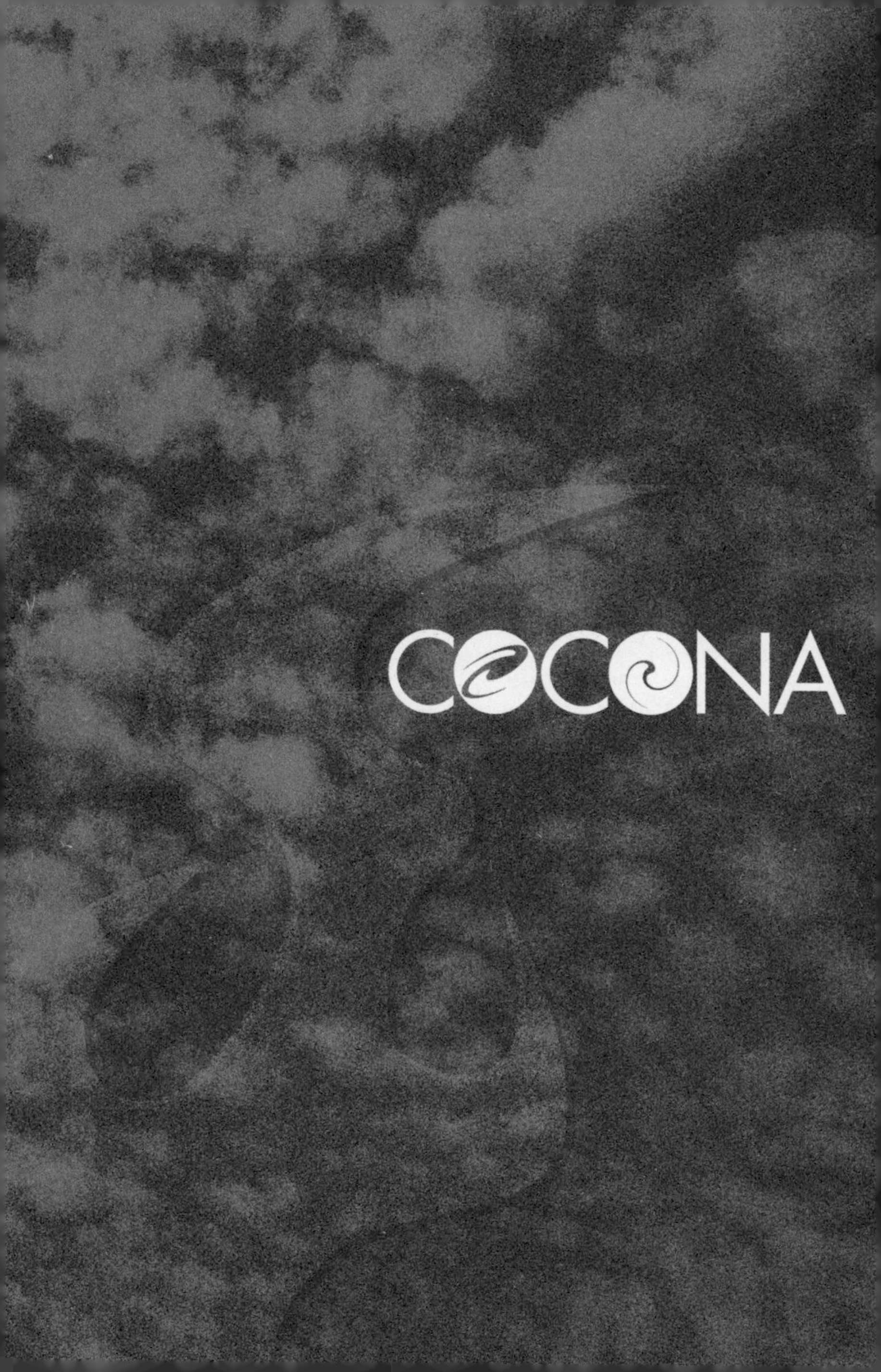
COCONA

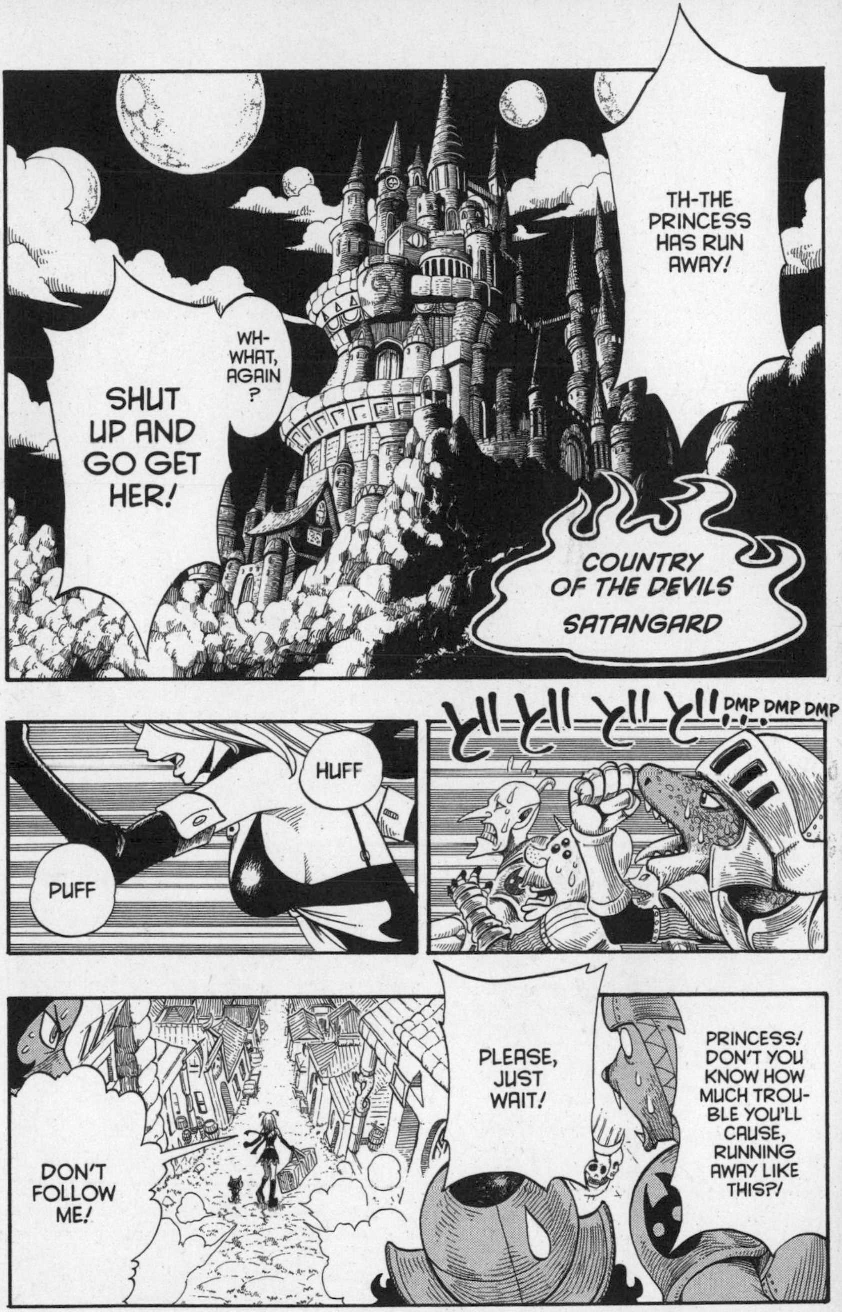

TH-THE PRINCESS HAS RUN AWAY!
WH-WHAT, AGAIN?
SHUT UP AND GO GET HER!
COUNTRY OF THE DEVILS
SATANGARD
ど!! ど!! ど!! ど!!
DMP DMP DMP
HUFF
PUFF
PRINCESS! DON'T YOU KNOW HOW MUCH TROUBLE YOU'LL CAUSE, RUNNING AWAY LIKE THIS?!
PLEASE, JUST WAIT!
DON'T FOLLOW ME!

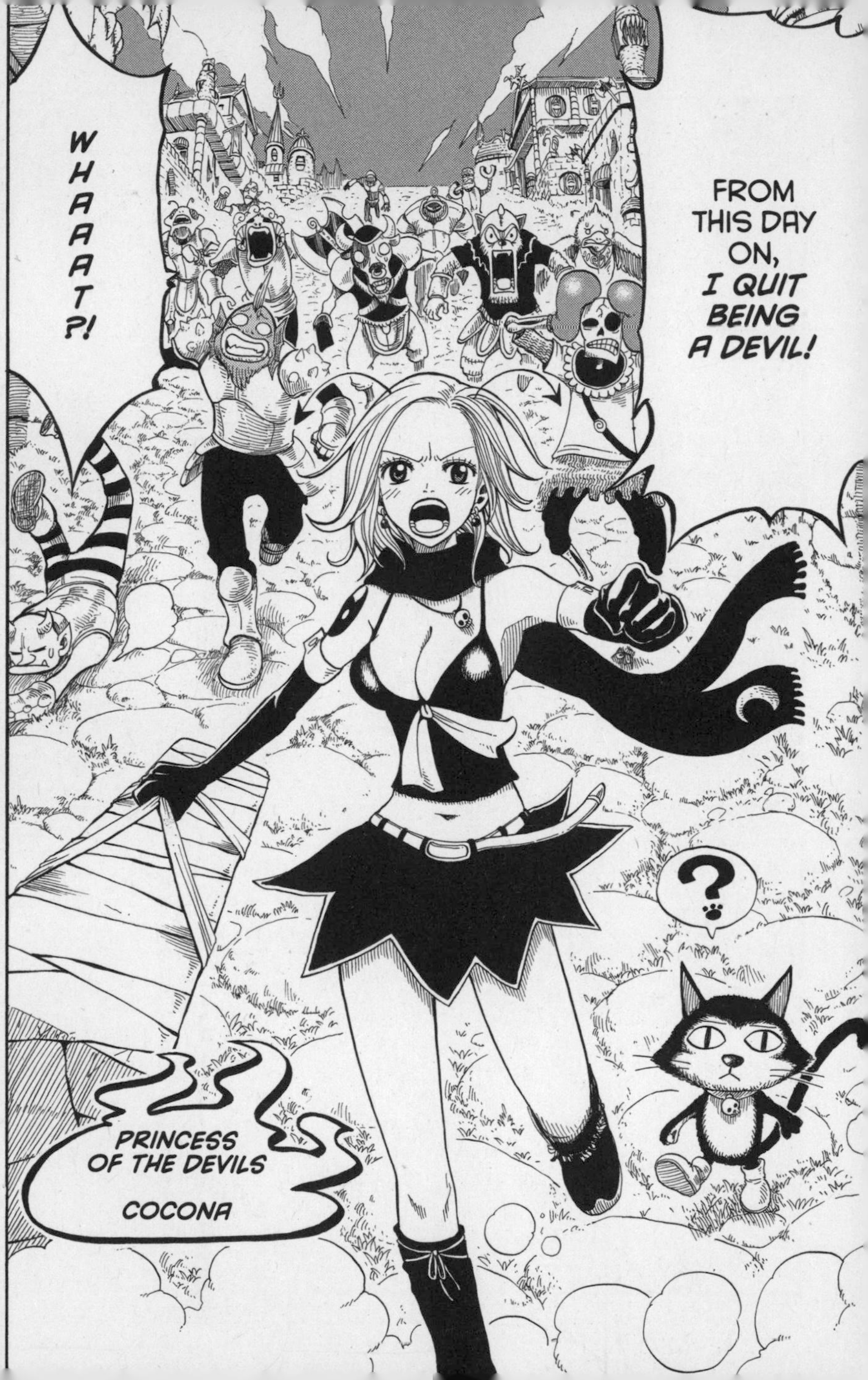
FROM THIS DAY ON, I QUIT BEING A DEVIL!
WHAAAT?!
?
PRINCESS OF THE DEVILS
COCONA

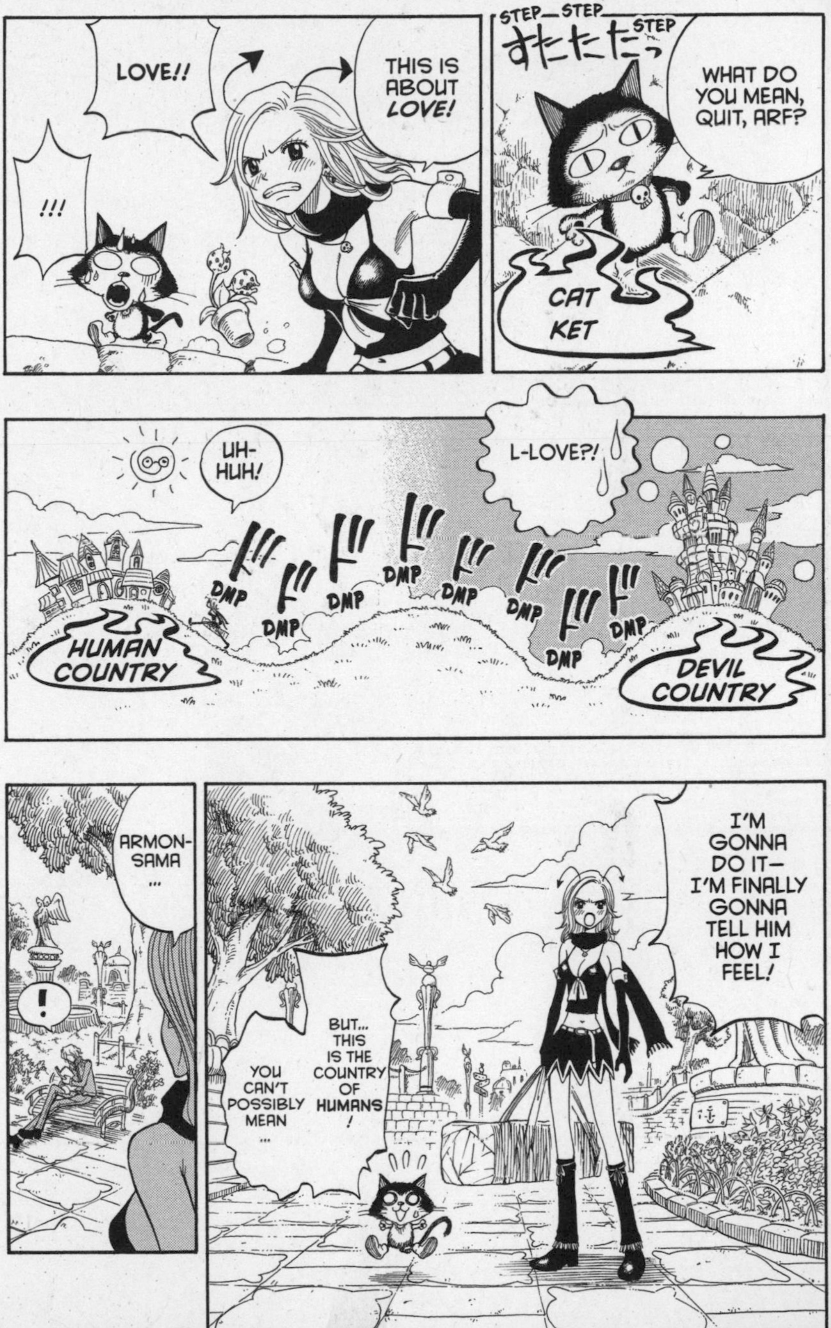
STEP STEP すたたたっ STEP
WHAT DO YOU MEAN, QUIT, ARF?
CAT KET
THIS IS ABOUT LOVE!
LOVE!!
!!!
L-LOVE?!
UH-HUH!
DMP DMP DMP DMP DMP DMP DMP DMP
DEVIL COUNTRY
HUMAN COUNTRY
I'M GONNA DO IT— I'M FINALLY GONNA TELL HIM HOW I FEEL!
BUT... THIS IS THE COUNTRY OF HUMANS!
YOU CAN'T POSSIBLY MEAN ...
ARMON-SAMA ...
!

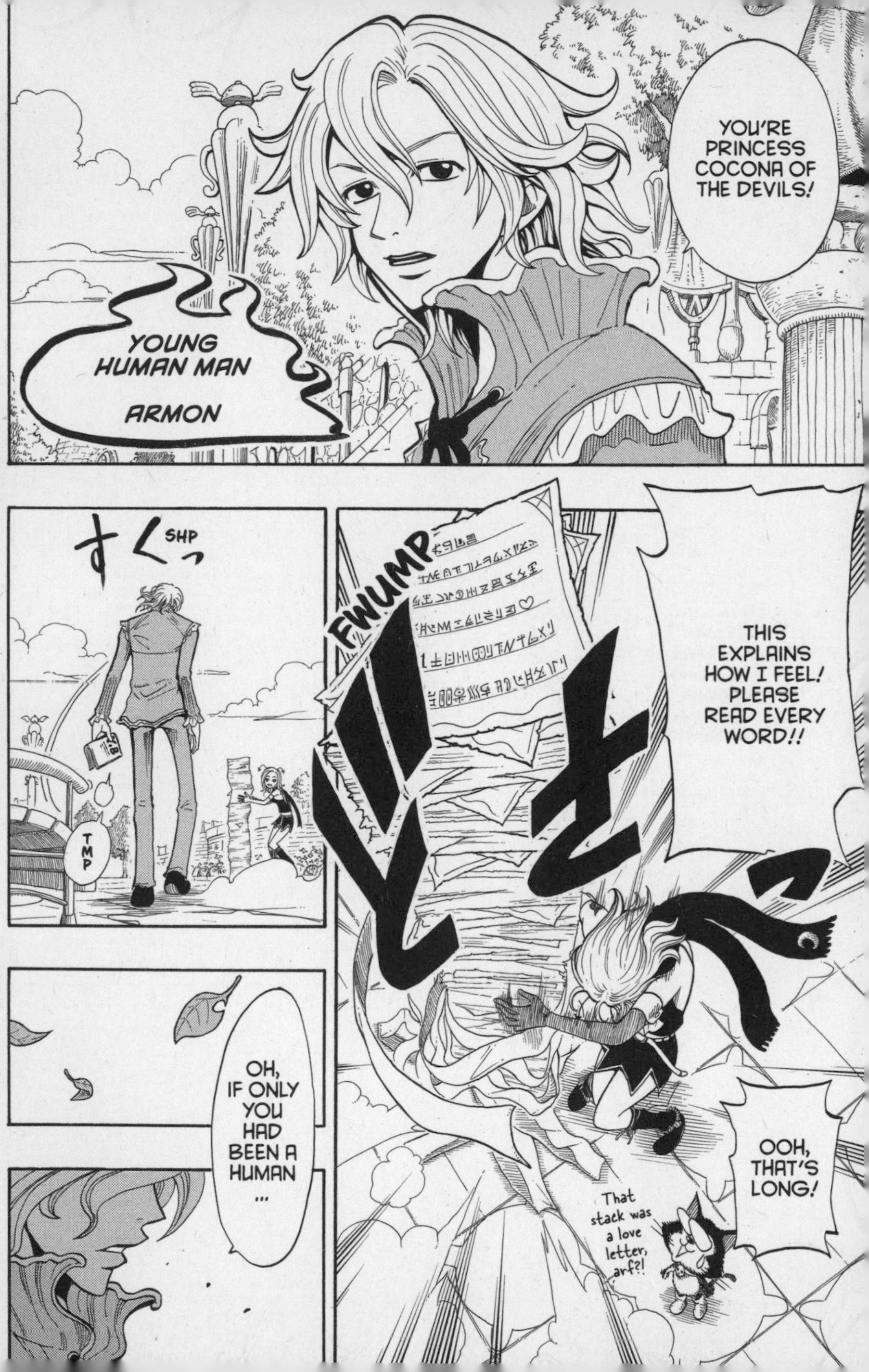
YOU'RE PRINCESS COCONA OF THE DEVILS!
YOUNG HUMAN MAN
ARMON
THIS EXPLAINS HOW I FEEL! PLEASE READ EVERY WORD!!
FWUMP
どさっ
OOH, THAT'S LONG!
That stack was a love letter, arf?!
すくっ SHP
TMP
OH, IF ONLY YOU HAD BEEN A HUMAN ...

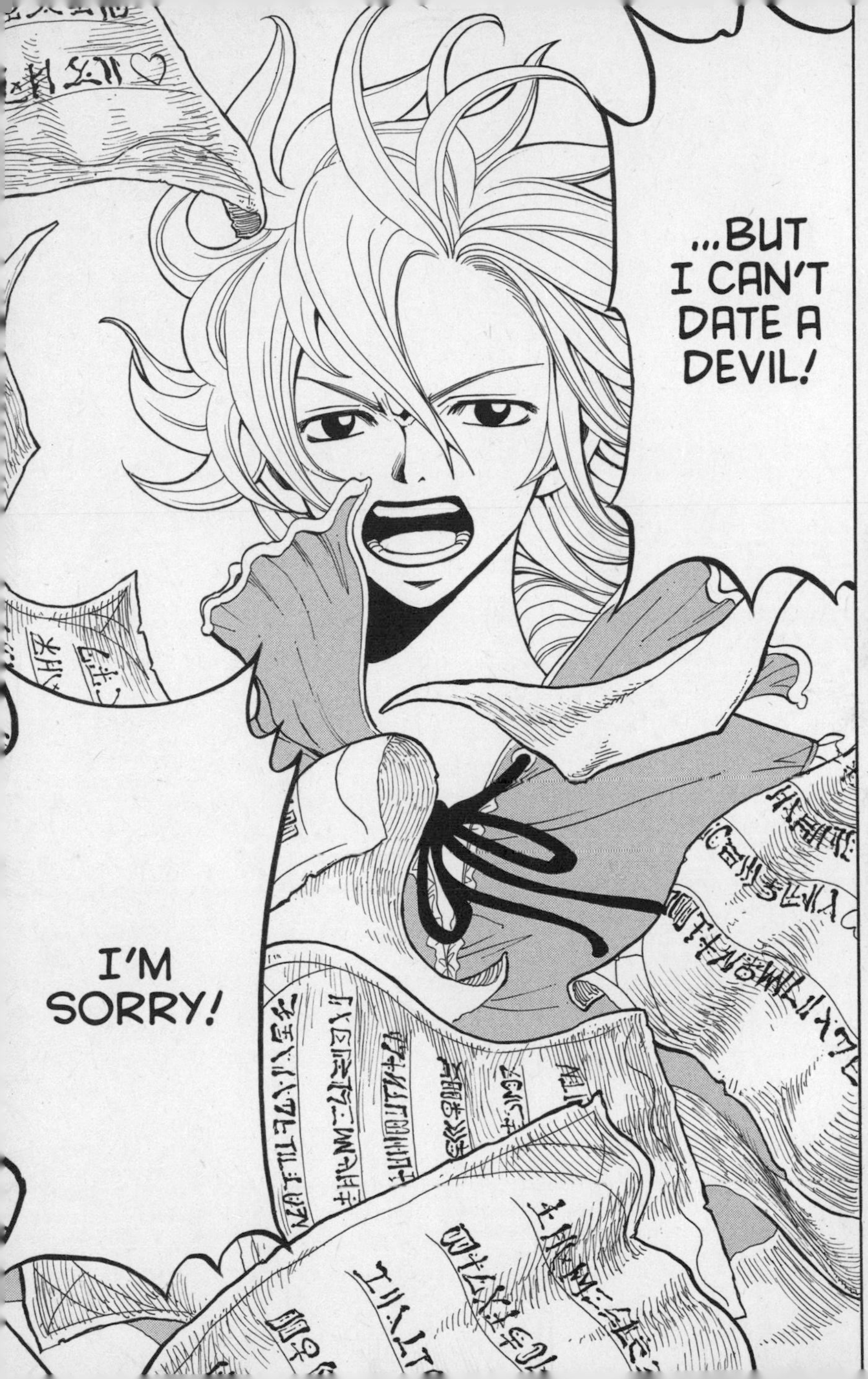
...BUT I CAN'T DATE A DEVIL!
I'M SORRY!

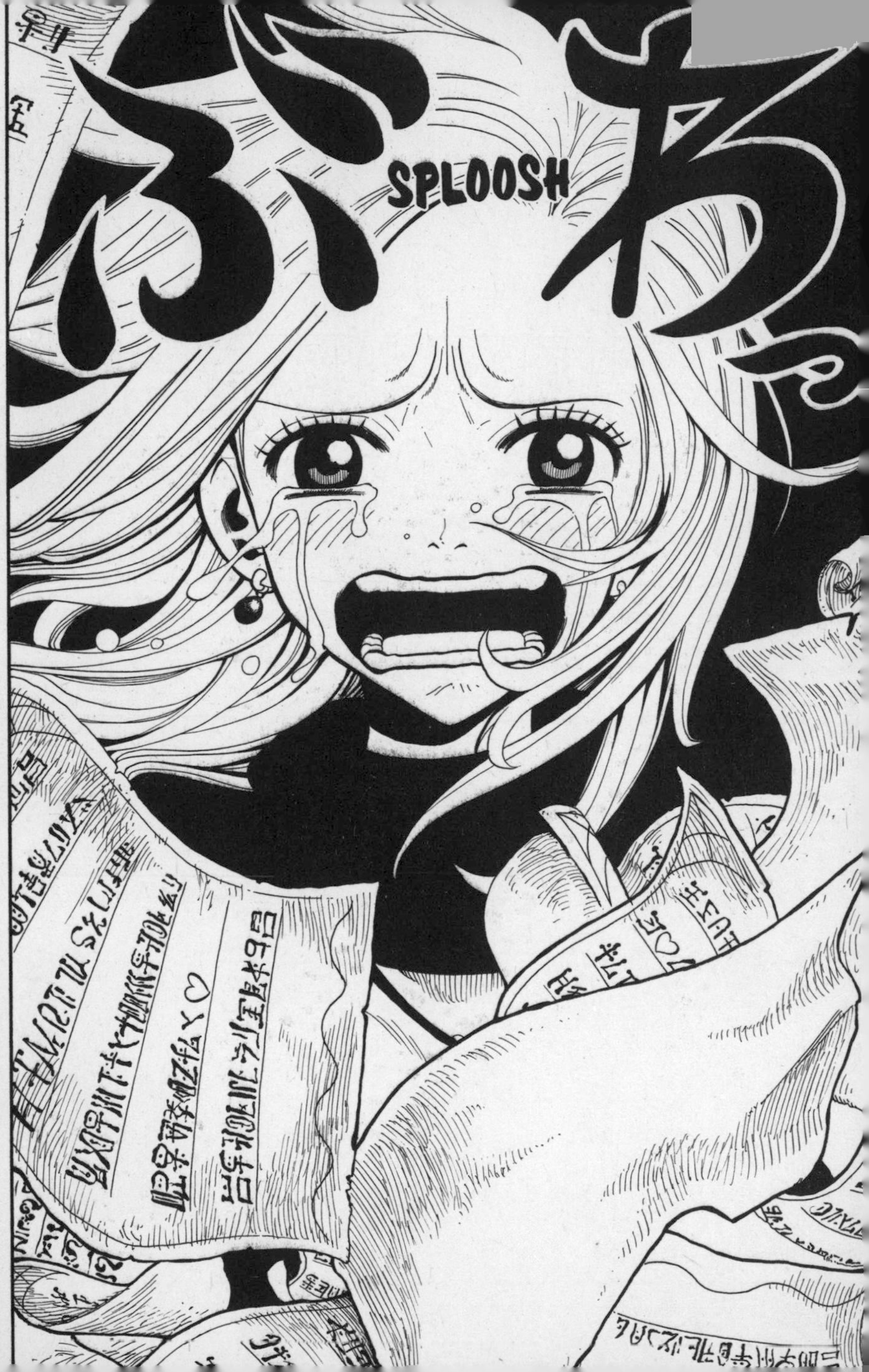
SPLOOSH

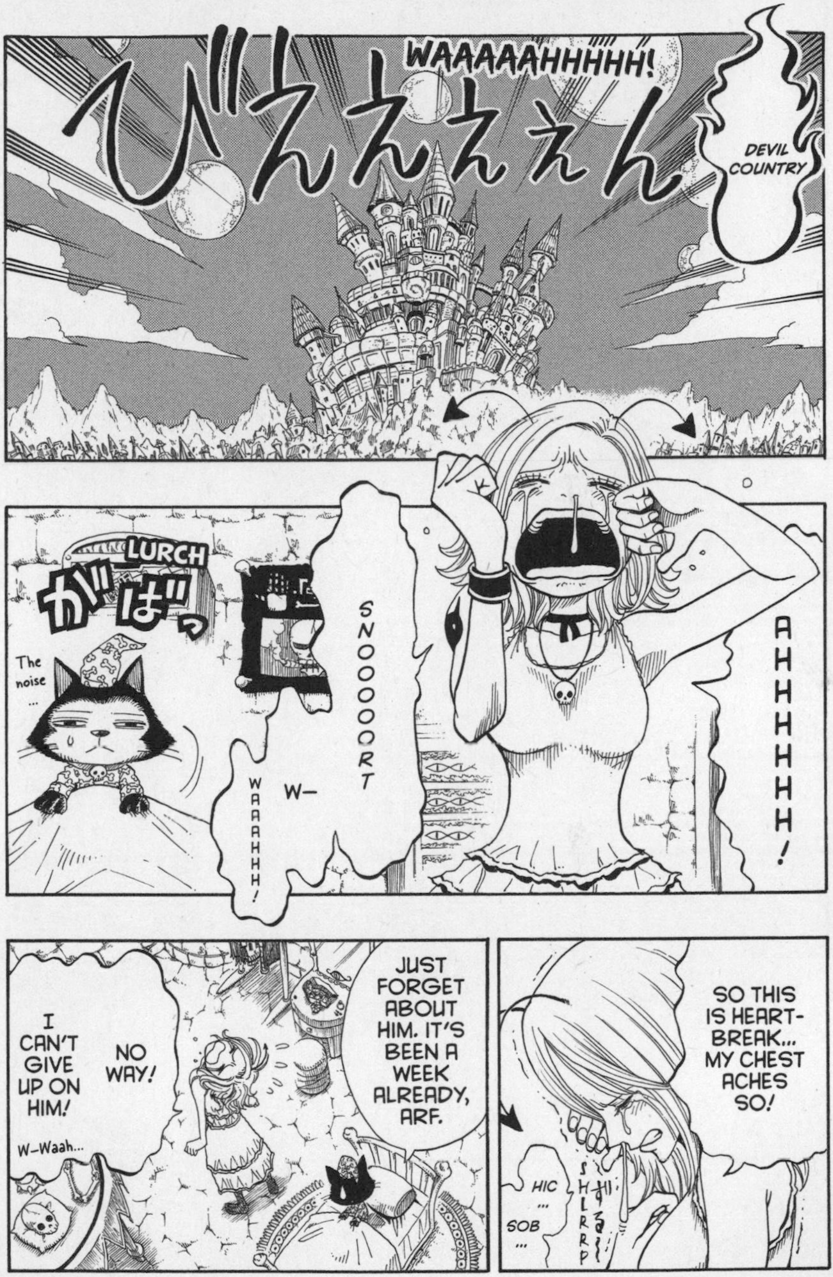

DEVIL COUNTRY
びえええええん
WAAAAAHHHHHH!
AHHHHHHHH!
SNOOOOOORT
W—
WAAAAHHHH!
がばっ
LURCH
The noise ...
SO THIS IS HEART-BREAK... MY CHEST ACHES SO!
ずるる~
SHLRRP
HIC ...
SOB ...
JUST FORGET ABOUT HIM. IT'S BEEN A WEEK ALREADY, ARF.
NO WAY!
I CAN'T GIVE UP ON HIM!
W-Waah...

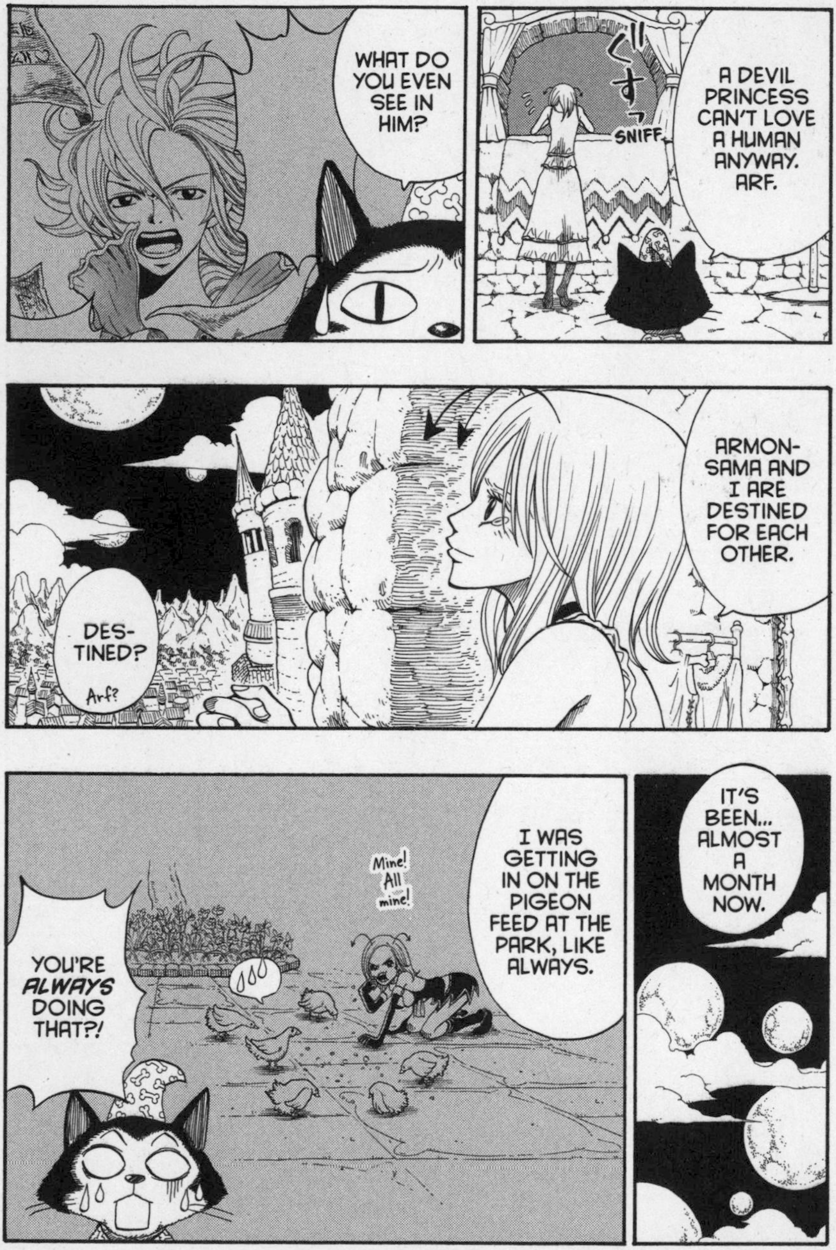
ぐすっ
SNIFF
A DEVIL PRINCESS CAN'T LOVE A HUMAN ANYWAY. ARF.
WHAT DO YOU EVEN SEE IN HIM?
ARMON-SAMA AND I ARE DESTINED FOR EACH OTHER.
DES-TINED?
Arf?
IT'S BEEN... ALMOST A MONTH NOW.
I WAS GETTING IN ON THE PIGEON FEED AT THE PARK, LIKE ALWAYS.
Mine! All mine!
YOU'RE *ALWAYS* DOING THAT?!

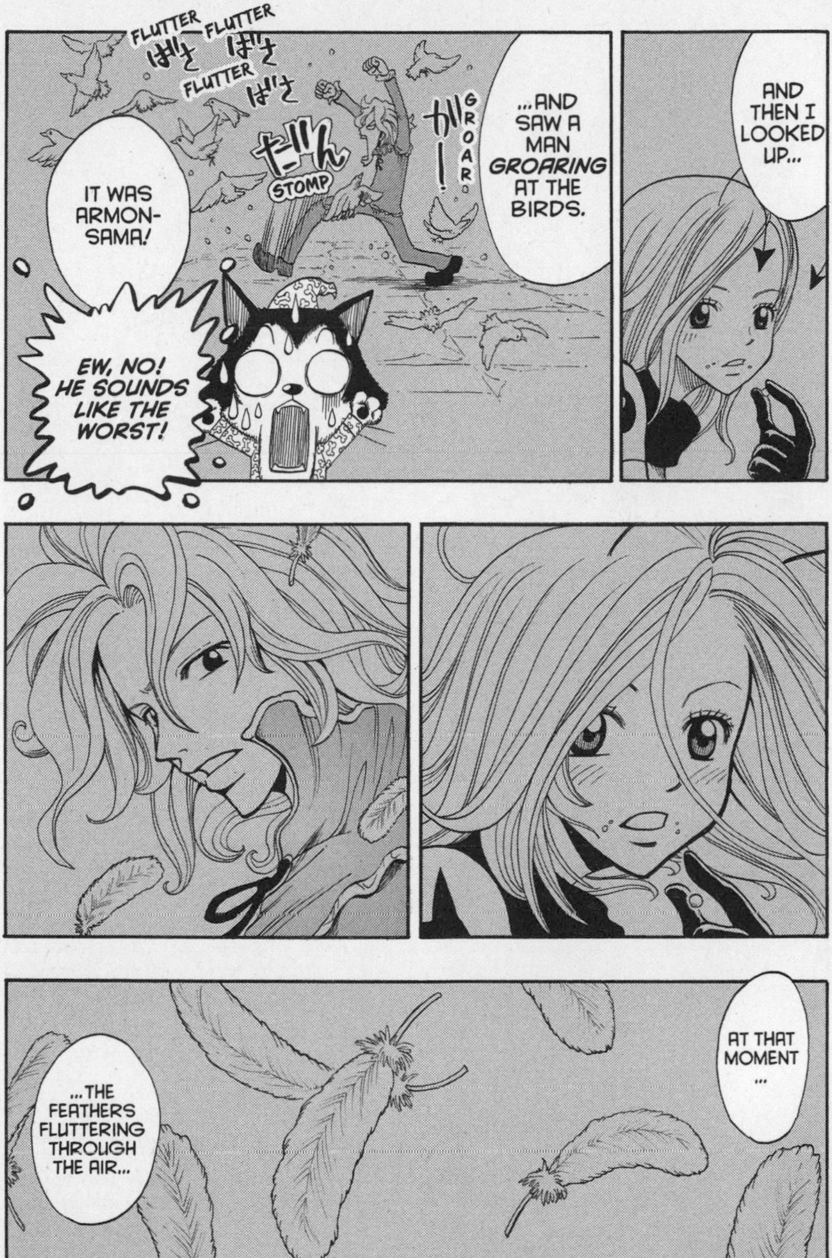
AND THEN I LOOKED UP...
...AND SAW A MAN GROARING AT THE BIRDS.
GROAR
がー!
FLUTTER FLUTTER
ばさ ばさ
FLUTTER
ばさ
STOMP
IT WAS ARMON-SAMA!
EW, NO! HE SOUNDS LIKE THE WORST!
AT THAT MOMENT ...
...THE FEATHERS FLUTTERING THROUGH THE AIR...

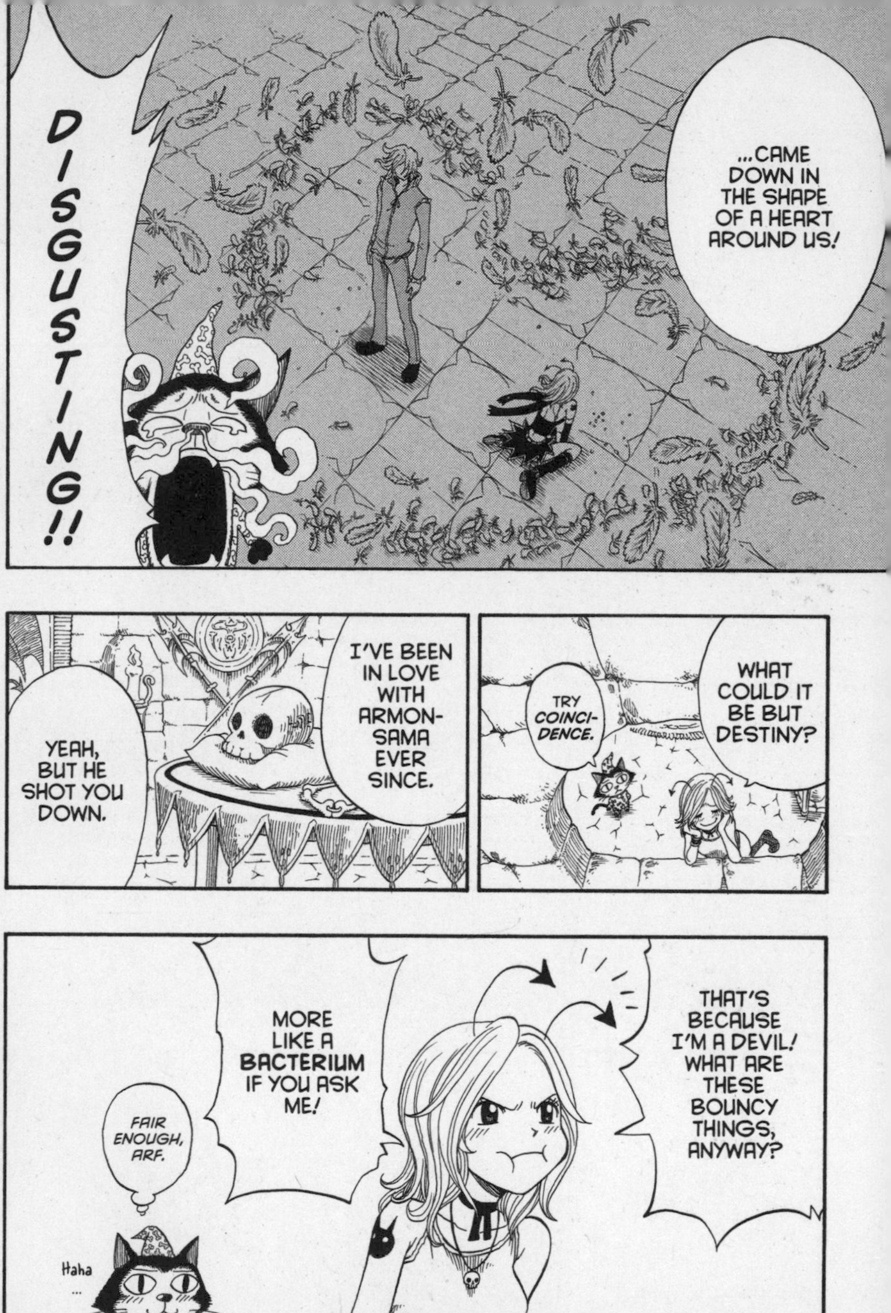
...CAME DOWN IN THE SHAPE OF A HEART AROUND US!
DISGUSTING!!
WHAT COULD IT BE BUT DESTINY?
TRY *COINCIDENCE*.
I'VE BEEN IN LOVE WITH ARMON-SAMA EVER SINCE.
YEAH, BUT HE SHOT YOU DOWN.
THAT'S BECAUSE I'M A DEVIL! WHAT ARE THESE BOUNCY THINGS, ANYWAY?
MORE LIKE A **BACTERIUM** IF YOU ASK ME!
FAIR ENOUGH, ARF.
Haha ...

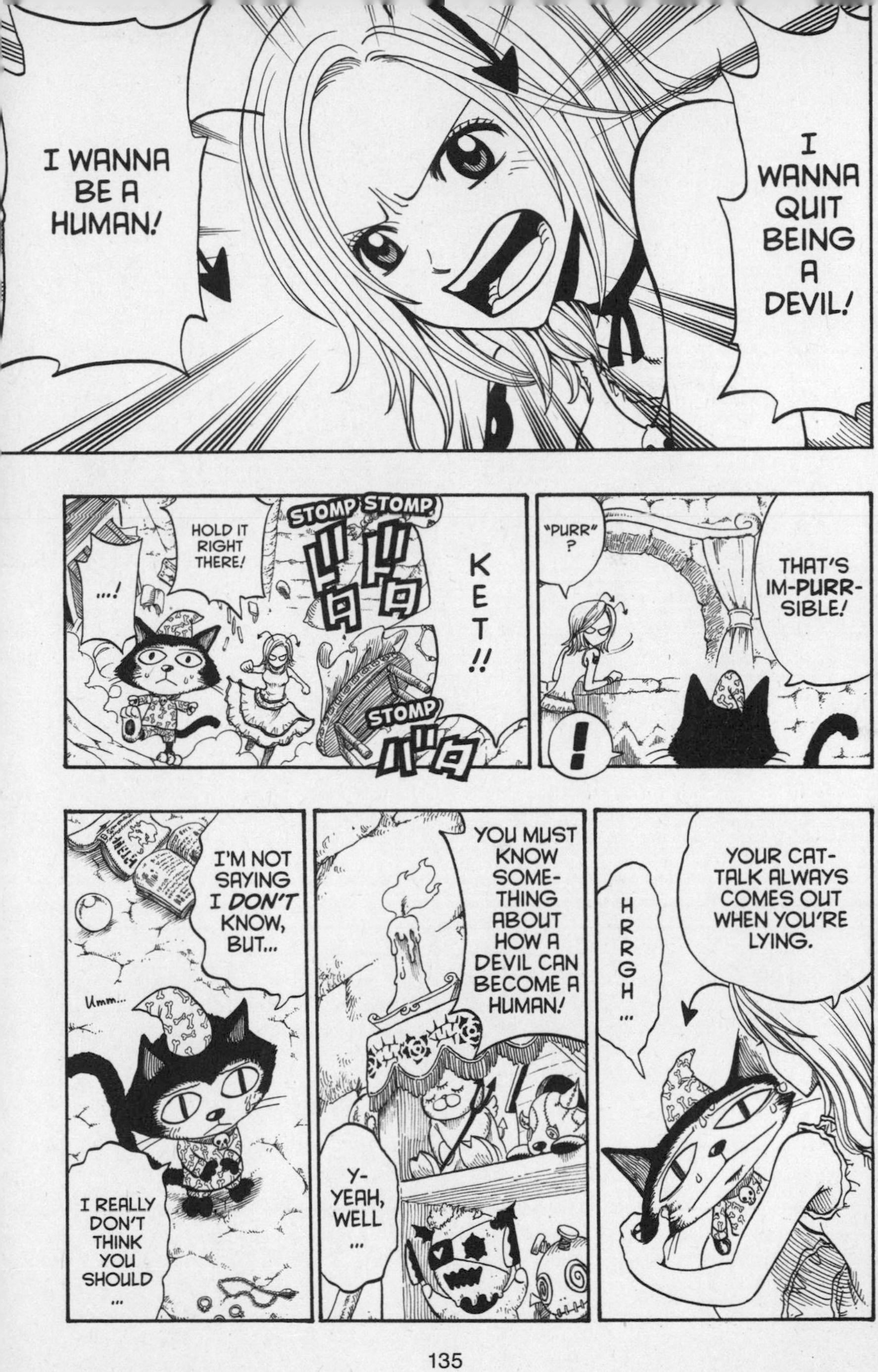
I WANNA QUIT BEING A DEVIL!
I WANNA BE A HUMAN!
THAT'S IM-PURR-SIBLE!
"PURR"?
!
STOMP STOMP
KET!!
HOLD IT RIGHT THERE!
...!
STOMP
YOUR CAT-TALK ALWAYS COMES OUT WHEN YOU'RE LYING.
HRRGH...
YOU MUST KNOW SOME-THING ABOUT HOW A DEVIL CAN BECOME A HUMAN!
Y-YEAH, WELL...
I'M NOT SAYING I *DON'T* KNOW, BUT...
Umm...
I REALLY DON'T THINK YOU SHOULD...

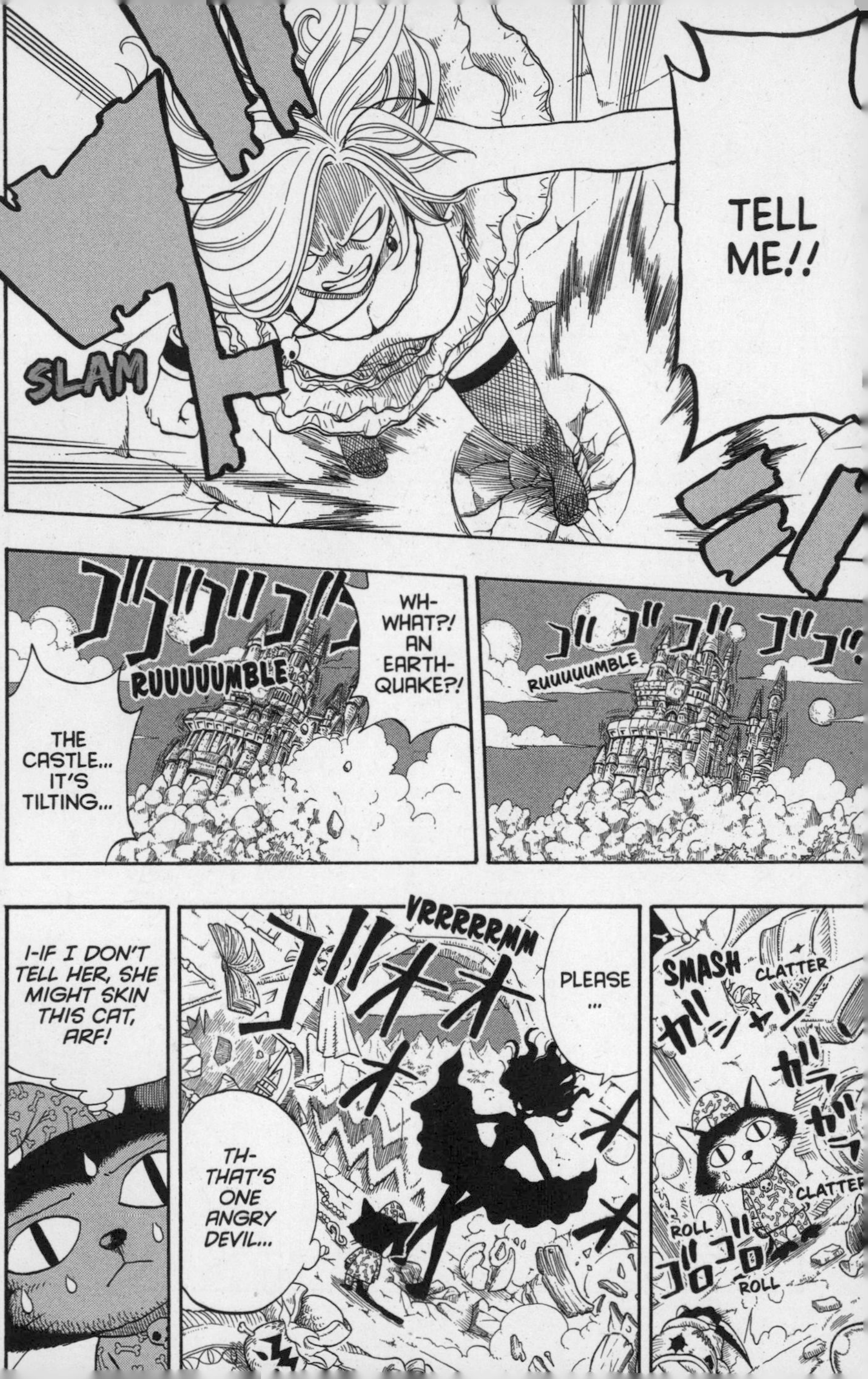
TELL ME!!
SLAM
RUUUUUMBLE
WH-WHAT?! AN EARTH-QUAKE?!
RUUUUUMBLE
THE CASTLE... IT'S TILTING...
SMASH
CLATTER
CLATTER
ROLL
ROLL
VRRRRRRMM
PLEASE ...
TH-THAT'S ONE ANGRY DEVIL...
I-IF I DON'T TELL HER, SHE MIGHT SKIN THIS CAT, ARF!

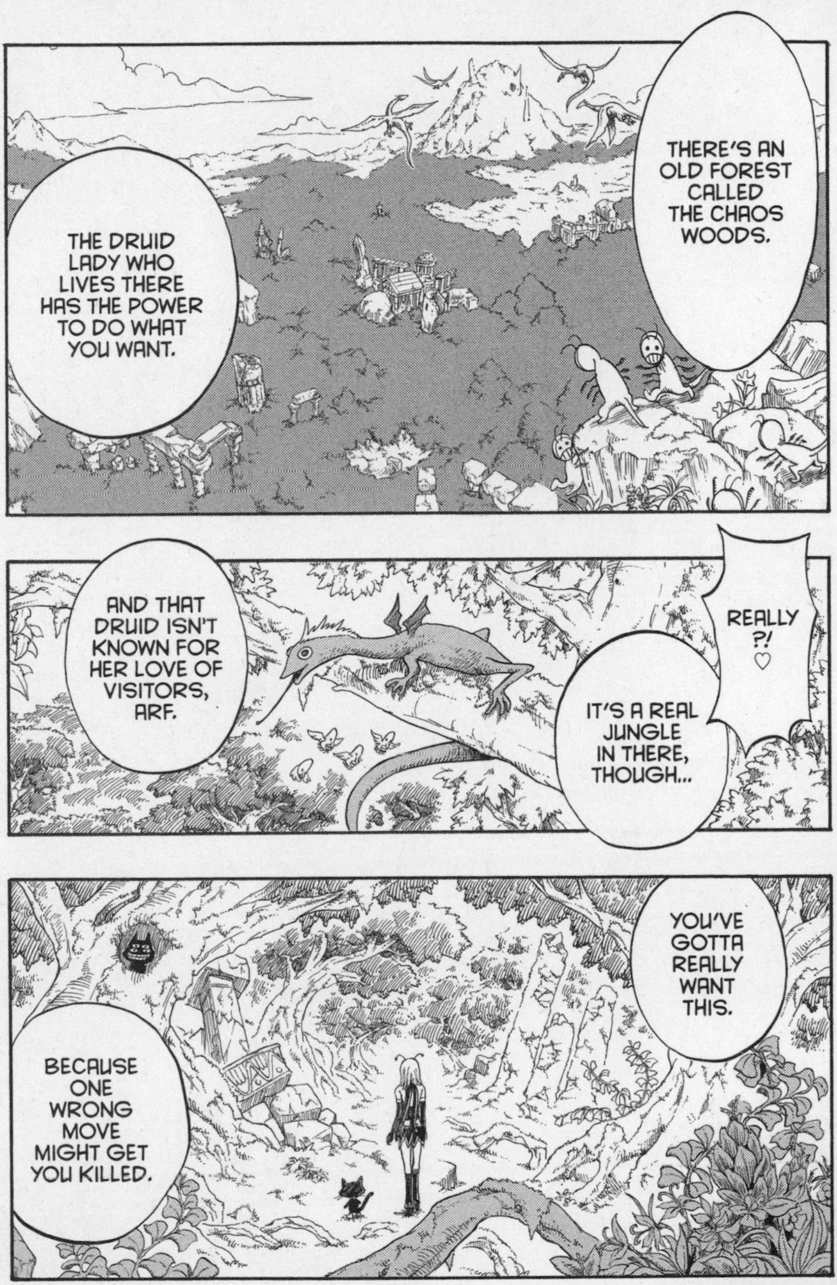
THERE'S AN OLD FOREST CALLED THE CHAOS WOODS.
THE DRUID LADY WHO LIVES THERE HAS THE POWER TO DO WHAT YOU WANT.
REALLY?! ♡
IT'S A REAL JUNGLE IN THERE, THOUGH...
AND THAT DRUID ISN'T KNOWN FOR HER LOVE OF VISITORS, ARF.
YOU'VE GOTTA REALLY WANT THIS.
BECAUSE ONE WRONG MOVE MIGHT GET YOU KILLED.

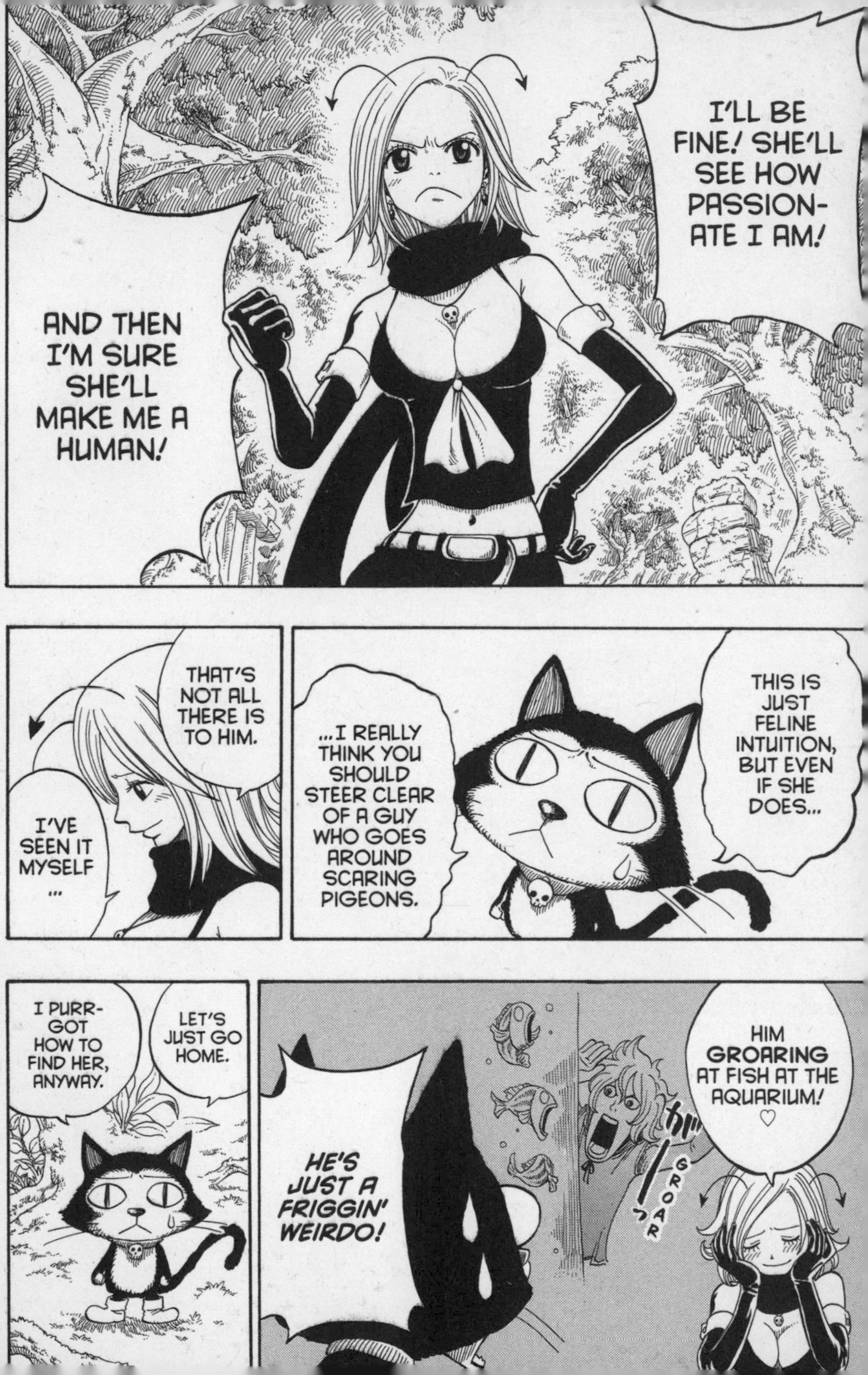
I'LL BE FINE! SHE'LL SEE HOW PASSION-ATE I AM!
AND THEN I'M SURE SHE'LL MAKE ME A HUMAN!
THIS IS JUST FELINE INTUITION, BUT EVEN IF SHE DOES...
...I REALLY THINK YOU SHOULD STEER CLEAR OF A GUY WHO GOES AROUND SCARING PIGEONS.
THAT'S NOT ALL THERE IS TO HIM.
I'VE SEEN IT MYSELF ...
HIM **GROARING** AT FISH AT THE AQUARIUM! ♡
GROAR
HE'S JUST A FRIGGIN' WEIRDO!
LET'S JUST GO HOME.
I PURR-GOT HOW TO FIND HER, ANYWAY.

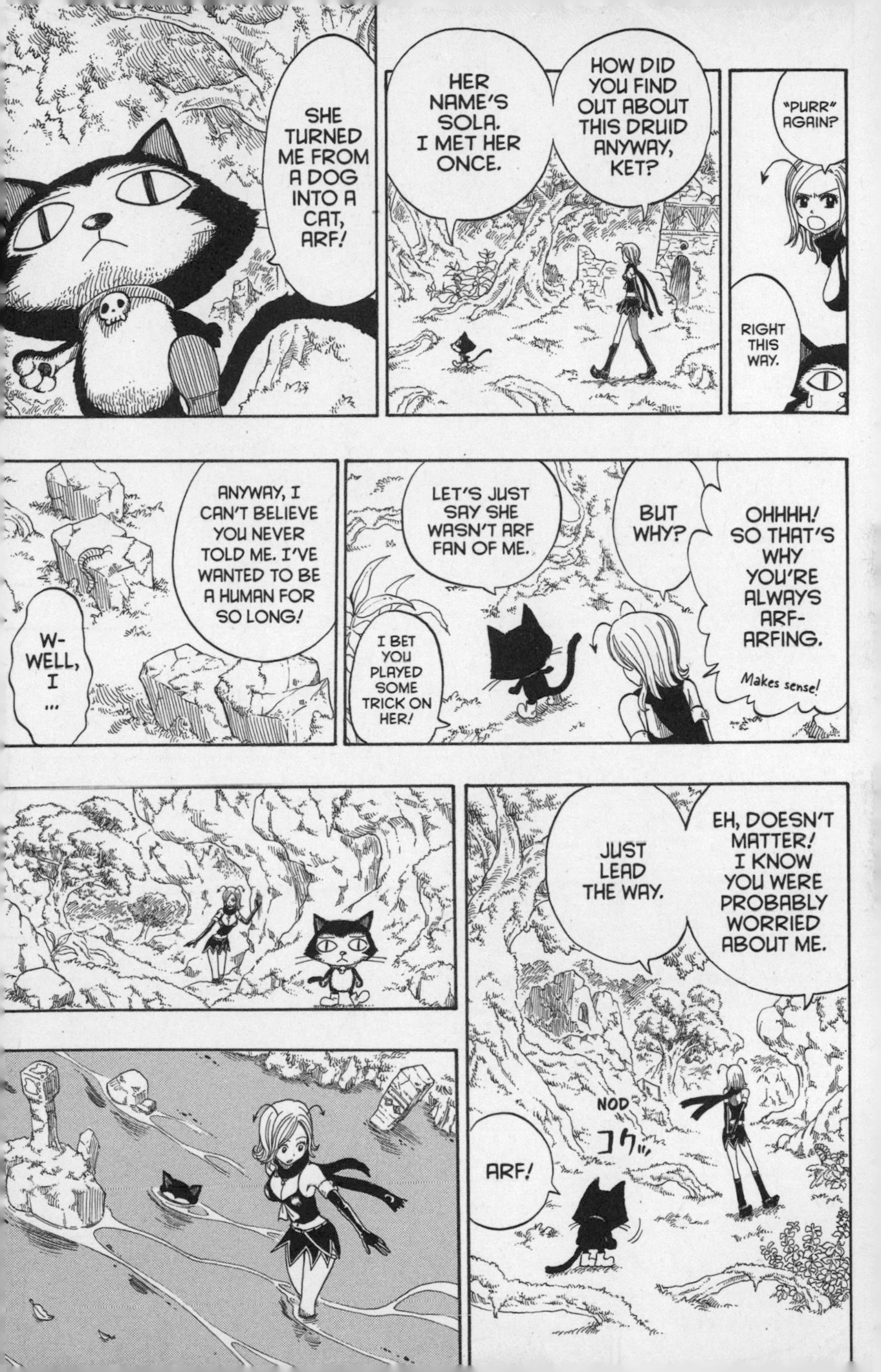
"PURR" AGAIN?
RIGHT THIS WAY.
HOW DID YOU FIND OUT ABOUT THIS DRUID ANYWAY, KET?
HER NAME'S SOLA. I MET HER ONCE.
SHE TURNED ME FROM A DOG INTO A CAT, ARF!
OHHHH! SO THAT'S WHY YOU'RE ALWAYS ARF-ARFING.
Makes sense!
BUT WHY?
LET'S JUST SAY SHE WASN'T ARF FAN OF ME.
I BET YOU PLAYED SOME TRICK ON HER!
ANYWAY, I CAN'T BELIEVE YOU NEVER TOLD ME. I'VE WANTED TO BE A HUMAN FOR SO LONG!
W-WELL, I ...
EH, DOESN'T MATTER! I KNOW YOU WERE PROBABLY WORRIED ABOUT ME.
JUST LEAD THE WAY.
NOD
コク
ARF!

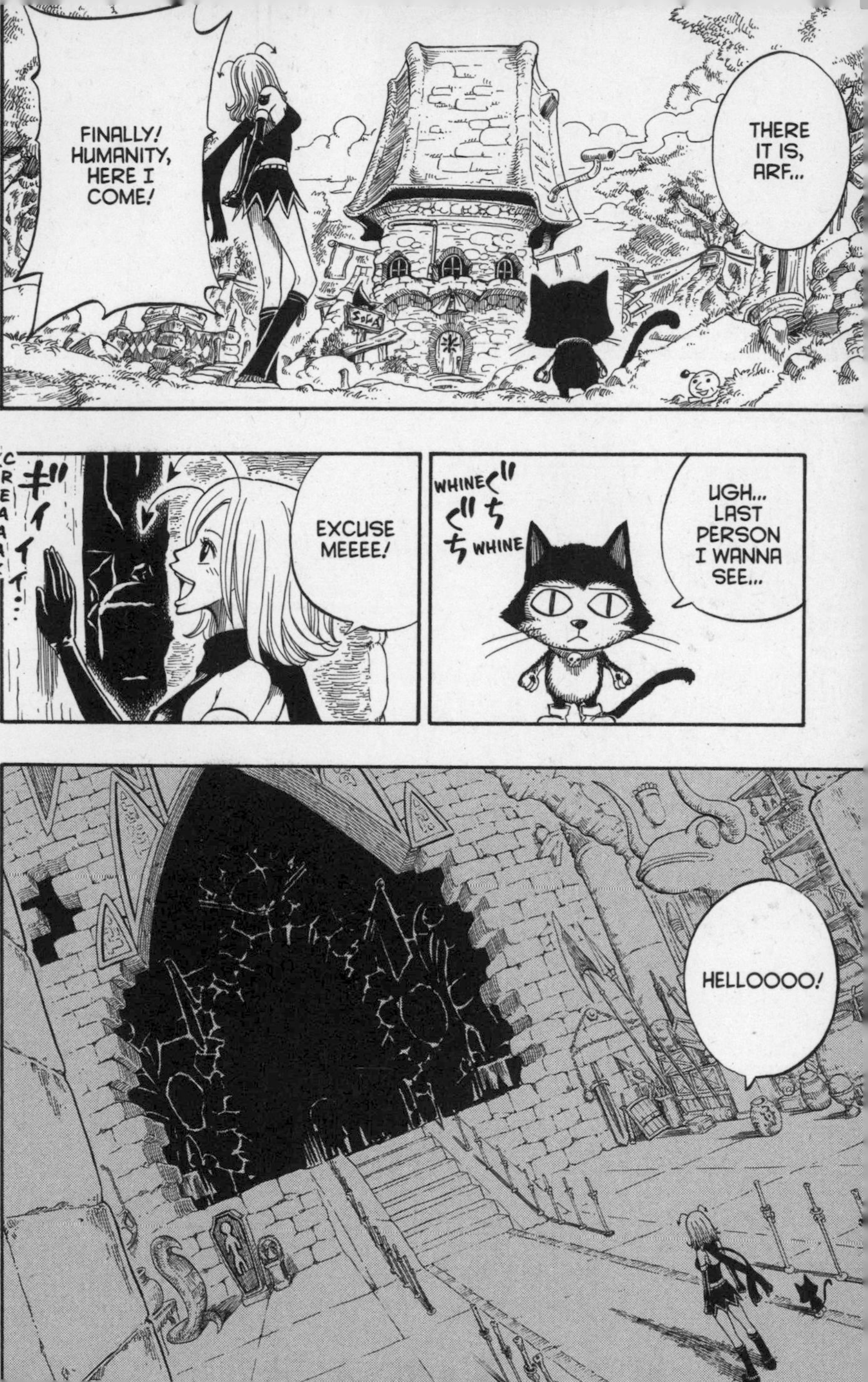
THERE IT IS, ARF...
FINALLY! HUMANITY, HERE I COME!
WHINE ぐち
ぐち WHINE
UGH... LAST PERSON I WANNA SEE...
EXCUSE MEEEE!
CREAAAK ギイイイ…
HELLOOOO!

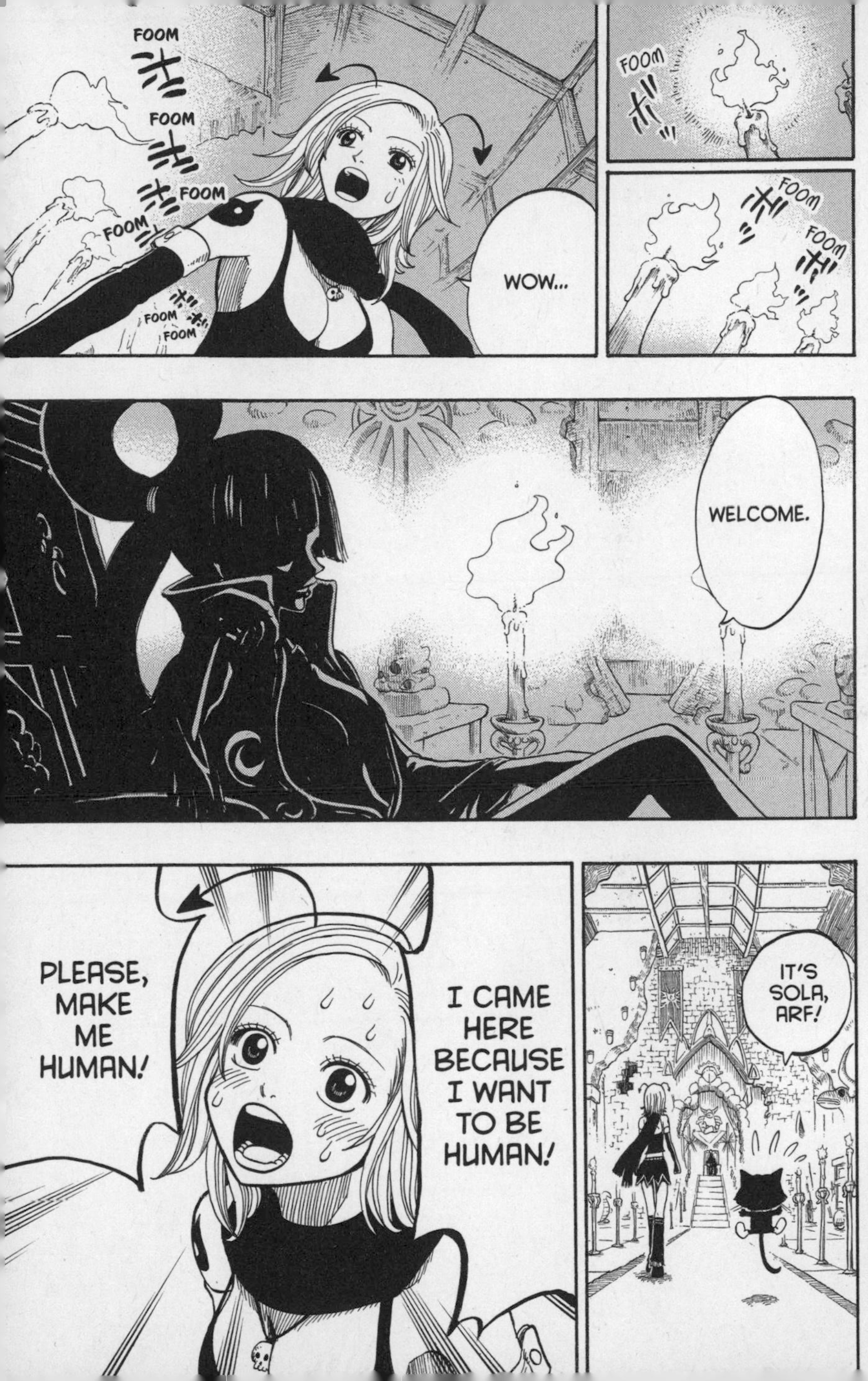
FOOM
FOOM
FOOM
FOOM
FOOM
FOOM
FOOM
FOOM
FOOM
WOW...
WELCOME.
IT'S SOLA, ARF!
I CAME HERE BECAUSE I WANT TO BE HUMAN!
PLEASE, MAKE ME HUMAN!

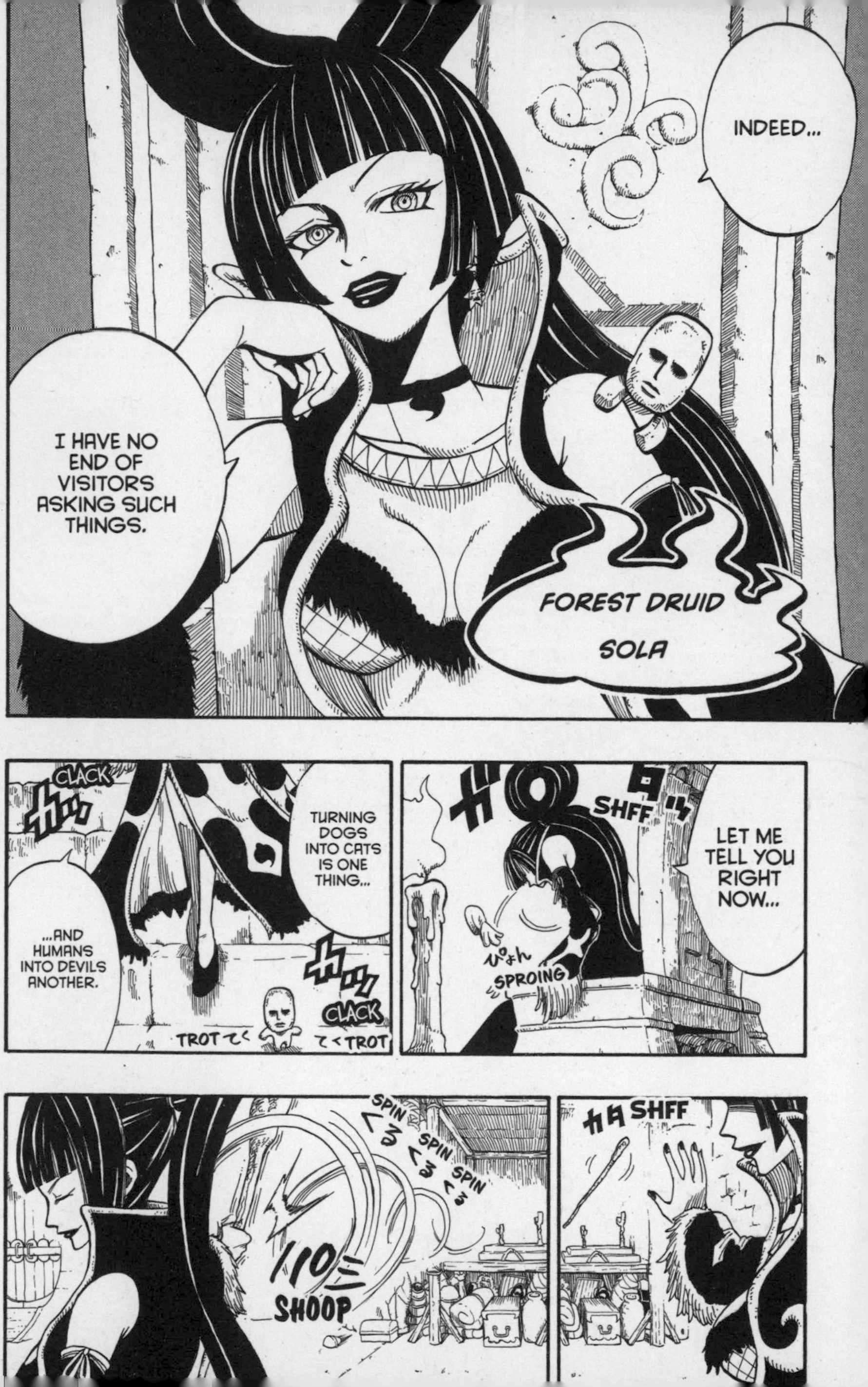

INDEED...
I HAVE NO END OF VISITORS ASKING SUCH THINGS.
FOREST DRUID SOLA
SHFF
LET ME TELL YOU RIGHT NOW...
ぴょん
SPROING
CLACK
TURNING DOGS INTO CATS IS ONE THING...
...AND HUMANS INTO DEVILS ANOTHER.
CLACK
TROT てく
てく TROT
カタ SHFF
SPIN くる
SPIN くる
SPIN くる
SHOOP

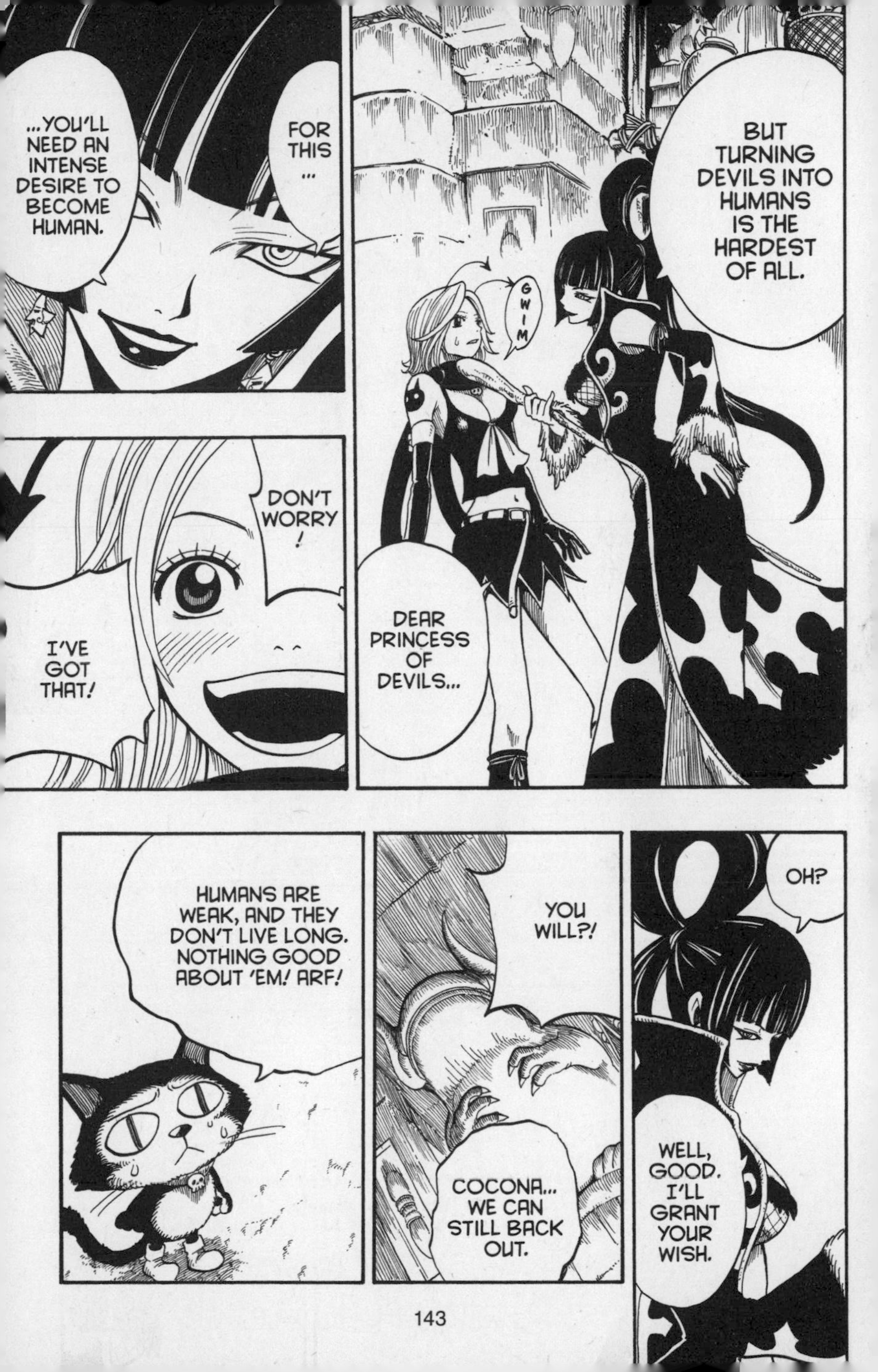
BUT TURNING DEVILS INTO HUMANS IS THE HARDEST OF ALL.
GWIM
DEAR PRINCESS OF DEVILS...
FOR THIS...
...YOU'LL NEED AN INTENSE DESIRE TO BECOME HUMAN.
DON'T WORRY!
I'VE GOT THAT!
OH?
WELL, GOOD. I'LL GRANT YOUR WISH.
YOU WILL?!
COCONA... WE CAN STILL BACK OUT.
HUMANS ARE WEAK, AND THEY DON'T LIVE LONG. NOTHING GOOD ABOUT 'EM! ARF!

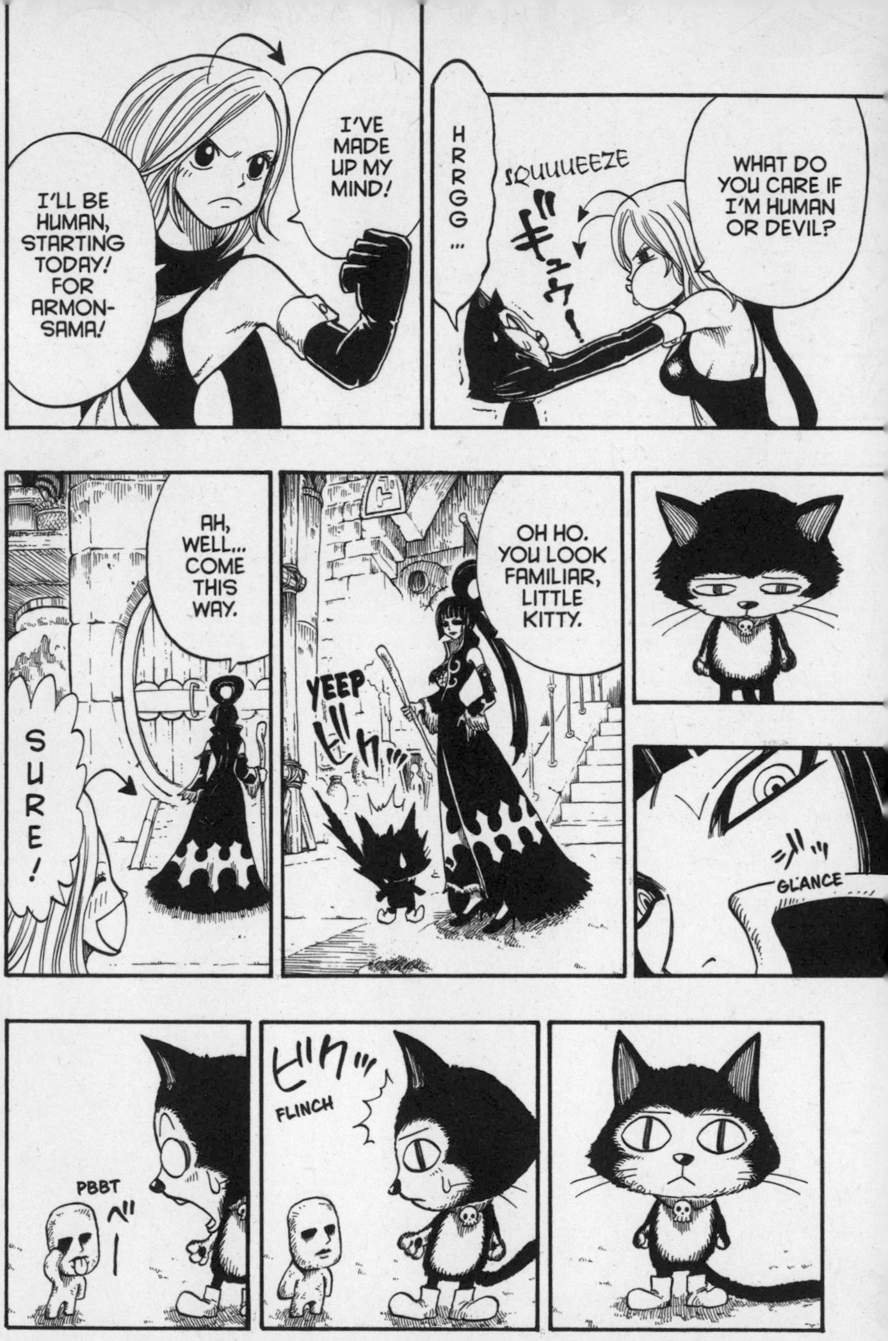
WHAT DO YOU CARE IF I'M HUMAN OR DEVIL?
SQUUUEEZE
HRRGG...
I'VE MADE UP MY MIND!
I'LL BE HUMAN, STARTING TODAY! FOR ARMON-SAMA!
GLANCE
OH HO. YOU LOOK FAMILIAR, LITTLE KITTY.
YEEP
AH, WELL... COME THIS WAY.
SURE!
FLINCH
PBBT

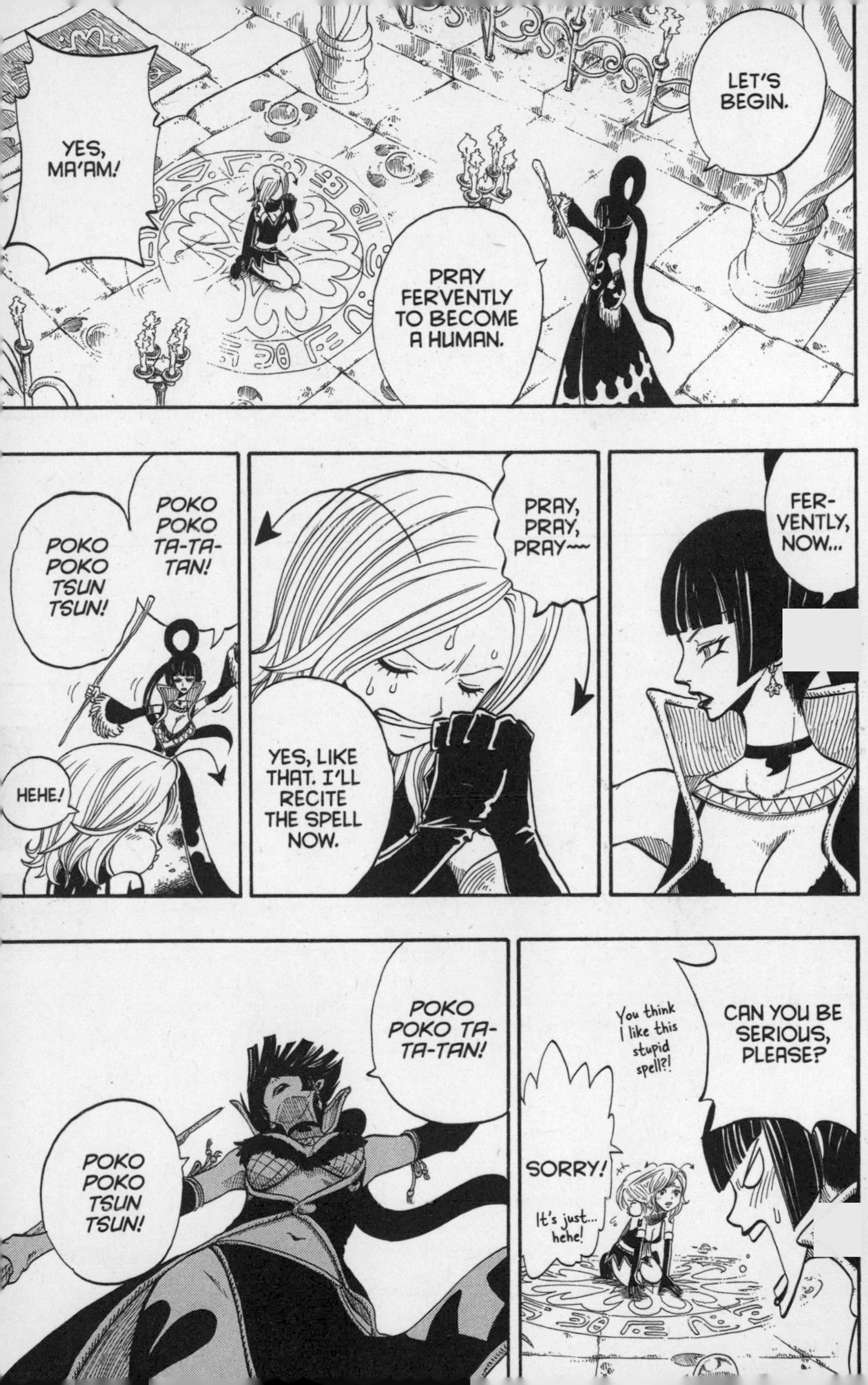
LET'S BEGIN.
PRAY FERVENTLY TO BECOME A HUMAN.
YES, MA'AM!
FER-VENTLY, NOW...
PRAY, PRAY, PRAY~~
YES, LIKE THAT. I'LL RECITE THE SPELL NOW.
POKO POKO TA-TA-TAN!
POKO POKO TSUN TSUN!
HEHE!
CAN YOU BE SERIOUS, PLEASE?
You think I like this stupid spell?!
SORRY!
It's just... hehe!
POKO POKO TA-TA-TAN!
POKO POKO TSUN TSUN!

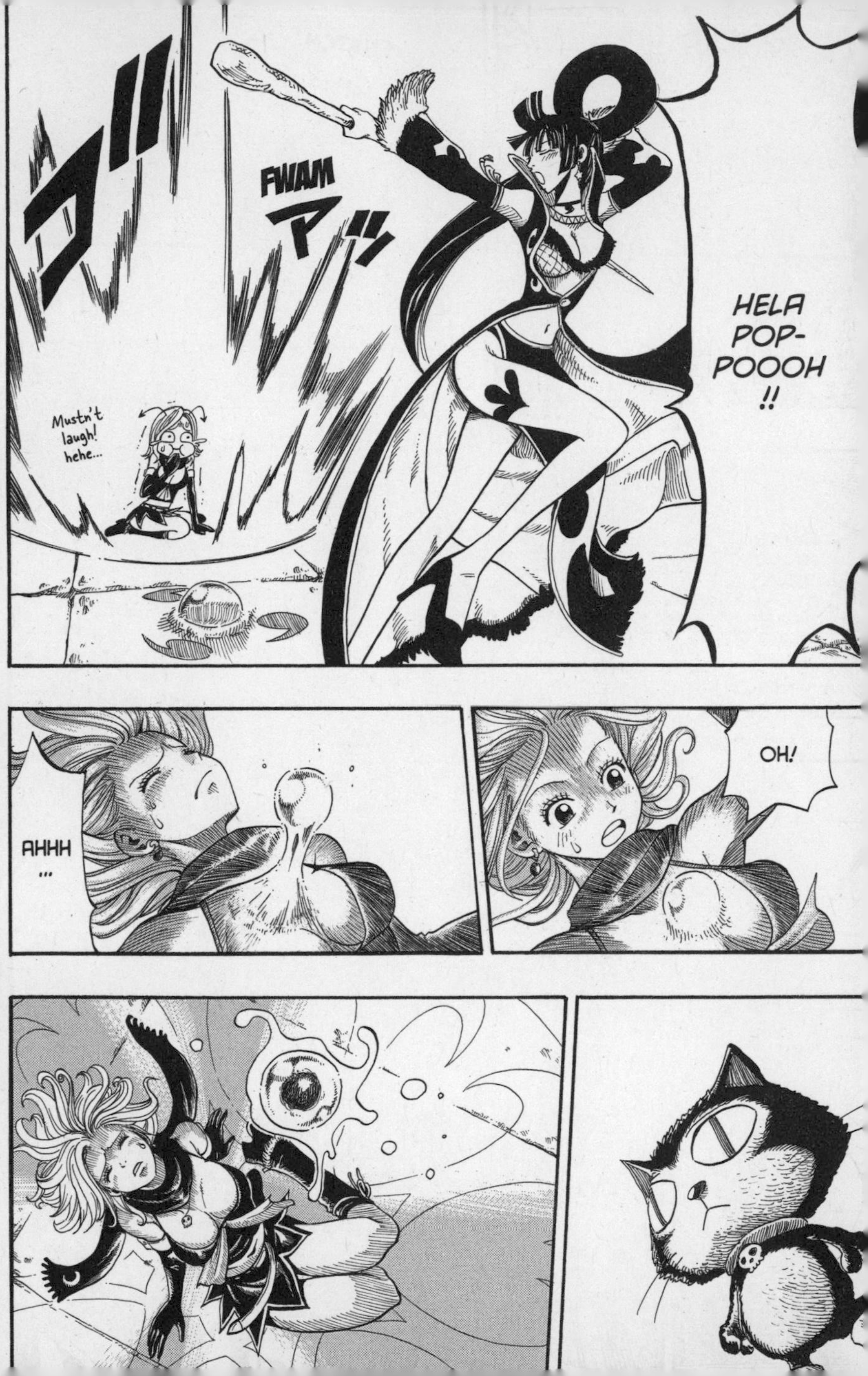
HELA POP-POOOH!!
FWAM
Mustn't laugh! hehe...
OH!
AHHH ...

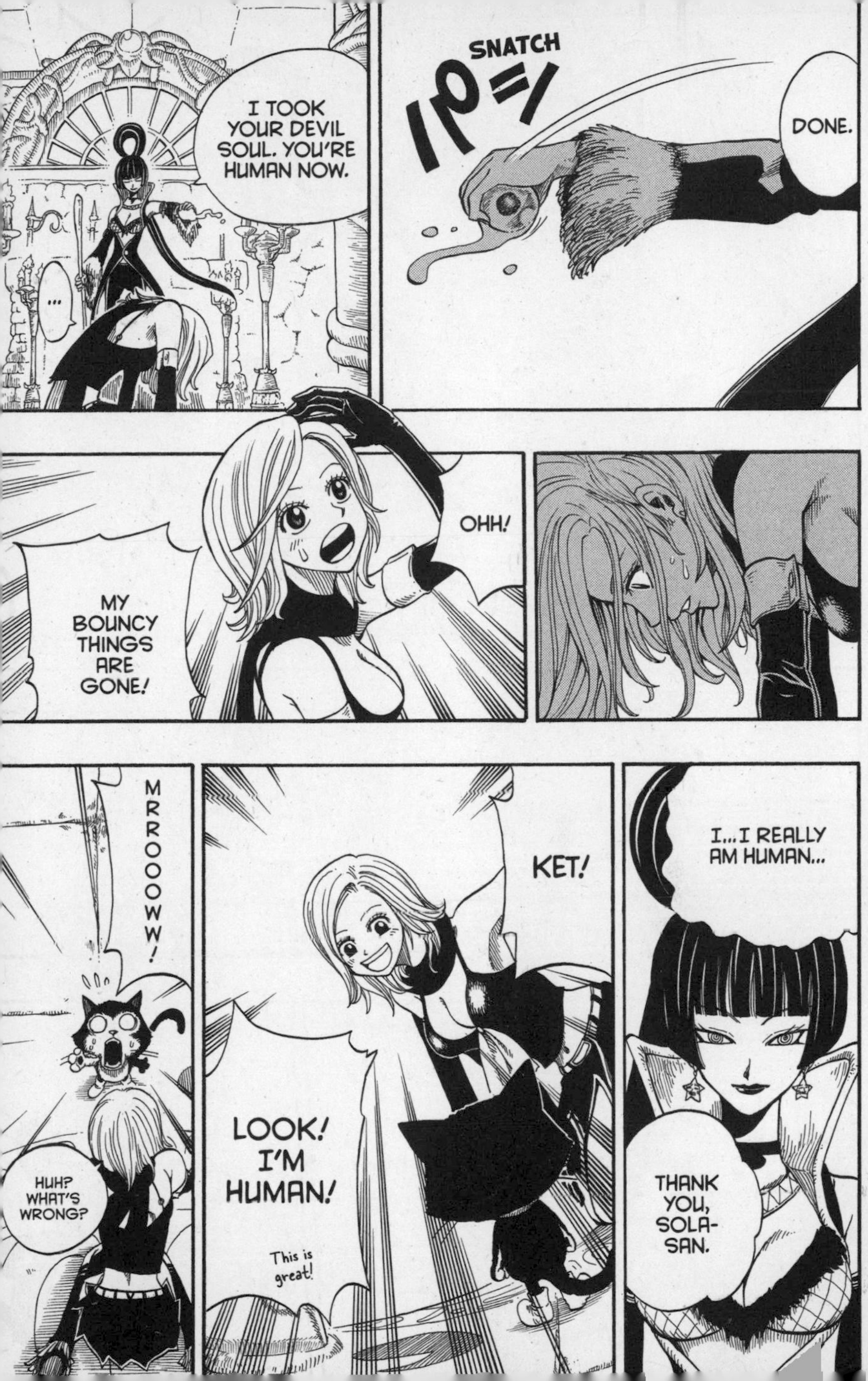
DONE.
SNATCH
I TOOK YOUR DEVIL SOUL. YOU'RE HUMAN NOW.
...
OHH!
MY BOUNCY THINGS ARE GONE!
I...I REALLY AM HUMAN...
THANK YOU, SOLA-SAN.
KET!
LOOK! I'M HUMAN!
This is great!
MRROOOOWW!
HUH? WHAT'S WRONG?

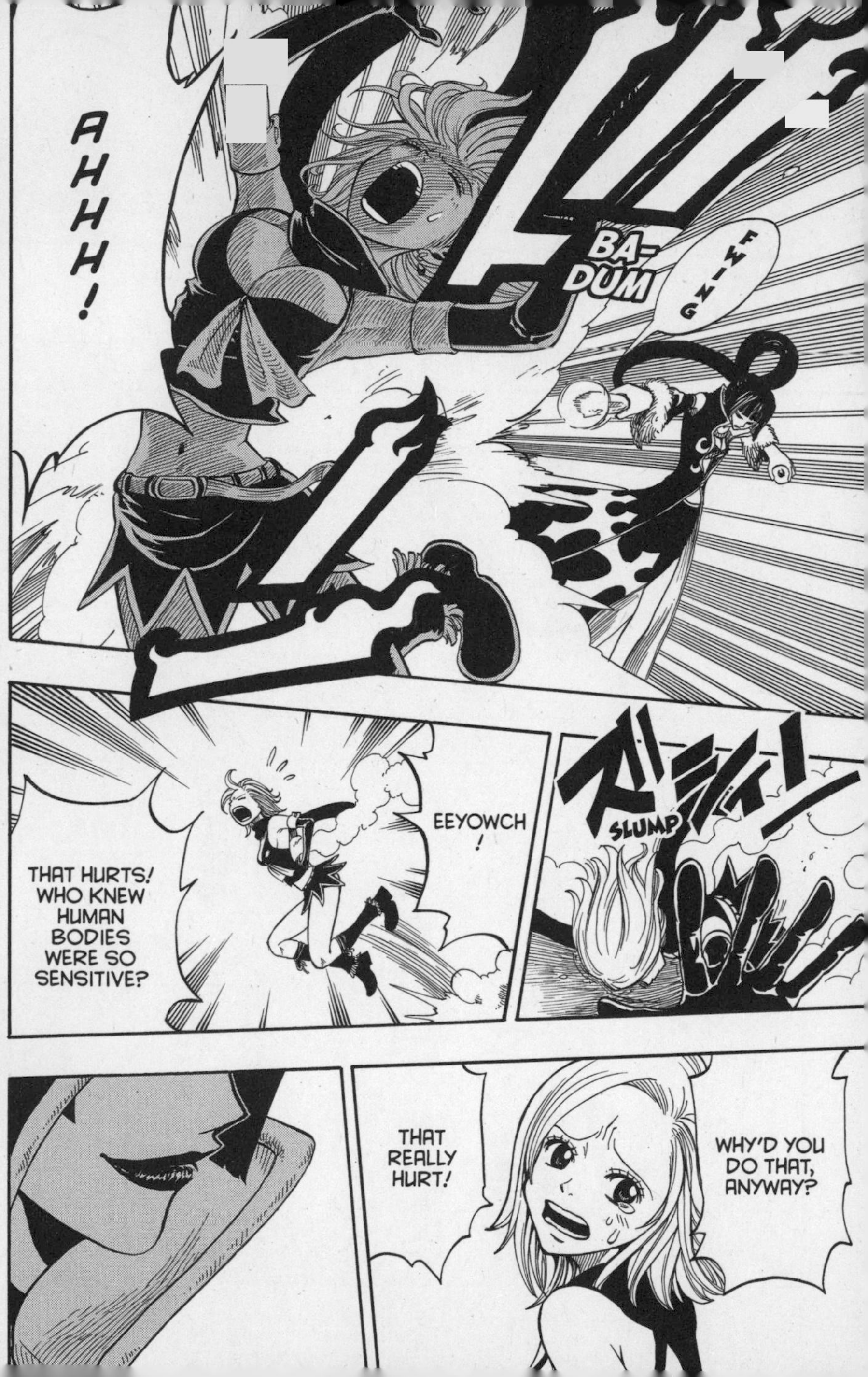
FWING
BA-DUM
AHHHH!
SLUMP
EEYOWCH!
THAT HURTS! WHO KNEW HUMAN BODIES WERE SO SENSITIVE?
WHY'D YOU DO THAT, ANYWAY?
THAT REALLY HURT!

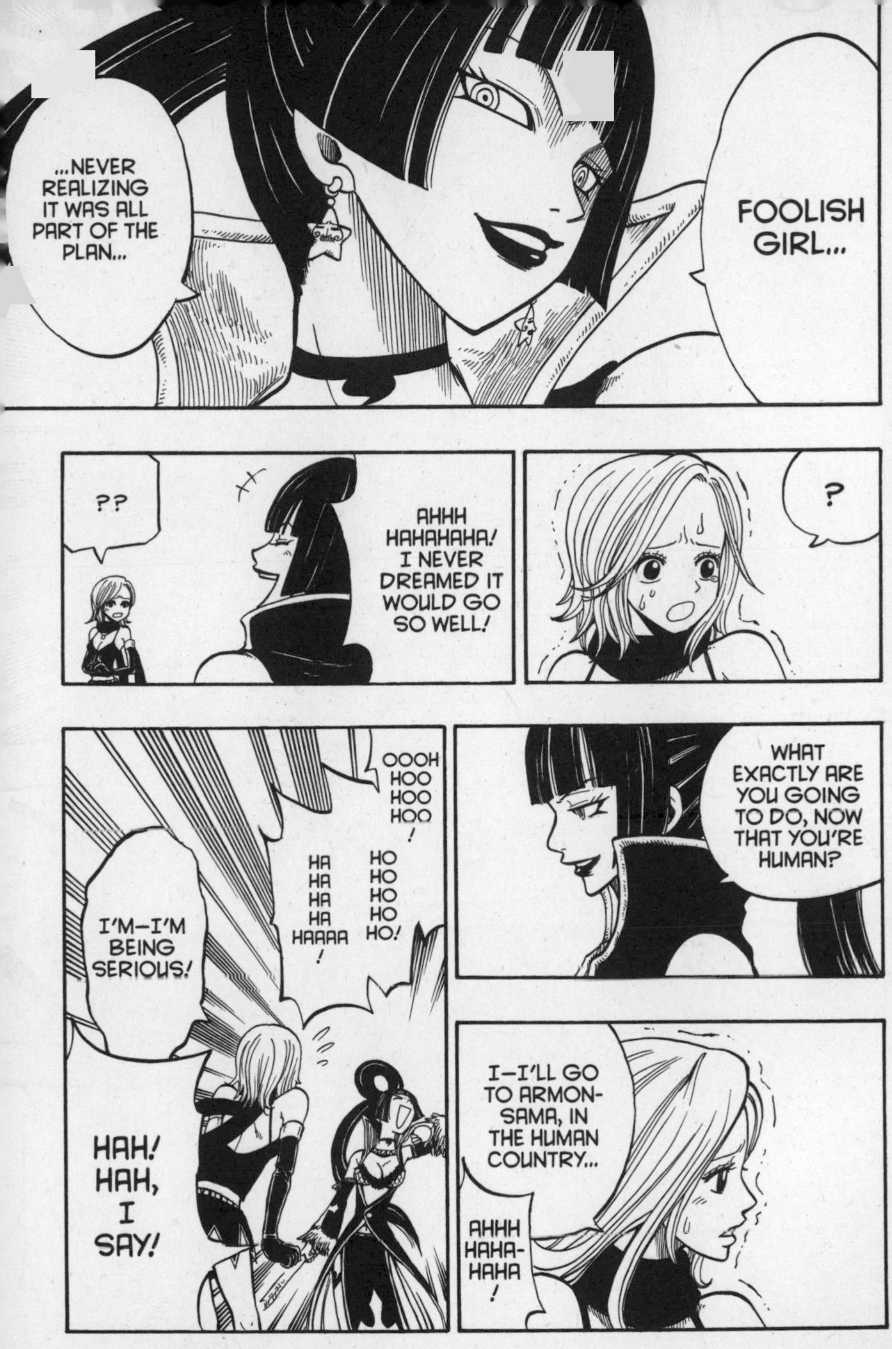
FOOLISH GIRL...
...NEVER REALIZING IT WAS ALL PART OF THE PLAN...
?
AHHH HAHAHAHA! I NEVER DREAMED IT WOULD GO SO WELL!
??
WHAT EXACTLY ARE YOU GOING TO DO, NOW THAT YOU'RE HUMAN?
I—I'LL GO TO ARMON-SAMA, IN THE HUMAN COUNTRY...
AHHH HAHA-HAHA!
OOOH HOO HOO HOO!
HO HO HO HO HO HO!
HA HA HA HA HAAAA!
I'M—I'M BEING SERIOUS!
HAH! HAH, I SAY!

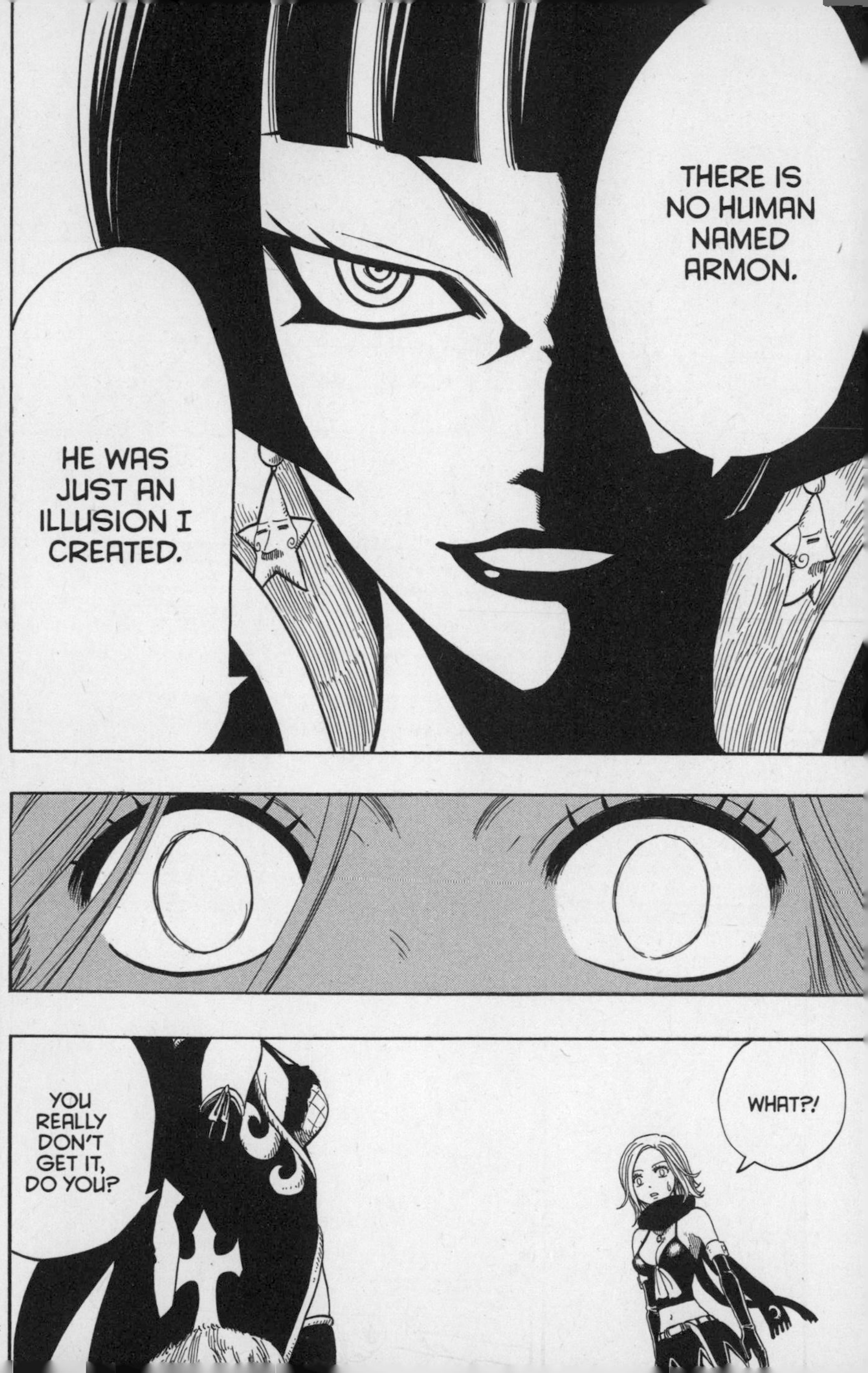
THERE IS NO HUMAN NAMED ARMON.
HE WAS JUST AN ILLUSION I CREATED.
WHAT?!
YOU REALLY DON'T GET IT, DO YOU?

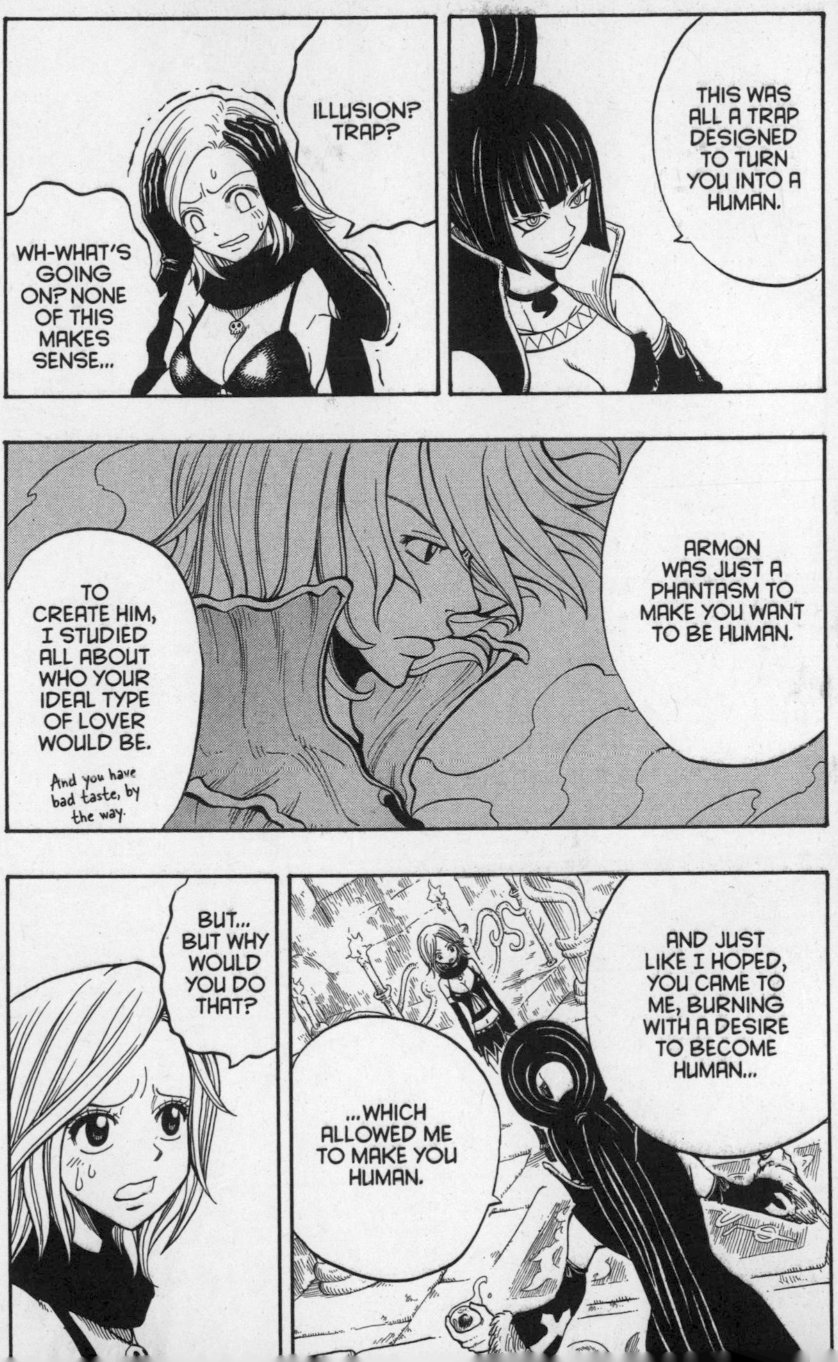
THIS WAS ALL A TRAP DESIGNED TO TURN YOU INTO A HUMAN.
ILLUSION? TRAP?
WH-WHAT'S GOING ON? NONE OF THIS MAKES SENSE...
ARMON WAS JUST A PHANTASM TO MAKE YOU WANT TO BE HUMAN.
TO CREATE HIM, I STUDIED ALL ABOUT WHO YOUR IDEAL TYPE OF LOVER WOULD BE.
And you have bad taste, by the way.
AND JUST LIKE I HOPED, YOU CAME TO ME, BURNING WITH A DESIRE TO BECOME HUMAN...
...WHICH ALLOWED ME TO MAKE YOU HUMAN.
BUT... BUT WHY WOULD YOU DO THAT?

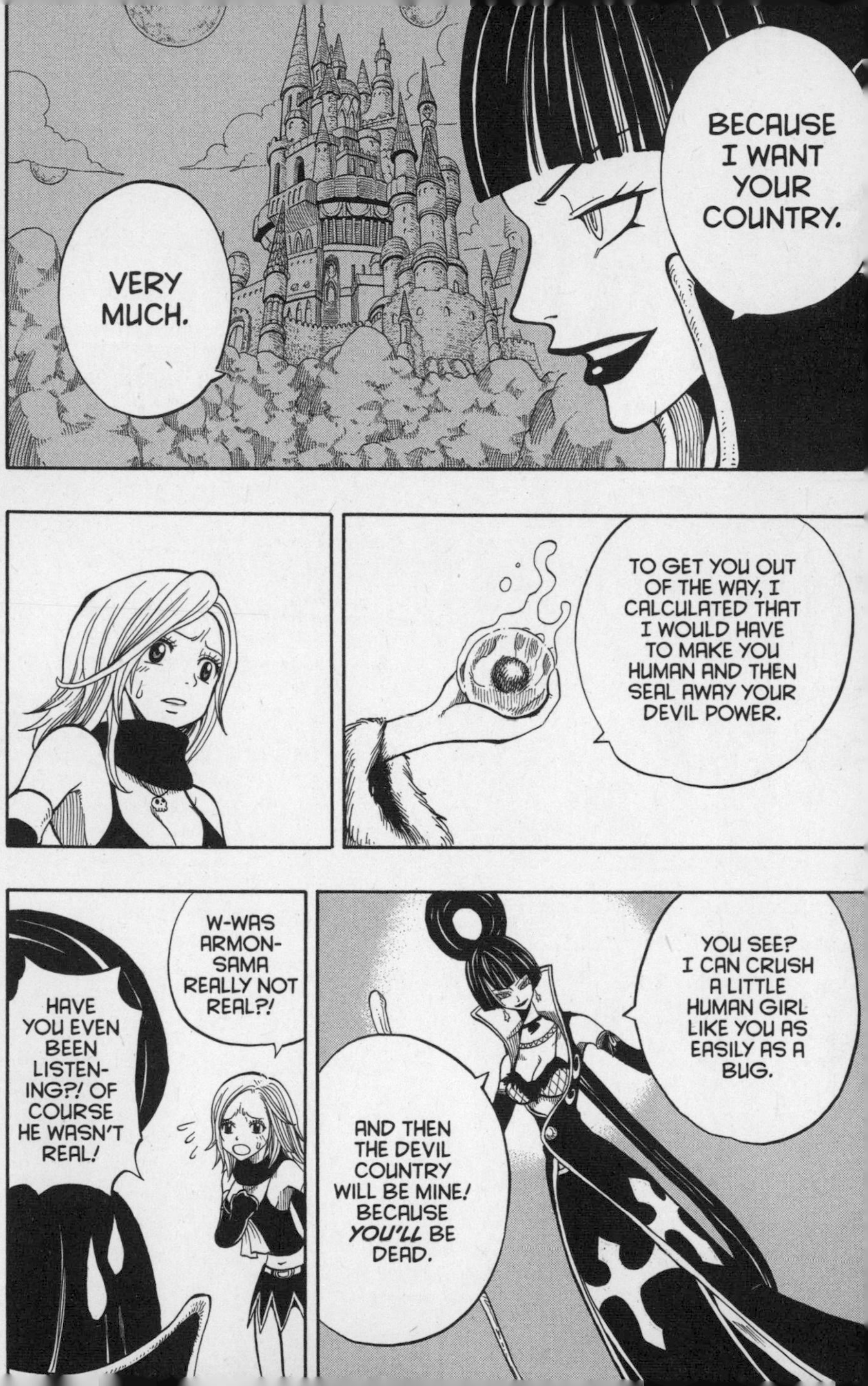
BECAUSE I WANT YOUR COUNTRY.
VERY MUCH.
TO GET YOU OUT OF THE WAY, I CALCULATED THAT I WOULD HAVE TO MAKE YOU HUMAN AND THEN SEAL AWAY YOUR DEVIL POWER.
YOU SEE? I CAN CRUSH A LITTLE HUMAN GIRL LIKE YOU AS EASILY AS A BUG.
AND THEN THE DEVIL COUNTRY WILL BE MINE! BECAUSE *YOU'LL* BE DEAD.
W-WAS ARMON-SAMA REALLY NOT REAL?!
HAVE YOU EVEN BEEN LISTENING?! OF COURSE HE WASN'T REAL!

SHOCK

SLUMP

I THOUGHT HE WAS MY DESTINED LOVE!

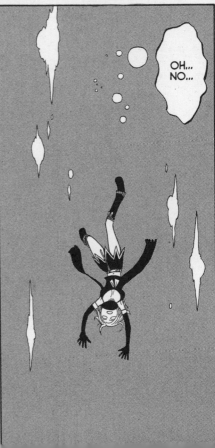
OH... NO...

KET ...!

SNIFF!

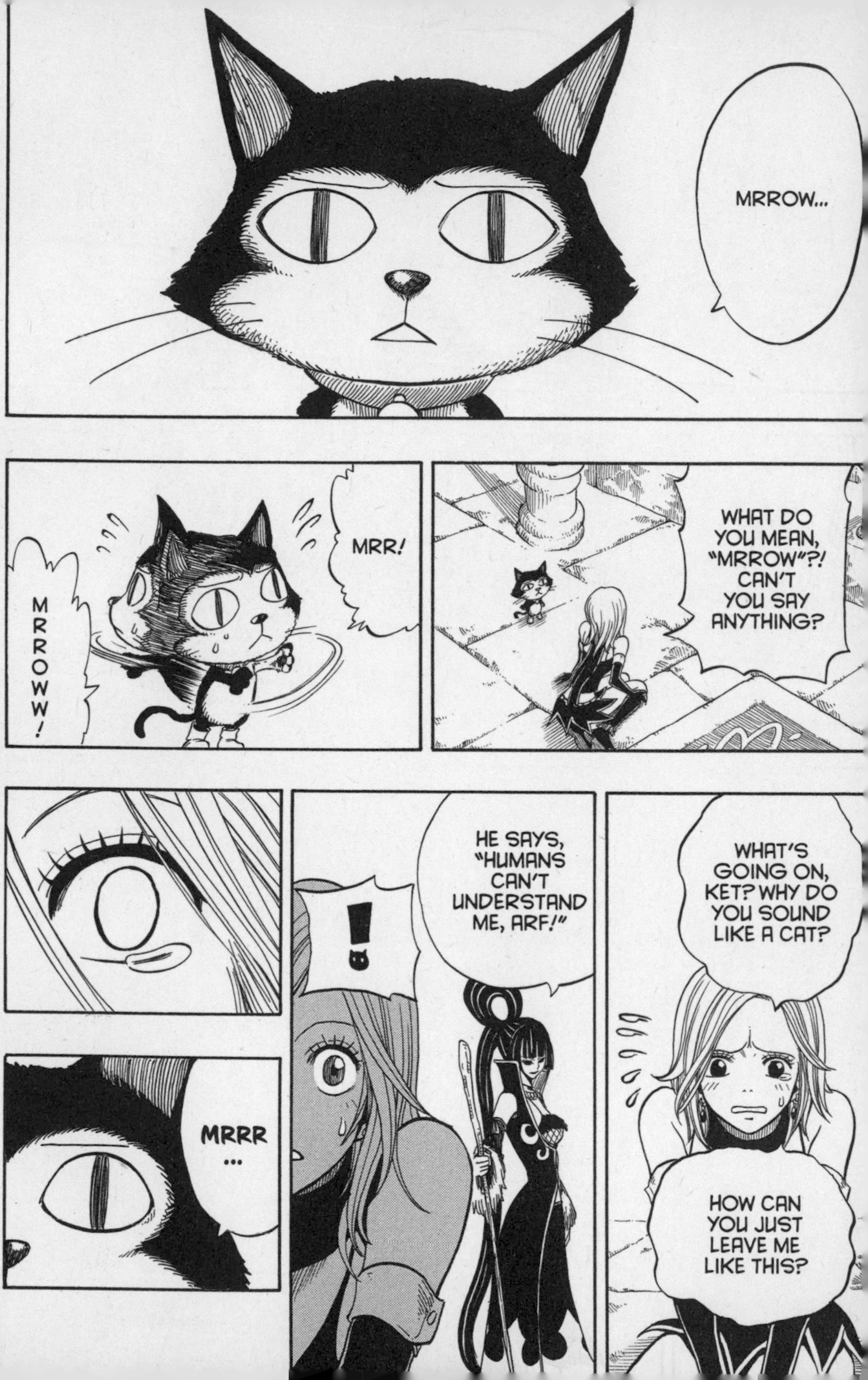
MRROW...
WHAT DO YOU MEAN, "MRROW"?! CAN'T YOU SAY ANYTHING?
MRR!
MRROWW!
WHAT'S GOING ON, KET? WHY DO YOU SOUND LIKE A CAT?
HOW CAN YOU JUST LEAVE ME LIKE THIS?
HE SAYS, "HUMANS CAN'T UNDERSTAND ME, ARF!"
!
MRRR ...

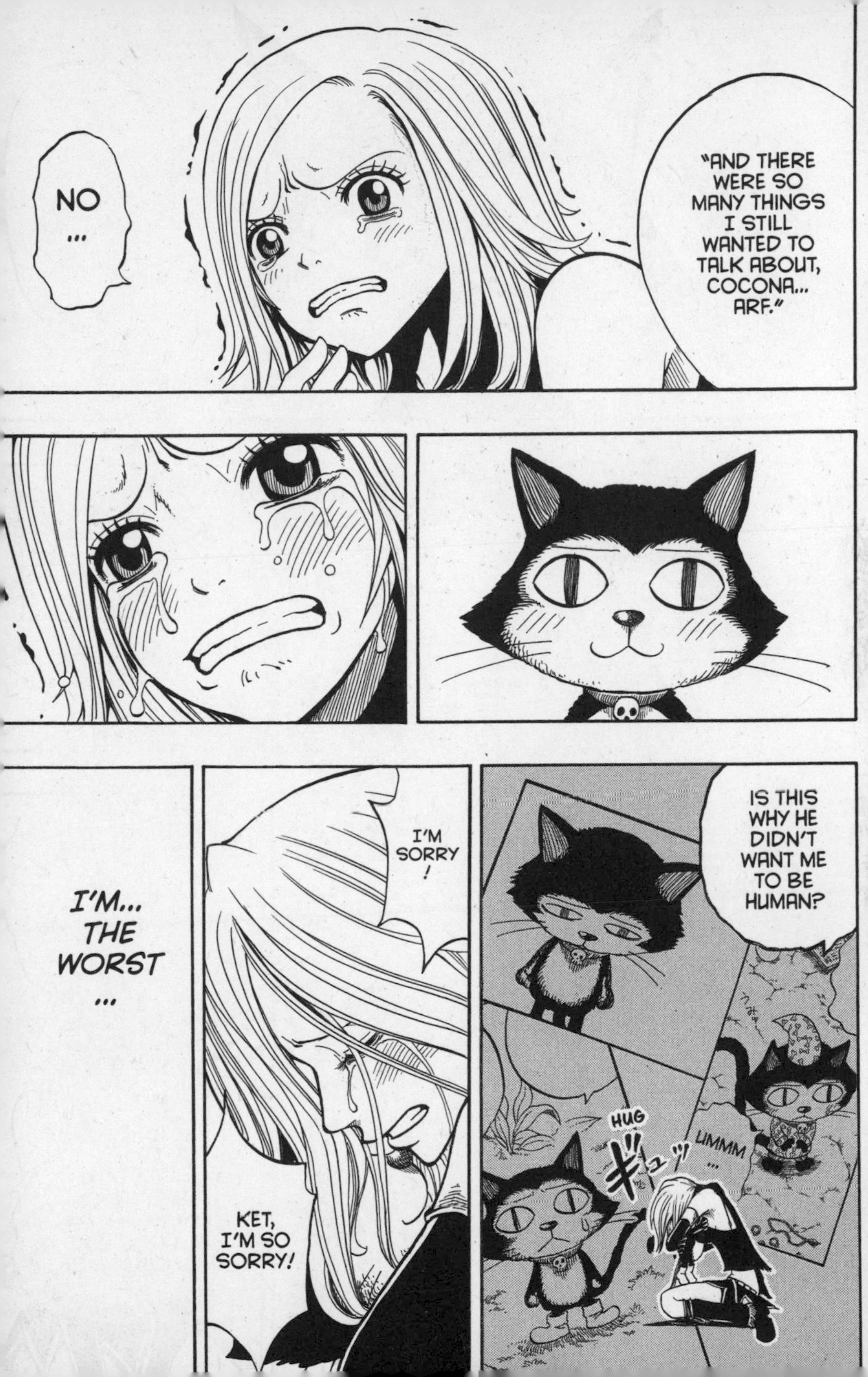
"AND THERE WERE SO MANY THINGS I STILL WANTED TO TALK ABOUT, COCONA... ARF."
NO ...
IS THIS WHY HE DIDN'T WANT ME TO BE HUMAN?
UMMM ...
HUG
I'M SORRY!
KET, I'M SO SORRY!
I'M... THE WORST ...

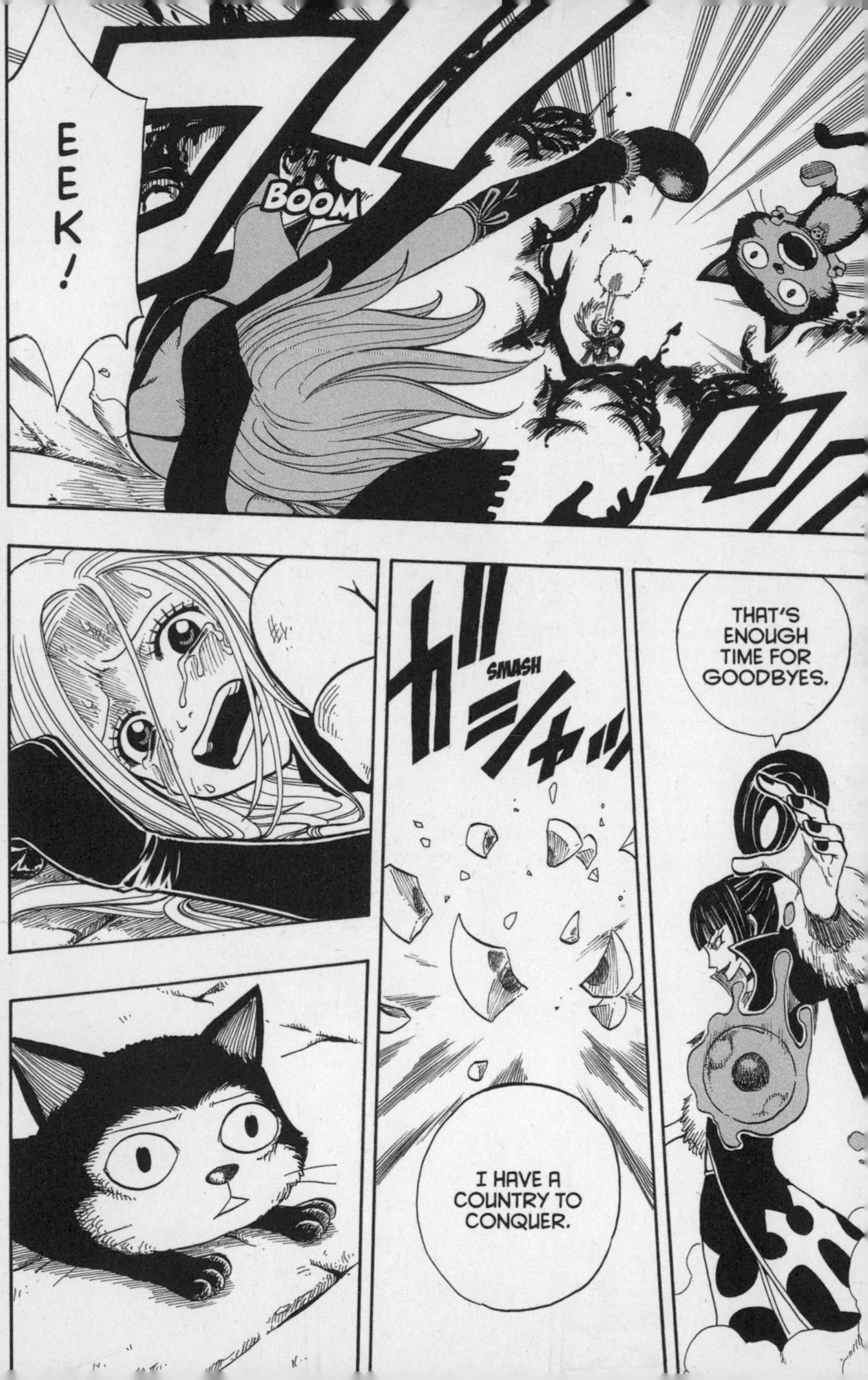
BOOM
EEK!
THAT'S ENOUGH TIME FOR GOODBYES.
SMASH
I HAVE A COUNTRY TO CONQUER.

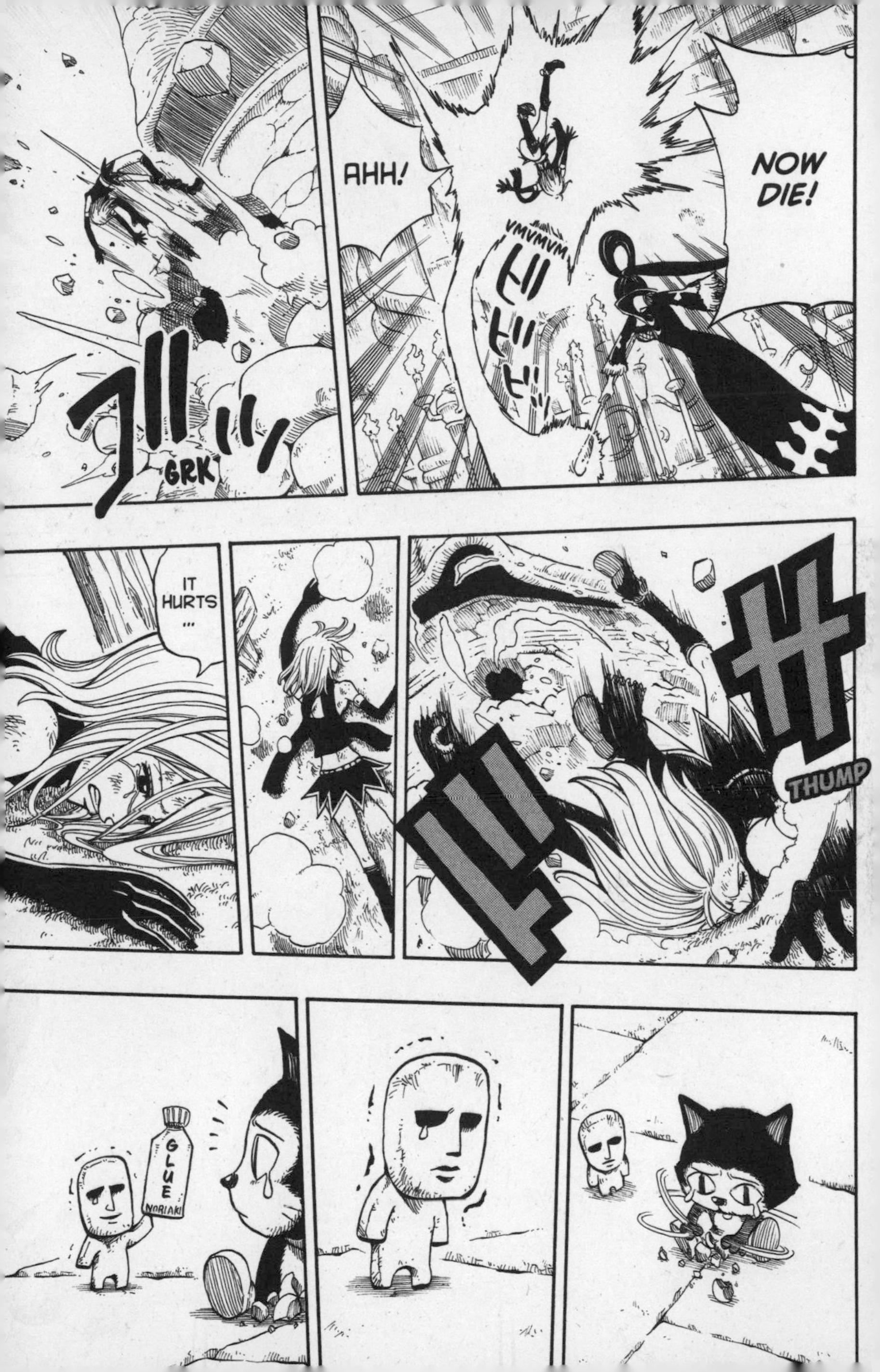
NOW DIE!
AHH!
VMVMVM
GRK
THUMP
IT HURTS ...
GLUE
NORIAKI

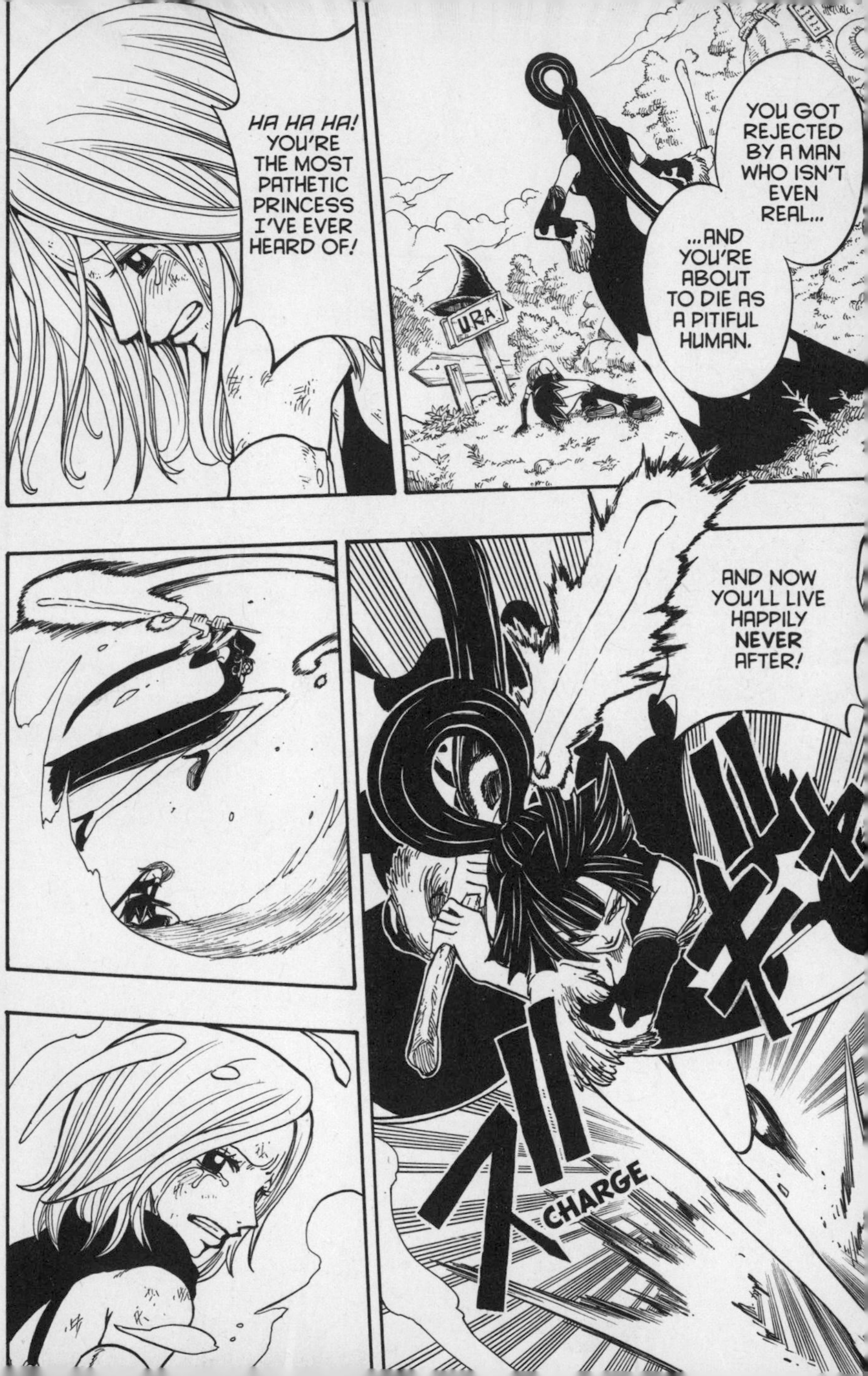
YOU GOT REJECTED BY A MAN WHO ISN'T EVEN REAL...
...AND YOU'RE ABOUT TO DIE AS A PITIFUL HUMAN.
URA
HA HA HA! YOU'RE THE MOST PATHETIC PRINCESS I'VE EVER HEARD OF!
AND NOW YOU'LL LIVE HAPPILY NEVER AFTER!
CHARGE

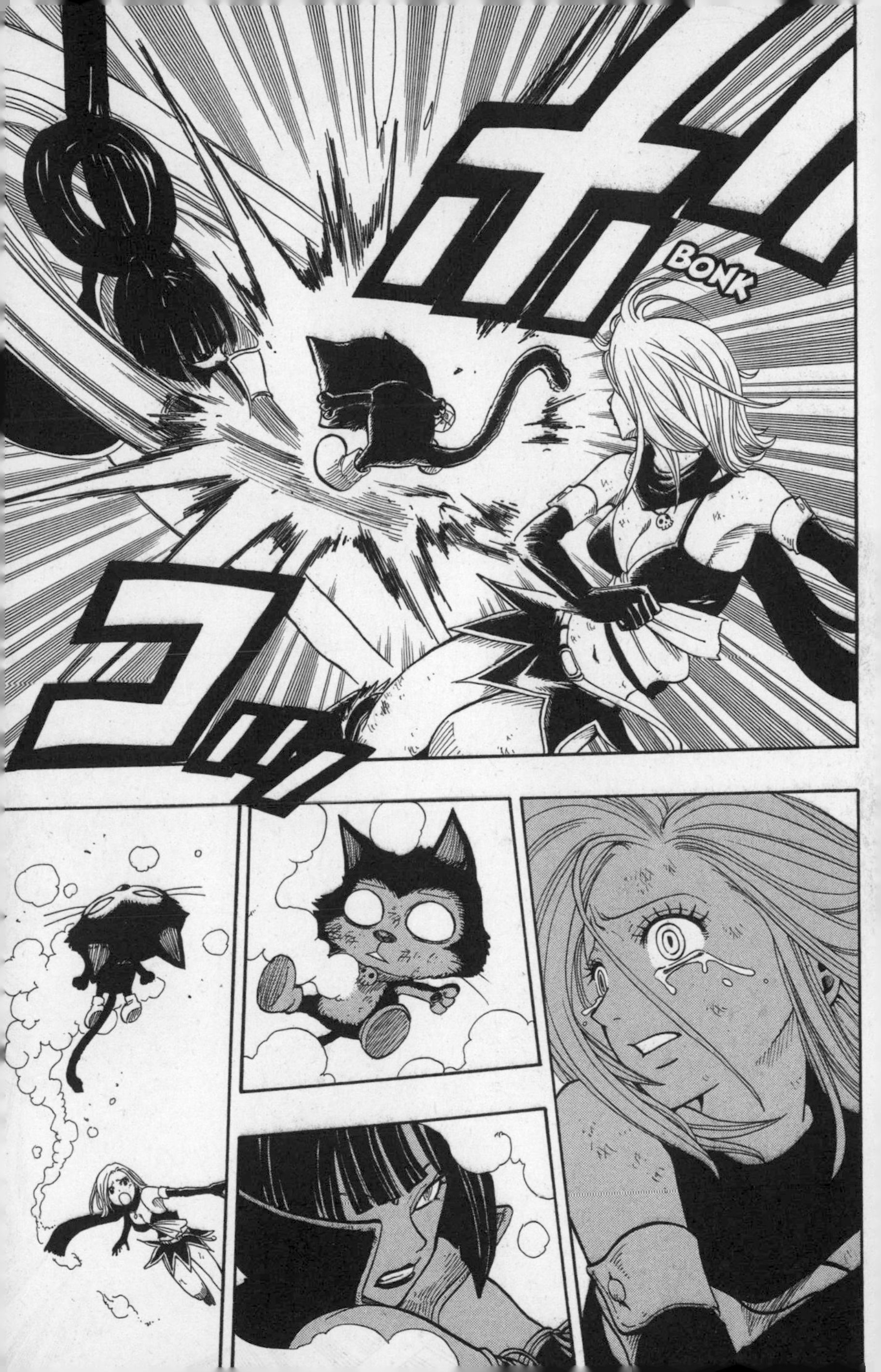
BONK

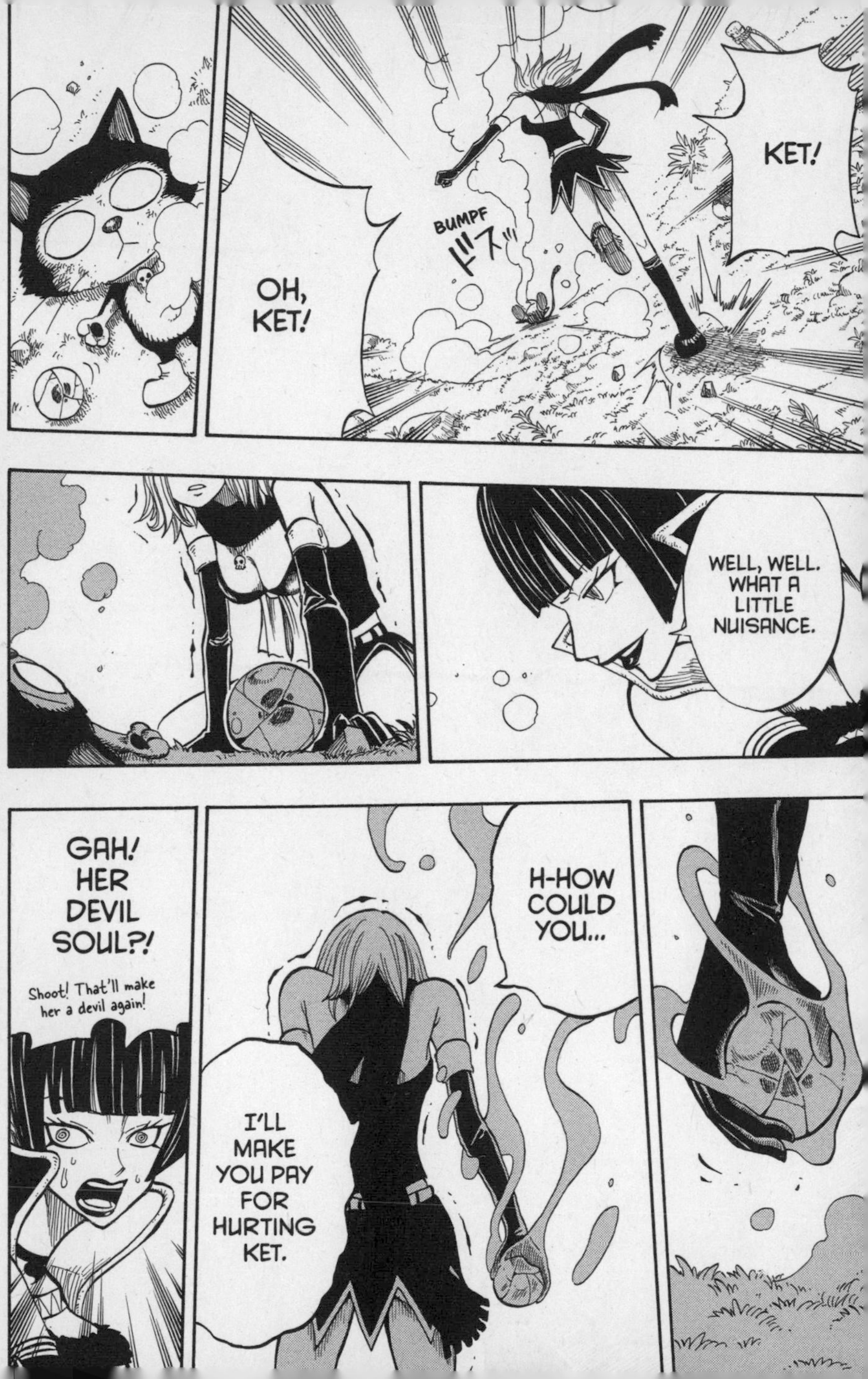
KET!
BUMPF
ドズ
OH, KET!
WELL, WELL. WHAT A LITTLE NUISANCE.
H-HOW COULD YOU...
I'LL MAKE YOU PAY FOR HURTING KET.
GAH! HER DEVIL SOUL?!
Shoot! That'll make her a devil again!

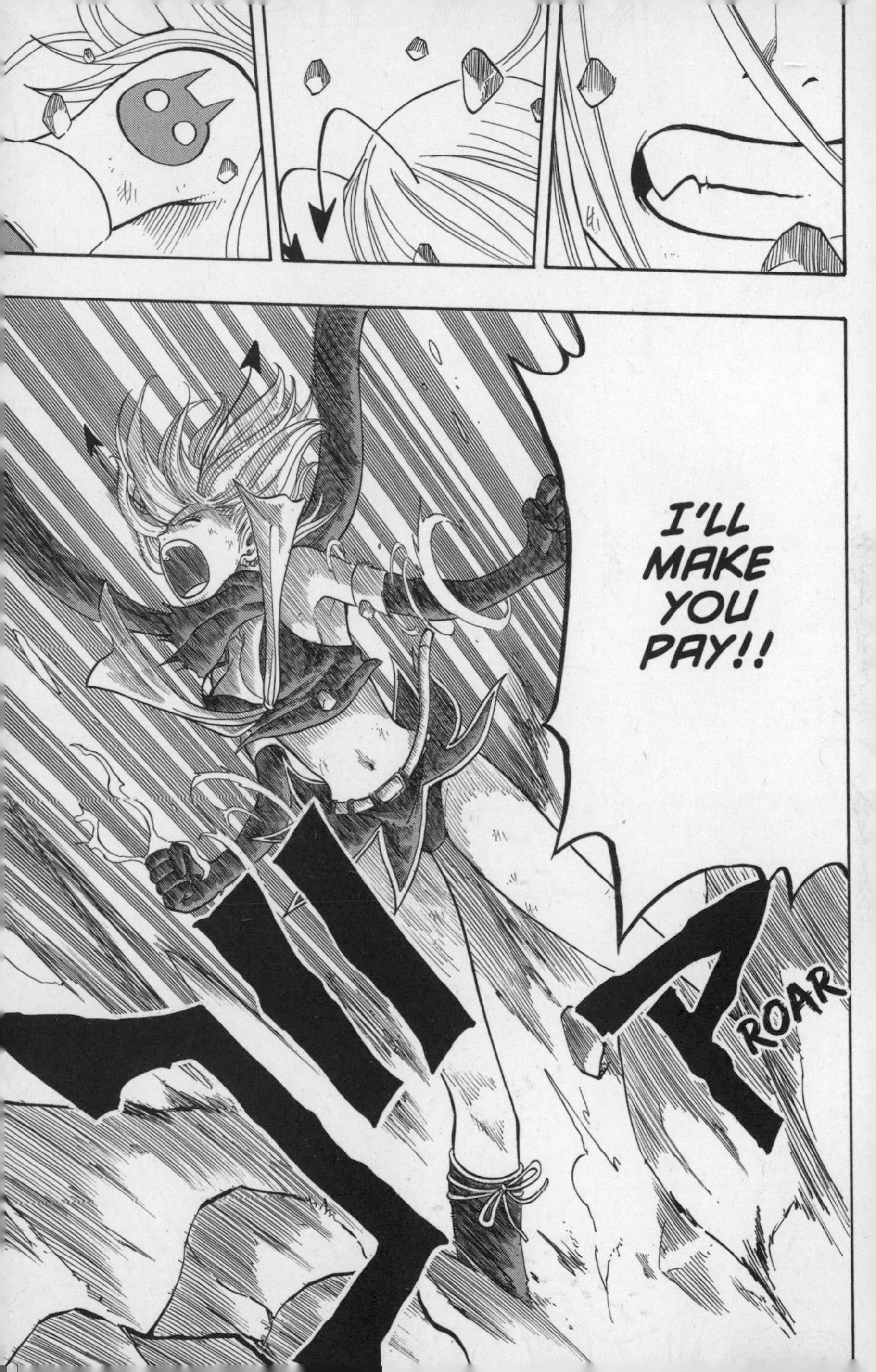
I'LL MAKE YOU PAY!!
ROAR

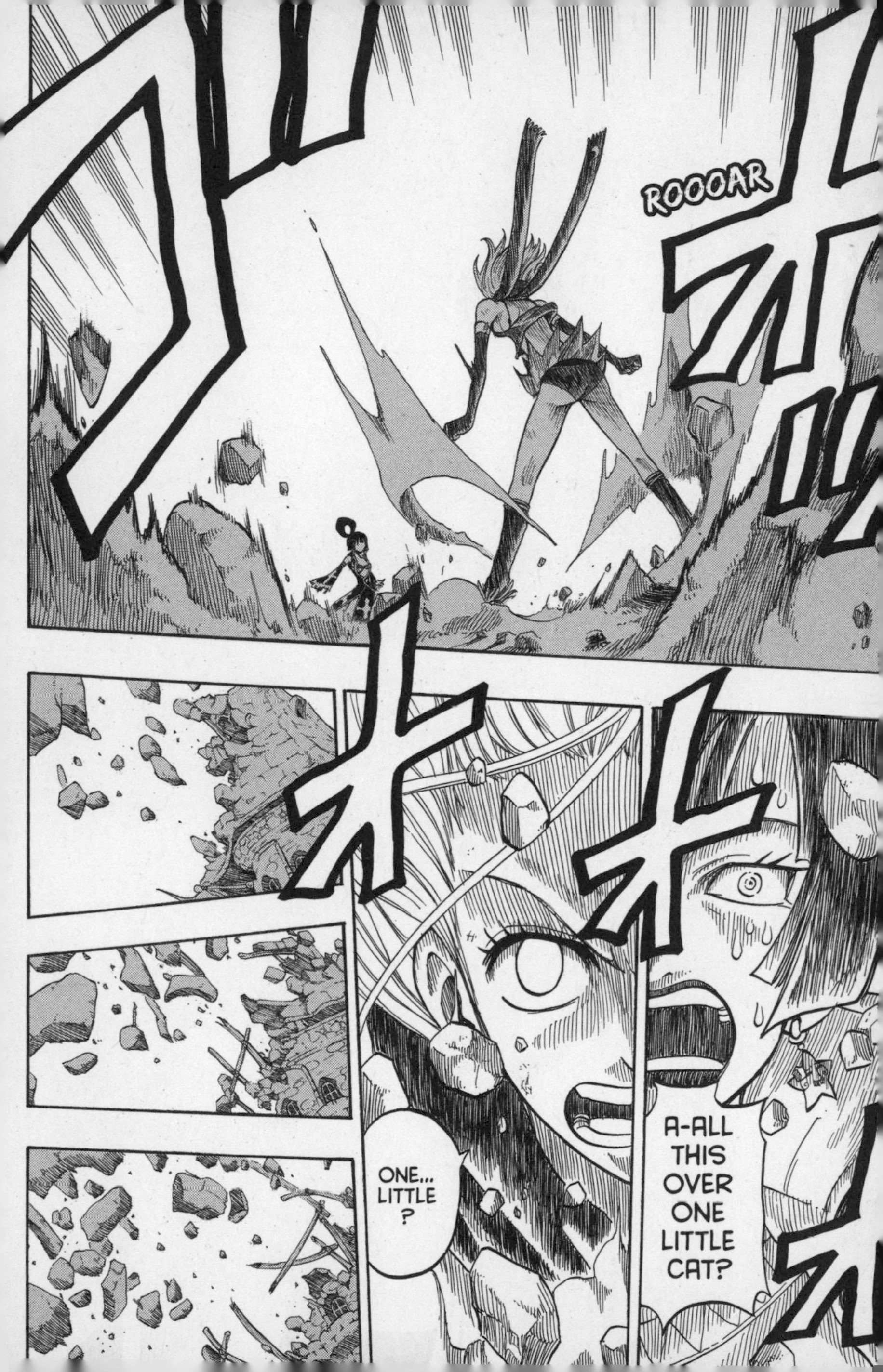
ROOOAR
A-ALL THIS OVER ONE LITTLE CAT?
ONE... LITTLE ?

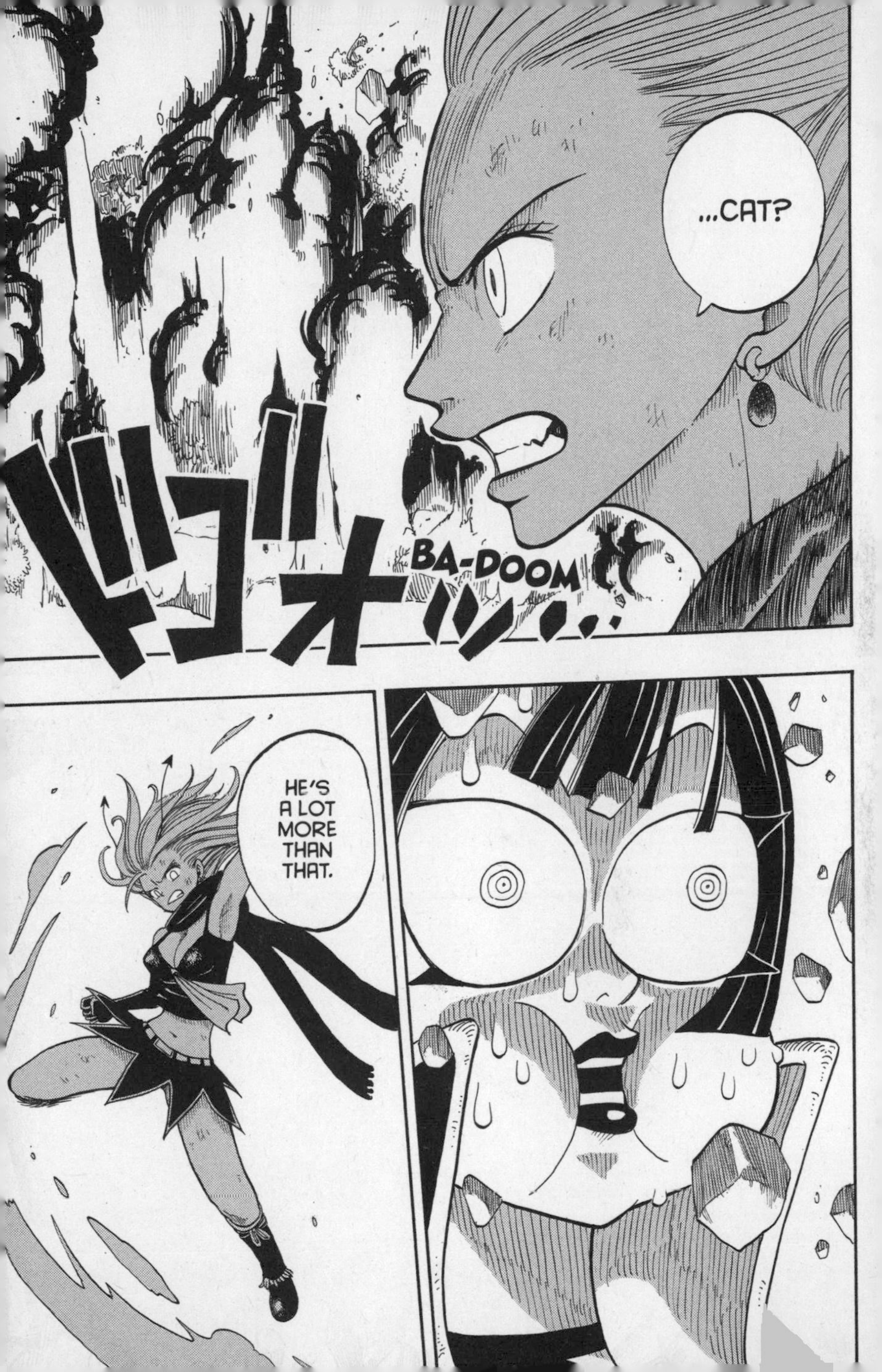
...CAT?
ドゴオッ BA-DOOM
HE'S A LOT MORE THAN THAT.

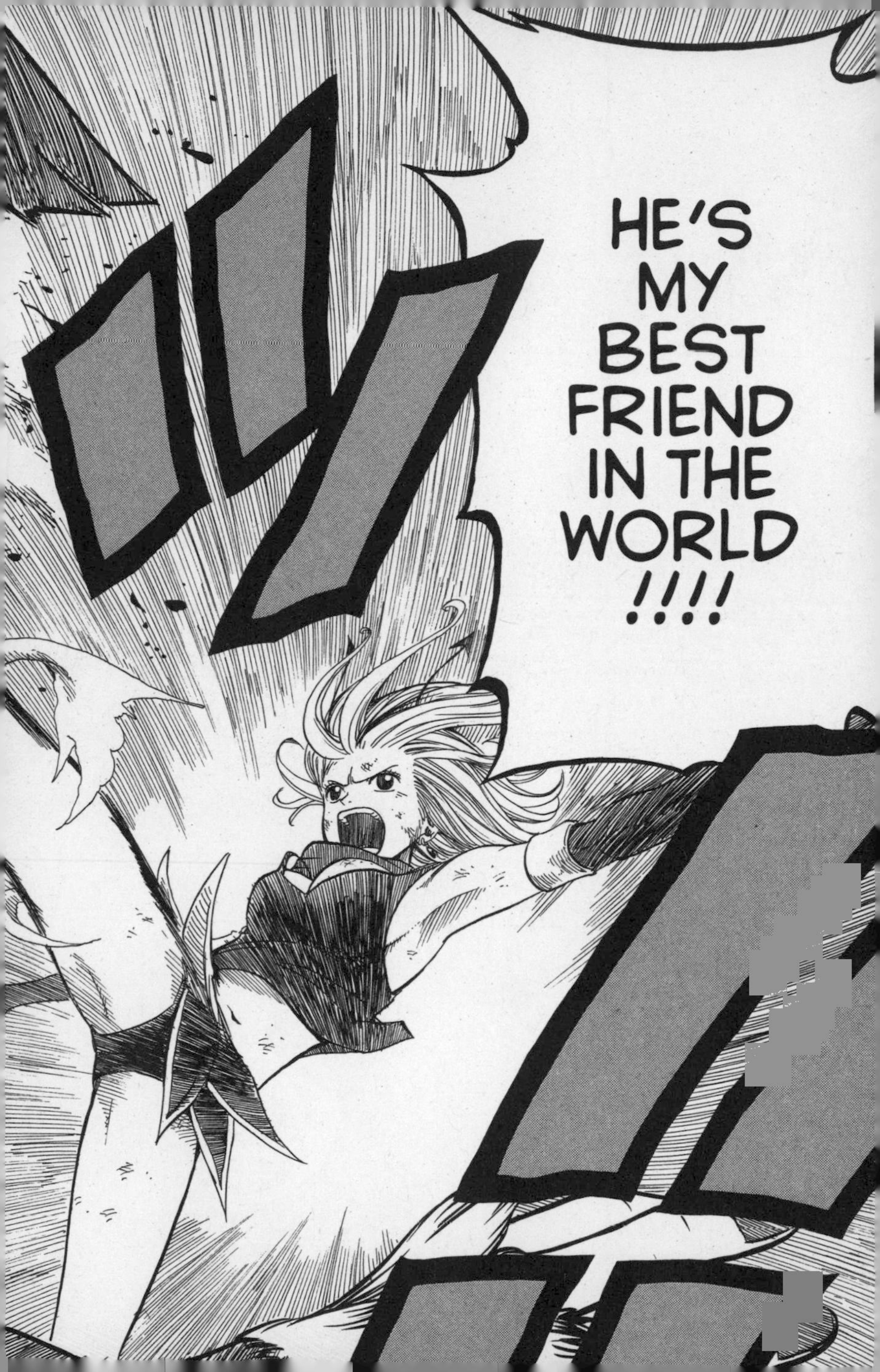
HE'S MY BEST FRIEND IN THE WORLD !!!!

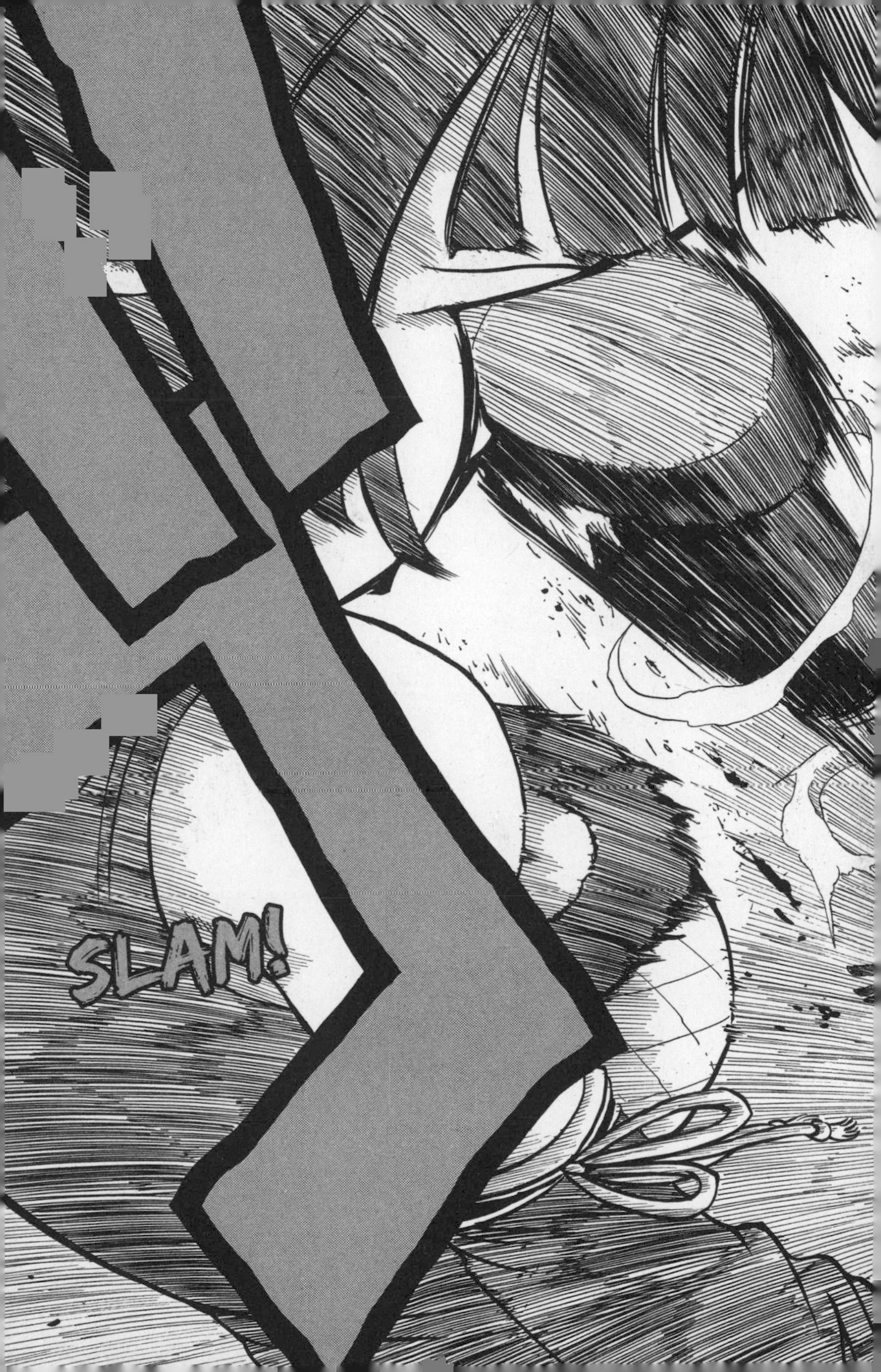
SLAM!

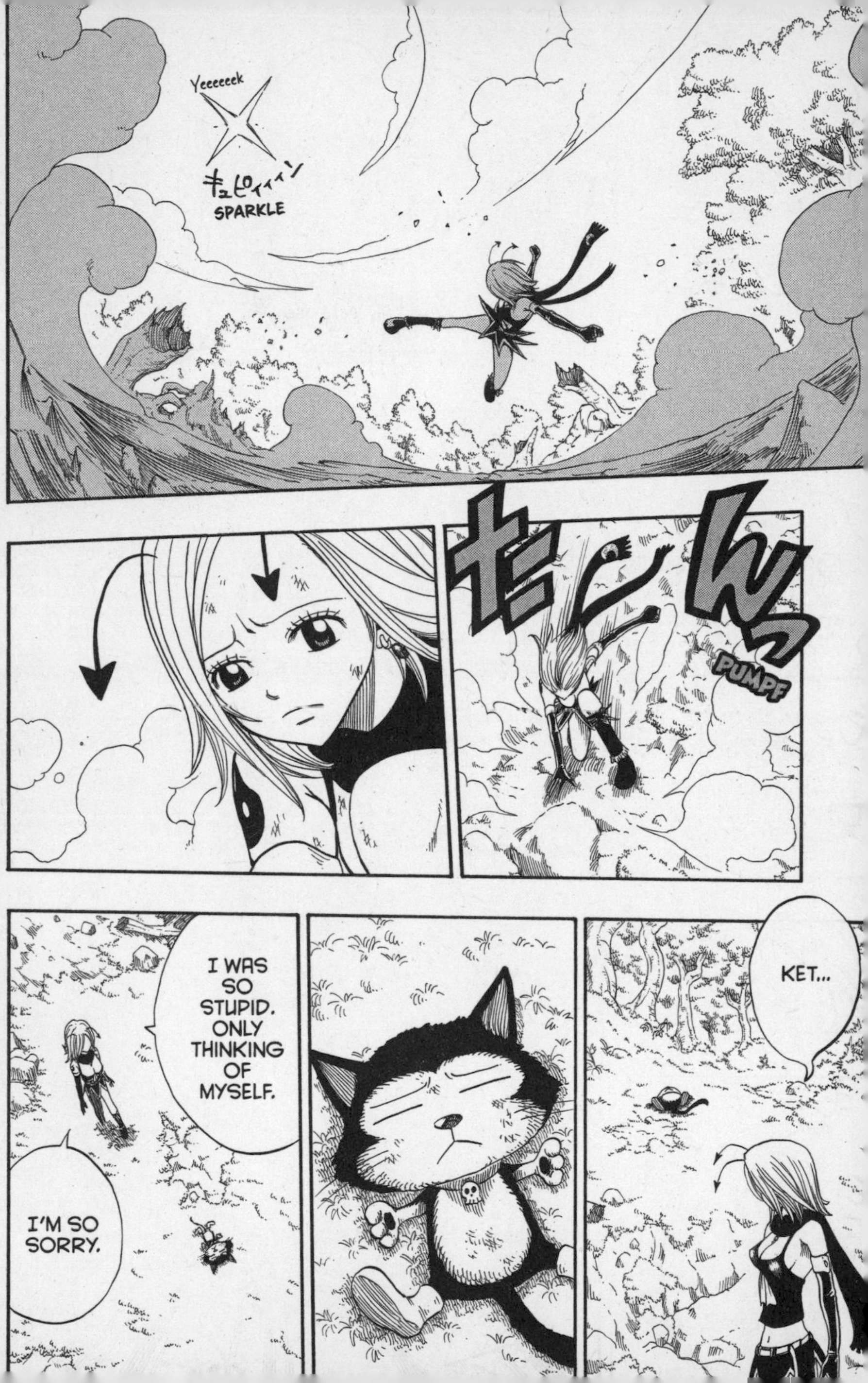
Yeeeeeek
キュピィイイン
SPARKLE
PUMPF
KET...
I WAS SO STUPID. ONLY THINKING OF MYSELF.
I'M SO SORRY.

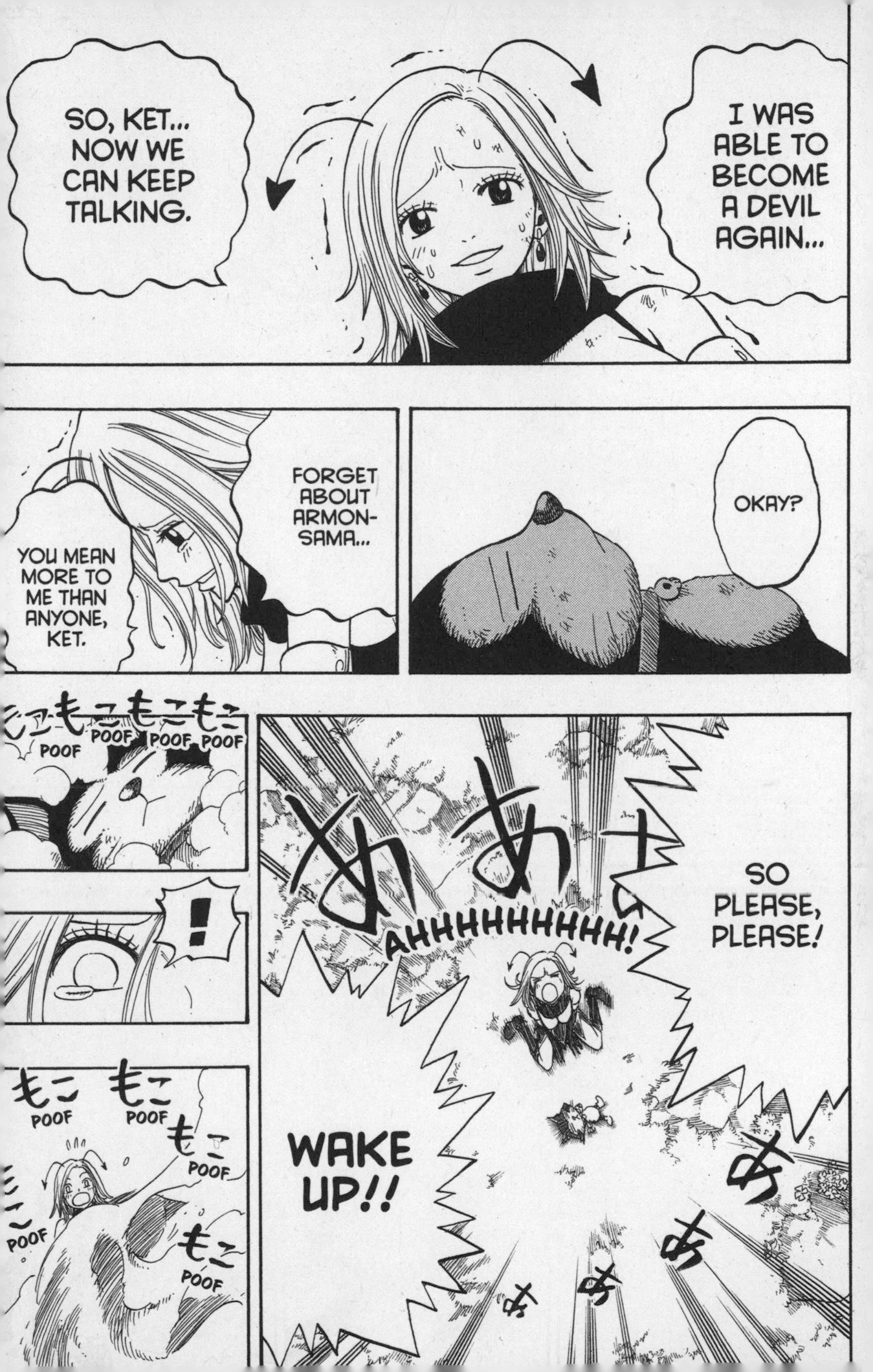
I WAS ABLE TO BECOME A DEVIL AGAIN...
SO, KET... NOW WE CAN KEEP TALKING.
OKAY?
FORGET ABOUT ARMON-SAMA...
YOU MEAN MORE TO ME THAN ANYONE, KET.
SO PLEASE, PLEASE!
AHHHHHHHHHH!
WAKE UP!!
POOF POOF POOF POOF
!
POOF POOF POOF POOF POOF

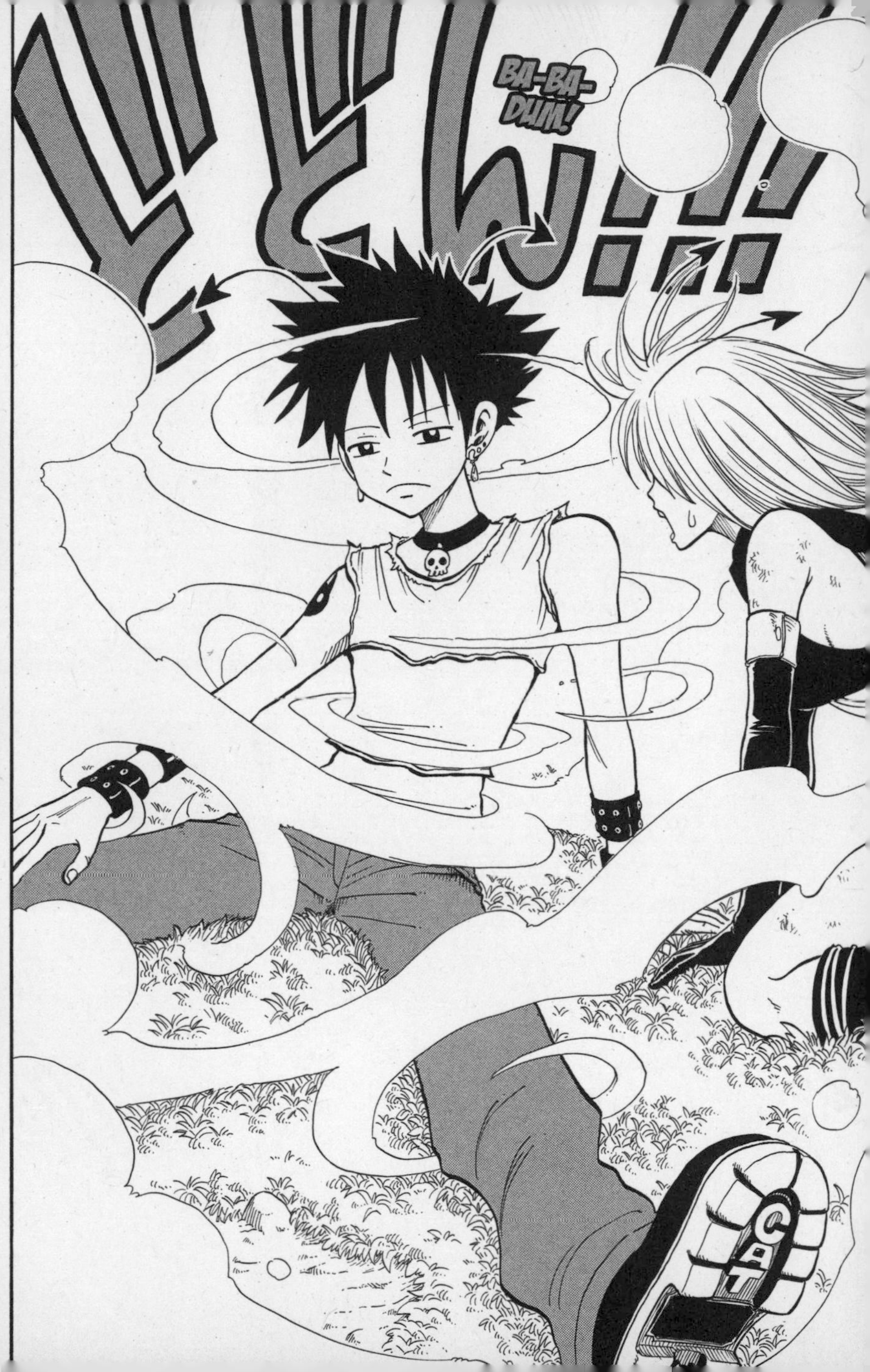
BA-BA-DUM!
CAT

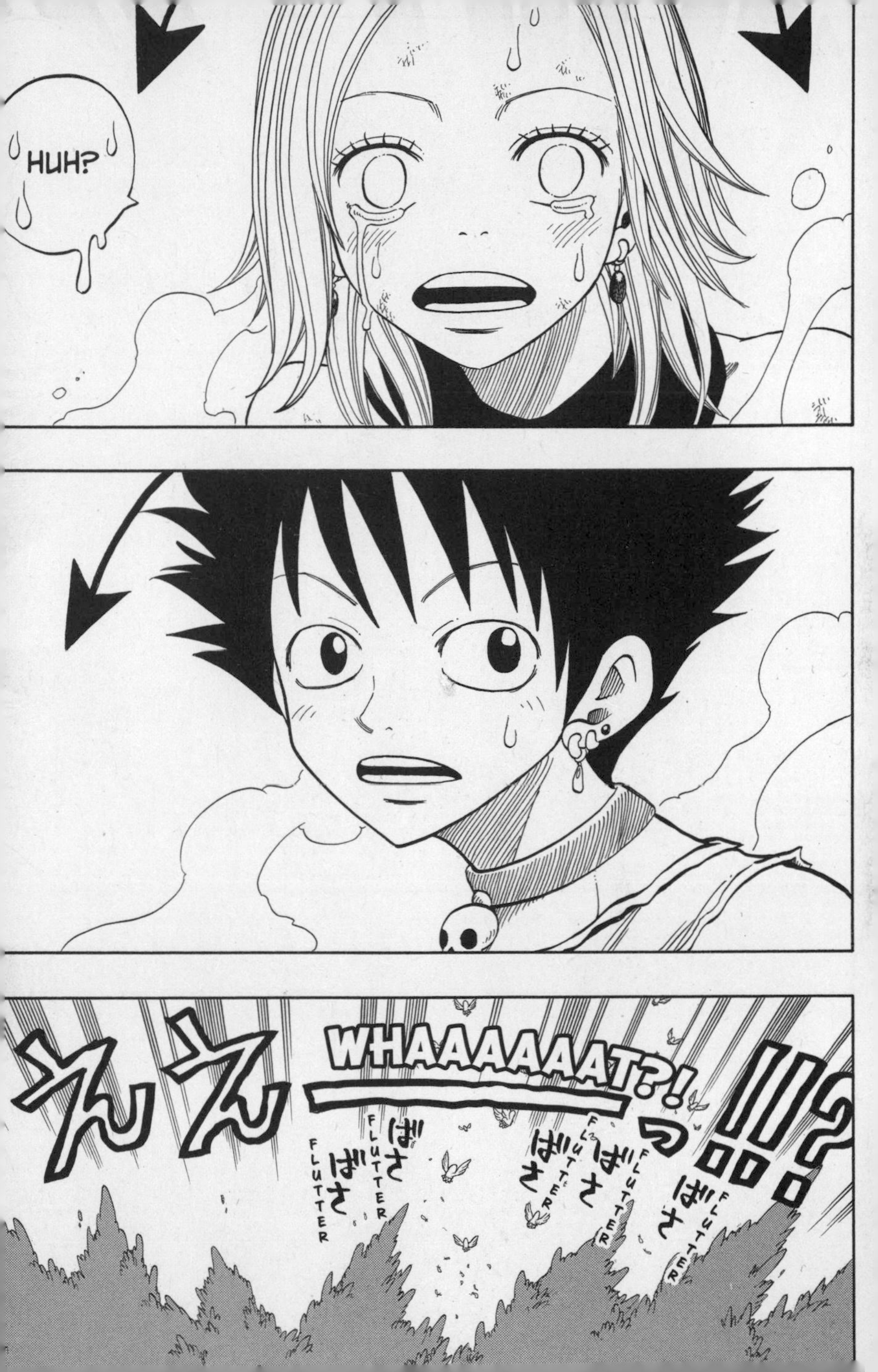
HUH?
WHAAAAAAAT?!
ばさ ばさ
FLUTTER
ばさ ばさ
FLUTTER
ばさ ばさ
FLUTTER
FLUTTER

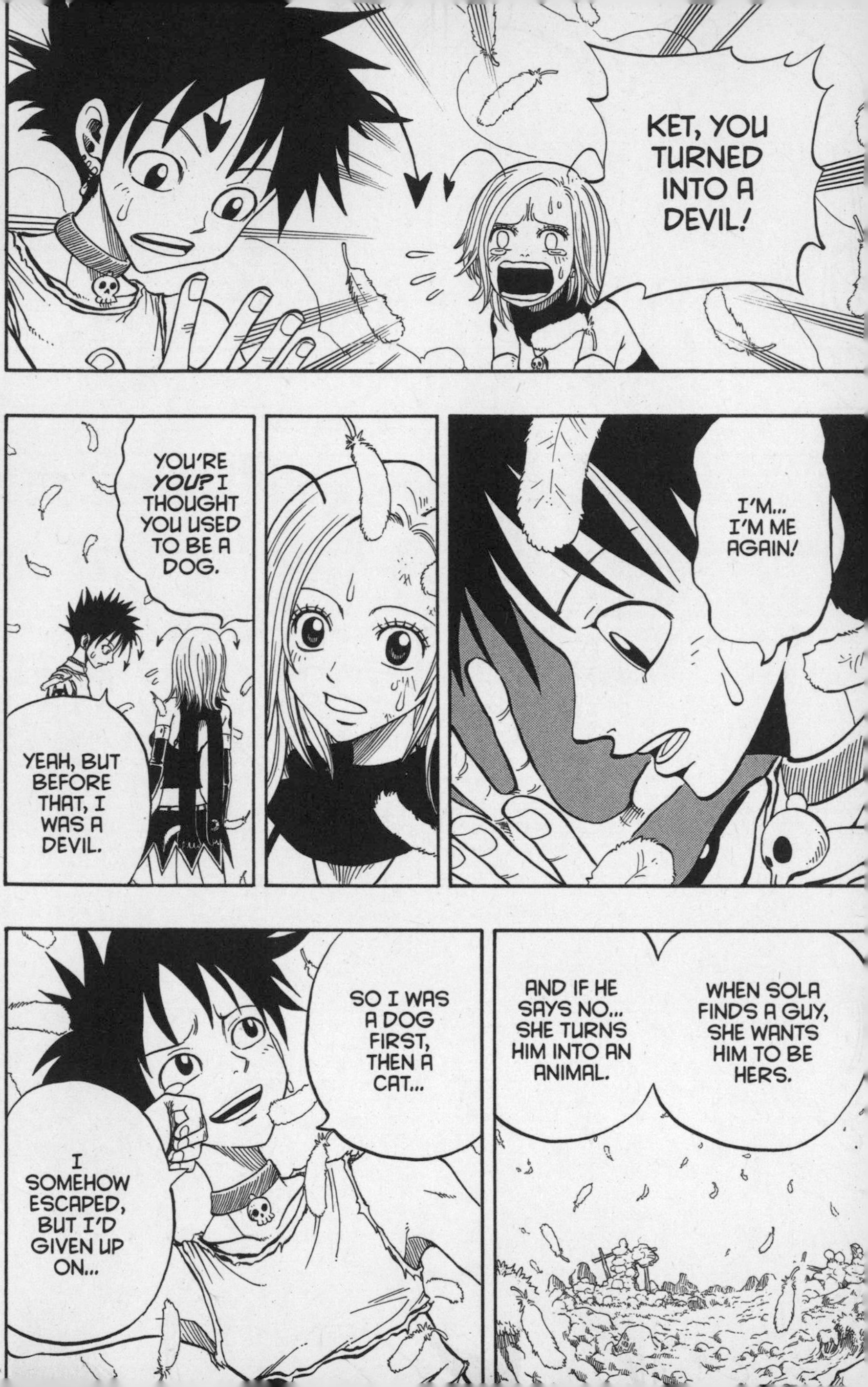
KET, YOU TURNED INTO A DEVIL!
I'M... I'M ME AGAIN!
YOU'RE *YOU?* I THOUGHT YOU USED TO BE A DOG.
YEAH, BUT BEFORE THAT, I WAS A DEVIL.
WHEN SOLA FINDS A GUY, SHE WANTS HIM TO BE HERS.
AND IF HE SAYS NO... SHE TURNS HIM INTO AN ANIMAL.
SO I WAS A DOG FIRST, THEN A CAT...
I SOMEHOW ESCAPED, BUT I'D GIVEN UP ON...

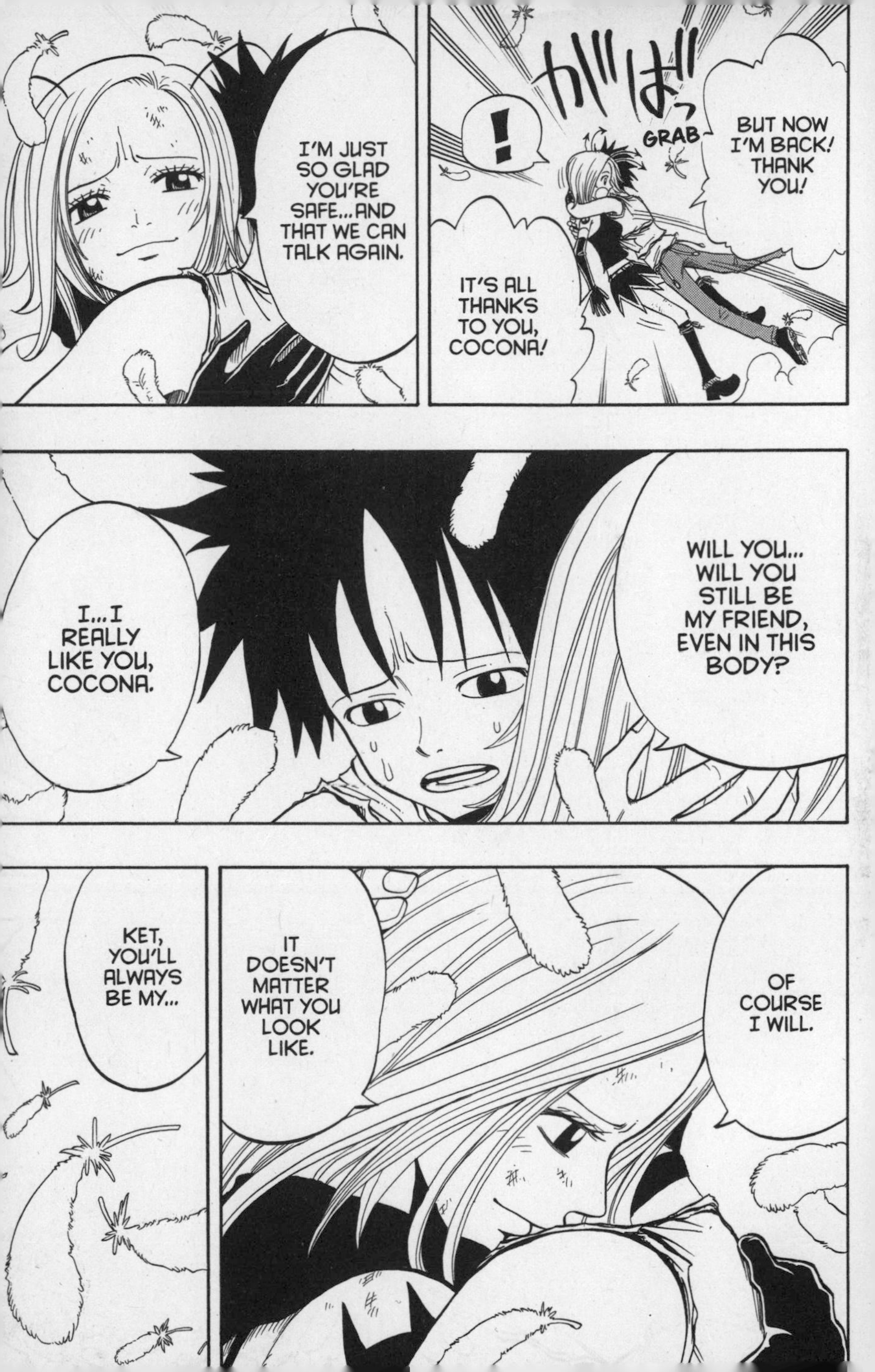
!
がばっ
GRAB
BUT NOW I'M BACK! THANK YOU!
IT'S ALL THANKS TO YOU, COCONA!
I'M JUST SO GLAD YOU'RE SAFE...AND THAT WE CAN TALK AGAIN.
WILL YOU... WILL YOU STILL BE MY FRIEND, EVEN IN THIS BODY?
I...I REALLY LIKE YOU, COCONA.
OF COURSE I WILL.
IT DOESN'T MATTER WHAT YOU LOOK LIKE.
KET, YOU'LL ALWAYS BE MY...

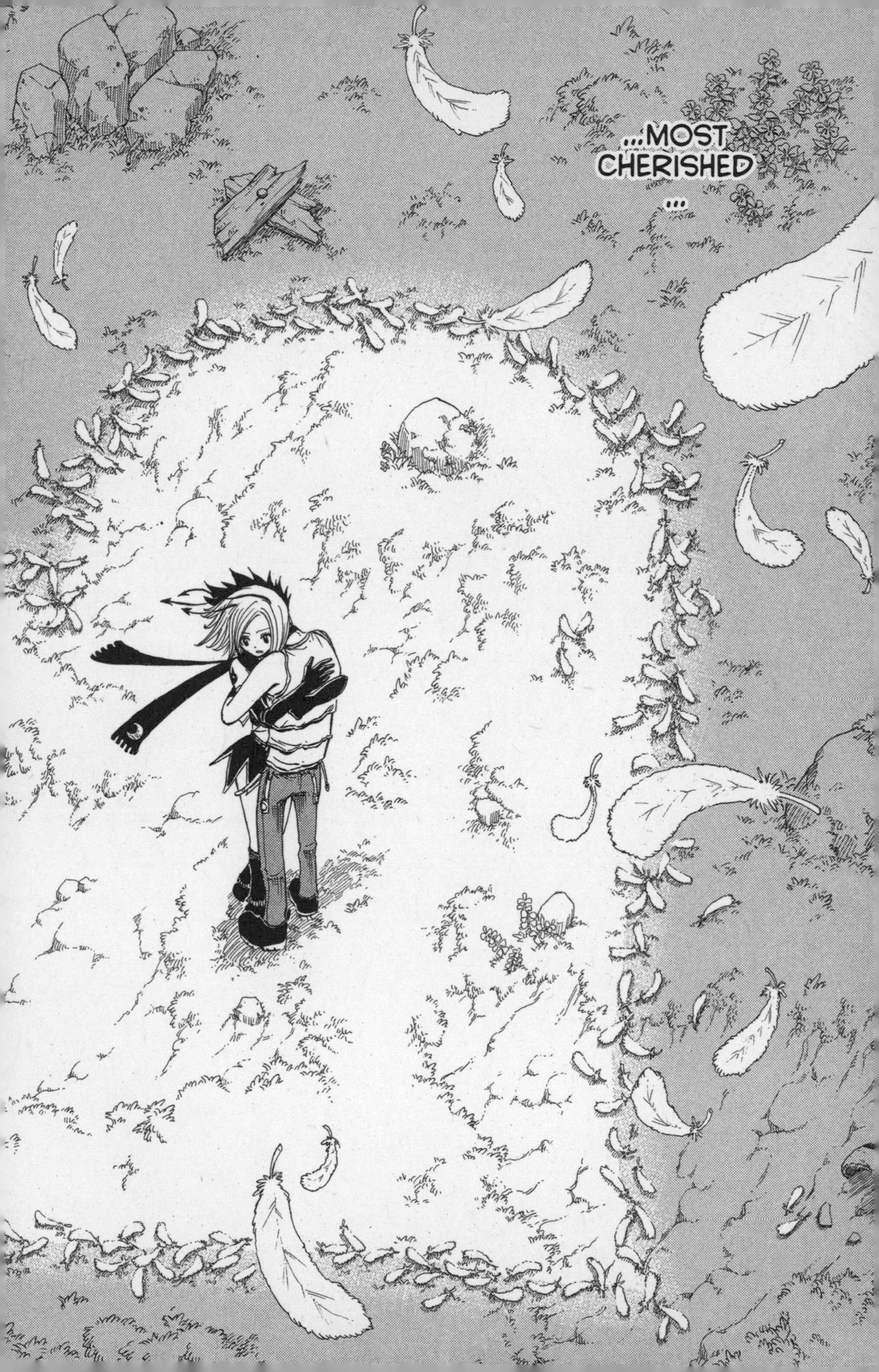
...MOST CHERISHED ...

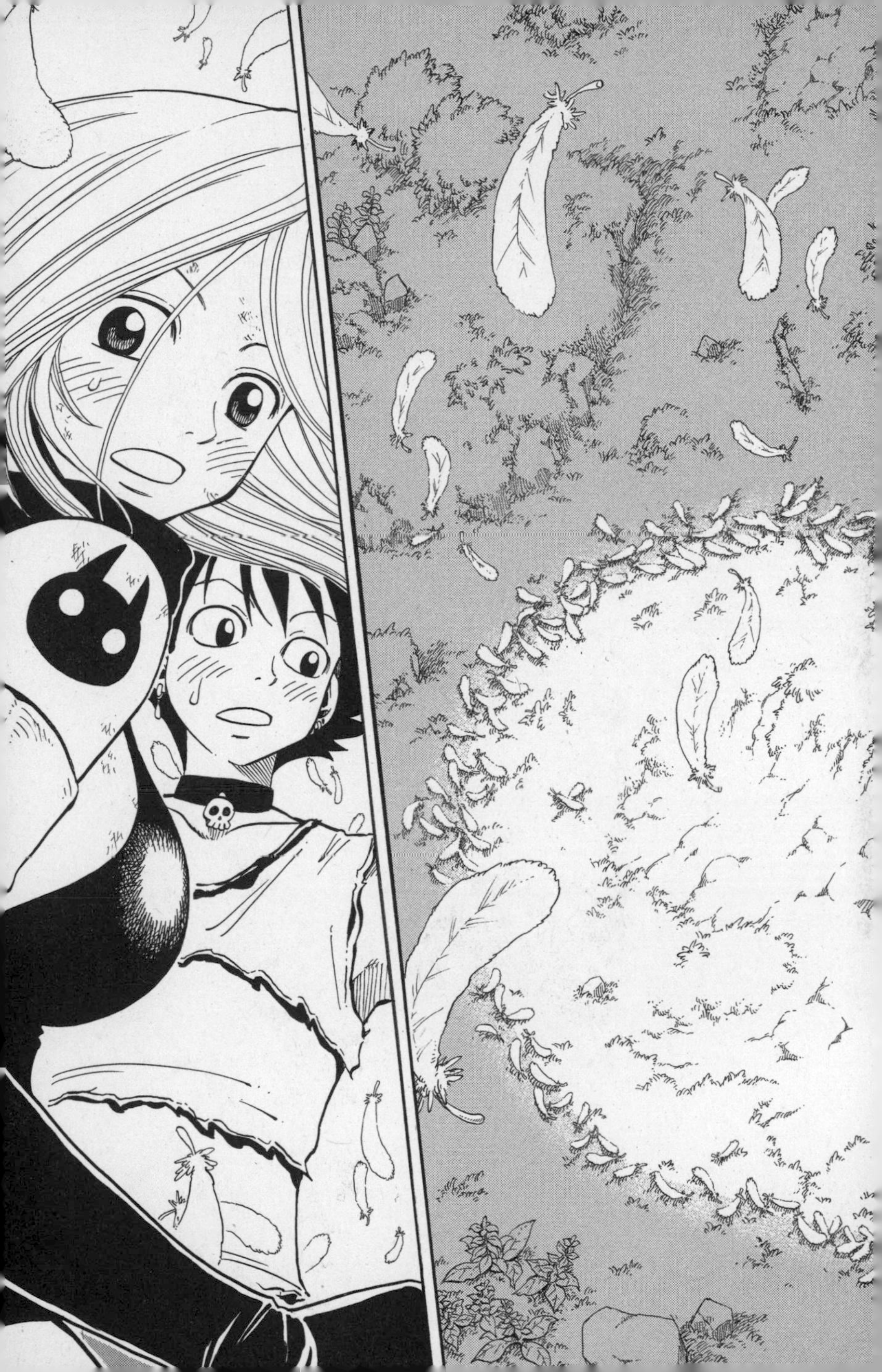

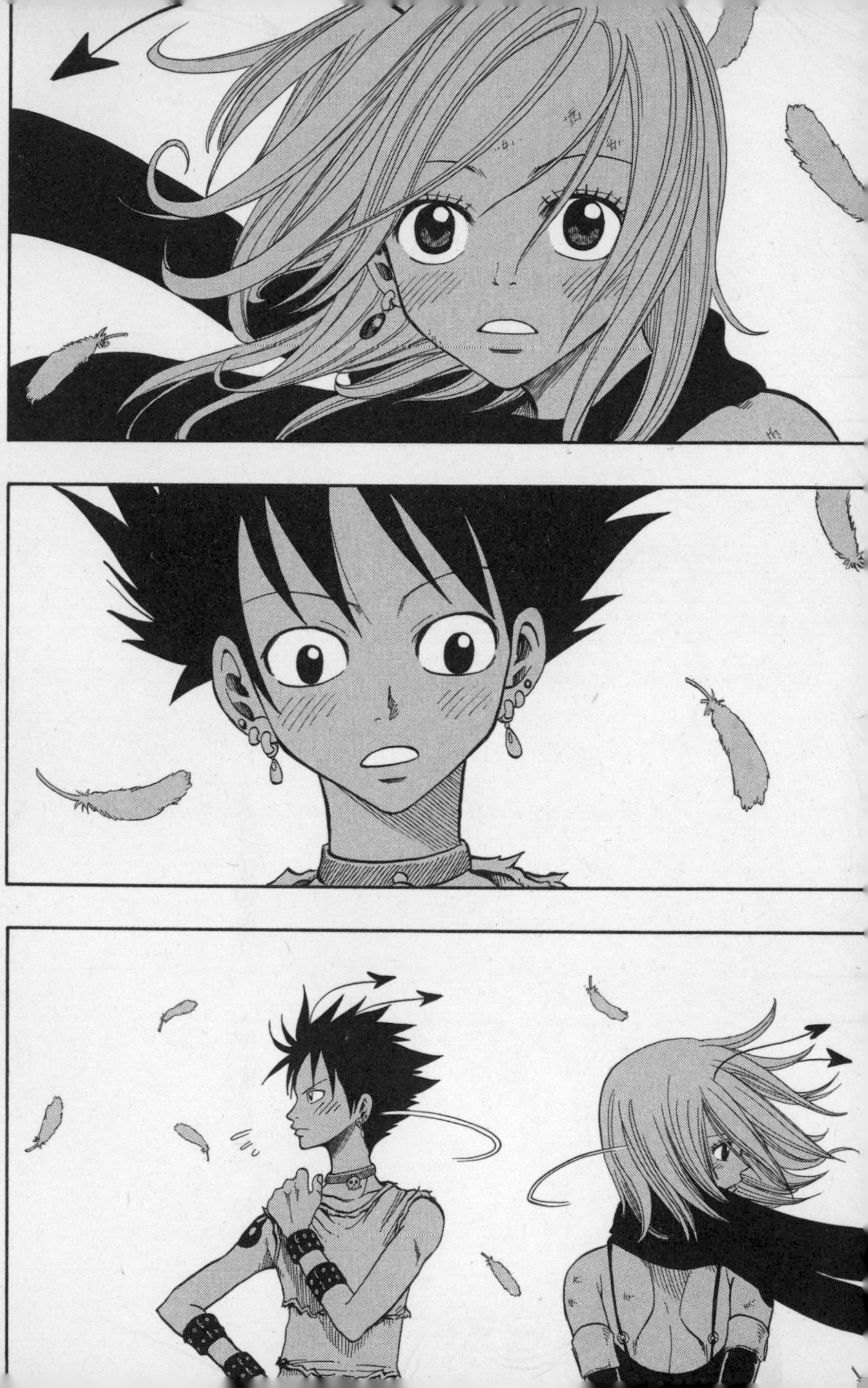

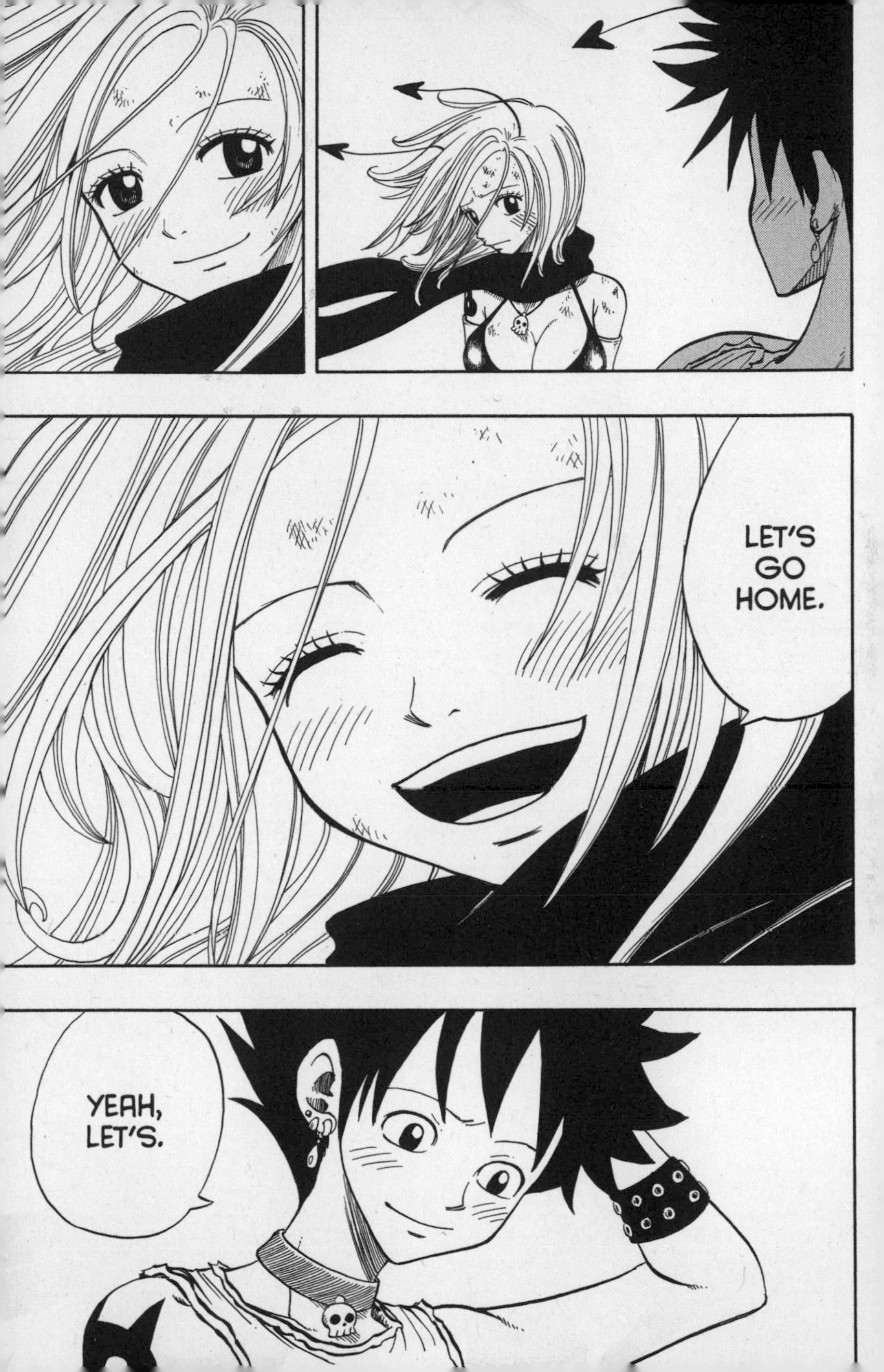
LET'S GO HOME.
YEAH, LET'S.

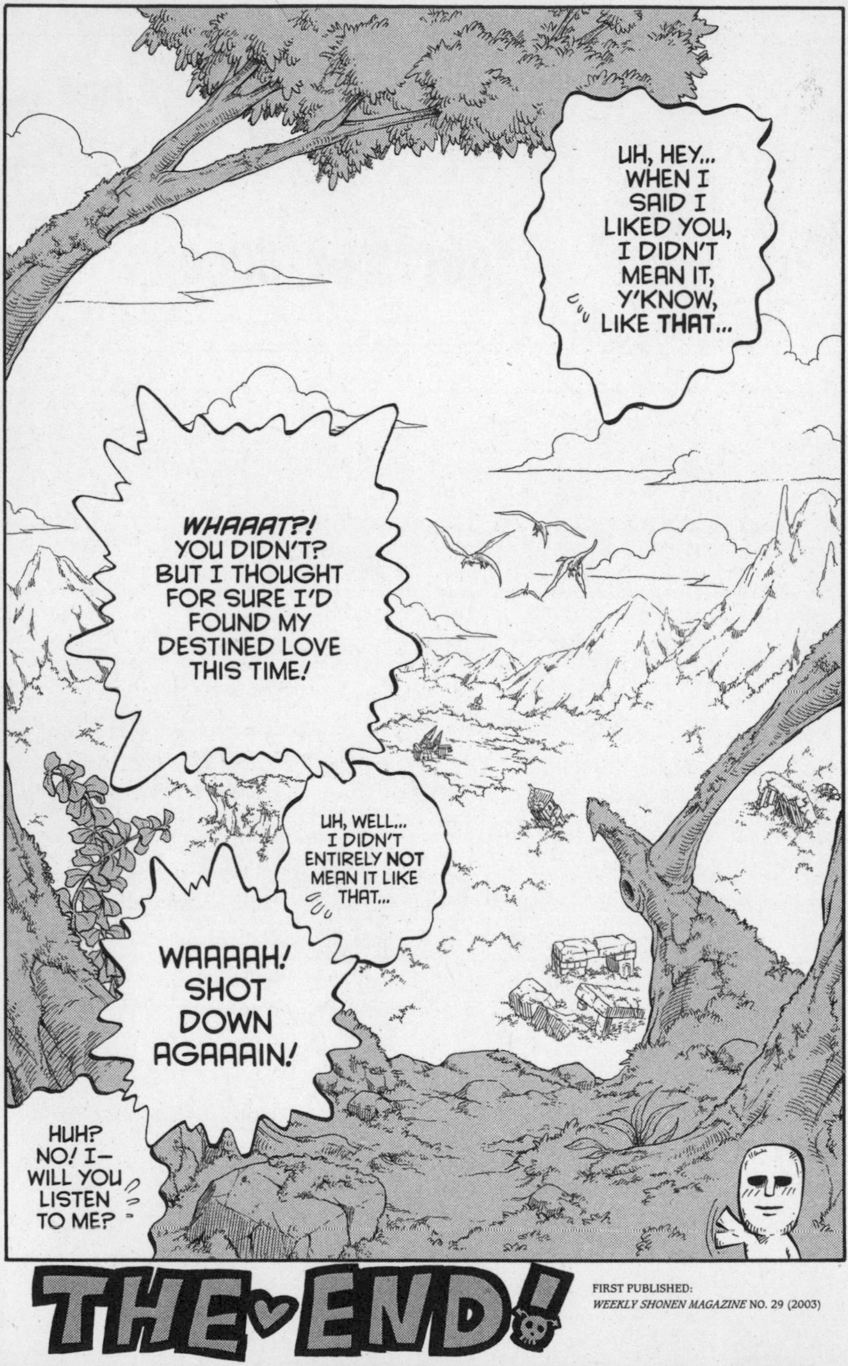
UH, HEY... WHEN I SAID I LIKED YOU, I DIDN'T MEAN IT, Y'KNOW, LIKE THAT...
WHAAAT?! YOU DIDN'T? BUT I THOUGHT FOR SURE I'D FOUND MY DESTINED LOVE THIS TIME!
UH, WELL... I DIDN'T ENTIRELY NOT MEAN IT LIKE THAT...
WAAAAH! SHOT DOWN AGAAAIN!
HUH? NO! I— WILL YOU LISTEN TO ME?

THE♥END!

FIRST PUBLISHED:
WEEKLY SHONEN MAGAZINE NO. 29 (2003)

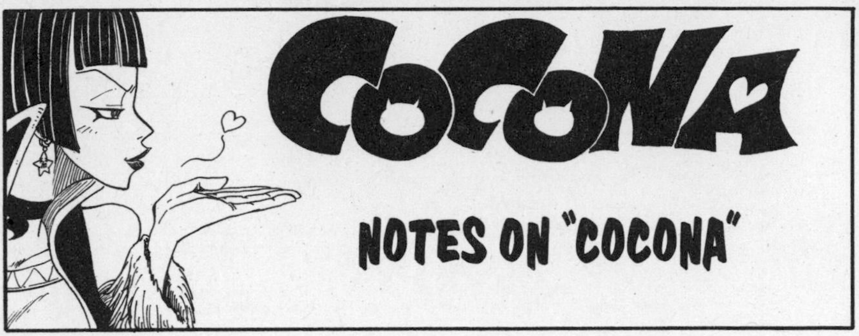

COCONA

NOTES ON "COCONA"

I set out to write a romantic comedy with this one, but what with all the romance and the comedy... Well, looking back on it, it's basically the story of this weird girl going on a rampage (heh). A little bit like the situation I described in "On 'Fairy tale,'" my drafts for "Cocona" were rejected two separate times before I finally finished it (sobs).

Anyway, what I really wanted to draw was **a fighting princess** and her **cat**. The initial concept for "Cocona" was **a robot manga (LOL)**! This was another thing that I thought might become an ongoing series. You know, a giant-robot fantasy about a beautiful princess and her fighting robot. **REJECTED!!** So next I thought, how about a beautiful princess and her gallant knight who travel through time? **REJECTED!!** For some reason, the last idea I had was about a devil princess who falls in love. And the cat? The truth is, I like drawing cats more than dogs, but somehow I've done two manga in a row featuring a dog...and I just wanted to draw me some cats. Meow!

Incidentally, the names come from the following: Cocona → Coconut
Armon → Almond
Sola → Soramame (fava beans in Japanese)

....**Wait, why beans?!**

Cocona Reject Files 1

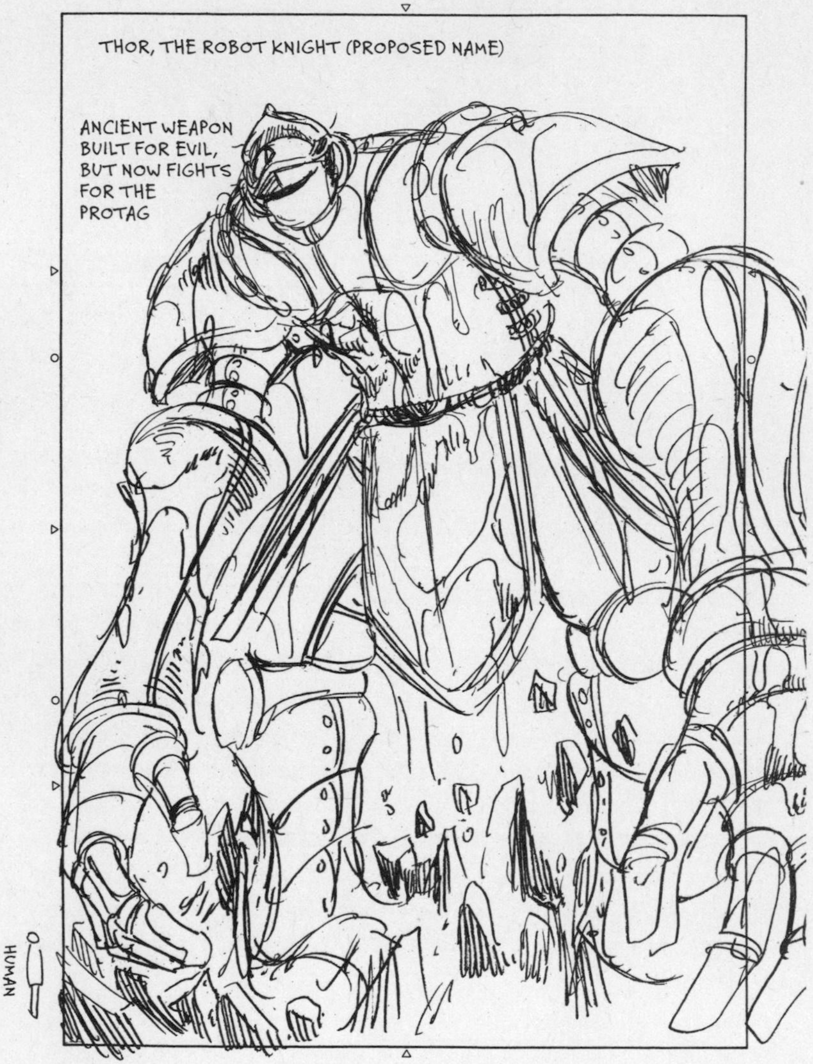
THOR, THE ROBOT KNIGHT (PROPOSED NAME)
ANCIENT WEAPON BUILT FOR EVIL, BUT NOW FIGHTS FOR THE PROTAG
HUMAN

(   )

A ROBOT STORY. THE MAIN CHARACTER RIDES INSIDE THOR, CONTROLLING HIM WITH MAGIC. IN CASE YOU DON'T KNOW, THOR IS A NORSE THUNDER GIANT. SOMETIMES HE'S PICTURED AS THIS CRAZY OLD MAN, BUT HE'S MY FAVORITE. *SIGH...* I'D LOVE TO DO A ROBOT STORY... SOMETIME...

Cocona Reject Files 2

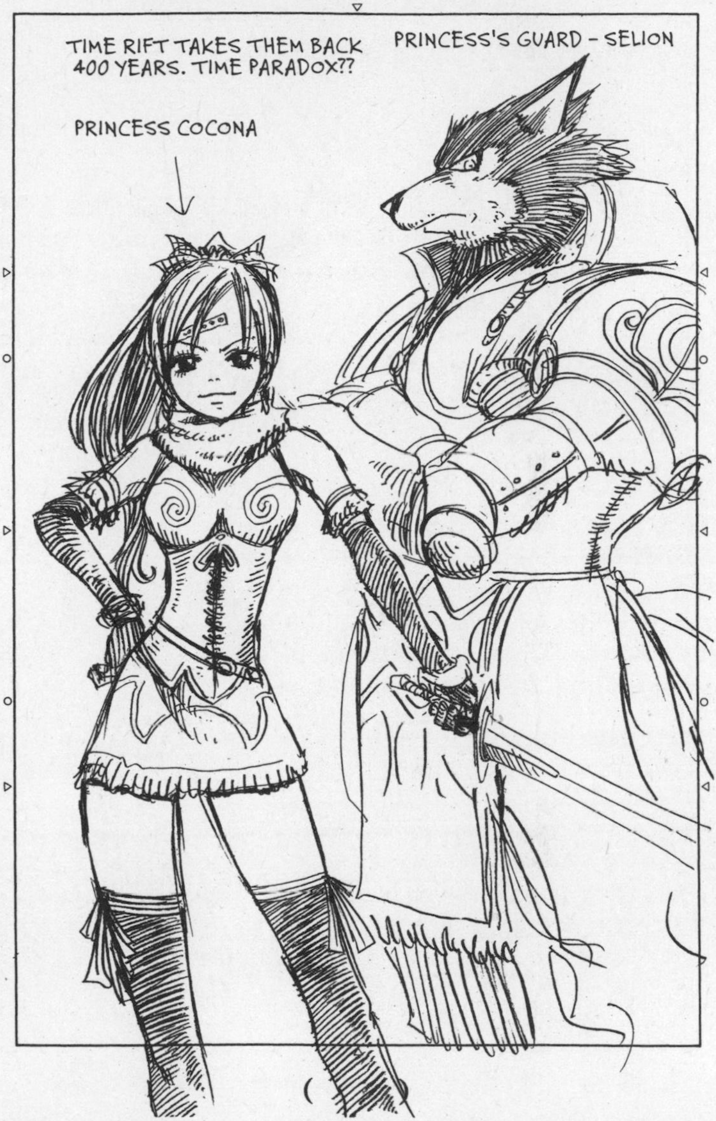
TIME RIFT TAKES THEM BACK 400 YEARS. TIME PARADOX??
PRINCESS'S GUARD - SELION
PRINCESS COCONA

THIS IS ONE IDEA THAT I ACTUALLY CONCEIVED AS A SHORT STORY, BUT FOR REASONS I DON'T FULLY UNDERSTAND, IT WAS REJECTED. PERSONALLY, I THOUGHT THE DRAFT WAS PRETTY INTERESTING, BUT MY EDITOR DIDN'T AGREE. REREADING IT NOW, I REALIZE HE WAS RIGHT (LOL).

BEFORE YOU READ PLUE'S ADVENTURE II...

Meet the characters

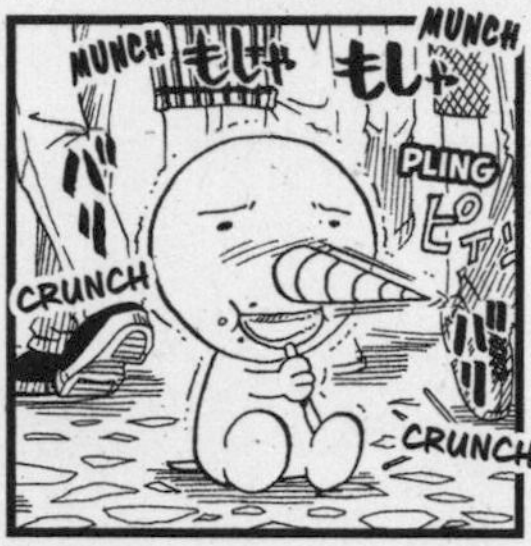
MUNCH
もしゃ
MUNCH
もしゃ
PLING
CRUNCH
CRUNCH

As you can see, our hero Plue loves candy! He may look strange at first sight, but he's actually a master of the sacred stone Rave. What a good dog! He travels the world with Rave Master Haru to bring peace to every corner of the land.

This is Plue's friend Griffon Kato, or Griff for short. Apparently he used to be evil. Plue rescued him during the time of resistance, so Griff calls him "Master Plue." Now he helps Plue on his quest as his cartographer.

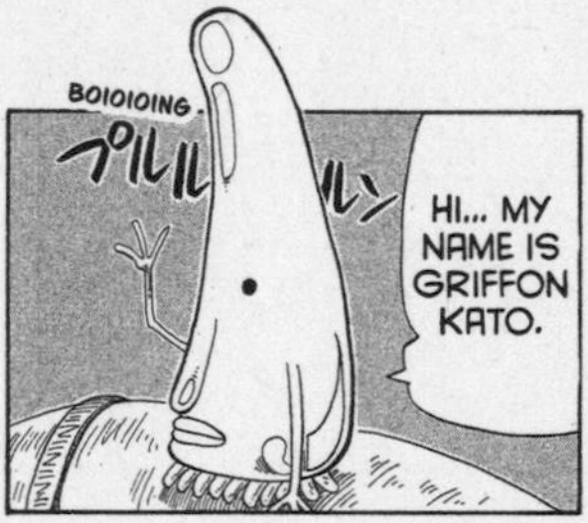
BOIOIOING
プルル
ルン
HI... MY NAME IS GRIFFON KATO.

Plue & Griff's Friends

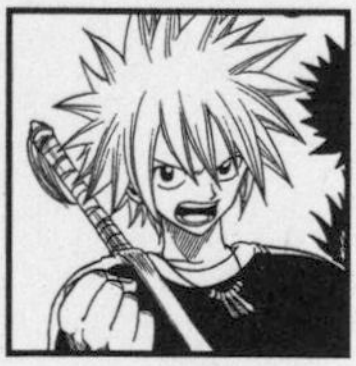

Rave Master
HARU
Kind young man

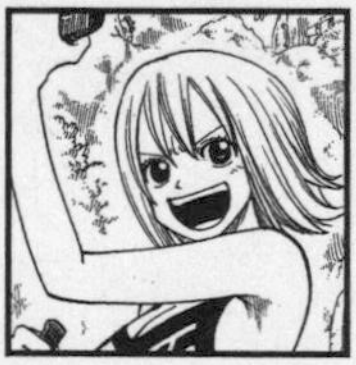

Girl with Amnesia
ELIE
Cheerful and cute

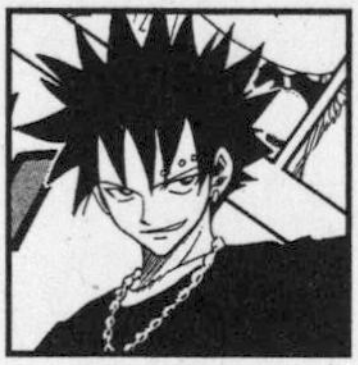

Silver Claimer
MUSICA
Leader of the Silver Rhythm thieves

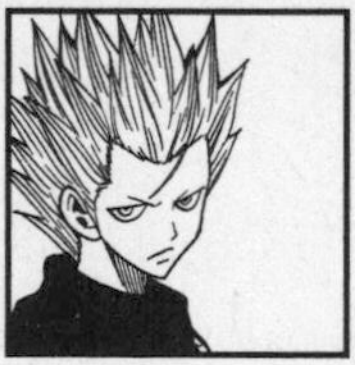

Dragon Person
LET
Demi-human from the Mystic Realm

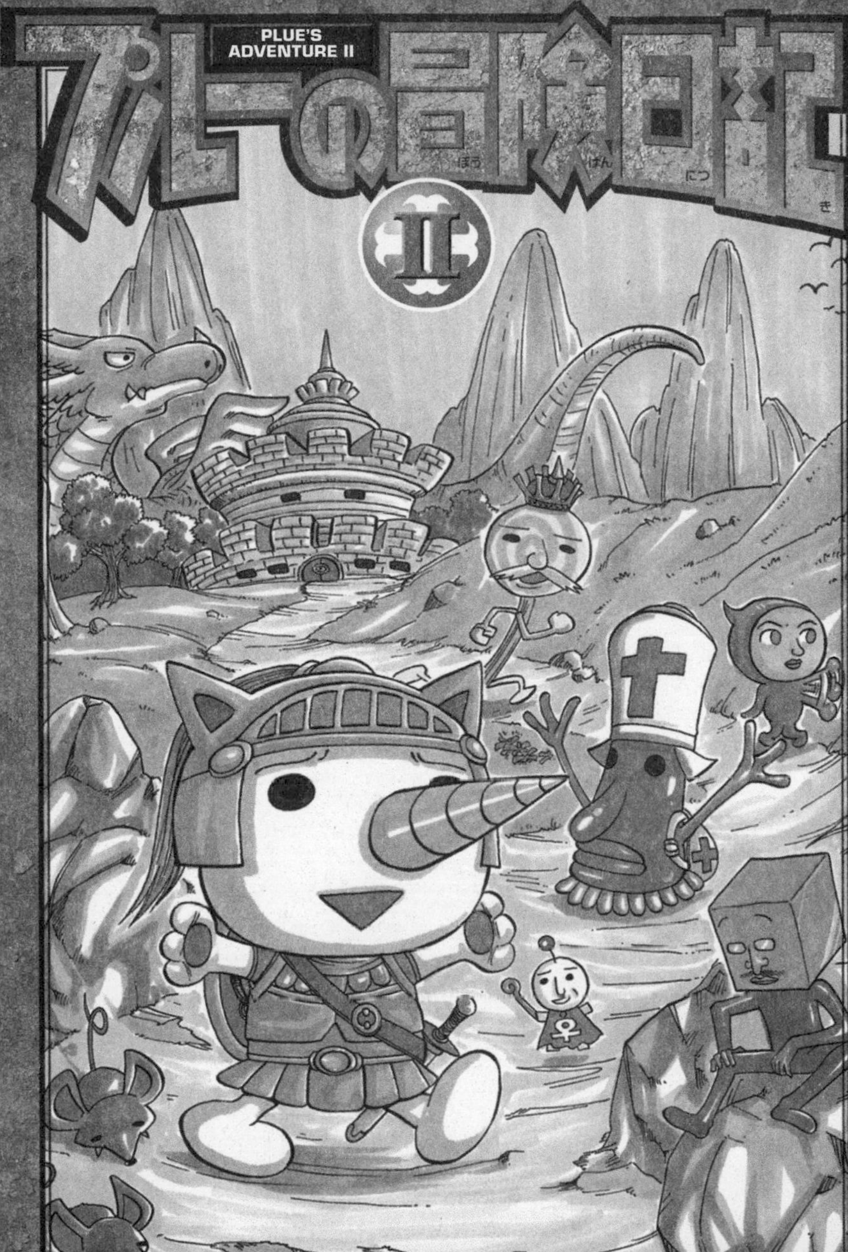
PLUE'S ADVENTURE II
プルーの冒険日記
II

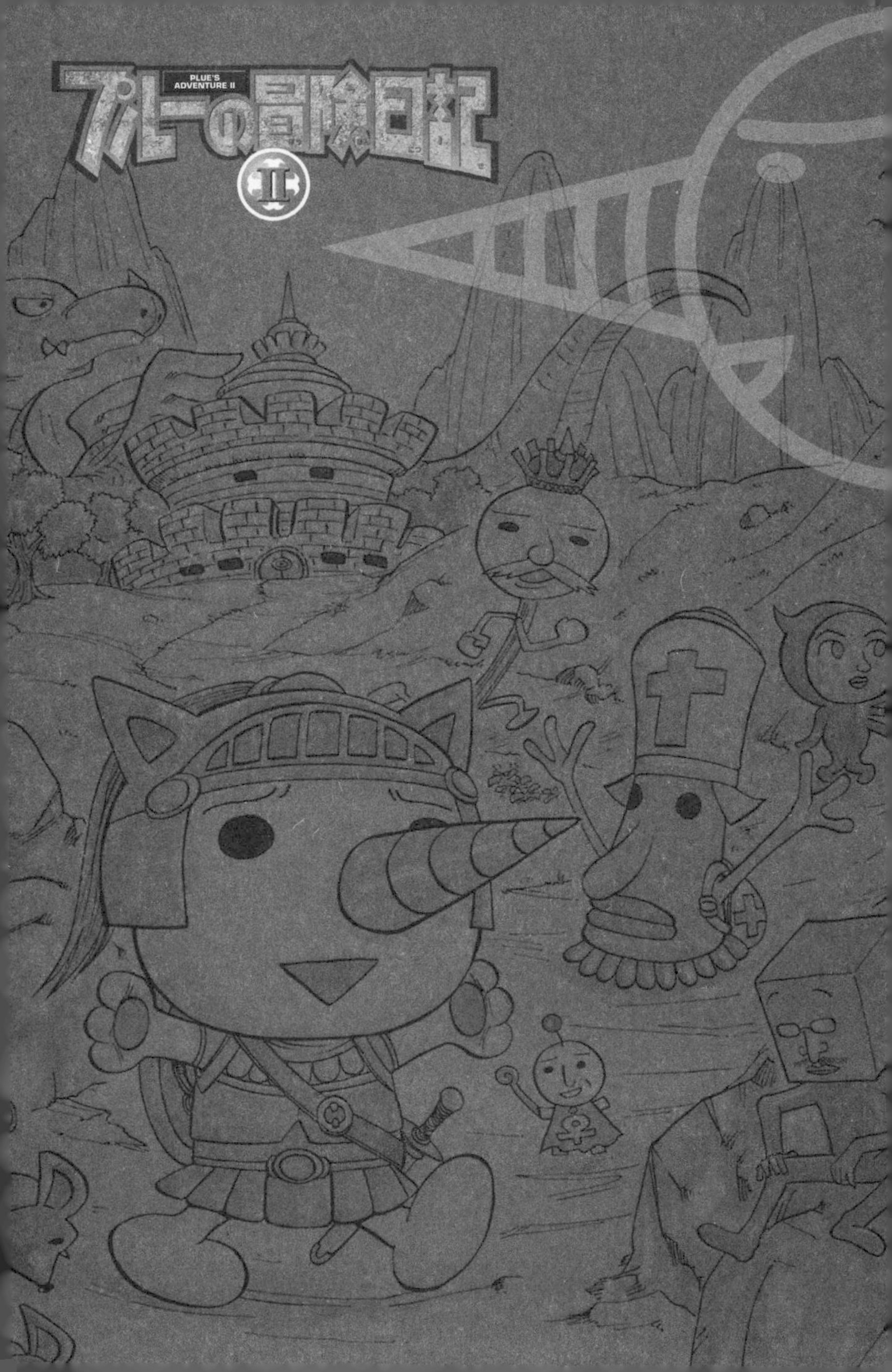
PLUE'S ADVENTURE II
プルーの冒険日記
II

PROLOGUE

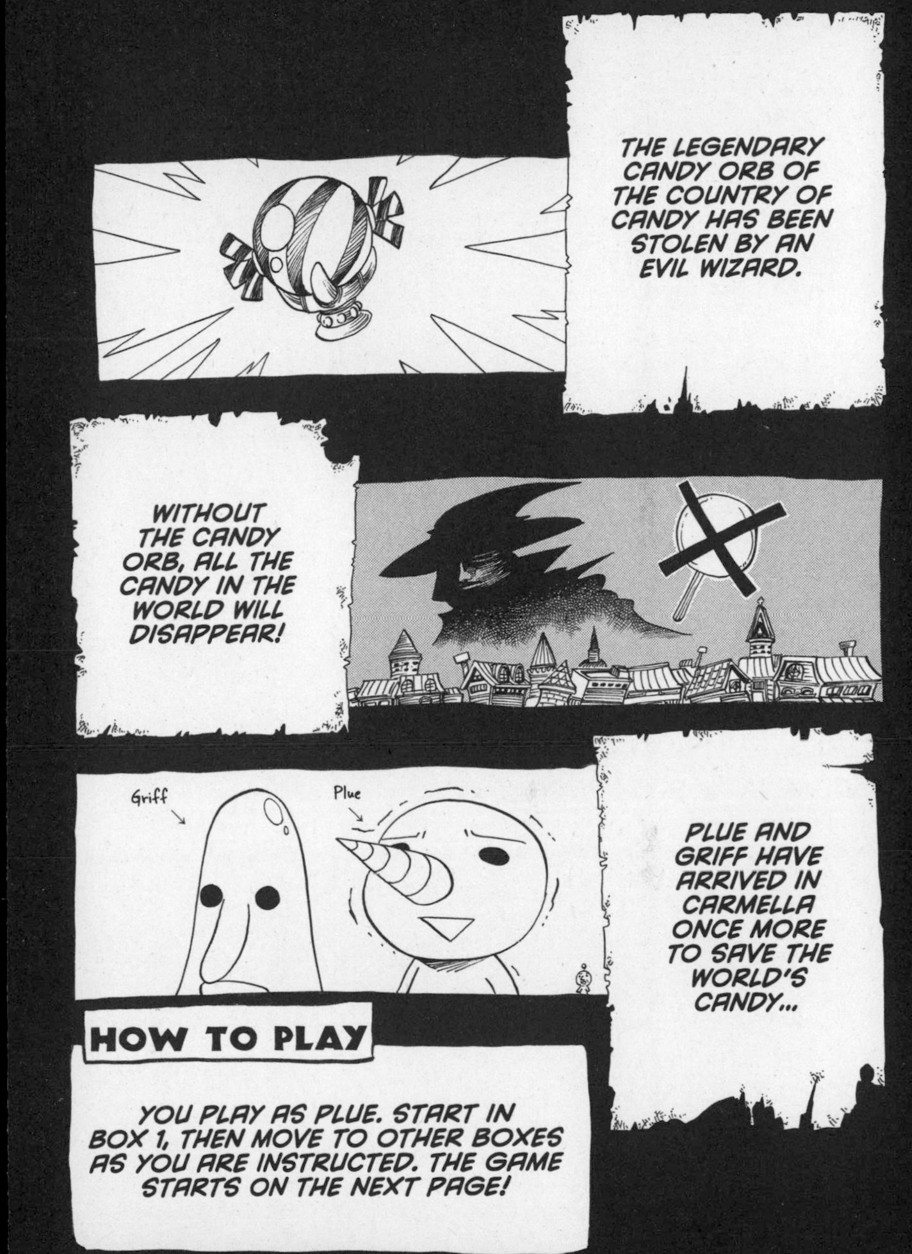
THE LEGENDARY CANDY ORB OF THE COUNTRY OF CANDY HAS BEEN STOLEN BY AN EVIL WIZARD.
WITHOUT THE CANDY ORB, ALL THE CANDY IN THE WORLD WILL DISAPPEAR!
PLUE AND GRIFF HAVE ARRIVED IN CARMELLA ONCE MORE TO SAVE THE WORLD'S CANDY...
Griff
Plue
HOW TO PLAY
YOU PLAY AS PLUE. START IN BOX 1, THEN MOVE TO OTHER BOXES AS YOU ARE INSTRUCTED. THE GAME STARTS ON THE NEXT PAGE!

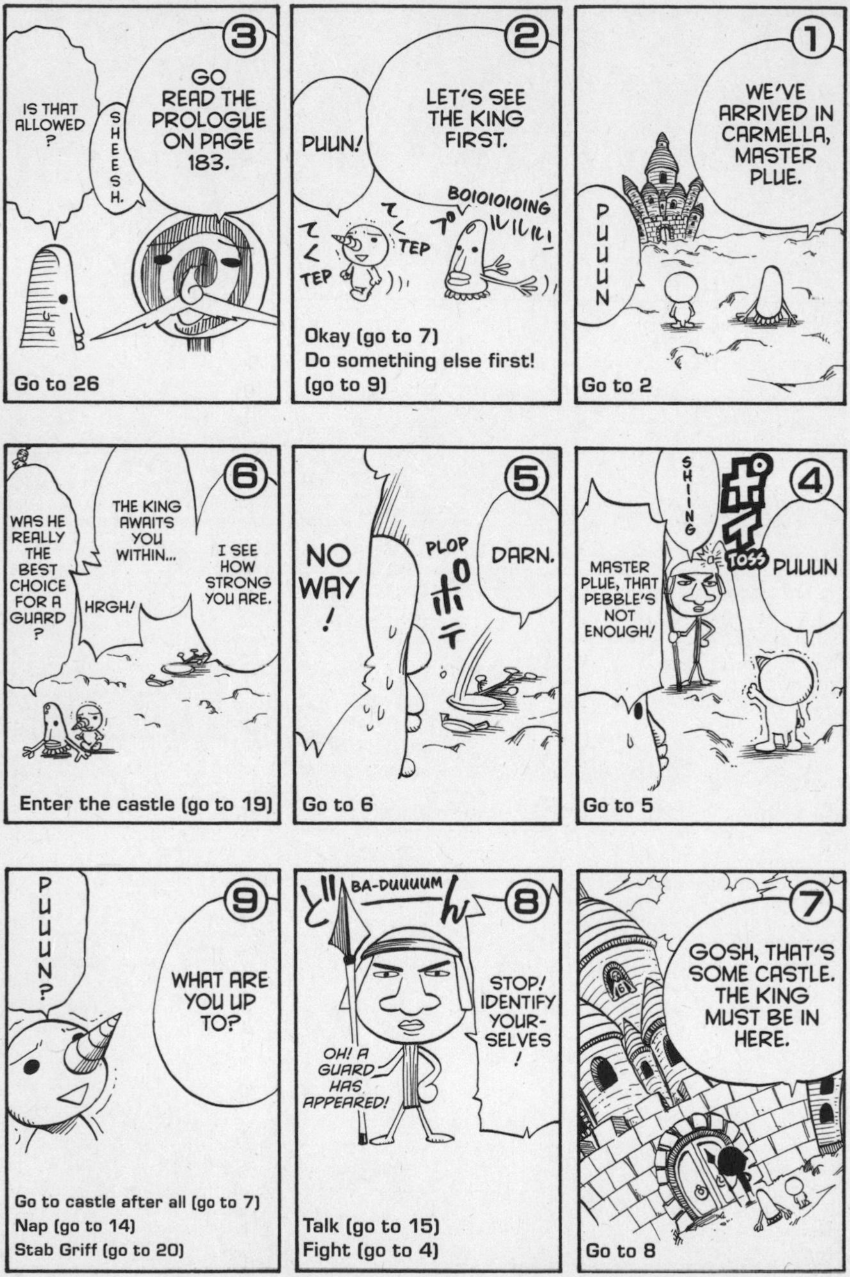
1
WE'VE ARRIVED IN CARMELLA, MASTER PLUE.
PUUUN
Go to 2
2
LET'S SEE THE KING FIRST.
PUUN!
BOIOIOIOING
プルルル!
てく
TEP
てく
TEP
Okay (go to 7)
Do something else first! (go to 9)
3
GO READ THE PROLOGUE ON PAGE 183.
SHEESH.
IS THAT ALLOWED?
Go to 26
4
PUUUN
ポイ
TOSS
SHIING
MASTER PLUE, THAT PEBBLE'S NOT ENOUGH!
Go to 5
5
DARN.
PLOP
ポテ
NO WAY!
Go to 6
6
I SEE HOW STRONG YOU ARE.
THE KING AWAITS YOU WITHIN...
HRGH!
WAS HE REALLY THE BEST CHOICE FOR A GUARD?
Enter the castle (go to 19)
7
GOSH, THAT'S SOME CASTLE. THE KING MUST BE IN HERE.
Go to 8
8
STOP! IDENTIFY YOUR-SELVES!
BA-DUUUUM
どん
OH! A GUARD HAS APPEARED!
Talk (go to 15)
Fight (go to 4)
9
WHAT ARE YOU UP TO?
PUUUN?
Go to castle after all (go to 7)
Nap (go to 14)
Stab Griff (go to 20)

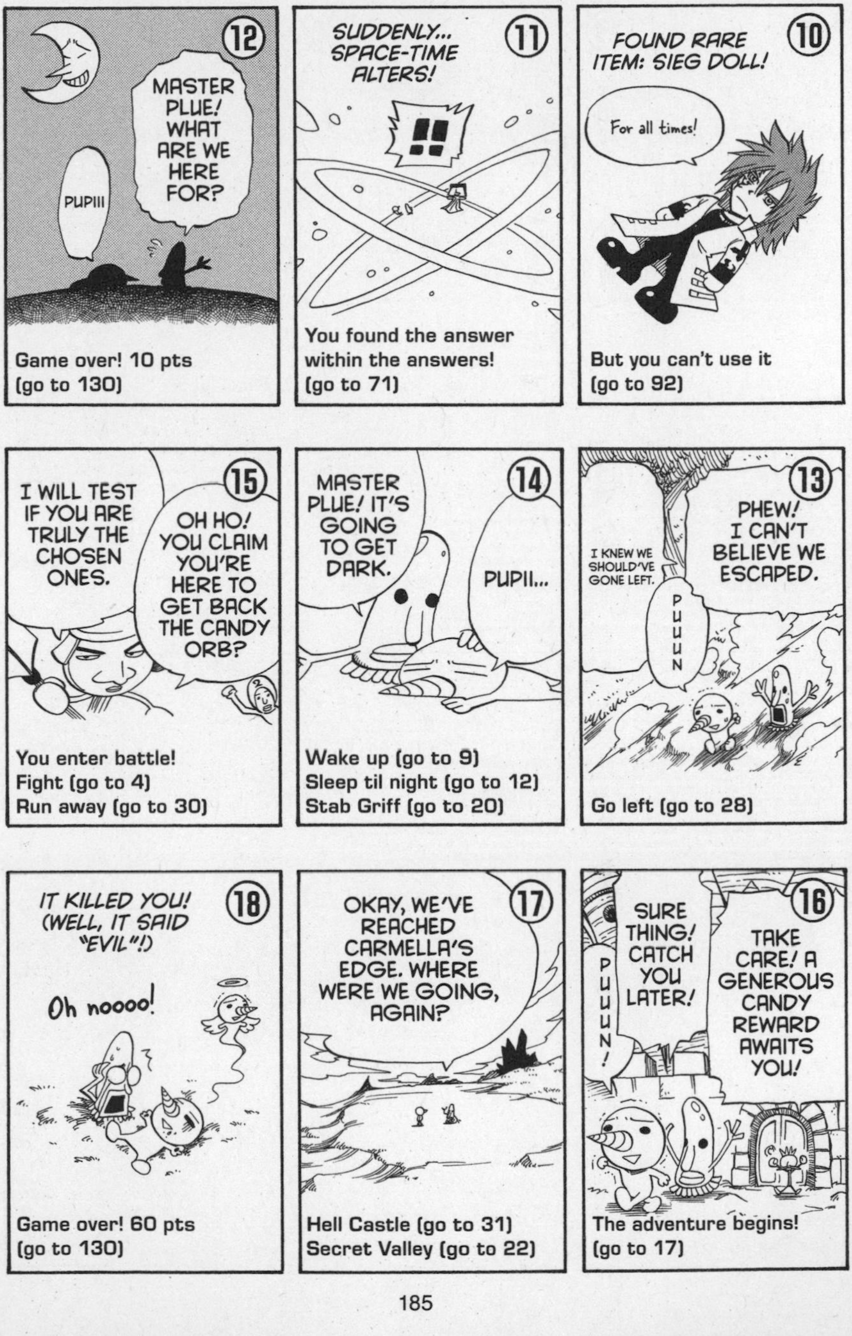
10
FOUND RARE ITEM: SIEG DOLL!
For all times!
But you can't use it
(go to 92)
11
SUDDENLY... SPACE-TIME ALTERS!
!!
You found the answer within the answers!
(go to 71)
12
MASTER PLUE! WHAT ARE WE HERE FOR?
PUPIII
Game over! 10 pts
(go to 130)
13
PHEW! I CAN'T BELIEVE WE ESCAPED.
I KNEW WE SHOULD'VE GONE LEFT.
PUUUN
Go left (go to 28)
14
PUPII...
MASTER PLUE! IT'S GOING TO GET DARK.
Wake up (go to 9)
Sleep til night (go to 12)
Stab Griff (go to 20)
15
OH HO! YOU CLAIM YOU'RE HERE TO GET BACK THE CANDY ORB?
I WILL TEST IF YOU ARE TRULY THE CHOSEN ONES.
You enter battle!
Fight (go to 4)
Run away (go to 30)
16
TAKE CARE! A GENEROUS CANDY REWARD AWAITS YOU!
SURE THING! CATCH YOU LATER!
PUUUUN!
The adventure begins!
(go to 17)
17
OKAY, WE'VE REACHED CARMELLA'S EDGE. WHERE WERE WE GOING, AGAIN?
Hell Castle (go to 31)
Secret Valley (go to 22)
18
IT KILLED YOU! (WELL, IT SAID "EVIL"!)
Oh noooo!
Game over! 60 pts
(go to 130)

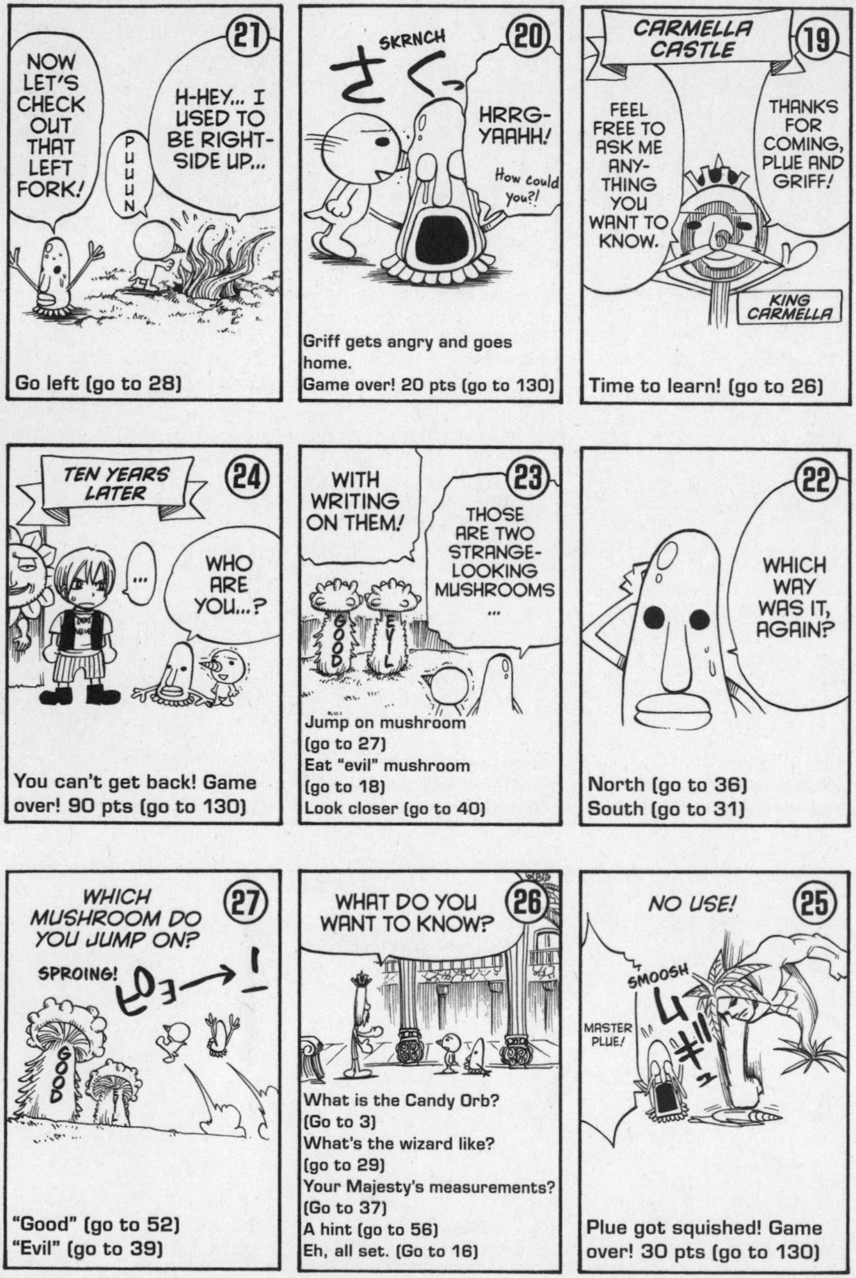
CARMELLA CASTLE
19
THANKS FOR COMING, PLUE AND GRIFF!
FEEL FREE TO ASK ME ANY-THING YOU WANT TO KNOW.
KING CARMELLA
Time to learn! (go to 26)
20
SKRNCH
さくっ
HRRG-YAAHH!
How could you?!
Griff gets angry and goes home.
Game over! 20 pts (go to 130)
21
H-HEY... I USED TO BE RIGHT-SIDE UP...
PUUUN
NOW LET'S CHECK OUT THAT LEFT FORK!
Go left (go to 28)
22
WHICH WAY WAS IT, AGAIN?
North (go to 36)
South (go to 31)
23
THOSE ARE TWO STRANGE-LOOKING MUSHROOMS ...
WITH WRITING ON THEM!
GOOD
EVIL
Jump on mushroom (go to 27)
Eat "evil" mushroom (go to 18)
Look closer (go to 40)
TEN YEARS LATER
24
WHO ARE YOU...?
...
You can't get back! Game over! 90 pts (go to 130)
25
NO USE!
SMOOSH
MASTER PLUE!
Plue got squished! Game over! 30 pts (go to 130)
26
WHAT DO YOU WANT TO KNOW?
What is the Candy Orb? (Go to 3)
What's the wizard like? (go to 29)
Your Majesty's measurements? (Go to 37)
A hint (go to 56)
Eh, all set. (Go to 16)
27
WHICH MUSHROOM DO YOU JUMP ON?
SPROING!
GOOD
"Good" (go to 52)
"Evil" (go to 39)

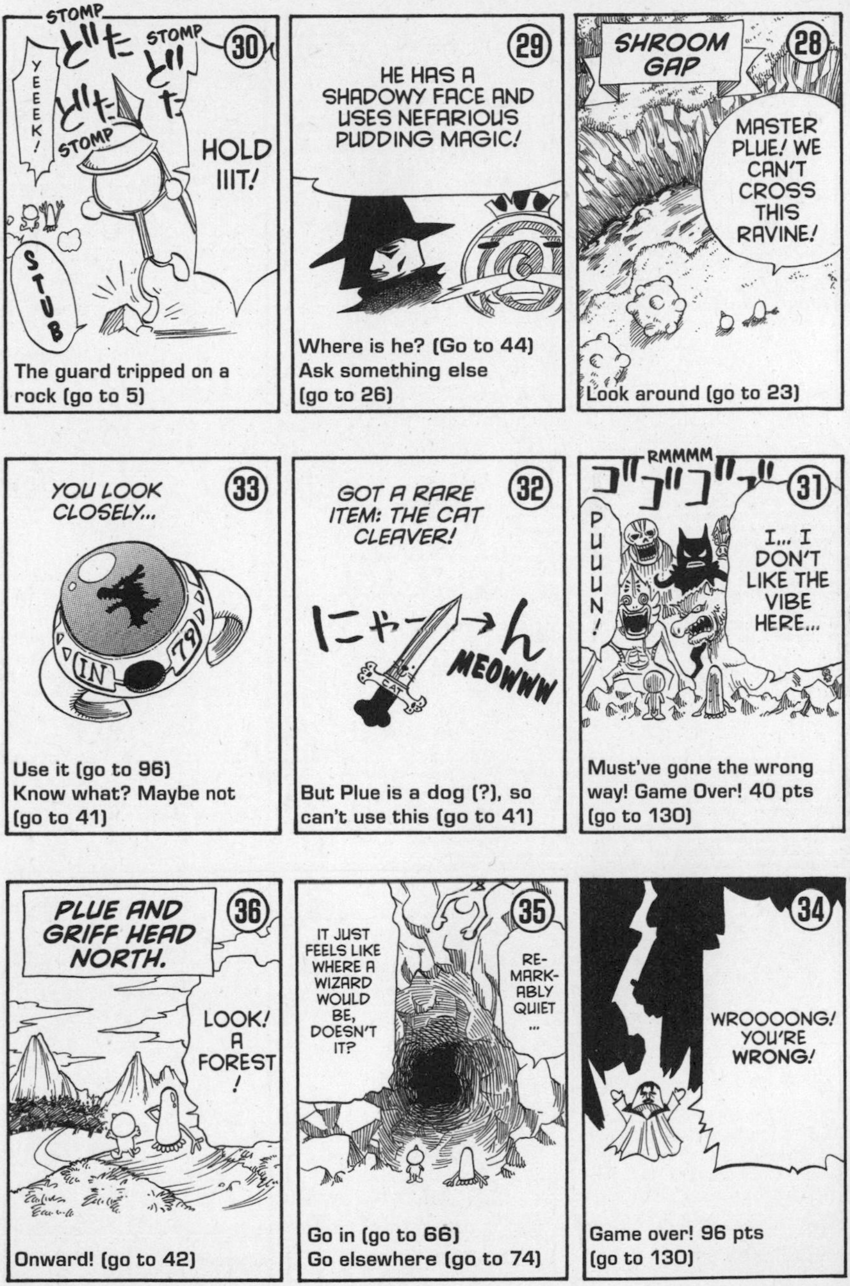
28
SHROOM GAP
MASTER PLUE! WE CAN'T CROSS THIS RAVINE!
Look around (go to 23)
29
HE HAS A SHADOWY FACE AND USES NEFARIOUS PUDDING MAGIC!
Where is he? (Go to 44)
Ask something else (go to 26)
30
STOMP
どた
STOMP
どた
STOMP
どた
YEEEEK!
HOLD IIIT!
STUB
The guard tripped on a rock (go to 5)
31
RMMMM
ゴゴゴゴ
I... I DON'T LIKE THE VIBE HERE...
PUUUUN!
Must've gone the wrong way! Game Over! 40 pts (go to 130)
32
GOT A RARE ITEM: THE CAT CLEAVER!
にゃーーん
MEOWWW
CAT
But Plue is a dog (?), so can't use this (go to 41)
33
YOU LOOK CLOSELY...
IN
79
Use it (go to 96)
Know what? Maybe not (go to 41)
34
WROOOONG! YOU'RE WRONG!
Game over! 96 pts (go to 130)
35
RE-MARK-ABLY QUIET ...
IT JUST FEELS LIKE WHERE A WIZARD WOULD BE, DOESN'T IT?
Go in (go to 66)
Go elsewhere (go to 74)
36
PLUE AND GRIFF HEAD NORTH.
LOOK! A FOREST!
Onward! (go to 42)

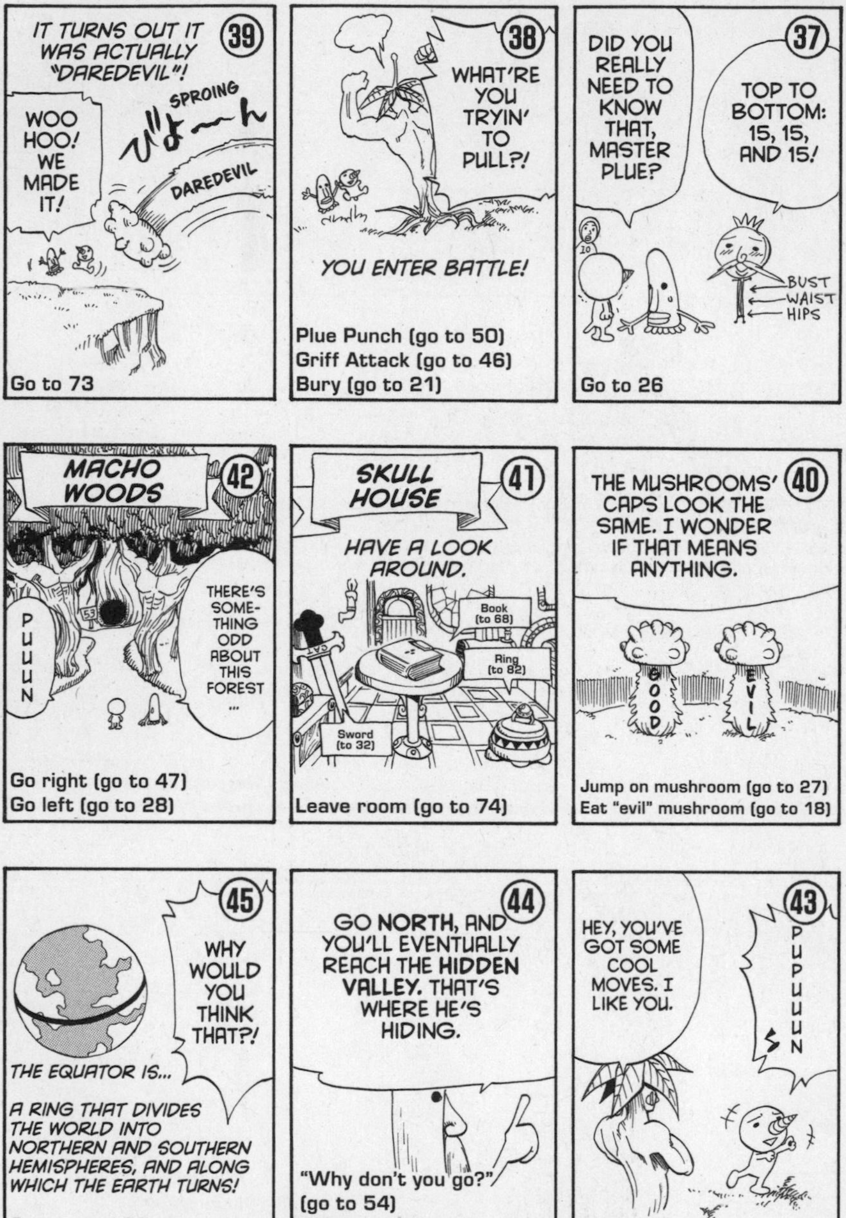
37
TOP TO BOTTOM: 15, 15, AND 15!
DID YOU REALLY NEED TO KNOW THAT, MASTER PLUE?
BUST
WAIST
HIPS
10
Go to 26
38
WHAT'RE YOU TRYIN' TO PULL?!
YOU ENTER BATTLE!
Plue Punch (go to 50)
Griff Attack (go to 46)
Bury (go to 21)
39
IT TURNS OUT IT WAS ACTUALLY "DAREDEVIL"!
SPROING
びよ〜〜ん
WOO HOO! WE MADE IT!
DAREDEVIL
Go to 73
40
THE MUSHROOMS' CAPS LOOK THE SAME. I WONDER IF THAT MEANS ANYTHING.
GOOD
EVIL
Jump on mushroom (go to 27)
Eat "evil" mushroom (go to 18)
41
SKULL HOUSE
HAVE A LOOK AROUND.
Book (to 68)
Ring (to 82)
CAT
Sword (to 32)
Leave room (go to 74)
42
MACHO WOODS
THERE'S SOMETHING ODD ABOUT THIS FOREST...
53
PUUUN
Go right (go to 47)
Go left (go to 28)
43
PUPUUUN
HEY, YOU'VE GOT SOME COOL MOVES. I LIKE YOU.
Go to 58
44
GO NORTH, AND YOU'LL EVENTUALLY REACH THE HIDDEN VALLEY. THAT'S WHERE HE'S HIDING.
"Why don't you go?" (go to 54)
Ask something else (go to 26)
45
WHY WOULD YOU THINK THAT?!
THE EQUATOR IS...
A RING THAT DIVIDES THE WORLD INTO NORTHERN AND SOUTHERN HEMISPHERES, AND ALONG WHICH THE EARTH TURNS!
Game over! 93 pts (go to 130)

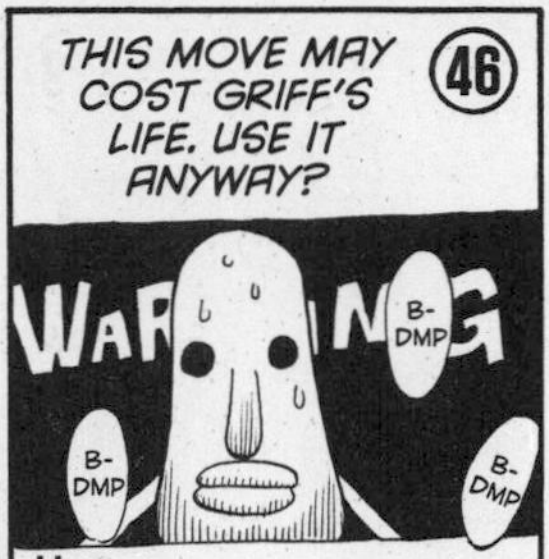
THIS MOVE MAY COST GRIFF'S LIFE. USE IT ANYWAY?
46
WAR ING
B-DMP
B-DMP
B-DMP

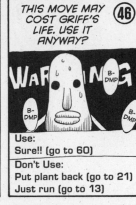

Use:
Sure!! (go to 60)

Don't Use:
Put plant back (go to 21)
Just run (go to 13)

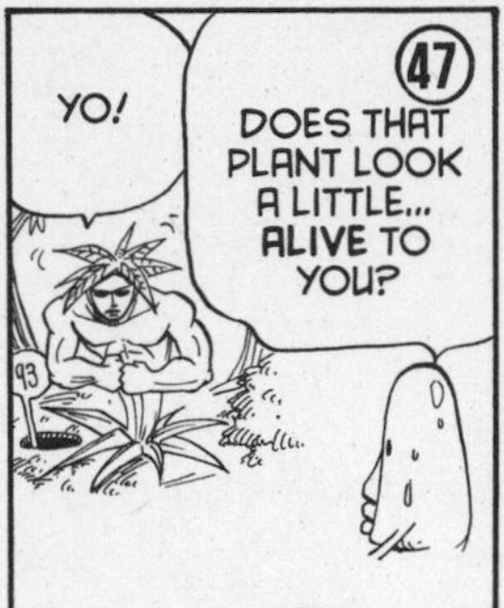
47
DOES THAT PLANT LOOK A LITTLE... ALIVE TO YOU?
YO!
93

Dance (go to 43)
Uproot (go to 38)
Go left instead (go to 28)

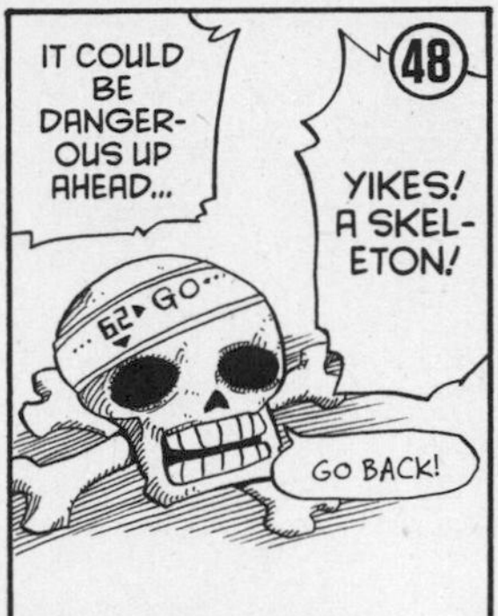
48
YIKES! A SKEL-ETON!
IT COULD BE DANGER-OUS UP AHEAD...
62▸GO
GO BACK!

Go back (go to 95)
Go forth (go to 31)

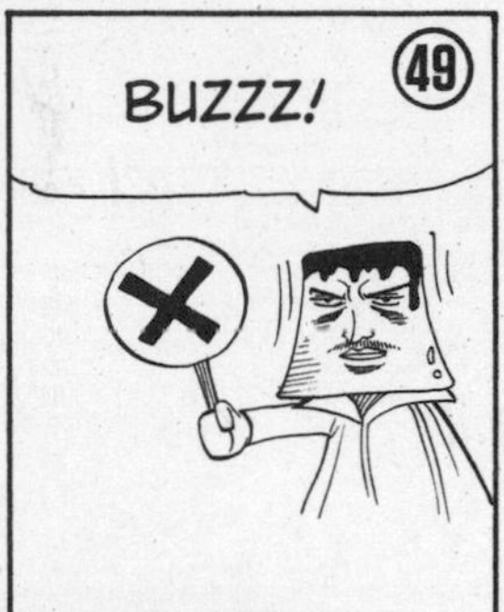
49
BUZZZ!

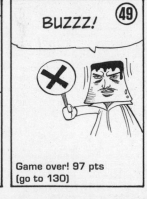

Game over! 97 pts
(go to 130)

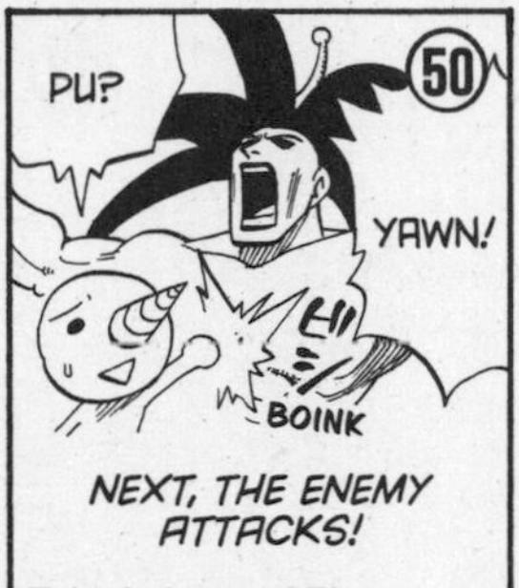
50
PU?
YAWN!
BOINK
NEXT, THE ENEMY ATTACKS!

Take it (go to 25)
Griff Attack (go to 46)
Bury (go to 21)

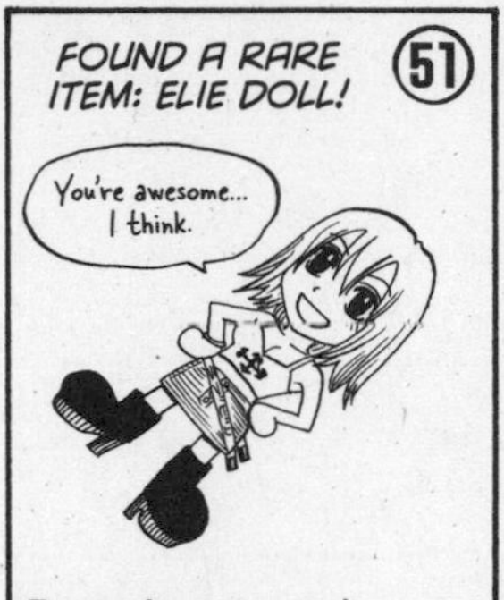
FOUND A RARE ITEM: ELIE DOLL!
51
You're awesome... I think.

Dunno how to use it, though (go to 101)

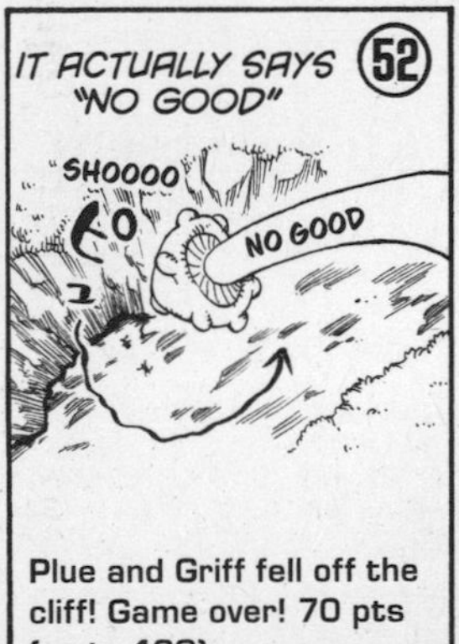
IT ACTUALLY SAYS "NO GOOD"
52
"SHOOOO
NO GOOD

Plue and Griff fell off the cliff! Game over! 70 pts
(go to 130)

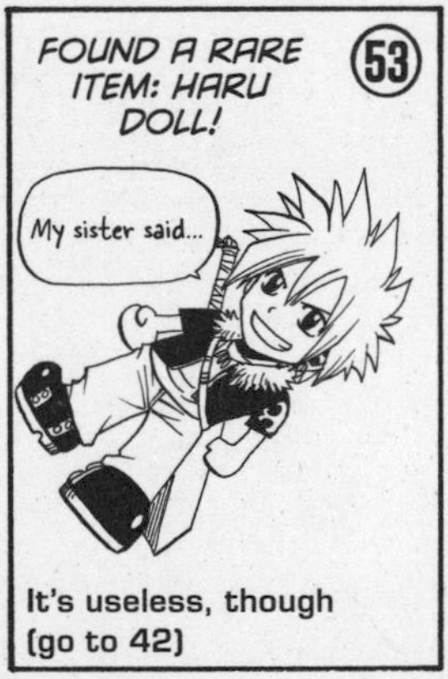
FOUND A RARE ITEM: HARU DOLL!
53
My sister said...

It's useless, though
(go to 42)

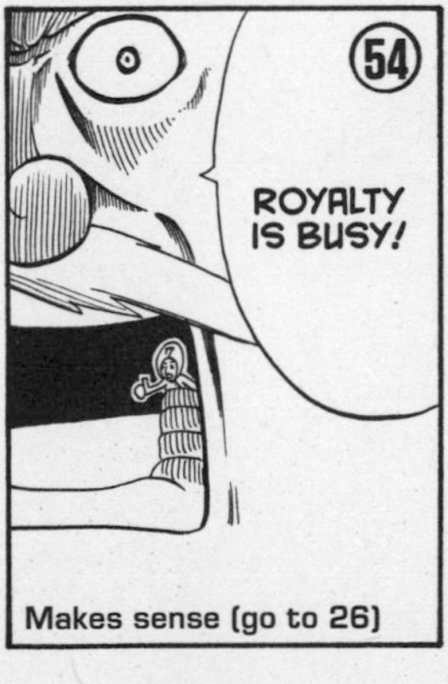
54
ROYALTY IS BUSY!

Makes sense (go to 26)

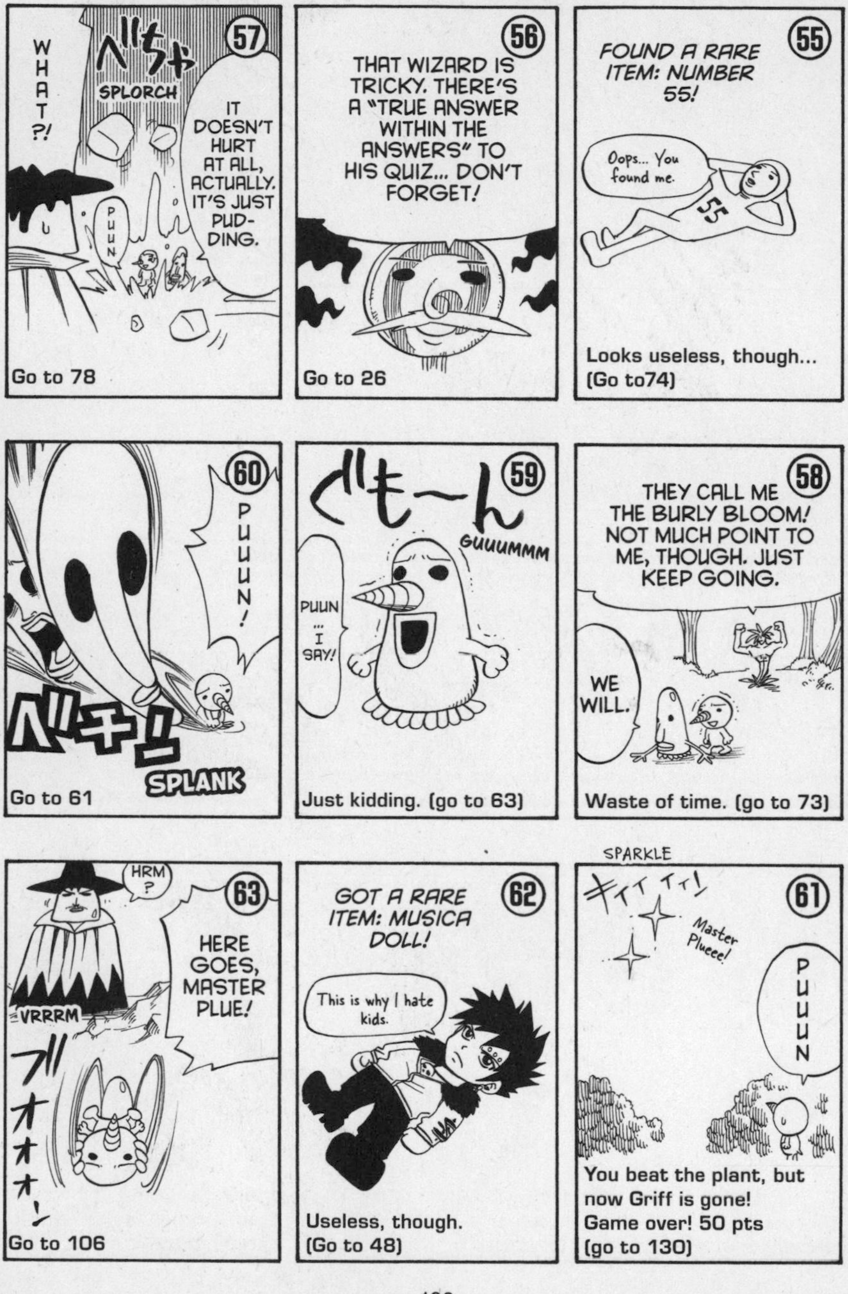
55
FOUND A RARE ITEM: NUMBER 55!
Oops... You found me.
55
Looks useless, though... (Go to74)
56
THAT WIZARD IS TRICKY. THERE'S A "TRUE ANSWER WITHIN THE ANSWERS" TO HIS QUIZ... DON'T FORGET!
Go to 26
57
べちゃ
SPLORCH
IT DOESN'T HURT AT ALL, ACTUALLY. IT'S JUST PUD-DING.
WHAT?!
PUUN
Go to 78
58
THEY CALL ME THE BURLY BLOOM! NOT MUCH POINT TO ME, THOUGH. JUST KEEP GOING.
WE WILL.
Waste of time. (go to 73)
59
ぐも~ん
GUUUMMM
PUUN... I SAY!
Just kidding. (go to 63)
60
PUUUUN!
ベチョ!
SPLANK
Go to 61
SPARKLE
キィィィィ!
61
Master Pluee!
PUUUN
You beat the plant, but now Griff is gone! Game over! 50 pts (go to 130)
62
GOT A RARE ITEM: MUSICA DOLL!
This is why I hate kids.
Useless, though. (Go to 48)
63
HRM?
HERE GOES, MASTER PLUE!
VRRRM
ブオオオ!
Go to 106

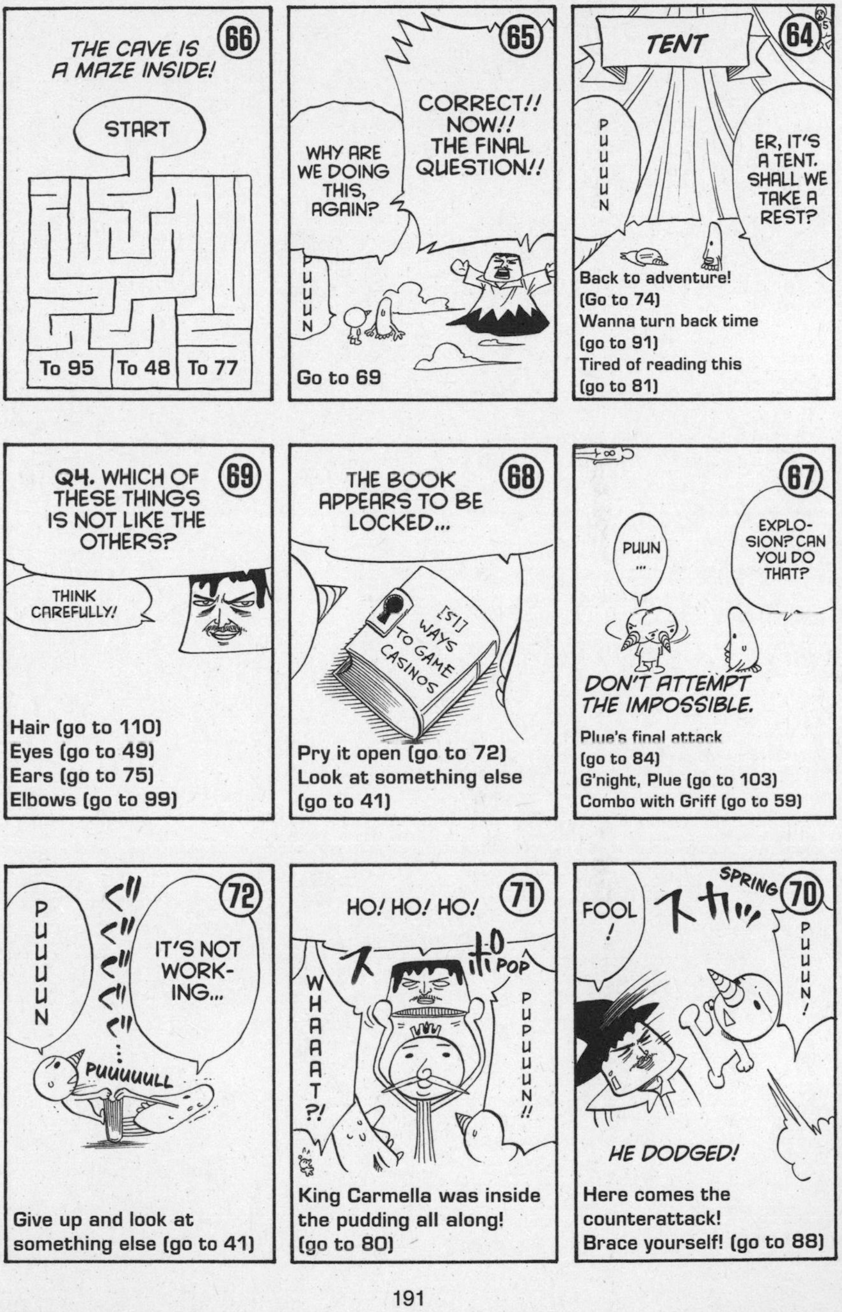
64
TENT
ER, IT'S A TENT. SHALL WE TAKE A REST?
PUUUUN
Back to adventure! (Go to 74)
Wanna turn back time (go to 91)
Tired of reading this (go to 81)
65
CORRECT!! NOW!! THE FINAL QUESTION!!
WHY ARE WE DOING THIS, AGAIN?
PUUUN
Go to 69
66
THE CAVE IS A MAZE INSIDE!
START
To 95
To 48
To 77
67
EXPLOSION? CAN YOU DO THAT?
PUUN ...
DON'T ATTEMPT THE IMPOSSIBLE.
Plue's final attack (go to 84)
G'night, Plue (go to 103)
Combo with Griff (go to 59)
68
THE BOOK APPEARS TO BE LOCKED...
WAYS TO GAME CASINOS
Pry it open (go to 72)
Look at something else (go to 41)
69
Q4. WHICH OF THESE THINGS IS NOT LIKE THE OTHERS?
THINK CAREFULLY!
Hair (go to 110)
Eyes (go to 49)
Ears (go to 75)
Elbows (go to 99)
70
SPRING
PUUUN!
FOOL!
HE DODGED!
Here comes the counterattack! Brace yourself! (go to 88)
71
HO! HO! HO!
POP
PUPUUUN!!
WHAAAT?!
King Carmella was inside the pudding all along! (go to 80)
72
IT'S NOT WORKING...
PUUUUN
PUUUUULL
Give up and look at something else (go to 41)

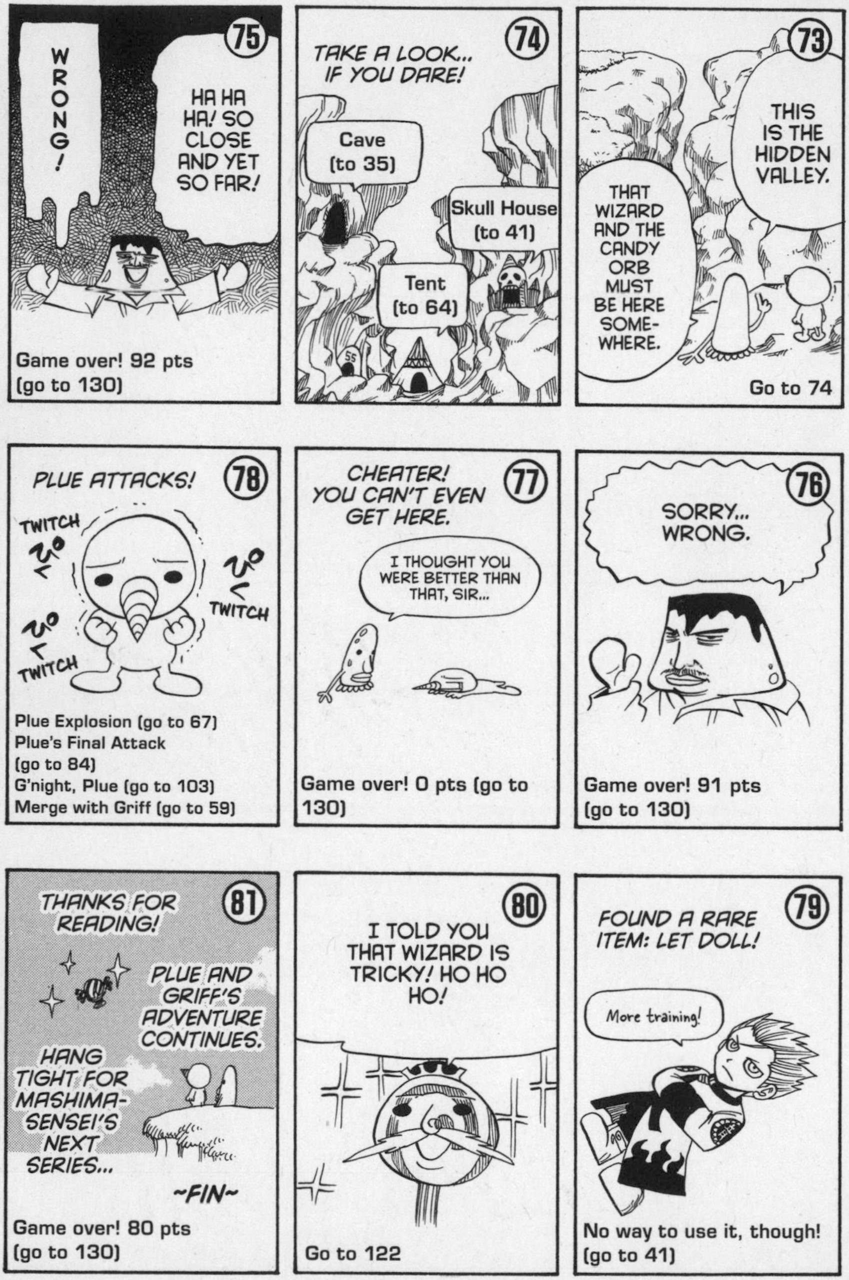
73
THIS IS THE HIDDEN VALLEY.
THAT WIZARD AND THE CANDY ORB MUST BE HERE SOME-WHERE.
Go to 74
74
TAKE A LOOK... IF YOU DARE!
Cave (to 35)
Skull House (to 41)
Tent (to 64)
55
75
WRONG!
HA HA HA! SO CLOSE AND YET SO FAR!
Game over! 92 pts (go to 130)
76
SORRY... WRONG.
Game over! 91 pts (go to 130)
77
CHEATER! YOU CAN'T EVEN GET HERE.
I THOUGHT YOU WERE BETTER THAN THAT, SIR...
Game over! 0 pts (go to 130)
78
PLUE ATTACKS!
TWITCH
TWITCH
TWITCH
Plue Explosion (go to 67)
Plue's Final Attack (go to 84)
G'night, Plue (go to 103)
Merge with Griff (go to 59)
79
FOUND A RARE ITEM: LET DOLL!
More training!
No way to use it, though! (go to 41)
80
I TOLD YOU THAT WIZARD IS TRICKY! HO HO HO!
Go to 122
81
THANKS FOR READING!
PLUE AND GRIFF'S ADVENTURE CONTINUES.
HANG TIGHT FOR MASHIMA-SENSEI'S NEXT SERIES...
~FIN~
Game over! 80 pts (go to 130)

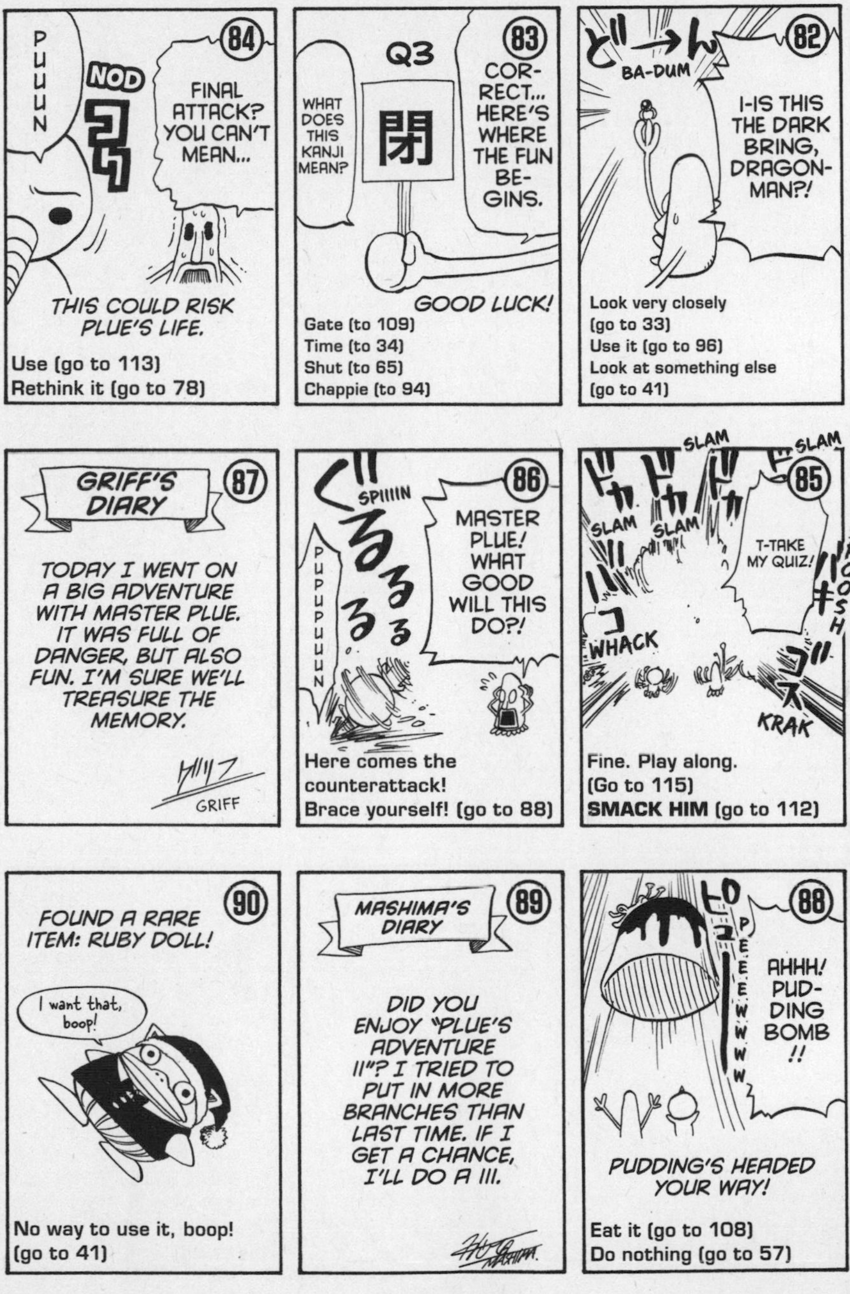
82
BA-DUM
I-IS THIS THE DARK BRING, DRAGON-MAN?!
Look very closely (go to 33)
Use it (go to 96)
Look at something else (go to 41)
83
Q3
CORRECT... HERE'S WHERE THE FUN BEGINS.
閉
WHAT DOES THIS KANJI MEAN?
GOOD LUCK!
Gate (to 109)
Time (to 34)
Shut (to 65)
Chappie (to 94)
84
FINAL ATTACK? YOU CAN'T MEAN...
NOD
PUUUN
THIS COULD RISK PLUE'S LIFE.
Use (go to 113)
Rethink it (go to 78)
85
SLAM
SLAM
SLAM
SLAM
T-TAKE MY QUIZ!
SPOOSH
WHACK
KRAK
Fine. Play along. (Go to 115)
SMACK HIM (go to 112)
86
MASTER PLUE! WHAT GOOD WILL THIS DO?!
SPIIIIN
PUPUPUUUN
Here comes the counterattack!
Brace yourself! (go to 88)
87
GRIFF'S DIARY
TODAY I WENT ON A BIG ADVENTURE WITH MASTER PLUE. IT WAS FULL OF DANGER, BUT ALSO FUN. I'M SURE WE'LL TREASURE THE MEMORY.
GRIFF
88
AHHH! PUDDING BOMB!!
PEEEWWWWW
PUDDING'S HEADED YOUR WAY!
Eat it (go to 108)
Do nothing (go to 57)
89
MASHIMA'S DIARY
DID YOU ENJOY "PLUE'S ADVENTURE II"? I TRIED TO PUT IN MORE BRANCHES THAN LAST TIME. IF I GET A CHANCE, I'LL DO A III.
90
FOUND A RARE ITEM: RUBY DOLL!
I want that, boop!
No way to use it, boop! (go to 41)

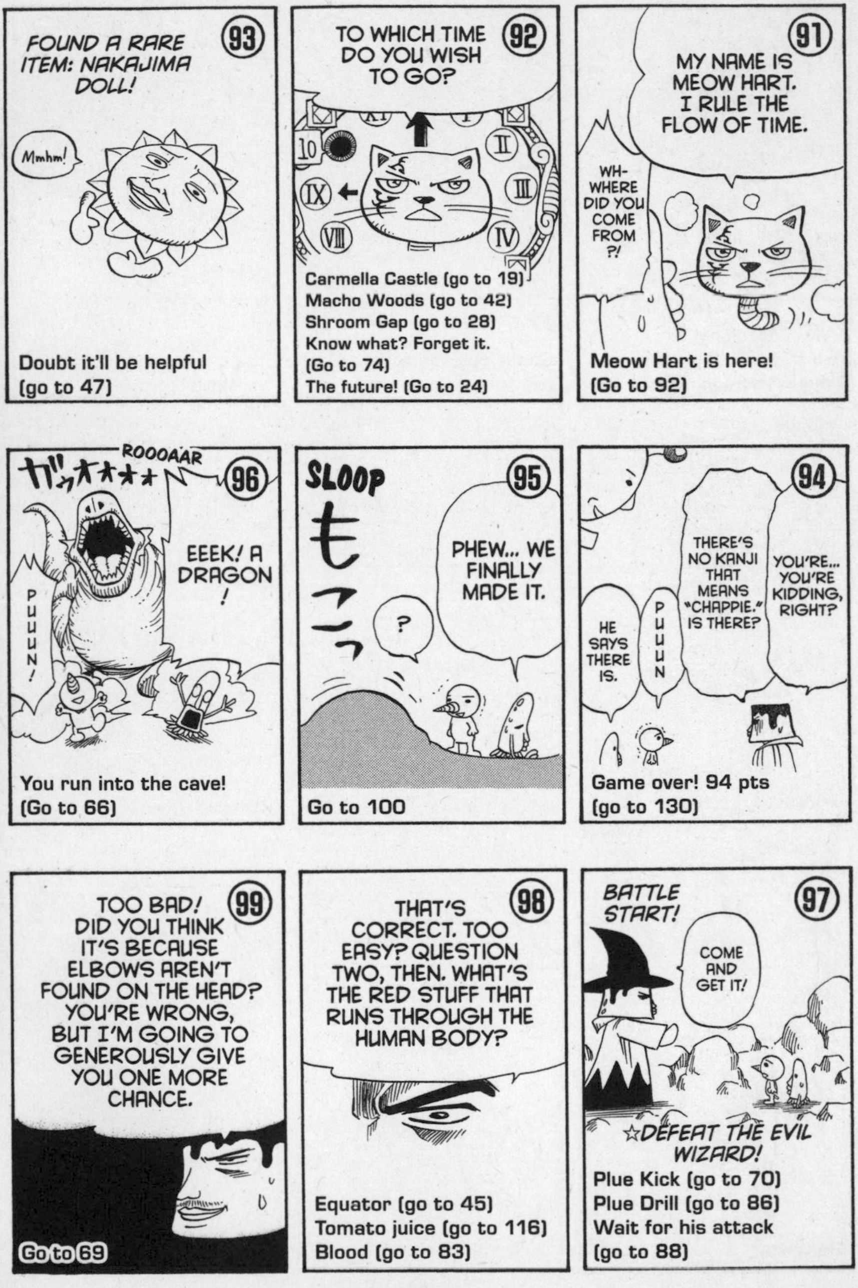
91
MY NAME IS MEOW HART. I RULE THE FLOW OF TIME.
WH-WHERE DID YOU COME FROM ?!
Meow Hart is here! (Go to 92)
92
TO WHICH TIME DO YOU WISH TO GO?
Carmella Castle (go to 19)
Macho Woods (go to 42)
Shroom Gap (go to 28)
Know what? Forget it. (Go to 74)
The future! (Go to 24)
93
FOUND A RARE ITEM: NAKAJIMA DOLL!
Mmhm!
Doubt it'll be helpful (go to 47)
94
YOU'RE... YOU'RE KIDDING, RIGHT?
THERE'S NO KANJI THAT MEANS "CHAPPIE." IS THERE?
PUUUN
HE SAYS THERE IS.
Game over! 94 pts (go to 130)
95
SLOOP
PHEW... WE FINALLY MADE IT.
?
Go to 100
96
ROOOAAR
EEEK! A DRAGON!
PUUUN!
You run into the cave! (Go to 66)
97
BATTLE START!
COME AND GET IT!
☆DEFEAT THE EVIL WIZARD!
Plue Kick (go to 70)
Plue Drill (go to 86)
Wait for his attack (go to 88)
98
THAT'S CORRECT. TOO EASY? QUESTION TWO, THEN. WHAT'S THE RED STUFF THAT RUNS THROUGH THE HUMAN BODY?
Equator (go to 45)
Tomato juice (go to 116)
Blood (go to 83)
99
TOO BAD! DID YOU THINK IT'S BECAUSE ELBOWS AREN'T FOUND ON THE HEAD? YOU'RE WRONG, BUT I'M GOING TO GENEROUSLY GIVE YOU ONE MORE CHANCE.
Go to 69

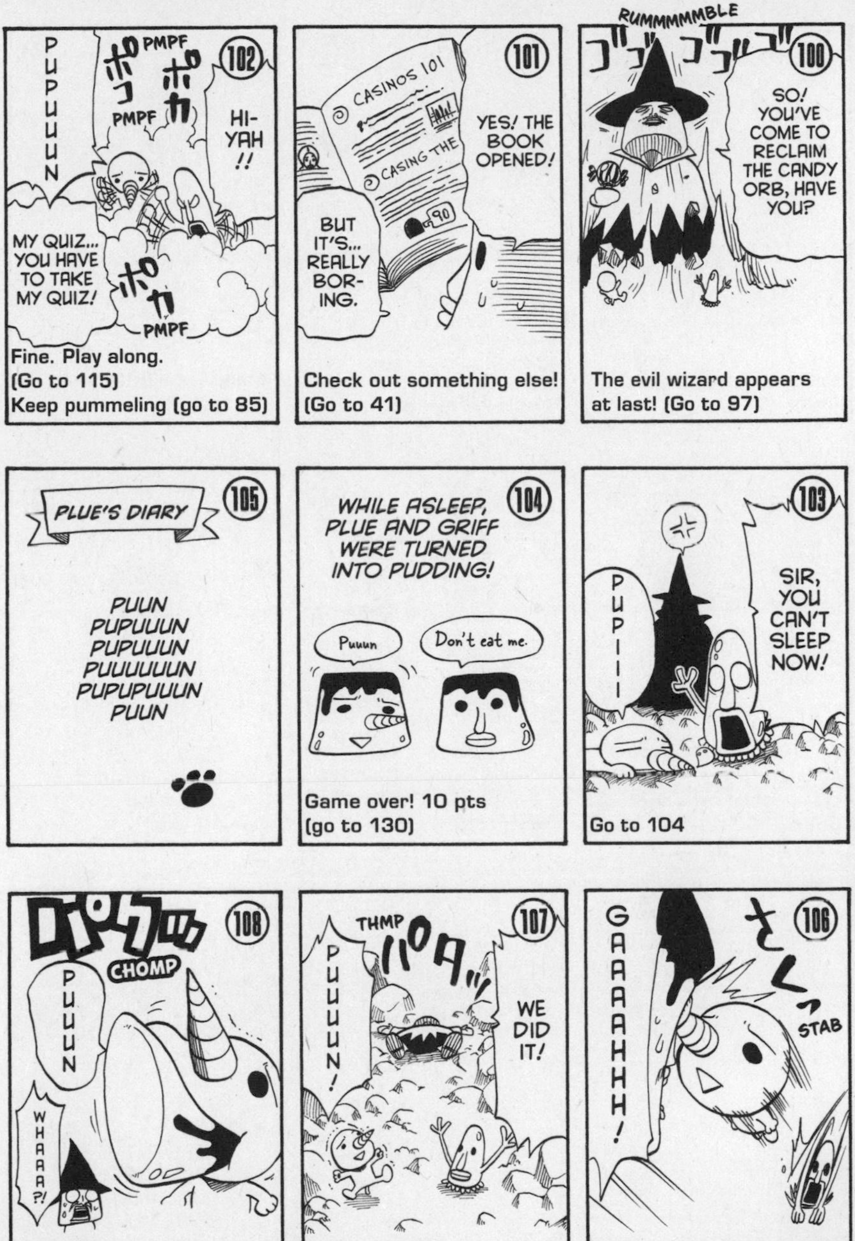
100
RUMMMMMBLE
SO! YOU'VE COME TO RECLAIM THE CANDY ORB, HAVE YOU?
The evil wizard appears at last! (Go to 97)
101
CASINOS 101
CASING THE
YES! THE BOOK OPENED!
BUT IT'S... REALLY BOR-ING.
Check out something else! (Go to 41)
102
PMPF
PMPF
PUPUUUUN
HI-YAH !!
MY QUIZ... YOU HAVE TO TAKE MY QUIZ!
PMPF
Fine. Play along. (Go to 115)
Keep pummeling (go to 85)
103
SIR, YOU CAN'T SLEEP NOW!
PUPIII
Go to 104
104
WHILE ASLEEP, PLUE AND GRIFF WERE TURNED INTO PUDDING!
Don't eat me.
Puuun
Game over! 10 pts (go to 130)
105
PLUE'S DIARY
PUUN PUPUUUN PUPUUUN PUUUUUUN PUPUPUUUN PUUN
106
STAB
GAAAAAHHH!
Go to 107
107
THMP
WE DID IT!
PUUUUN!
Go to 119
108
CHOMP
PUUUN
WHAAAA?!
Go to 78

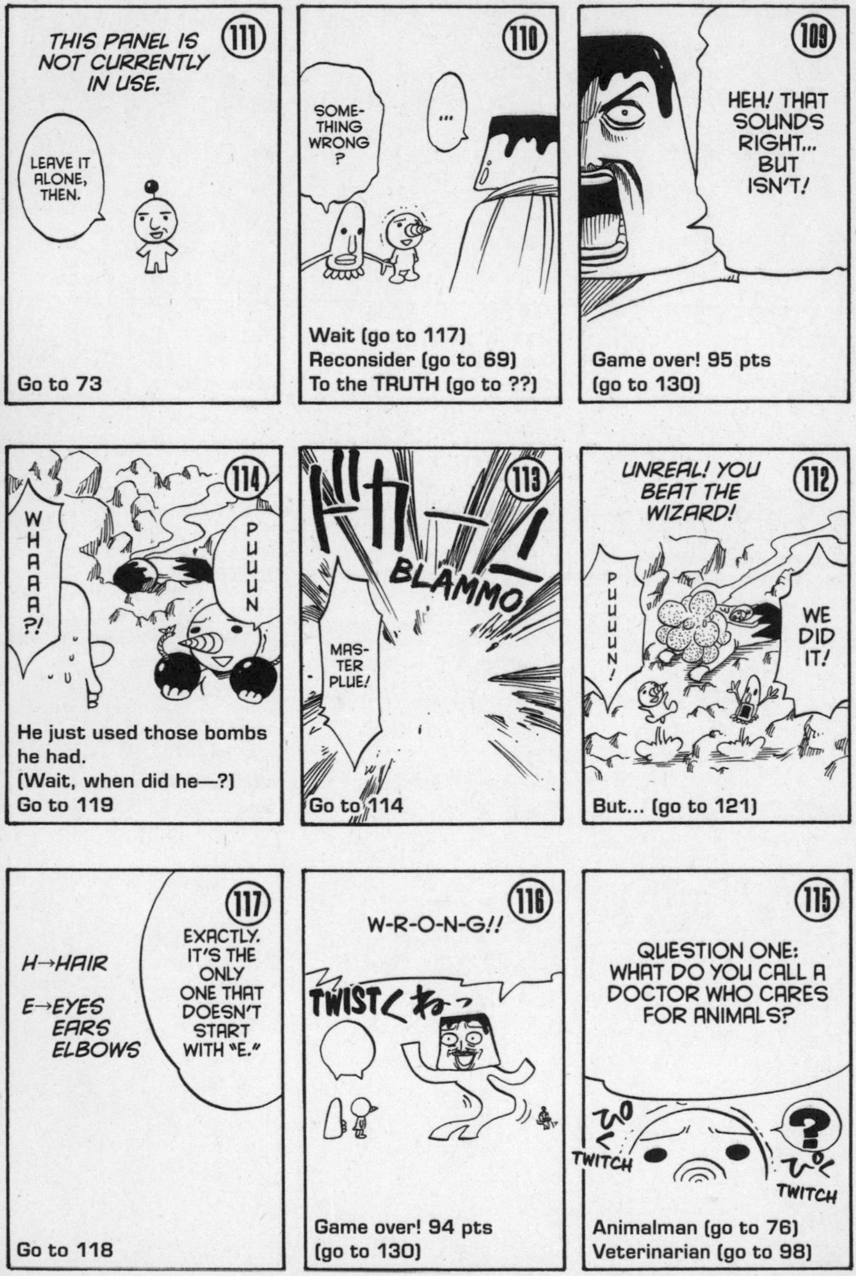
109
HEH! THAT SOUNDS RIGHT... BUT ISN'T!
Game over! 95 pts (go to 130)
110
...
SOME-THING WRONG ?
Wait (go to 117)
Reconsider (go to 69)
To the TRUTH (go to ??)
111
THIS PANEL IS NOT CURRENTLY IN USE.
LEAVE IT ALONE, THEN.
Go to 73
112
UNREAL! YOU BEAT THE WIZARD!
WE DID IT!
PUUUUN!
But... (go to 121)
113
BLAMMO
MAS-TER PLUE!
Go to 114
114
PUUUN
WHAAAA?!
He just used those bombs he had.
(Wait, when did he—?)
Go to 119
115
QUESTION ONE: WHAT DO YOU CALL A DOCTOR WHO CARES FOR ANIMALS?
?
TWITCH
TWITCH
Animalman (go to 76)
Veterinarian (go to 98)
116
W-R-O-N-G!!
TWIST
Game over! 94 pts (go to 130)
117
EXACTLY. IT'S THE ONLY ONE THAT DOESN'T START WITH "E."
H→HAIR
E→EYES EARS ELBOWS
Go to 118

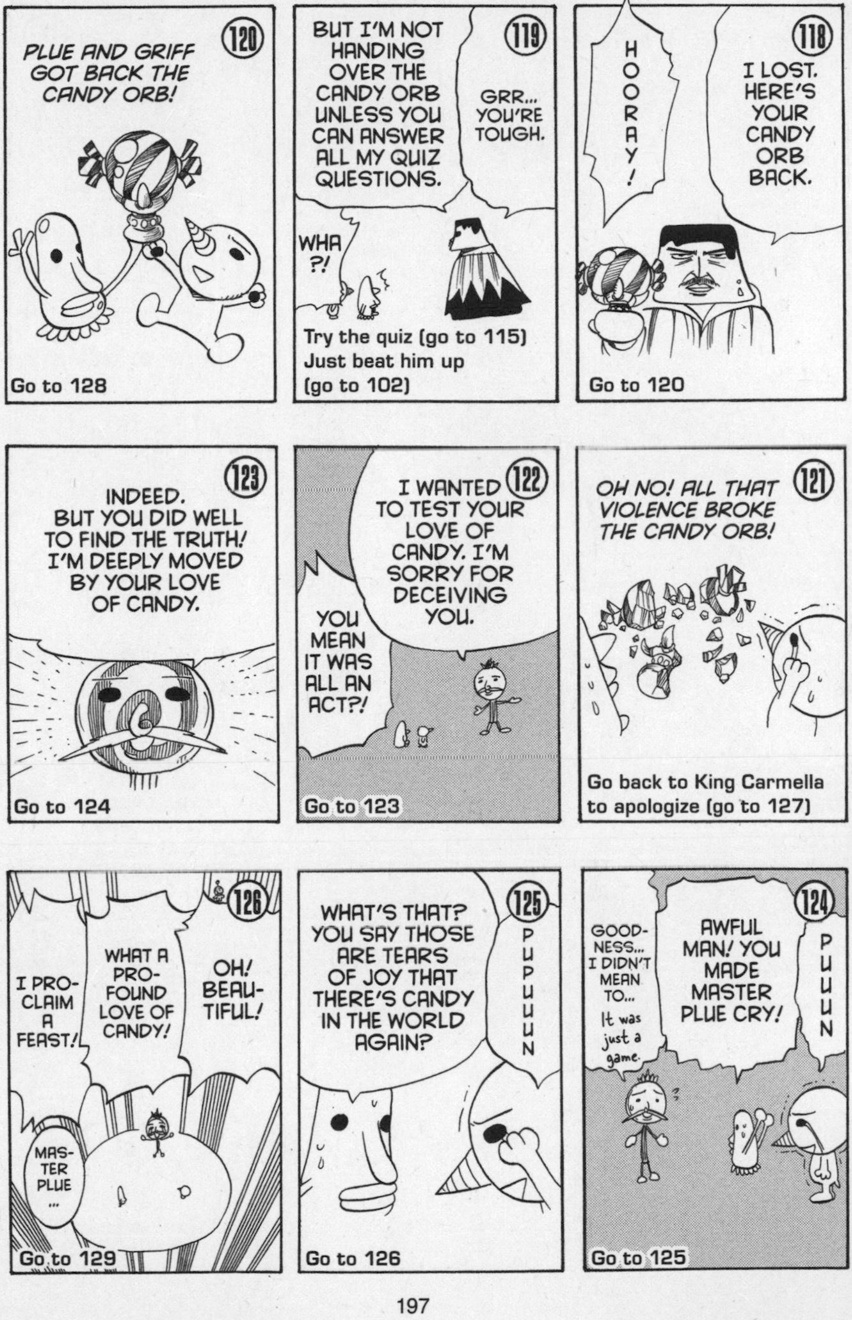
118
I LOST. HERE'S YOUR CANDY ORB BACK.
HOORAY!
Go to 120
119
GRR... YOU'RE TOUGH.
BUT I'M NOT HANDING OVER THE CANDY ORB UNLESS YOU CAN ANSWER ALL MY QUIZ QUESTIONS.
WHA?!
Try the quiz (go to 115)
Just beat him up (go to 102)
120
PLUE AND GRIFF GOT BACK THE CANDY ORB!
Go to 128
121
OH NO! ALL THAT VIOLENCE BROKE THE CANDY ORB!
Go back to King Carmella to apologize (go to 127)
122
I WANTED TO TEST YOUR LOVE OF CANDY. I'M SORRY FOR DECEIVING YOU.
YOU MEAN IT WAS ALL AN ACT?!
Go to 123
123
INDEED. BUT YOU DID WELL TO FIND THE TRUTH! I'M DEEPLY MOVED BY YOUR LOVE OF CANDY.
Go to 124
124
PUUUN
AWFUL MAN! YOU MADE MASTER PLUE CRY!
GOODNESS... I DIDN'T MEAN TO...
It was just a game.
Go to 125
125
PUPUUUN
WHAT'S THAT? YOU SAY THOSE ARE TEARS OF JOY THAT THERE'S CANDY IN THE WORLD AGAIN?
Go to 126
126
OH! BEAUTIFUL!
WHAT A PROFOUND LOVE OF CANDY!
I PROCLAIM A FEAST!
MASTER PLUE...
Go to 129

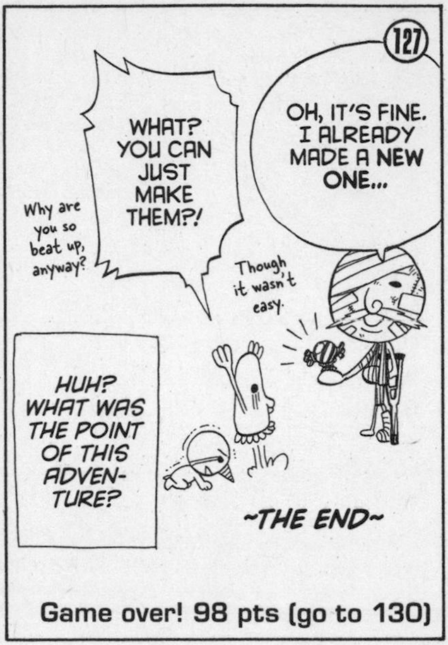
127
OH, IT'S FINE. I ALREADY MADE A NEW ONE...
WHAT? YOU CAN JUST MAKE THEM?!
Why are you so beat up, anyway?
Though it wasn't easy.
HUH? WHAT WAS THE POINT OF THIS ADVENTURE?
~THE END~
Game over! 98 pts (go to 130)

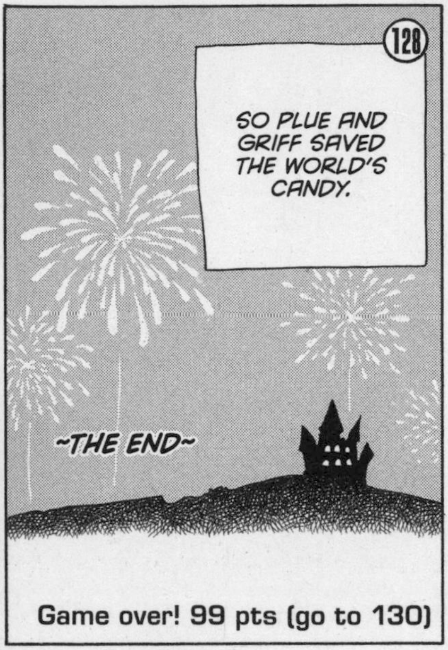
128
SO PLUE AND GRIFF SAVED THE WORLD'S CANDY.
~THE END~
Game over! 99 pts (go to 130)

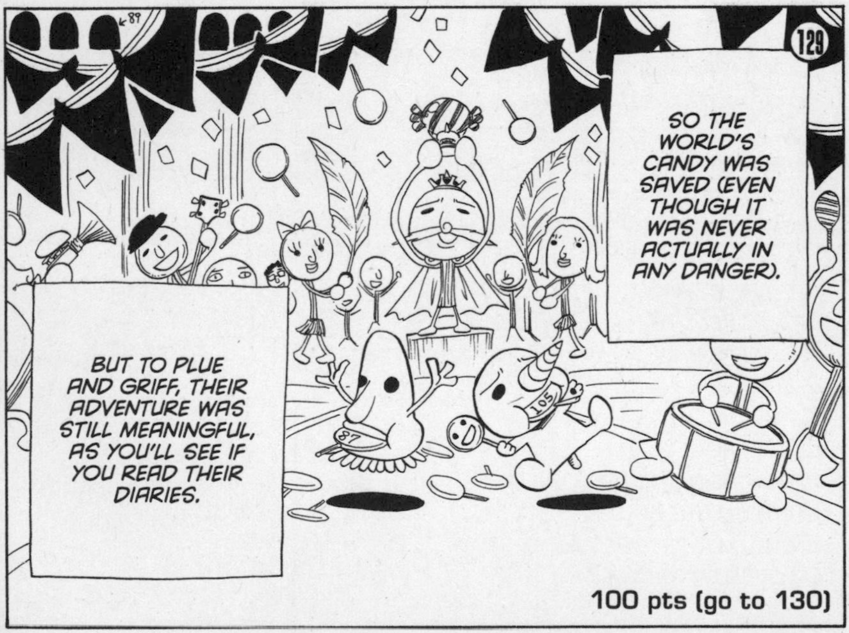
129
SO THE WORLD'S CANDY WAS SAVED (EVEN THOUGH IT WAS NEVER ACTUALLY IN ANY DANGER).
BUT TO PLUE AND GRIFF, THEIR ADVENTURE WAS STILL MEANINGFUL, AS YOU'LL SEE IF YOU READ THEIR DIARIES.
100 pts (go to 130)

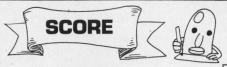

SCORE

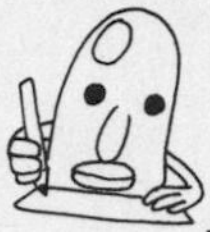

		TITLE
0 PTS	☐	WARP PLUE
10 PTS	☐	NAP PLUE
20 PTS	☐	KILLER PLUE
30 PTS	☐	SMOOSHED PLUE
40 PTS	☐	LI'L LOST PLUE
50 PTS	☐	HOME RUN PLUE
60 PTS	☐	SHROOM PLUE
70 PTS	☐	FALLEN PLUE
80 PTS	☐	SAYONARA PLUE
90 PTS	☐	FUTURE PLUE
91-97 PTS	☐	QUIZ PLUE
98 PTS	☐	POINTLESS PLUE
99 PTS	☐	HAPPY PLUE
100 PTS	☐	MASTER PLUE

Hint on getting 100 points

Remember King Carmella's hint! "The answer within the answers." Could the pudding quiz hold some hidden meaning?

BONUS HINT

Sometimes in this game you can move even without specific instructions. Do you see a hole? Any numbers by it?

ACHIEVEMENT CHECKLIST

- ☐ GOT 98 POINTS
- ☐ GOT 99 POINTS
- ☐ GOT 100 POINTS
- ☐ FOUND THE CAT CLEAVER
- ☐ FOUND NUMBER MAN 55
- ☐ MET THE BURLY BLOOM
- ☐ MET MEOW HART
- ☐ GOT THE HARU DOLL
- ☐ GOT THE ELLIE DOLL
- ☐ GOT THE MUSICA DOLL
- ☐ GOT THE LET DOLL
- ☐ GOT THE SIEG DOLL
- ☐ GOT THE RUBY DOLL
- ☐ GOT THE NAKAJIMA DOLL
- ☐ GOT ALL THE DOLLS!
- ☐ GOT ALL THE POINTS BESIDES 0!
- ☐ FOUND EDITOR MR. M-KI

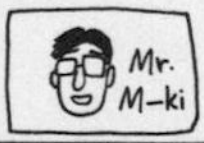
Mr.
M-ki

- ☐ FOUND NUMBER MAN 1
- ☐ FOUND NUMBER MAN 2
- ☐ FOUND NUMBER MAN 3
- ☐ FOUND NUMBER MAN 4
- ☐ FOUND NUMBER MAN 5
- ☐ FOUND NUMBER MAN 6
- ☐ FOUND NUMBER MAN 7
- ☐ FOUND NUMBER MAN 8
- ☐ FOUND NUMBER MAN 9
- ☐ FOUND NUMBER MAN 10

- ☐ READ PLUE'S DIARY
- ☐ READ GRIFF'S DIARY
- ☐ READ MASHIMA'S DIARY
- ☐ NOTICED NOT EVERY PANEL IS ACTUALLY USED
- ☐ FOUND THREE DUDES
- ☐ FOUND FIVE DUDES
- ☐ FOUND TEN DUDES

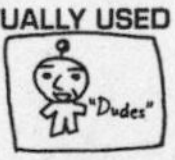
"Dudes"

FIRST PUBLISHED: *WEEKLY SHONEN MAGAZINE* NO. 6 (2002)

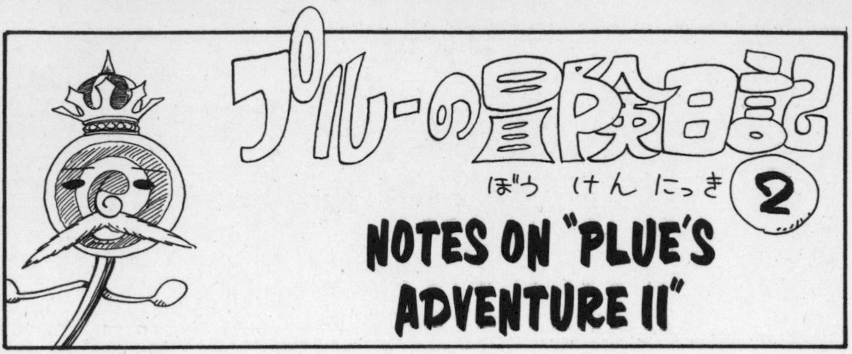

プルーの冒険日記 ②

ぼうけんにっき

NOTES ON "PLUE'S ADVENTURE II"

"II"? I know what you're thinking: "What?! Is there a I?!" As it happens, "Plue's Adventure I" appeared in volume 16 of *Rave Master*. It was surprisingly well-received, so I made another! That's pretty much the story. Honestly, you could probably skip it (haha). For that matter, if you don't know the story of *Rave Master*, I'm not sure how much you're going to care about this piece. I'm just mentioning that because, you know, this is a Hiro Mashima short story collection, and I'd like to think the people buying it are apt to be fans of mine, but hey, maybe someone's never read *Rave Master*, but they're like, "Eh, I'll give this a try," and then suddenly, bam...II.

So consider this a *Rave Master* extra. It might have been best included in a Rave Master collection someplace, but things just didn't work out that way and it wound up here instead.

It's less a short story than a sort of bonus piece. A *Hiro Mashima's Playground* bonus! You can just kind of flip through it when you have a few minutes to kill. By the way, it's not easy to check off all the achievements. It's not a job for the faint of heart!

PARK MANAGER'S AFTERWORD

"How was it? I'm Hiro Mizuno...I mean, Mashima!" **Hah!** I'll bet you kids today don't even get that joke. Eh, just forget it then (LOL). Hello, and, where appropriate, nice to meet you. Thanks so much for reading all the way to the end. What did you think? Phew! Releasing a short story collection gave me a chance to look back at some older work, and...it's embarrassing (grin). Worst one of this bunch? "Magician," no doubt. It **SUCKS!! (LOL)**

Look, I don't exactly consider myself a top-flight artist even now, but back when I did that story? Ugh. How did it ever win a prize? Good luck, maybe.

It is interesting, though, to be able to see how my art has evolved, as represented by the stories in this book. Plue in "Magician" and Plue in "Plue's Adventure II" are practically different people (dogs??)! Okay, eyes, back to a normal size now. Anyway, even if the art stinks and the stories are pathetic, I put all the ability I had at the time into each piece; every story is the result of my blood and sweat and tears and snot. If you enjoyed them, great; if they made you laugh, wonderful; and if they served as a cautionary tale to deter you from becoming a manga artist, so much the better. If you remember even one panel, even one line, and carry it with you, I'll be happy. See you in part 2!

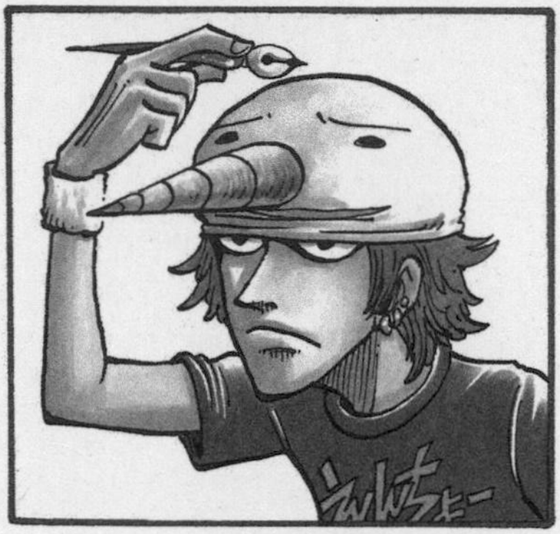
えんちょー

*SHIRT: MANAGER

Thank you all so much for visiting *Hiro Mashima's Playground!* I'm the park manager, Hiro Mashima. Some readers may be asking what "Hiro Mashima's Playground" even means... But they'll have to wait till part 2 for the answer! Both parts are coming out at once anyway, so just go ahead and read it all. In one fell swoop! So, these works of mine are all quite old, but please check them out!

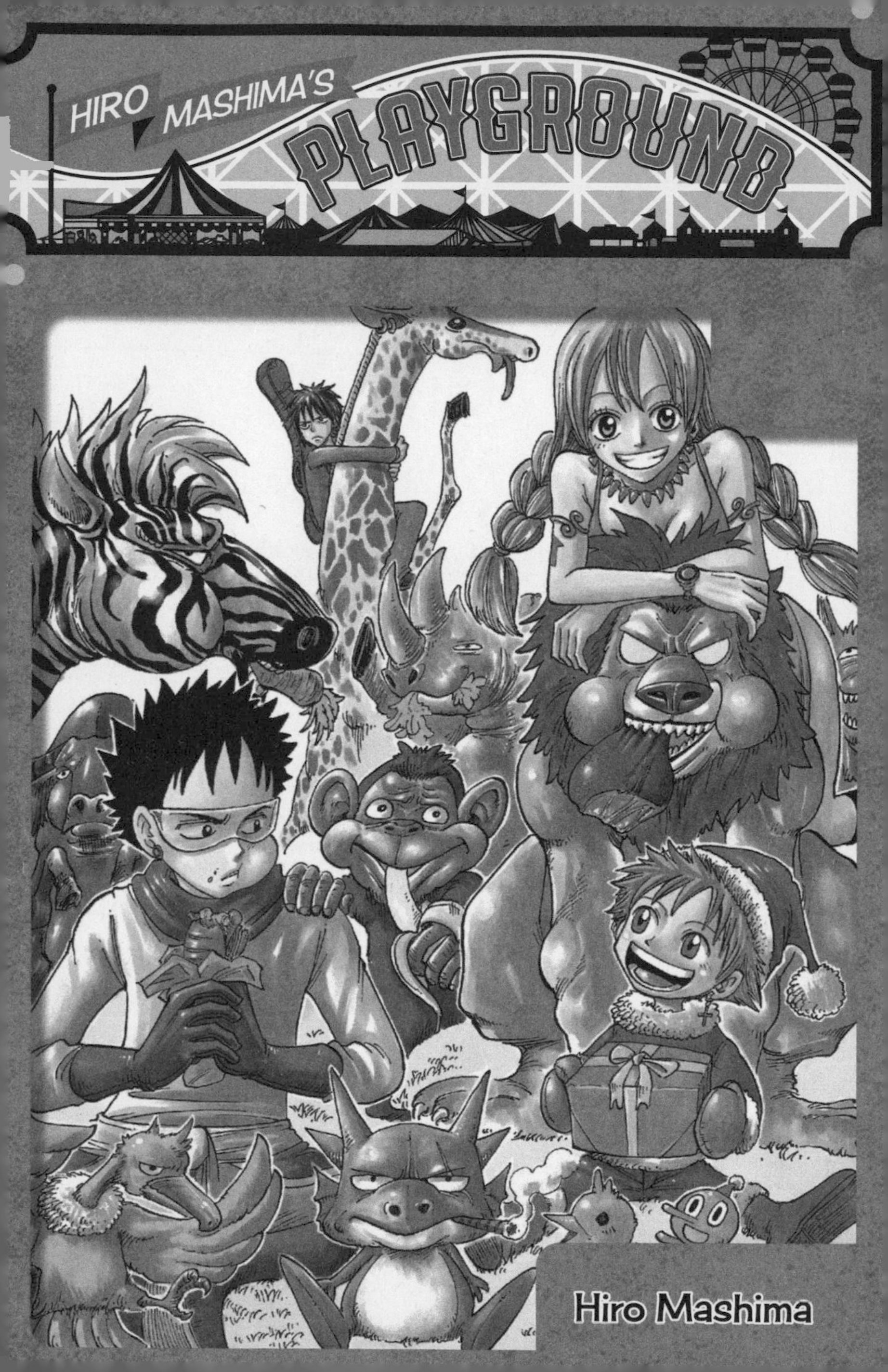
HIRO MASHIMA'S
PLAYGROUND
Hiro Mashima

Short Stories by Hiro Mashima

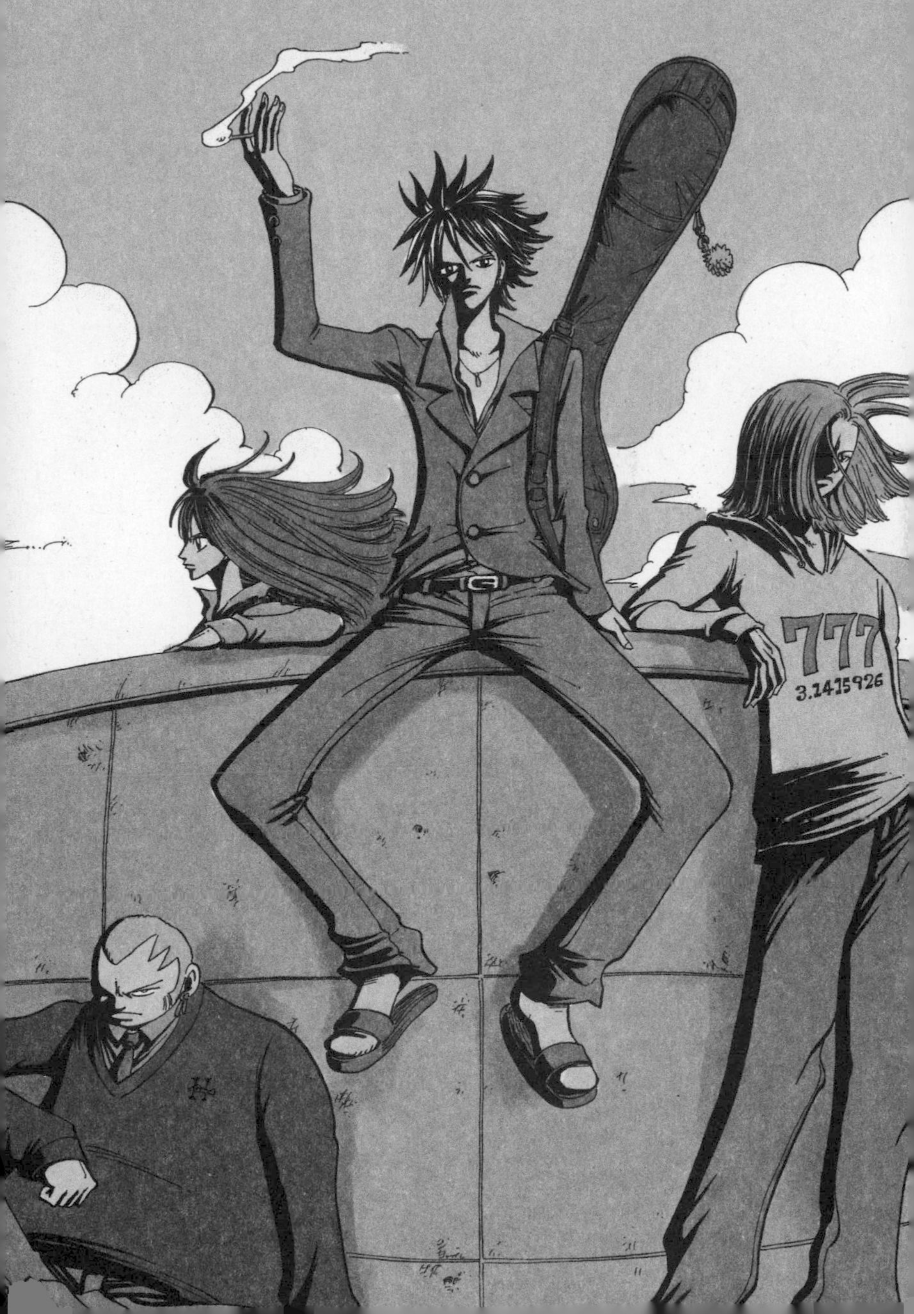
777
3.1415926

HIRO MASHIMA'S PLAYGROUND PART 2

HAVE A LOOK AT THESE CONTENTS, EH?

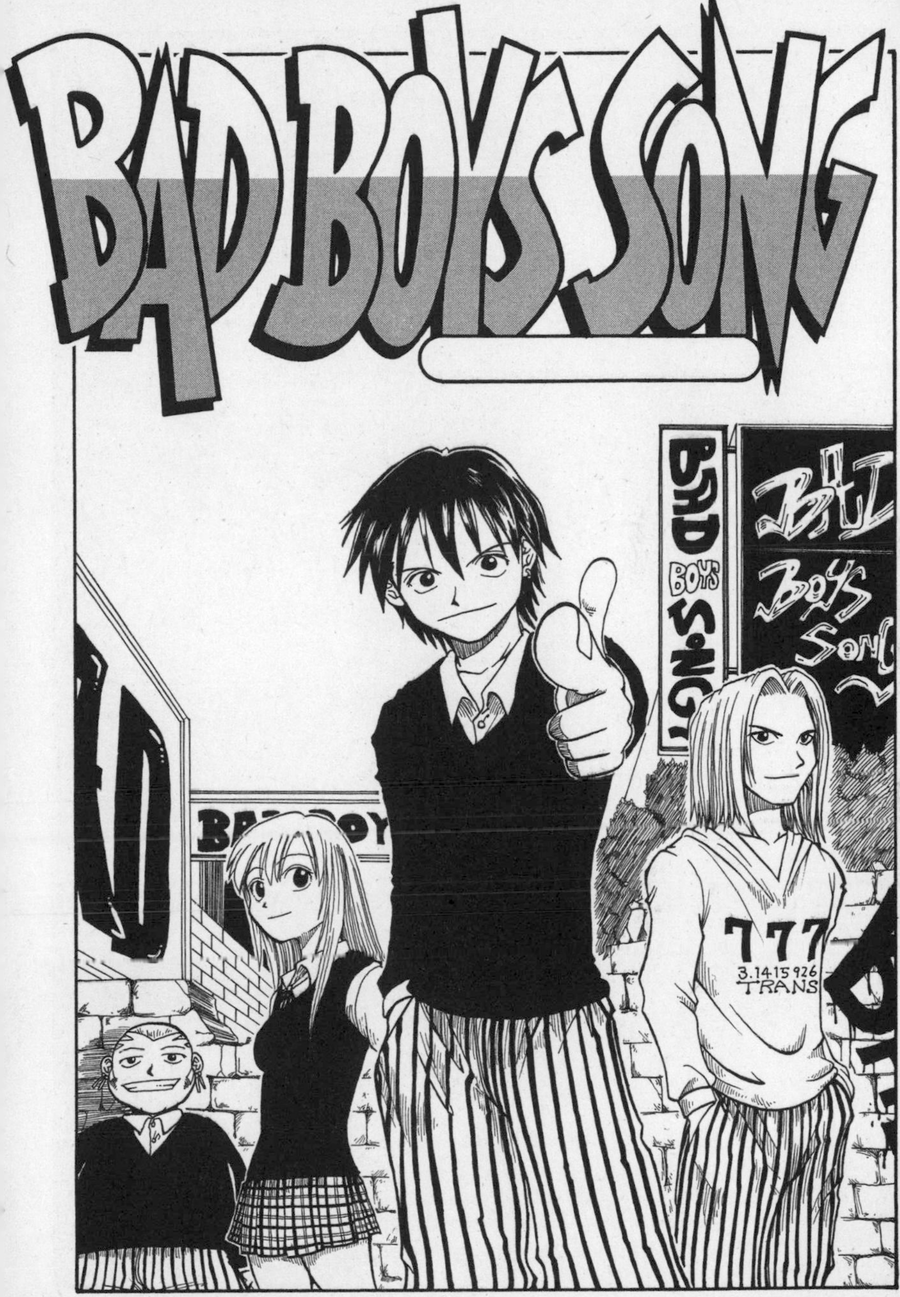
BAD BOYS SONG
BAD BOYS SONG
777
3.1415926
TRANS

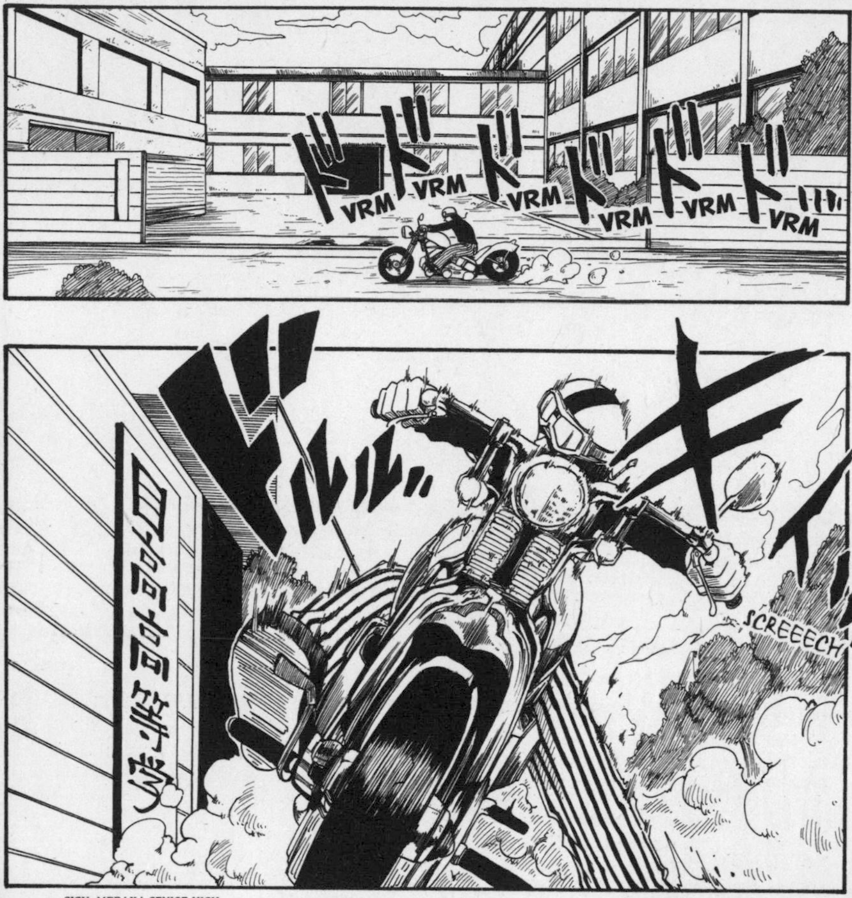
VRM
VRM
VRM
VRM
VRM
VRM
SCREEEECH

SIGN: MEDAKA SENIOR HIGH

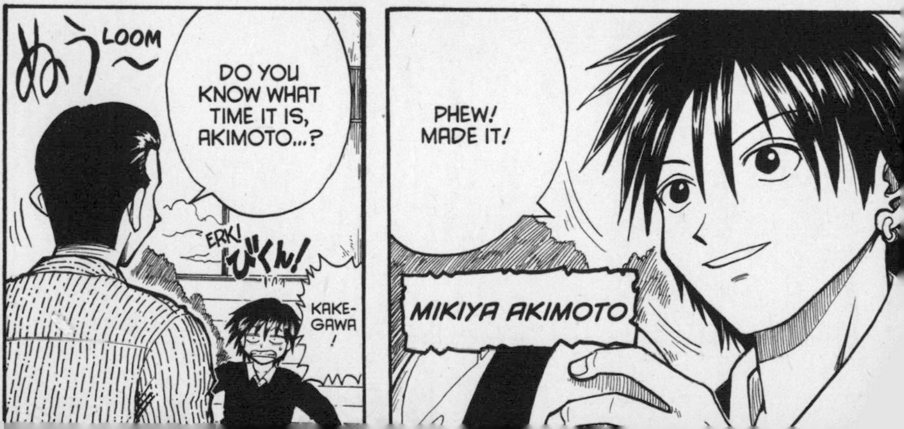
PHEW! MADE IT!
MIKIYA AKIMOTO
ぬう LOOM
DO YOU KNOW WHAT TIME IT IS, AKIMOTO...?
ERK! びくん!
KAKE-GAWA!

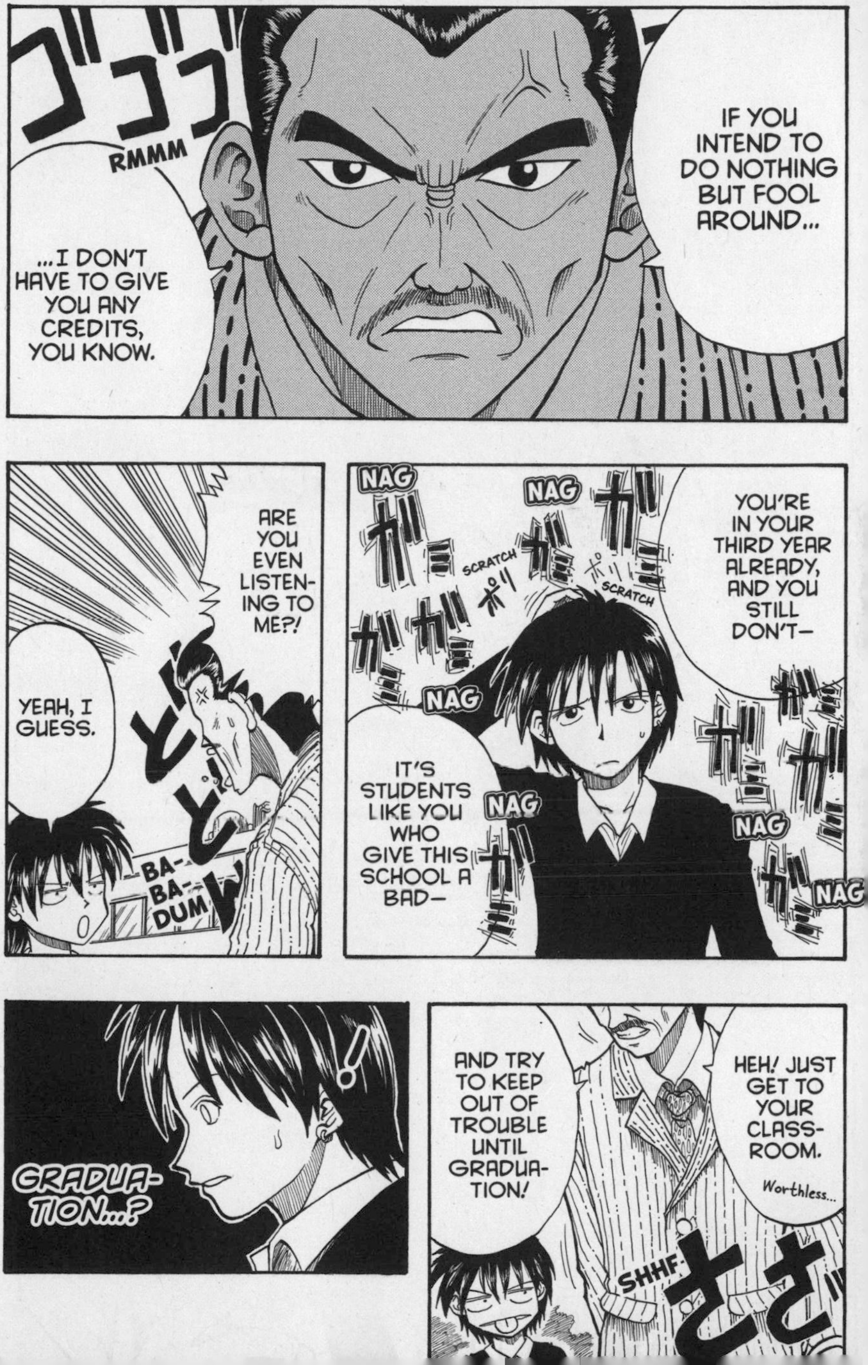
IF YOU INTEND TO DO NOTHING BUT FOOL AROUND...
ゴゴゴ
RMMM
...I DON'T HAVE TO GIVE YOU ANY CREDITS, YOU KNOW.
NAG
NAG
YOU'RE IN YOUR THIRD YEAR ALREADY, AND YOU STILL DON'T—
SCRATCH
ポリ
SCRATCH
NAG
IT'S STUDENTS LIKE YOU WHO GIVE THIS SCHOOL A BAD—
NAG
NAG
NAG
ARE YOU EVEN LISTENING TO ME?!
YEAH, I GUESS.
BA-BA-DUM
HEH! JUST GET TO YOUR CLASSROOM.
Worthless...
AND TRY TO KEEP OUT OF TROUBLE UNTIL GRADUATION!
SHHF
GRADUATION...?

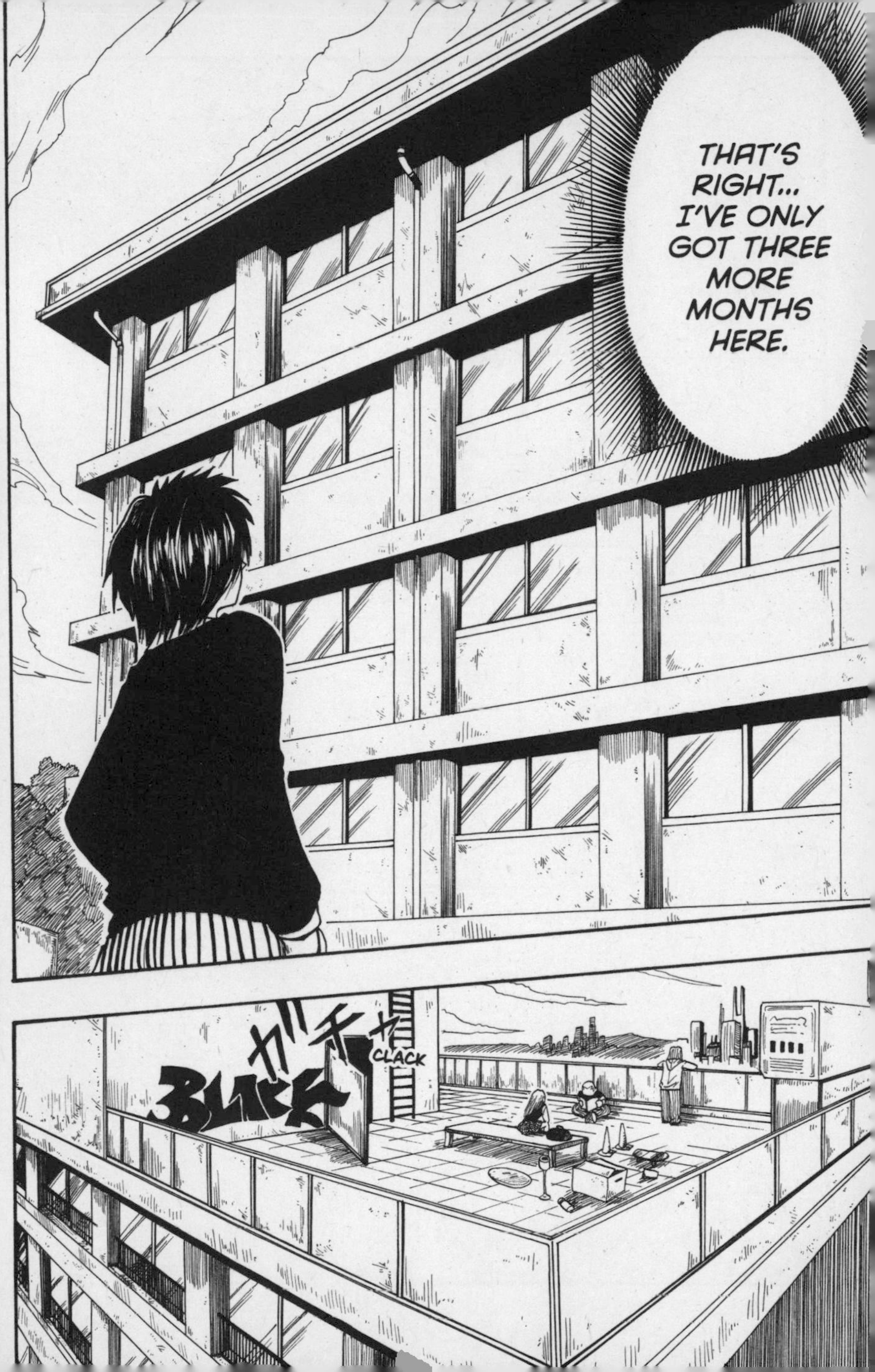
THAT'S RIGHT... I'VE ONLY GOT THREE MORE MONTHS HERE.
カチャ
CLACK

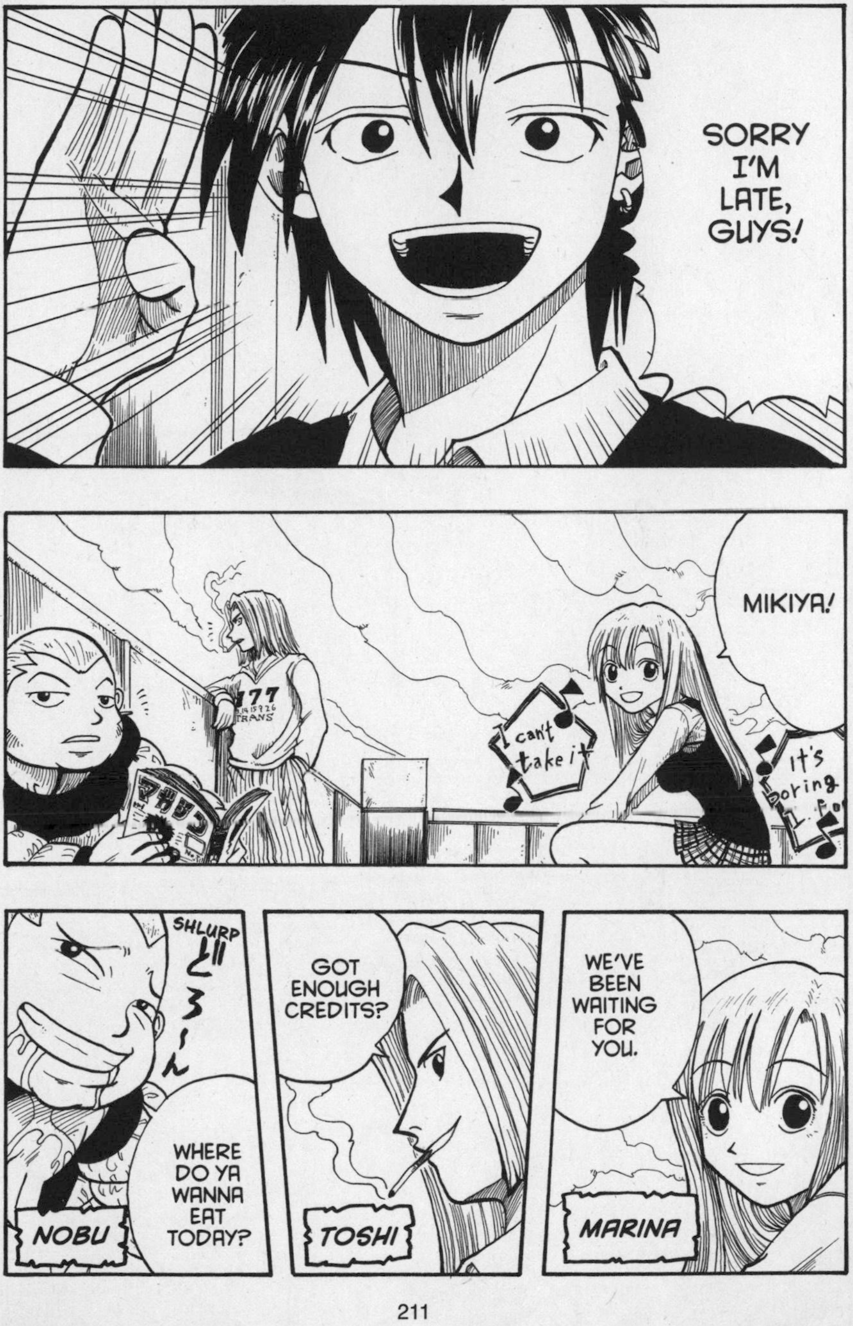
SORRY I'M LATE, GUYS!
MIKIYA!
I can't take it
WE'VE BEEN WAITING FOR YOU.
MARINA
GOT ENOUGH CREDITS?
TOSHI
SHLURP
どろ～ん
WHERE DO YA WANNA EAT TODAY?
NOBU

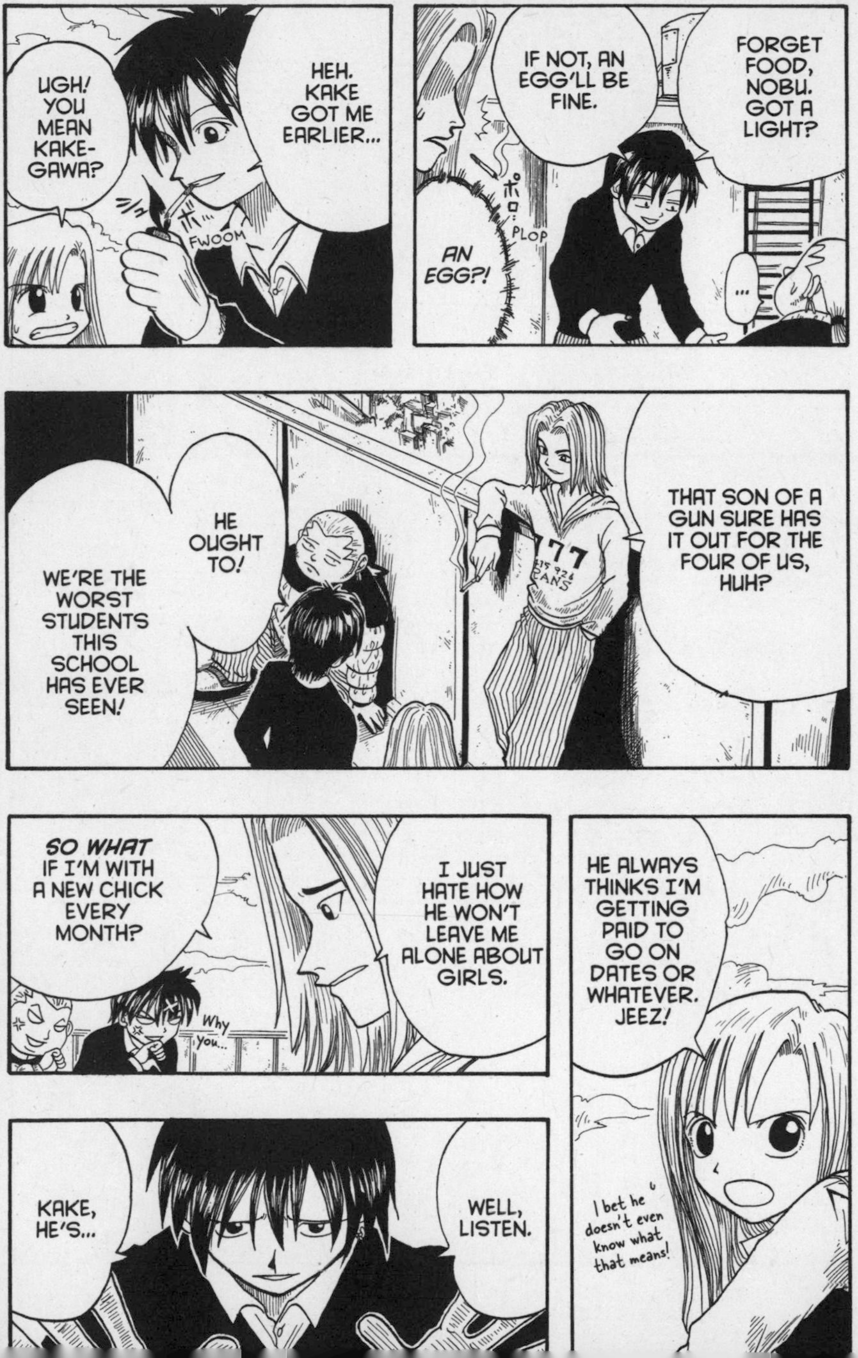
FORGET FOOD, NOBU. GOT A LIGHT?
IF NOT, AN EGG'LL BE FINE.
...
ポロ PLOP
AN EGG?!
HEH. KAKE GOT ME EARLIER...
UGH! YOU MEAN KAKE-GAWA?
ボ FWOOM
THAT SON OF A GUN SURE HAS IT OUT FOR THE FOUR OF US, HUH?
HE OUGHT TO!
WE'RE THE WORST STUDENTS THIS SCHOOL HAS EVER SEEN!
HE ALWAYS THINKS I'M GETTING PAID TO GO ON DATES OR WHATEVER. JEEZ!
I bet he doesn't even know what that means!
I JUST HATE HOW HE WON'T LEAVE ME ALONE ABOUT GIRLS.
SO WHAT IF I'M WITH A NEW CHICK EVERY MONTH?
Why you...
WELL, LISTEN.
KAKE, HE'S...

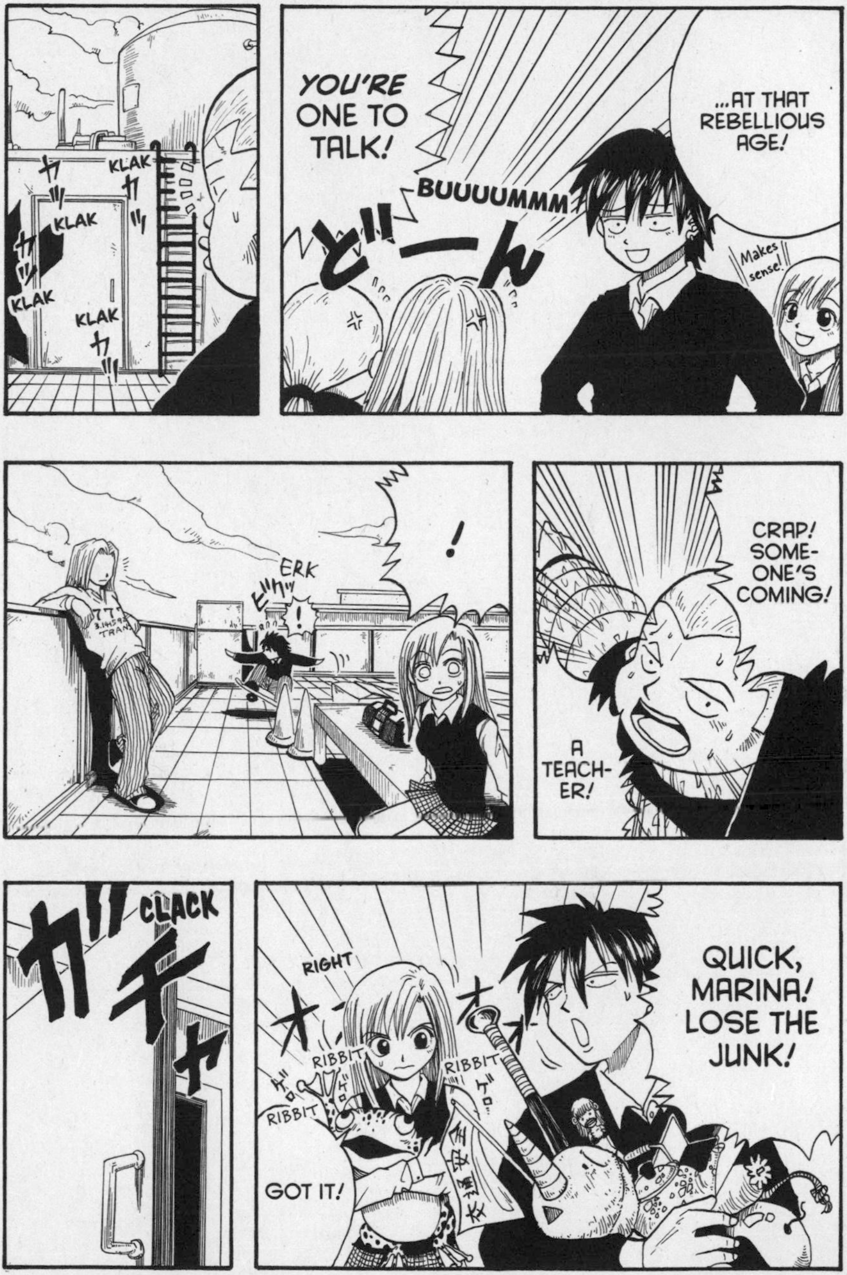
...AT THAT REBELLIOUS AGE!
Makes sense!
YOU'RE ONE TO TALK!
BUUUUMMM
KLAK
KLAK
KLAK
KLAK
CRAP! SOME-ONE'S COMING!
A TEACH-ER!
!
ERK
!
QUICK, MARINA! LOSE THE JUNK!
RIGHT
RIBBIT
RIBBIT
RIBBIT
GOT IT!
CLACK

FLAG: DRIVE SAFE

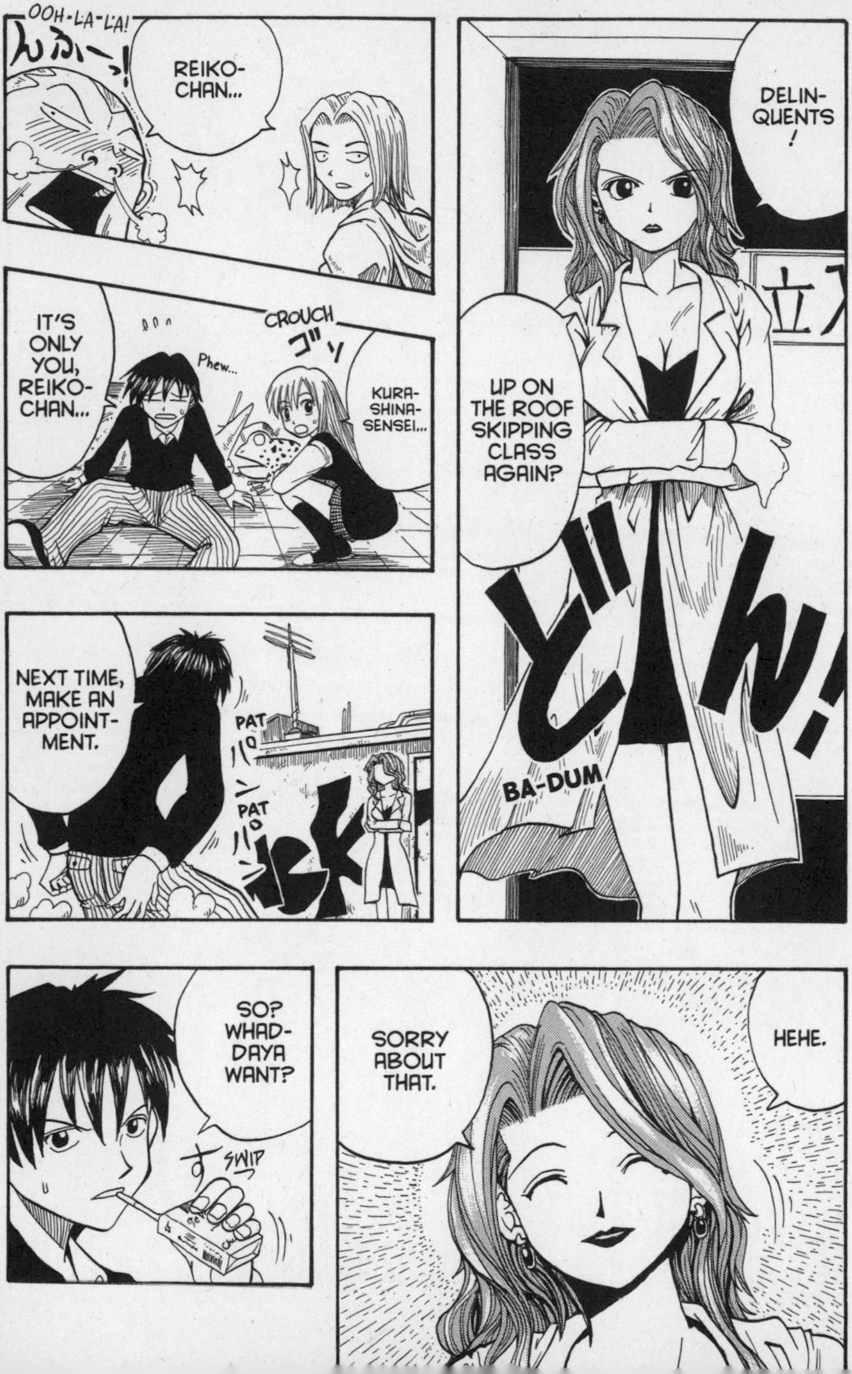
DELIN-QUENTS!
UP ON THE ROOF SKIPPING CLASS AGAIN?
どん!!
BA-DUM
REIKO-CHAN...
OOH-LA-LA!
んふー!
CROUCH
ゴッ
KURA-SHINA-SENSEI...
Phew...
IT'S ONLY YOU, REIKO-CHAN...
PAT
パ
PAT
パ
NEXT TIME, MAKE AN APPOINT-MENT.
HEHE.
SORRY ABOUT THAT.
SO? WHAD-DAYA WANT?
SWIP
す

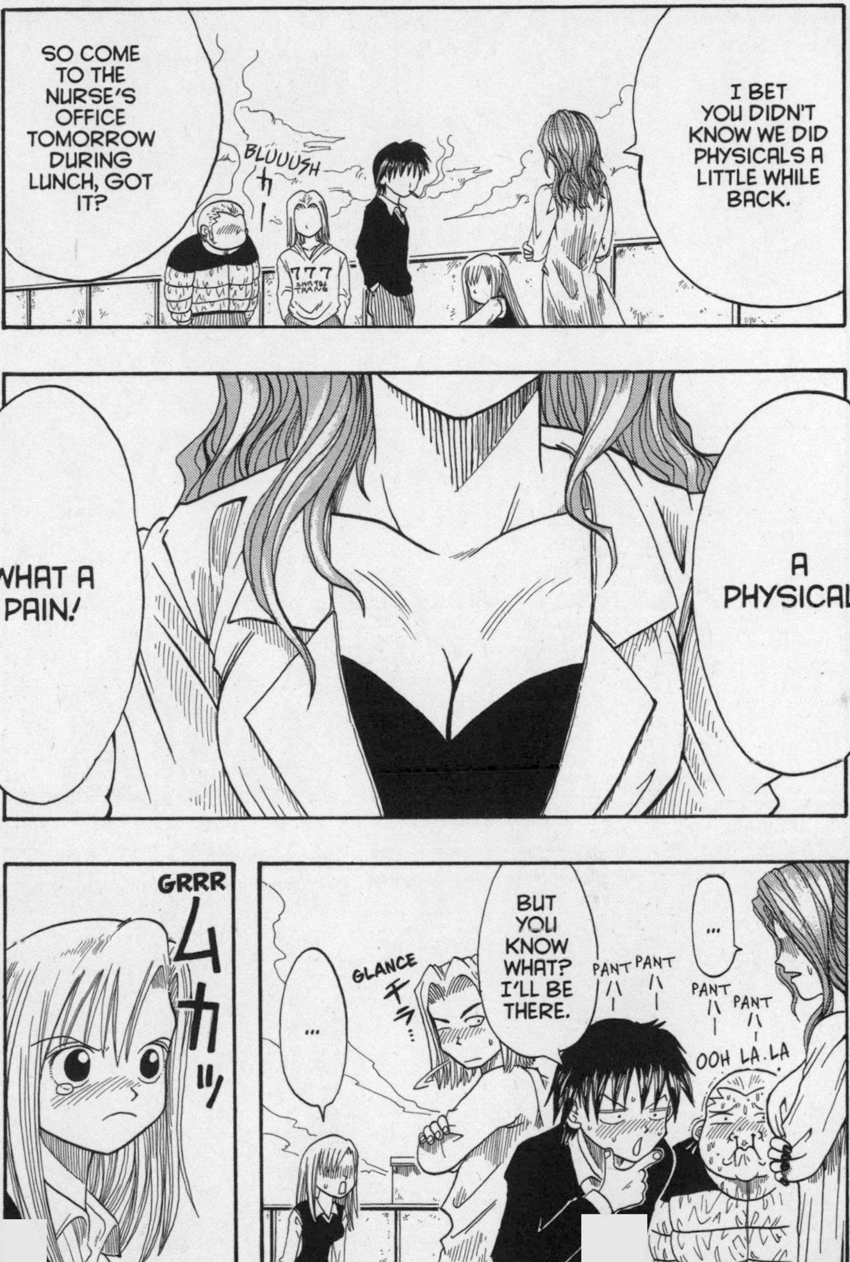
I BET YOU DIDN'T KNOW WE DID PHYSICALS A LITTLE WHILE BACK.
BLUUUSH
カ
SO COME TO THE NURSE'S OFFICE TOMORROW DURING LUNCH, GOT IT?
A PHYSICAL?
WHAT A PAIN!
...
PANT PANT
PANT PANT
OOH LA LA
BUT YOU KNOW WHAT? I'LL BE THERE.
GLANCE
チラ...
...
GRRR
ムカッ

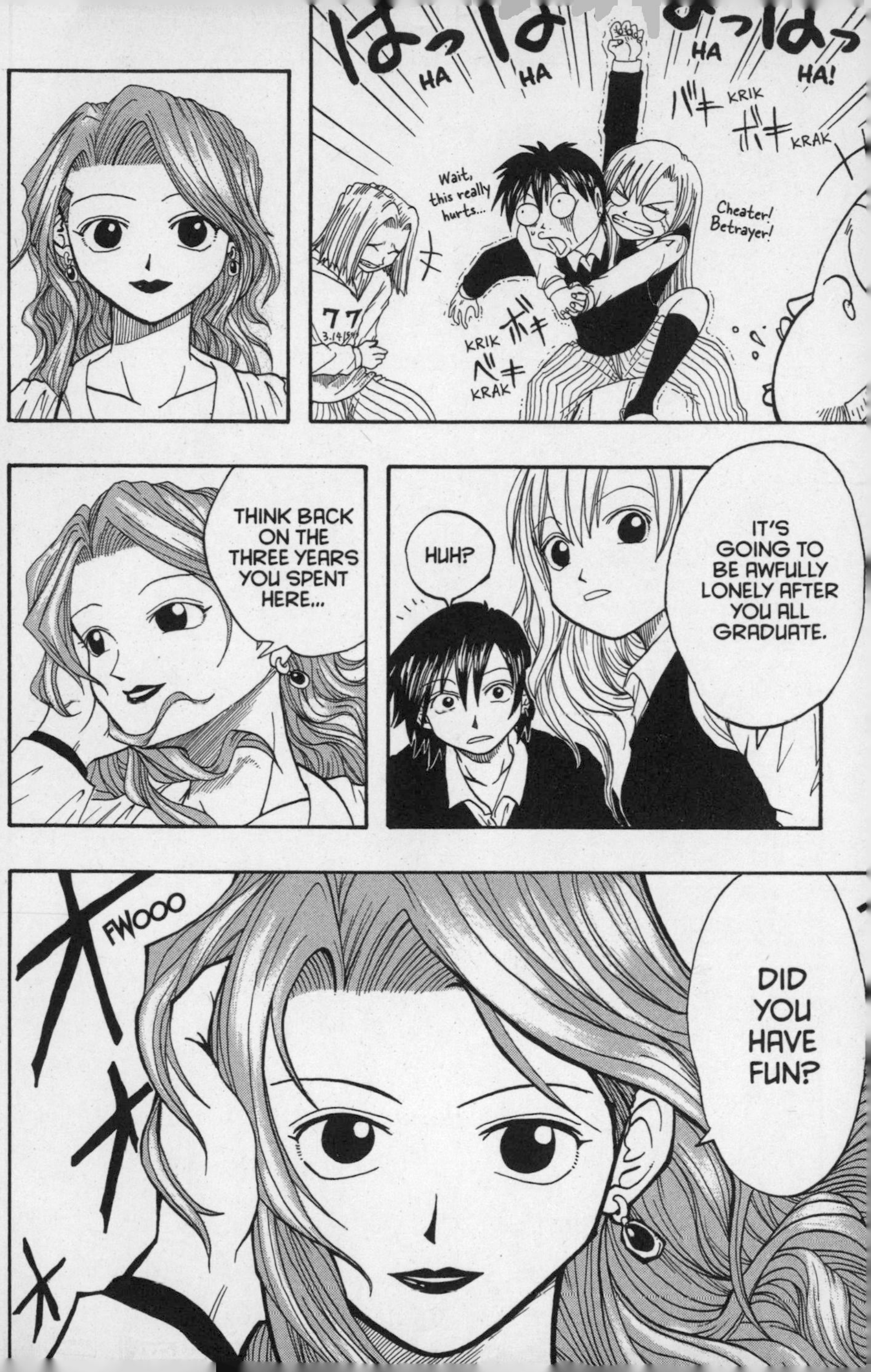
HA!
HA
HA
HA
バキ KRIK
ボキ KRAK
Cheater! Betrayer!
Wait, this really hurts...
ボキ KRIK
ベキ KRAK
IT'S GOING TO BE AWFULLY LONELY AFTER YOU ALL GRADUATE.
HUH?
THINK BACK ON THE THREE YEARS YOU SPENT HERE...
DID YOU HAVE FUN?
FWOOO

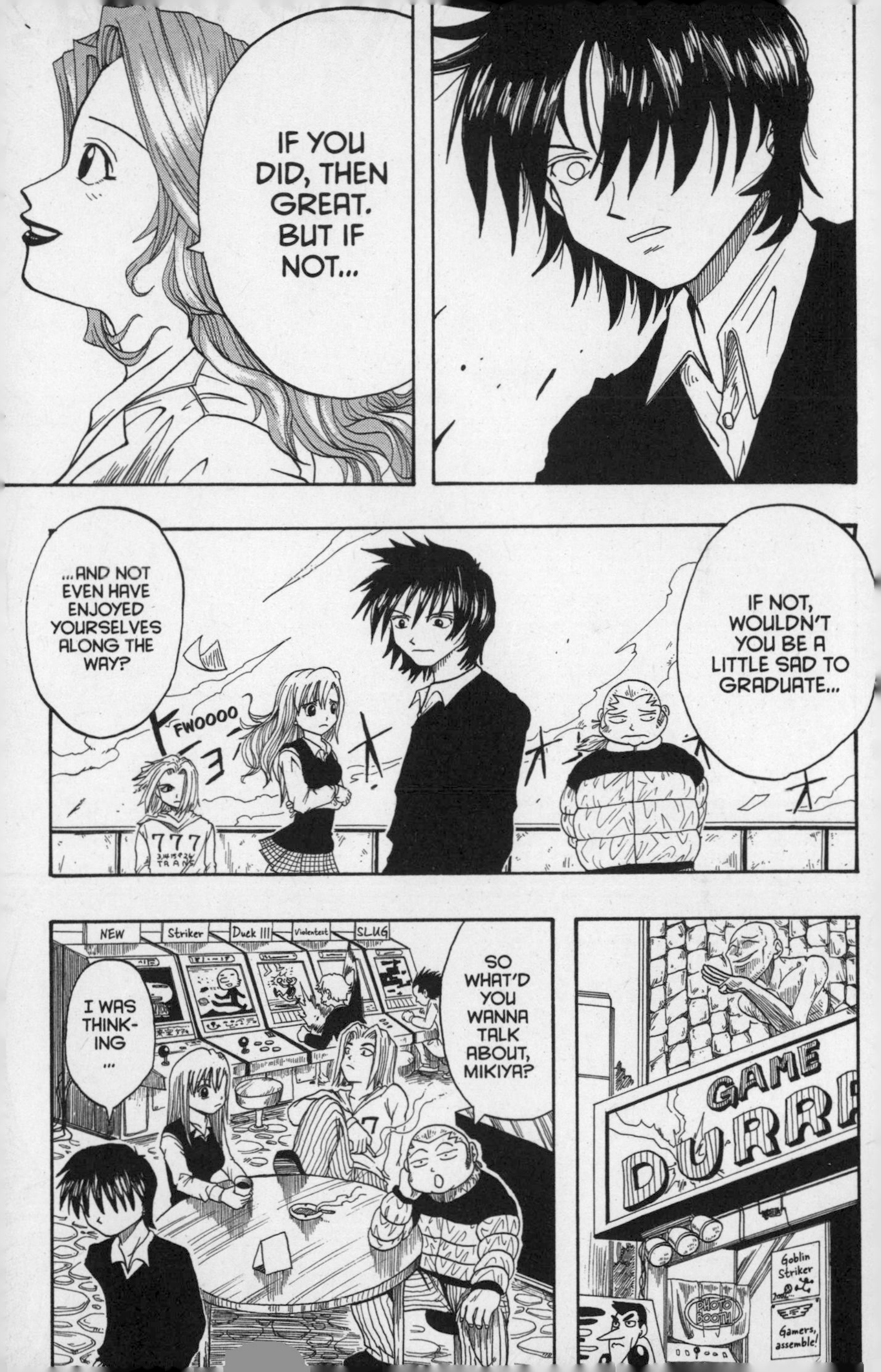
IF YOU DID, THEN GREAT. BUT IF NOT...
IF NOT, WOULDN'T YOU BE A LITTLE SAD TO GRADUATE...
...AND NOT EVEN HAVE ENJOYED YOURSELVES ALONG THE WAY?
FWOOOO
GAME DURRR
Goblin Striker
PHOTO BOOTH
Gamers, assemble!
NEW
Striker
Duck III
Violentest
SLUG
SO WHAT'D YOU WANNA TALK ABOUT, MIKIYA?
I WAS THINK-ING...

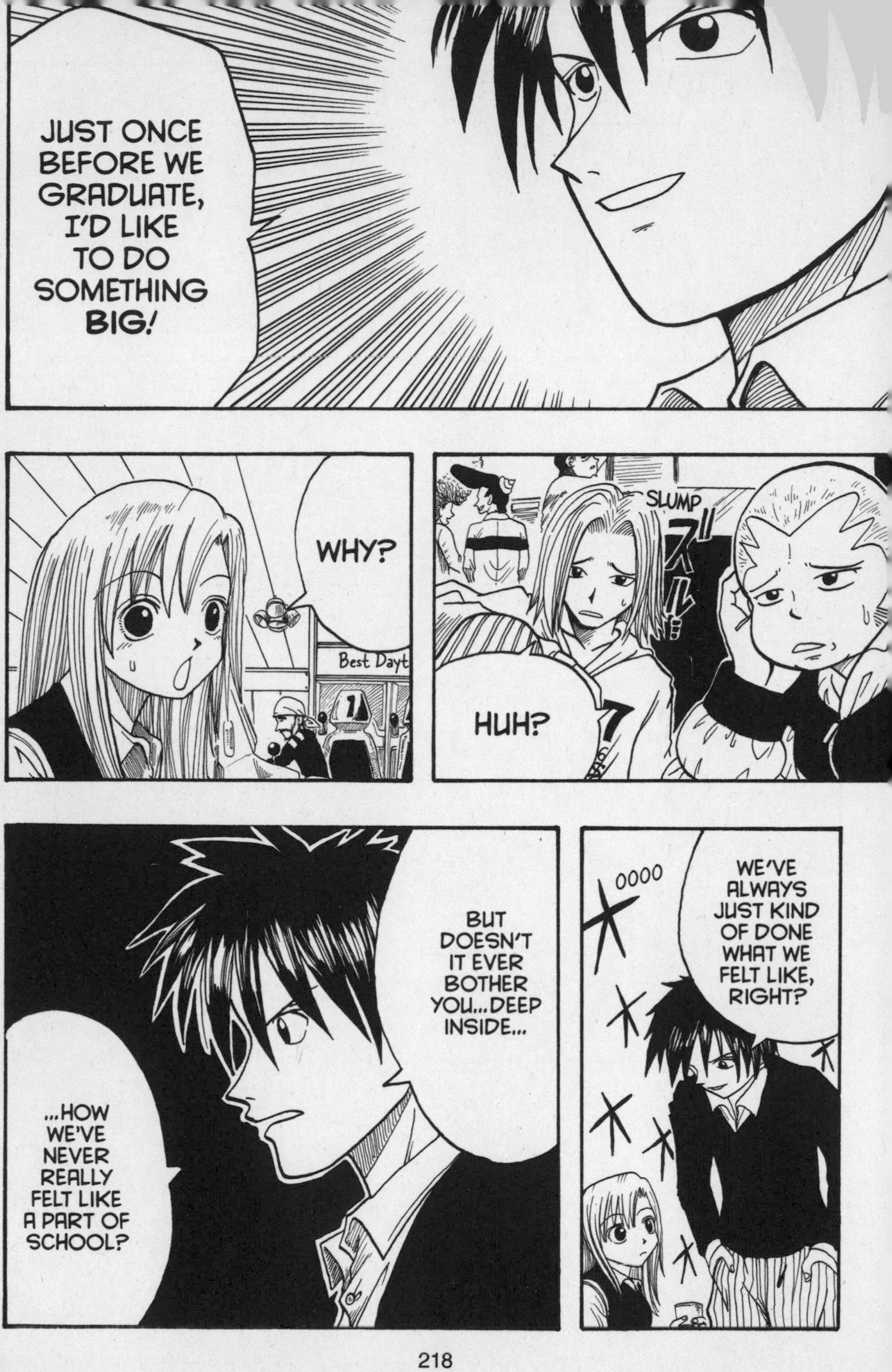
JUST ONCE BEFORE WE GRADUATE, I'D LIKE TO DO SOMETHING **BIG!**
SLUMP
HUH?
WHY?
OOOO
WE'VE ALWAYS JUST KIND OF DONE WHAT WE FELT LIKE, RIGHT?
BUT DOESN'T IT EVER BOTHER YOU...DEEP INSIDE...
...HOW WE'VE NEVER REALLY FELT LIKE A PART OF SCHOOL?

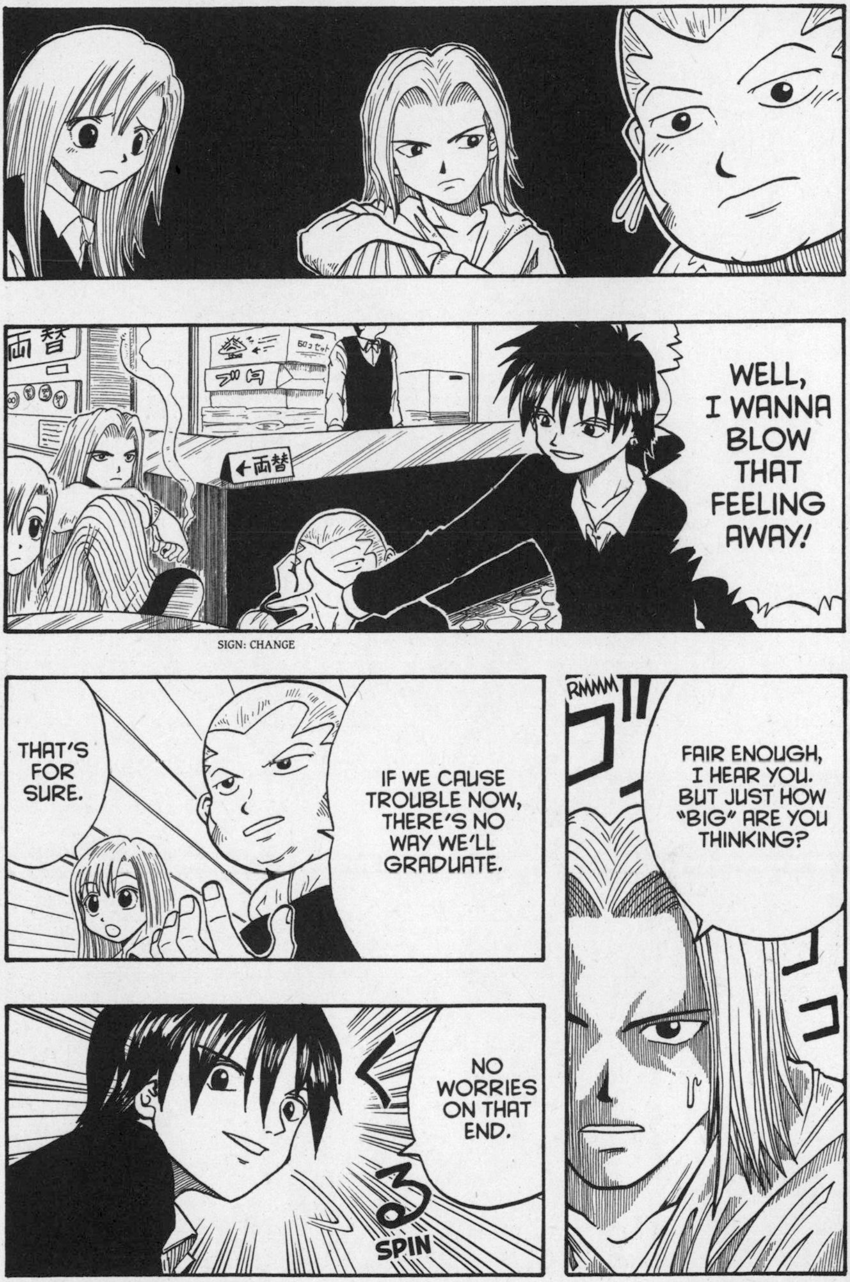
両替
← 両替
WELL, I WANNA BLOW THAT FEELING AWAY!
RMMM
FAIR ENOUGH, I HEAR YOU. BUT JUST HOW "BIG" ARE YOU THINKING?
IF WE CAUSE TROUBLE NOW, THERE'S NO WAY WE'LL GRADUATE.
THAT'S FOR SURE.
NO WORRIES ON THAT END.
SPIN
SIGN: CHANGE

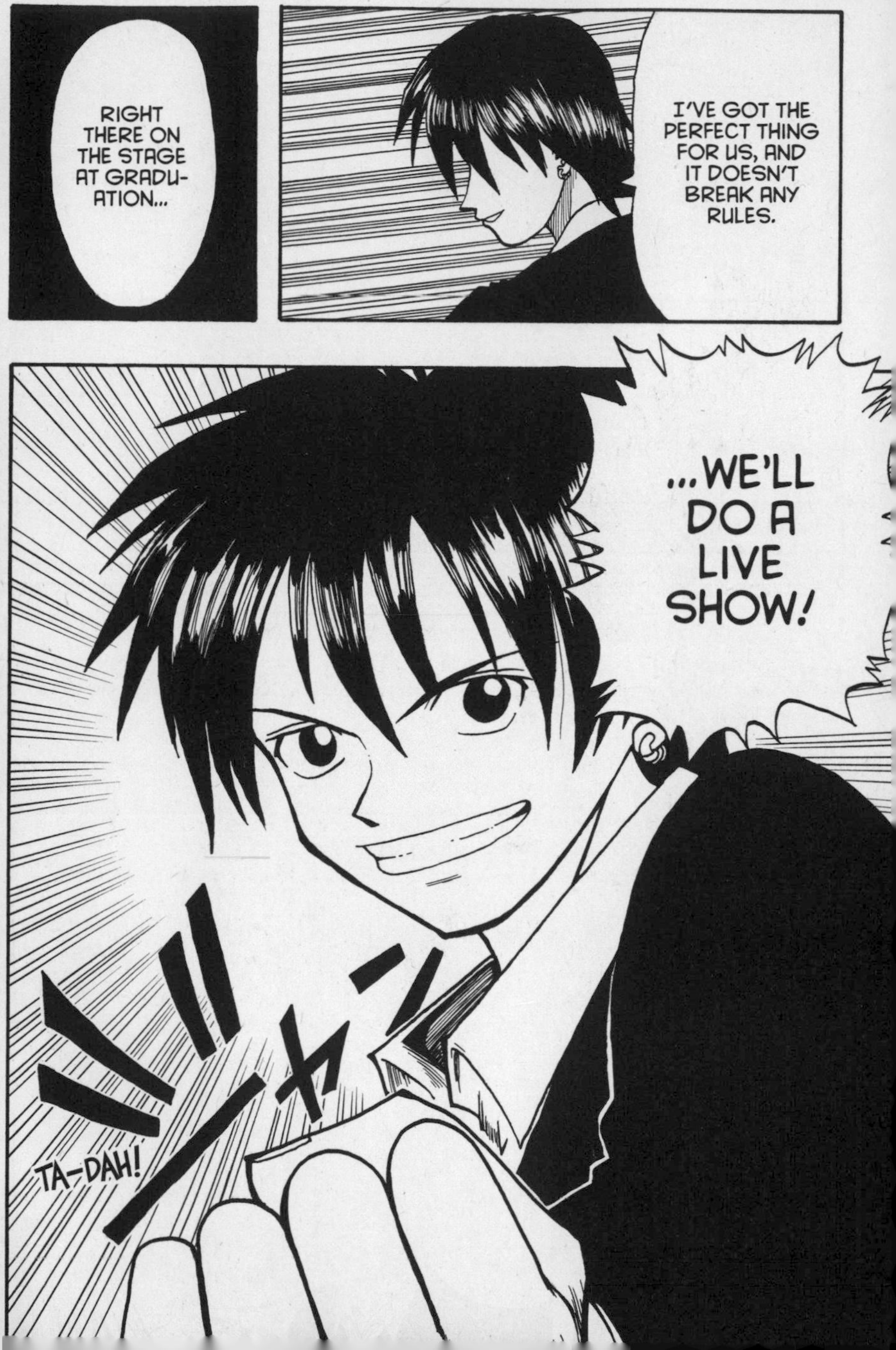
I'VE GOT THE PERFECT THING FOR US, AND IT DOESN'T BREAK ANY RULES.
RIGHT THERE ON THE STAGE AT GRADU-ATION...
...WE'LL DO A LIVE SHOW!
TA-DAH!

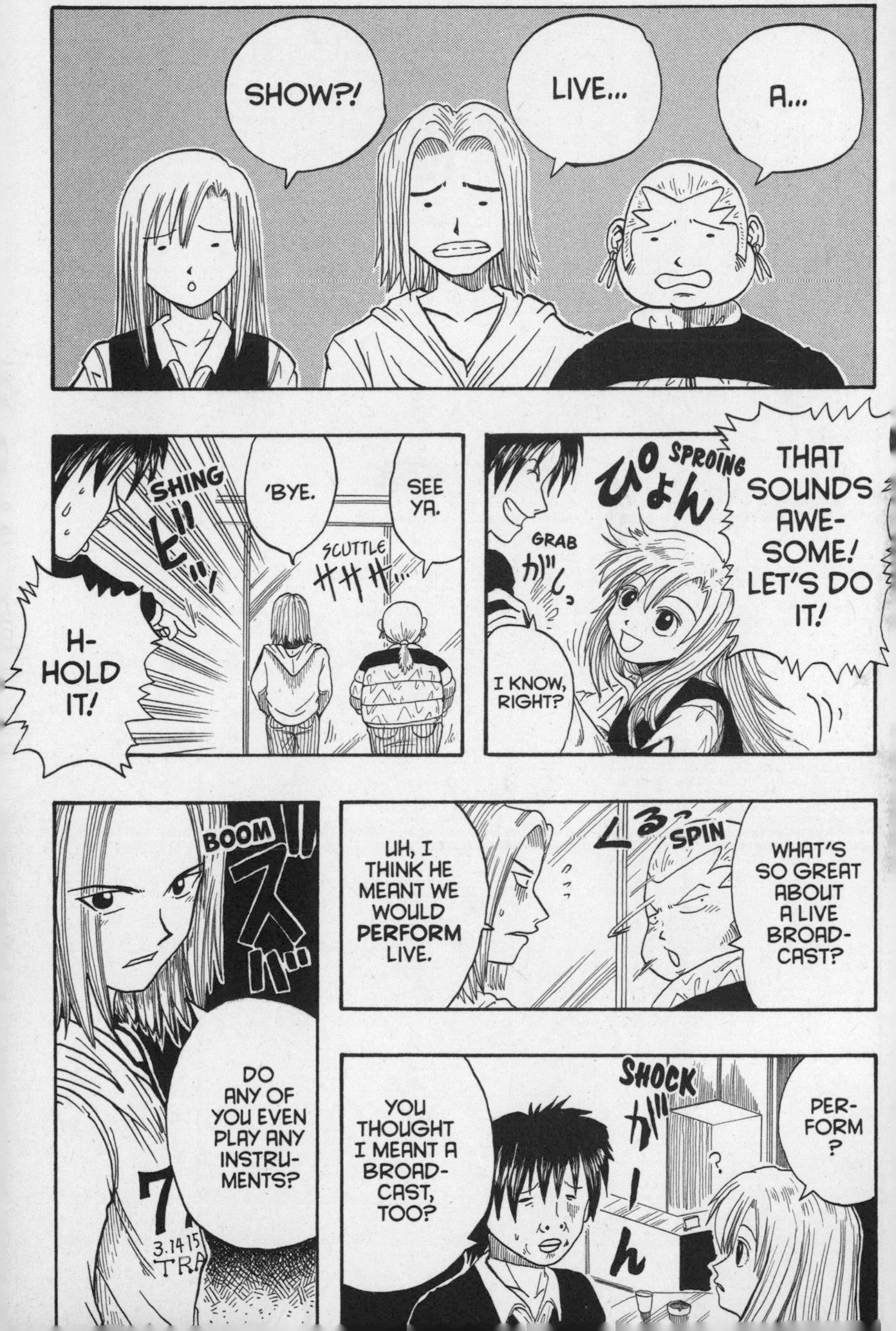
A...
LIVE...
SHOW?!
THAT SOUNDS AWE-SOME! LET'S DO IT!
SPROING
ぴょん
GRAB
がしっ
I KNOW, RIGHT?
SEE YA.
'BYE.
SCUTTLE
SHING
H-HOLD IT!
WHAT'S SO GREAT ABOUT A LIVE BROADCAST?
SPIN
くるっ
UH, I THINK HE MEANT WE WOULD PERFORM LIVE.
PER-FORM?
SHOCK
YOU THOUGHT I MEANT A BROAD-CAST, TOO?
BOOM
DO ANY OF YOU EVEN PLAY ANY INSTRU-MENTS?
7
3.14 15
TRA

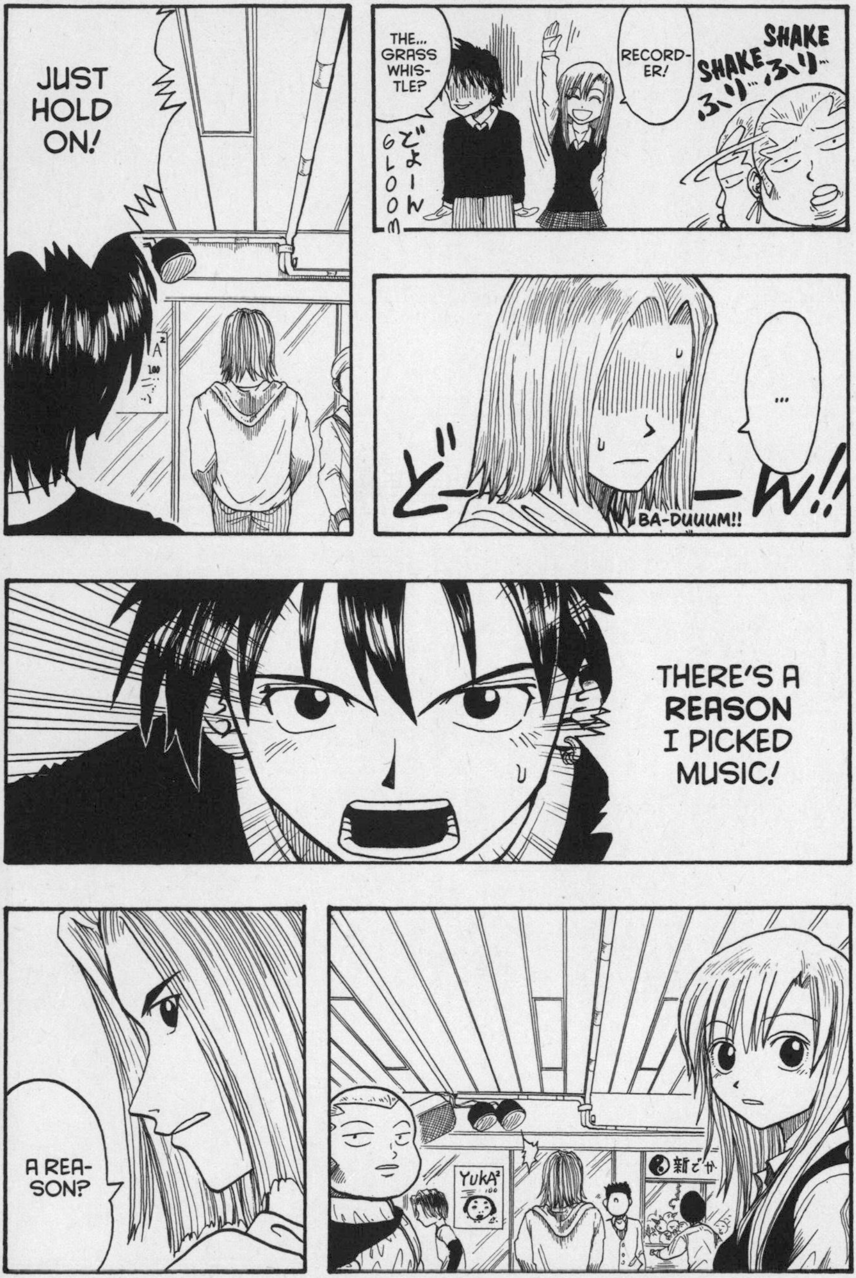
SHAKE
SHAKE
ふりふり
RECORDER-ER!
THE... GRASS WHIS-TLE?
どよーん
GLOOM
...
どーーん!!
BA-DUUUM!!
JUST HOLD ON!
THERE'S A REASON I PICKED MUSIC!
新でか
YUKA²
100
A REA-SON?

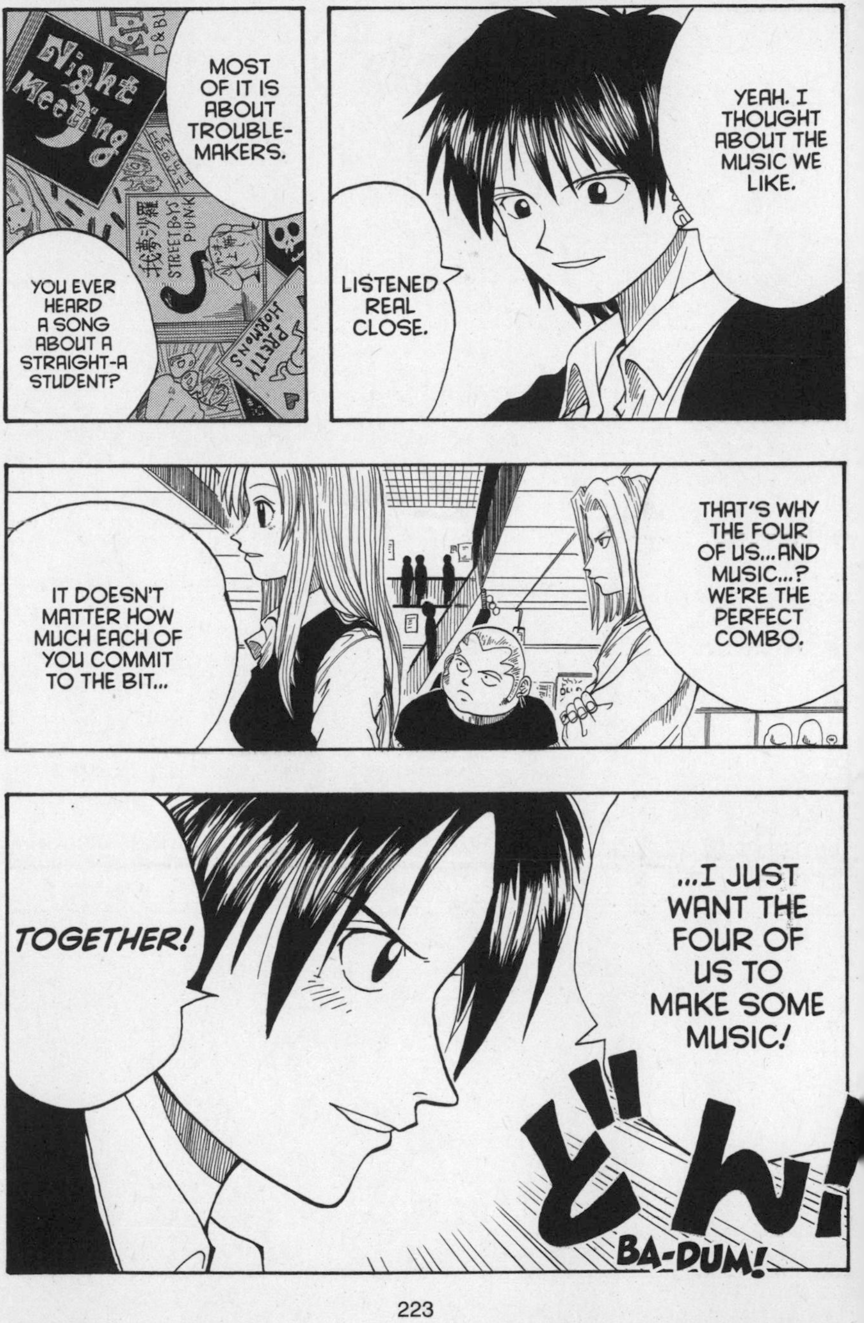
YEAH. I THOUGHT ABOUT THE MUSIC WE LIKE.
LISTENED REAL CLOSE.
MOST OF IT IS ABOUT TROUBLE-MAKERS.
Night Meeting
YOU EVER HEARD A SONG ABOUT A STRAIGHT-A STUDENT?
THAT'S WHY THE FOUR OF US...AND MUSIC...? WE'RE THE PERFECT COMBO.
IT DOESN'T MATTER HOW MUCH EACH OF YOU COMMIT TO THE BIT...
...I JUST WANT THE FOUR OF US TO MAKE SOME MUSIC!
TOGETHER!
どん!
BA-DUM!

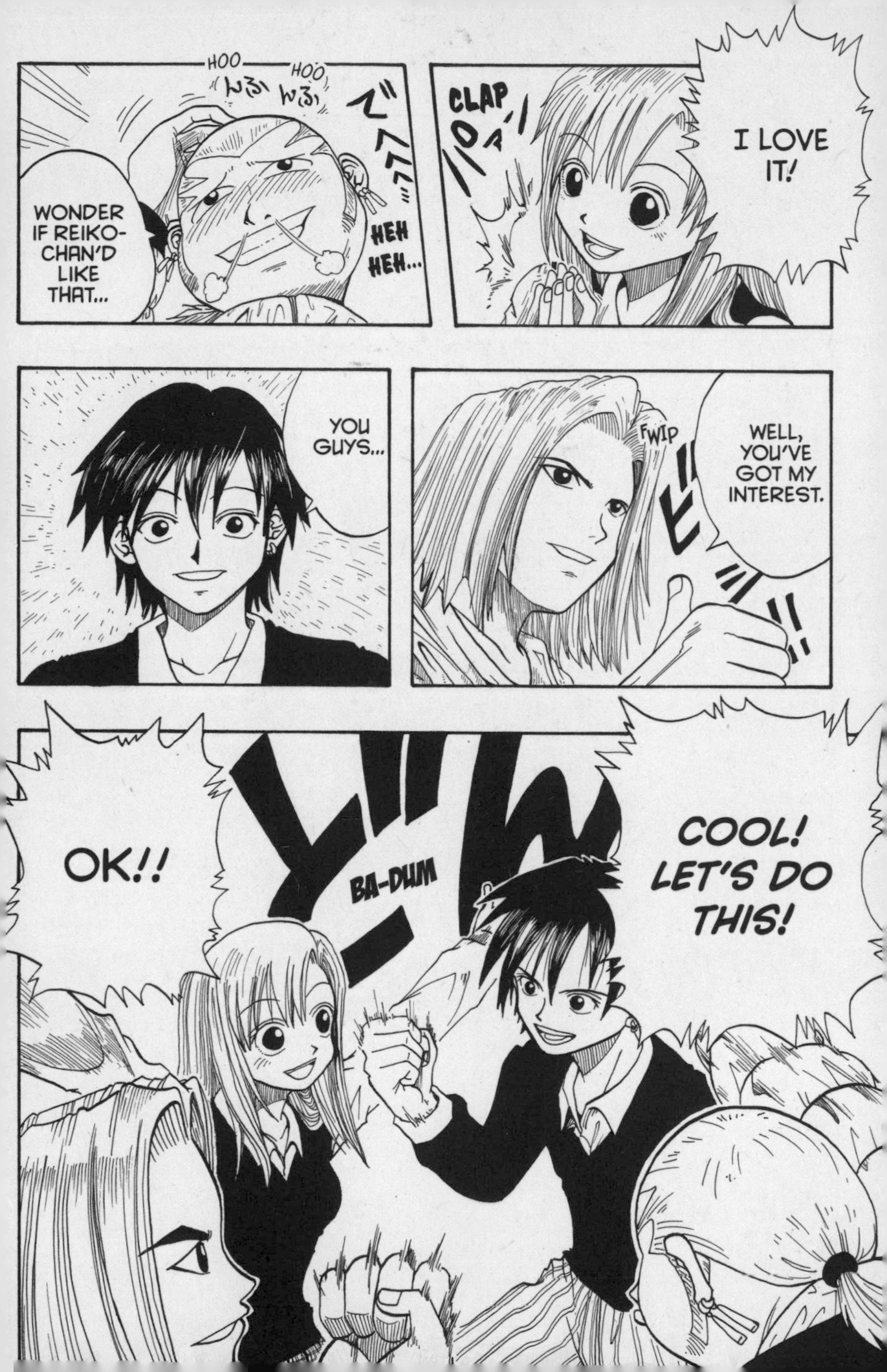
CLAP
I LOVE IT!
HOO
HOO
HEH HEH...
WONDER IF REIKO-CHAN'D LIKE THAT...
FWIP
WELL, YOU'VE GOT MY INTEREST.
YOU GUYS...
COOL! LET'S DO THIS!
BA-DUM
OK!!

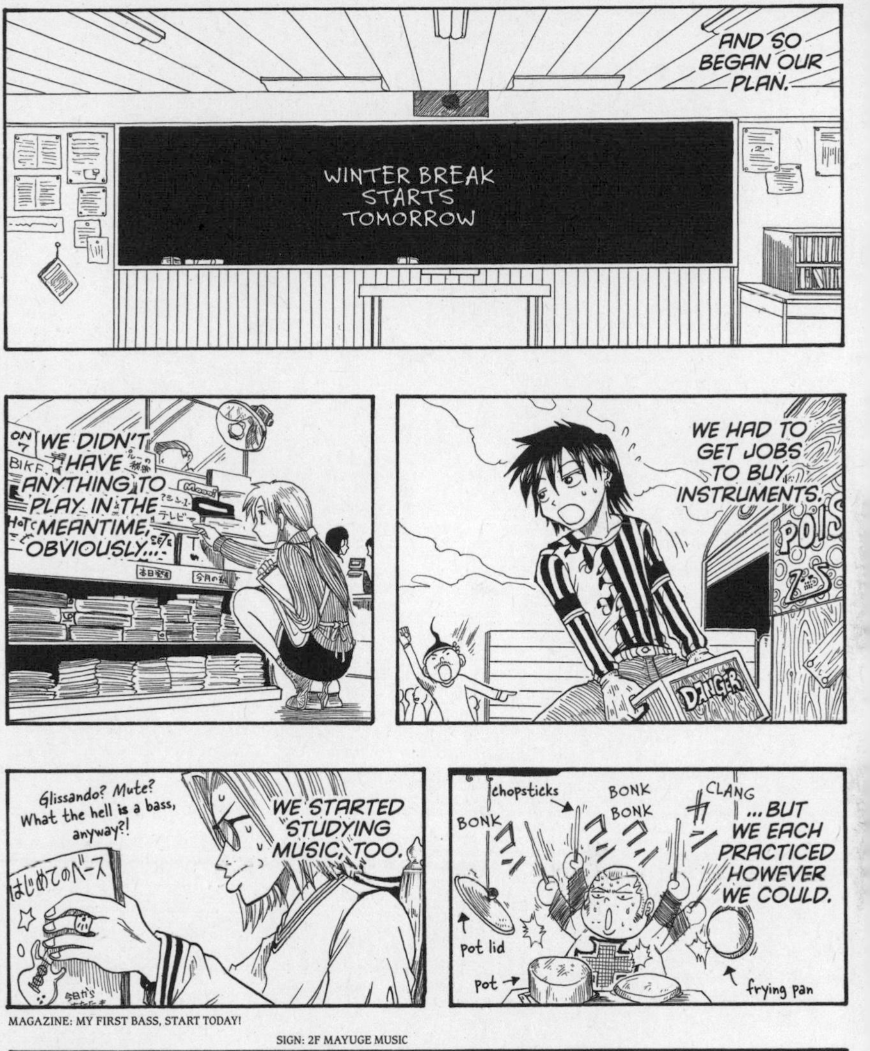
AND SO BEGAN OUR PLAN.
WINTER BREAK STARTS TOMORROW
WE HAD TO GET JOBS TO BUY INSTRUMENTS.
DANGER
WE DIDN'T HAVE ANYTHING TO PLAY IN THE MEANTIME, OBVIOUSLY...
CLANG
...BUT WE EACH PRACTICED HOWEVER WE COULD.
BONK
BONK
chopsticks
BONK
pot lid
frying pan
pot
WE STARTED STUDYING MUSIC, TOO.
Glissando? Mute? What the hell is a bass, anyway?!
はじめてのベース

MAGAZINE: MY FIRST BASS, START TODAY!

SIGN: 2F MAYUGE MUSIC

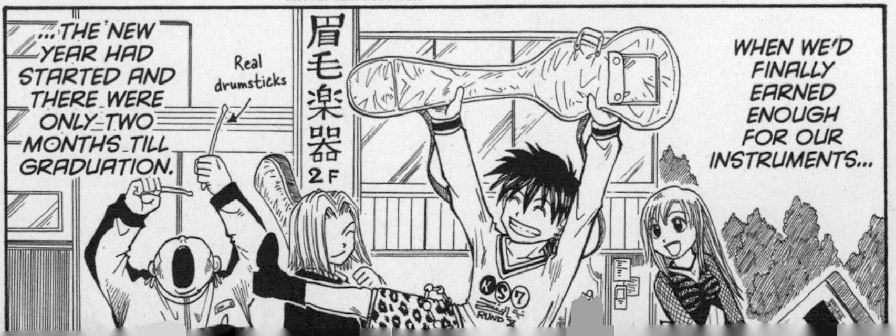
WHEN WE'D FINALLY EARNED ENOUGH FOR OUR INSTRUMENTS...
眉毛楽器 2F
Real drumsticks
...THE NEW YEAR HAD STARTED AND THERE WERE ONLY TWO MONTHS TILL GRADUATION.

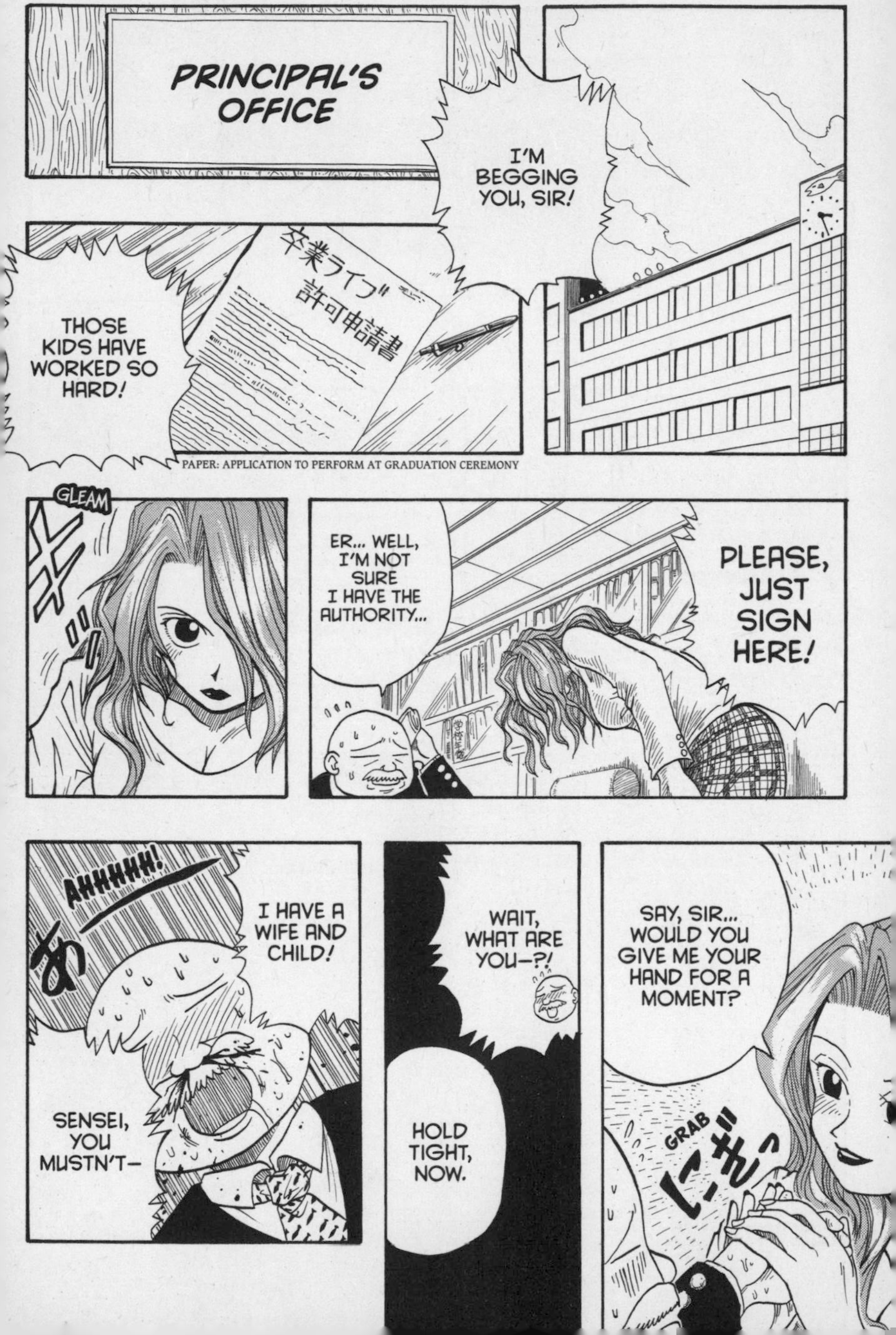
I'M BEGGING YOU, SIR!
PRINCIPAL'S OFFICE
卒業ライブ許可申請書
THOSE KIDS HAVE WORKED SO HARD!
PAPER: APPLICATION TO PERFORM AT GRADUATION CEREMONY
PLEASE, JUST SIGN HERE!
ER... WELL, I'M NOT SURE I HAVE THE AUTHORITY...
GLEAM
SAY, SIR... WOULD YOU GIVE ME YOUR HAND FOR A MOMENT?
GRAB
にぎっ
WAIT, WHAT ARE YOU—?!
HOLD TIGHT, NOW.
AHHHHH!
あ
I HAVE A WIFE AND CHILD!
SENSEI, YOU MUSTN'T—

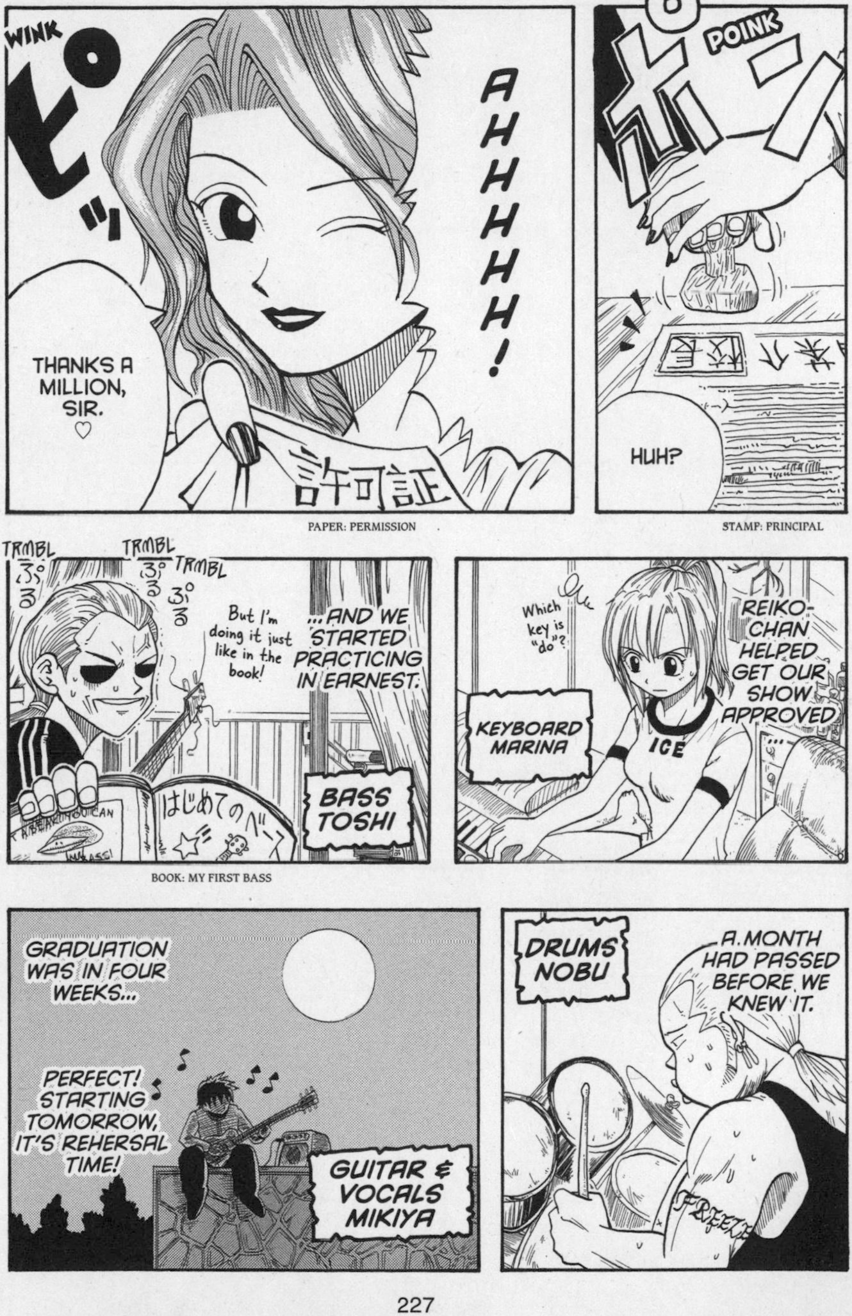
POINK
HUH?
STAMP: PRINCIPAL
WINK
AHHHHHH!
THANKS A MILLION, SIR. ♡
PAPER: PERMISSION
REIKO-CHAN HELPED GET OUR SHOW APPROVED...
Which key is "do"?
KEYBOARD MARINA
...AND WE STARTED PRACTICING IN EARNEST.
But I'm doing it just like in the book!
TRMBL
TRMBL
TRMBL
BASS TOSHI
BOOK: MY FIRST BASS
A MONTH HAD PASSED BEFORE WE KNEW IT.
DRUMS NOBU
GRADUATION WAS IN FOUR WEEKS...
PERFECT! STARTING TOMORROW, IT'S REHEARSAL TIME!
GUITAR & VOCALS MIKIYA

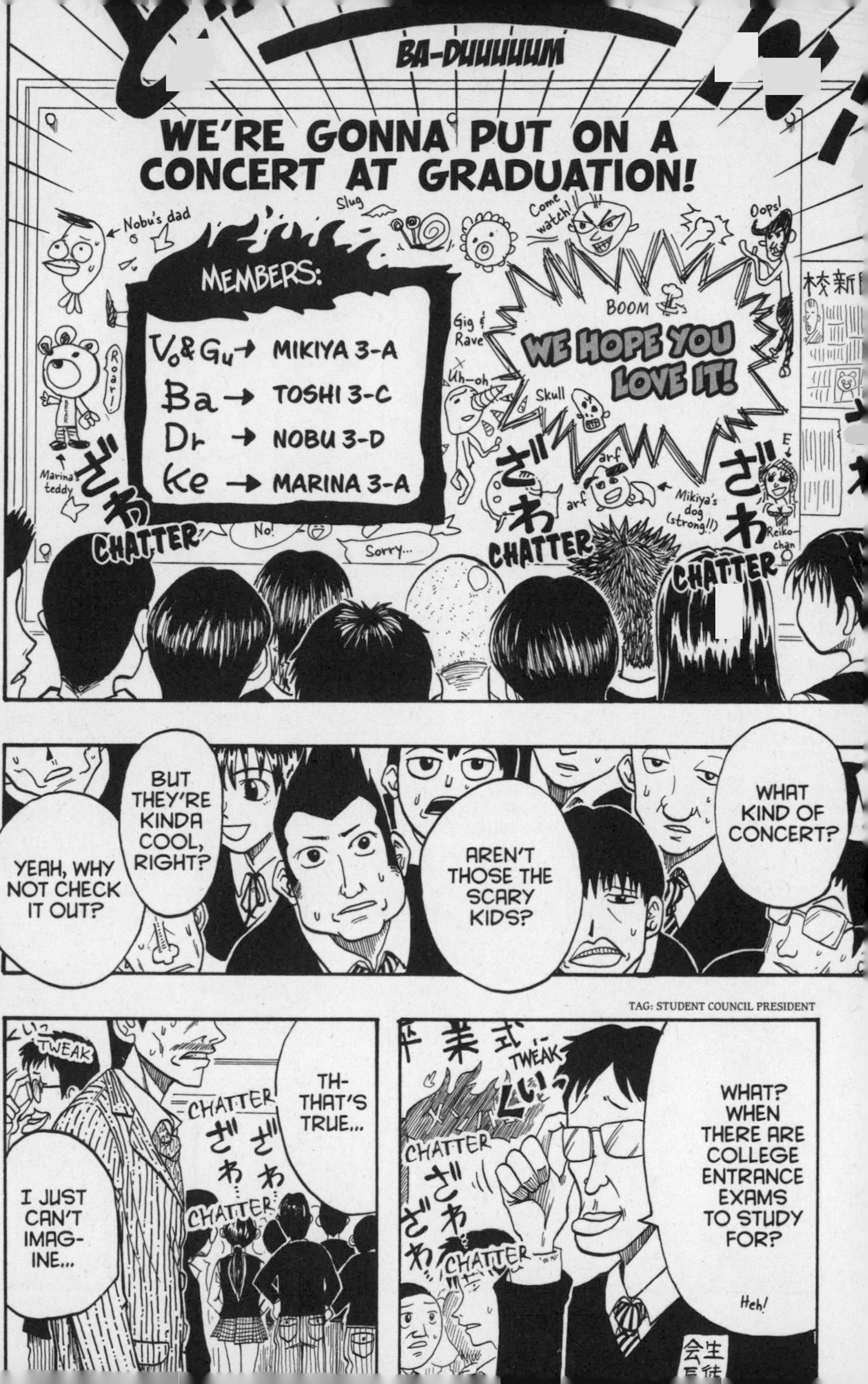
BA-DUUUUUM
WE'RE GONNA PUT ON A CONCERT AT GRADUATION!
MEMBERS:
Vo & Gu → MIKIYA 3-A
Ba → TOSHI 3-C
Dr → NOBU 3-D
Ke → MARINA 3-A
WE HOPE YOU LOVE IT!
Nobu's dad
Slug
Come watch!
Oops!
BOOM
Gig & Rave
Uh-oh
Skull
Roar!
Marina's teddy
arf
arf
Mikiya's dog (strong!!)
Reiko-chan
No!
Sorry...
ざわ
CHATTER
ざわ
CHATTER
ざわ
CHATTER
WHAT KIND OF CONCERT?
AREN'T THOSE THE SCARY KIDS?
BUT THEY'RE KINDA COOL, RIGHT?
YEAH, WHY NOT CHECK IT OUT?
TAG: STUDENT COUNCIL PRESIDENT
TWEAK
CHATTER
ざわ ざわ
CHATTER
WHAT? WHEN THERE ARE COLLEGE ENTRANCE EXAMS TO STUDY FOR?
Heh!
TWEAK
TH-THAT'S TRUE...
CHATTER
ざわ ざわ
CHATTER
I JUST CAN'T IMAGINE...

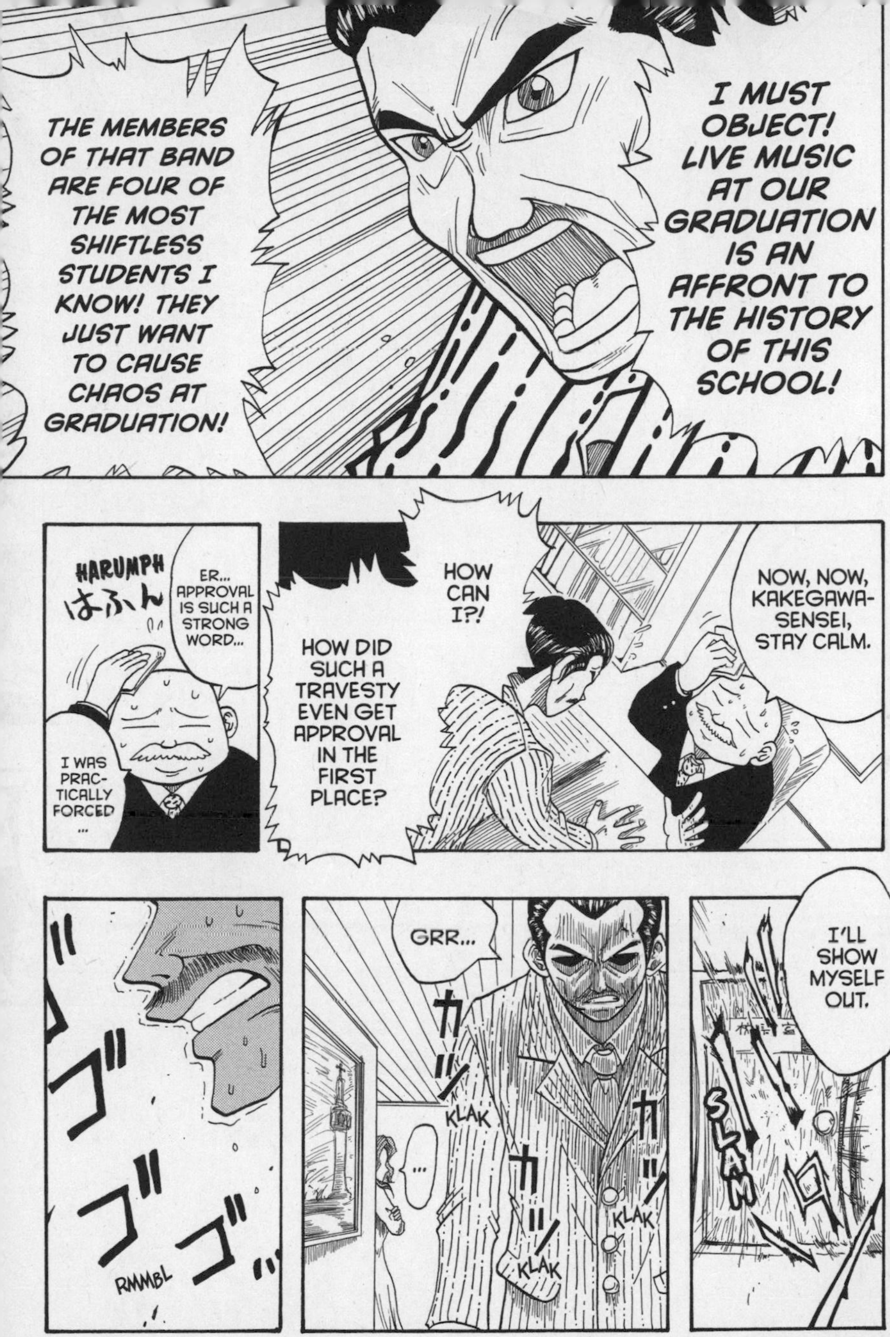
I MUST OBJECT! LIVE MUSIC AT OUR GRADUATION IS AN AFFRONT TO THE HISTORY OF THIS SCHOOL!
THE MEMBERS OF THAT BAND ARE FOUR OF THE MOST SHIFTLESS STUDENTS I KNOW! THEY JUST WANT TO CAUSE CHAOS AT GRADUATION!
NOW, NOW, KAKEGAWA-SENSEI, STAY CALM.
HOW CAN I?!
HOW DID SUCH A TRAVESTY EVEN GET APPROVAL IN THE FIRST PLACE?
ER... APPROVAL IS SUCH A STRONG WORD...
HARUMPH
はふん
I WAS PRACTICALLY FORCED ...
I'LL SHOW MYSELF OUT.
SLAM
GRR...
KLAK
...
KLAK
KLAK
RMMBL

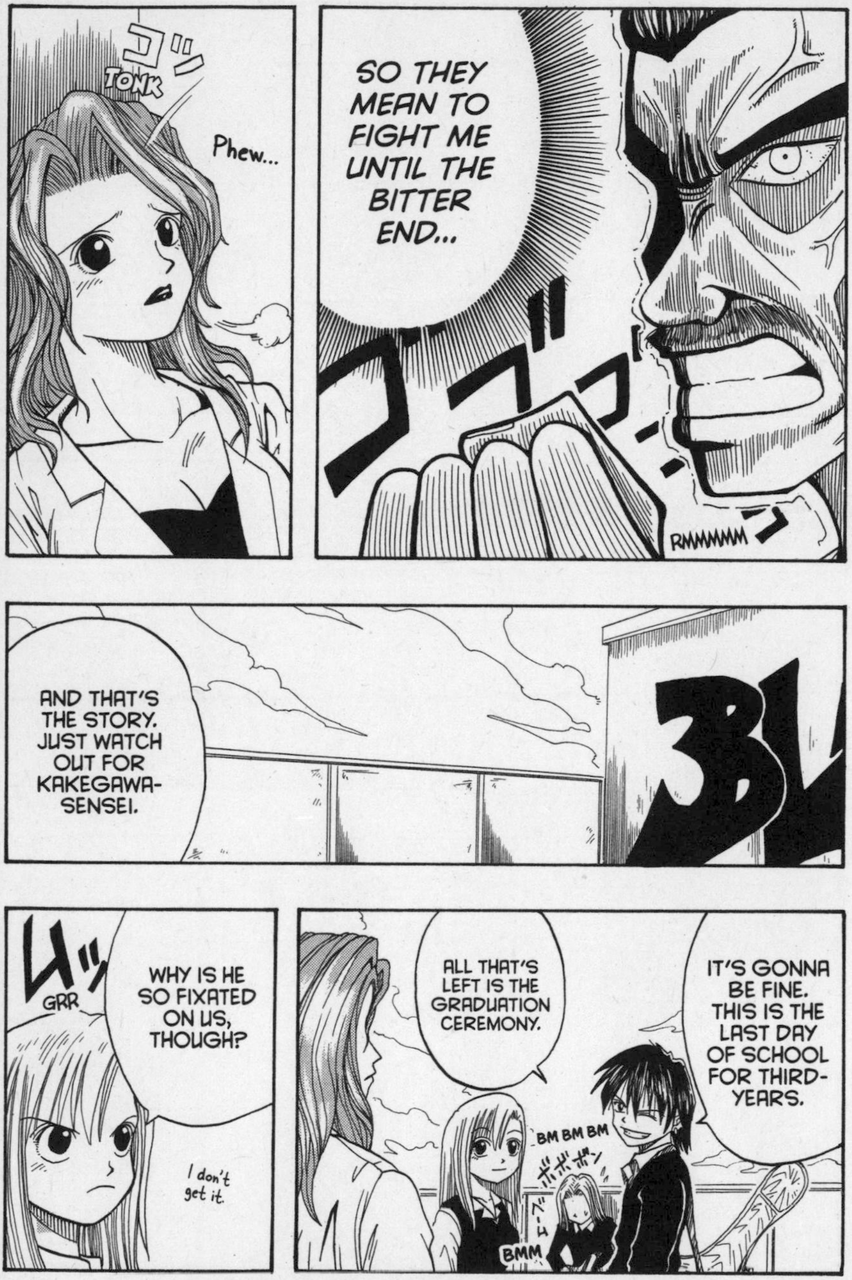

SO THEY MEAN TO FIGHT ME UNTIL THE BITTER END...
ゴゴゴ
RMMMMM
ゴッ
TONK
Phew...
AND THAT'S THE STORY. JUST WATCH OUT FOR KAKEGAWA-SENSEI.
3B
IT'S GONNA BE FINE. THIS IS THE LAST DAY OF SCHOOL FOR THIRD-YEARS.
ALL THAT'S LEFT IS THE GRADUATION CEREMONY.
BM BM BM
ボボボーン
ベーム
BMM
ムッ
GRR
WHY IS HE SO FIXATED ON US, THOUGH?
I don't get it.

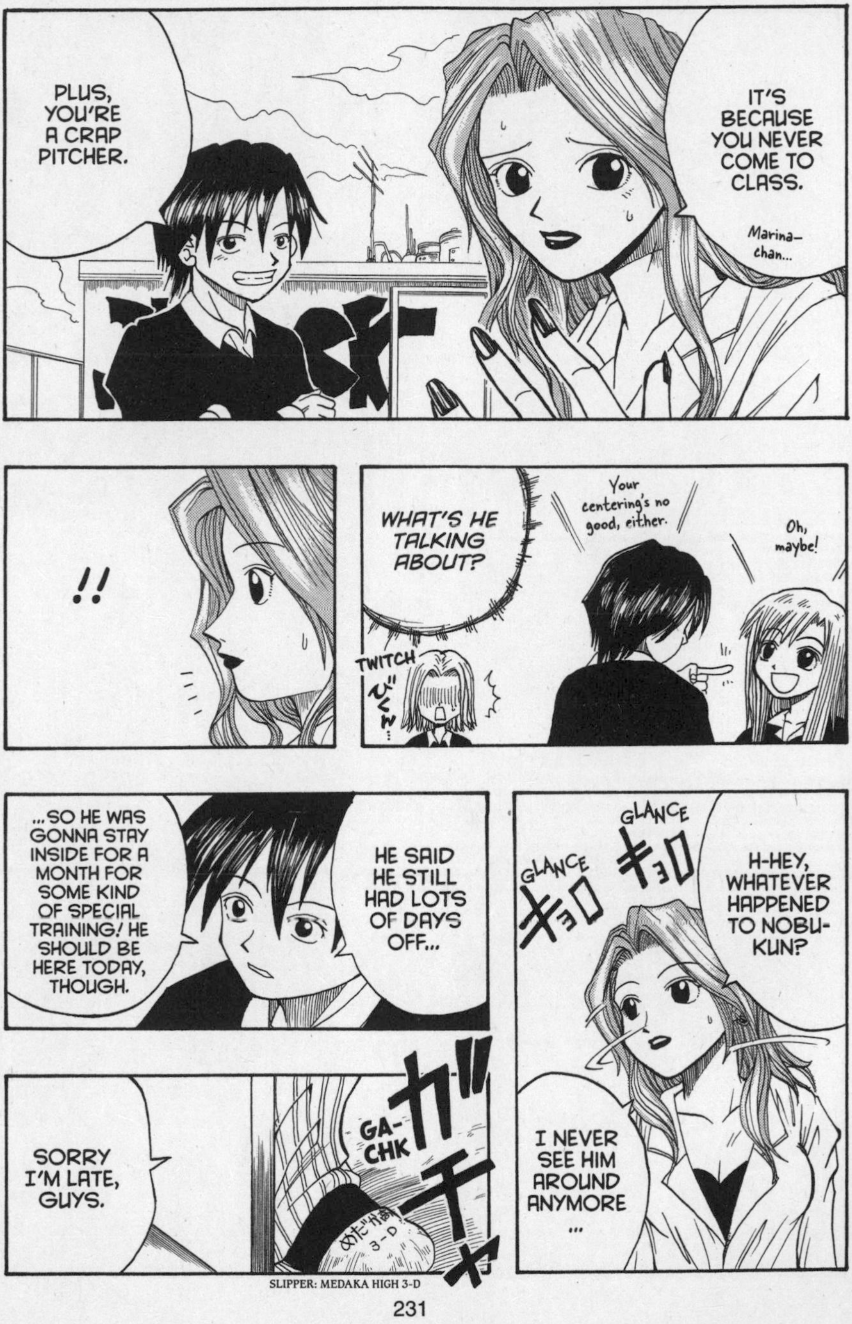
IT'S BECAUSE YOU NEVER COME TO CLASS.
Marina-chan...
PLUS, YOU'RE A CRAP PITCHER.
Oh, maybe!
Your centering's no good, either.
WHAT'S HE TALKING ABOUT?
TWITCH
!!
GLANCE
GLANCE
H-HEY, WHATEVER HAPPENED TO NOBU-KUN?
I NEVER SEE HIM AROUND ANYMORE ...
HE SAID HE STILL HAD LOTS OF DAYS OFF...
...SO HE WAS GONNA STAY INSIDE FOR A MONTH FOR SOME KIND OF SPECIAL TRAINING! HE SHOULD BE HERE TODAY, THOUGH.
GA-CHK
SORRY I'M LATE, GUYS.

SLIPPER: MEDAKA HIGH 3-D

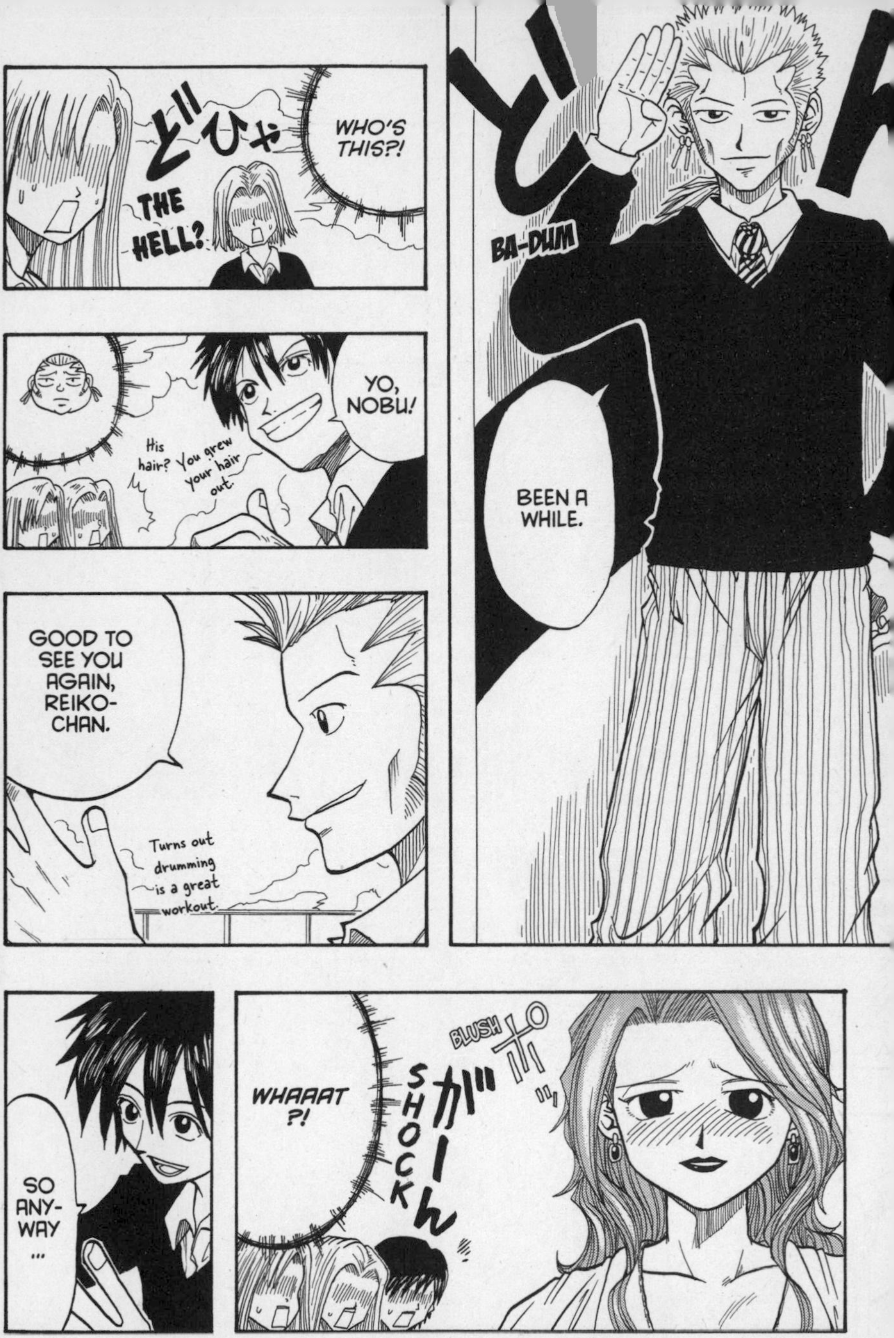
BA-DUM
BEEN A WHILE.
WHO'S THIS?!
どひゃ
THE HELL?
YO, NOBU!
His hair? You grew your hair out.
GOOD TO SEE YOU AGAIN, REIKO-CHAN.
Turns out drumming is a great workout.
BLUSH
SHOCK
WHAAAT ?!
SO ANYWAY ...

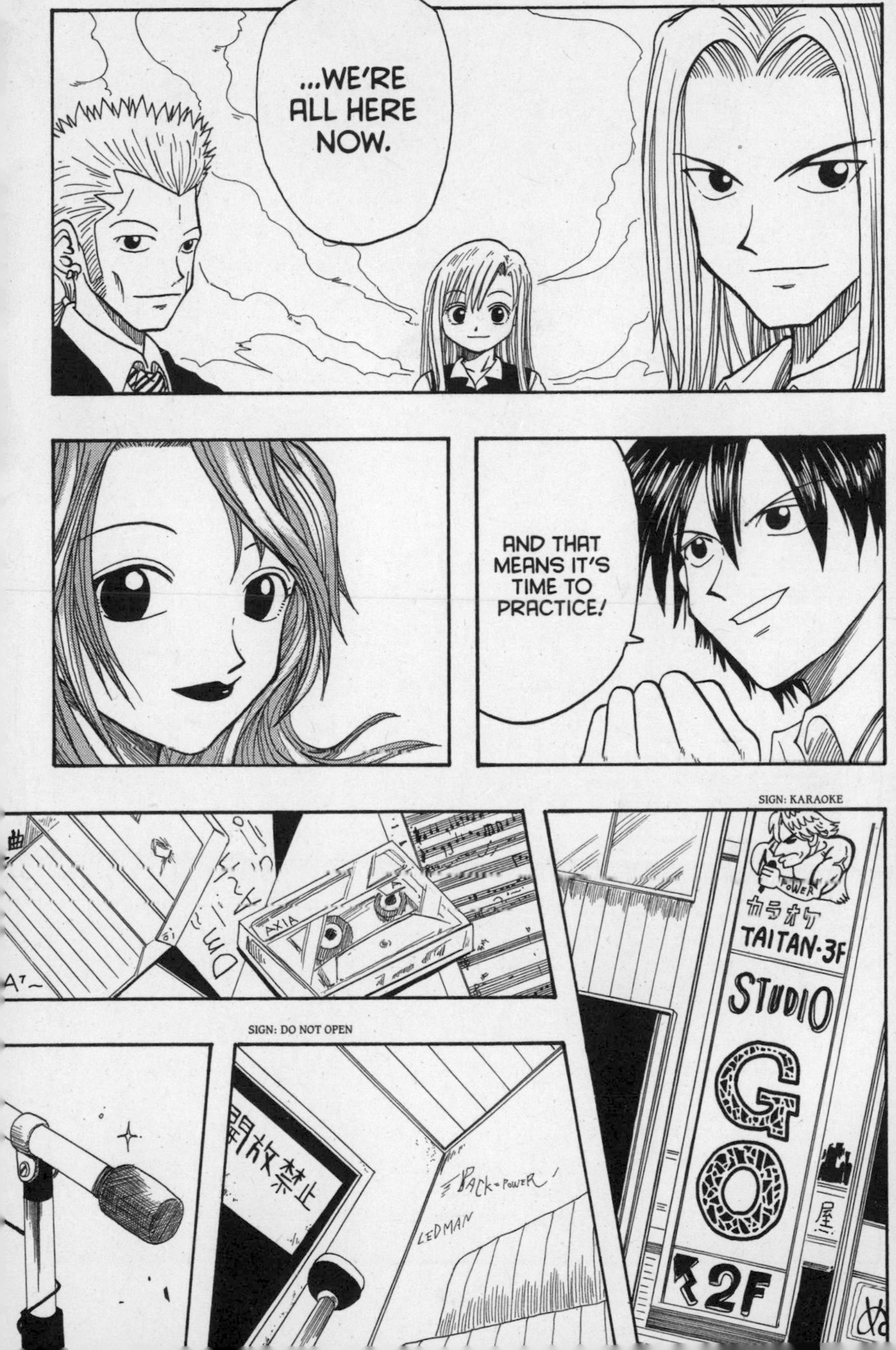
...WE'RE ALL HERE NOW.
AND THAT MEANS IT'S TIME TO PRACTICE!
SIGN: KARAOKE
POWER
カラオケ
TAITAN-3F
STUDIO
GO
2F
AXIA
SIGN: DO NOT OPEN
開放禁止
PACK = POWER
LEDMAN

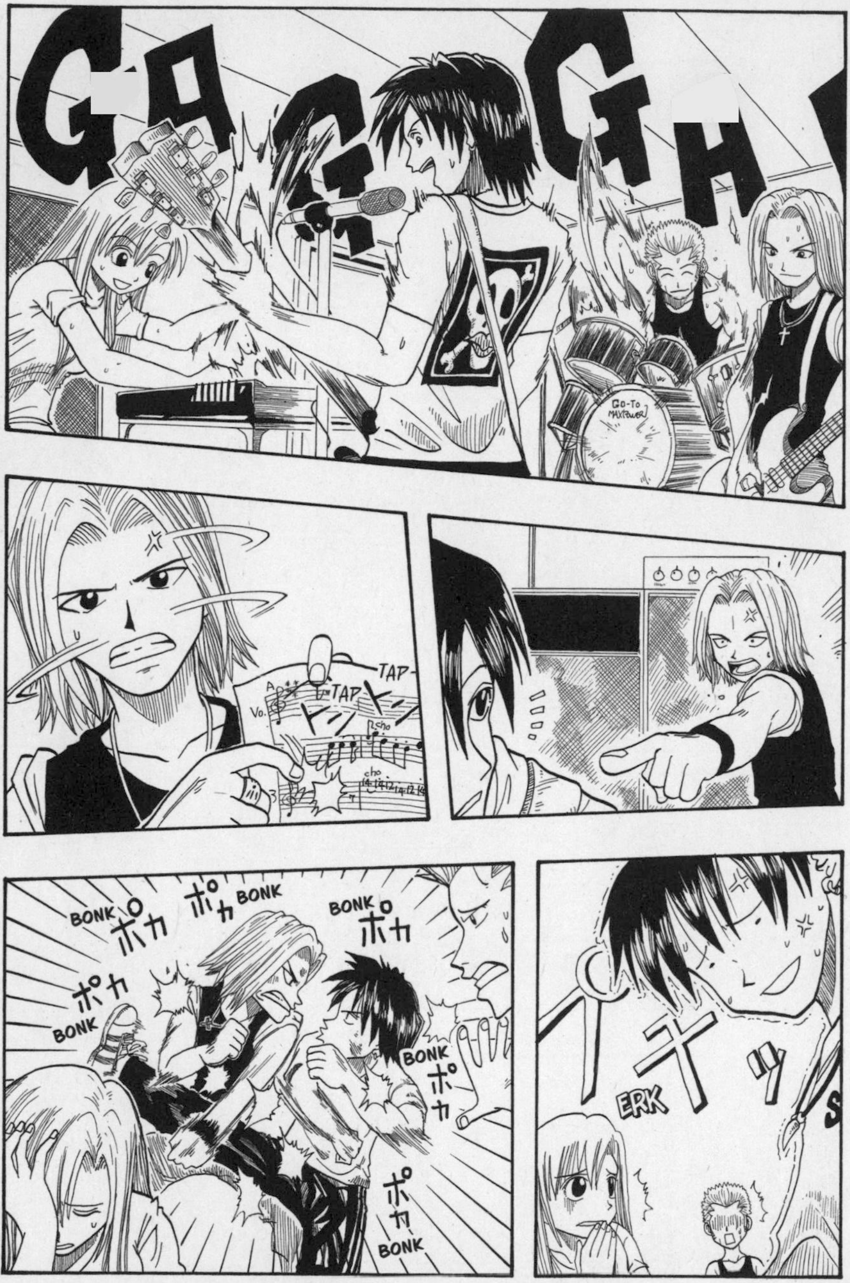
GA GA GA
GO-TO MAXPOWER
TAP-
TAP
トン トン
ピキッ
ERK
BONK ポカ
ポカ BONK
BONK ポカ
ポカ BONK
BONK ポカ
ポカ BONK

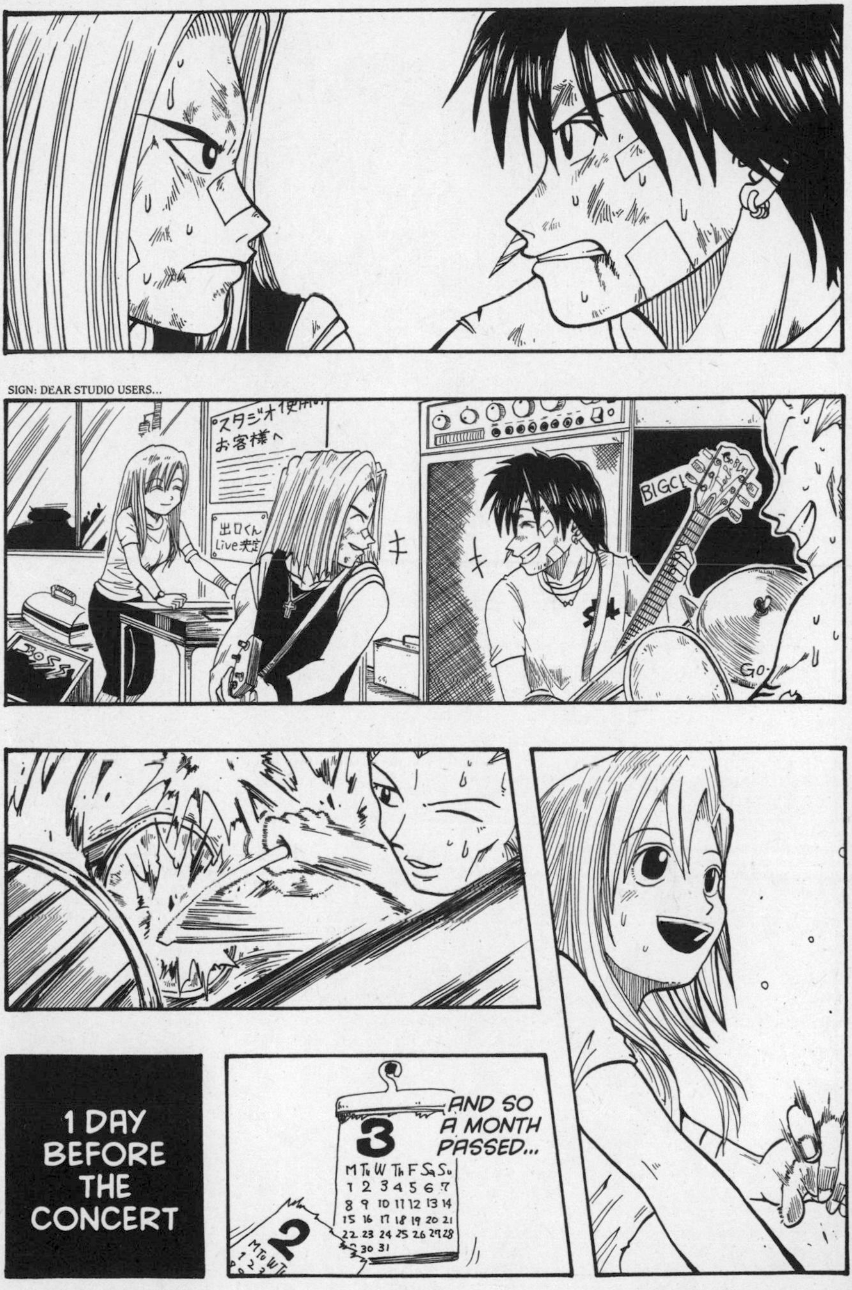
SIGN: DEAR STUDIO USERS...
スタジオ使用の
お客様へ
GO-
AND SO A MONTH PASSED...
1 DAY BEFORE THE CONCERT

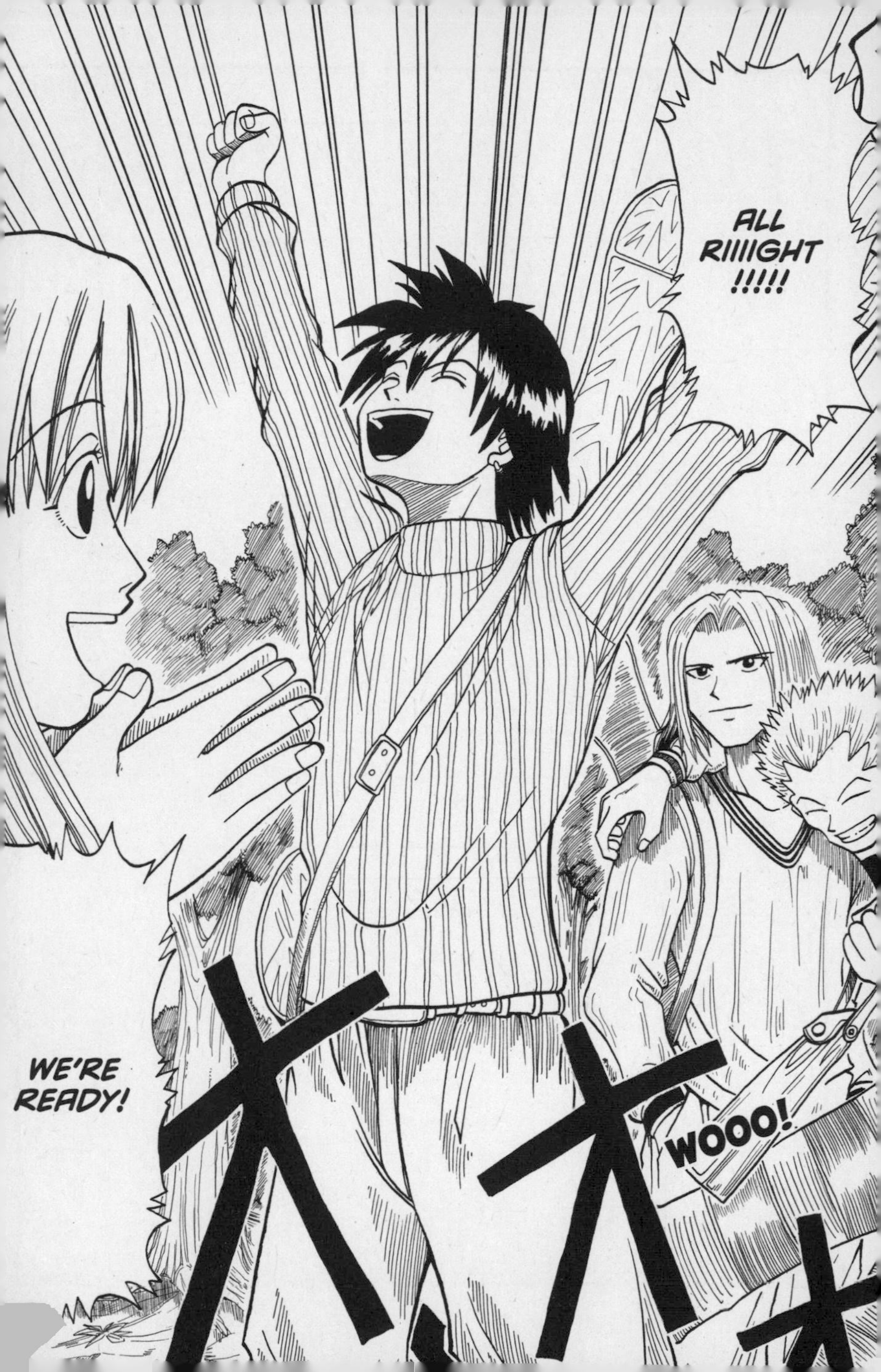
ALL RIIIIGHT !!!!!
WOOO!
WE'RE READY!

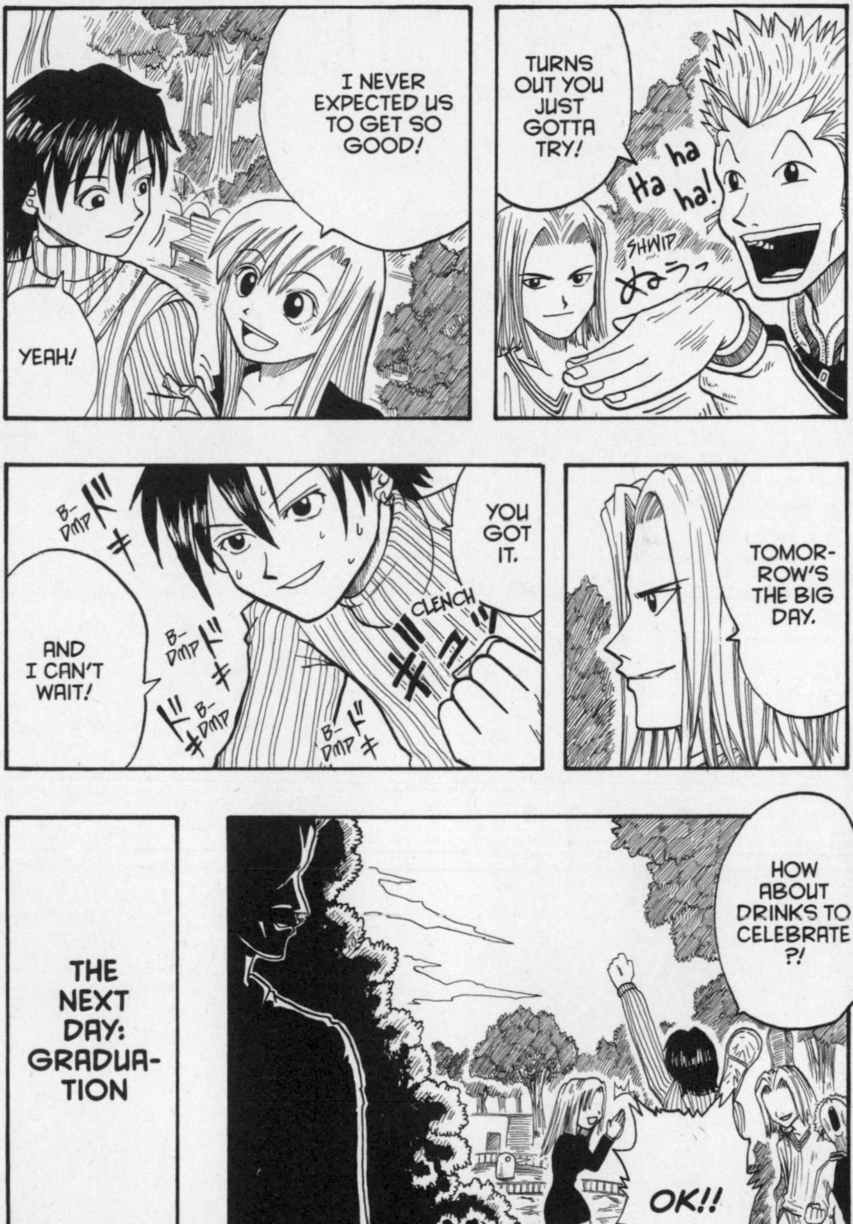
TURNS OUT YOU JUST GOTTA TRY!
Ha ha ha!
SHWIP
ぬらっ
I NEVER EXPECTED US TO GET SO GOOD!
YEAH!
TOMORROW'S THE BIG DAY.
YOU GOT IT.
CLENCH
B-DMP ドキ
B-DMP ドキ
AND I CAN'T WAIT!
B-DMP ドキ
B-DMP ドキ
HOW ABOUT DRINKS TO CELEBRATE?!
OK!!
THE NEXT DAY: GRADUATION

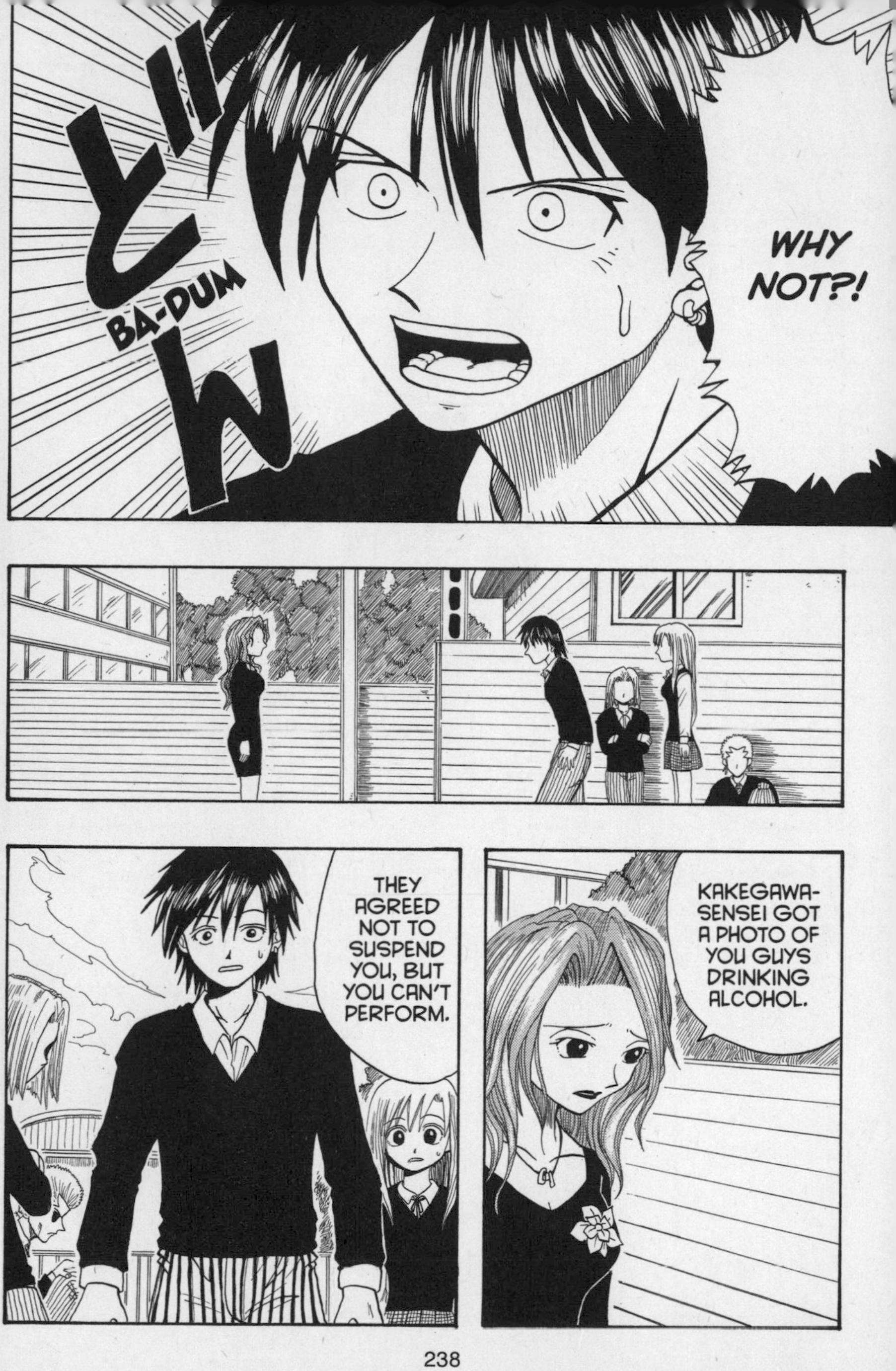
WHY NOT?!
BA-DUM
KAKEGAWA-SENSEI GOT A PHOTO OF YOU GUYS DRINKING ALCOHOL.
THEY AGREED NOT TO SUSPEND YOU, BUT YOU CAN'T PERFORM.

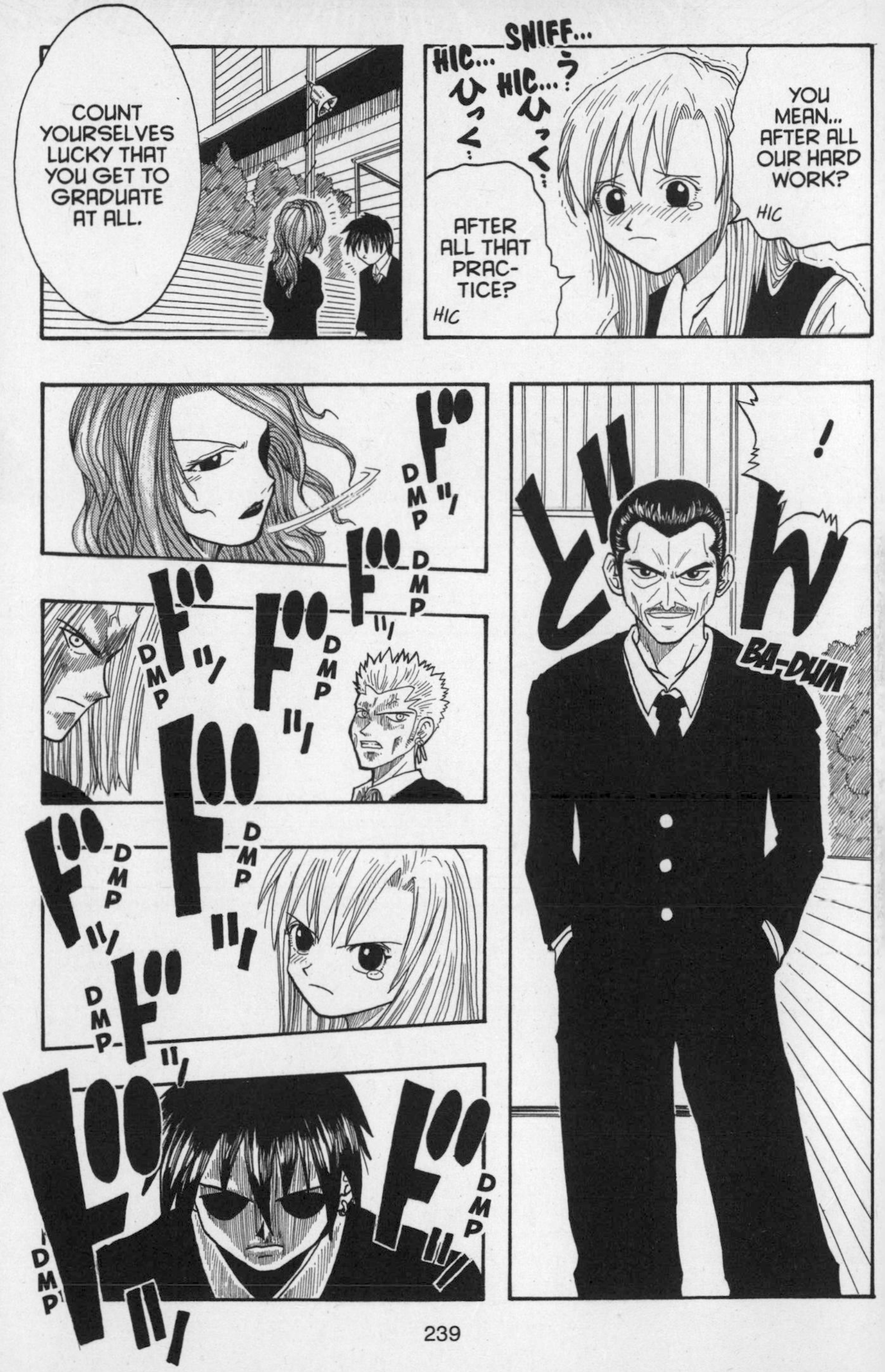
SNIFF...
YOU MEAN... AFTER ALL OUR HARD WORK?
HIC
HIC...
HIC...
AFTER ALL THAT PRAC-TICE?
HIC
COUNT YOURSELVES LUCKY THAT YOU GET TO GRADUATE AT ALL.
!
BA-DUM
DMP
DMP
DMP
DMP
DMP
DMP
DMP
DMP
DMP

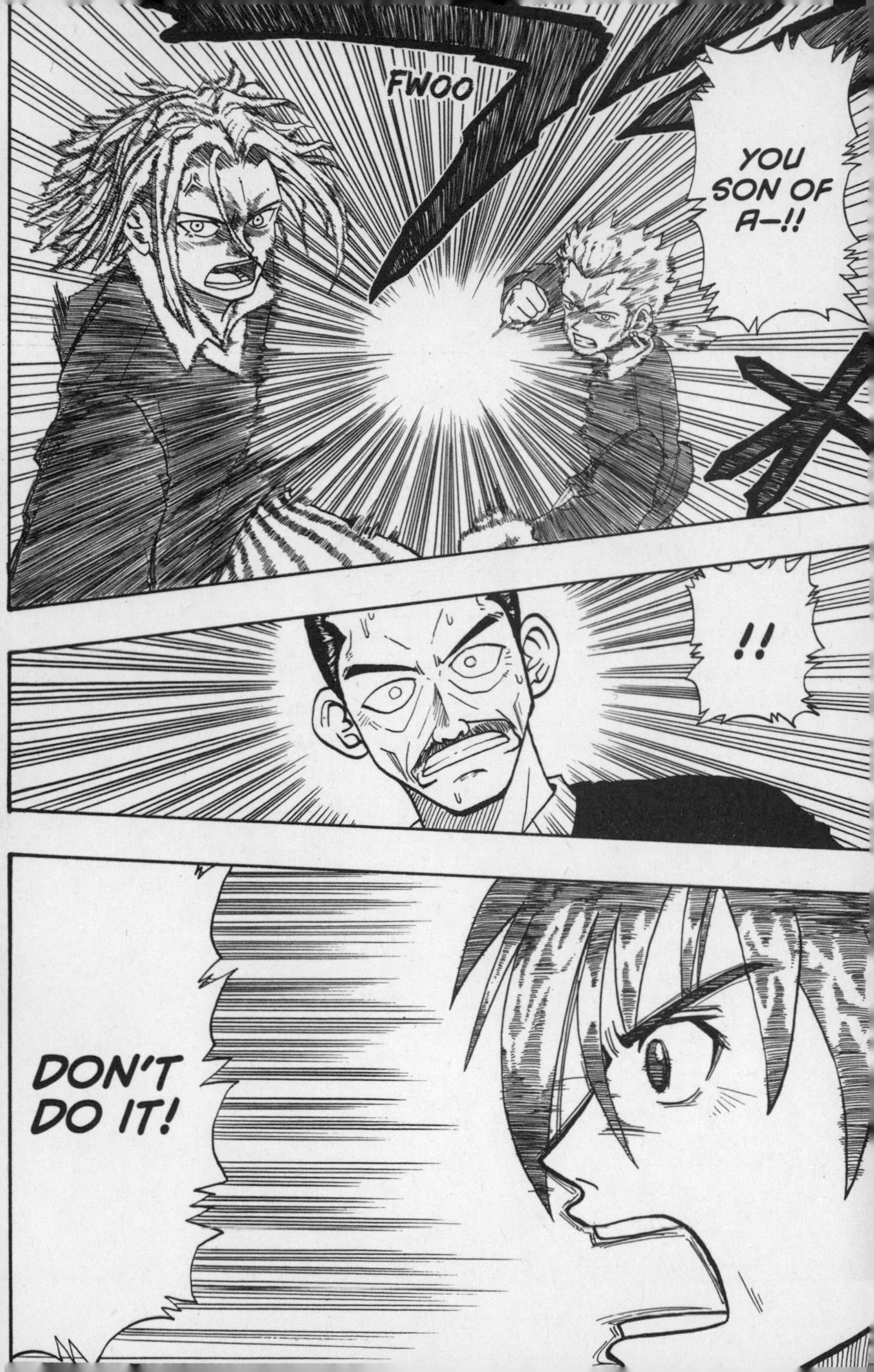
YOU SON OF A-!!
FWOO
!!
DON'T DO IT!

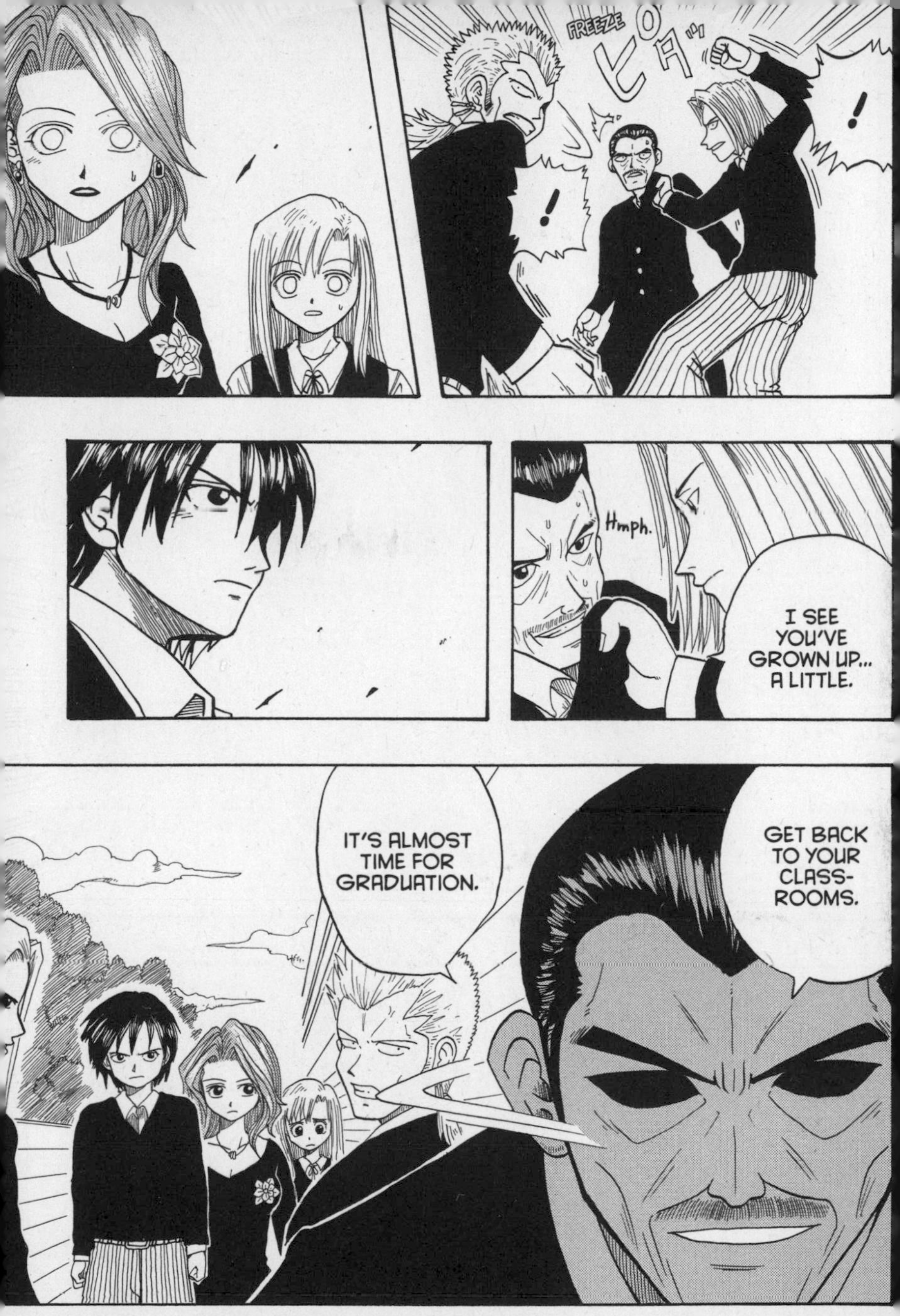
FREEZE
Hmph.
I SEE YOU'VE GROWN UP... A LITTLE.
GET BACK TO YOUR CLASS-ROOMS.
IT'S ALMOST TIME FOR GRADUATION.

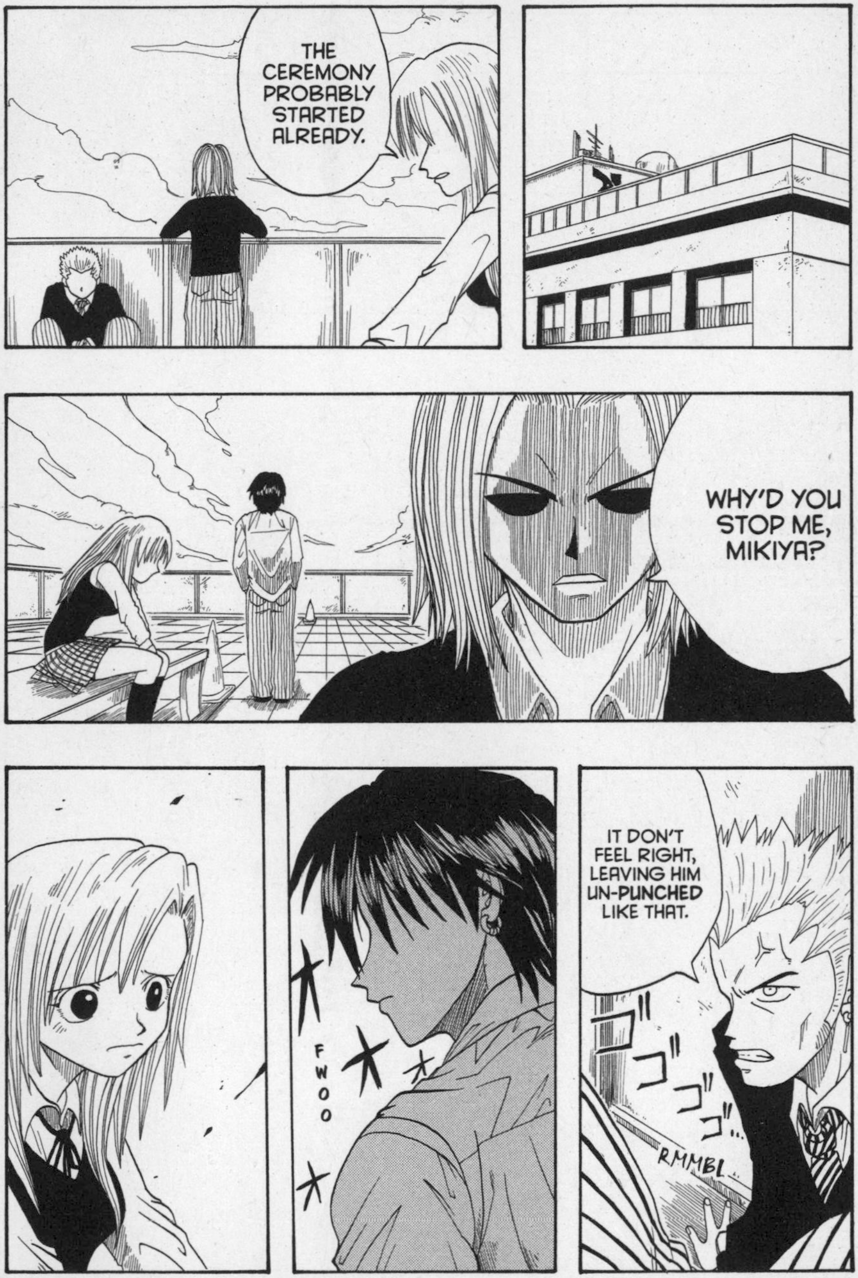

THE CEREMONY PROBABLY STARTED ALREADY.
WHY'D YOU STOP ME, MIKIYA?
IT DON'T FEEL RIGHT, LEAVING HIM UN-PUNCHED LIKE THAT.
ゴゴゴゴ…
RMMBL..
FWOO

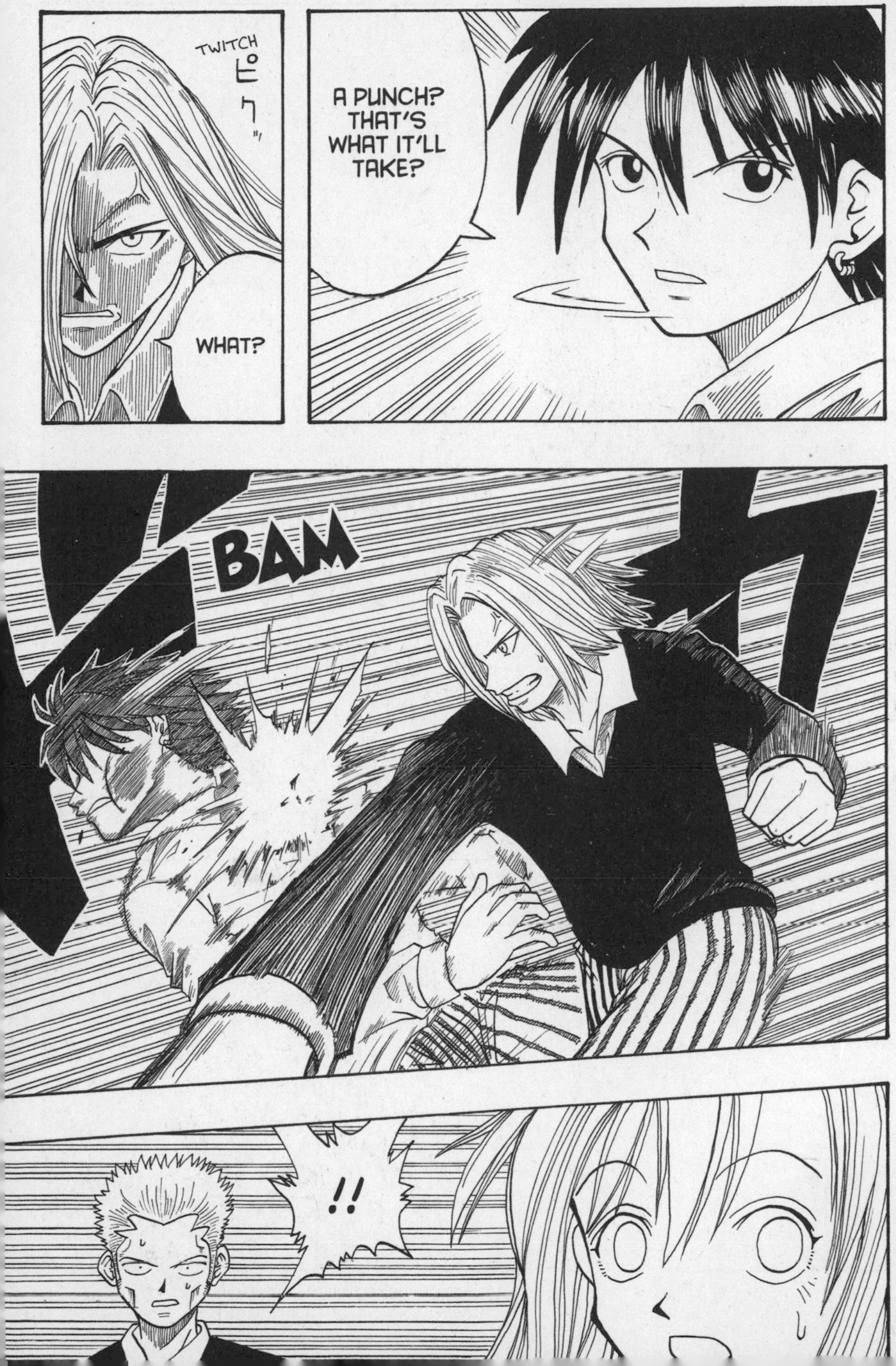
A PUNCH? THAT'S WHAT IT'LL TAKE?
TWITCH
ピク
WHAT?
BAM
!!

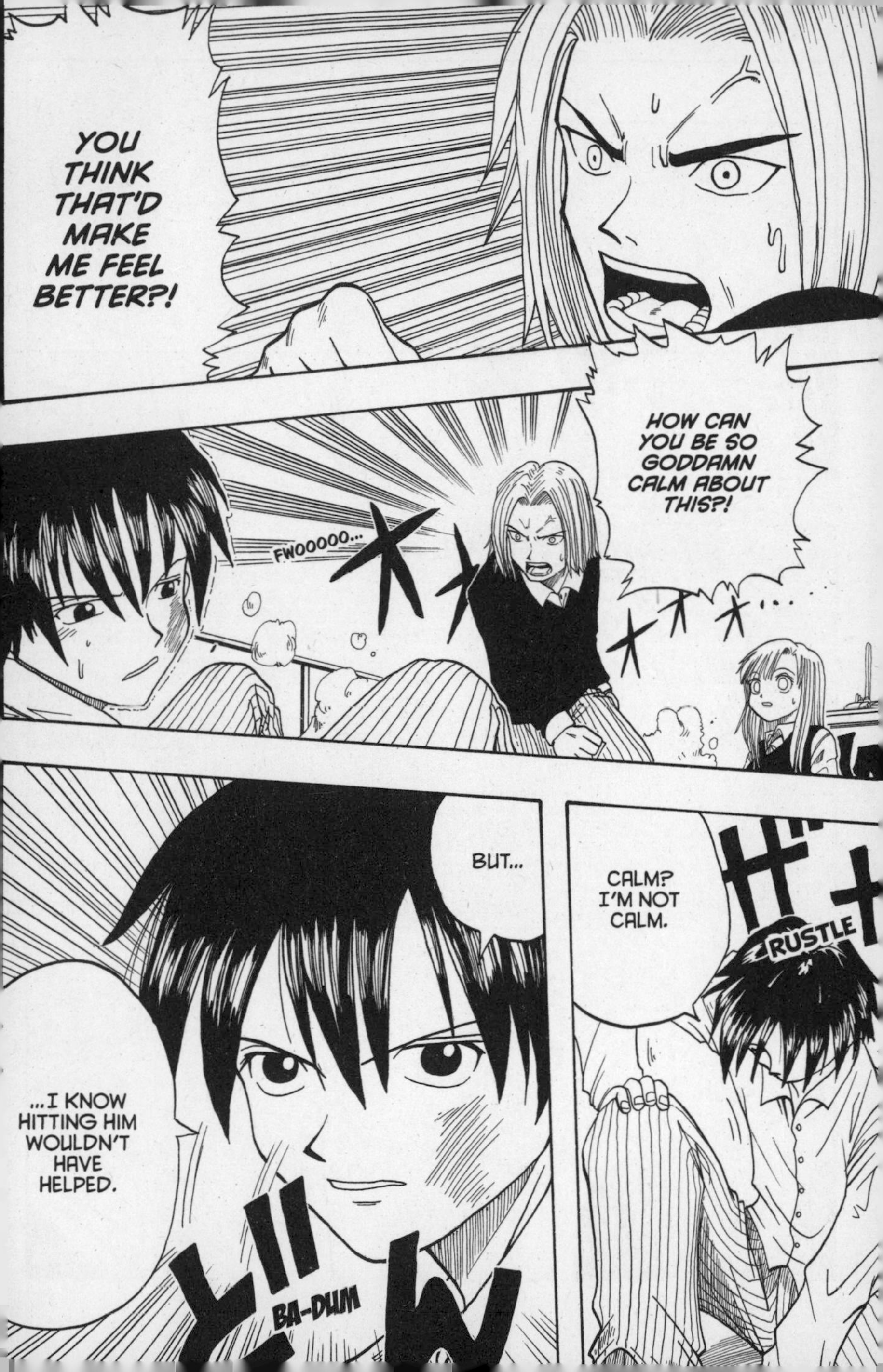
YOU THINK THAT'D MAKE ME FEEL BETTER?!
HOW CAN YOU BE SO GODDAMN CALM ABOUT THIS?!
FWOOOOO...
CALM? I'M NOT CALM.
RUSTLE
BUT...
...I KNOW HITTING HIM WOULDN'T HAVE HELPED.
BA-DUM

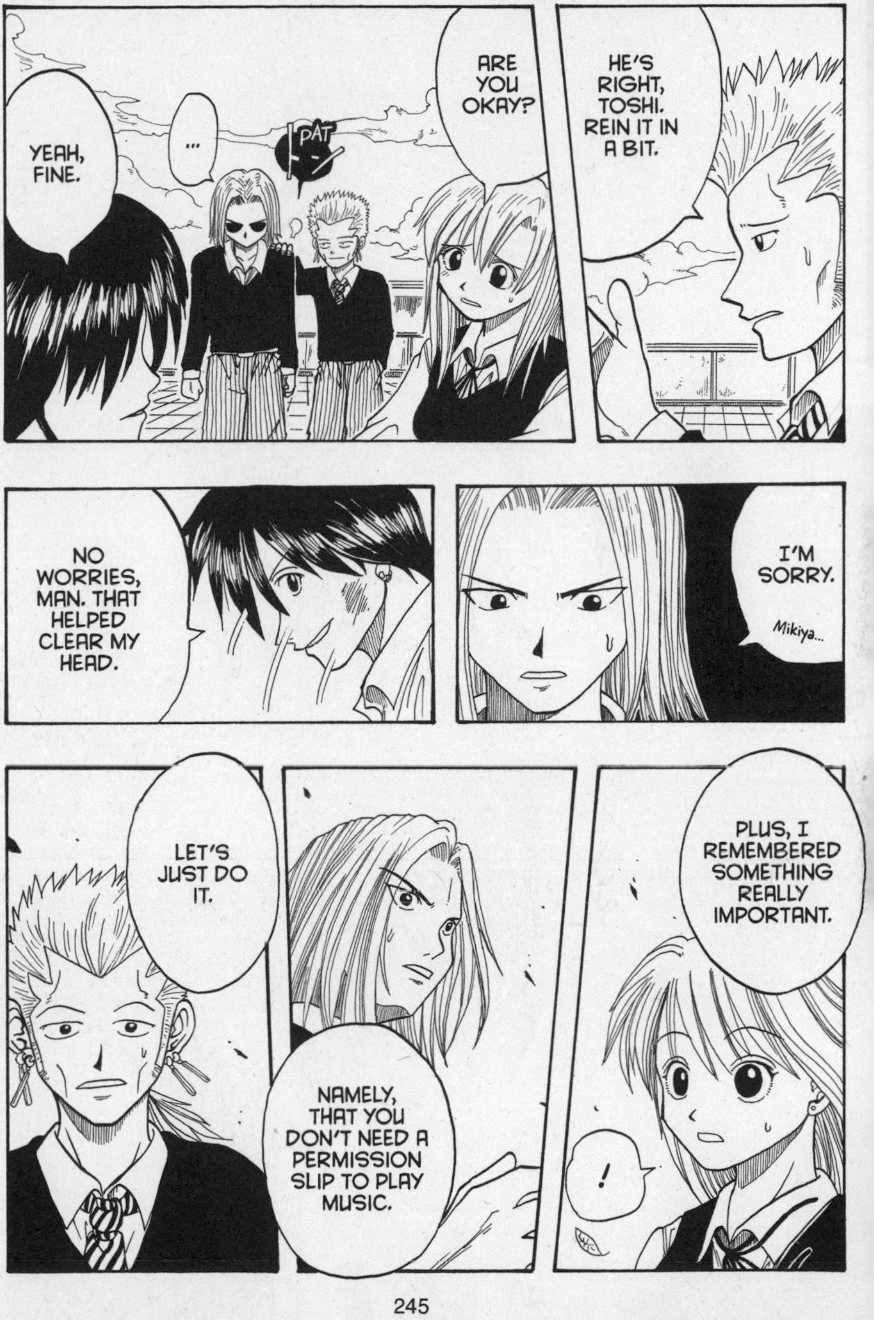
HE'S RIGHT, TOSHI. REIN IT IN A BIT.
ARE YOU OKAY?
PAT
...
YEAH, FINE.
I'M SORRY.
Mikiya...
NO WORRIES, MAN. THAT HELPED CLEAR MY HEAD.
PLUS, I REMEMBERED SOMETHING REALLY IMPORTANT.
!
NAMELY, THAT YOU DON'T NEED A PERMISSION SLIP TO PLAY MUSIC.
LET'S JUST DO IT.

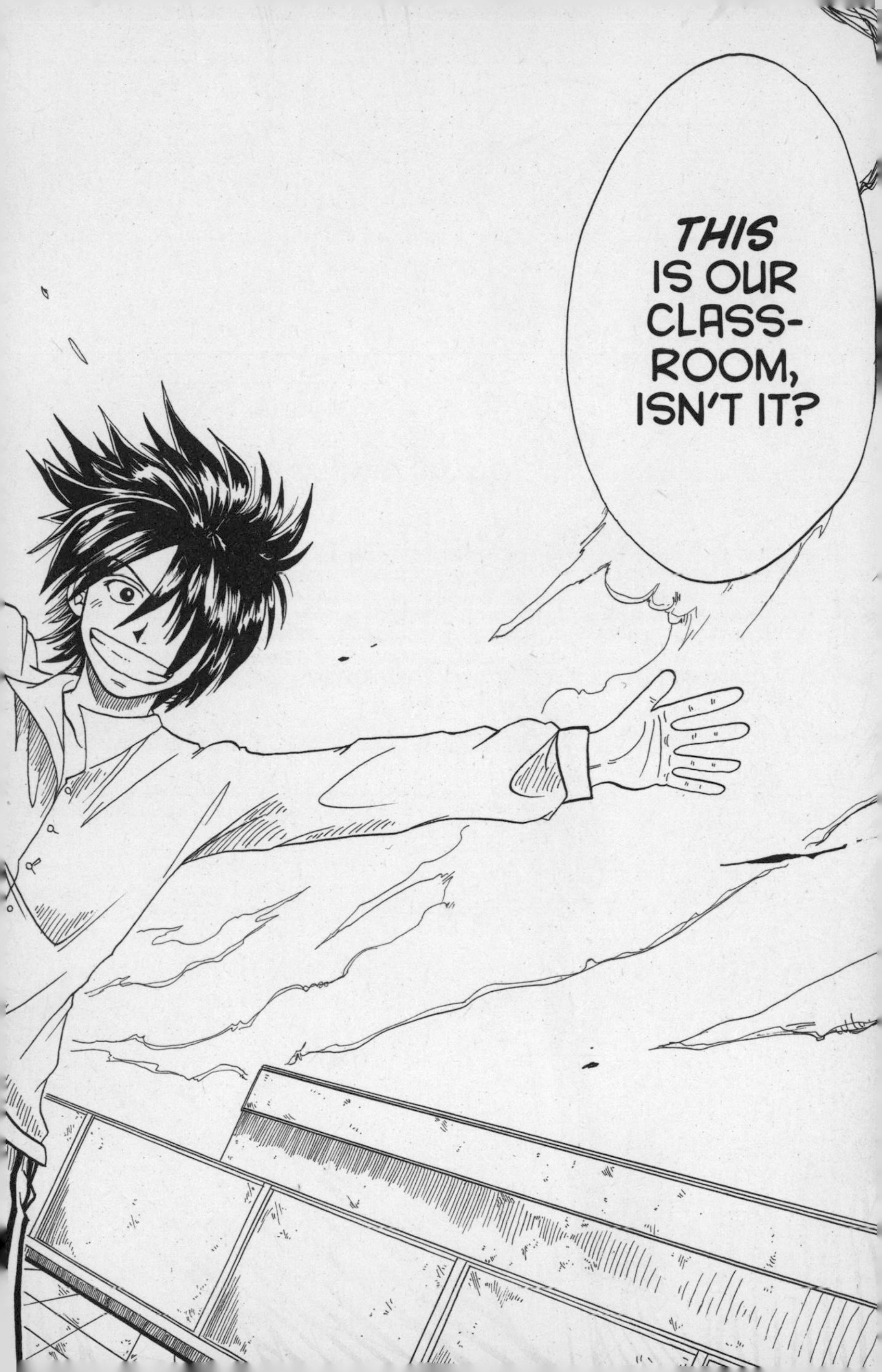
THIS IS OUR CLASS-ROOM, ISN'T IT?

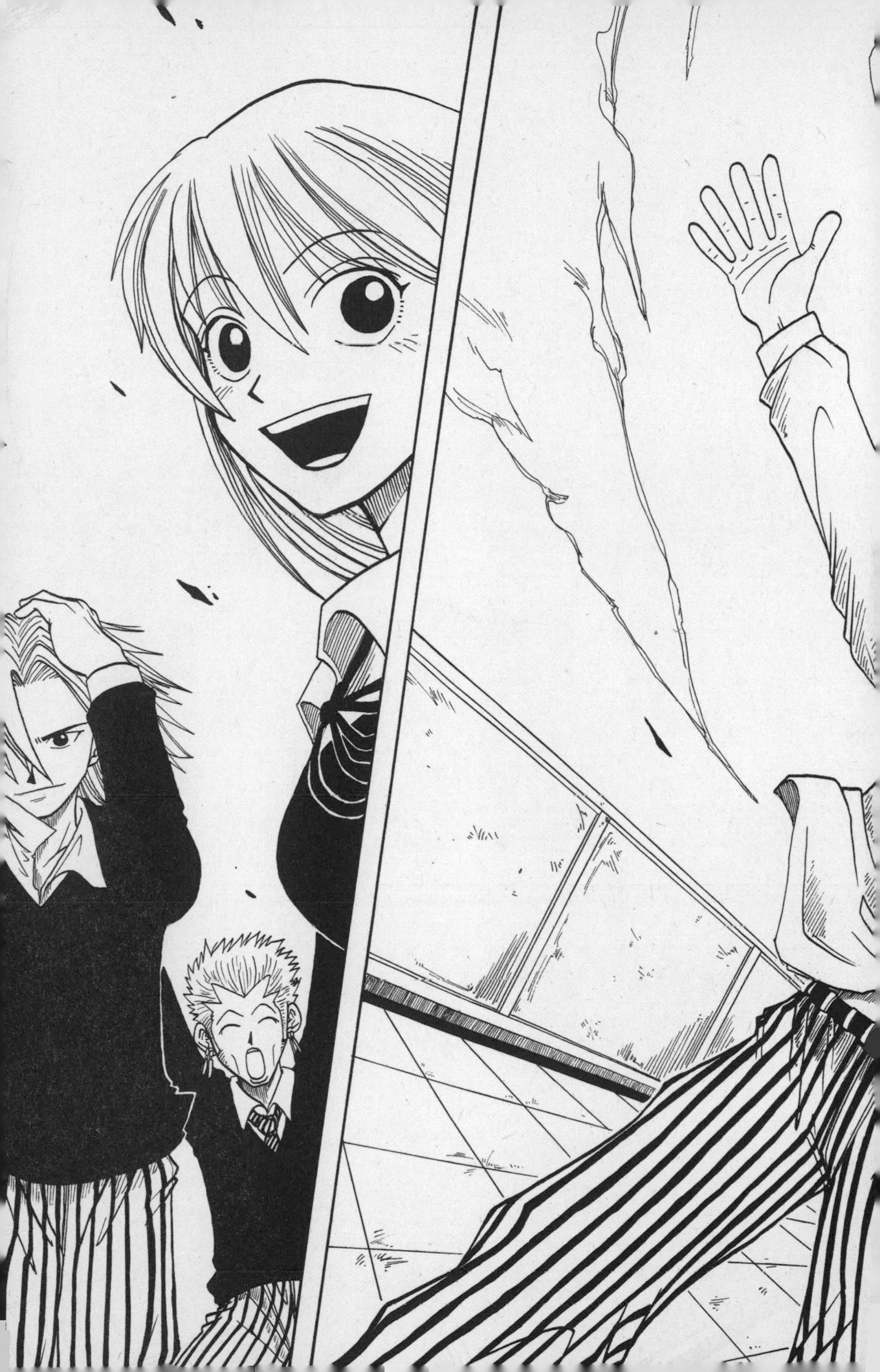

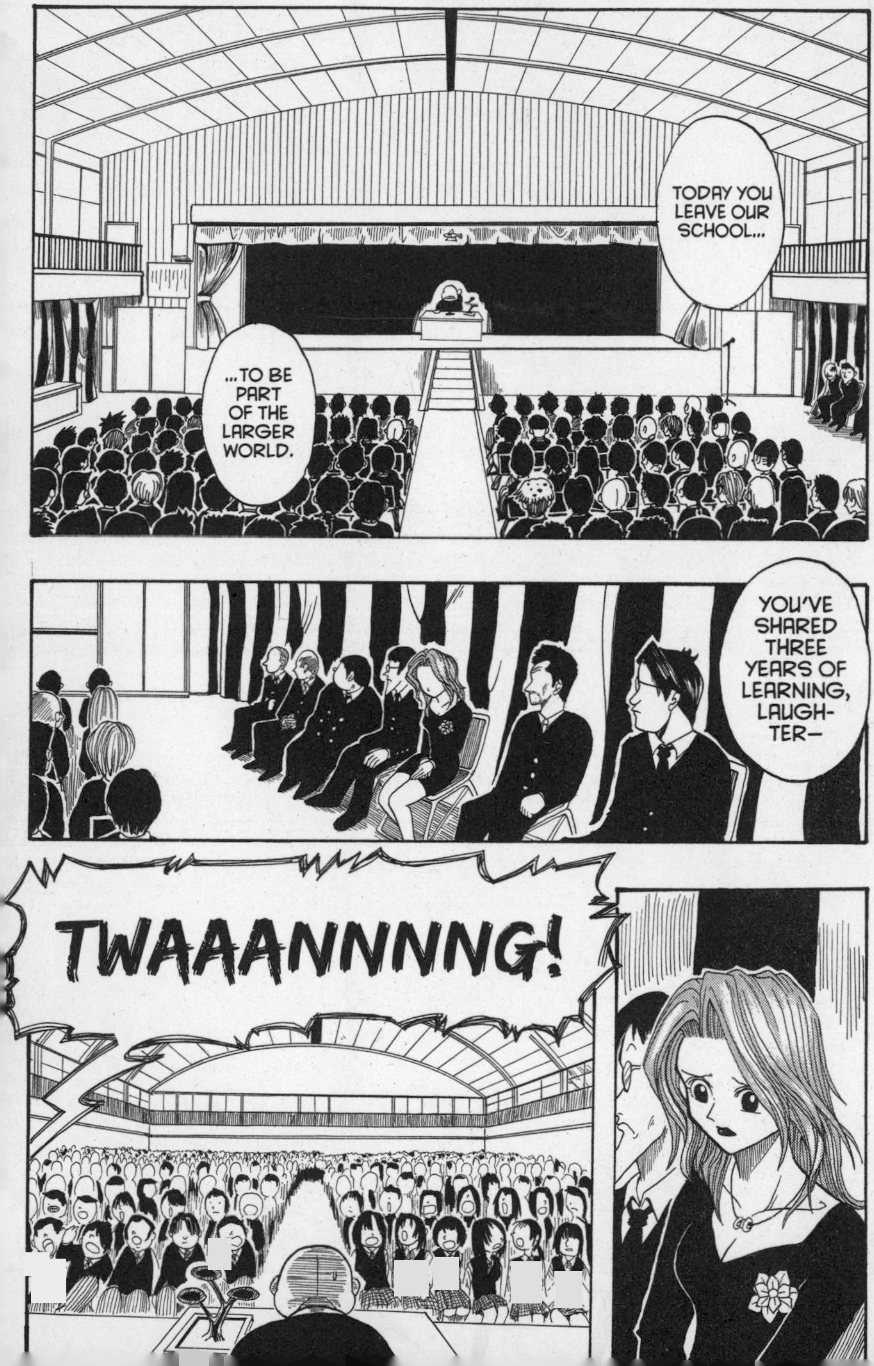
TODAY YOU LEAVE OUR SCHOOL...
...TO BE PART OF THE LARGER WORLD.
YOU'VE SHARED THREE YEARS OF LEARNING, LAUGH- TER—
TWAAANNNNG!

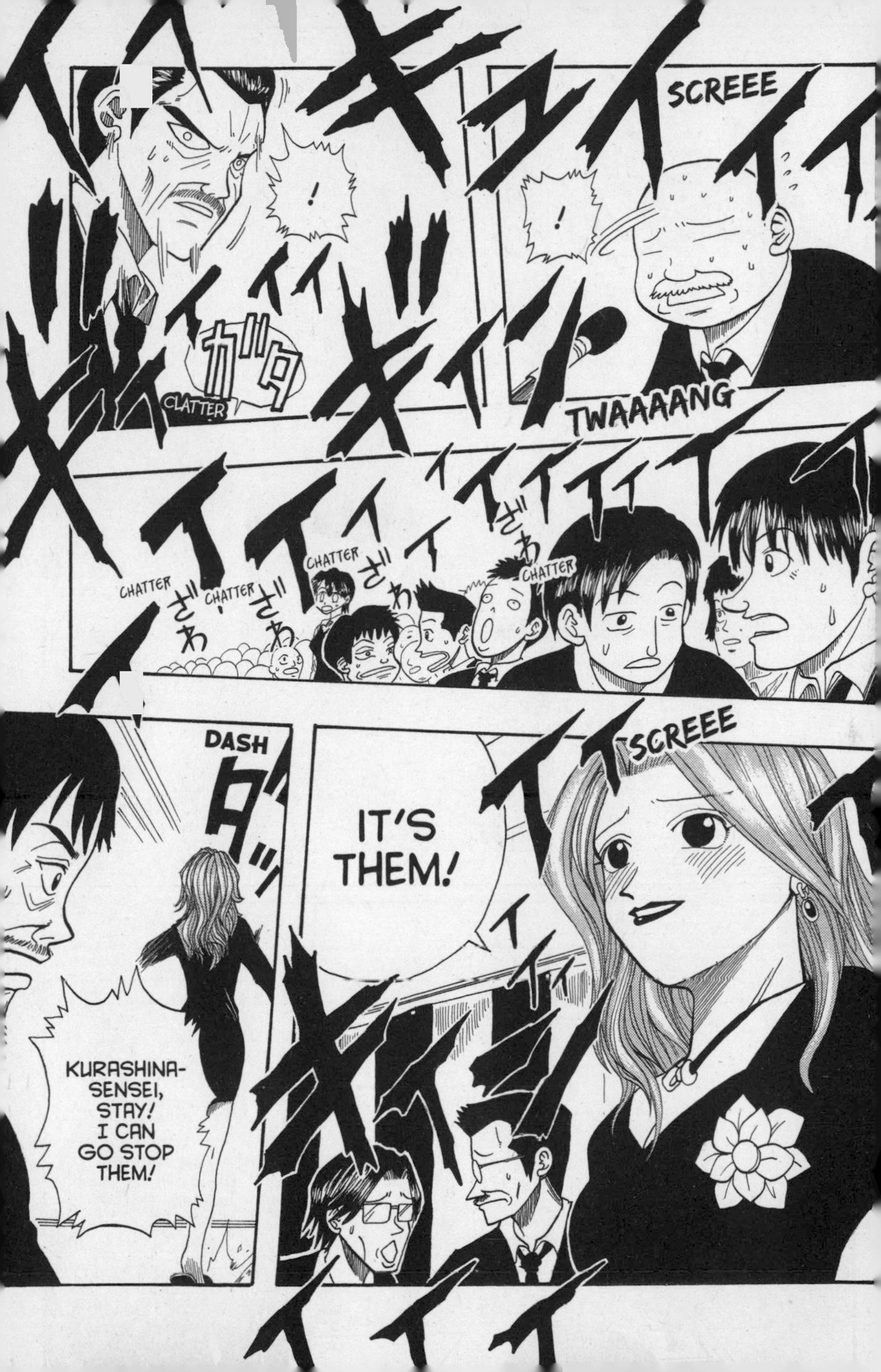
SCREEE
!
!
ガタ
CLATTER
TWAAAANG
CHATTER
ざわ
CHATTER
ざわ
CHATTER
ざわ
CHATTER
ざわ
SCREEE
IT'S THEM!
DASH
ダッ
KURASHINA-SENSEI, STAY! I CAN GO STOP THEM!

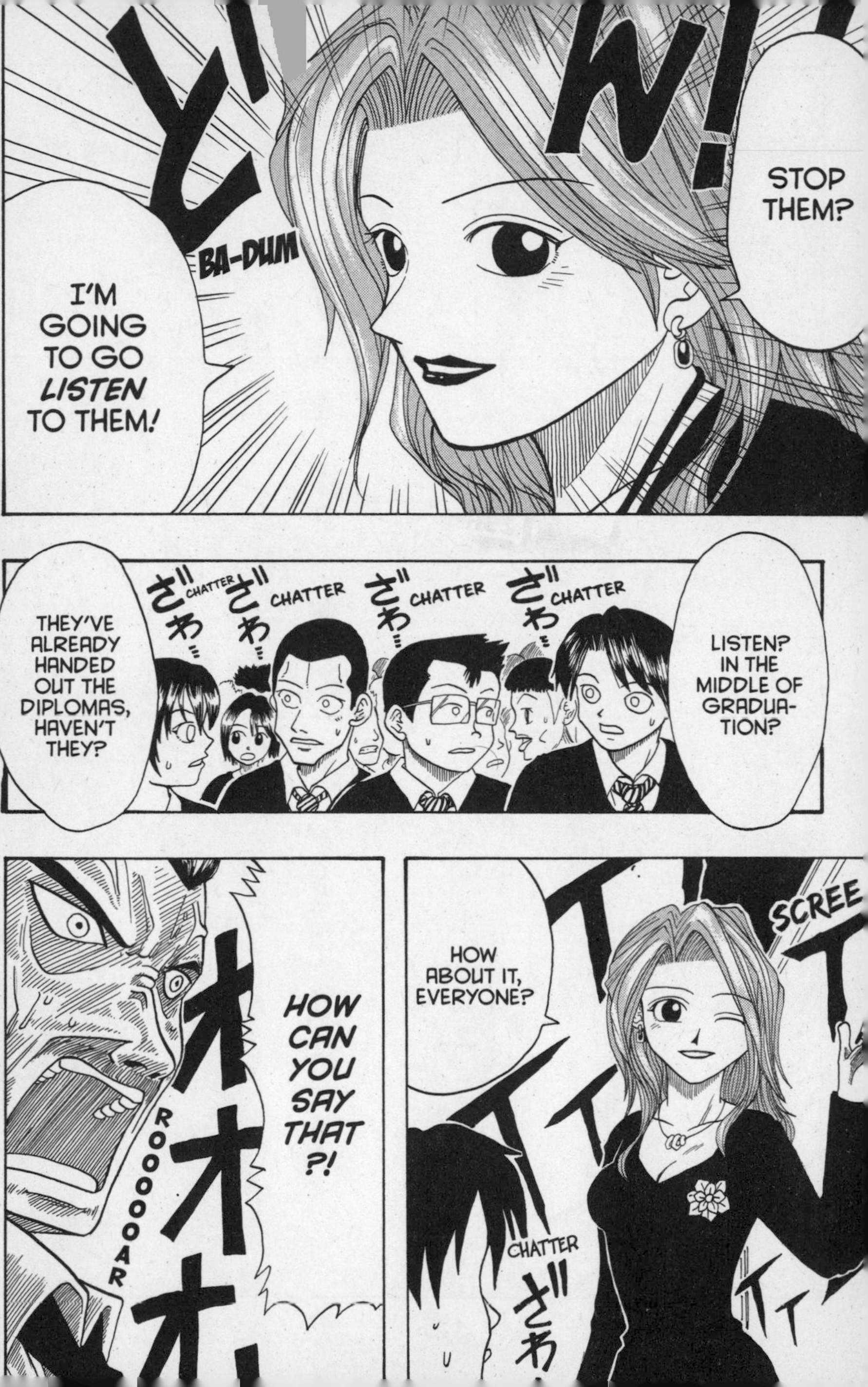
STOP THEM?
どん!
BA-DUM
I'M GOING TO GO LISTEN TO THEM!
LISTEN? IN THE MIDDLE OF GRADUATION?
ざわ CHATTER
ざわ CHATTER
ざわ CHATTER
ざわ CHATTER
THEY'VE ALREADY HANDED OUT THE DIPLOMAS, HAVEN'T THEY?
SCREE
HOW ABOUT IT, EVERYONE?
CHATTER
ざわ
HOW CAN YOU SAY THAT?!
ROOOOOOAR
オオオ

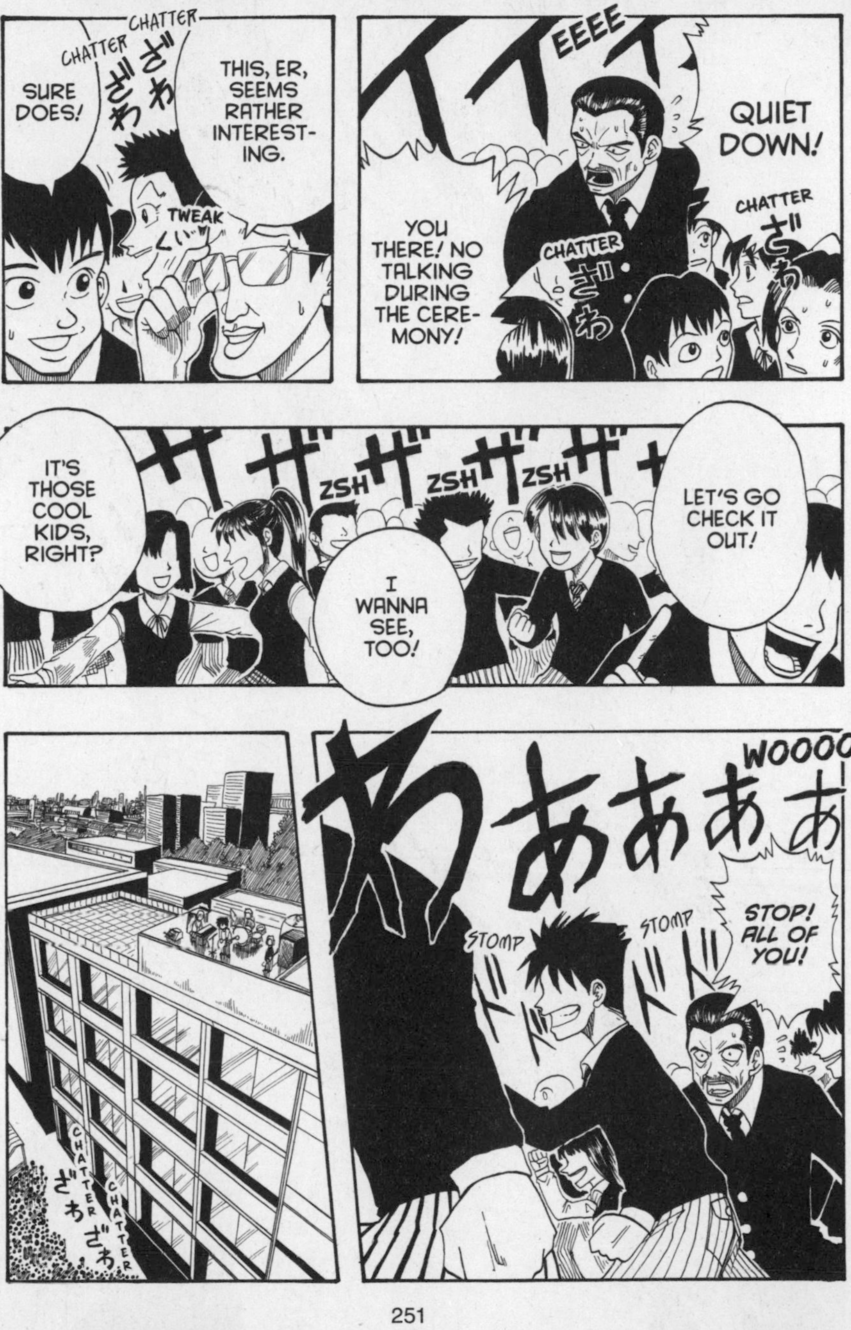
EEEE
イイ
QUIET DOWN!
YOU THERE! NO TALKING DURING THE CEREMONY!
CHATTER
ざわ
CHATTER
ざわ
THIS, ER, SEEMS RATHER INTERESTING.
CHATTER
CHATTER
ざわ ざわ
SURE DOES!
TWEAK
くいっ
LET'S GO CHECK IT OUT!
ZSH
ZSH
ZSH
ザザザザザ
I WANNA SEE, TOO!
IT'S THOSE COOL KIDS, RIGHT?
WOOOO!
わあああああ
STOP! ALL OF YOU!
STOMP
STOMP
ドドドド
CHATTER
CHATTER
ざわ ざわ

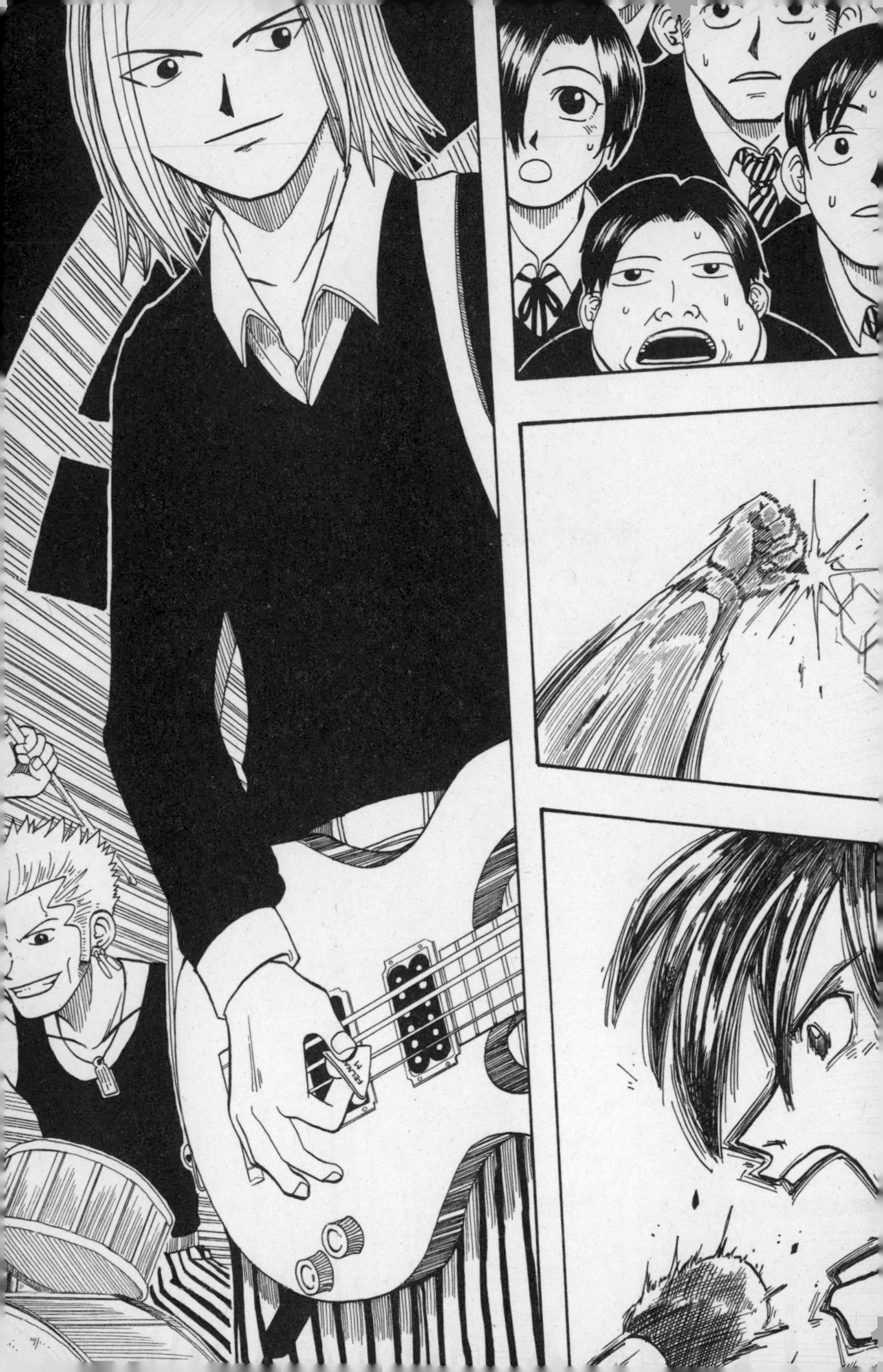

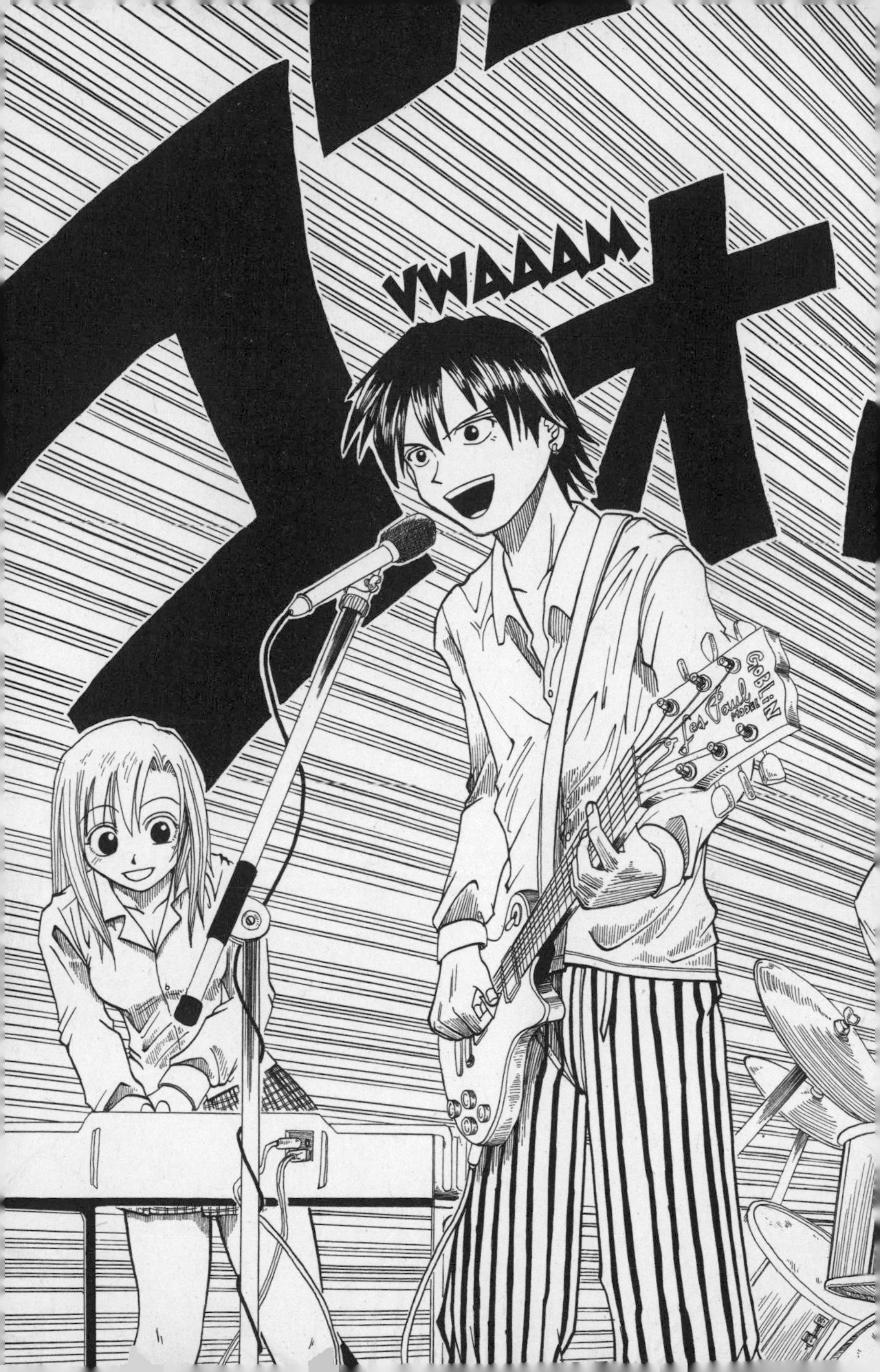
VWAAAM
GOBLIN
Les Paul
MODEL

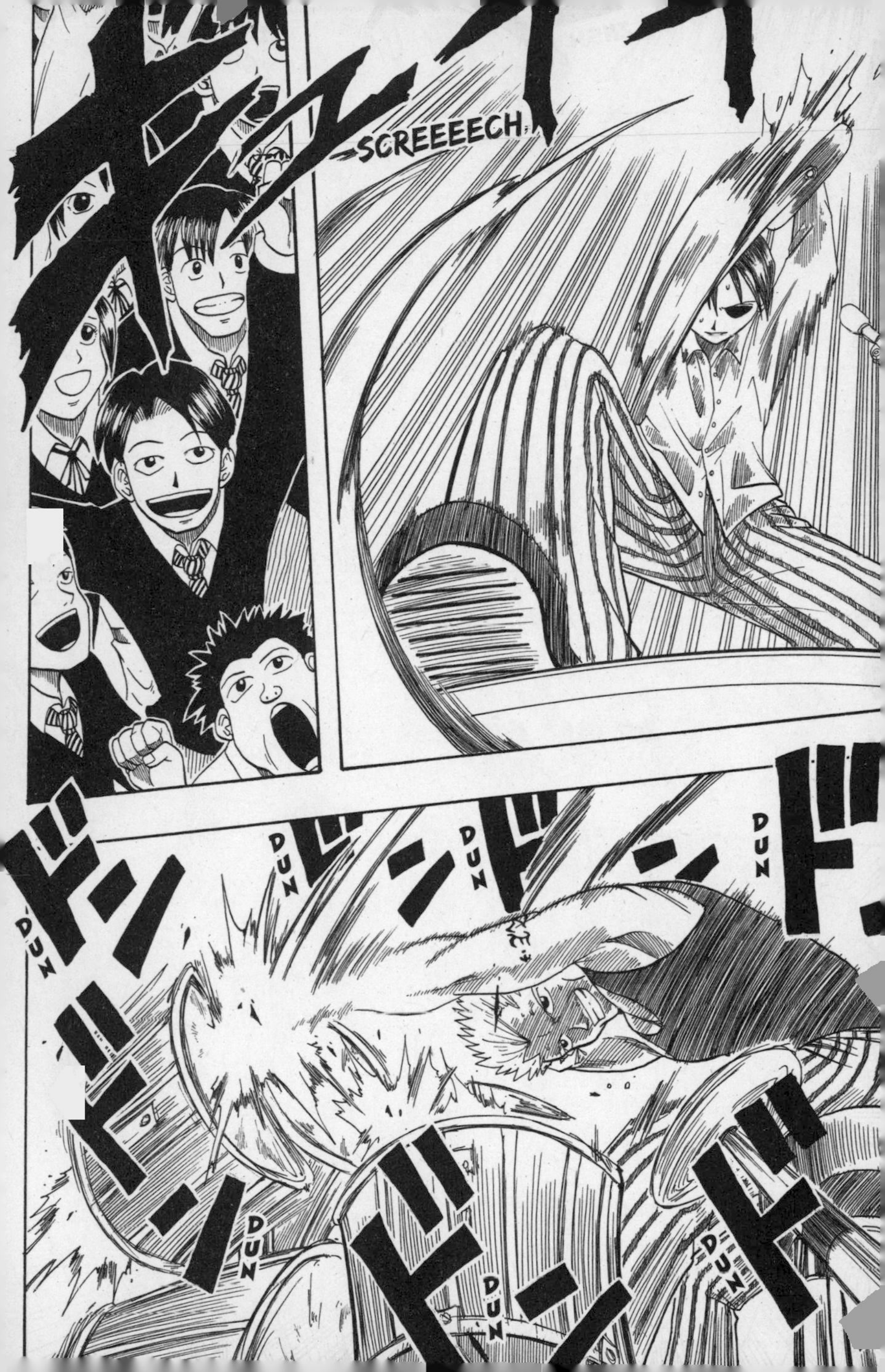
SCREEEEECH
DUN
DUN
DUN
DUN
DUN
DUN
DUN

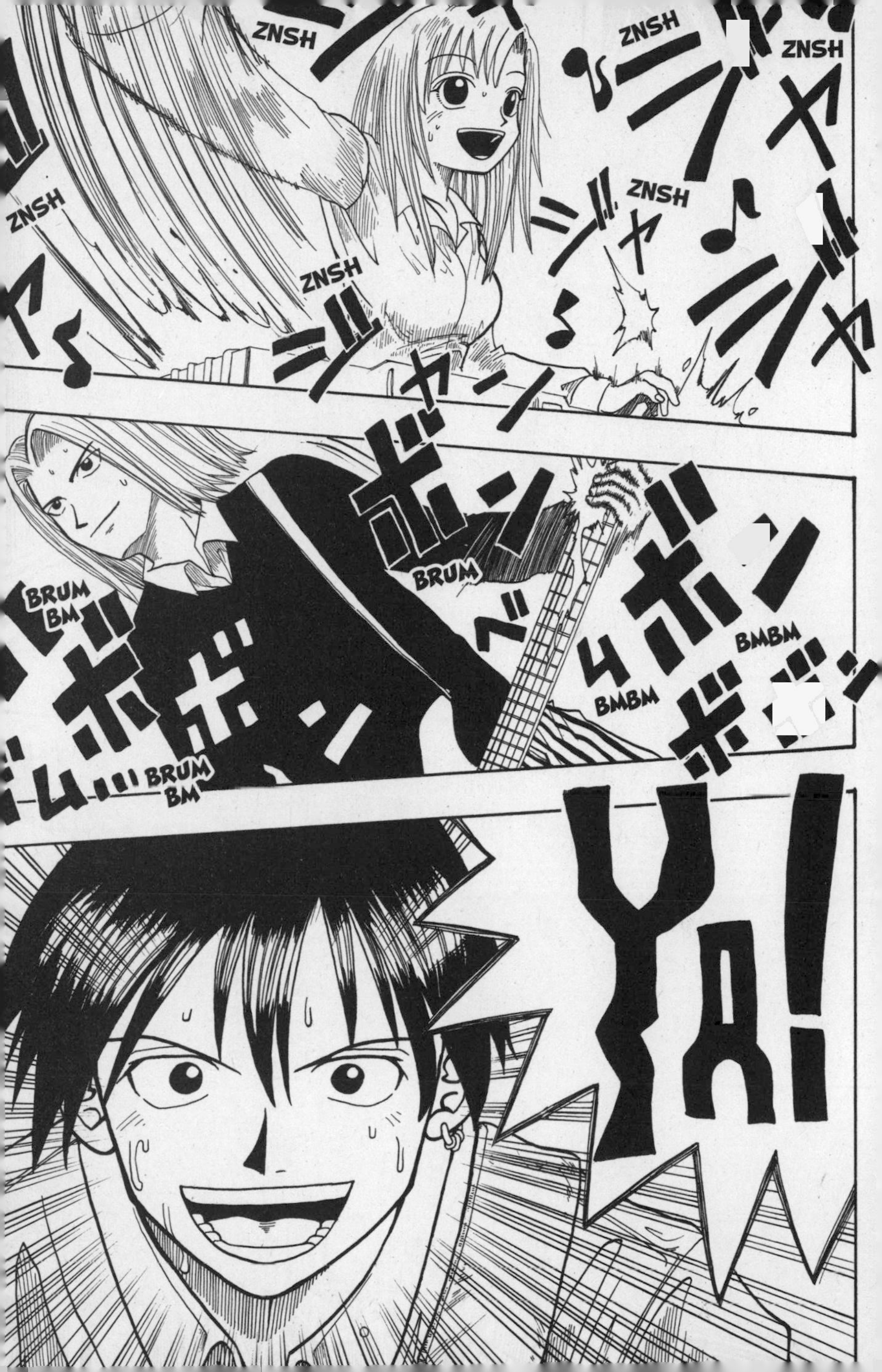
ZNSH
ZNSH
ZNSH
ZNSH
ZNSH
ZNSH
BMBM
BMBM
BRUM
BRUM BM
BRUM BM
YA!

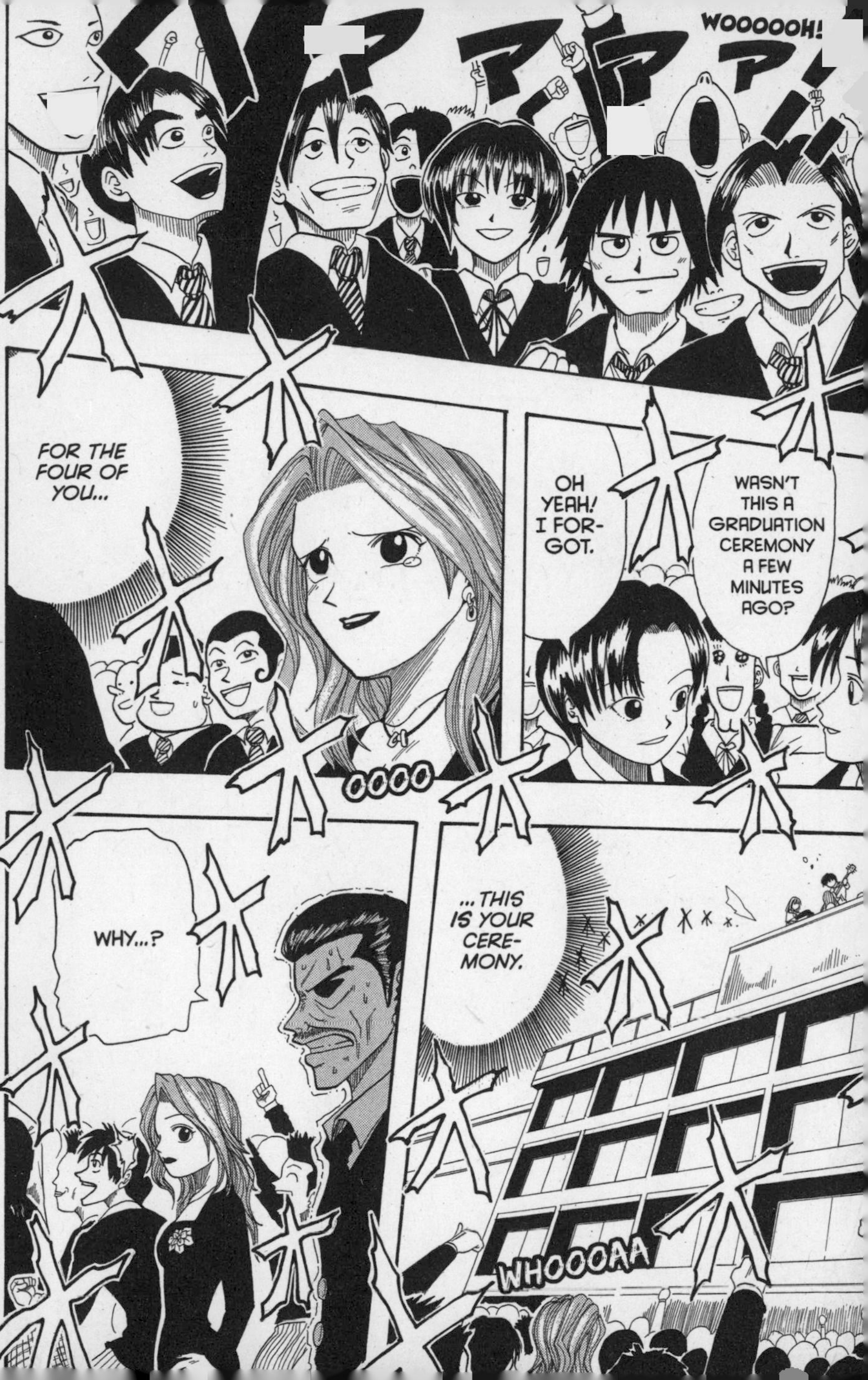
WOOOOOH!
WASN'T THIS A GRADUATION CEREMONY A FEW MINUTES AGO?
OH YEAH! I FOR-GOT.
FOR THE FOUR OF YOU...
OOOO
...THIS IS YOUR CERE-MONY.
WHOOOAA
WHY...?

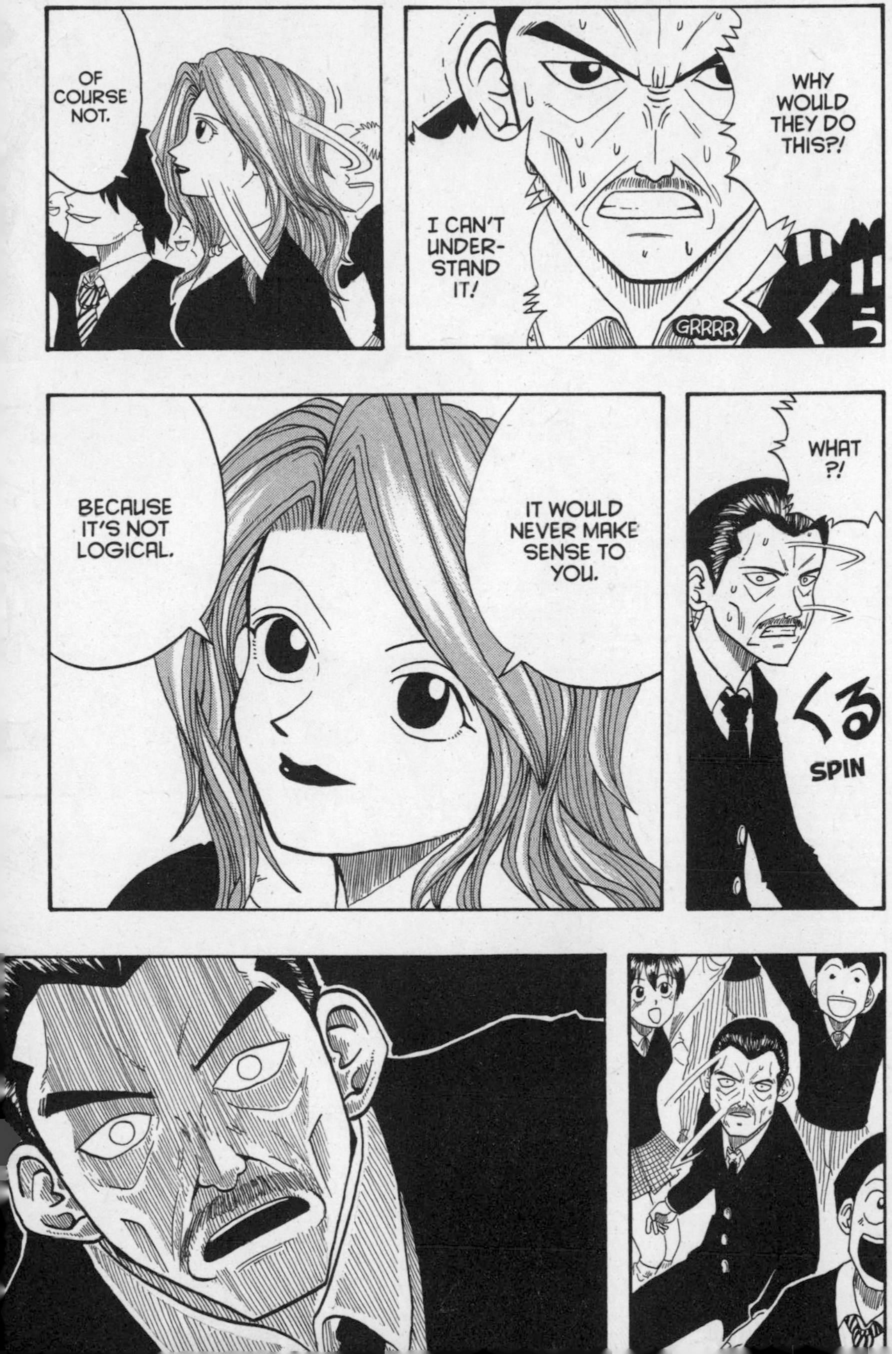
WHY WOULD THEY DO THIS?!
I CAN'T UNDER-STAND IT!
GRRRR
OF COURSE NOT.
WHAT ?!
くる
SPIN
IT WOULD NEVER MAKE SENSE TO YOU.
BECAUSE IT'S NOT LOGICAL.

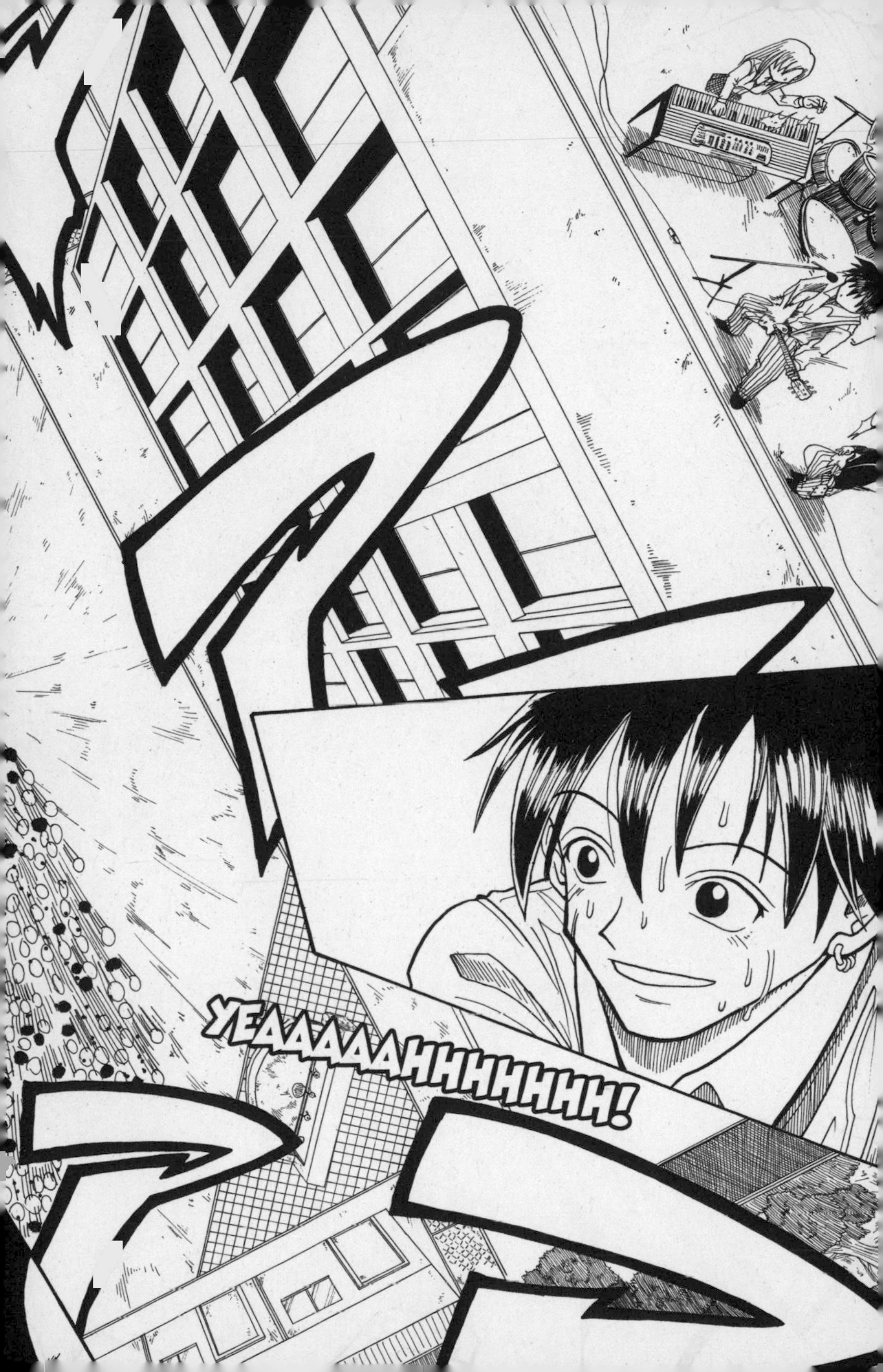
YEAAAAAHHHHHHHH!

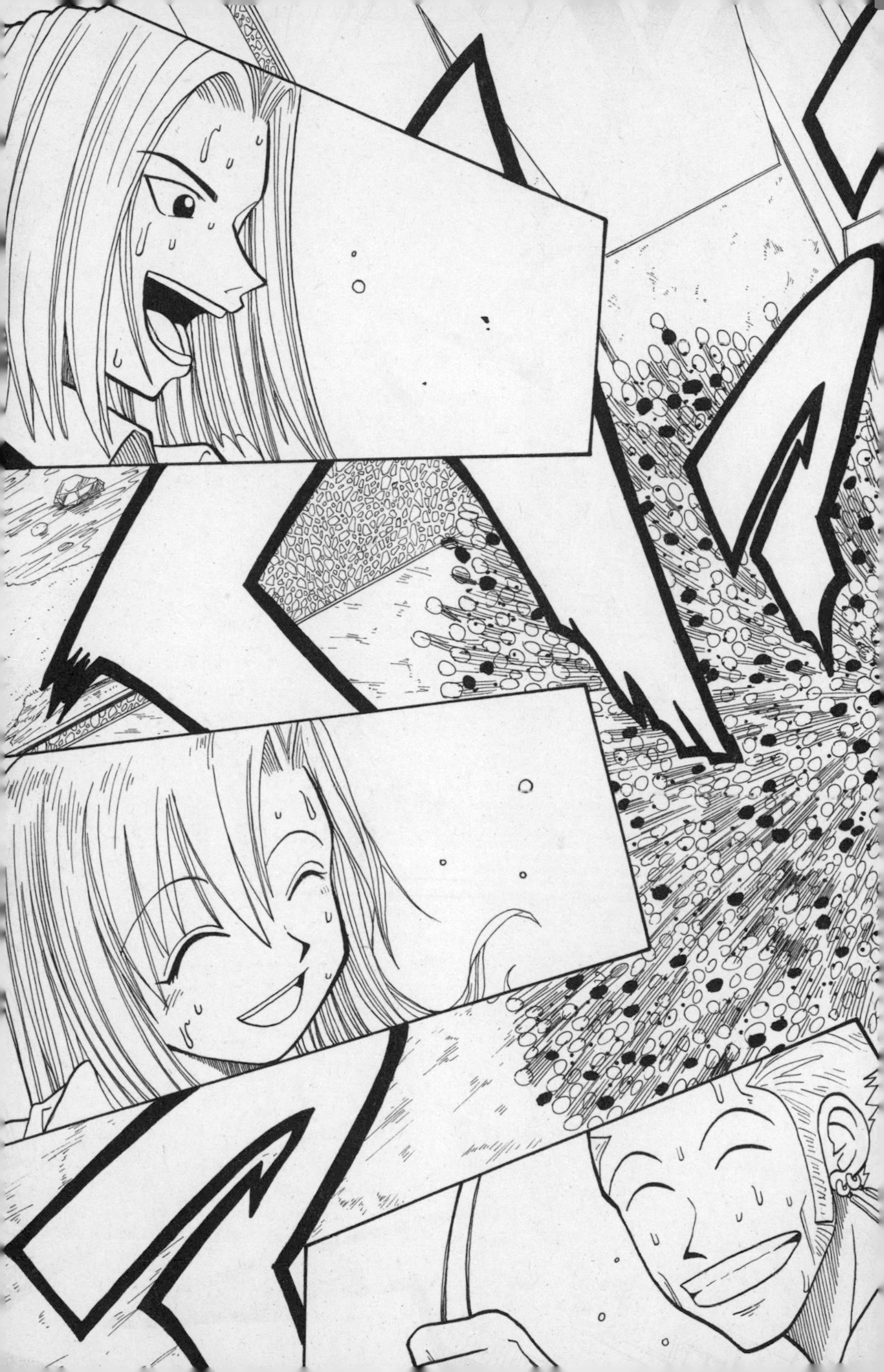

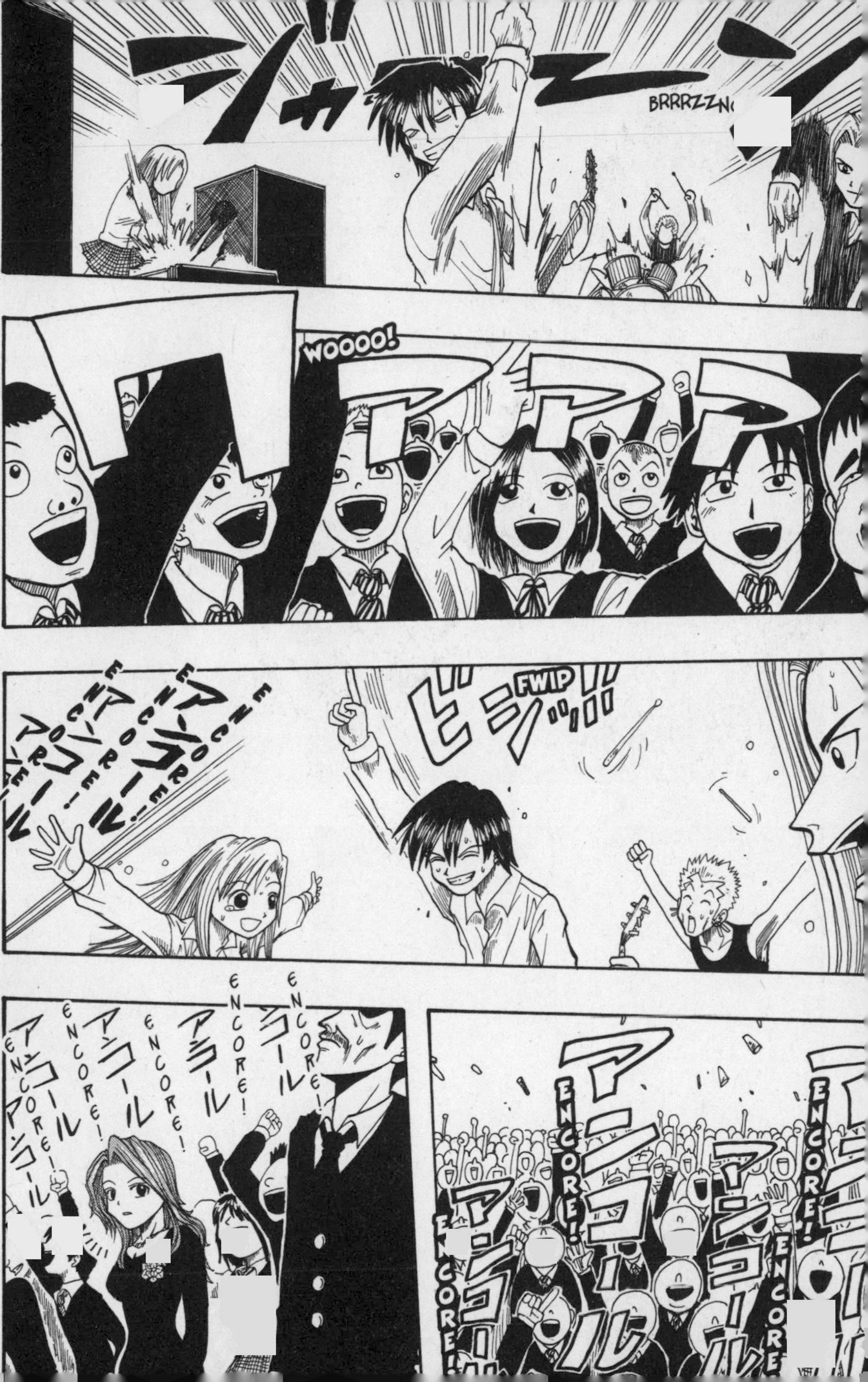

BRRRZZN
WOOOO!
FWIP
ENCORE!
ENCORE!
ENCORE!
ENCORE!
ENCORE!
ENCORE!
ENCORE!
ENCORE!
ENCORE!
ENCORE!
ENCORE!

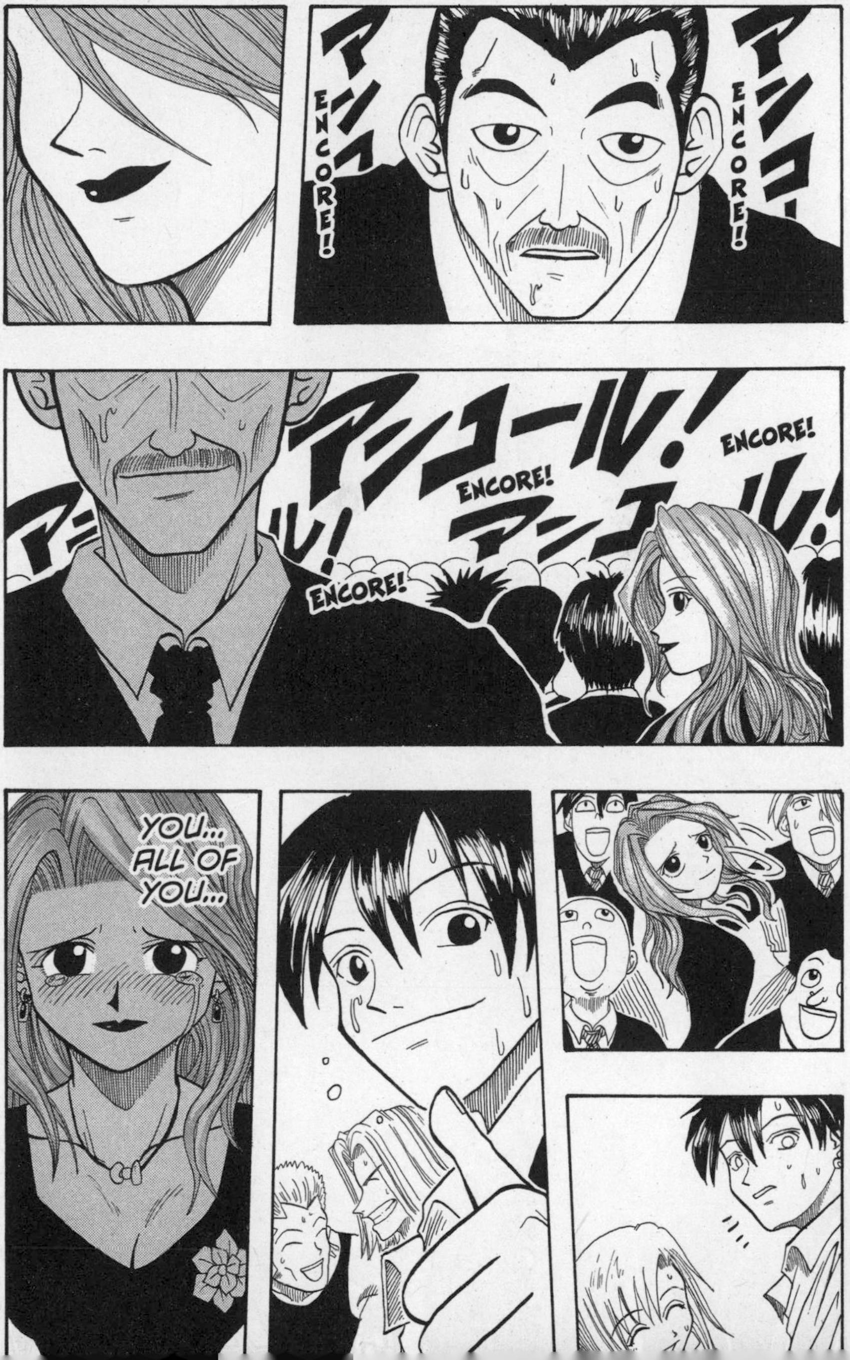
ENCORE!
ENCORE!
アンコール!
ENCORE!
ENCORE!
ENCORE!
YOU... ALL OF YOU...

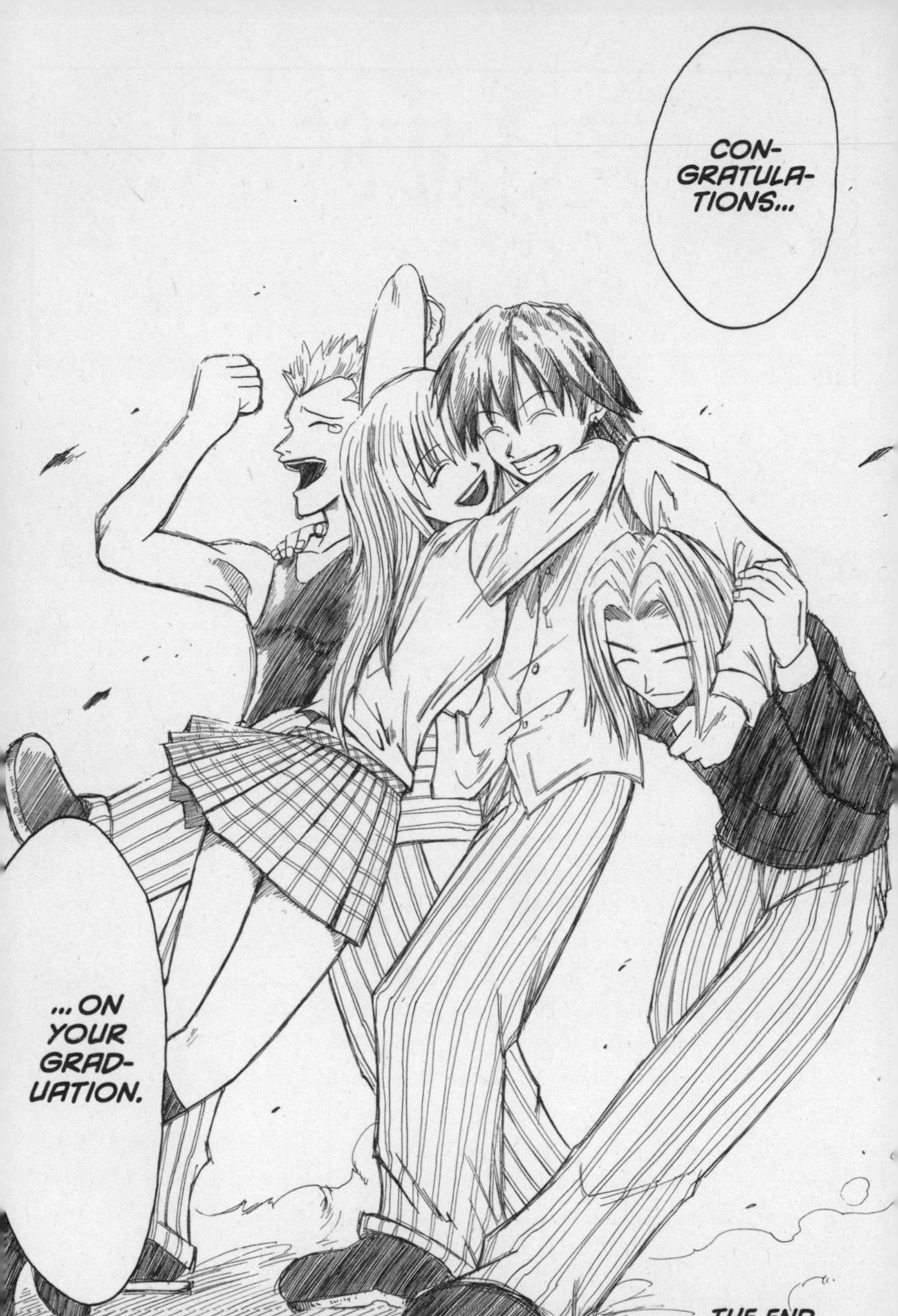
CON-GRATULA-TIONS...
...ON YOUR GRAD-UATION.
THE END

FIRST PUBLISHED: *WEEKLY SHONEN MAGAZINE* NO. 31 AUG 1998 (MAGAZINE FRESH)

BAD BOYS SONG

ON "BAD BOYS SONG"

Geeeez, I wanna redraw this one! (LOL) This was the only story I hesitated to include in this collection.

So first off, how did I end up with this story? Honestly... I was just **killing time!! (LMAO)** Seriously, though, at the time I was drawing manga like my life depended on it. This, however, was the piece I did while waiting for the results of the Rookie Prize. That, of course, was won by "Magician," which you can see in Part 1. But I actually finished that story well ahead of the deadline, and was left with a lot of time to twiddle my thumbs. "Bad Boys Song" was published in a magazine called "Magazine FRESH." So although I drew this after "Magician," this one technically ran first. So I don't actually know which one is my debut work (LOL)...

This story draws inspiration from my own high school days (which is not to say it's true!). I cribbed the title (verbatim!) from "Bad Boys," a story by one of my favorite authors, Hiroshi Tanaka. This is my only set-in-real-ish-life story, for now. Like I said, I would love to redraw it. If I got that chance, I would make it so the protagonist can **fly through the sky,** the heroine **carries a machine gun,** and the drums and bass **combine to form a crazy guardian beast!** What's that? Give it up, you say...?

ON BACK WHEN I WAS IN A BAND, AND STUFF

I touched on this in one of the extras in Part 1, but during my high school days, I was in a band called Night Meeting. I first started playing guitar when I saw one of the upperclassmen do a live show and thought, "That's so cool!!" Playing in a band seemed like a much better way to get girls than drawing manga. And so I bought a (very, very cheap) guitar. I kept quietly doing comics on the side. At first, I just couldn't get the hang of the instrument, and I was left feeling all like, "This stupid thing!" But the better I got at it, the more interesting it was. (I'm sure art will be the same way!) Once the band got going, we did live shows at a rate of about one every two or three months. To put it bluntly, our band pretty much sucked, me most of all (sobs). But, carried along on sheer enthusiasm, during our senior year we started to think, "Hey, why not go pro?" To find out just how good we were, we entered a regional contest...which we lost. I can see why. (To review: We sucked.) What's more, we didn't actually feel that bad about it. It helped us realize we hadn't been serious. We had just been doing it for the fun of it! In the end, the band broke up when we all graduated high school. I went to Tokyo in hopes of making my dream of becoming a manga artist. But I'm still friends with the other band members, and we always go out for a drink whenever I visit my hometown.

But I'll let you in on a secret—those three years in a band taught me something else: Even if you suck, as long as you love what you're doing, people will enjoy it. I think manga might be the same way. I'm not the world's greatest artist, but I hope to bring my readers joy through my unfettered love of the craft...or at least through having decent characters and stories.

So please keep reading my manga. And remember the love!

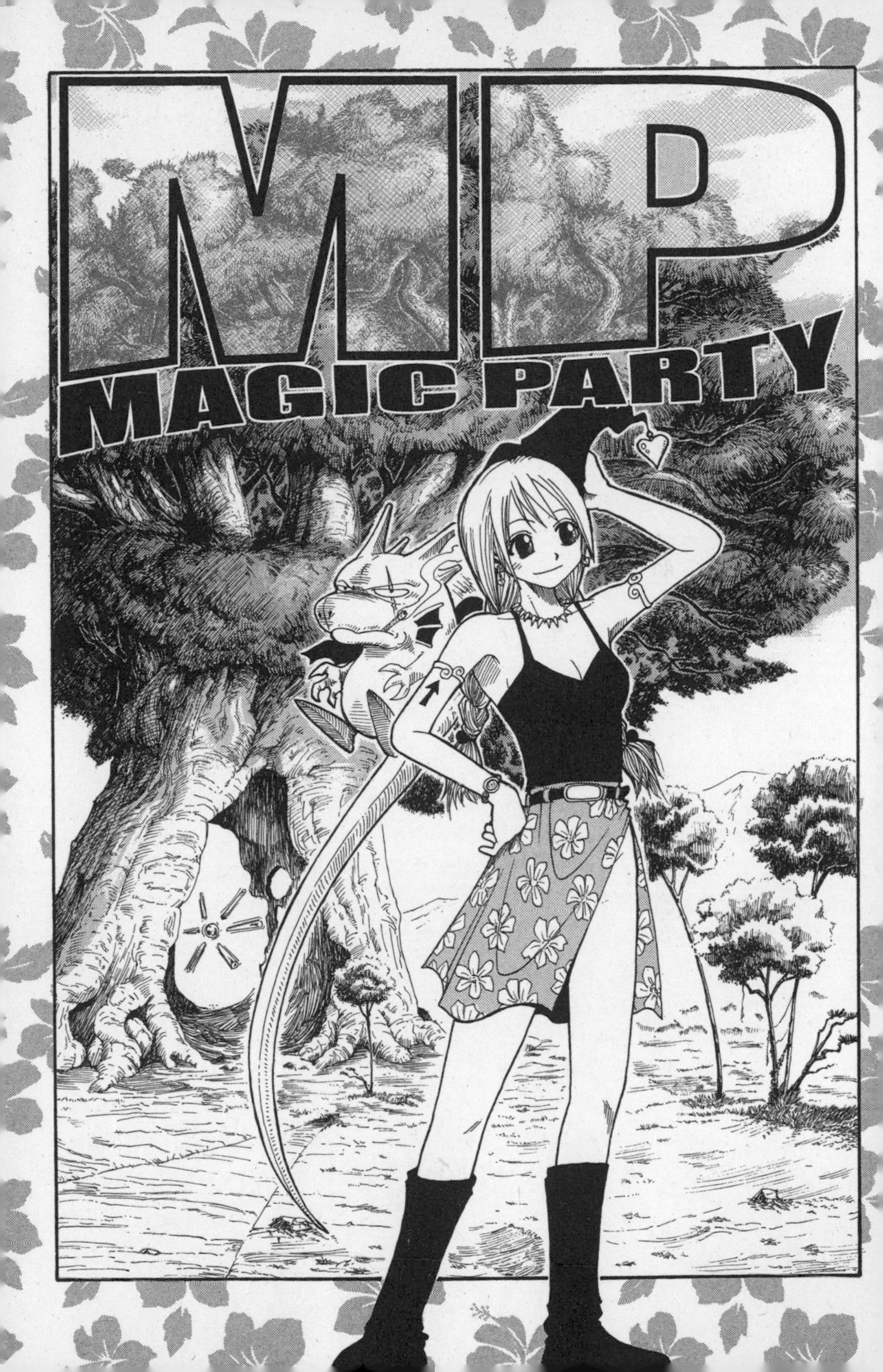
MP
MAGIC PARTY

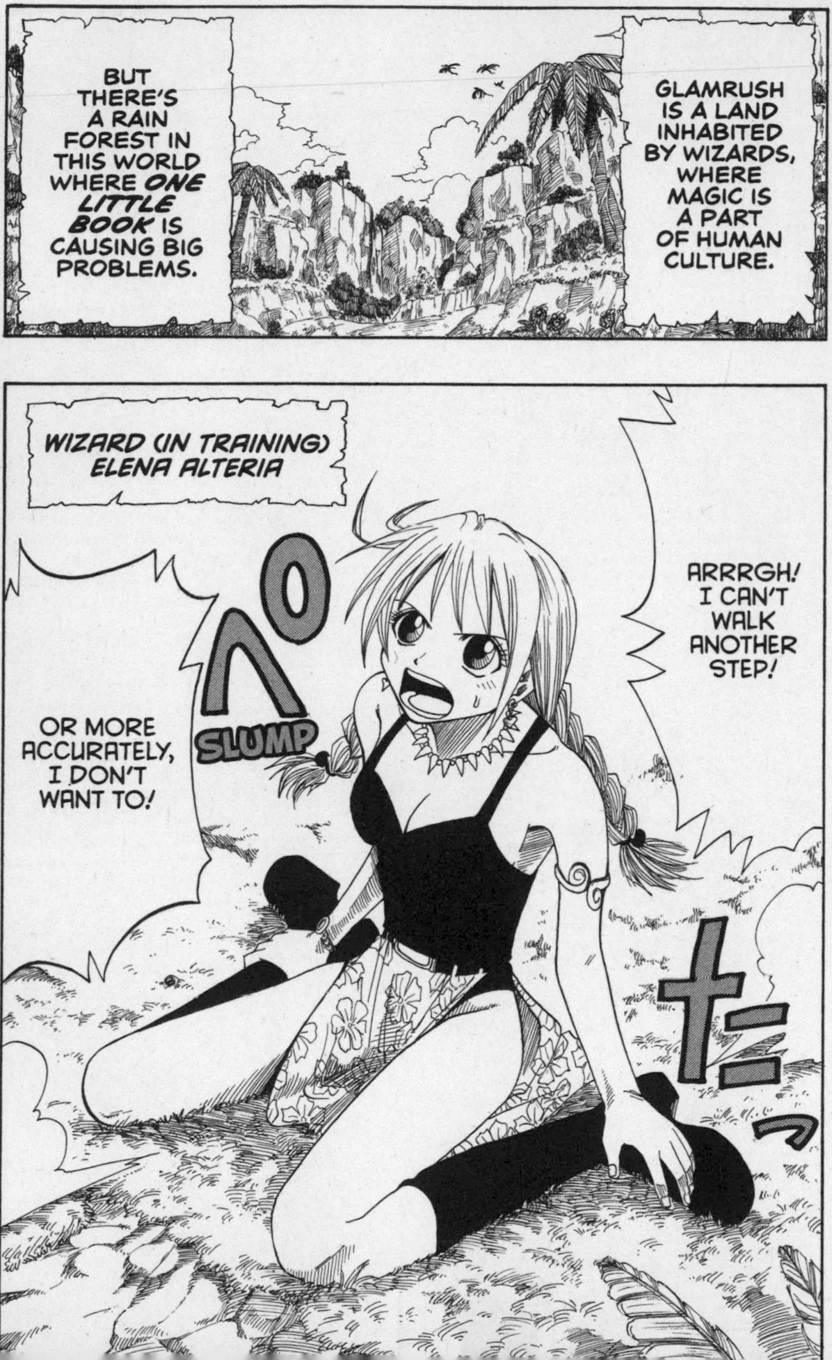
GLAMRUSH IS A LAND INHABITED BY WIZARDS, WHERE MAGIC IS A PART OF HUMAN CULTURE.
BUT THERE'S A RAIN FOREST IN THIS WORLD WHERE ONE LITTLE BOOK IS CAUSING BIG PROBLEMS.
WIZARD (IN TRAINING) ELENA ALTERIA
ARRRGH! I CAN'T WALK ANOTHER STEP!
SLUMP
OR MORE ACCURATELY, I DON'T WANT TO!

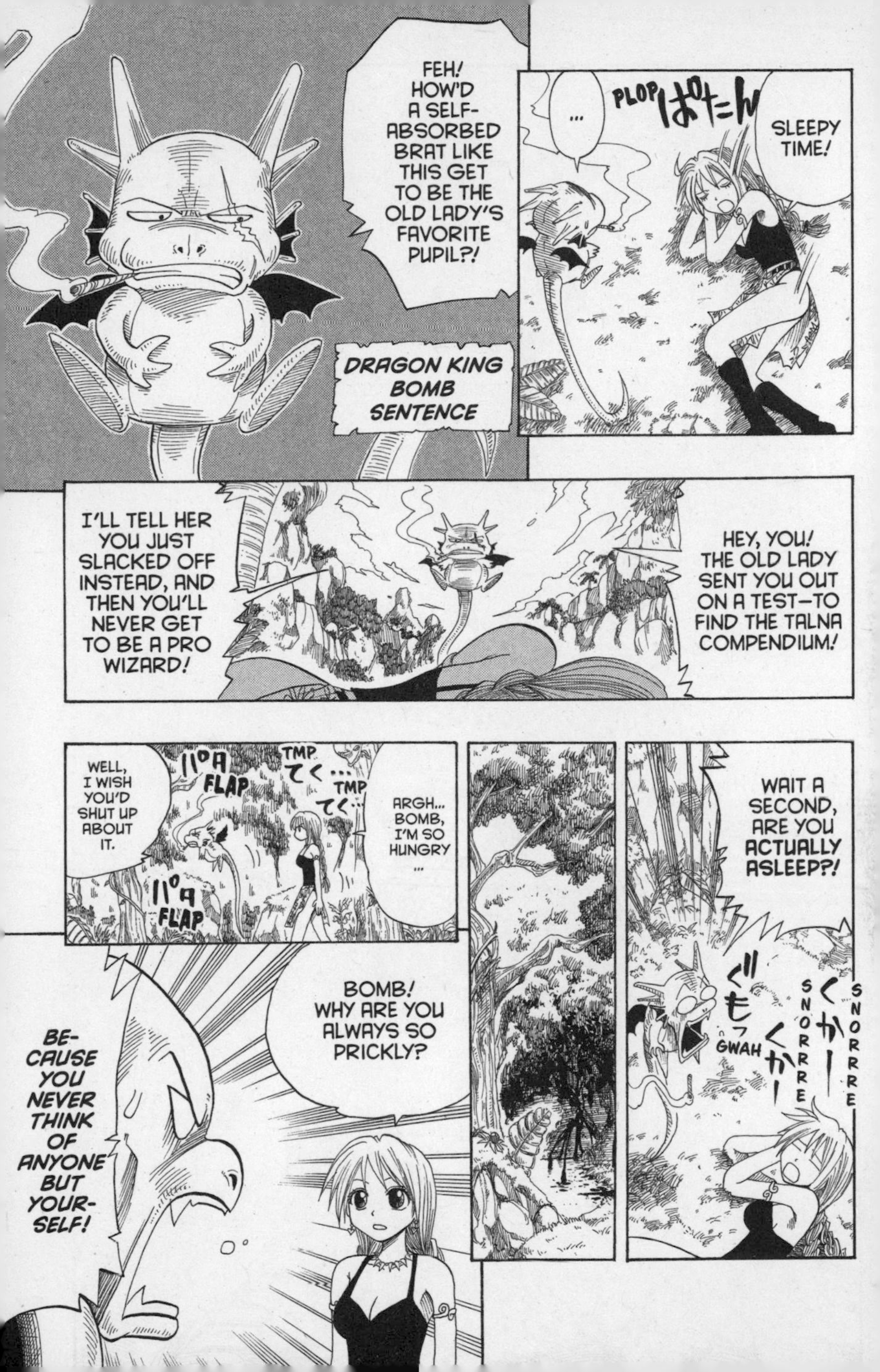

SLEEPY TIME!
PLOP ぱたん
...
FEH! HOW'D A SELF-ABSORBED BRAT LIKE THIS GET TO BE THE OLD LADY'S FAVORITE PUPIL?!
DRAGON KING BOMB SENTENCE
HEY, YOU! THE OLD LADY SENT YOU OUT ON A TEST—TO FIND THE TALNA COMPENDIUM!
I'LL TELL HER YOU JUST SLACKED OFF INSTEAD, AND THEN YOU'LL NEVER GET TO BE A PRO WIZARD!
WAIT A SECOND, ARE YOU ACTUALLY ASLEEP?!
くかー SNORRE
くかー SNORRE
ぐもっ GWAH
ARGH... BOMB, I'M SO HUNGRY ...
TMP てく...
TMP てく...
パタ FLAP
WELL, I WISH YOU'D SHUT UP ABOUT IT.
パタ FLAP
BOMB! WHY ARE YOU ALWAYS SO PRICKLY?
BE-CAUSE YOU NEVER THINK OF ANYONE BUT YOUR-SELF!

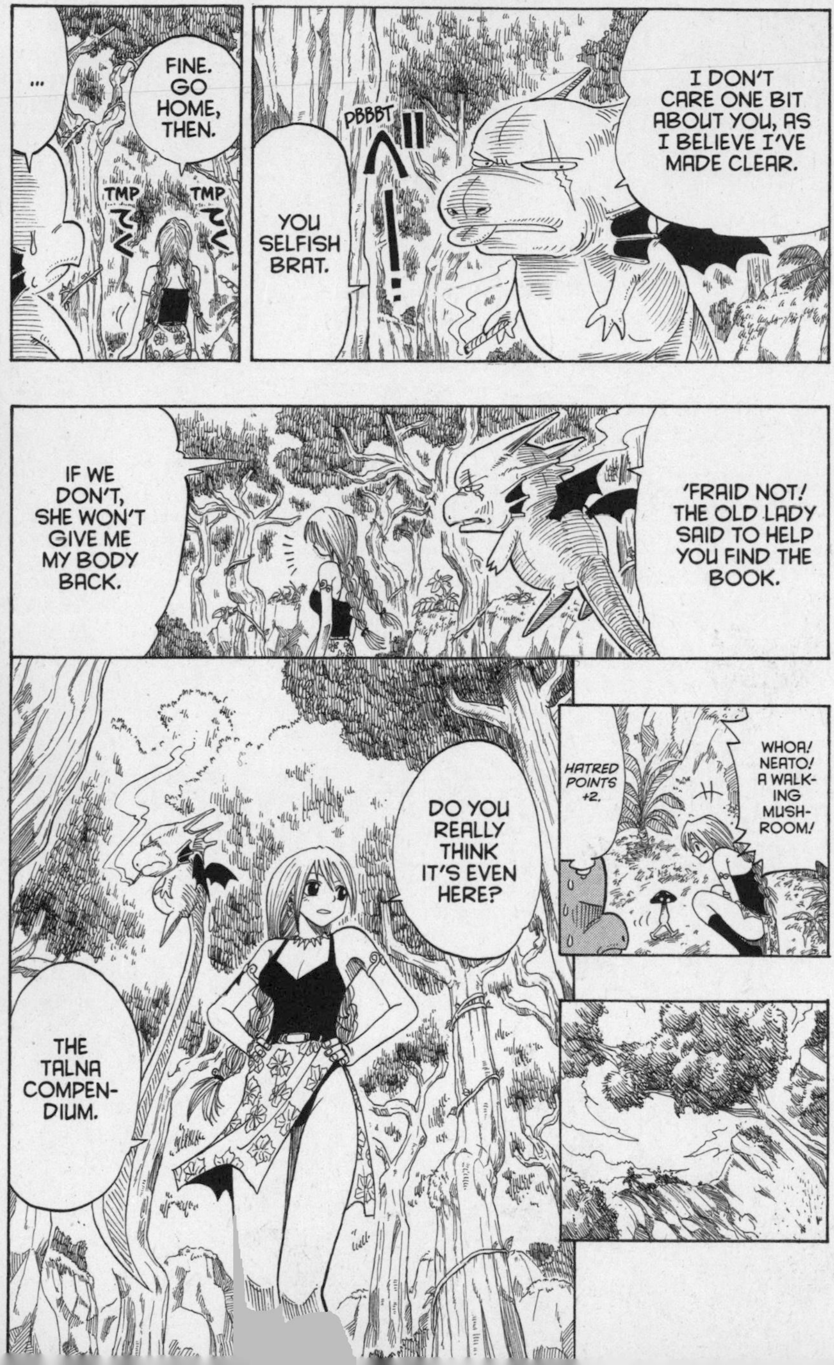

I DON'T CARE ONE BIT ABOUT YOU, AS I BELIEVE I'VE MADE CLEAR.
PBBBT
YOU SELFISH BRAT.
FINE. GO HOME, THEN.
TMP
TMP
...
'FRAID NOT! THE OLD LADY SAID TO HELP YOU FIND THE BOOK.
IF WE DON'T, SHE WON'T GIVE ME MY BODY BACK.
WHOA! NEATO! A WALKING-MUSHROOM!
HATRED POINTS +2.
DO YOU REALLY THINK IT'S EVEN HERE?
THE TALNA COMPENDIUM.

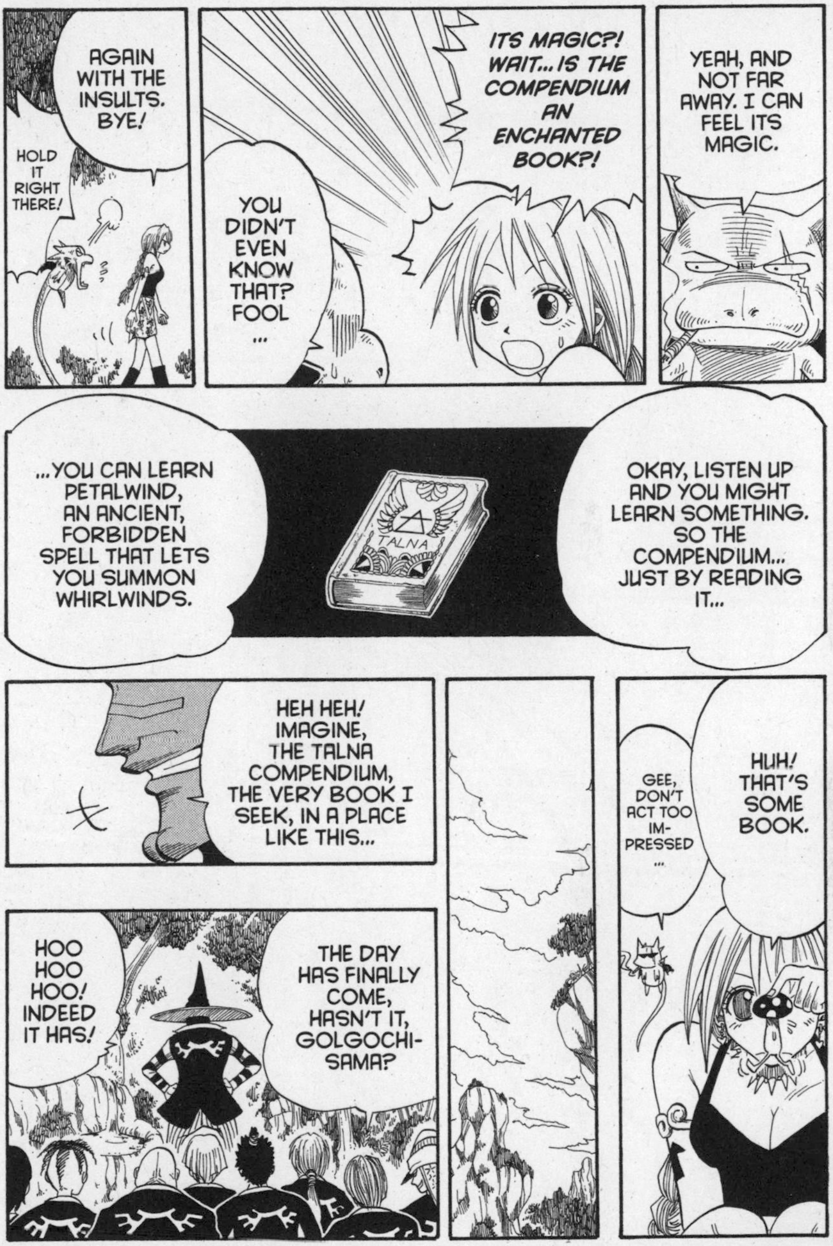

YEAH, AND NOT FAR AWAY. I CAN FEEL ITS MAGIC.
ITS MAGIC?! WAIT... IS THE COMPENDIUM AN ENCHANTED BOOK?!
YOU DIDN'T EVEN KNOW THAT? FOOL ...
AGAIN WITH THE INSULTS. BYE!
HOLD IT RIGHT THERE!
OKAY, LISTEN UP AND YOU MIGHT LEARN SOMETHING. SO THE COMPENDIUM... JUST BY READING IT...
TALNA
...YOU CAN LEARN PETALWIND, AN ANCIENT, FORBIDDEN SPELL THAT LETS YOU SUMMON WHIRLWINDS.
HUH! THAT'S SOME BOOK.
GEE, DON'T ACT TOO IM- PRESSED ...
HEH HEH! IMAGINE, THE TALNA COMPENDIUM, THE VERY BOOK I SEEK, IN A PLACE LIKE THIS...
THE DAY HAS FINALLY COME, HASN'T IT, GOLGOCHI-SAMA?
HOO HOO HOO! INDEED IT HAS!

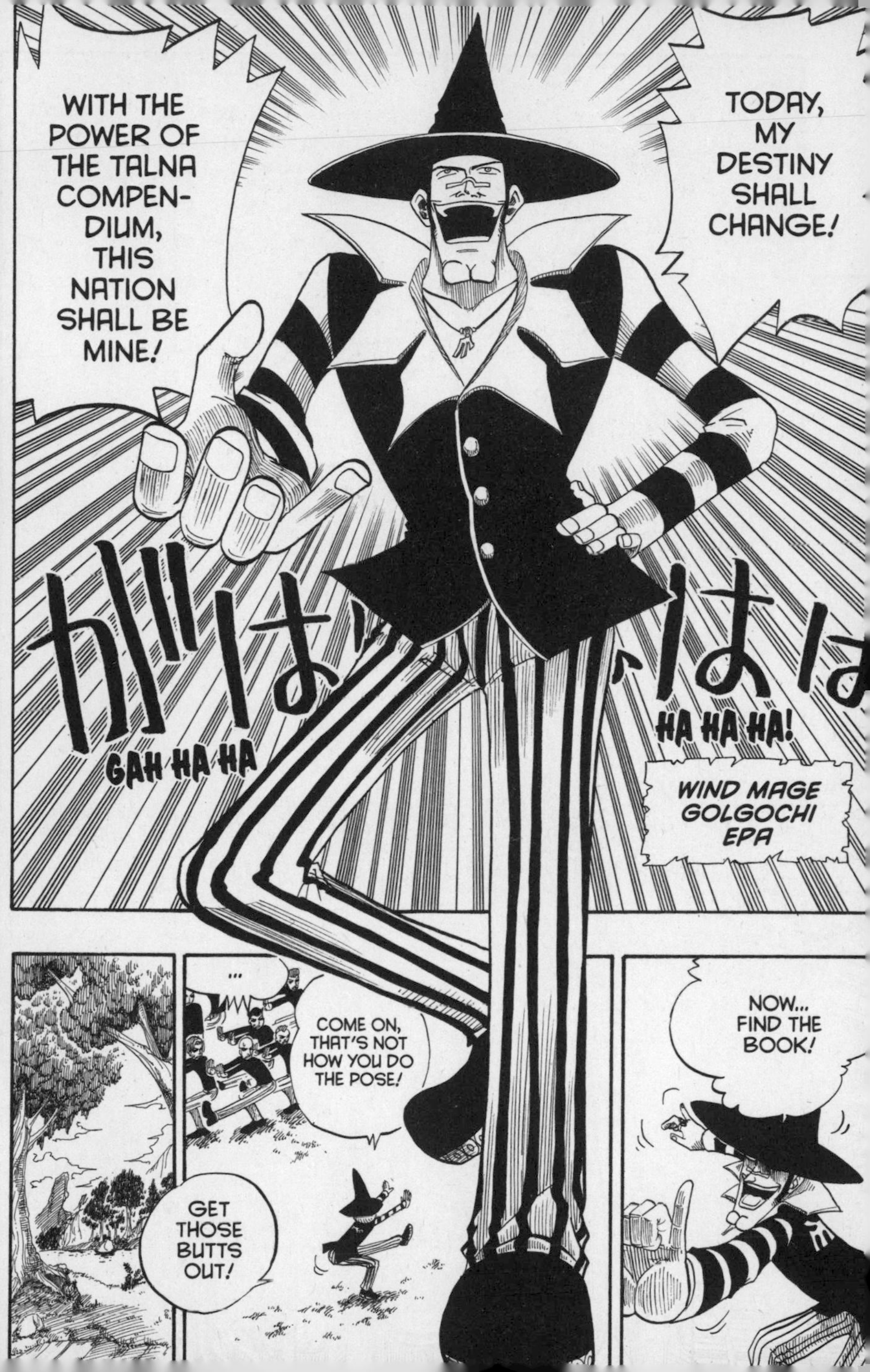
TODAY, MY DESTINY SHALL CHANGE!
WITH THE POWER OF THE TALNA COMPEN-DIUM, THIS NATION SHALL BE MINE!
GAH HA HA
HA HA HA!
WIND MAGE GOLGOCHI EPA
NOW... FIND THE BOOK!
...
COME ON, THAT'S NOT HOW YOU DO THE POSE!
GET THOSE BUTTS OUT!

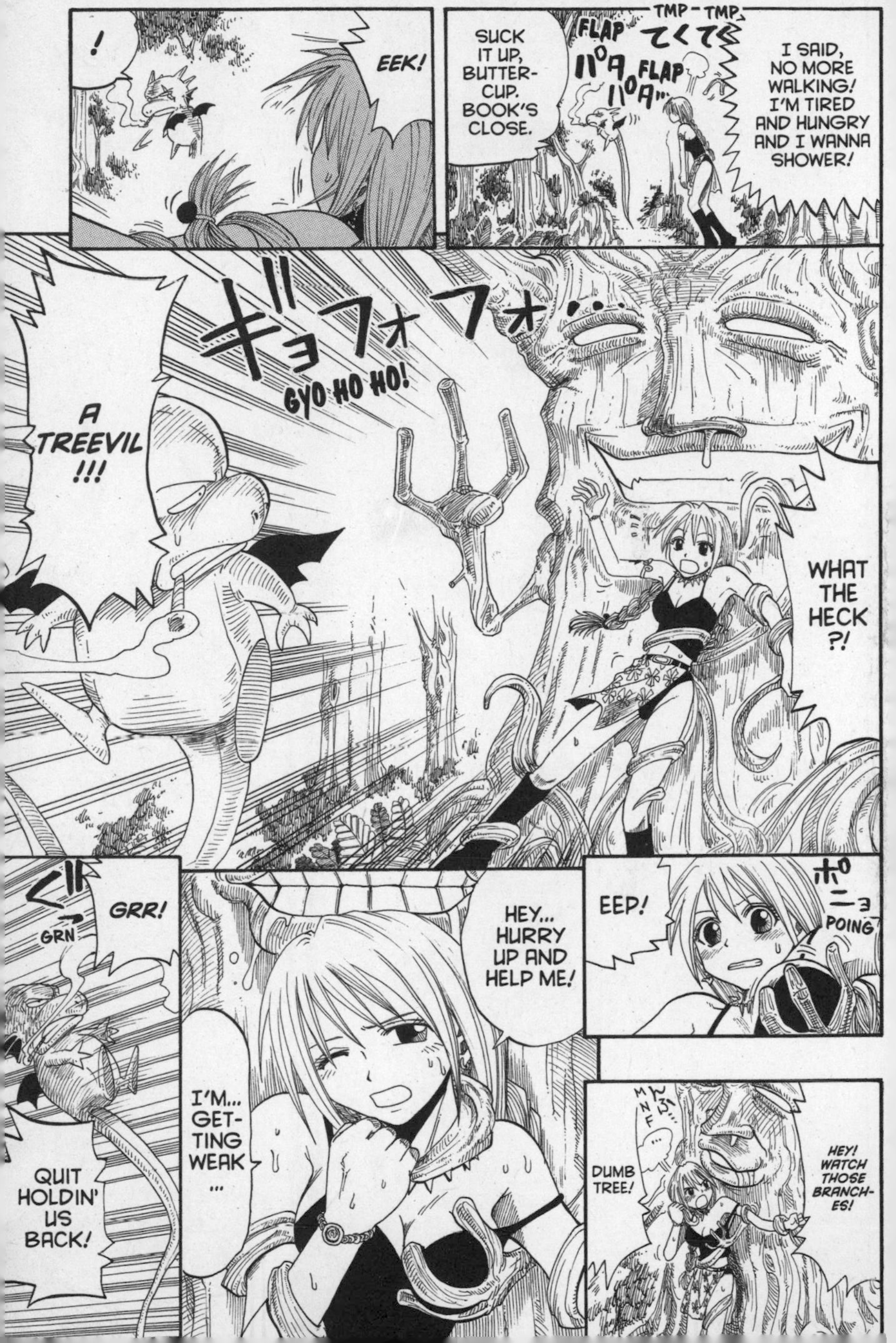
I SAID, NO MORE WALKING! I'M TIRED AND HUNGRY AND I WANNA SHOWER!
TMP-TMP てくて
FLAP パタ FLAP パタ...
SUCK IT UP, BUTTER-CUP. BOOK'S CLOSE.
EEK!
!
WHAT THE HECK?!
ギョフォフォ…
GYO HO HO!
A TREEVIL!!!
POING
EEP!
HEY! WATCH THOSE BRANCH-ES!
MNF
...
DUMB TREE!
HEY... HURRY UP AND HELP ME!
I'M... GET-TING WEAK ...
GRR!
GRN
QUIT HOLDIN' US BACK!

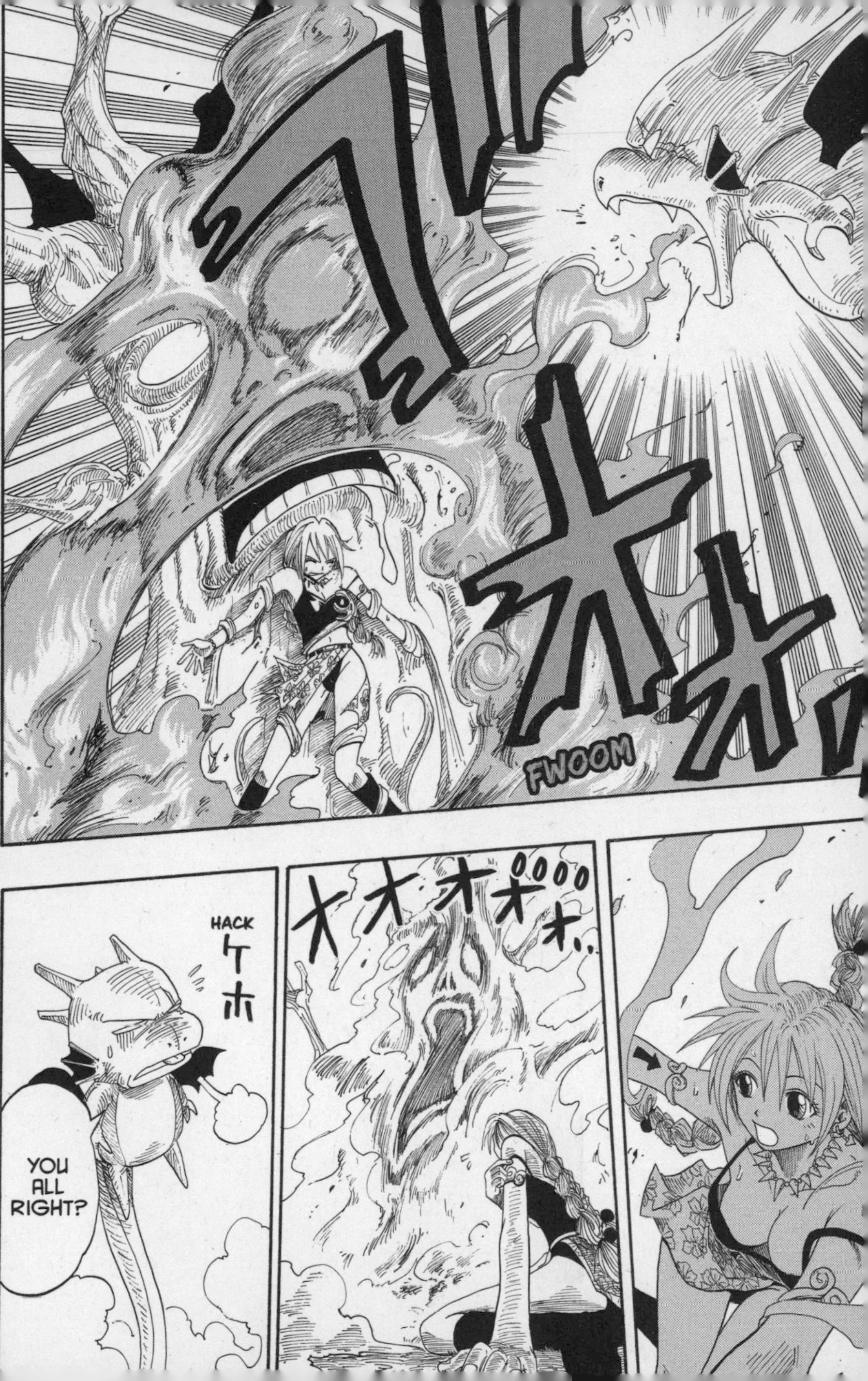
FWOOM
OOOO
HACK
ケホ
YOU ALL RIGHT?

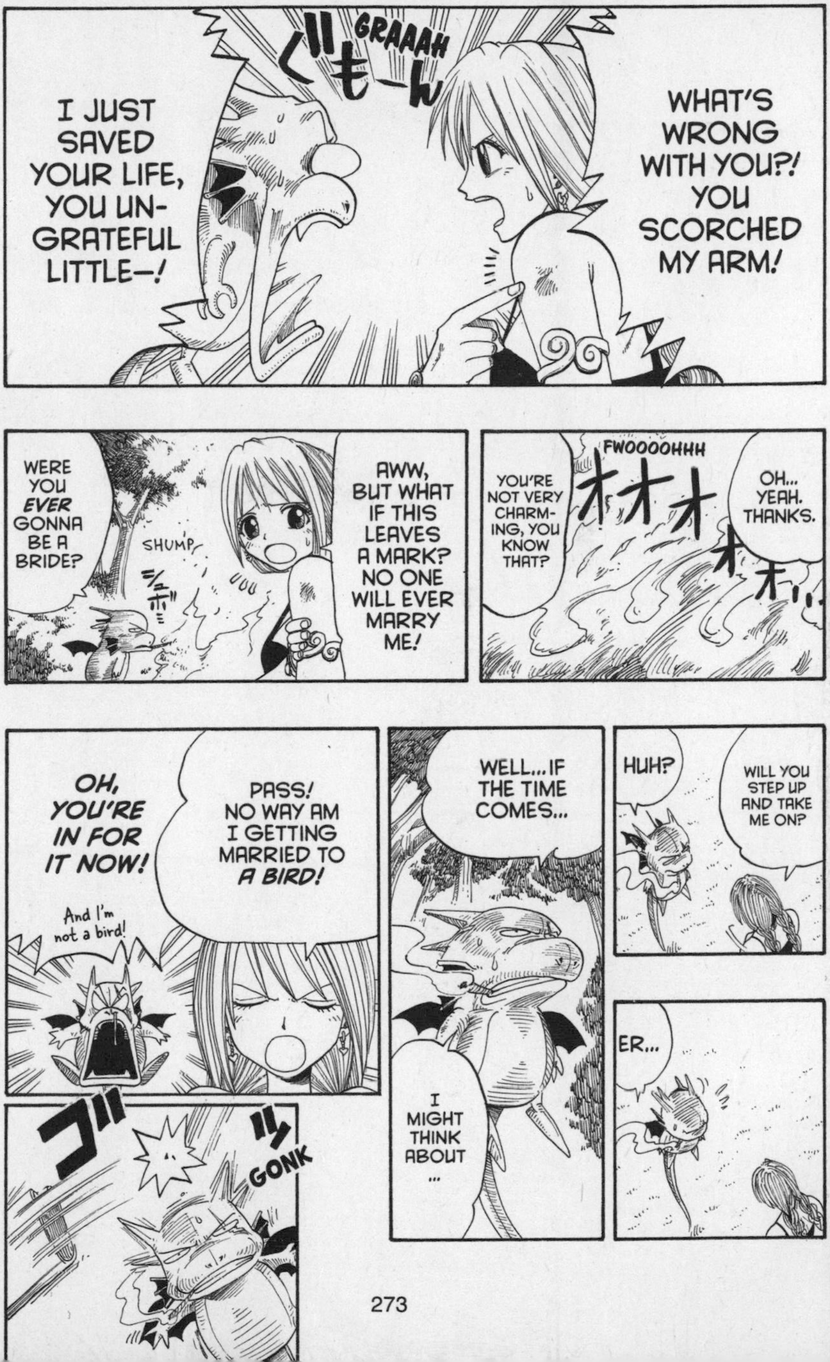
WHAT'S WRONG WITH YOU?! YOU SCORCHED MY ARM!
GRAAAH
I JUST SAVED YOUR LIFE, YOU UN-GRATEFUL LITTLE—!
OH... YEAH. THANKS.
FWOOOOHHH
YOU'RE NOT VERY CHARMING, YOU KNOW THAT?
AWW, BUT WHAT IF THIS LEAVES A MARK? NO ONE WILL EVER MARRY ME!
SHUMP
WERE YOU *EVER* GONNA BE A BRIDE?
WILL YOU STEP UP AND TAKE ME ON?
HUH?
ER...
WELL...IF THE TIME COMES...
I MIGHT THINK ABOUT ...
PASS! NO WAY AM I GETTING MARRIED TO *A BIRD!*
OH, YOU'RE IN FOR IT NOW!
And I'm not a bird!
GONK

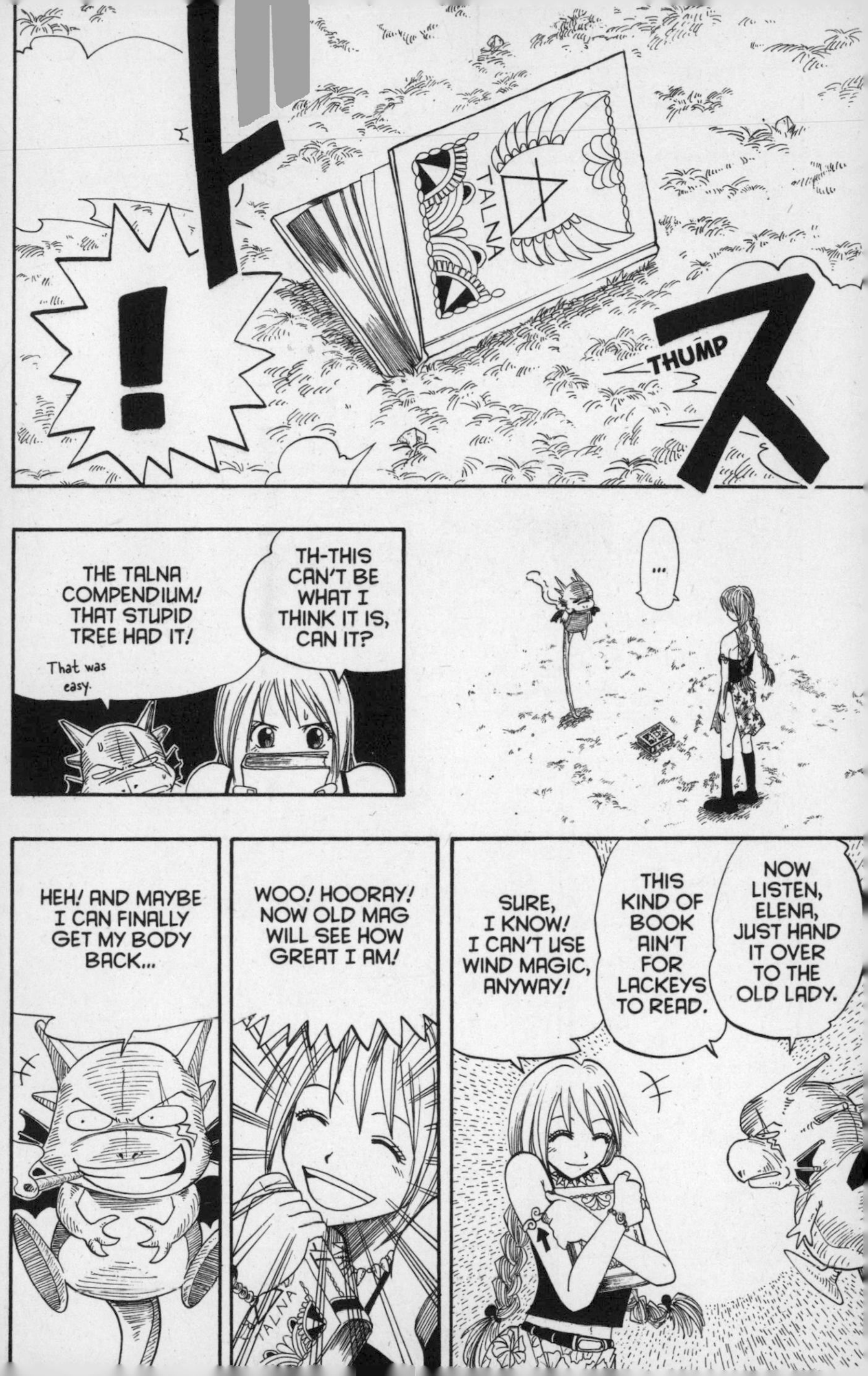
TALNA
THUMP
!
...
TH-THIS CAN'T BE WHAT I THINK IT IS, CAN IT?
THE TALNA COMPENDIUM! THAT STUPID TREE HAD IT!
That was easy.
NOW LISTEN, ELENA, JUST HAND IT OVER TO THE OLD LADY.
THIS KIND OF BOOK AIN'T FOR LACKEYS TO READ.
SURE, I KNOW! I CAN'T USE WIND MAGIC, ANYWAY!
WOO! HOORAY! NOW OLD MAG WILL SEE HOW GREAT I AM!
HEH! AND MAYBE I CAN FINALLY GET MY BODY BACK...

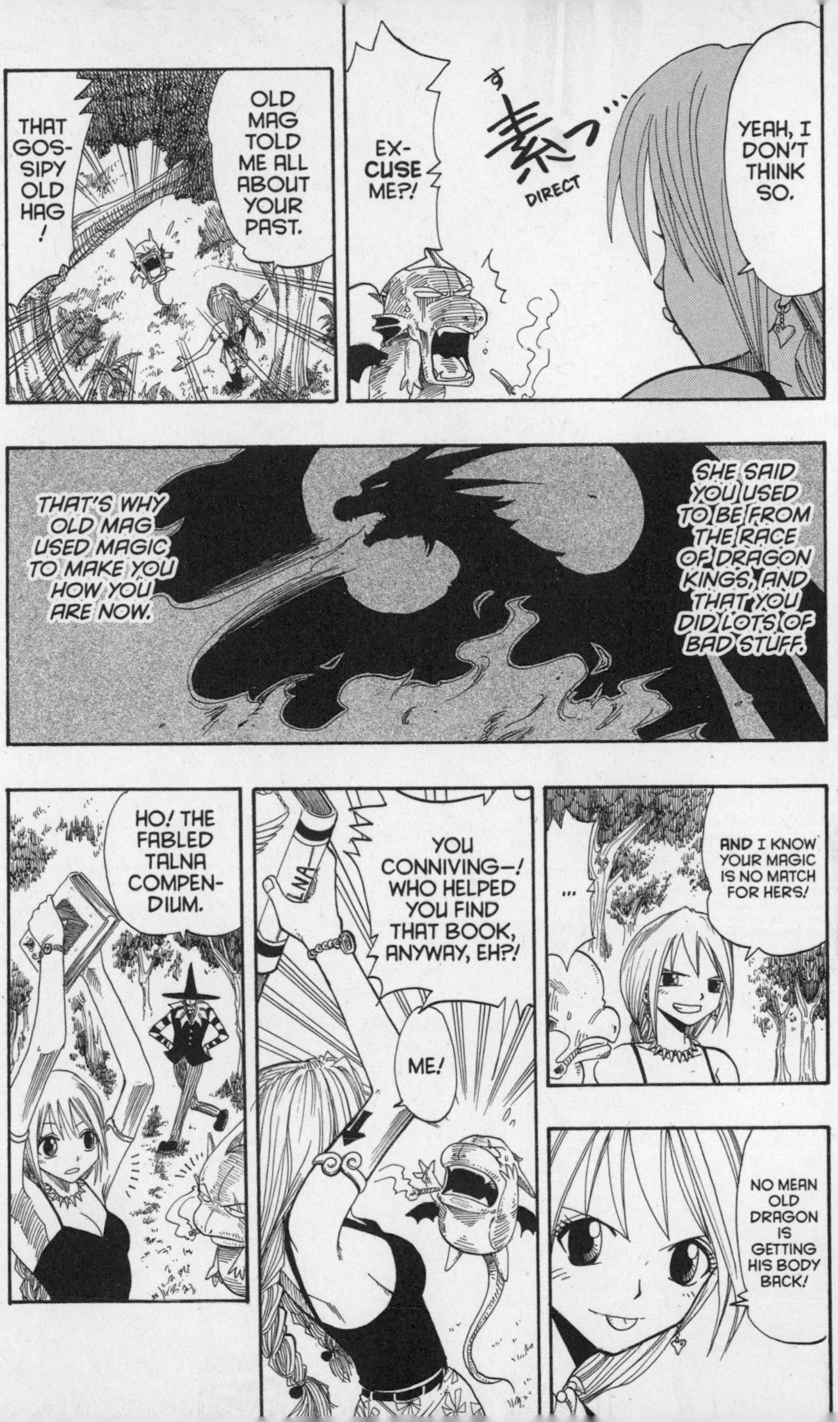
YEAH, I DON'T THINK SO.
素っ
DIRECT
EX-CUSE ME?!
OLD MAG TOLD ME ALL ABOUT YOUR PAST.
THAT GOS-SIPY OLD HAG!
SHE SAID YOU USED TO BE FROM THE RACE OF DRAGON KINGS, AND THAT YOU DID LOTS OF BAD STUFF.
THAT'S WHY OLD MAG USED MAGIC TO MAKE YOU HOW YOU ARE NOW.
AND I KNOW YOUR MAGIC IS NO MATCH FOR HERS!
...
NO MEAN OLD DRAGON IS GETTING HIS BODY BACK!
YOU CONNIVING—! WHO HELPED YOU FIND THAT BOOK, ANYWAY, EH?!
ME!
HO! THE FABLED TALNA COMPEN-DIUM.

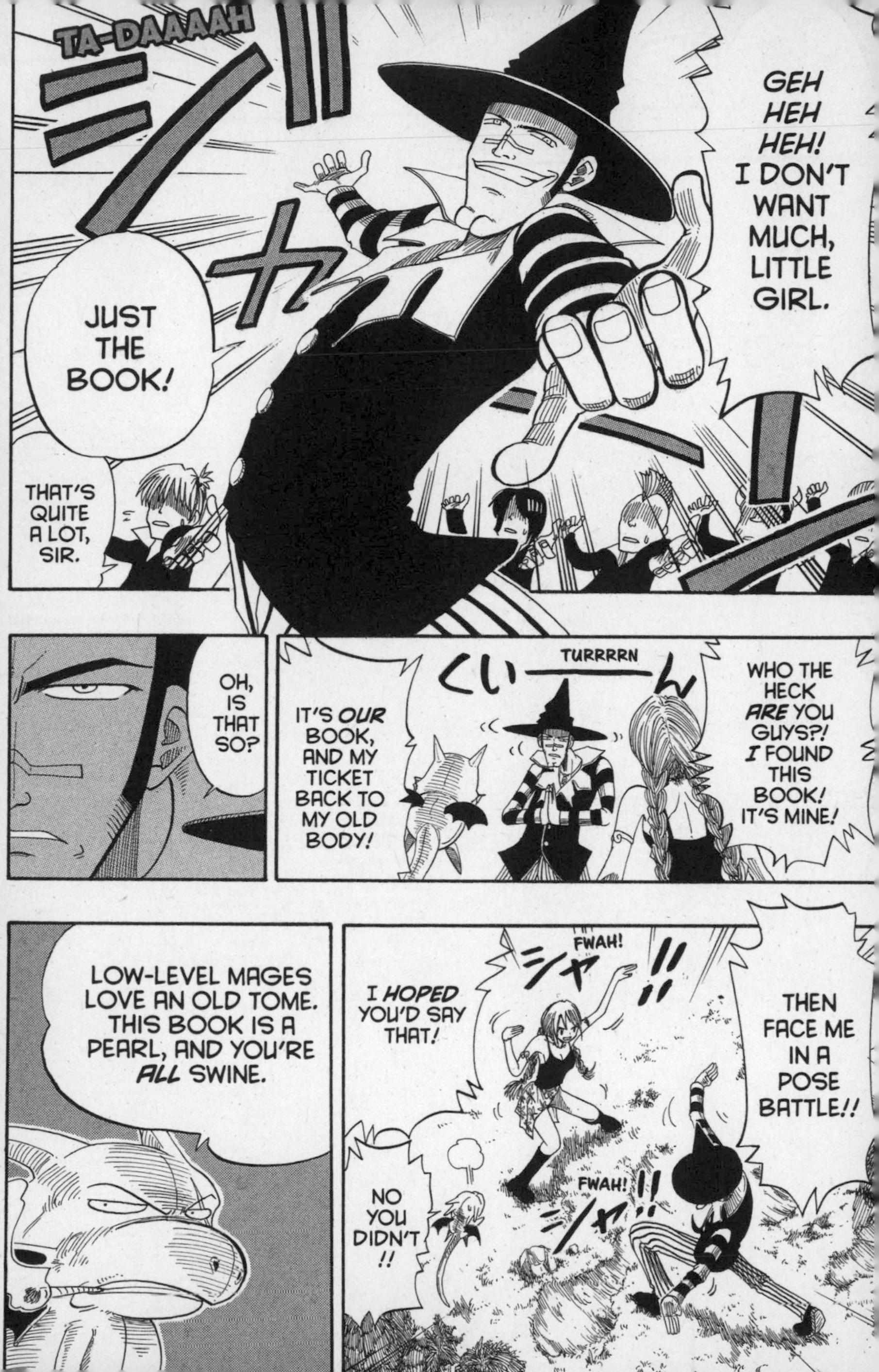
GEH HEH HEH! I DON'T WANT MUCH, LITTLE GIRL.
TA-DAAAAH
JUST THE BOOK!
THAT'S QUITE A LOT, SIR.
TURRRRN
WHO THE HECK *ARE* YOU GUYS?! *I* FOUND THIS BOOK! IT'S MINE!
IT'S *OUR* BOOK, AND MY TICKET BACK TO MY OLD BODY!
OH, IS THAT SO?
THEN FACE ME IN A POSE BATTLE!!
FWAH!
I *HOPED* YOU'D SAY THAT!
FWAH!
NO YOU DIDN'T!!
LOW-LEVEL MAGES LOVE AN OLD TOME. THIS BOOK IS A PEARL, AND YOU'RE *ALL* SWINE.

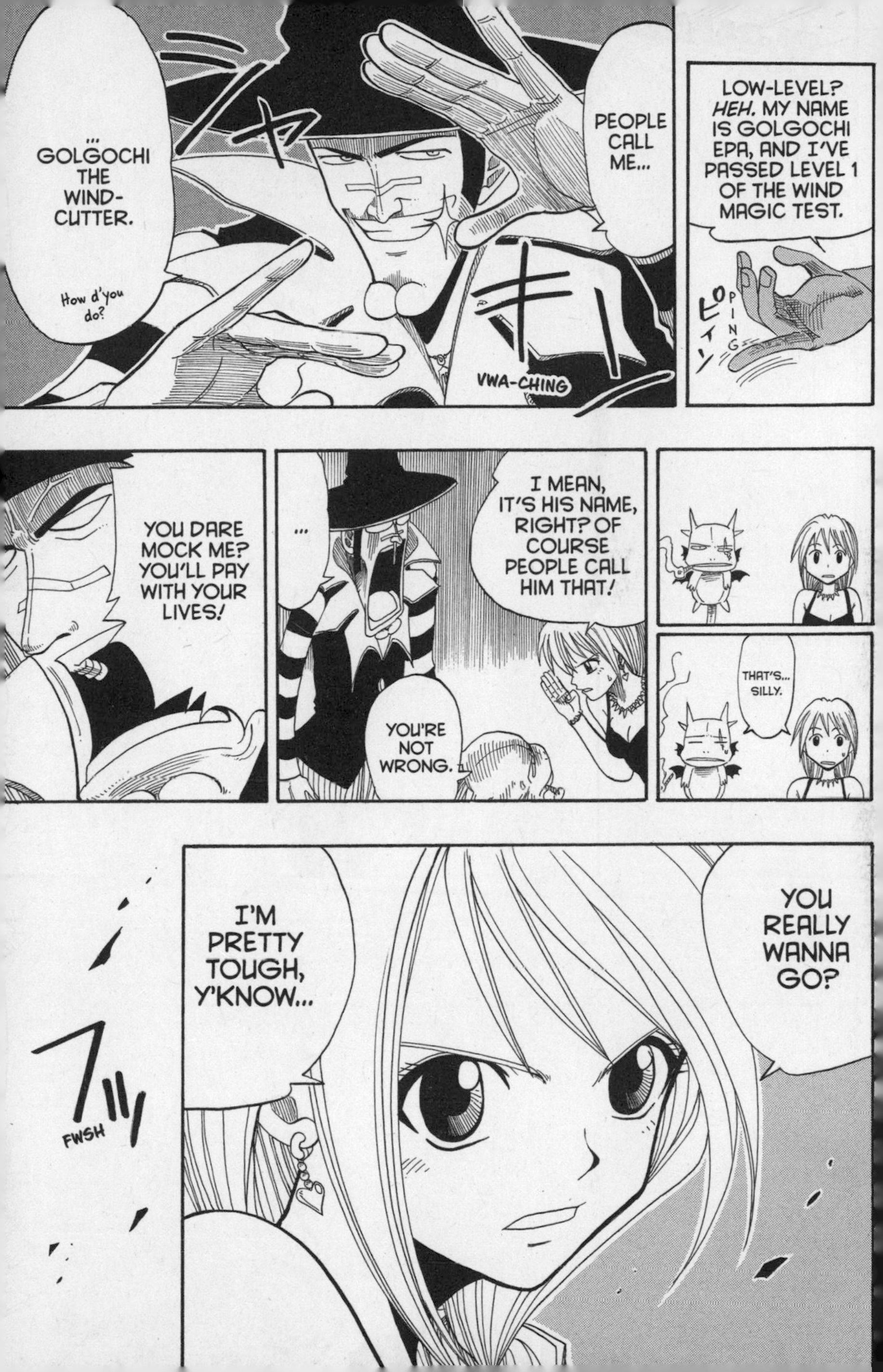
LOW-LEVEL? HEH. MY NAME IS GOLGOCHI EPA, AND I'VE PASSED LEVEL 1 OF THE WIND MAGIC TEST.
PING
PEOPLE CALL ME...
... GOLGOCHI THE WIND-CUTTER.
How d'you do?
VWA-CHING
THAT'S... SILLY.
I MEAN, IT'S HIS NAME, RIGHT? OF COURSE PEOPLE CALL HIM THAT!
...
YOU'RE NOT WRONG.
YOU DARE MOCK ME? YOU'LL PAY WITH YOUR LIVES!
YOU REALLY WANNA GO?
I'M PRETTY TOUGH, Y'KNOW...
FWSH

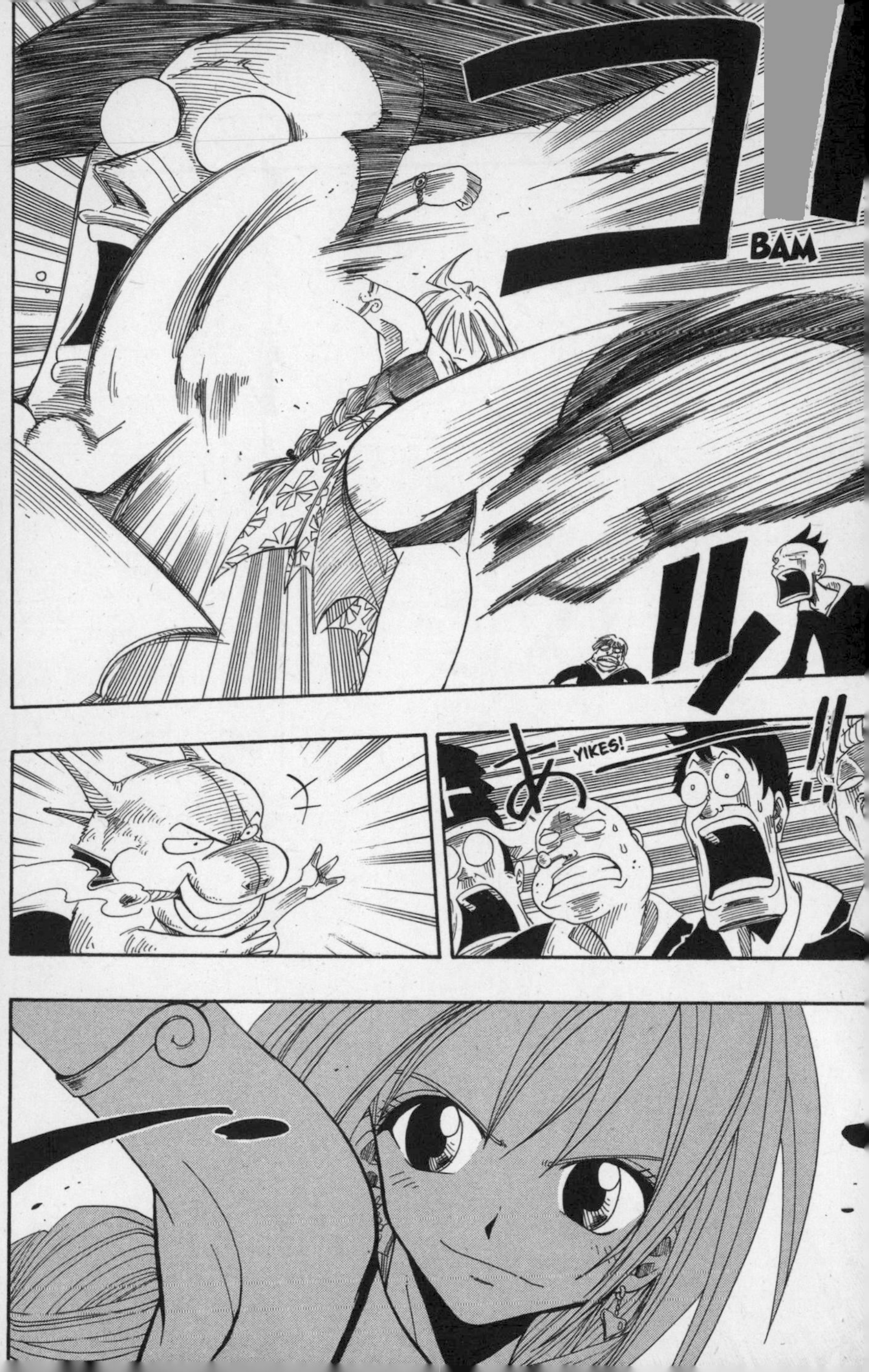
BAM
あ
YIKES!

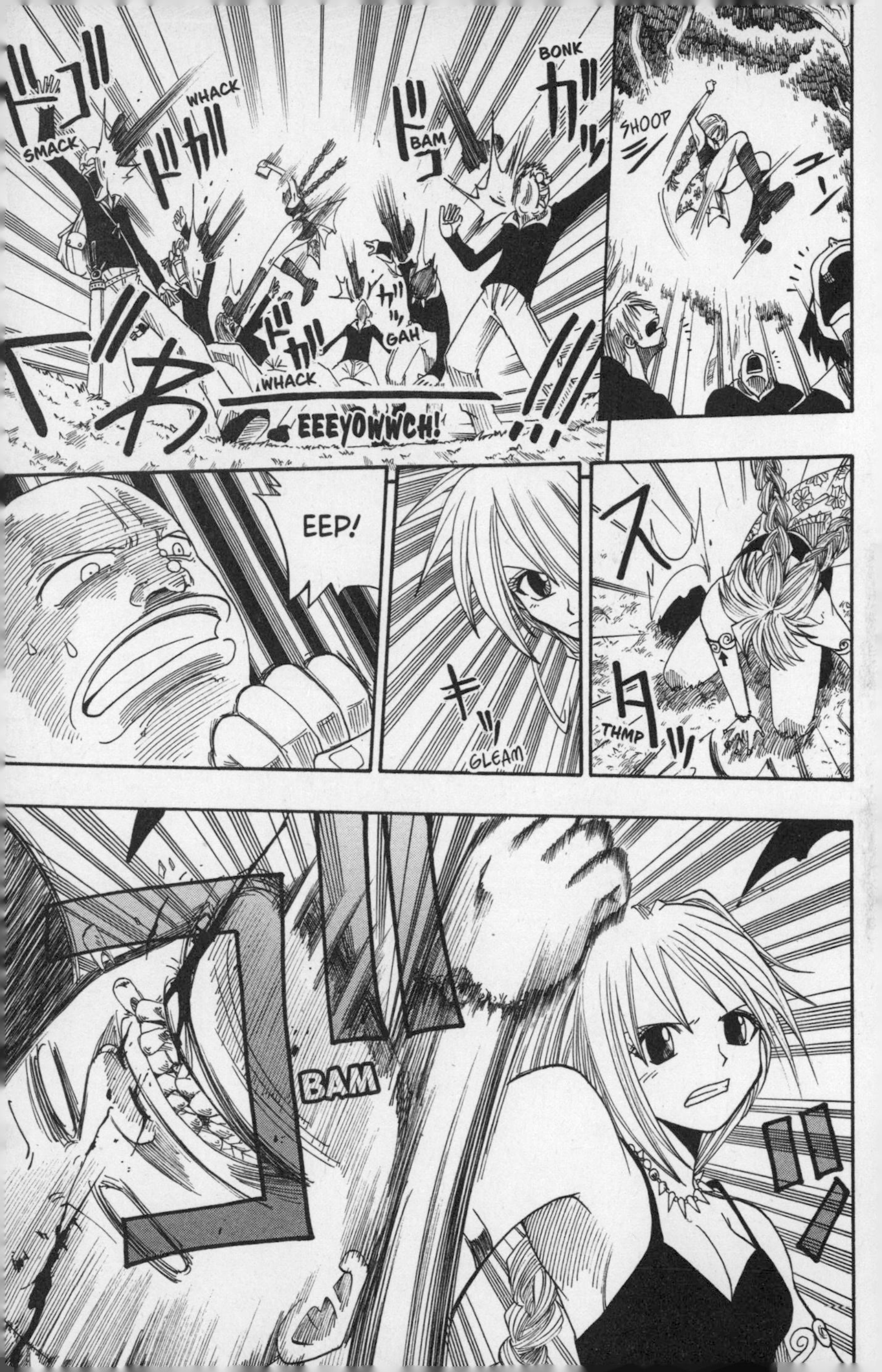
SHOOP
BONK
BAM
WHACK
SMACK
GAH
WHACK
EEEYOWWCH!
THMP
GLEAM
EEP!
BAM

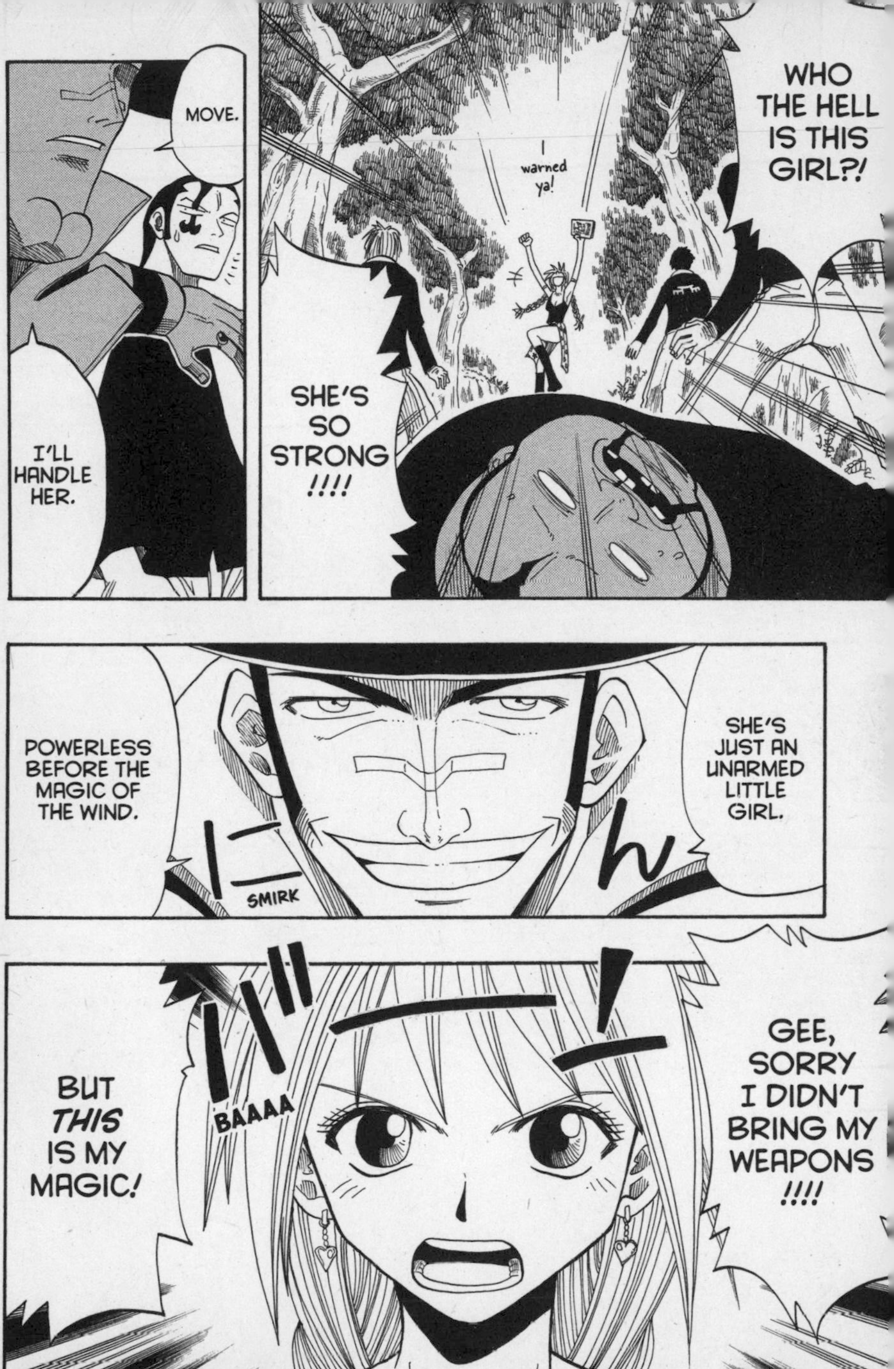
WHO THE HELL IS THIS GIRL?!
I warned ya!
SHE'S SO STRONG!!!!
MOVE.
I'LL HANDLE HER.
SHE'S JUST AN UNARMED LITTLE GIRL.
POWERLESS BEFORE THE MAGIC OF THE WIND.
SMIRK
GEE, SORRY I DIDN'T BRING MY WEAPONS!!!!
BUT *THIS* IS MY MAGIC!
BAAAA

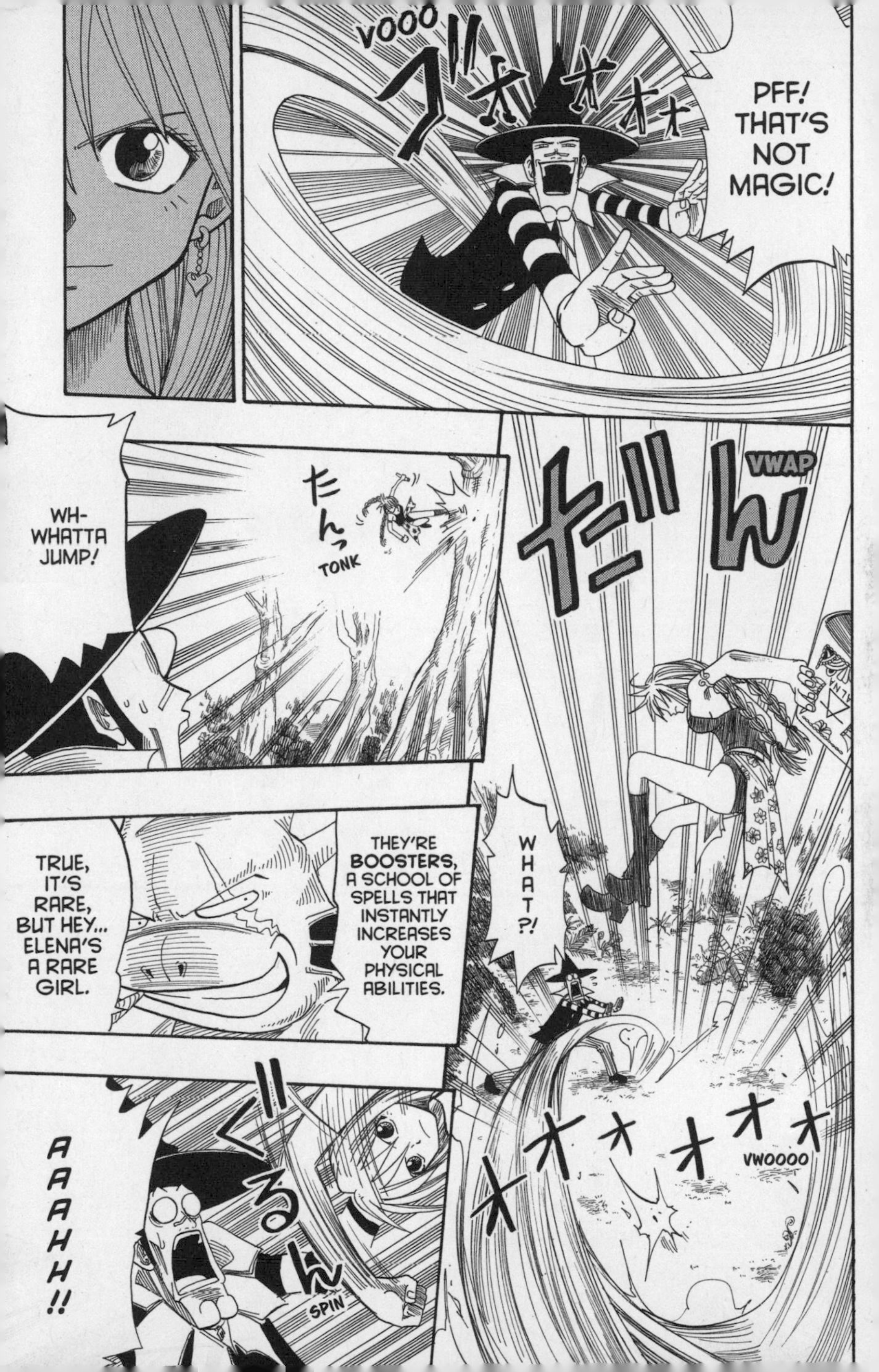
VOOO
PFF! THAT'S NOT MAGIC!
VWAP
WHAT?!
TONK
WH- WHATTA JUMP!
THEY'RE **BOOSTERS**, A SCHOOL OF SPELLS THAT INSTANTLY INCREASES YOUR PHYSICAL ABILITIES.
TRUE, IT'S RARE, BUT HEY... ELENA'S A RARE GIRL.
VWOOOO
SPIN
AAAAHH!!

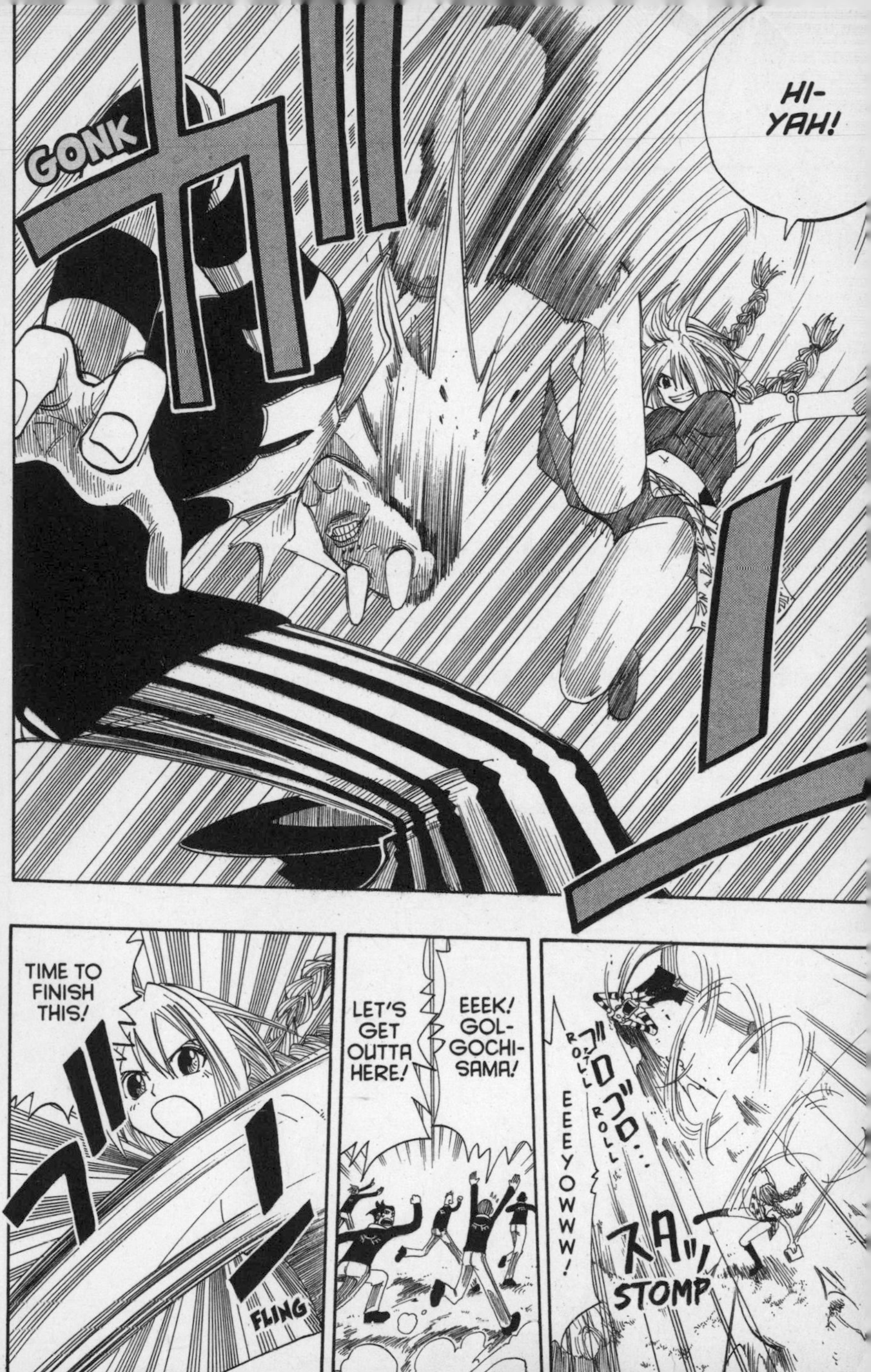
HI-YAH!
GONK
ROLL ROLL...
EEEEYOWWW!
STOMP
EEEK! GOL-GOCHI-SAMA!
LET'S GET OUTTA HERE!
TIME TO FINISH THIS!
FLING

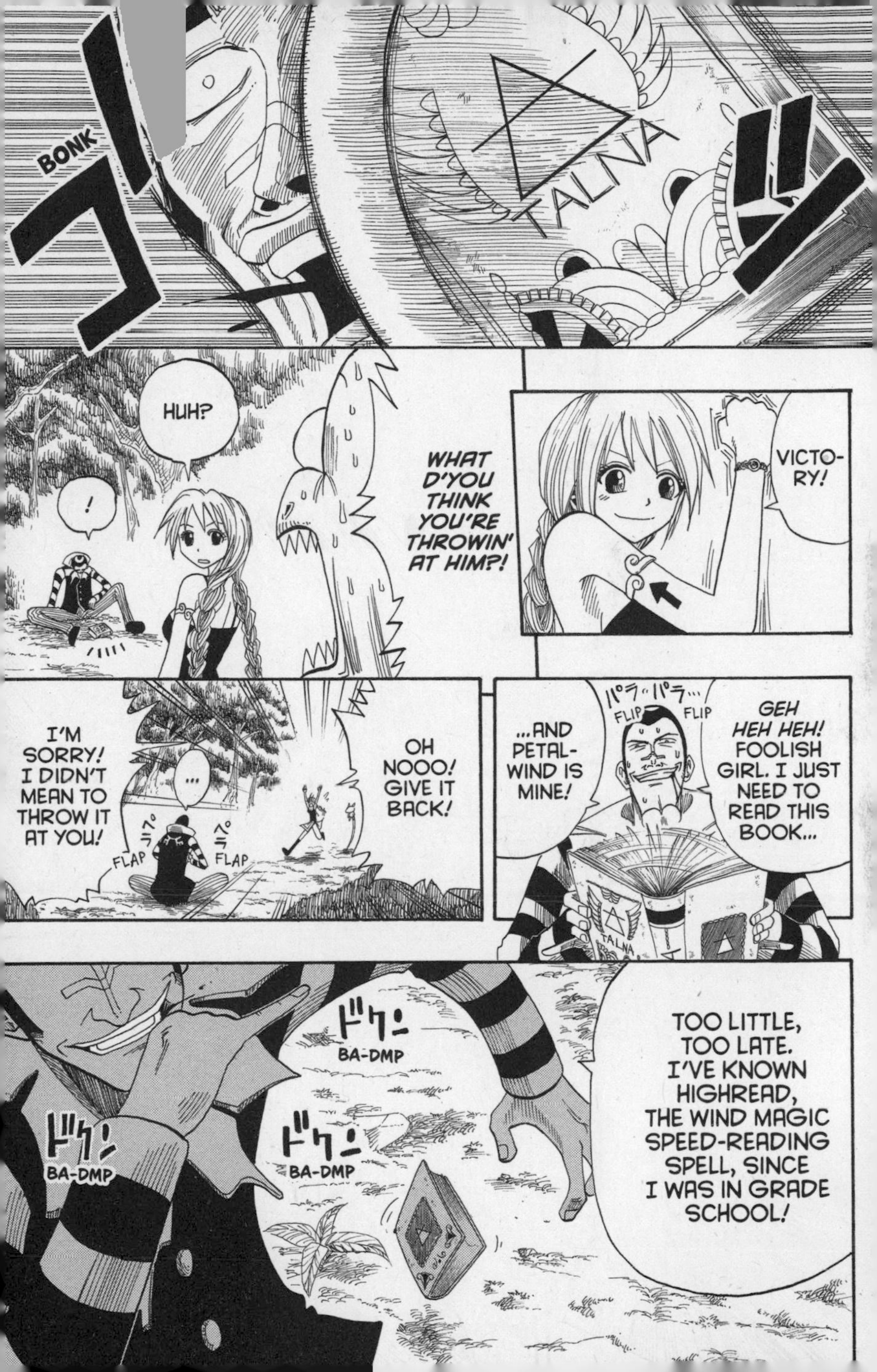
BONK
TALNA
VICTO-RY!
WHAT D'YOU THINK YOU'RE THROWIN' AT HIM?!
HUH?
!
GEH HEH HEH! FOOLISH GIRL. I JUST NEED TO READ THIS BOOK...
パラ FLIP パラ FLIP
...AND PETAL-WIND IS MINE!
TALNA
OH NOOO! GIVE IT BACK!
...
I'M SORRY! I DIDN'T MEAN TO THROW IT AT YOU!
ペラ FLAP
FLAP
TOO LITTLE, TOO LATE. I'VE KNOWN HIGHREAD, THE WIND MAGIC SPEED-READING SPELL, SINCE I WAS IN GRADE SCHOOL!
ドクン BA-DMP
ドクン BA-DMP
ドクン BA-DMP

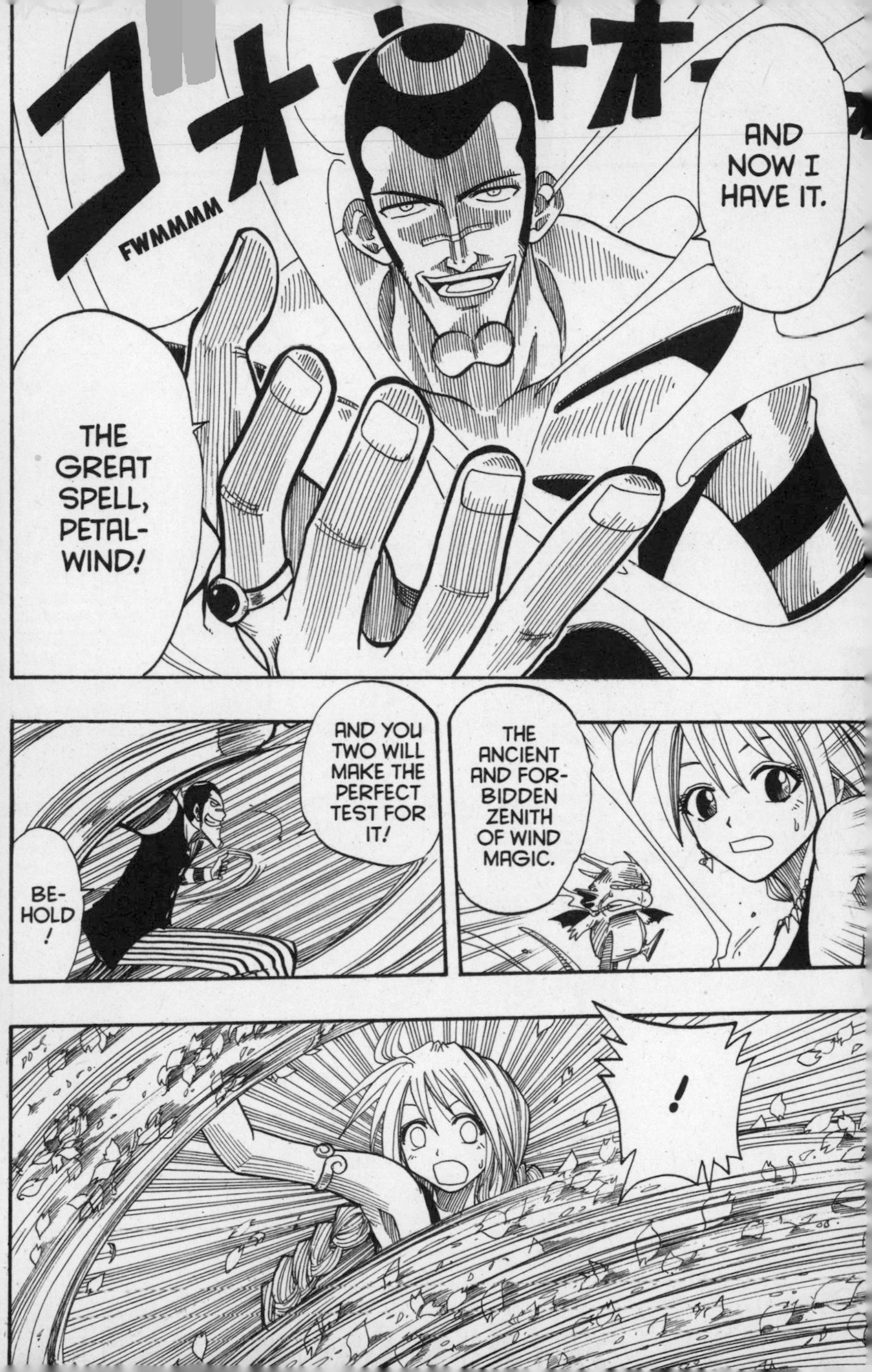
AND NOW I HAVE IT.
FWMMMM
THE GREAT SPELL, PETAL-WIND!
THE ANCIENT AND FOR-BIDDEN ZENITH OF WIND MAGIC.
AND YOU TWO WILL MAKE THE PERFECT TEST FOR IT!
BE-HOLD!
!

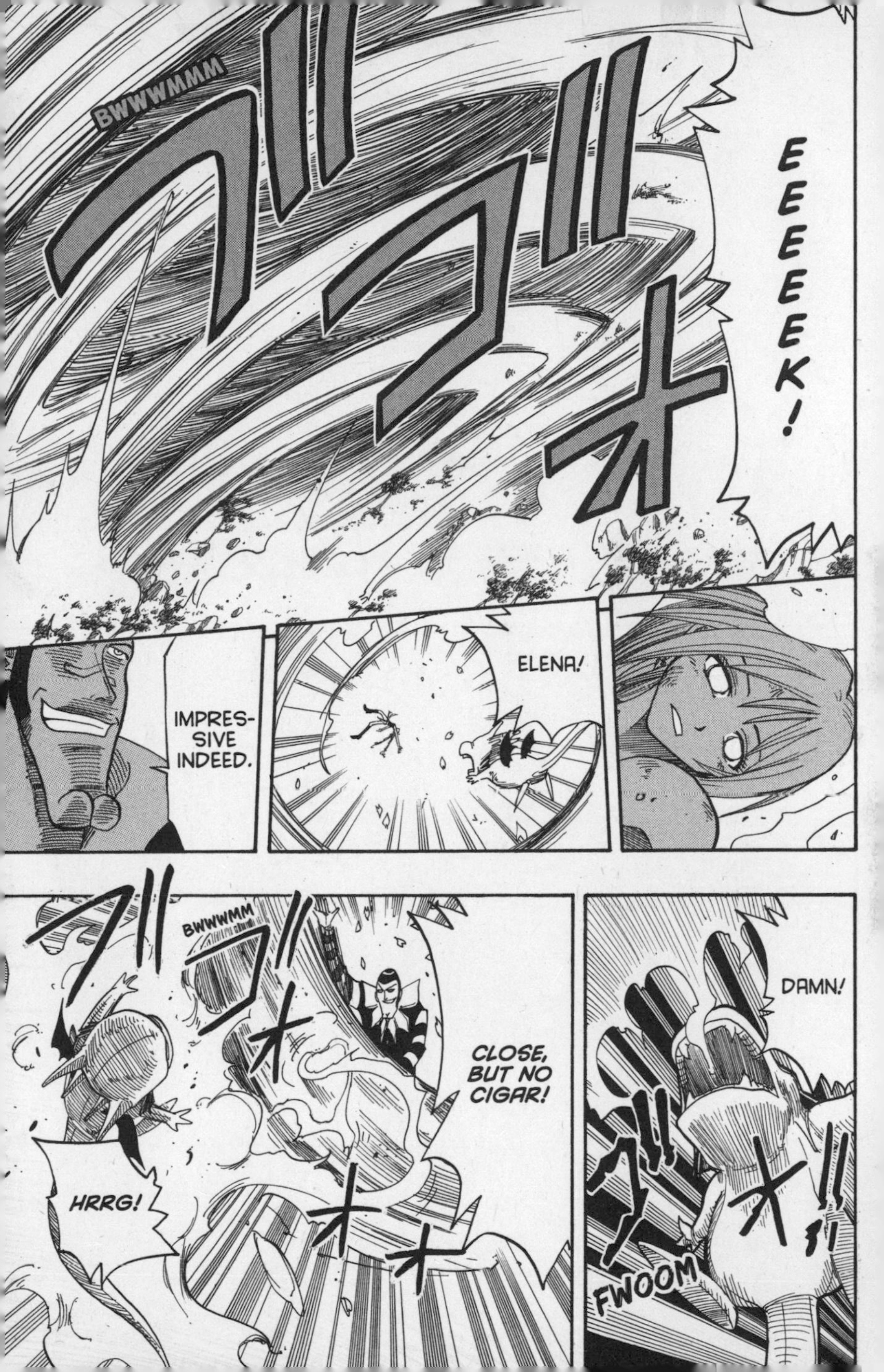
EEEEEK!
BWWWMMM
ELENA!
IMPRES-
SIVE
INDEED.
DAMN!
FWOOM
BWWWMM
CLOSE, BUT NO CIGAR!
HRRG!

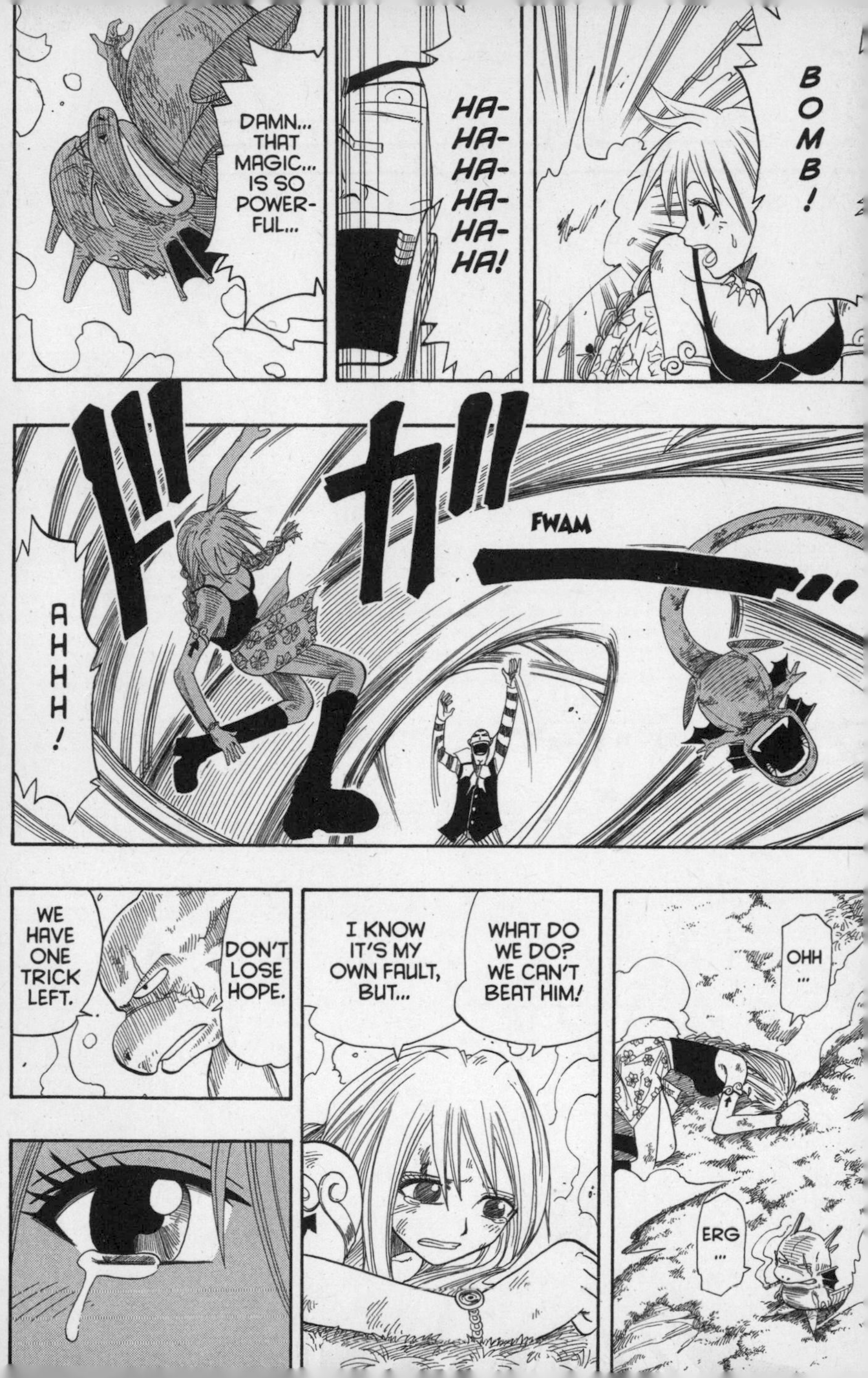
BOMB!
HA-HA-HA-HA-HA-HA!
DAMN... THAT MAGIC... IS SO POWERFUL...
FWAM
ドガー…
AHHHH!
OHH ...
ERG ...
WHAT DO WE DO? WE CAN'T BEAT HIM!
I KNOW IT'S MY OWN FAULT, BUT...
DON'T LOSE HOPE.
WE HAVE ONE TRICK LEFT.

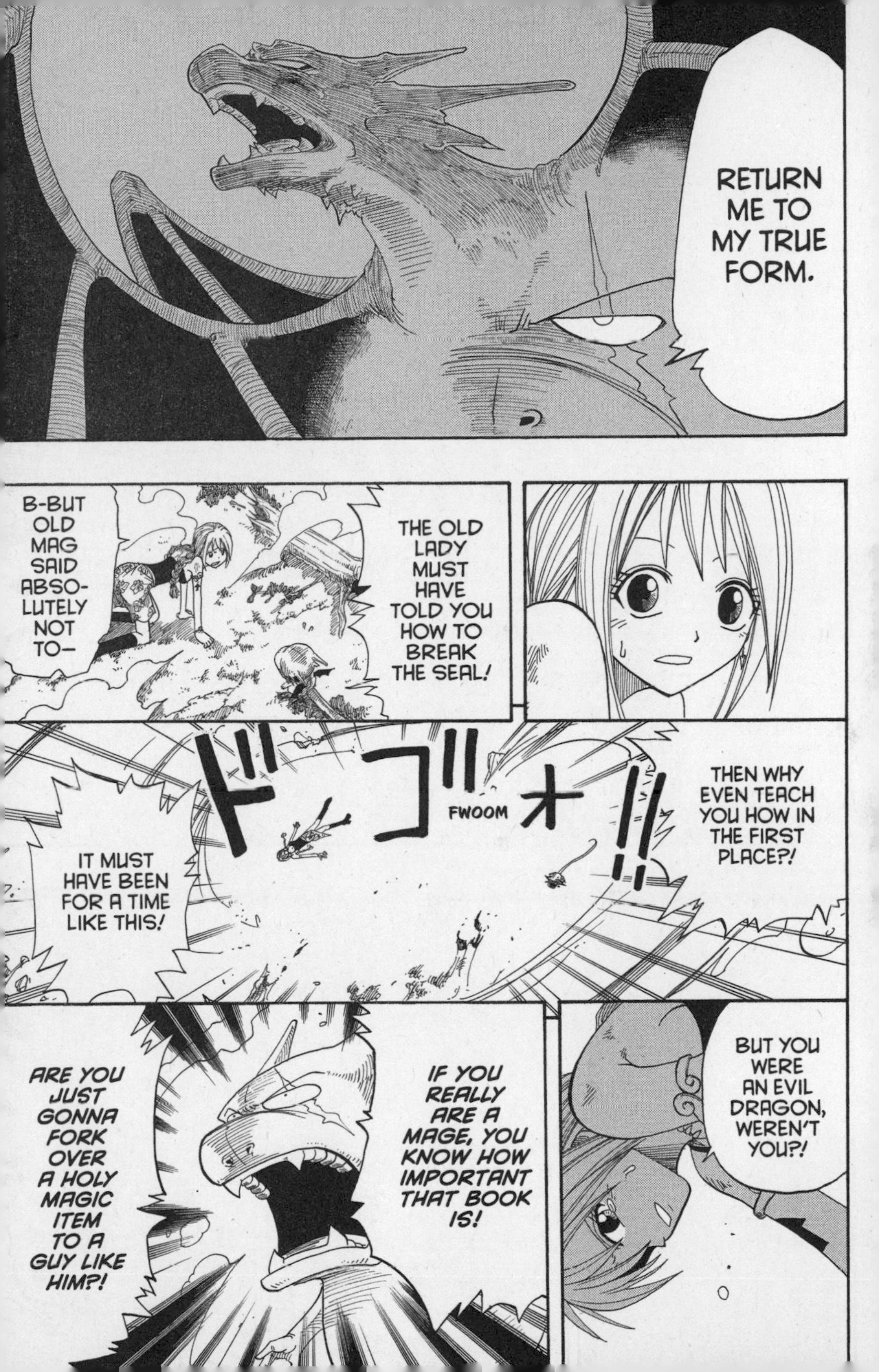
RETURN ME TO MY TRUE FORM.
THE OLD LADY MUST HAVE TOLD YOU HOW TO BREAK THE SEAL!
B-BUT OLD MAG SAID ABSO-LUTELY NOT TO—
ドゴォ!!
FWOOM
THEN WHY EVEN TEACH YOU HOW IN THE FIRST PLACE?!
IT MUST HAVE BEEN FOR A TIME LIKE THIS!
BUT YOU WERE AN EVIL DRAGON, WEREN'T YOU?!
IF YOU REALLY ARE A MAGE, YOU KNOW HOW IMPORTANT THAT BOOK IS!
ARE YOU JUST GONNA FORK OVER A HOLY MAGIC ITEM TO A GUY LIKE HIM?!

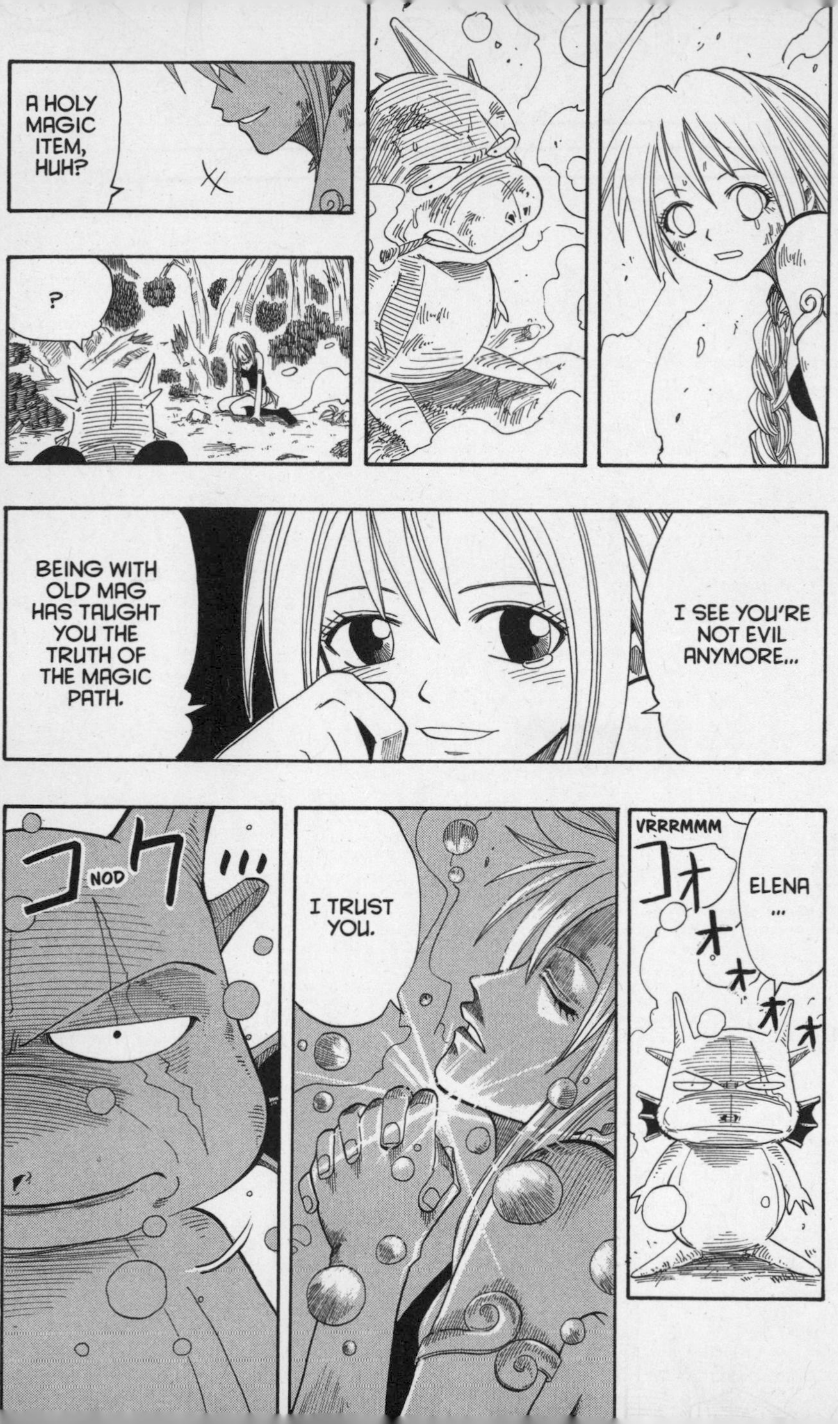
A HOLY MAGIC ITEM, HUH?
?
I SEE YOU'RE NOT EVIL ANYMORE...
BEING WITH OLD MAG HAS TAUGHT YOU THE TRUTH OF THE MAGIC PATH.
VRRRMMM
コォォォォォ
ELENA ...
I TRUST YOU.
コクッ
NOD

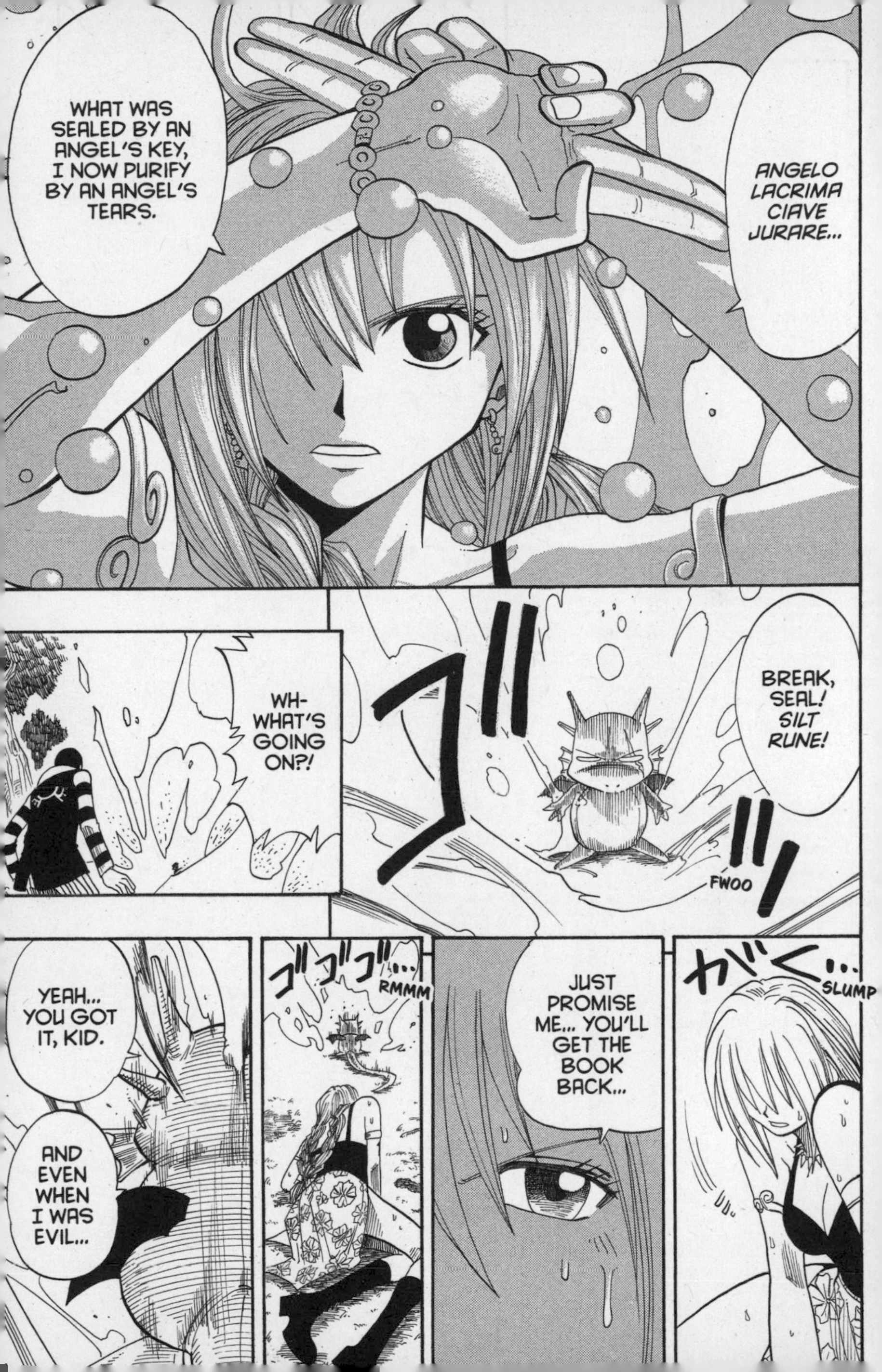
ANGELO LACRIMA CIAVE JURARE...
WHAT WAS SEALED BY AN ANGEL'S KEY, I NOW PURIFY BY AN ANGEL'S TEARS.
BREAK, SEAL! SILT RUNE!
ゴッ
FWOO
WH- WHAT'S GOING ON?!
がく...
SLUMP
JUST PROMISE ME... YOU'LL GET THE BOOK BACK...
ゴゴゴ...
RMMM
YEAH... YOU GOT IT, KID.
AND EVEN WHEN I WAS EVIL...

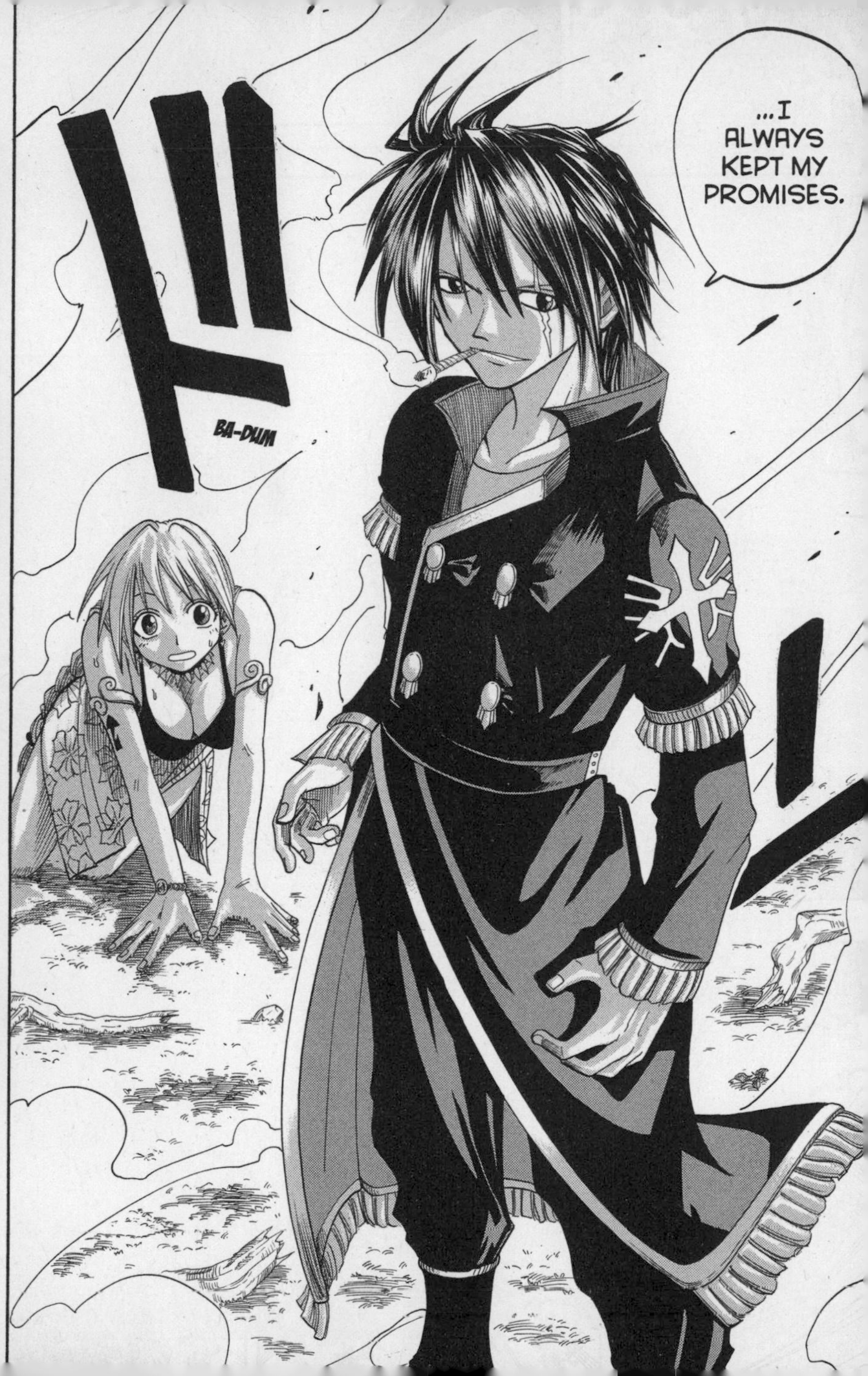
...I ALWAYS KEPT MY PROMISES.
BA-DUM

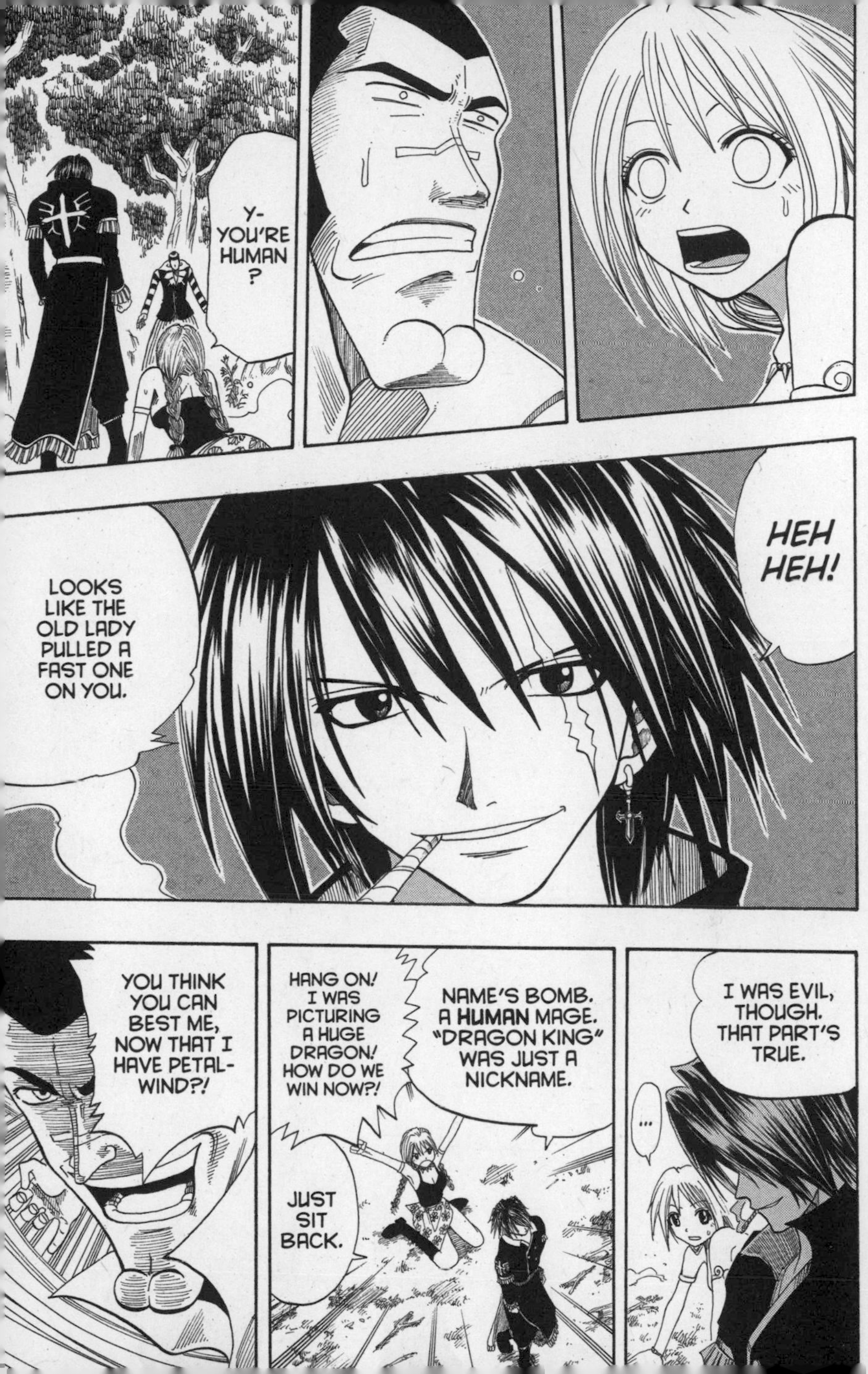
Y- YOU'RE HUMAN?
HEH HEH!
LOOKS LIKE THE OLD LADY PULLED A FAST ONE ON YOU.
I WAS EVIL, THOUGH. THAT PART'S TRUE.
...
NAME'S BOMB. A **HUMAN** MAGE. "DRAGON KING" WAS JUST A NICKNAME.
HANG ON! I WAS PICTURING A HUGE DRAGON! HOW DO WE WIN NOW?!
JUST SIT BACK.
YOU THINK YOU CAN BEST ME, NOW THAT I HAVE PETAL-WIND?!

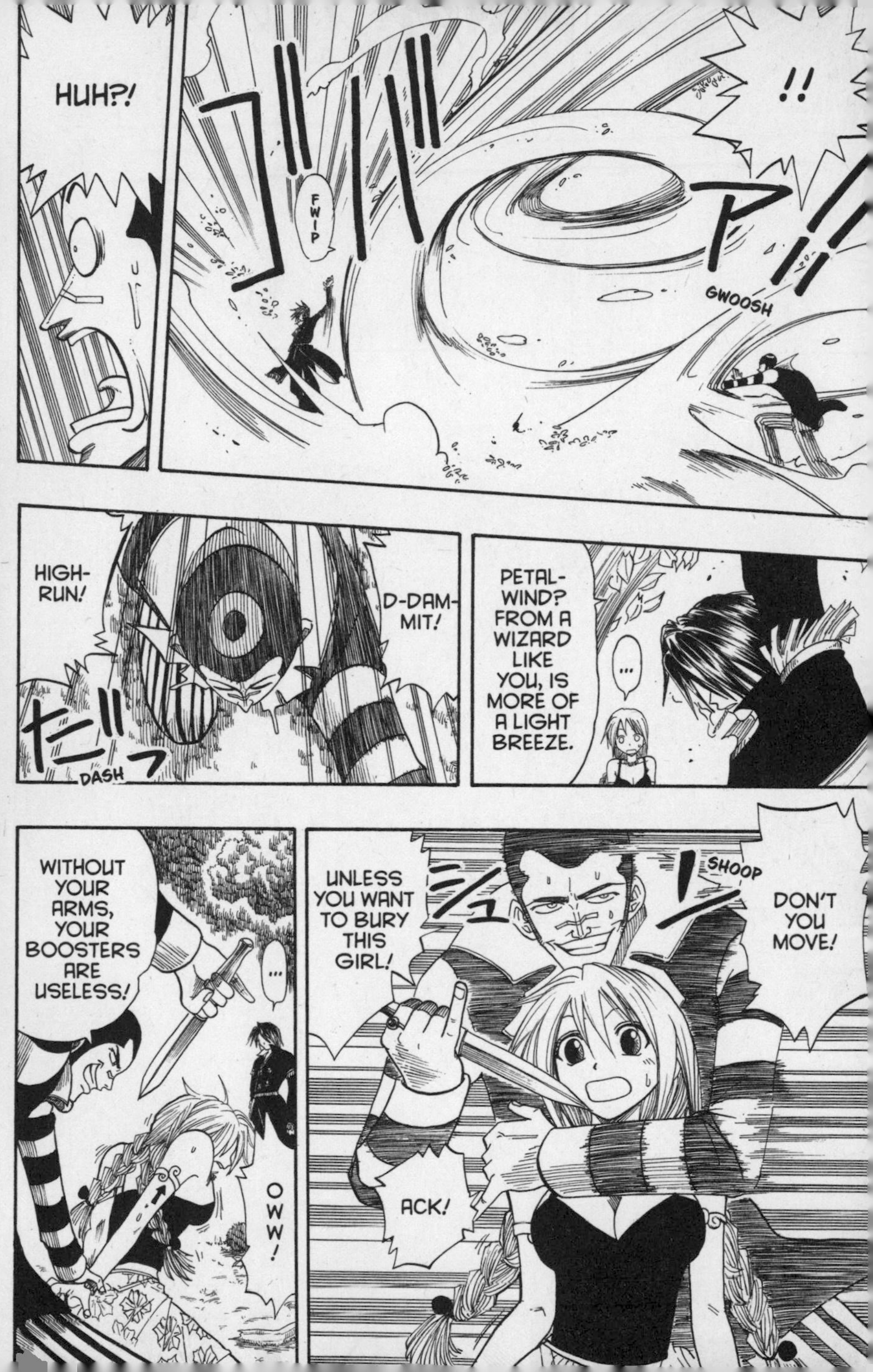
!!
GWOOSH
FWIP
HUH?!
PETAL-WIND? FROM A WIZARD LIKE YOU, IS MORE OF A LIGHT BREEZE.
...
D-DAM-MIT!
HIGH-RUN!
DASH
SHOOP
DON'T YOU MOVE!
UNLESS YOU WANT TO BURY THIS GIRL!
ACK!
WITHOUT YOUR ARMS, YOUR BOOSTERS ARE USELESS!
...
OWW!

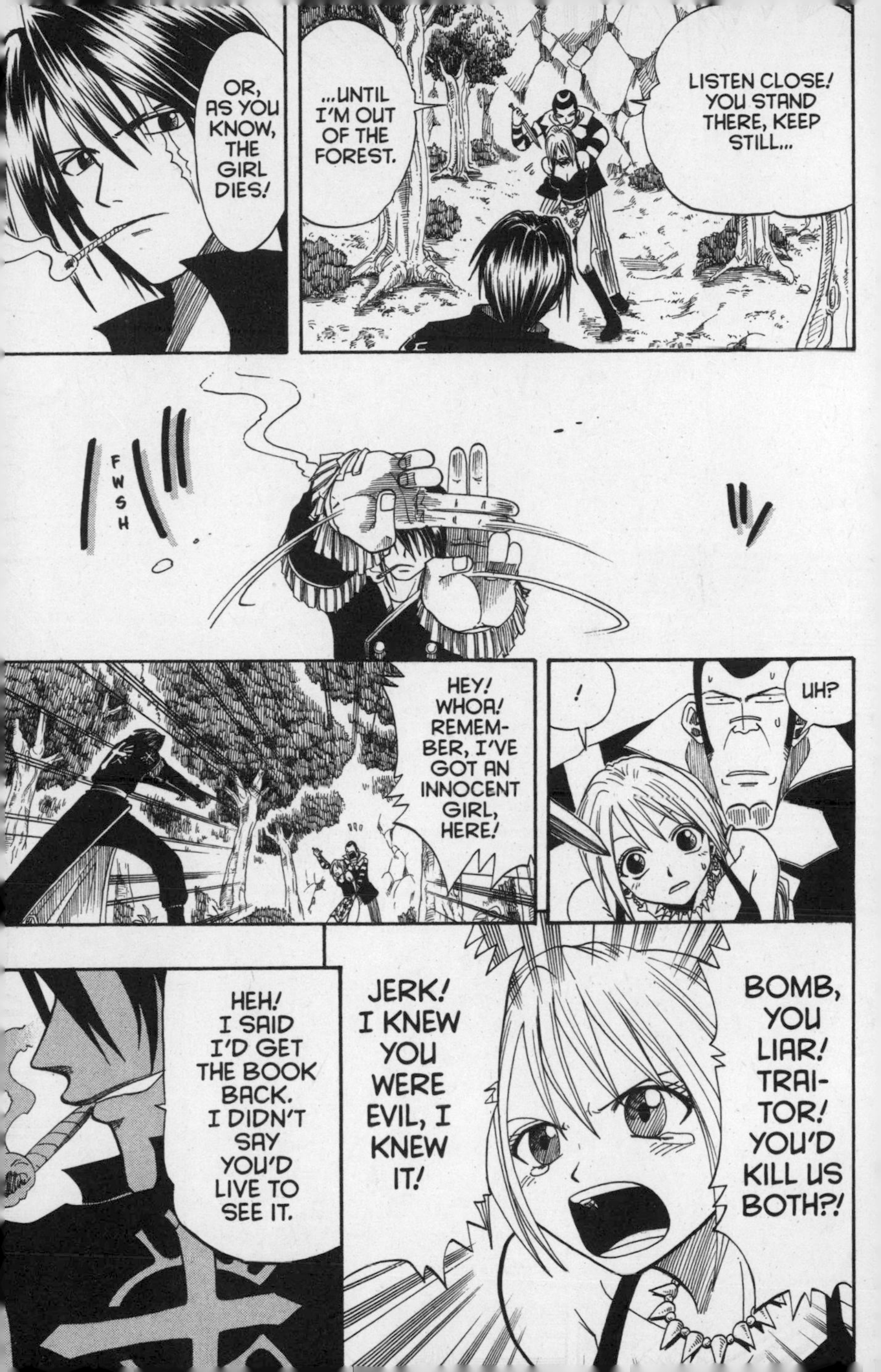
LISTEN CLOSE! YOU STAND THERE, KEEP STILL...
...UNTIL I'M OUT OF THE FOREST.
OR, AS YOU KNOW, THE GIRL DIES!
FWSH
!
UH?
HEY! WHOA! REMEMBER, I'VE GOT AN INNOCENT GIRL, HERE!
BOMB, YOU LIAR! TRAITOR! YOU'D KILL US BOTH?!
JERK! I KNEW YOU WERE EVIL, I KNEW IT!
HEH! I SAID I'D GET THE BOOK BACK. I DIDN'T SAY YOU'D LIVE TO SEE IT.

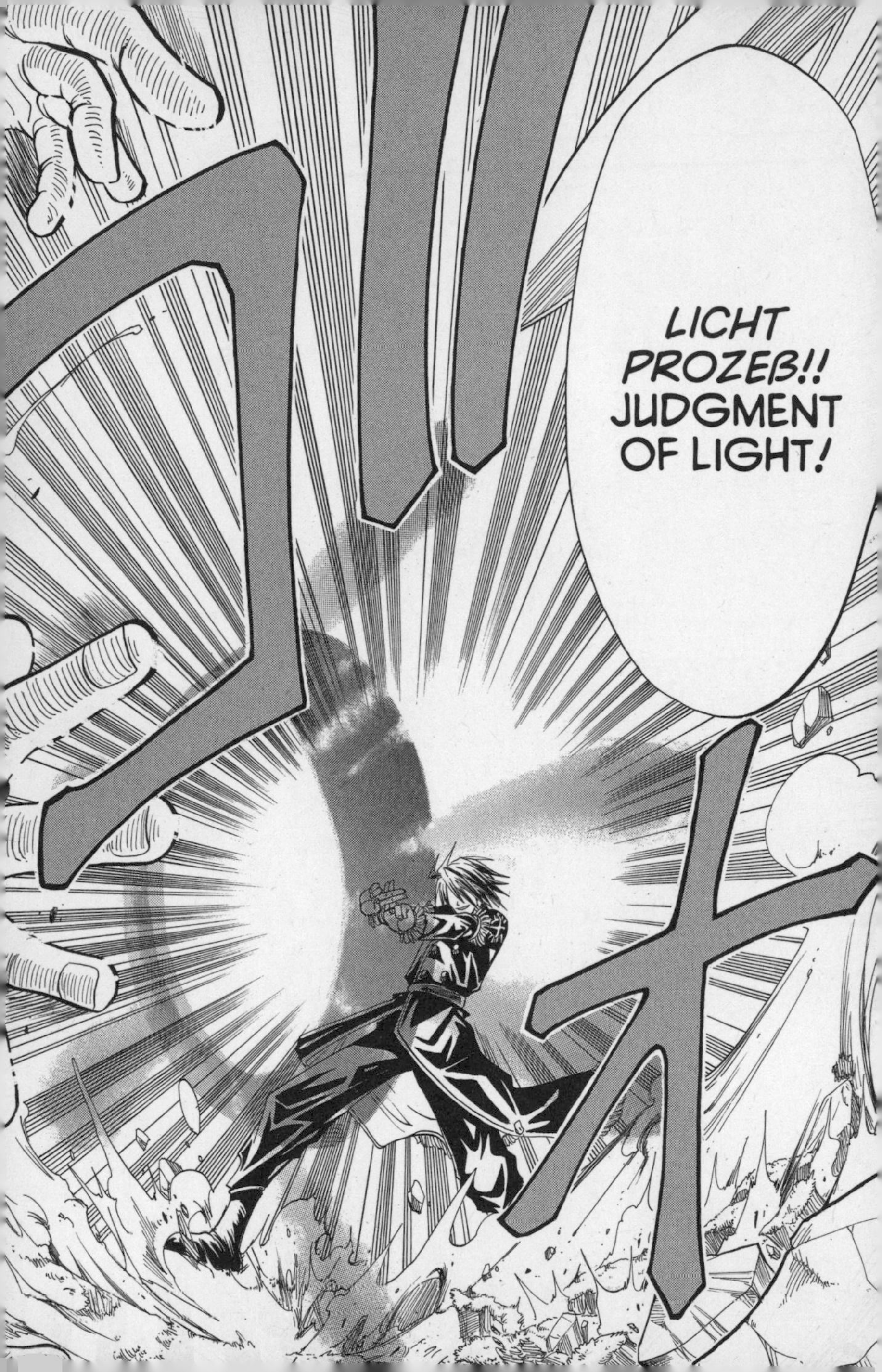
LICHT PROZEß!! JUDGMENT OF LIGHT!

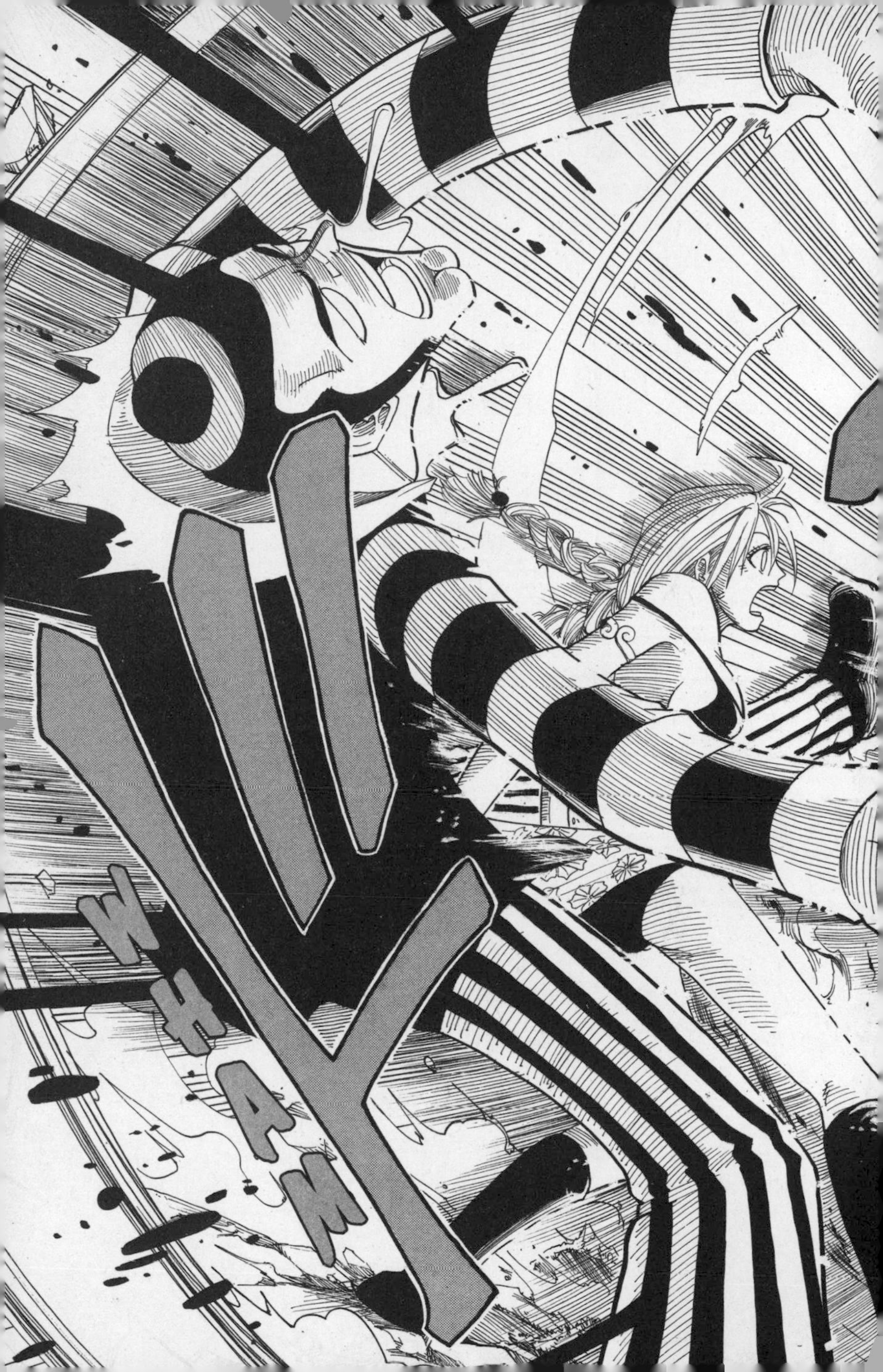
WHAM

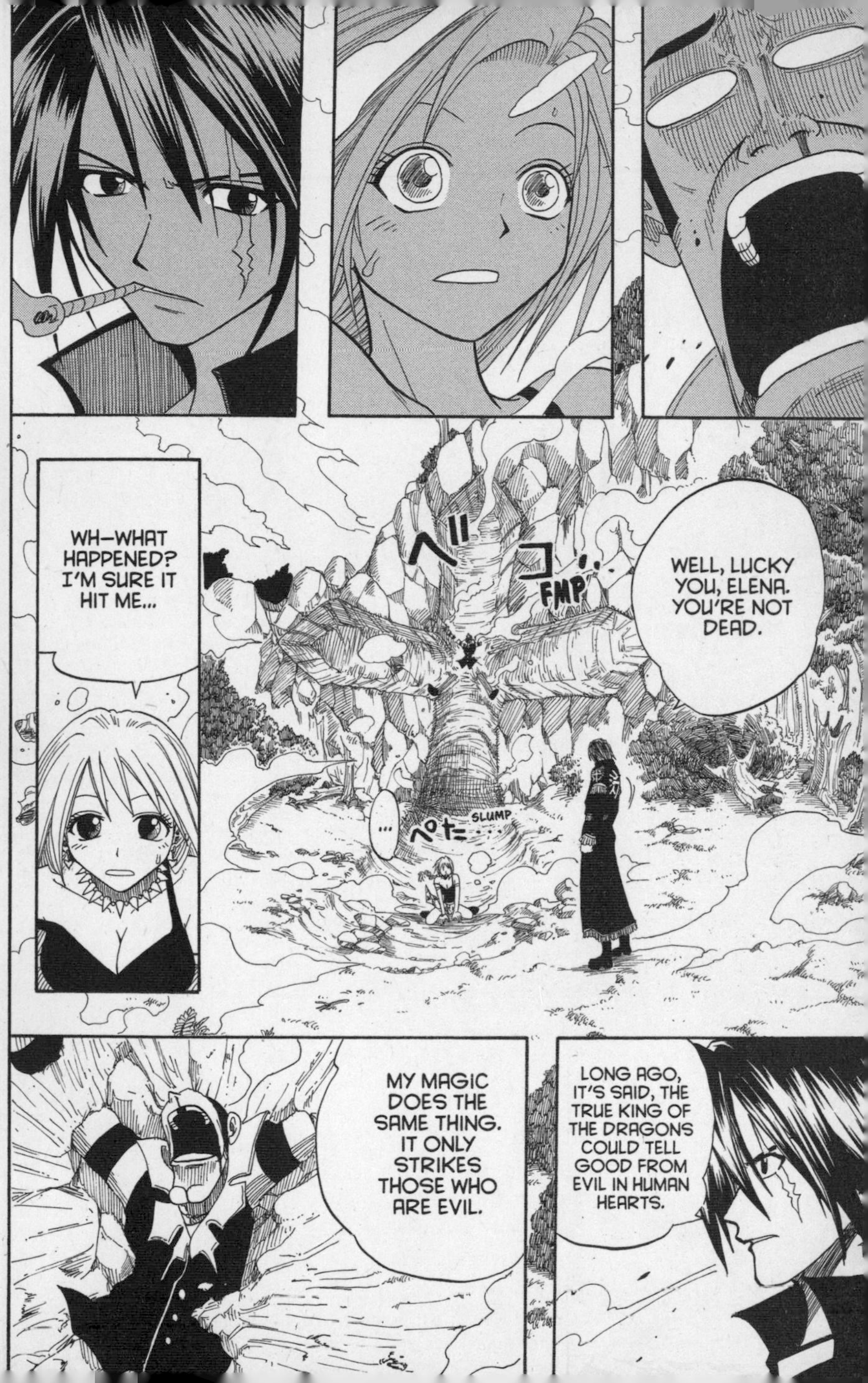
WELL, LUCKY YOU, ELENA. YOU'RE NOT DEAD.
FMP
WH—WHAT HAPPENED? I'M SURE IT HIT ME...
...
SLUMP
LONG AGO, IT'S SAID, THE TRUE KING OF THE DRAGONS COULD TELL GOOD FROM EVIL IN HUMAN HEARTS.
MY MAGIC DOES THE SAME THING. IT ONLY STRIKES THOSE WHO ARE EVIL.

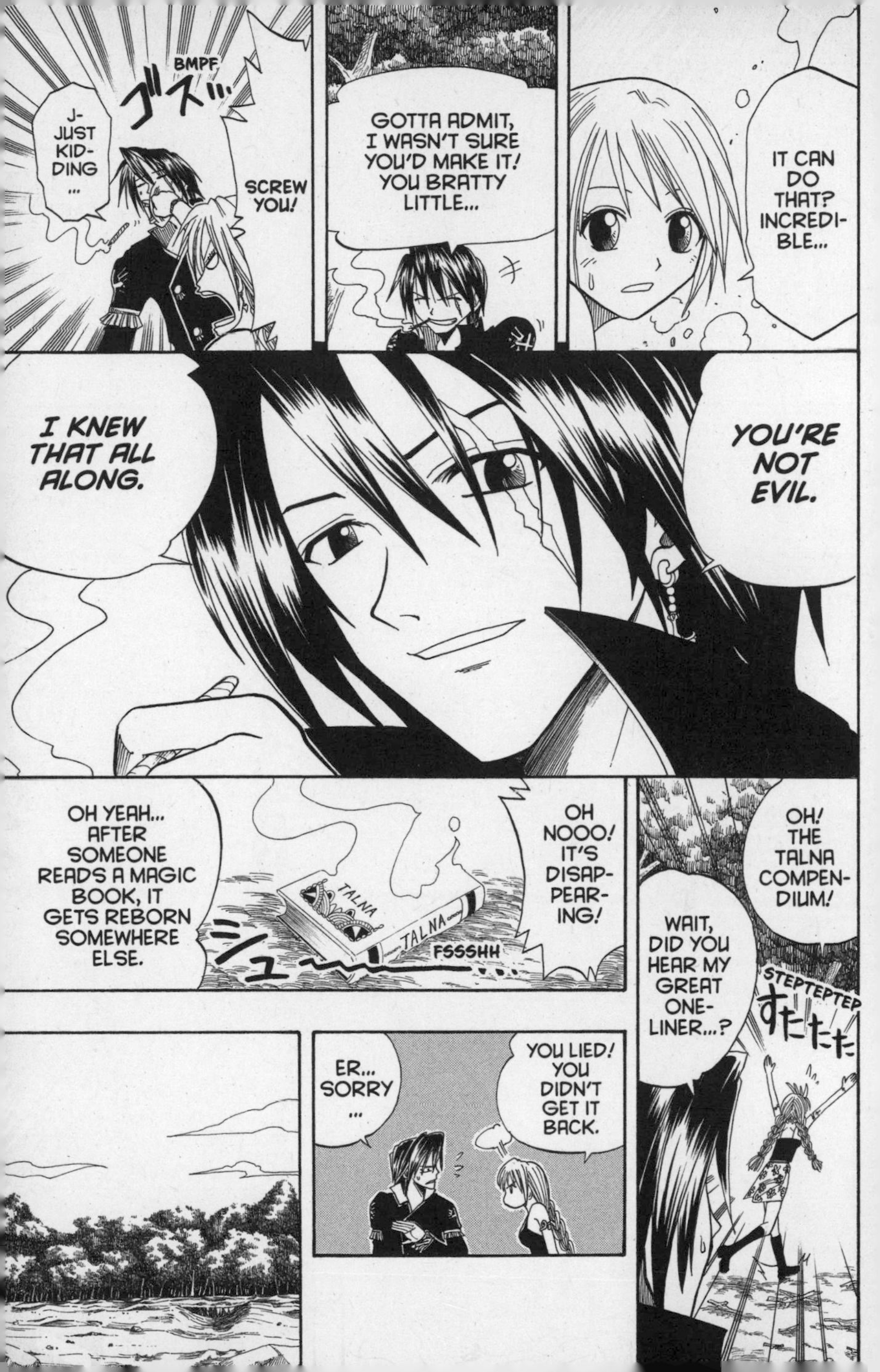
IT CAN DO THAT? INCREDIBLE...
GOTTA ADMIT, I WASN'T SURE YOU'D MAKE IT! YOU BRATTY LITTLE...
SCREW YOU!
BMPF
ゴスッ
J-JUST KID-DING...
YOU'RE NOT EVIL.
I KNEW THAT ALL ALONG.
OH! THE TALNA COMPEN-DIUM!
WAIT, DID YOU HEAR MY GREAT ONE-LINER...?
STEPTEPTEP
すたたた
OH NOOO! IT'S DISAP-PEAR-ING!
OH YEAH... AFTER SOMEONE READS A MAGIC BOOK, IT GETS REBORN SOMEWHERE ELSE.
TALNA
TALNA
シュ~
FSSSHH
YOU LIED! YOU DIDN'T GET IT BACK.
ER... SORRY...

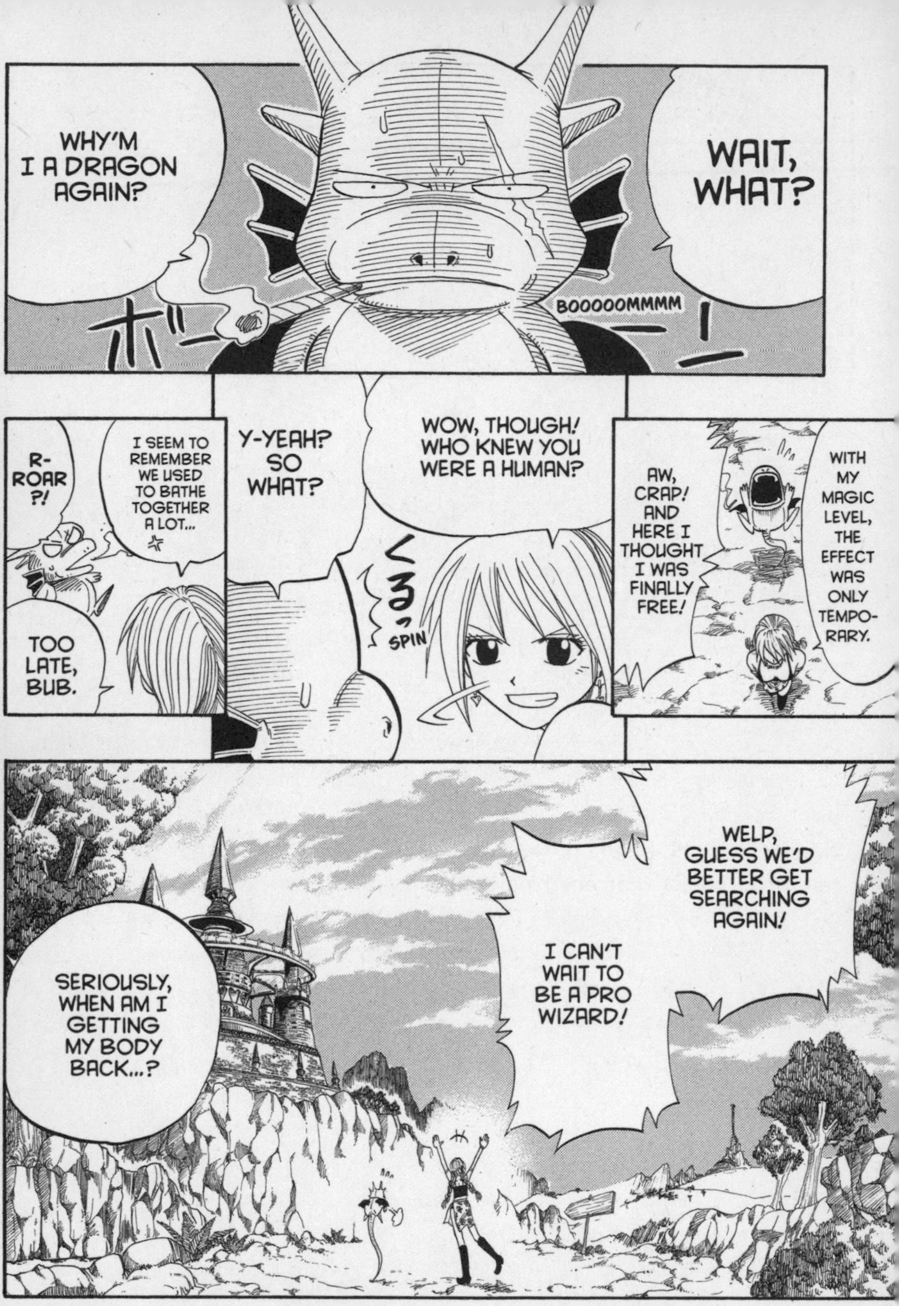

WAIT, WHAT?
WHY'M I A DRAGON AGAIN?
ボー
BOOOOOMMMM
WITH MY MAGIC LEVEL, THE EFFECT WAS ONLY TEMPORARY.
AW, CRAP! AND HERE I THOUGHT I WAS FINALLY FREE!
WOW, THOUGH! WHO KNEW YOU WERE A HUMAN?
Y-YEAH? SO WHAT?
くるっ
SPIN
I SEEM TO REMEMBER WE USED TO BATHE TOGETHER A LOT...
R-ROAR?!
TOO LATE, BUB.
WELP, GUESS WE'D BETTER GET SEARCHING AGAIN!
I CAN'T WAIT TO BE A PRO WIZARD!
SERIOUSLY, WHEN AM I GETTING MY BODY BACK...?

FIRST PUBLISHED:
WEEKLY SHONEN MAGAZINE NO. 4 SEP 2000
(MAGAZINE FRESH)

THE END

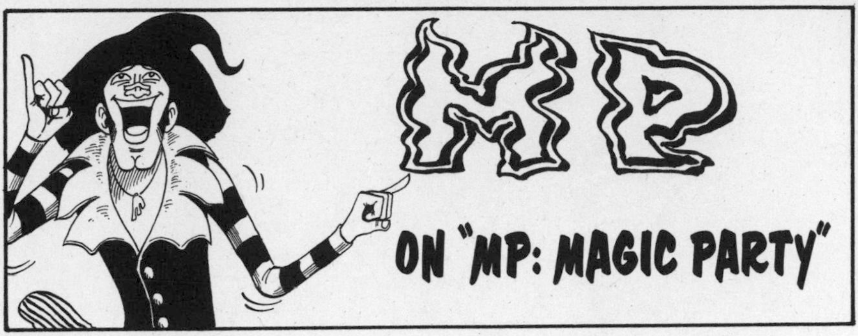
MP
ON "MP: MAGIC PARTY"

You might recognize the seed of the plot from "Cocona" in Part 1 (LOL). And "Magician," for that matter (yow!!). I love **transformation** and I love **magic**. That kind of miraculous element just seems so fantasy-like to me, y'know? I had initially intended this story for serialization. It was going to be a series where a magic-school dropout (Elena) grew up over time. But then Harry someone-or-other showed up on the scene, and I decided not to do a wizard-school plot. Even though I suspect there are a few of us (myself included) privately exclaiming, "*I* was doing wizard schools before they were cool!!" (Sigh.) Oh well... that other book is three times – no, ten times–cooler than anything I came up with for my wizard-school idea, so I guess they deserved it. I decided to keep the characters and world, drop the school, and do it as a short story instead. The result was "MP: Magic Party." Incidentally, "Magic Party" was going to be the name of the awesome graduation bash the wizard school threw every year. I took inspiration from the common RPG magical-power metric. Please don't be mad...

Oh, by the way, when I submitted the draft, my editor got upset because "Elena's panties are black." I mean, yes, they are... Sure, I guess upon reflection, I should've gone with white ones.

MP IDEA FILES (1)

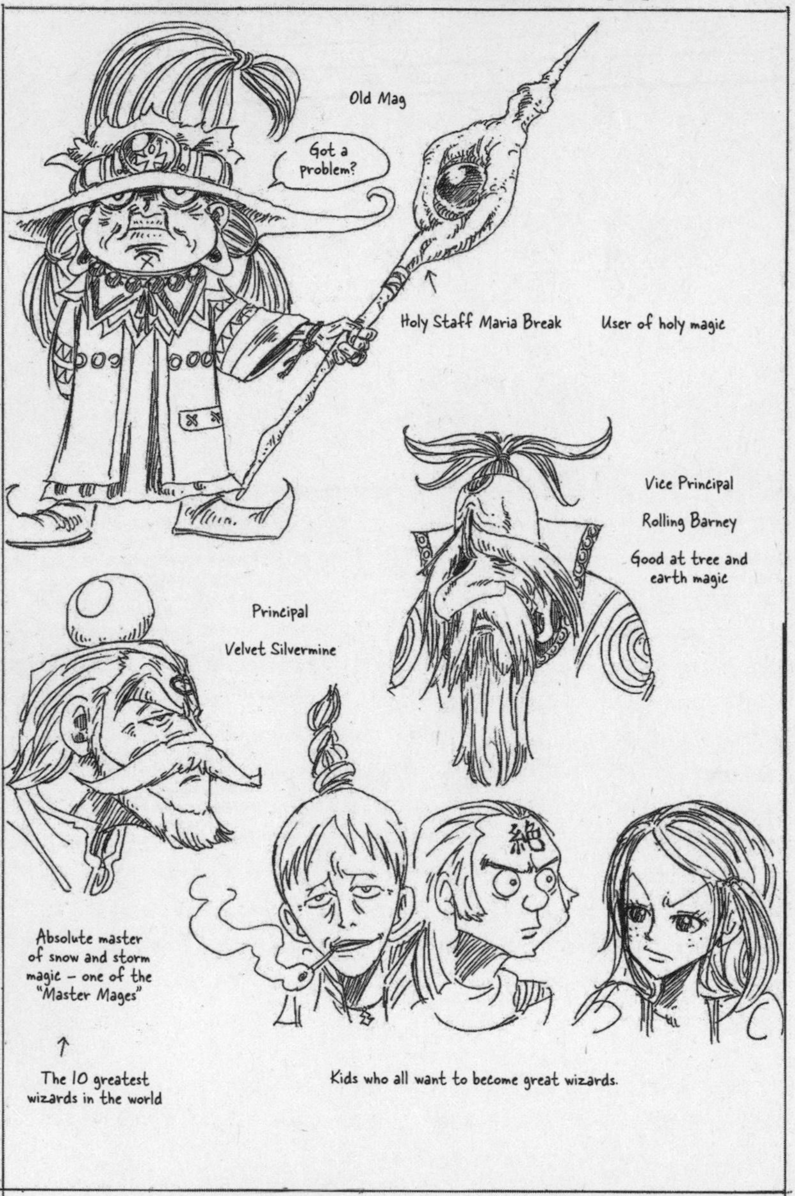
Old Mag
Got a problem?
Holy Staff Maria Break
User of holy magic
Vice Principal
Rolling Barney
Good at tree and earth magic
Principal
Velvet Silvermine
Absolute master of snow and storm magic – one of the "Master Mages"
The 10 greatest wizards in the world
Kids who all want to become great wizards.

IT'S A SCHOOL STORY. THEY HAVE FIELD DAYS, CULTURE FESTIVALS, SCHOOL TRIPS. IT'S VERY SLAPSTICK. SLAPSTICK, I SWEAR...

MP IDEA FILES (2)

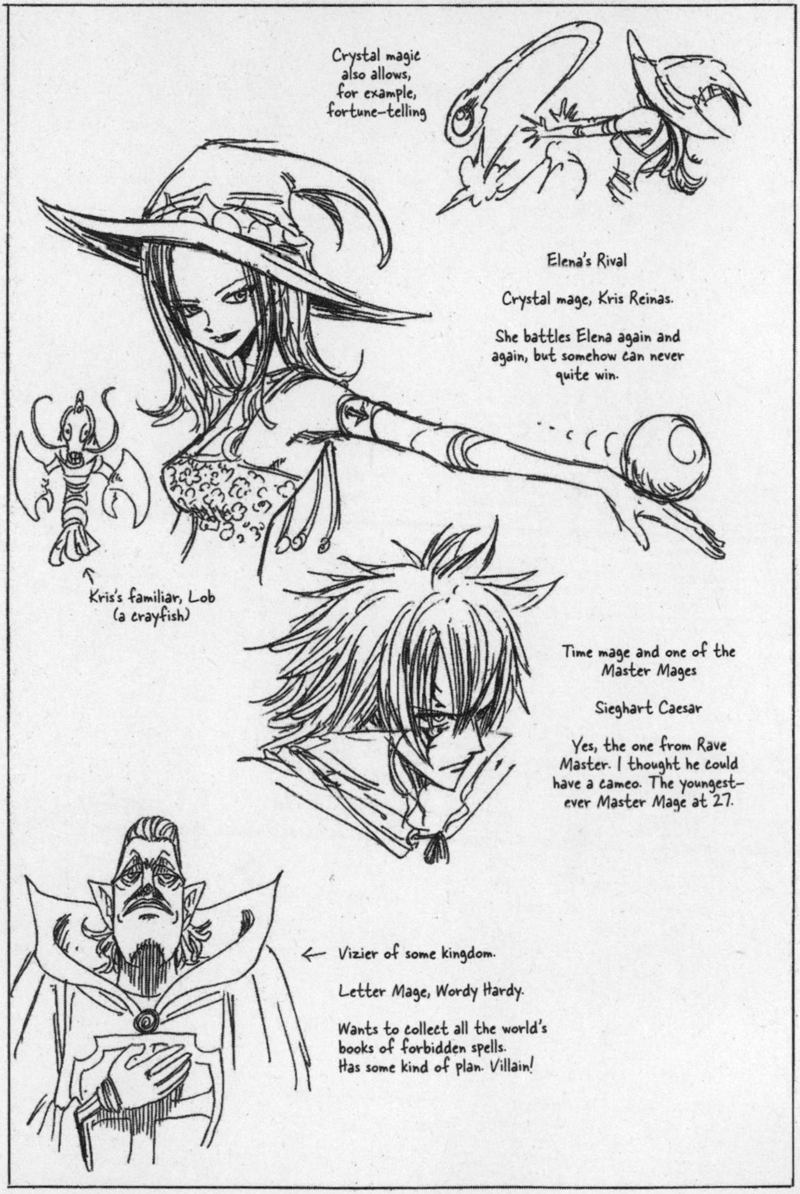
Crystal magic also allows, for example, fortune-telling
Elena's Rival
Crystal mage, Kris Reinas.
She battles Elena again and again, but somehow can never quite win.
Kris's familiar, Lob (a crayfish)
Time mage and one of the Master Mages
Sieghart Caesar
Yes, the one from Rave Master. I thought he could have a cameo. The youngest-ever Master Mage at 27.
Vizier of some kingdom.
Letter Mage, Wordy Hardy.
Wants to collect all the world's books of forbidden spells. Has some kind of plan. Villain!

I FIGURED ELENA AND HER SCHOOL CHUMS WOULD BATTLE WORDY HARDY AT SOME POINT.

MP IDEA FILES (3)

Summon the Ecliptic Twelve!!

12 of the most dangerous summoning spells.
In order to achieve her final goal, Elena sets out on a journey to enlist the aid of these dozen Starspirits.

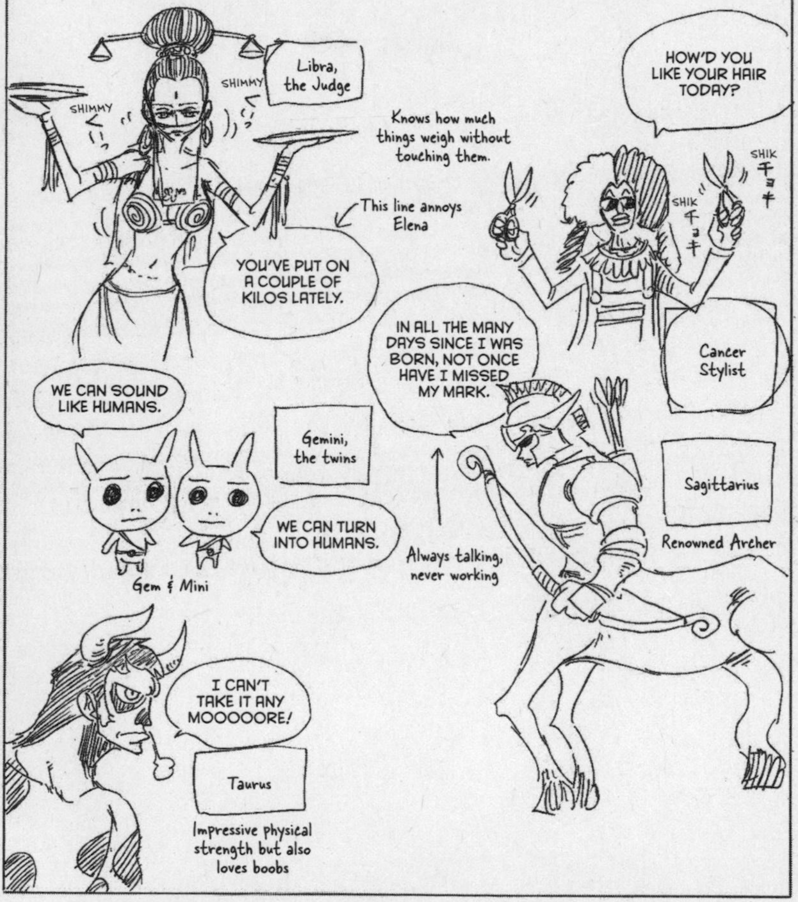
HOW'D YOU LIKE YOUR HAIR TODAY?
SHIK
SHIK
Cancer Stylist
Libra, the Judge
SHIMMY
SHIMMY
Knows how much things weigh without touching them.
This line annoys Elena
YOU'VE PUT ON A COUPLE OF KILOS LATELY.
IN ALL THE MANY DAYS SINCE I WAS BORN, NOT ONCE HAVE I MISSED MY MARK.
Sagittarius
Renowned Archer
Always talking, never working
Gemini, the twins
WE CAN SOUND LIKE HUMANS.
WE CAN TURN INTO HUMANS.
Gem & Mini
I CAN'T TAKE IT ANY MOOOOORE!
Taurus
Impressive physical strength but also loves boobs

HOLD ON, THESE CLOWNS DON'T LOOK DANGEROUS AT ALL. (LOL) BUT BRINGING THEM ALL TOGETHER MUST AMOUNT TO INCREDIBLE POWER! RIGHT?!

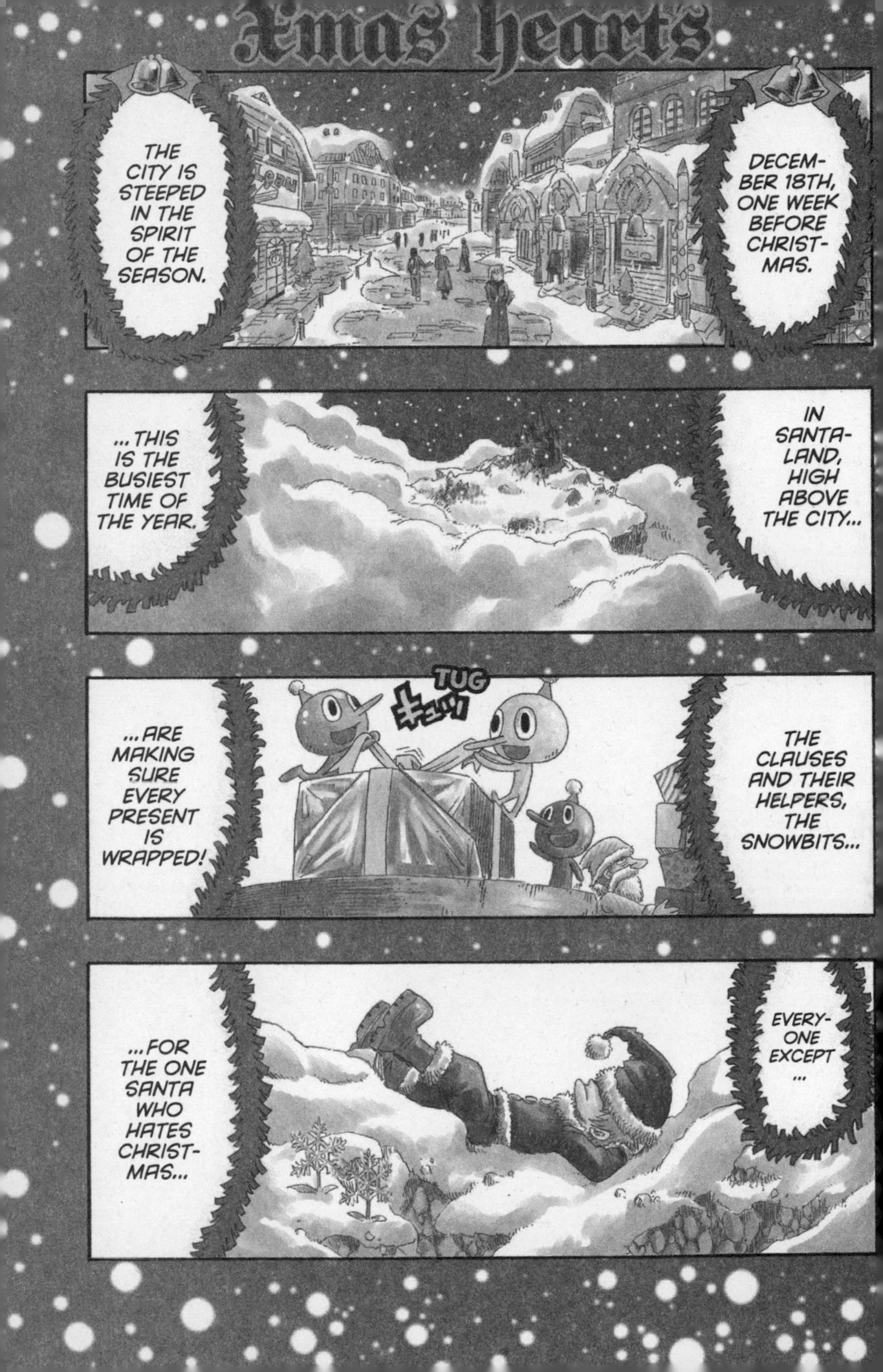
Xmas hearts
DECEMBER 18TH, ONE WEEK BEFORE CHRISTMAS.
THE CITY IS STEEPED IN THE SPIRIT OF THE SEASON.
IN SANTALAND, HIGH ABOVE THE CITY...
...THIS IS THE BUSIEST TIME OF THE YEAR.
THE CLAUSES AND THEIR HELPERS, THE SNOWBITS...
TUG
...ARE MAKING SURE EVERY PRESENT IS WRAPPED!
EVERYONE EXCEPT...
...FOR THE ONE SANTA WHO HATES CHRISTMAS...

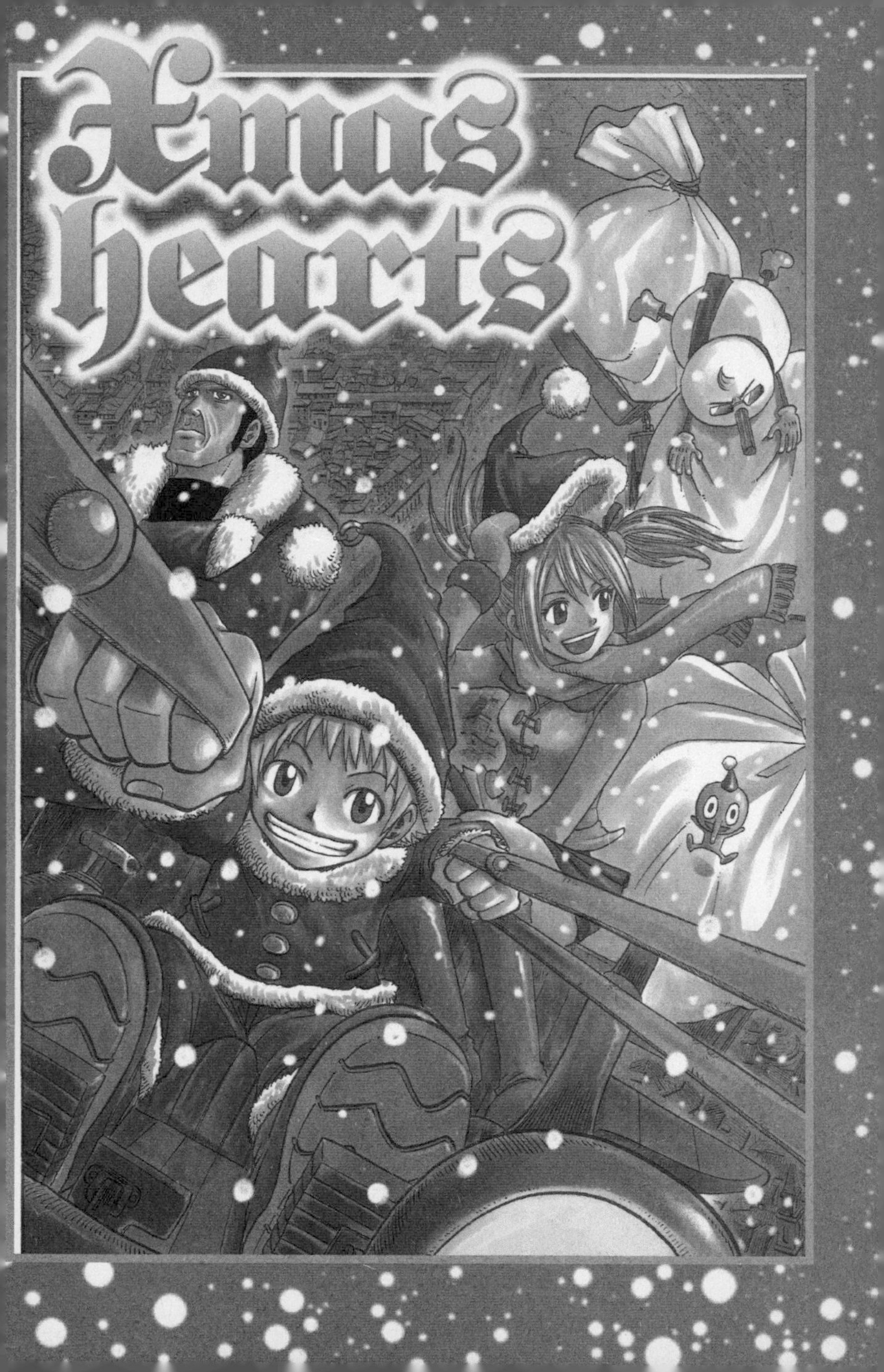
Xmas hearts

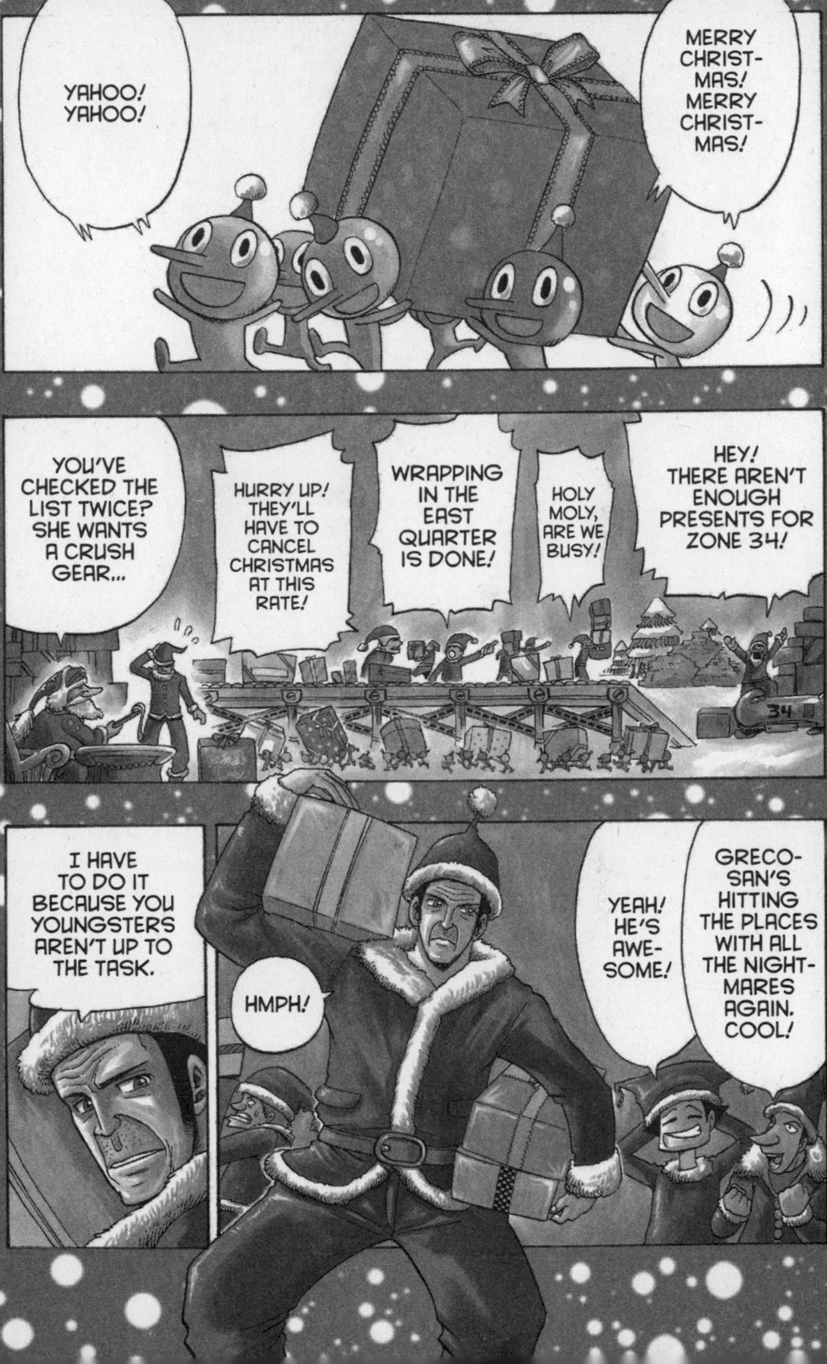
MERRY CHRIST-MAS! MERRY CHRIST-MAS!
YAHOO! YAHOO!
HEY! THERE AREN'T ENOUGH PRESENTS FOR ZONE 34!
HOLY MOLY, ARE WE BUSY!
WRAPPING IN THE EAST QUARTER IS DONE!
HURRY UP! THEY'LL HAVE TO CANCEL CHRISTMAS AT THIS RATE!
YOU'VE CHECKED THE LIST TWICE? SHE WANTS A CRUSH GEAR...
GRECO-SAN'S HITTING THE PLACES WITH ALL THE NIGHT-MARES AGAIN. COOL!
YEAH! HE'S AWE-SOME!
HMPH!
I HAVE TO DO IT BECAUSE YOU YOUNGSTERS AREN'T UP TO THE TASK.

Xmas hearts

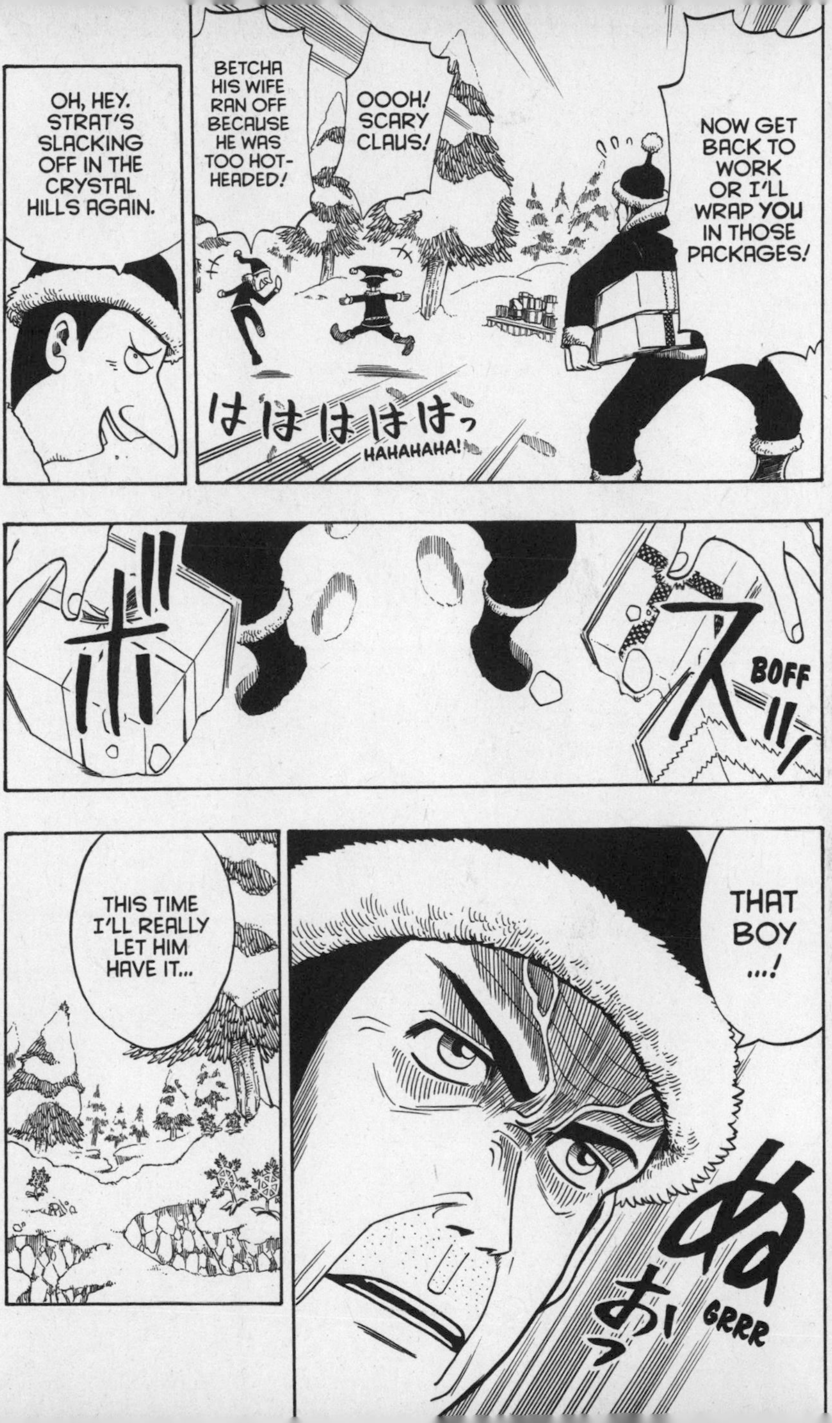
NOW GET BACK TO WORK OR I'LL WRAP YOU IN THOSE PACKAGES!
OOOH! SCARY CLAUS!
BETCHA HIS WIFE RAN OFF BECAUSE HE WAS TOO HOT-HEADED!
はははははっ
HAHAHAHA!
OH, HEY. STRAT'S SLACKING OFF IN THE CRYSTAL HILLS AGAIN.
ボス!!
BOFF
THAT BOY ...!
ぬおっ!
GRRR
THIS TIME I'LL REALLY LET HIM HAVE IT...

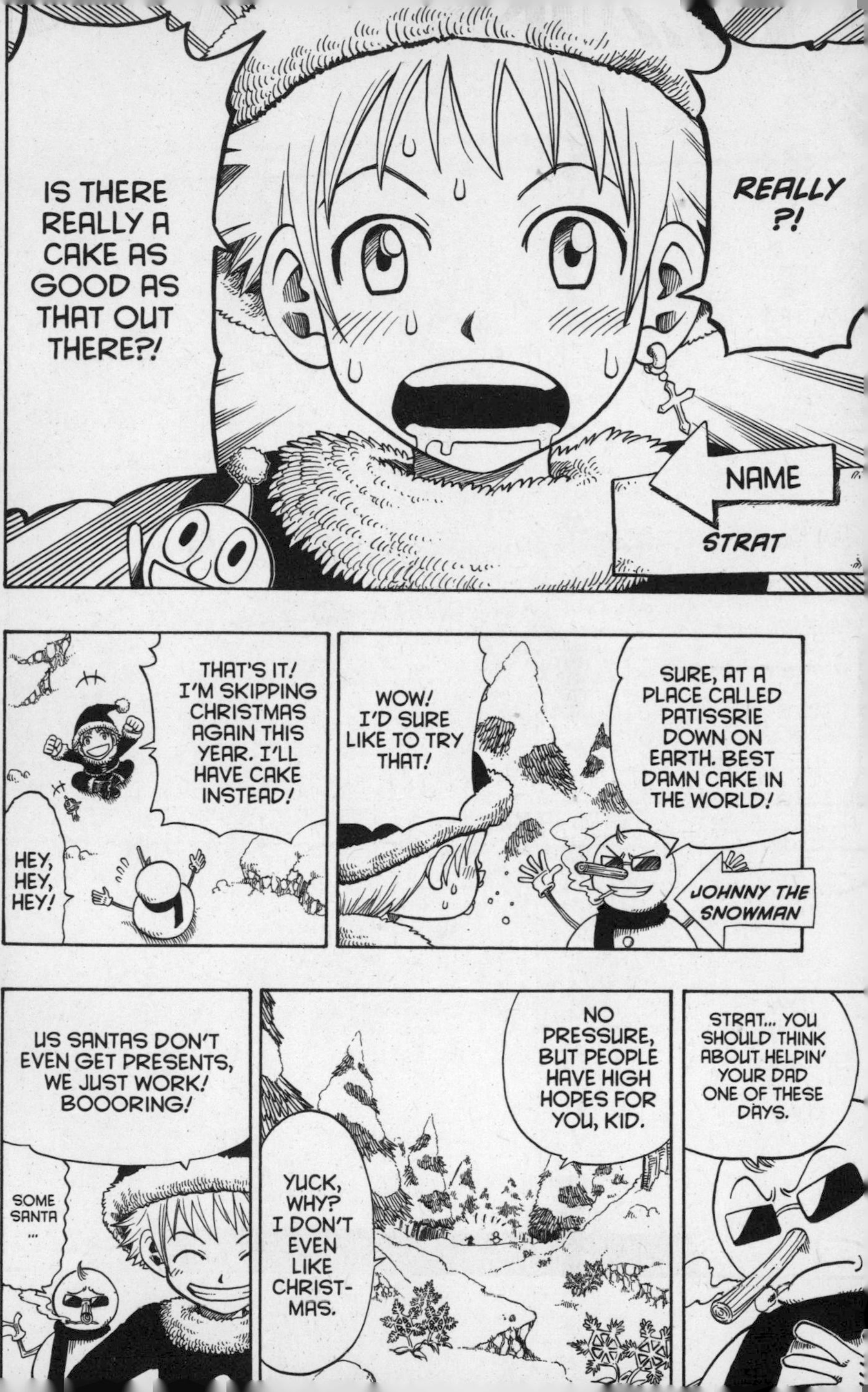
REALLY ?!
IS THERE REALLY A CAKE AS GOOD AS THAT OUT THERE?!
NAME
STRAT
SURE, AT A PLACE CALLED PATISSRIE DOWN ON EARTH. BEST DAMN CAKE IN THE WORLD!
WOW! I'D SURE LIKE TO TRY THAT!
JOHNNY THE SNOWMAN
THAT'S IT! I'M SKIPPING CHRISTMAS AGAIN THIS YEAR. I'LL HAVE CAKE INSTEAD!
HEY, HEY, HEY!
STRAT... YOU SHOULD THINK ABOUT HELPIN' YOUR DAD ONE OF THESE DAYS.
NO PRESSURE, BUT PEOPLE HAVE HIGH HOPES FOR YOU, KID.
YUCK, WHY? I DON'T EVEN LIKE CHRIST-MAS.
US SANTAS DON'T EVEN GET PRESENTS, WE JUST WORK! BOOORING!
SOME SANTA ...

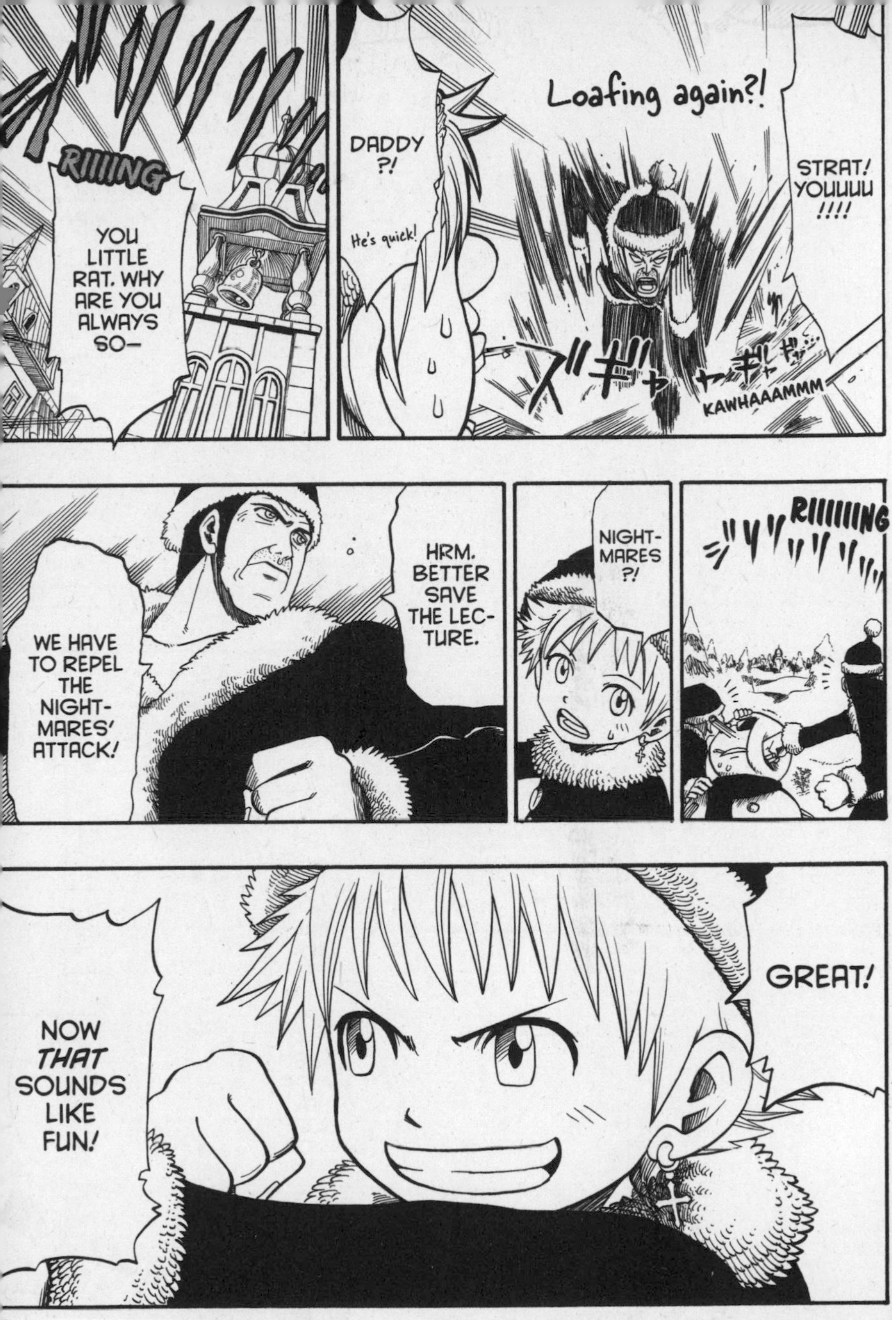

Loafing again?!
STRAT! YOUUUU!!!!
DADDY ?!
He's quick!
KAWHAAAMMM
RIIIING
YOU LITTLE RAT. WHY ARE YOU ALWAYS SO—
RIIIIIIING
NIGHT-MARES ?!
HRM. BETTER SAVE THE LEC-TURE.
WE HAVE TO REPEL THE NIGHT-MARES' ATTACK!
GREAT!
NOW *THAT* SOUNDS LIKE FUN!

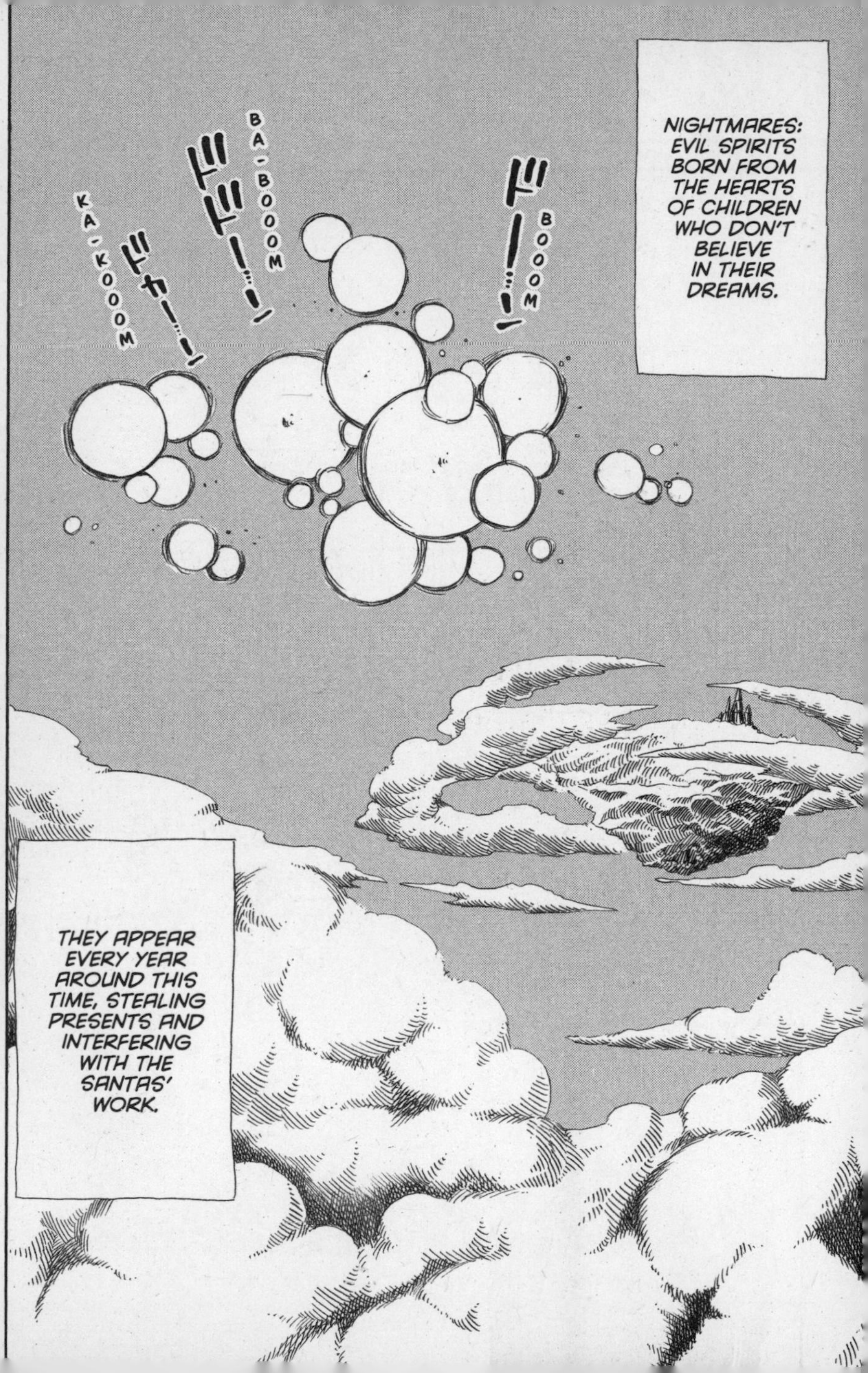
NIGHTMARES: EVIL SPIRITS BORN FROM THE HEARTS OF CHILDREN WHO DON'T BELIEVE IN THEIR DREAMS.
BOOOM
BA-BOOOM
KA-KOOOM
THEY APPEAR EVERY YEAR AROUND THIS TIME, STEALING PRESENTS AND INTERFERING WITH THE SANTAS' WORK.

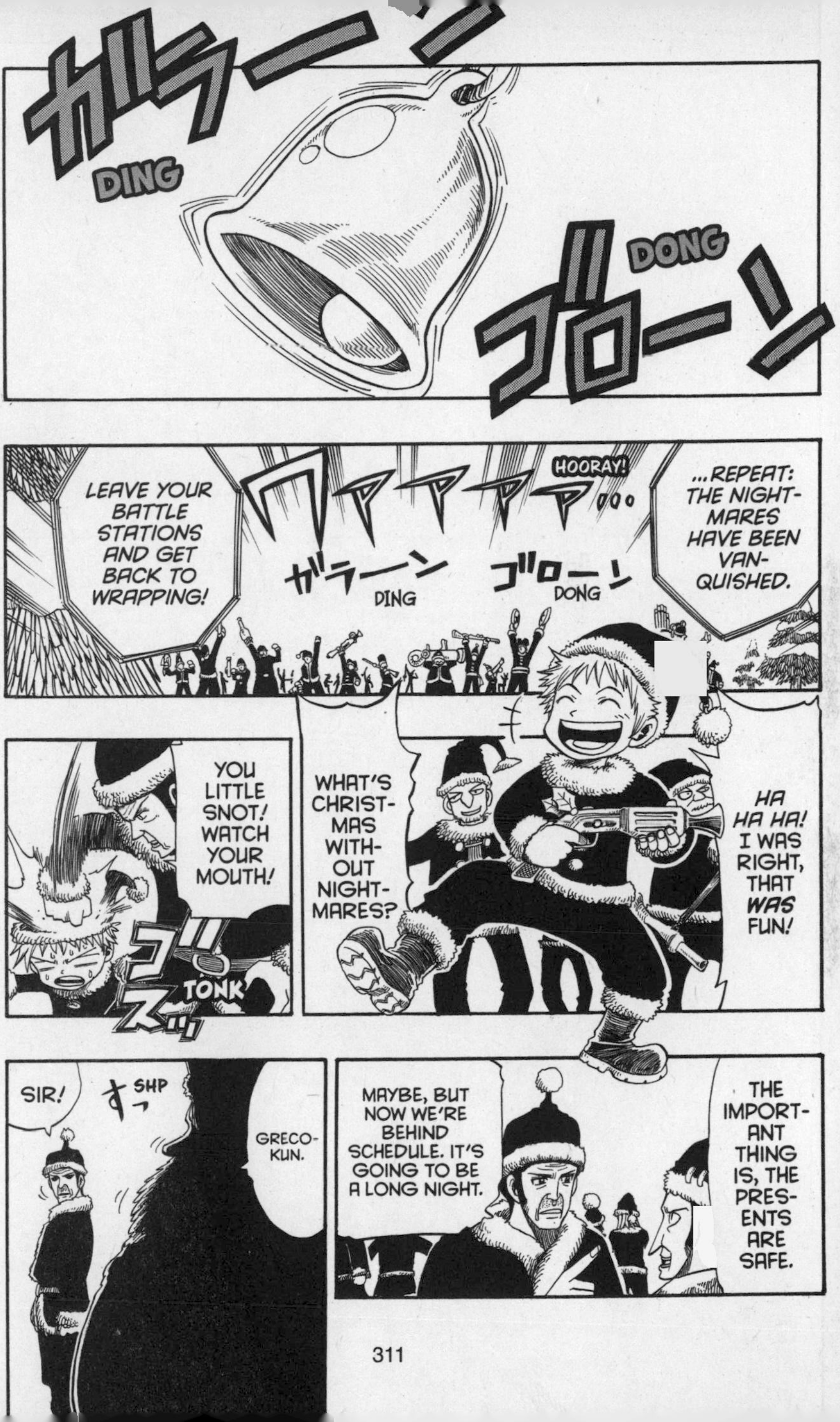
DING
DONG
...REPEAT: THE NIGHT-MARES HAVE BEEN VAN-QUISHED.
HOORAY!
ゴローン
DONG
ガラーン
DING
LEAVE YOUR BATTLE STATIONS AND GET BACK TO WRAPPING!
HA HA HA! I WAS RIGHT, THAT *WAS* FUN!
WHAT'S CHRIST-MAS WITH-OUT NIGHT-MARES?
YOU LITTLE SNOT! WATCH YOUR MOUTH!
TONK
THE IMPORT-ANT THING IS, THE PRES-ENTS ARE SAFE.
MAYBE, BUT NOW WE'RE BEHIND SCHEDULE. IT'S GOING TO BE A LONG NIGHT.
GRECO-KUN.
す
SHP
SIR!

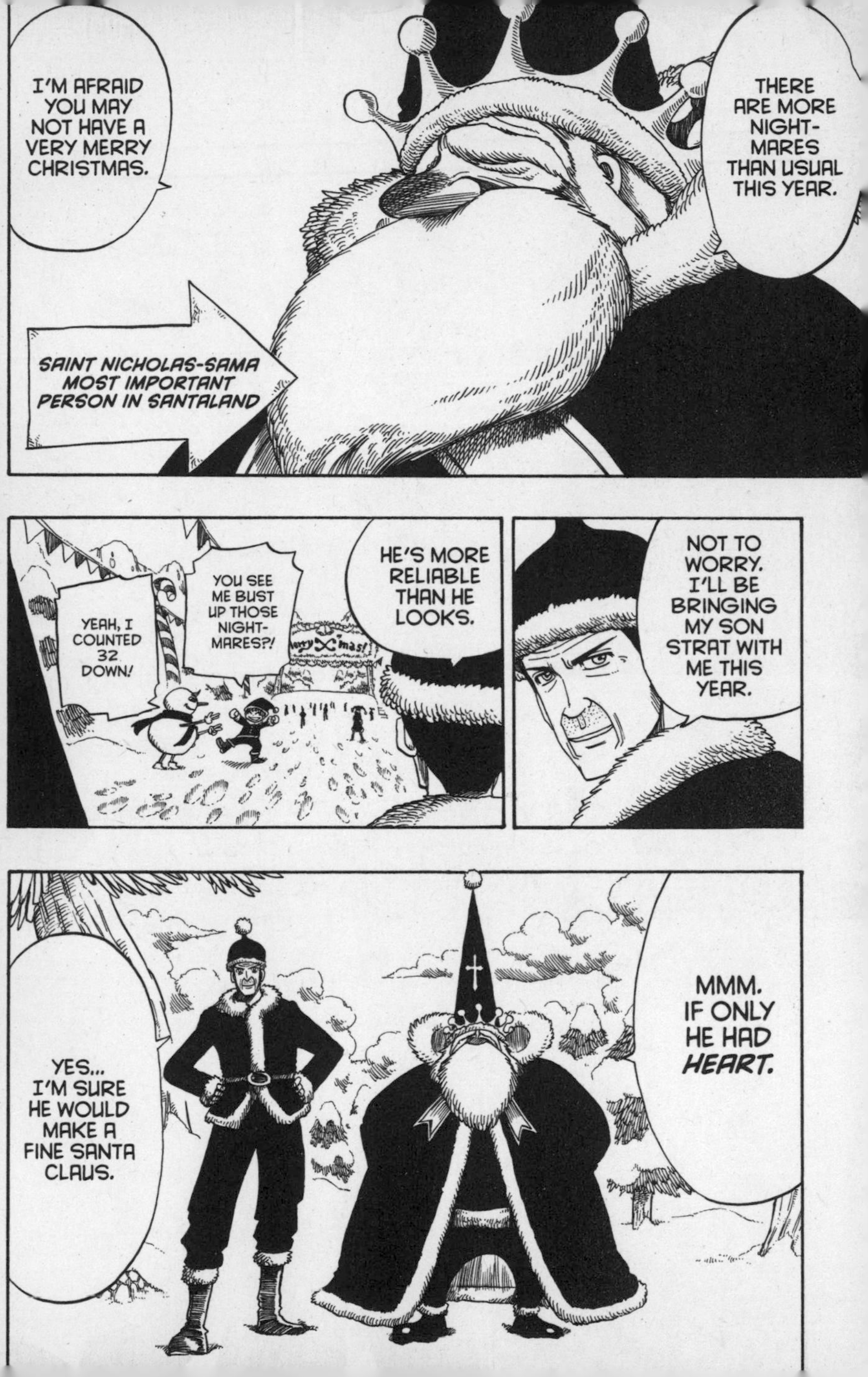
THERE ARE MORE NIGHT-MARES THAN USUAL THIS YEAR.
I'M AFRAID YOU MAY NOT HAVE A VERY MERRY CHRISTMAS.
SAINT NICHOLAS-SAMA MOST IMPORTANT PERSON IN SANTALAND
NOT TO WORRY. I'LL BE BRINGING MY SON STRAT WITH ME THIS YEAR.
HE'S MORE RELIABLE THAN HE LOOKS.
YOU SEE ME BUST UP THOSE NIGHT-MARES?!
YEAH, I COUNTED 32 DOWN!
MMM. IF ONLY HE HAD *HEART.*
YES... I'M SURE HE WOULD MAKE A FINE SANTA CLAUS.

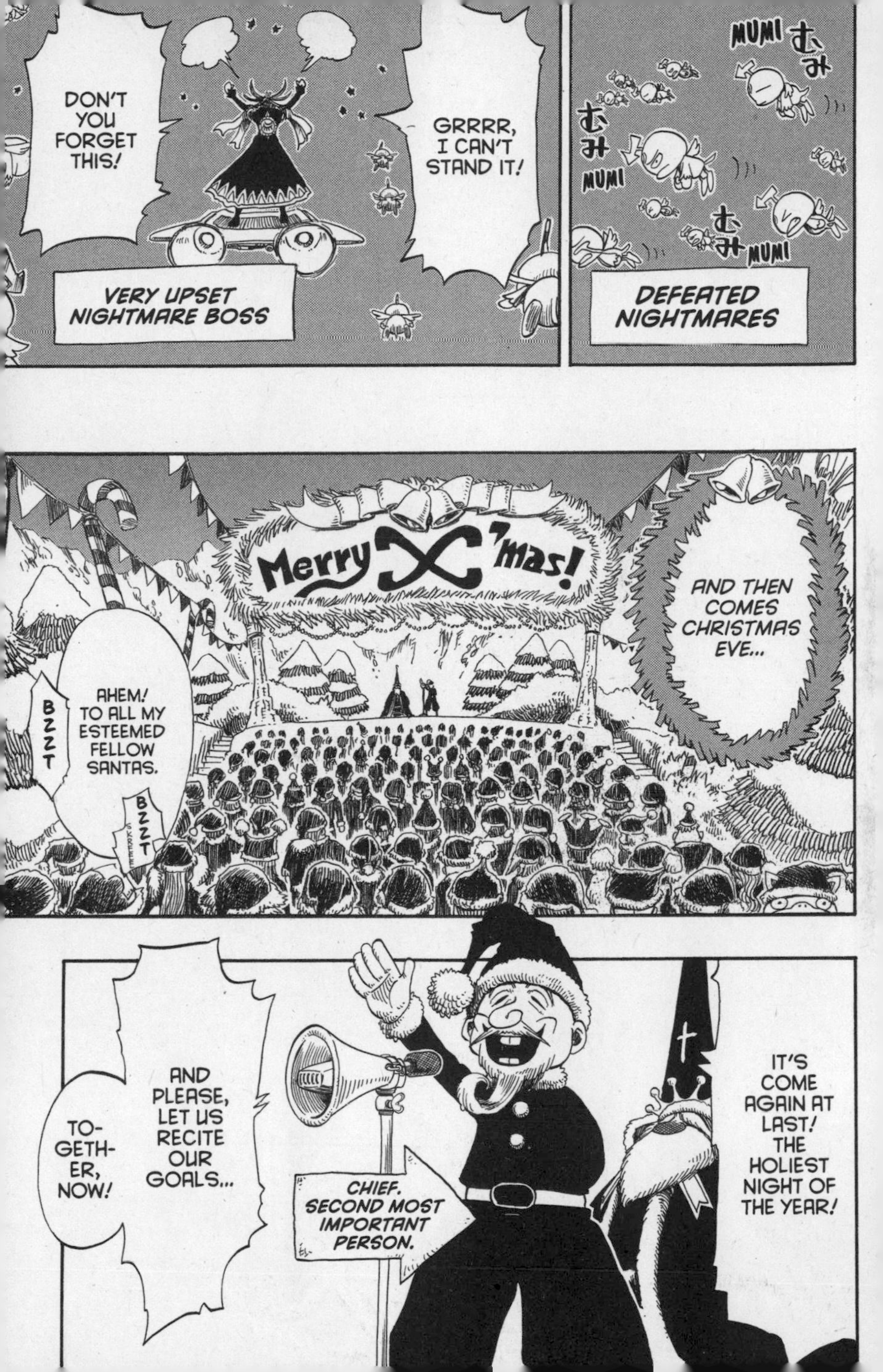
MUMI むみ
むみ MUMI
むみ MUMI
DEFEATED NIGHTMARES
GRRRR, I CAN'T STAND IT!
DON'T YOU FORGET THIS!
VERY UPSET NIGHTMARE BOSS
AND THEN COMES CHRISTMAS EVE...
Merry X'mas!
AHEM! TO ALL MY ESTEEMED FELLOW SANTAS.
BZZT
BZZT
IT'S COME AGAIN AT LAST! THE HOLIEST NIGHT OF THE YEAR!
CHIEF. SECOND MOST IMPORTANT PERSON.
AND PLEASE, LET US RECITE OUR GOALS...
TO-GETH-ER, NOW!

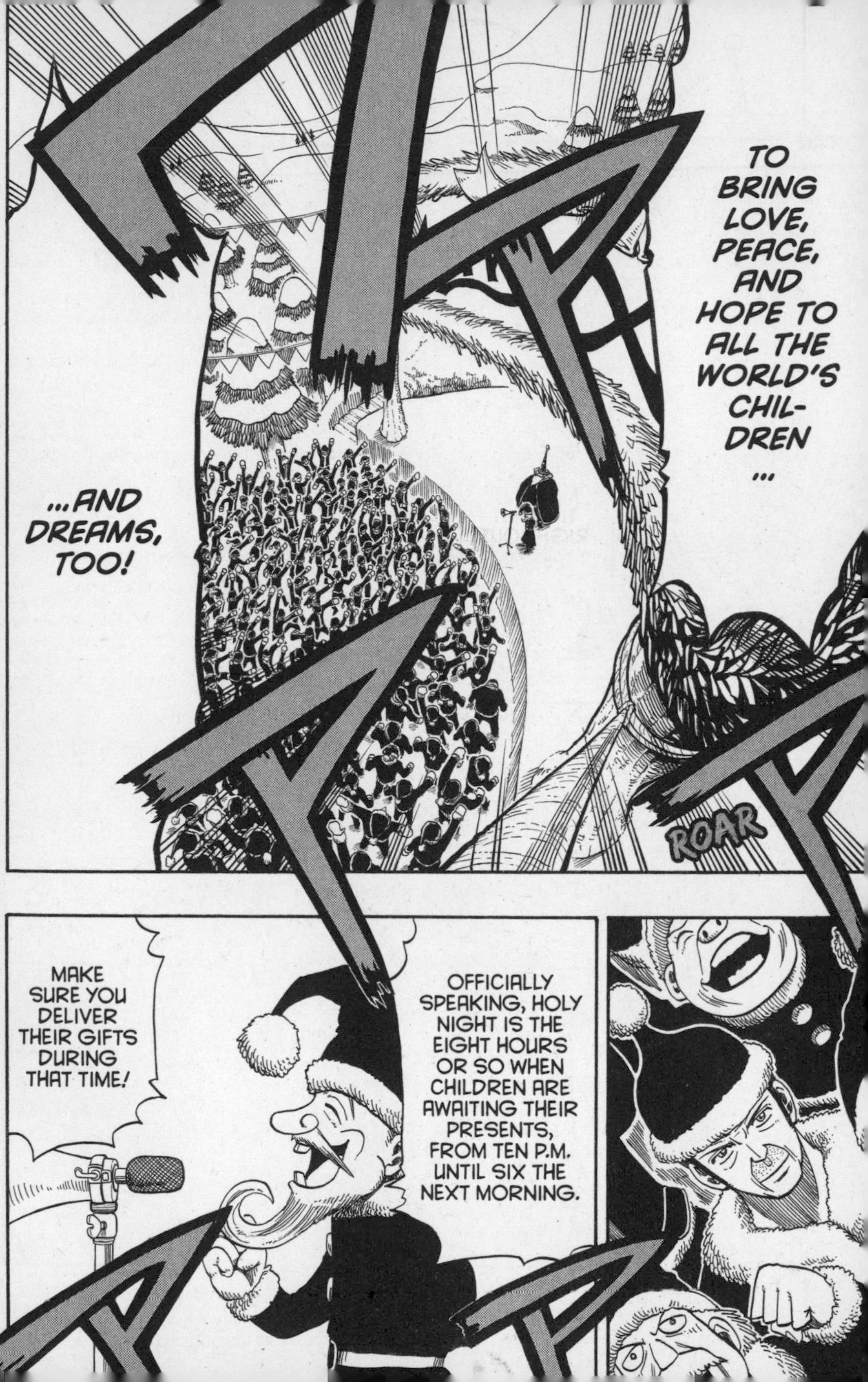
TO BRING LOVE, PEACE, AND HOPE TO ALL THE WORLD'S CHIL-DREN ...
...AND DREAMS, TOO!
ROAR
OFFICIALLY SPEAKING, HOLY NIGHT IS THE EIGHT HOURS OR SO WHEN CHILDREN ARE AWAITING THEIR PRESENTS, FROM TEN P.M. UNTIL SIX THE NEXT MORNING.
MAKE SURE YOU DELIVER THEIR GIFTS DURING THAT TIME!

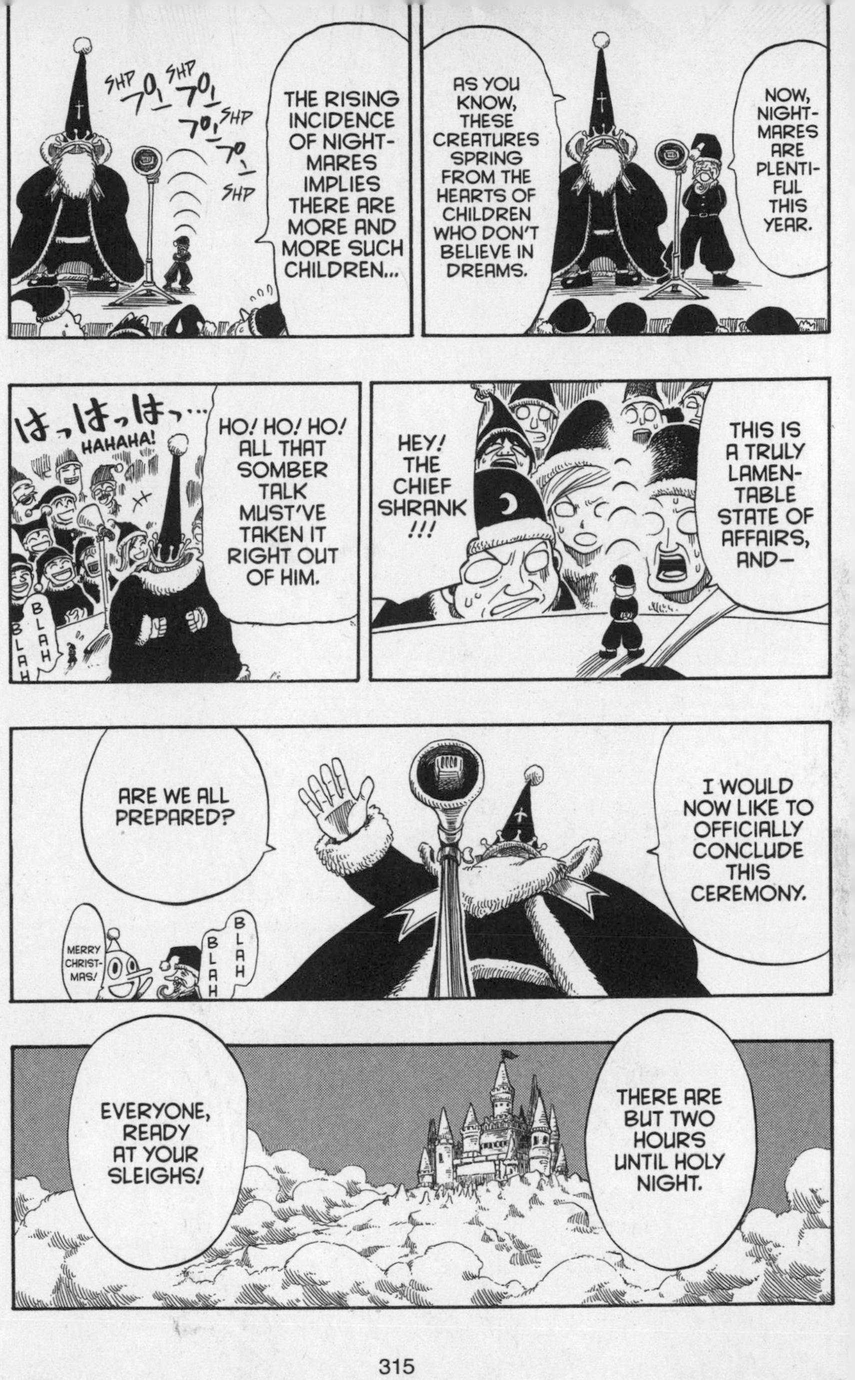
NOW, NIGHT-MARES ARE PLENTI-FUL THIS YEAR.
AS YOU KNOW, THESE CREATURES SPRING FROM THE HEARTS OF CHILDREN WHO DON'T BELIEVE IN DREAMS.
THE RISING INCIDENCE OF NIGHT-MARES IMPLIES THERE ARE MORE AND MORE SUCH CHILDREN...
SHP SHP SHP SHP
THIS IS A TRULY LAMEN-TABLE STATE OF AFFAIRS, AND—
HEY! THE CHIEF SHRANK!!!
HO! HO! HO! ALL THAT SOMBER TALK MUST'VE TAKEN IT RIGHT OUT OF HIM.
はっはっはっ…
HAHAHA!
BLAH BLAH
I WOULD NOW LIKE TO OFFICIALLY CONCLUDE THIS CEREMONY.
ARE WE ALL PREPARED?
BLAH BLAH
MERRY CHRISTMAS!
THERE ARE BUT TWO HOURS UNTIL HOLY NIGHT.
EVERYONE, READY AT YOUR SLEIGHS!

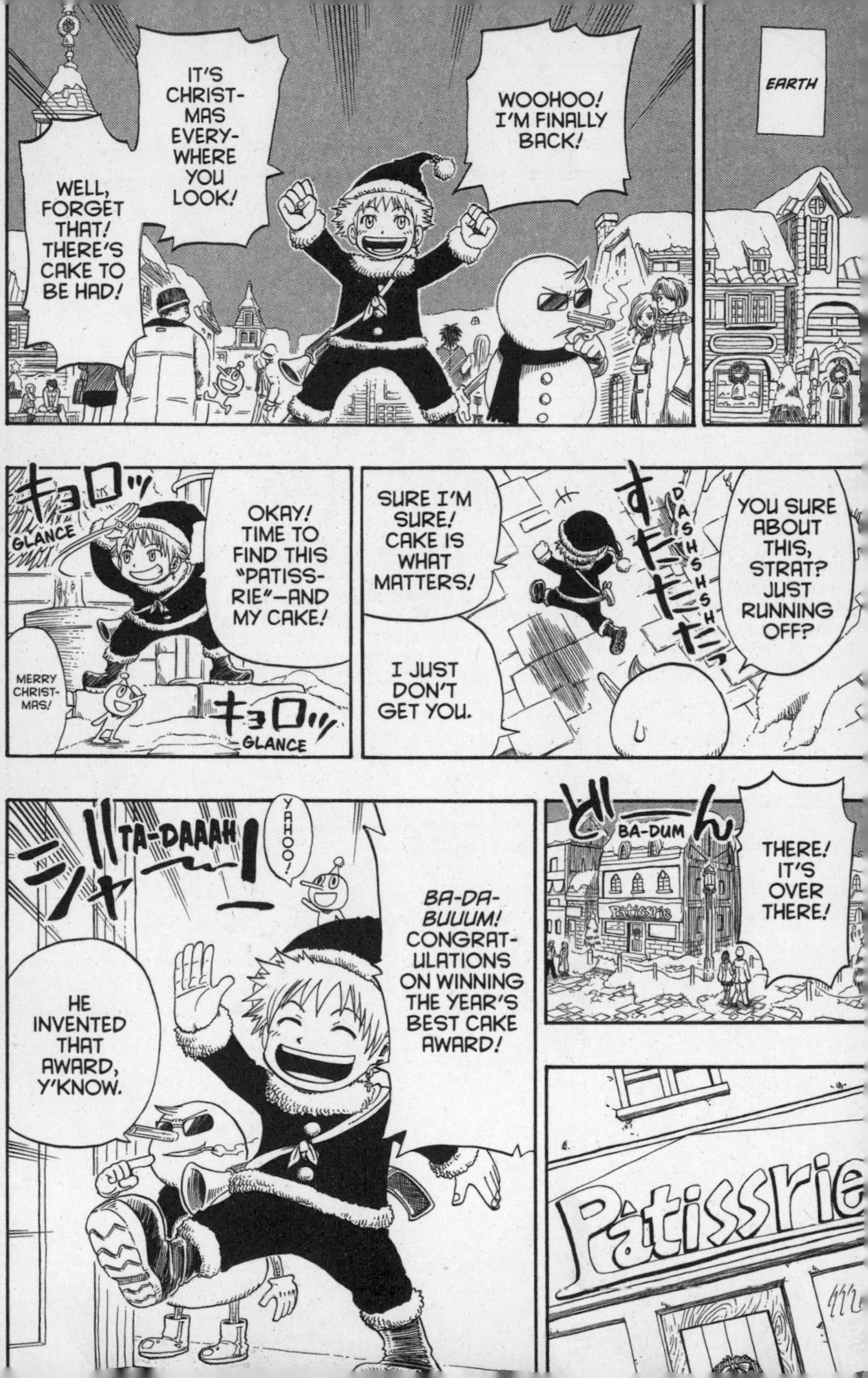
EARTH
WOOHOO! I'M FINALLY BACK!
IT'S CHRISTMAS EVERYWHERE YOU LOOK!
WELL, FORGET THAT! THERE'S CAKE TO BE HAD!
YOU SURE ABOUT THIS, STRAT? JUST RUNNING OFF?
DASHSHSHSH
SURE I'M SURE! CAKE IS WHAT MATTERS!
I JUST DON'T GET YOU.
OKAY! TIME TO FIND THIS "PATISSRIE"—AND MY CAKE!
キョロッ
GLANCE
MERRY CHRISTMAS!
キョロッ
GLANCE
THERE! IT'S OVER THERE!
BA-DUM
Patissrie
Patissrie
TA-DAAAH
YAHOO!
BA-DA-BUUUM! CONGRATULATIONS ON WINNING THE YEAR'S BEST CAKE AWARD!
HE INVENTED THAT AWARD, Y'KNOW.

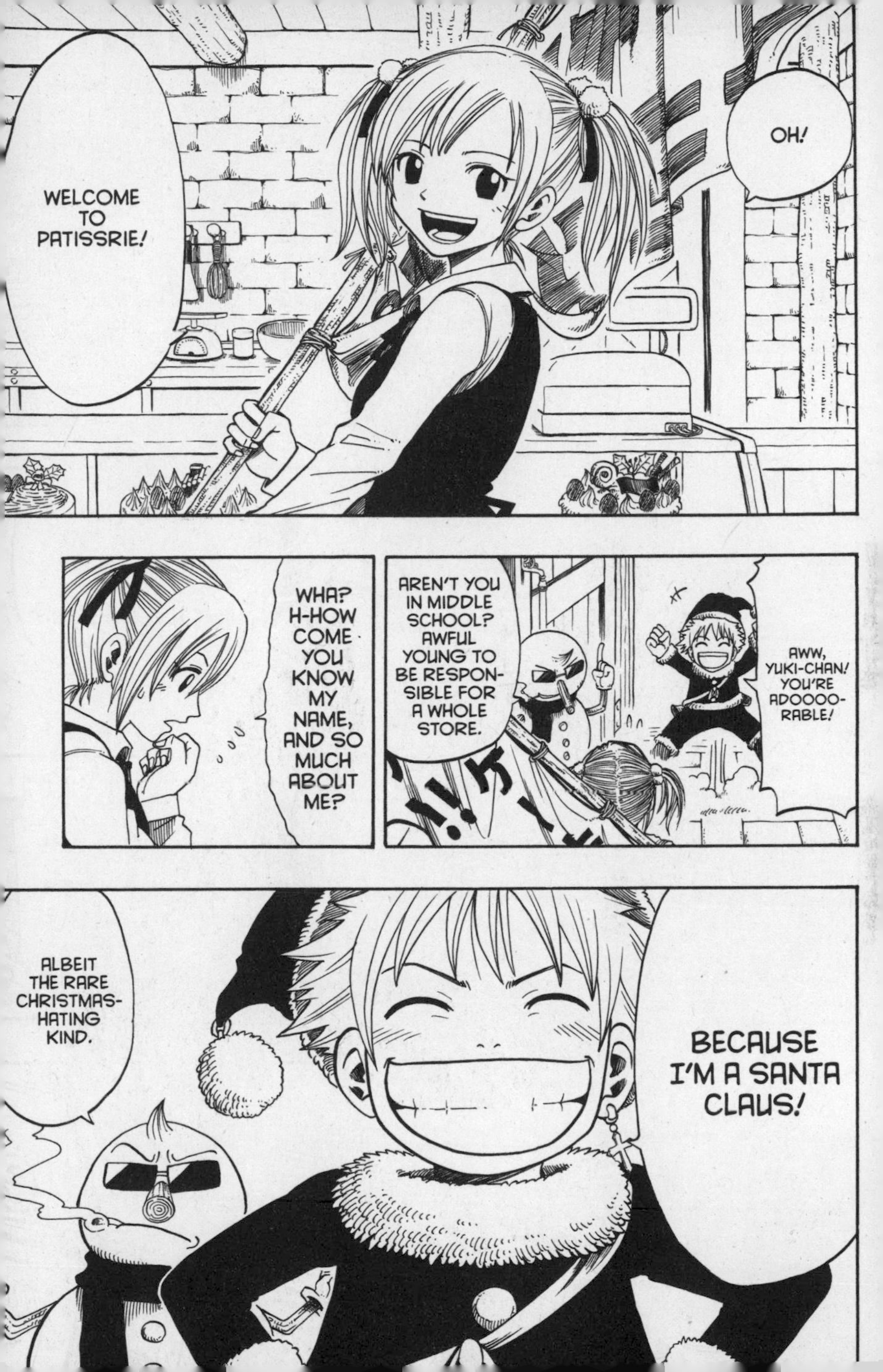
OH!
WELCOME TO PATISSRIE!
AWW, YUKI-CHAN! YOU'RE ADOOOO-RABLE!
AREN'T YOU IN MIDDLE SCHOOL? AWFUL YOUNG TO BE RESPONSIBLE FOR A WHOLE STORE.
WHA? H-HOW COME YOU KNOW MY NAME, AND SO MUCH ABOUT ME?
BECAUSE I'M A SANTA CLAUS!
ALBEIT THE RARE CHRISTMAS-HATING KIND.

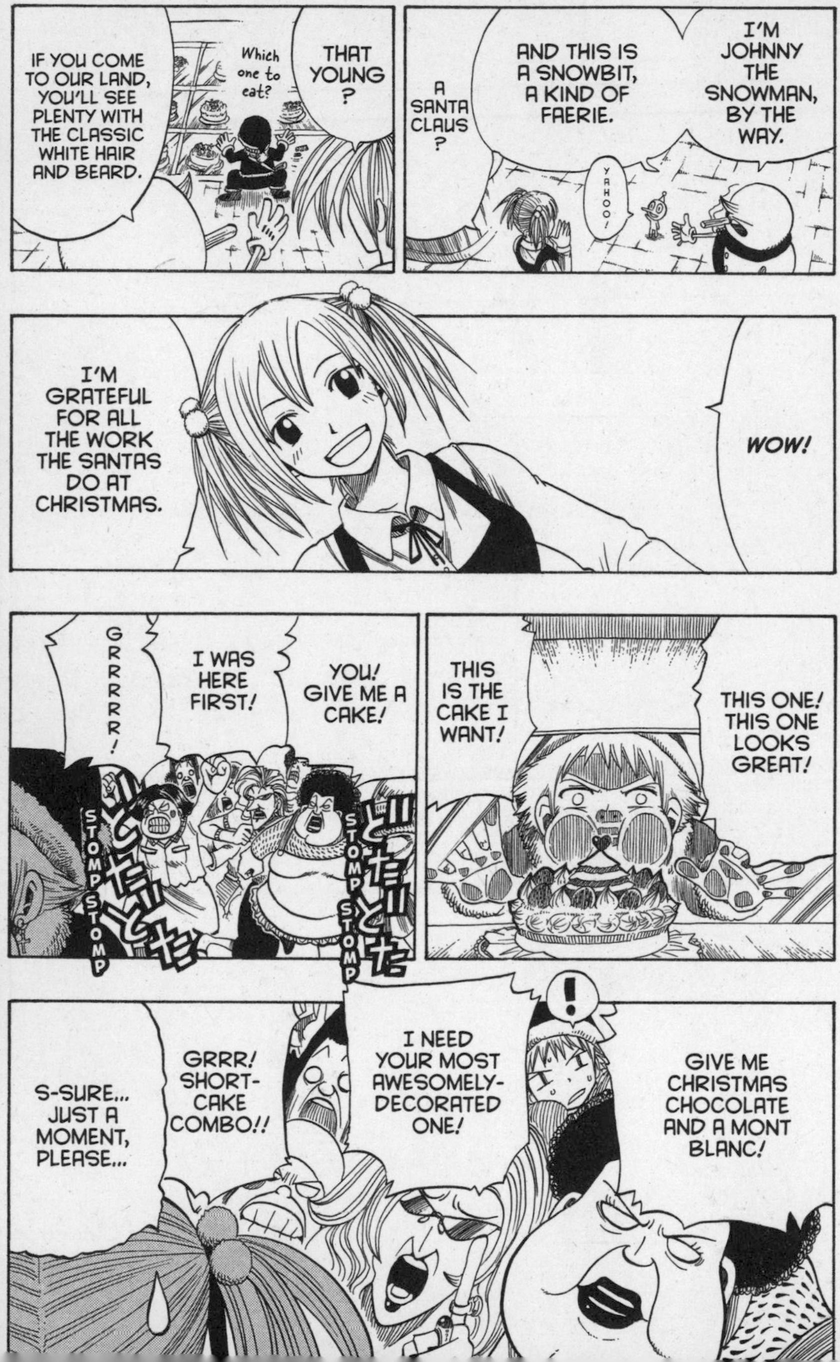
I'M JOHNNY THE SNOWMAN, BY THE WAY.
AND THIS IS A SNOWBIT, A KIND OF FAERIE.
YAHOO!
A SANTA CLAUS?
THAT YOUNG?
Which one to eat?
IF YOU COME TO OUR LAND, YOU'LL SEE PLENTY WITH THE CLASSIC WHITE HAIR AND BEARD.
WOW!
I'M GRATEFUL FOR ALL THE WORK THE SANTAS DO AT CHRISTMAS.
THIS ONE! THIS ONE LOOKS GREAT!
THIS IS THE CAKE I WANT!
YOU! GIVE ME A CAKE!
I WAS HERE FIRST!
GRRRRR!
STOMP STOMP
STOMP STOMP
!
GIVE ME CHRISTMAS CHOCOLATE AND A MONT BLANC!
I NEED YOUR MOST AWESOMELY-DECORATED ONE!
GRRR! SHORT-CAKE COMBO!!
S-SURE... JUST A MOMENT, PLEASE...

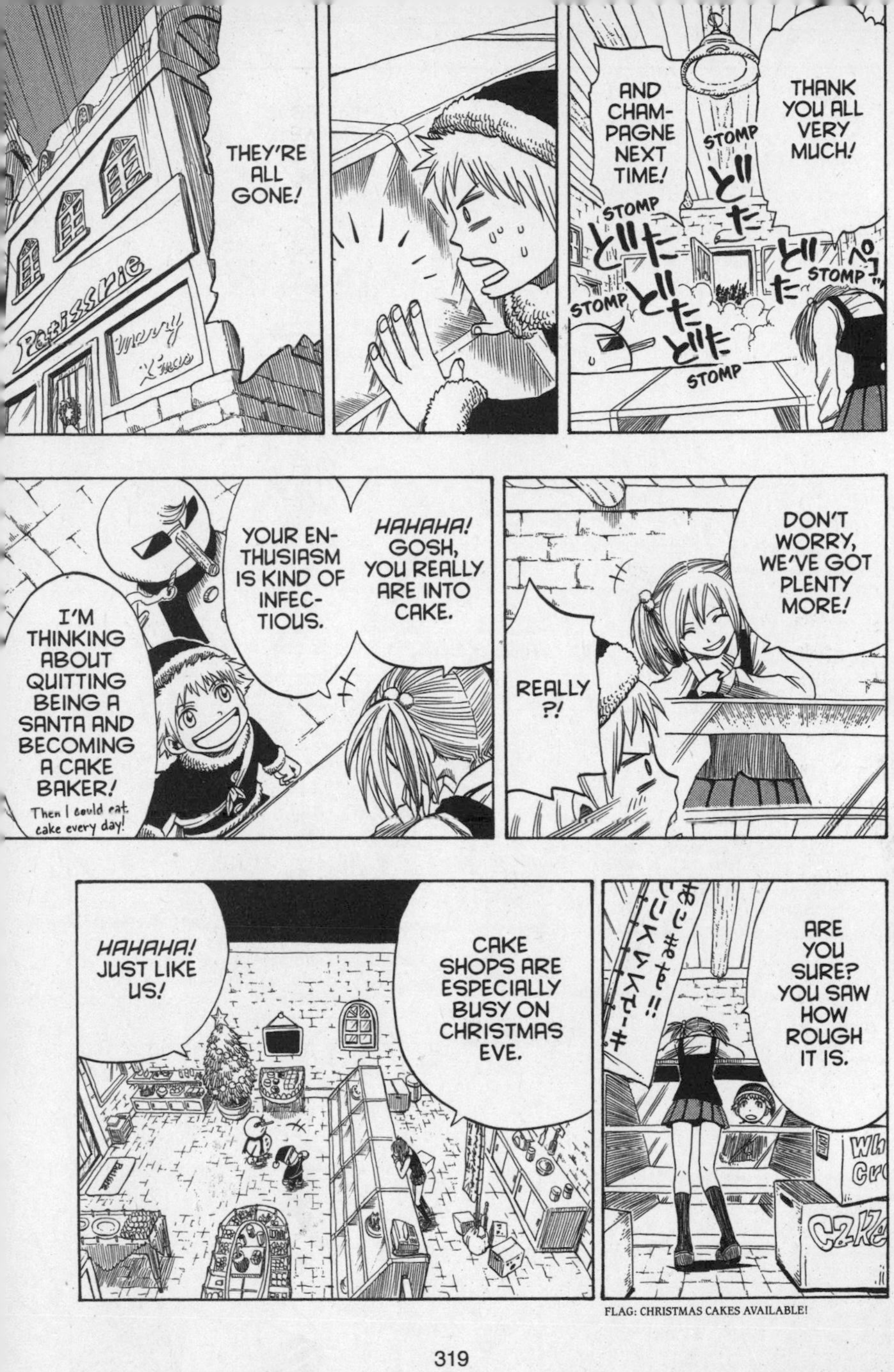
THANK YOU ALL VERY MUCH!
AND CHAMPAGNE NEXT TIME!
STOMP
STOMP
STOMP
STOMP
STOMP
THEY'RE ALL GONE!
DON'T WORRY, WE'VE GOT PLENTY MORE!
REALLY?!
HAHAHA! GOSH, YOU REALLY ARE INTO CAKE.
YOUR ENTHUSIASM IS KIND OF INFECTIOUS.
I'M THINKING ABOUT QUITTING BEING A SANTA AND BECOMING A CAKE BAKER!
Then I could eat cake every day!
ARE YOU SURE? YOU SAW HOW ROUGH IT IS.
CAKE SHOPS ARE ESPECIALLY BUSY ON CHRISTMAS EVE.
HAHAHA! JUST LIKE US!

FLAG: CHRISTMAS CAKES AVAILABLE!

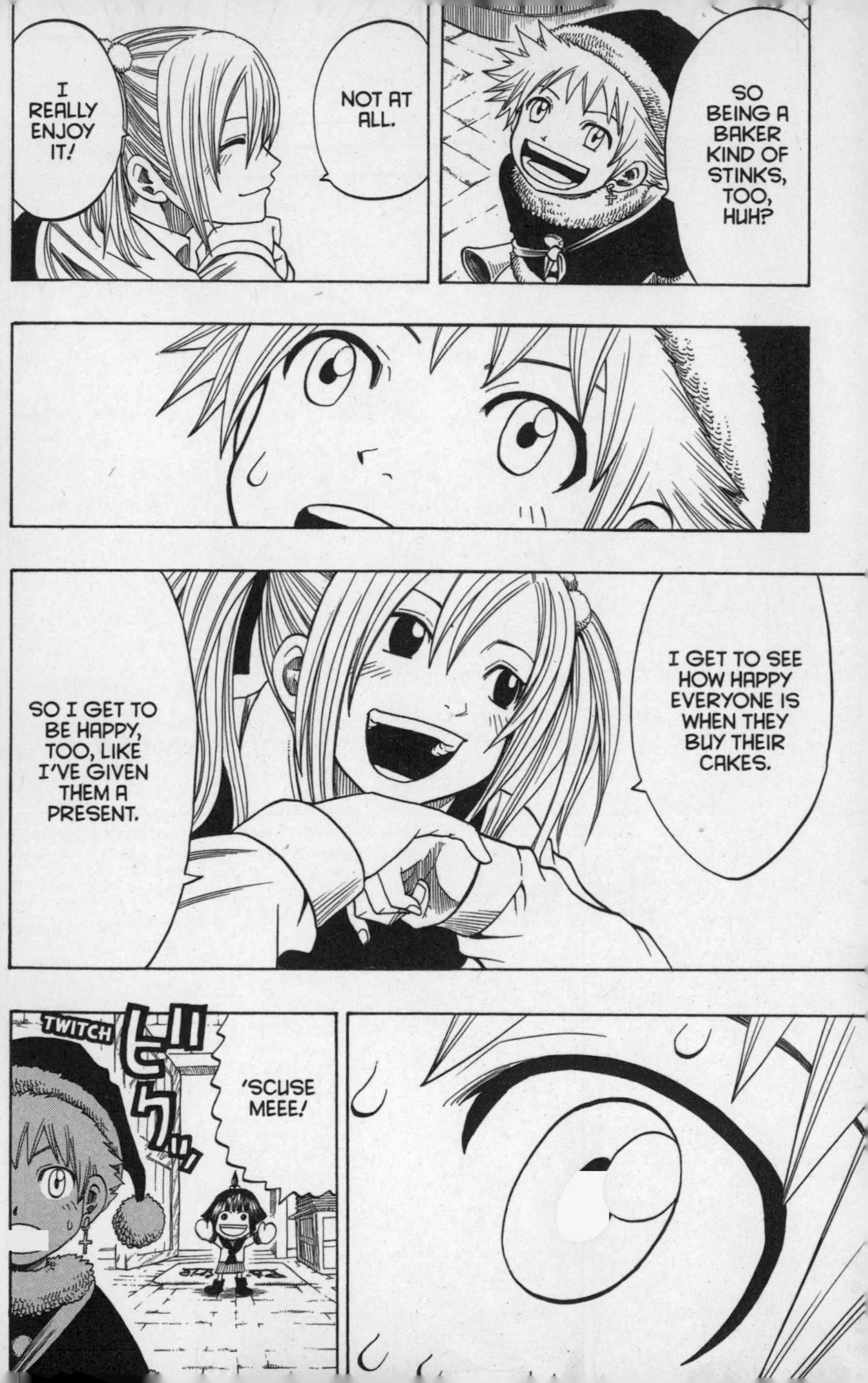
SO BEING A BAKER KIND OF STINKS, TOO, HUH?
NOT AT ALL.
I REALLY ENJOY IT!
I GET TO SEE HOW HAPPY EVERYONE IS WHEN THEY BUY THEIR CAKES.
SO I GET TO BE HAPPY, TOO, LIKE I'VE GIVEN THEM A PRESENT.
'SCUSE MEEE!
TWITCH

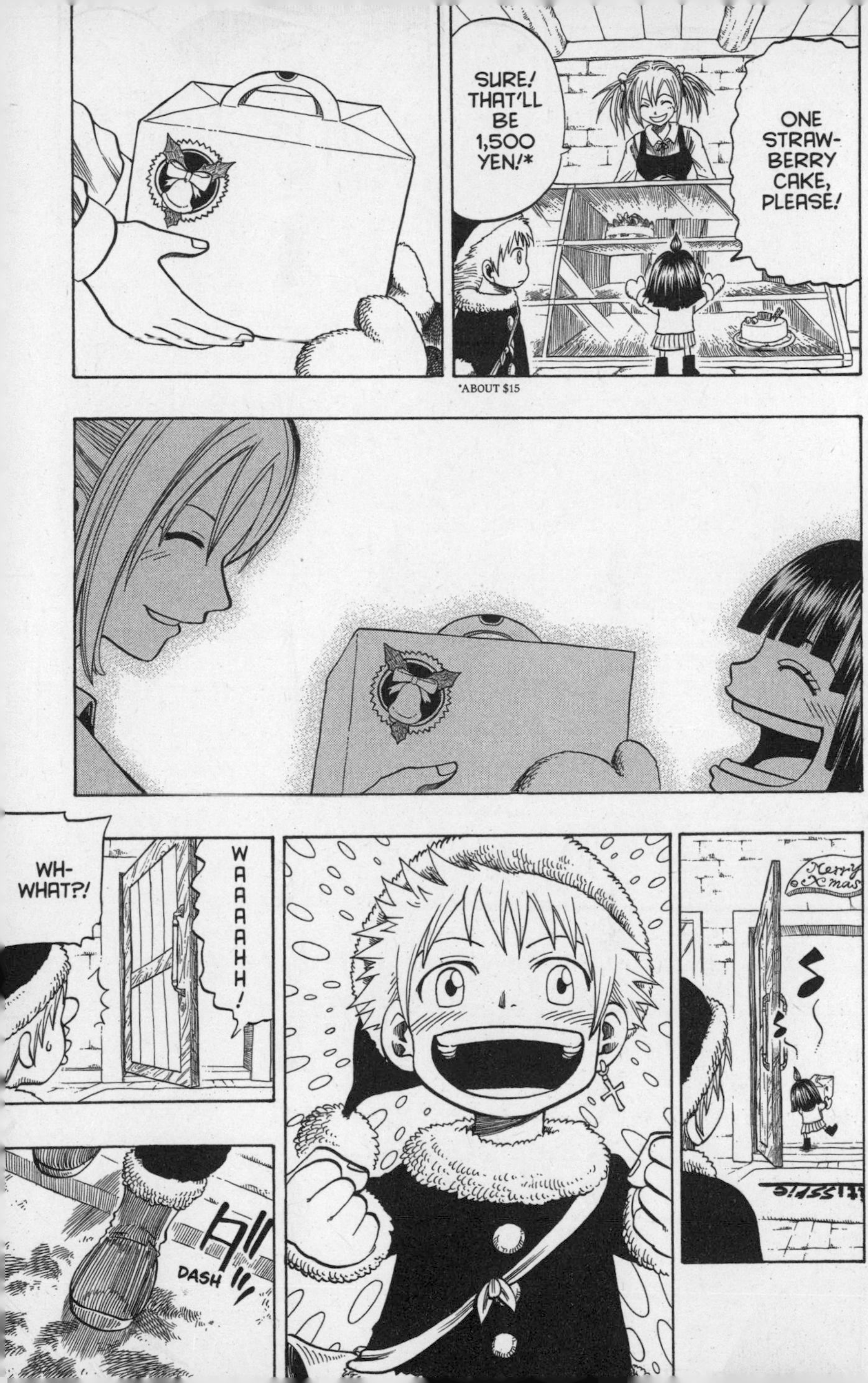
ONE STRAW-BERRY CAKE, PLEASE!
SURE! THAT'LL BE 1,500 YEN!*
Merry X'mas
WAAAAAHH!
WH-WHAT?!
DASH
*ABOUT $15

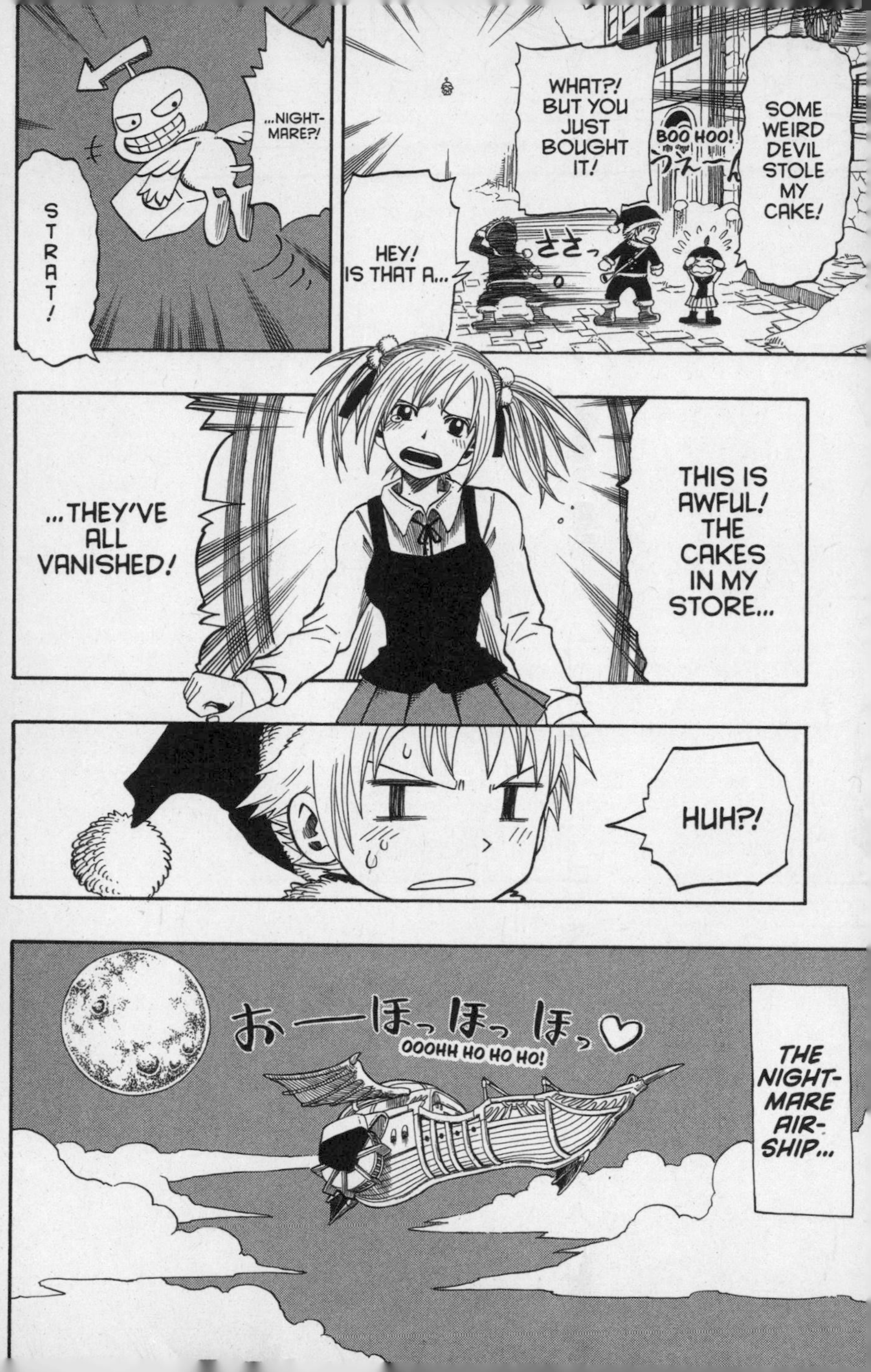
SOME WEIRD DEVIL STOLE MY CAKE!
BOO HOO!
WHAT?! BUT YOU JUST BOUGHT IT!
HEY! IS THAT A...
さささっ
...NIGHT-MARE?!
STRAT!
THIS IS AWFUL! THE CAKES IN MY STORE...
...THEY'VE ALL VANISHED!
HUH?!
THE NIGHT-MARE AIR-SHIP...
おーほっほっほっ♡
OOOHH HO HO HO!

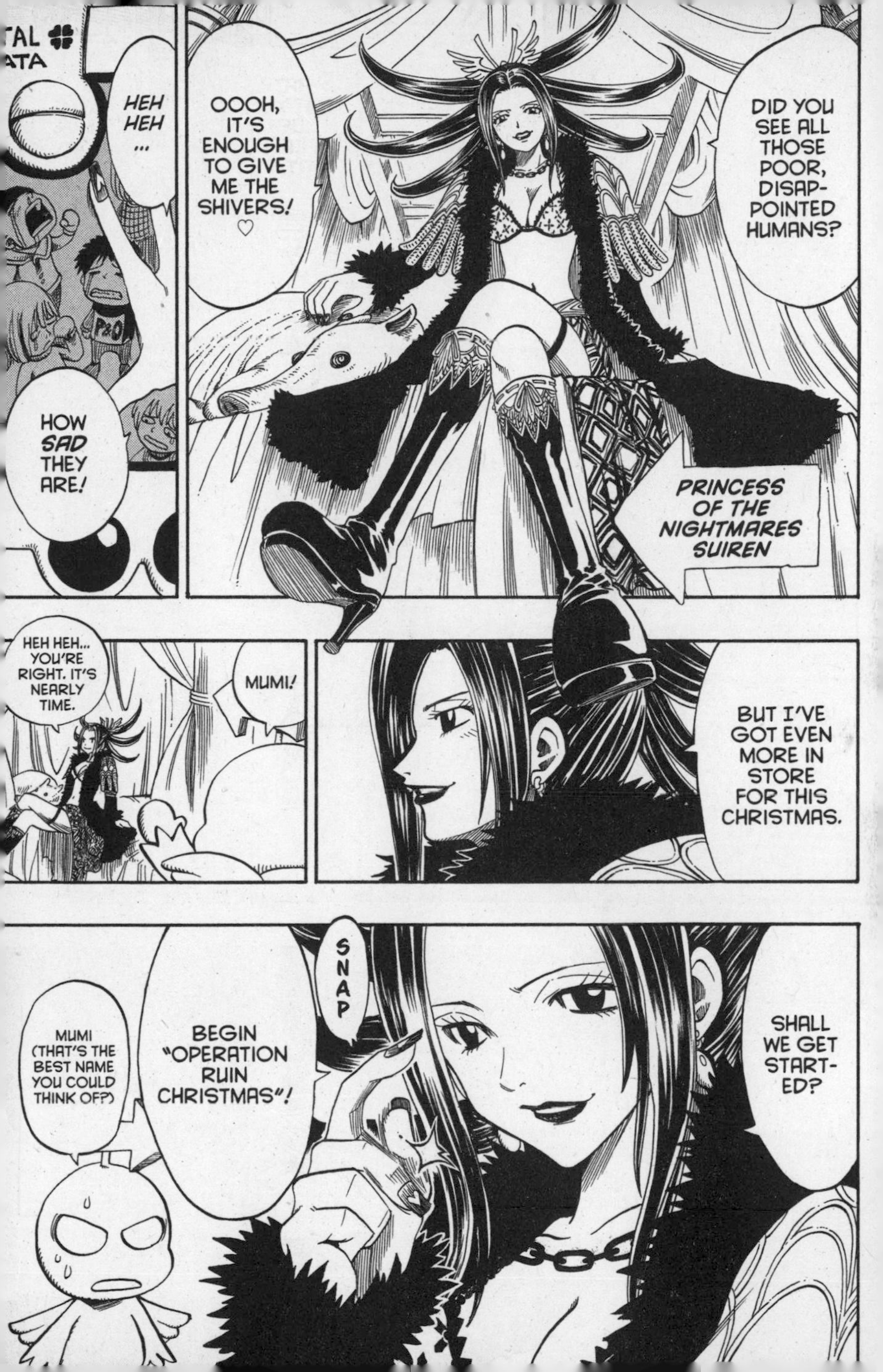
DID YOU SEE ALL THOSE POOR, DISAPPOINTED HUMANS?
OOOH, IT'S ENOUGH TO GIVE ME THE SHIVERS! ♡
PRINCESS OF THE NIGHTMARES SUIREN
HEH HEH ...
HOW SAD THEY ARE!
BUT I'VE GOT EVEN MORE IN STORE FOR THIS CHRISTMAS.
MUMI!
HEH HEH... YOU'RE RIGHT. IT'S NEARLY TIME.
SHALL WE GET STARTED?
SNAP
BEGIN "OPERATION RUIN CHRISTMAS"!
MUMI (THAT'S THE BEST NAME YOU COULD THINK OF?)

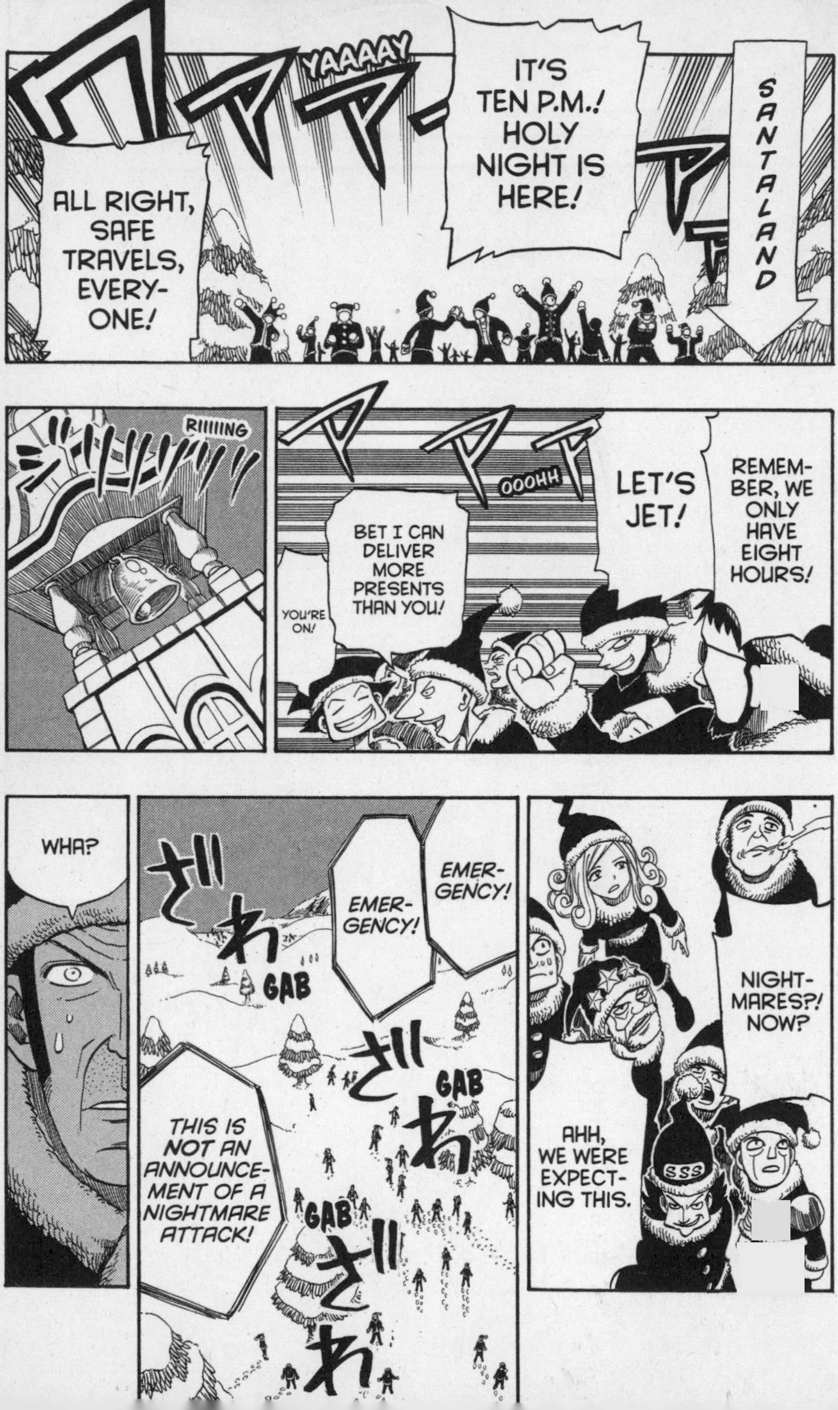
SANTALAND
IT'S TEN P.M.! HOLY NIGHT IS HERE!
YAAAAY
ALL RIGHT, SAFE TRAVELS, EVERYONE!
REMEMBER, WE ONLY HAVE EIGHT HOURS!
LET'S JET!
OOOHH
BET I CAN DELIVER MORE PRESENTS THAN YOU!
YOU'RE ON!
RIIIIING
NIGHTMARES?! NOW?
AHH, WE WERE EXPECTING THIS.
EMERGENCY!
EMERGENCY!
GAB
GAB
GAB
THIS IS NOT AN ANNOUNCEMENT OF A NIGHTMARE ATTACK!
WHA?

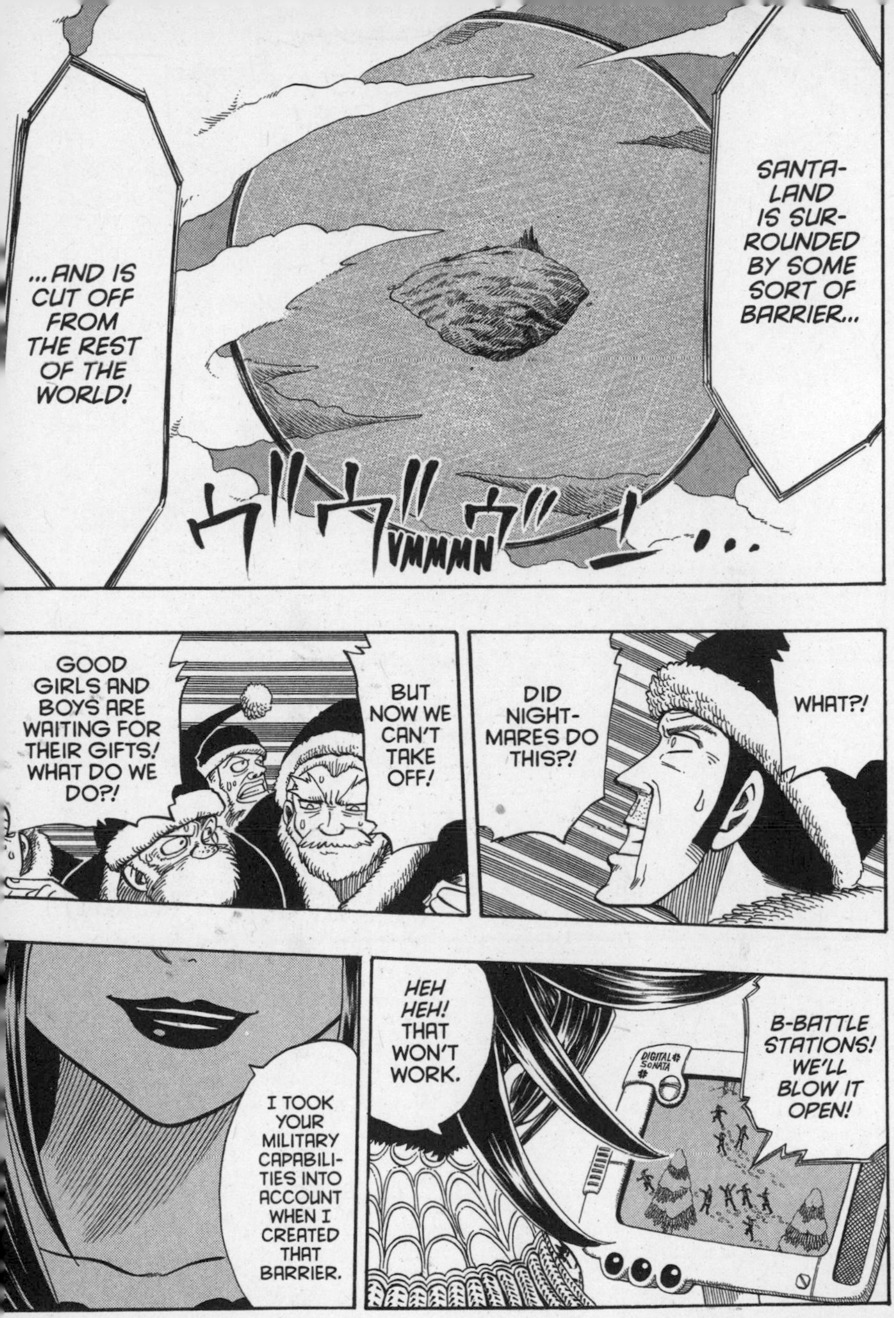
SANTA-LAND IS SURROUNDED BY SOME SORT OF BARRIER...
...AND IS CUT OFF FROM THE REST OF THE WORLD!
VMMMN
WHAT?!
DID NIGHTMARES DO THIS?!
BUT NOW WE CAN'T TAKE OFF!
GOOD GIRLS AND BOYS ARE WAITING FOR THEIR GIFTS! WHAT DO WE DO?!
B-BATTLE STATIONS! WE'LL BLOW IT OPEN!
DIGITAL SONATA
HEH HEH! THAT WON'T WORK.
I TOOK YOUR MILITARY CAPABILITIES INTO ACCOUNT WHEN I CREATED THAT BARRIER.

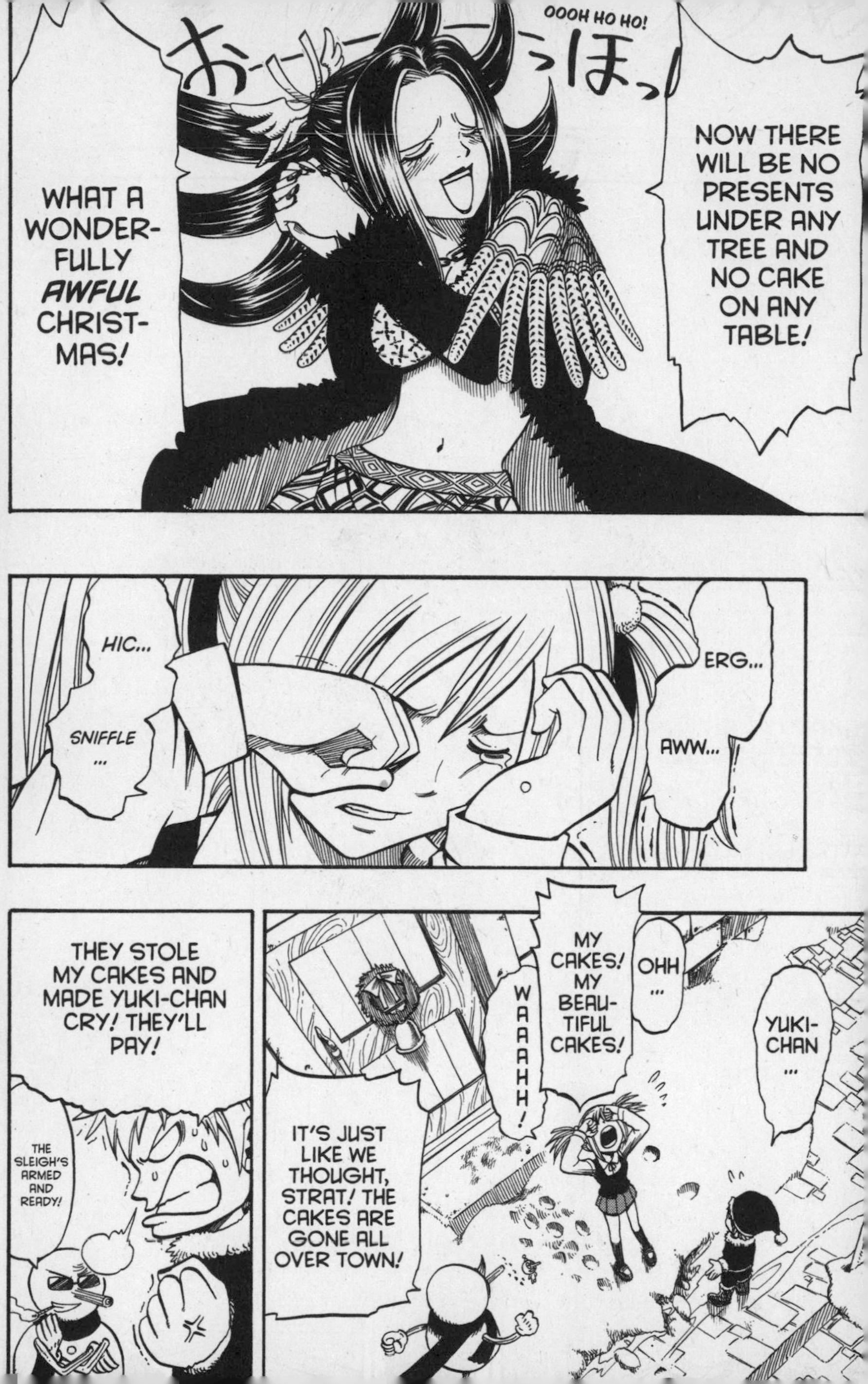
OOOH HO HO!
おーーーっほっ
NOW THERE WILL BE NO PRESENTS UNDER ANY TREE AND NO CAKE ON ANY TABLE!
WHAT A WONDER-FULLY *AWFUL* CHRIST-MAS!
ERG...
AWW...
HIC...
SNIFFLE ...
YUKI-CHAN ...
OHH ...
MY CAKES! MY BEAU-TIFUL CAKES!
WAAAAHH!
IT'S JUST LIKE WE THOUGHT, STRAT! THE CAKES ARE GONE ALL OVER TOWN!
THEY STOLE MY CAKES AND MADE YUKI-CHAN CRY! THEY'LL PAY!
THE SLEIGH'S ARMED AND READY!

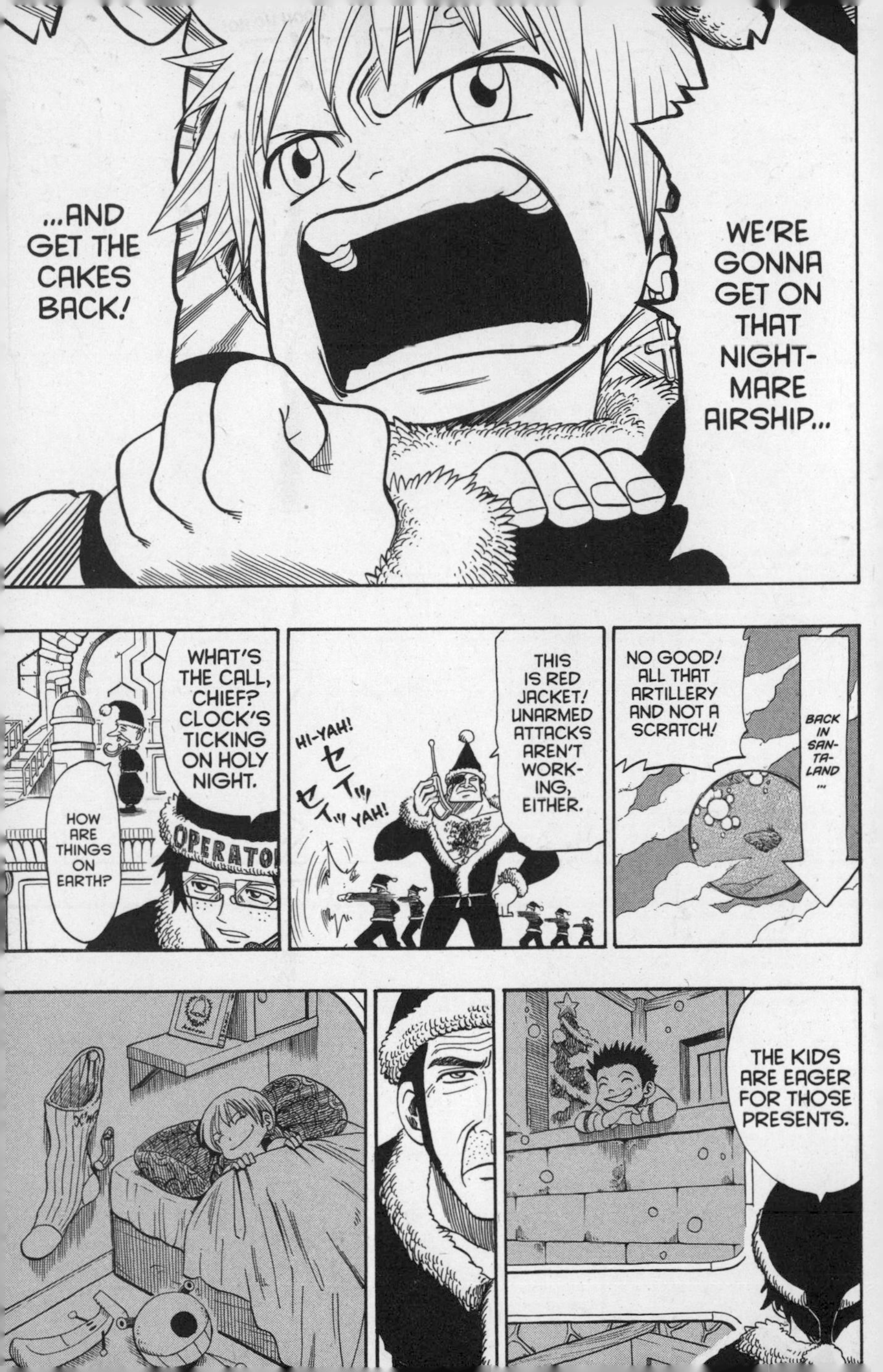
WE'RE GONNA GET ON THAT NIGHT-MARE AIRSHIP...
...AND GET THE CAKES BACK!
BACK IN SAN-TA-LAND ...
NO GOOD! ALL THAT ARTILLERY AND NOT A SCRATCH!
THIS IS RED JACKET! UNARMED ATTACKS AREN'T WORK-ING, EITHER.
HI-YAH! セイッ セイッ YAH!
WHAT'S THE CALL, CHIEF? CLOCK'S TICKING ON HOLY NIGHT.
HOW ARE THINGS ON EARTH?
OPERATO
THE KIDS ARE EAGER FOR THOSE PRESENTS.

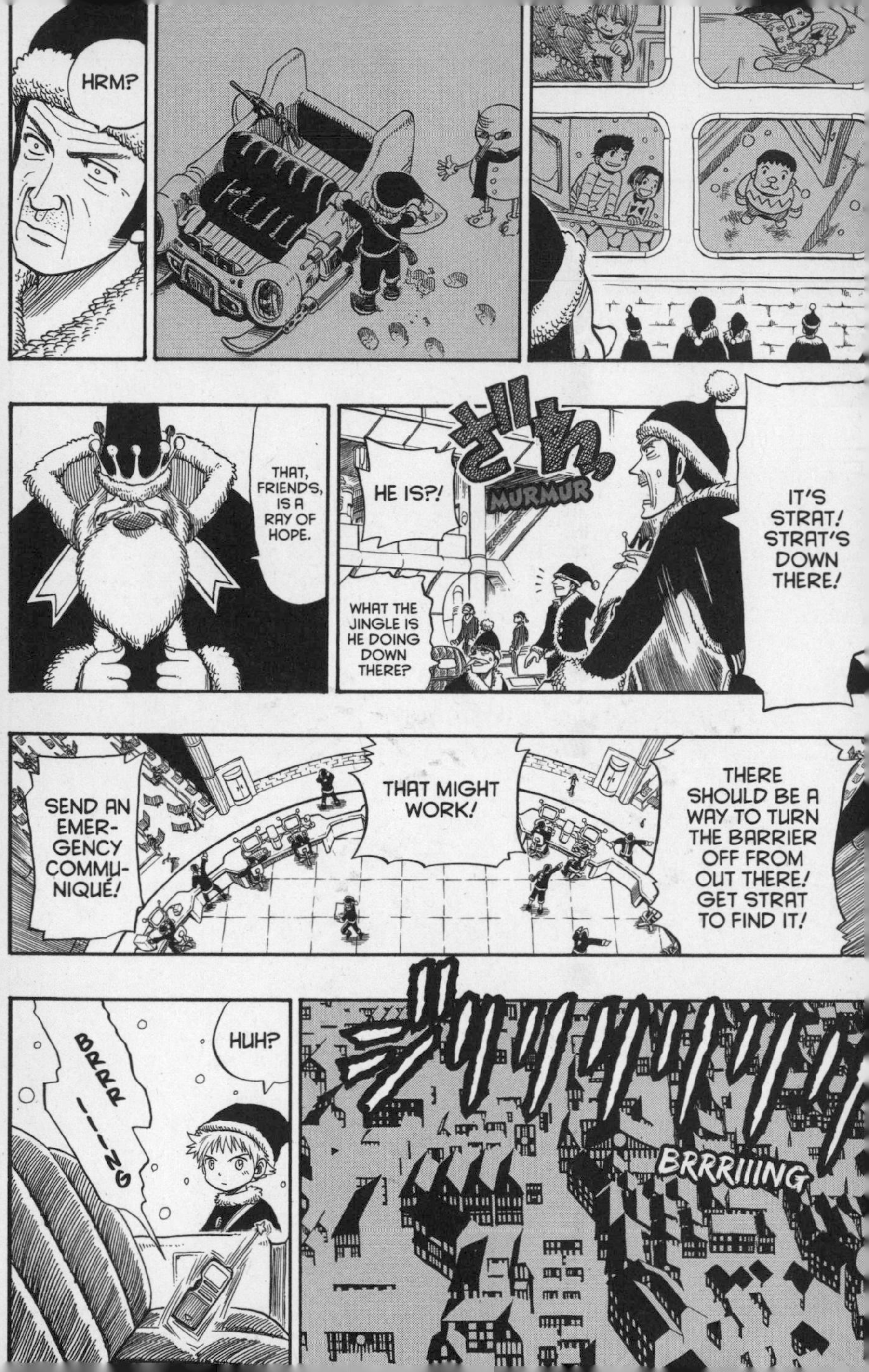
HRM?
IT'S STRAT! STRAT'S DOWN THERE!
HE IS?!
ざわ
MURMUR
WHAT THE JINGLE IS HE DOING DOWN THERE?
THAT, FRIENDS, IS A RAY OF HOPE.
THERE SHOULD BE A WAY TO TURN THE BARRIER OFF FROM OUT THERE! GET STRAT TO FIND IT!
THAT MIGHT WORK!
SEND AN EMERGENCY COMMUNIQUÉ!
BRRRIIING
BRRR IIING
HUH?

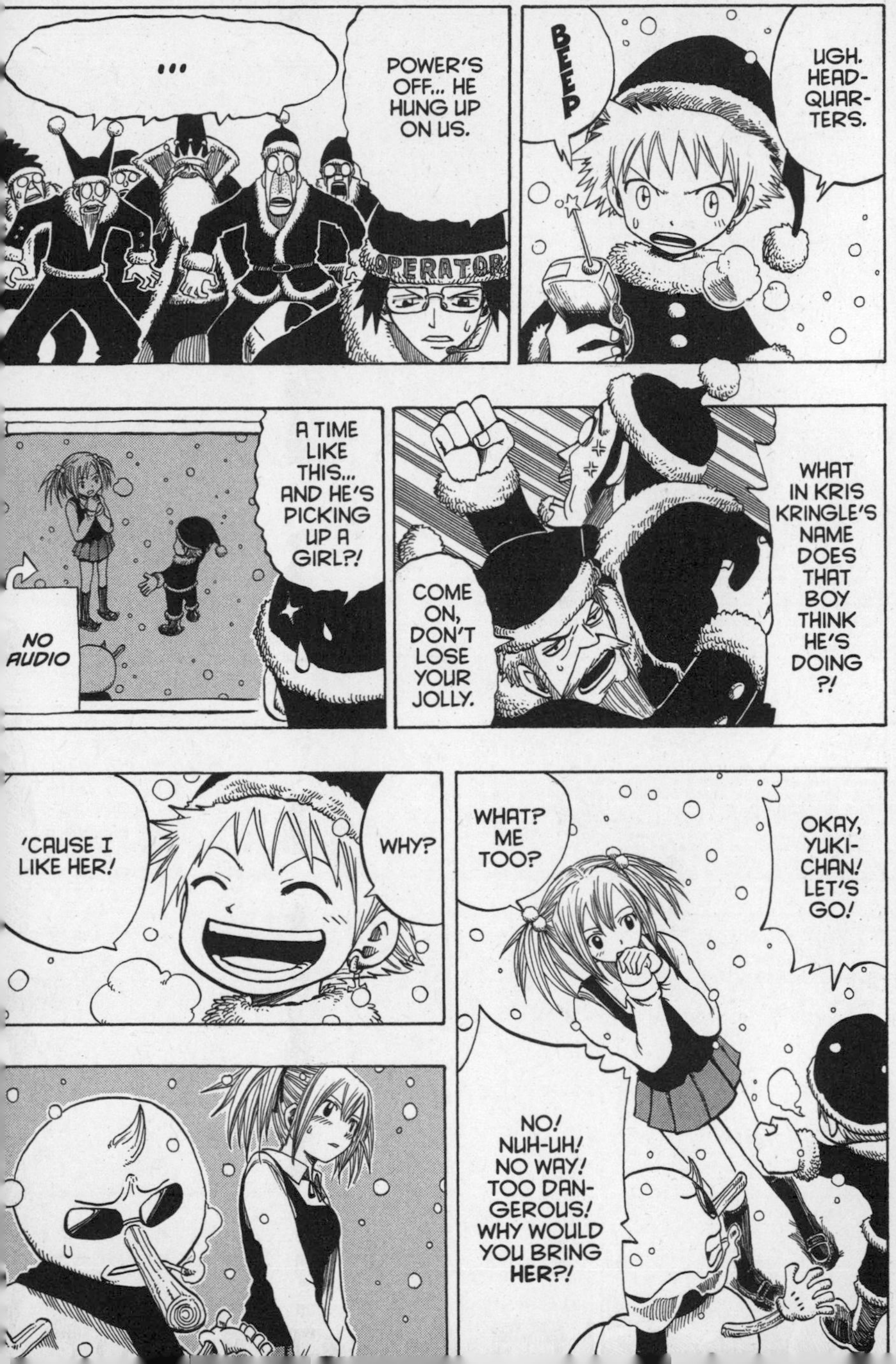
UGH. HEAD-QUARTERS.
BEEP
POWER'S OFF... HE HUNG UP ON US.
...
WHAT IN KRIS KRINGLE'S NAME DOES THAT BOY THINK HE'S DOING?!
COME ON, DON'T LOSE YOUR JOLLY.
A TIME LIKE THIS... AND HE'S PICKING UP A GIRL?!
NO AUDIO
OKAY, YUKI-CHAN! LET'S GO!
WHAT? ME TOO?
NO! NUH-UH! NO WAY! TOO DAN-GEROUS! WHY WOULD YOU BRING HER?!
WHY?
'CAUSE I LIKE HER!

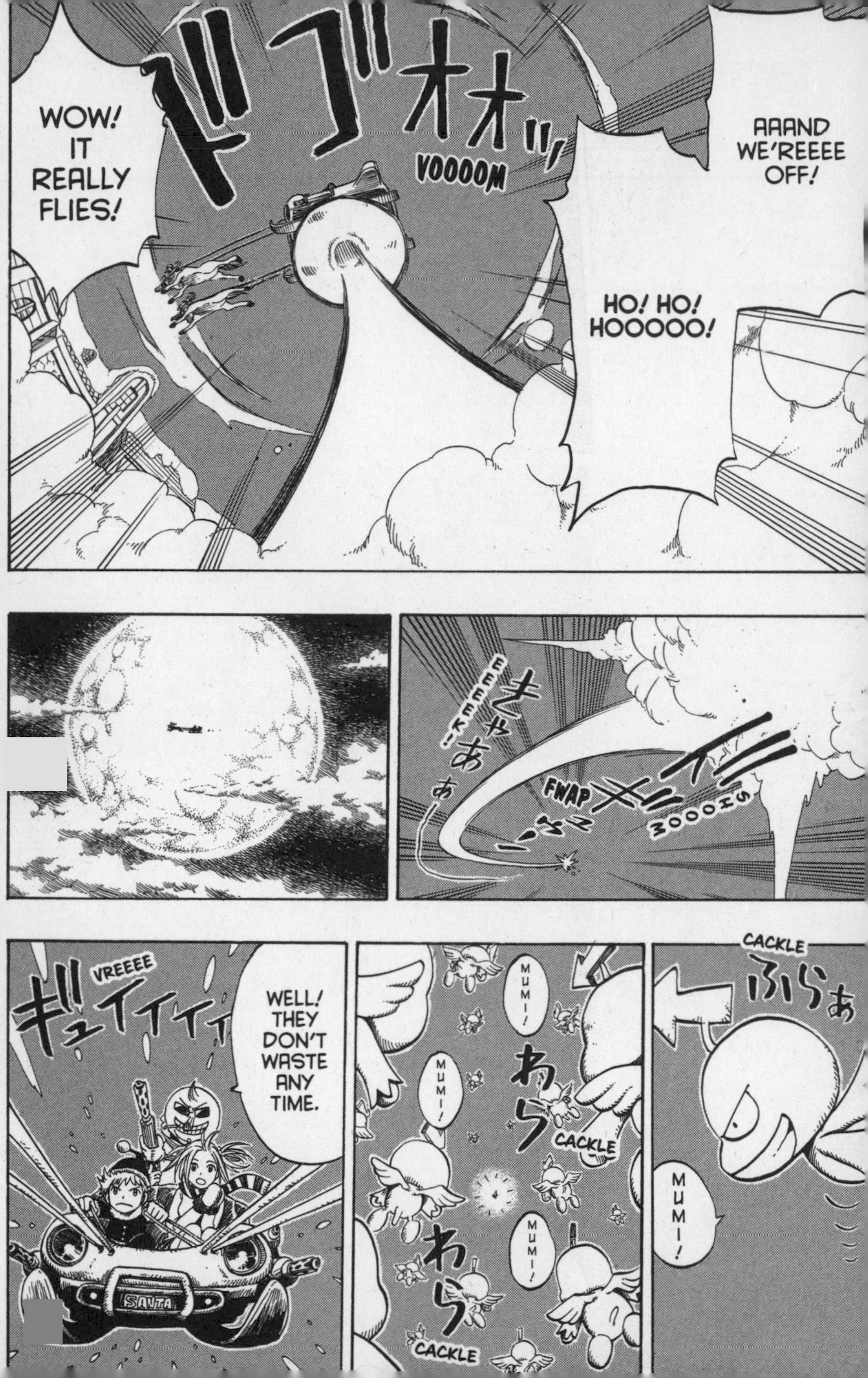
AAAND WE'REEEE OFF!
HO! HO! HOOOOO!
VOOOOM
WOW! IT REALLY FLIES!
EEEEEK-!
FWAP
CACKLE
MUMI!
MUMI!
MUMI!
CACKLE
MUMI!
CACKLE
WELL! THEY DON'T WASTE ANY TIME.
VREEEE
SANTA

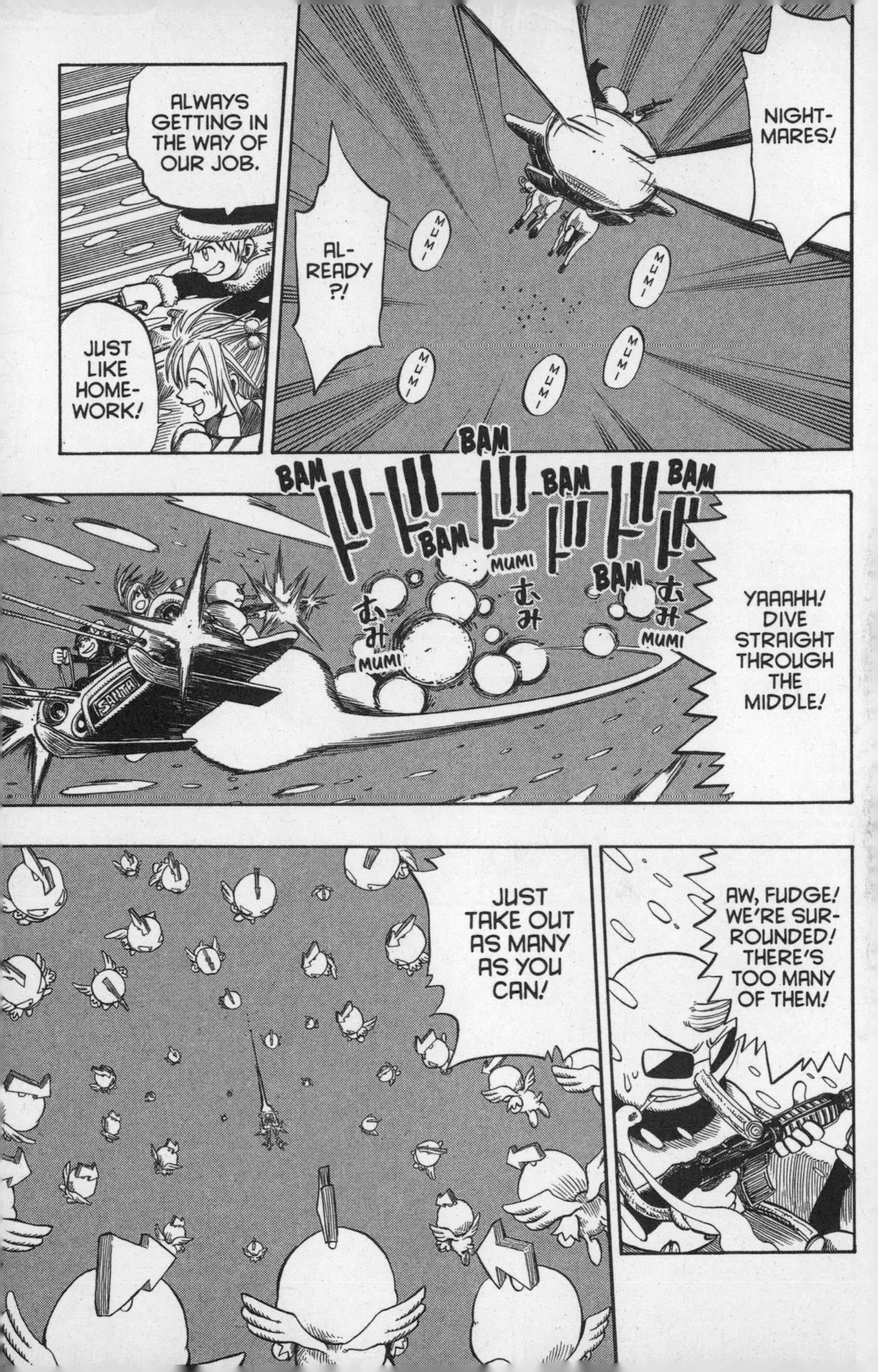
NIGHT-MARES!
AL-READY?!
MUMI
MUMI
MUMI
MUMI
MUMI
ALWAYS GETTING IN THE WAY OF OUR JOB.
JUST LIKE HOME-WORK!
BAM
ドドド
BAM
BAM
BAM
BAM
BAM
MUMI
むみ
MUMI
むみ
MUMI
むみ
MUMI
YAAAHH! DIVE STRAIGHT THROUGH THE MIDDLE!
AW, FUDGE! WE'RE SUR-ROUNDED! THERE'S TOO MANY OF THEM!
JUST TAKE OUT AS MANY AS YOU CAN!

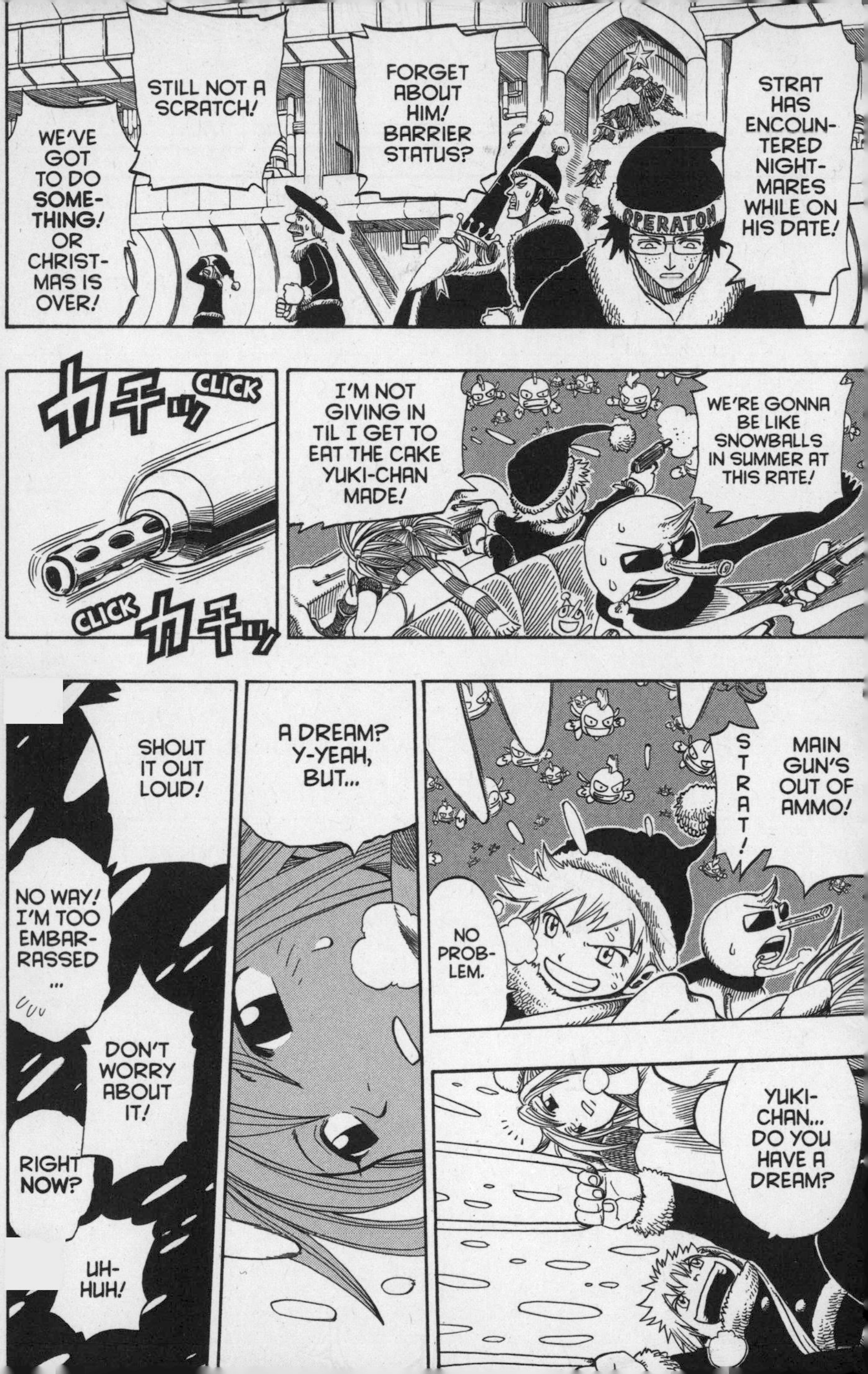
STRAT HAS ENCOUNTERED NIGHTMARES WHILE ON HIS DATE!
OPERATON
FORGET ABOUT HIM! BARRIER STATUS?
STILL NOT A SCRATCH!
WE'VE GOT TO DO SOMETHING! OR CHRISTMAS IS OVER!
WE'RE GONNA BE LIKE SNOWBALLS IN SUMMER AT THIS RATE!
I'M NOT GIVING IN TIL I GET TO EAT THE CAKE YUKI-CHAN MADE!
カチッ CLICK
CLICK カチッ
MAIN GUN'S OUT OF AMMO!
STRAT!
NO PROBLEM.
YUKI-CHAN... DO YOU HAVE A DREAM?
OPERATON
A DREAM? Y-YEAH, BUT...
SHOUT IT OUT LOUD!
NO WAY! I'M TOO EMBARRASSED...
DON'T WORRY ABOUT IT!
RIGHT NOW?
UH-HUH!

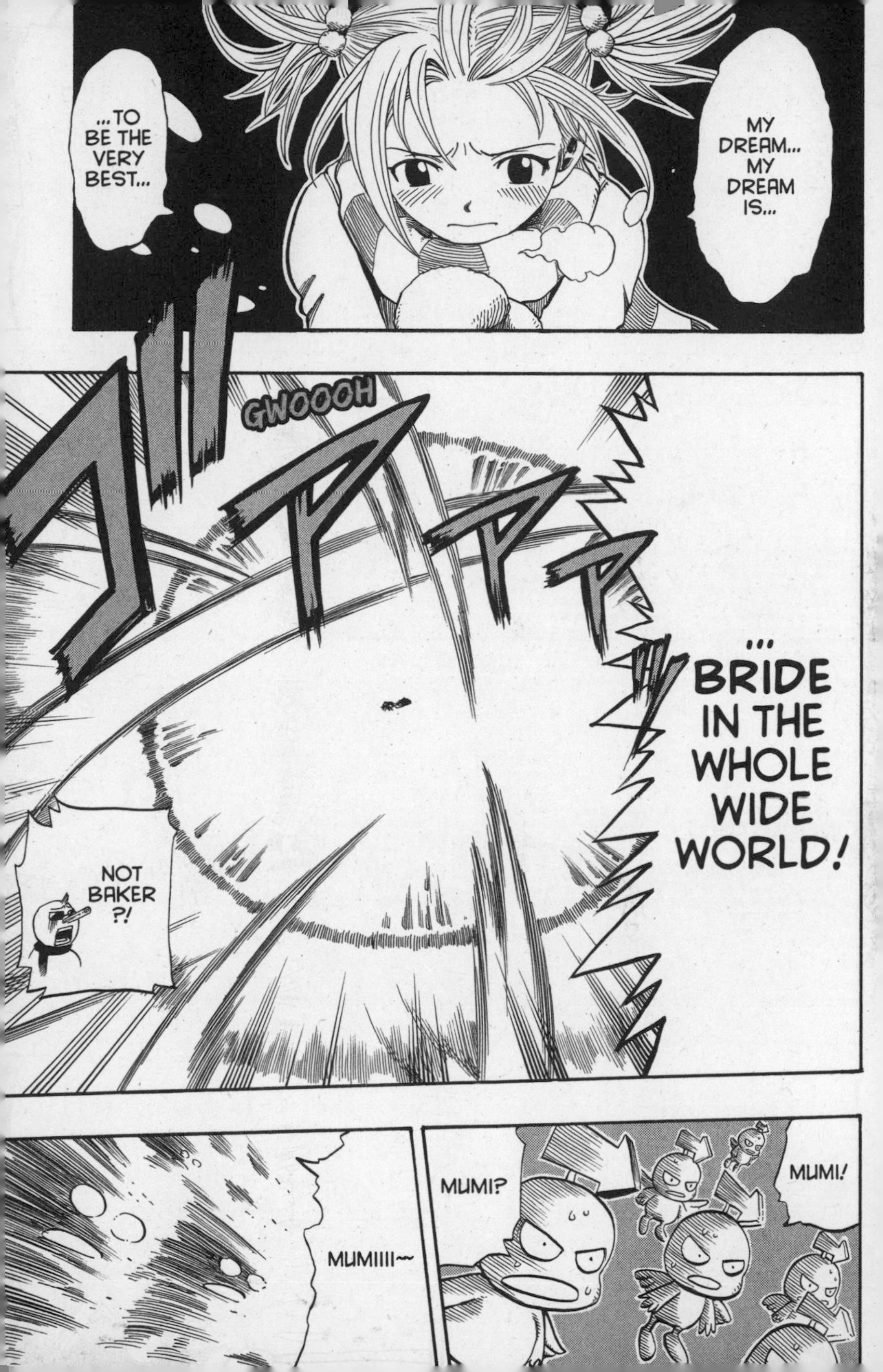
MY DREAM... MY DREAM IS...
...TO BE THE VERY BEST...
...BRIDE IN THE WHOLE WIDE WORLD!
GWOOOH
NOT BAKER ?!
MUMI!
MUMI?
MUMIIII~

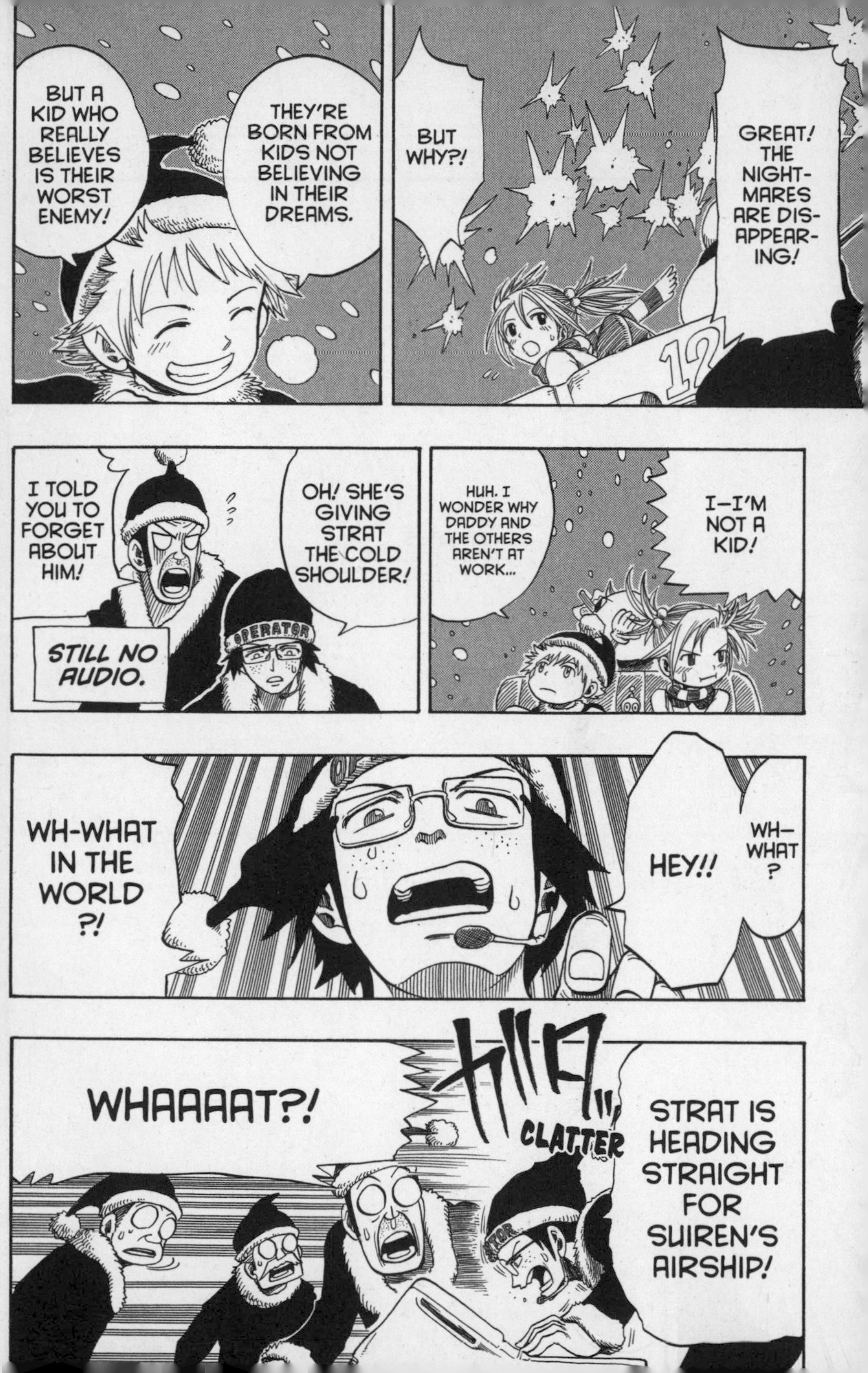
GREAT! THE NIGHTMARES ARE DISAPPEARING!
BUT WHY?!
THEY'RE BORN FROM KIDS NOT BELIEVING IN THEIR DREAMS.
BUT A KID WHO REALLY BELIEVES IS THEIR WORST ENEMY!
I—I'M NOT A KID!
HUH. I WONDER WHY DADDY AND THE OTHERS AREN'T AT WORK...
OH! SHE'S GIVING STRAT THE COLD SHOULDER!
I TOLD YOU TO FORGET ABOUT HIM!
STILL NO AUDIO.
WH—WHAT?
HEY!!
WH-WHAT IN THE WORLD?!
STRAT IS HEADING STRAIGHT FOR SUIREN'S AIRSHIP!
CLATTER
WHAAAAT?!

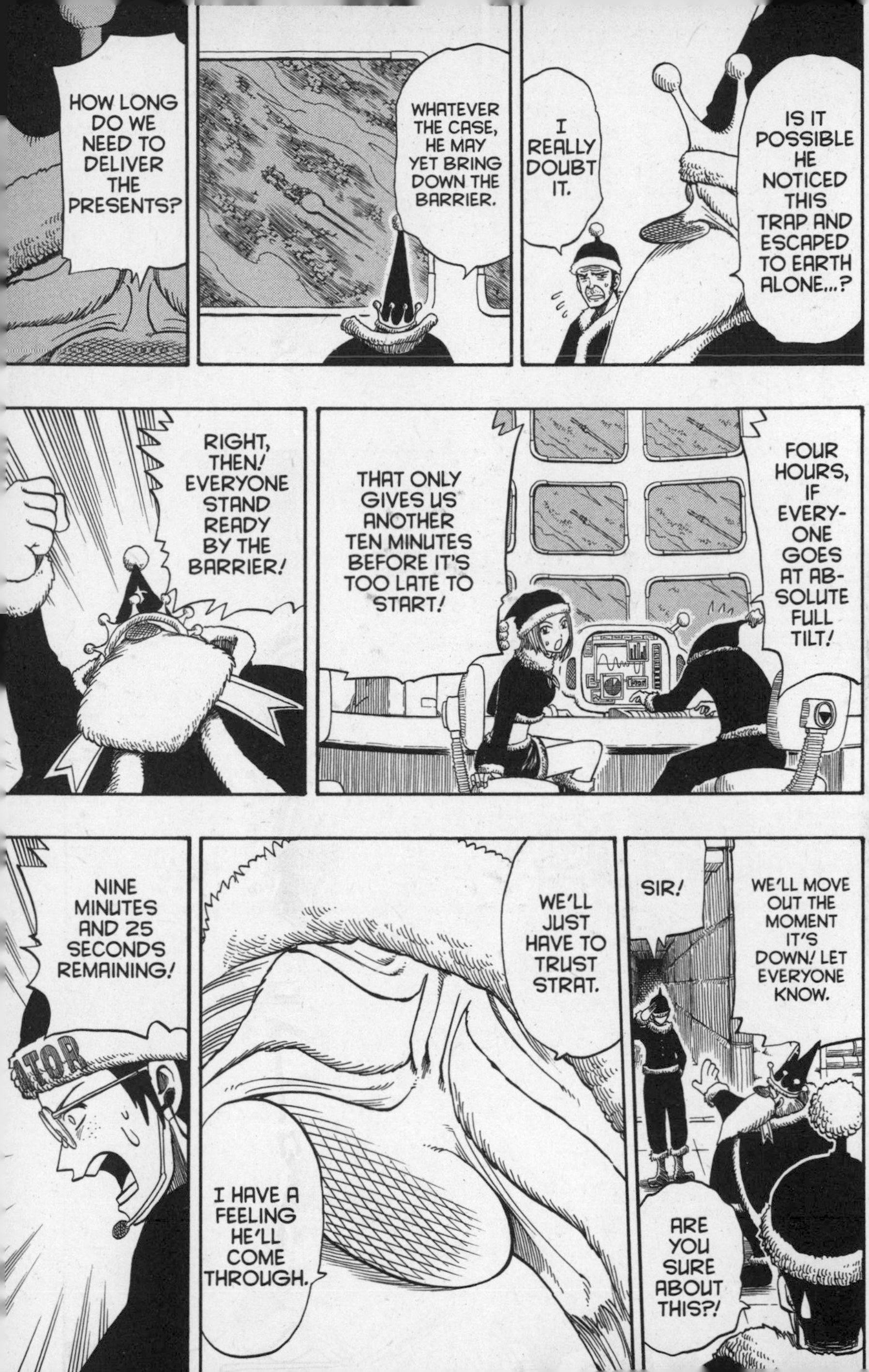
IS IT POSSIBLE HE NOTICED THIS TRAP AND ESCAPED TO EARTH ALONE...?
I REALLY DOUBT IT.
WHATEVER THE CASE, HE MAY YET BRING DOWN THE BARRIER.
HOW LONG DO WE NEED TO DELIVER THE PRESENTS?
FOUR HOURS, IF EVERY-ONE GOES AT AB-SOLUTE FULL TILT!
THAT ONLY GIVES US ANOTHER TEN MINUTES BEFORE IT'S TOO LATE TO START!
RIGHT, THEN! EVERYONE STAND READY BY THE BARRIER!
WE'LL MOVE OUT THE MOMENT IT'S DOWN! LET EVERYONE KNOW.
SIR!
ARE YOU SURE ABOUT THIS?!
WE'LL JUST HAVE TO TRUST STRAT.
I HAVE A FEELING HE'LL COME THROUGH.
NINE MINUTES AND 25 SECONDS REMAINING!

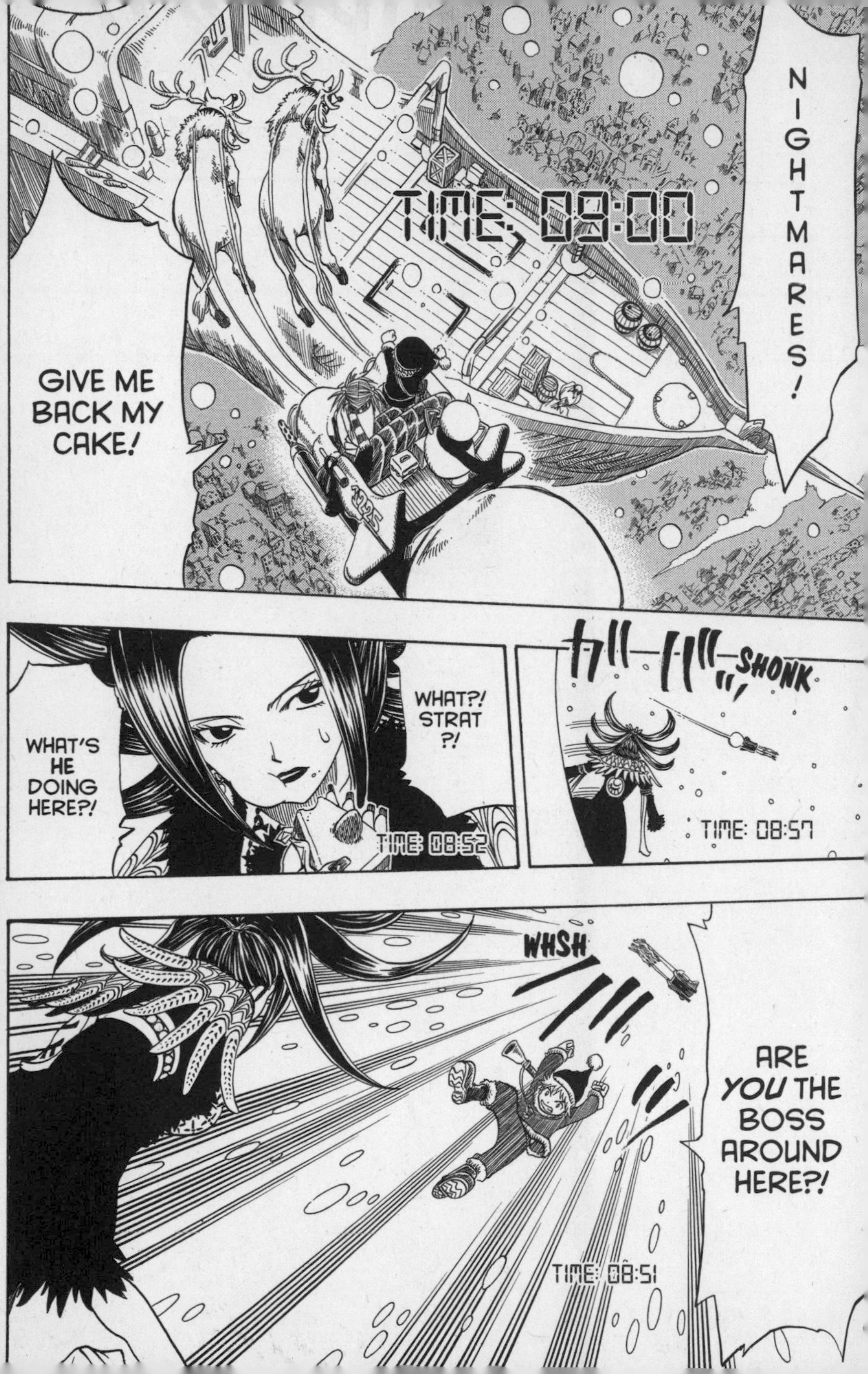
NIGHTMARES!
TIME: 09:00
GIVE ME BACK MY CAKE!
SHONK
TIME: 08:57
WHAT?! STRAT?!
WHAT'S HE DOING HERE?!
TIME: 08:52
WHSH
ARE *YOU* THE BOSS AROUND HERE?!
TIME: 08:51

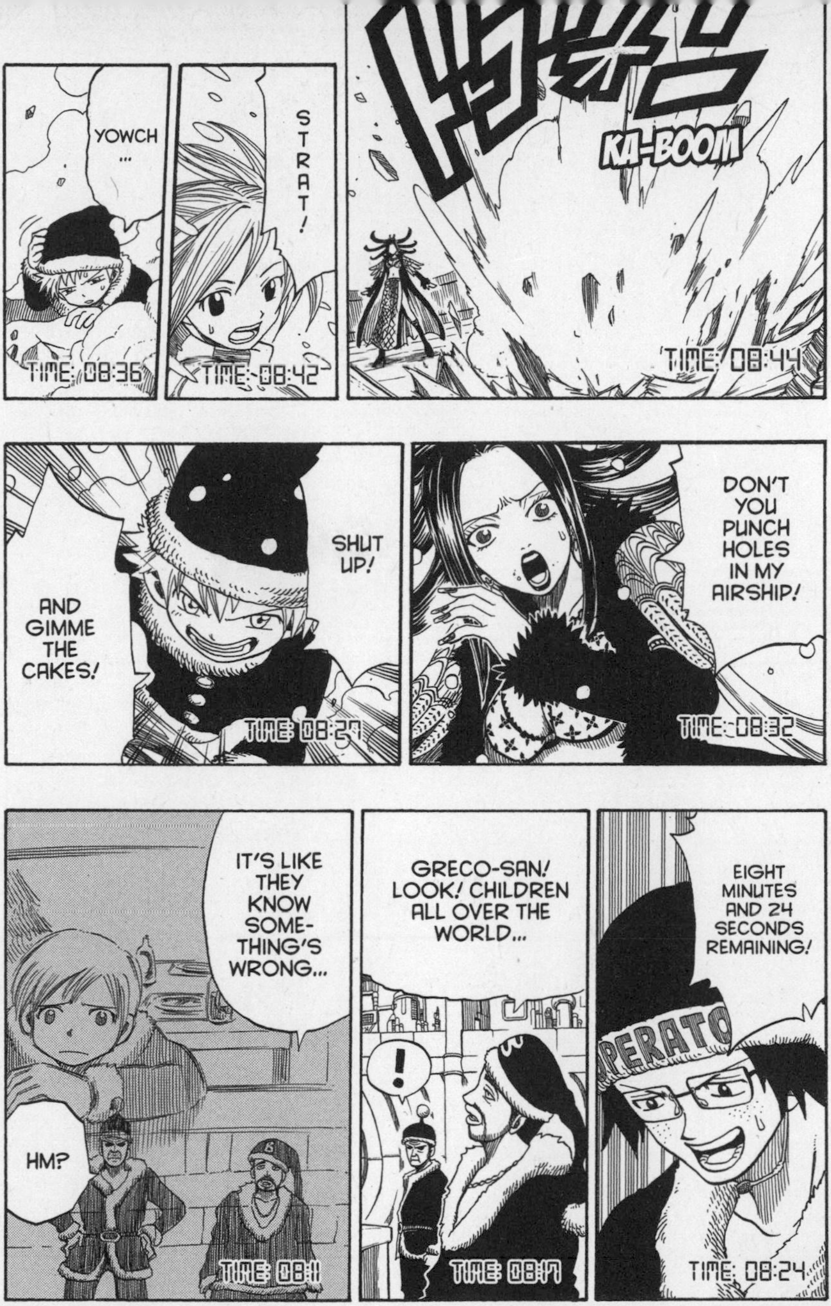
KA-BOOM
TIME: 08:44
STRAT!
TIME: 08:42
YOWCH ...
TIME: 08:36
DON'T YOU PUNCH HOLES IN MY AIRSHIP!
TIME: 08:32
SHUT UP!
AND GIMME THE CAKES!
TIME: 08:27
EIGHT MINUTES AND 24 SECONDS REMAINING!
PERATO
TIME: 08:24
GRECO-SAN! LOOK! CHILDREN ALL OVER THE WORLD...
!
TIME: 08:17
IT'S LIKE THEY KNOW SOME-THING'S WRONG...
HM?
TIME: 08:11

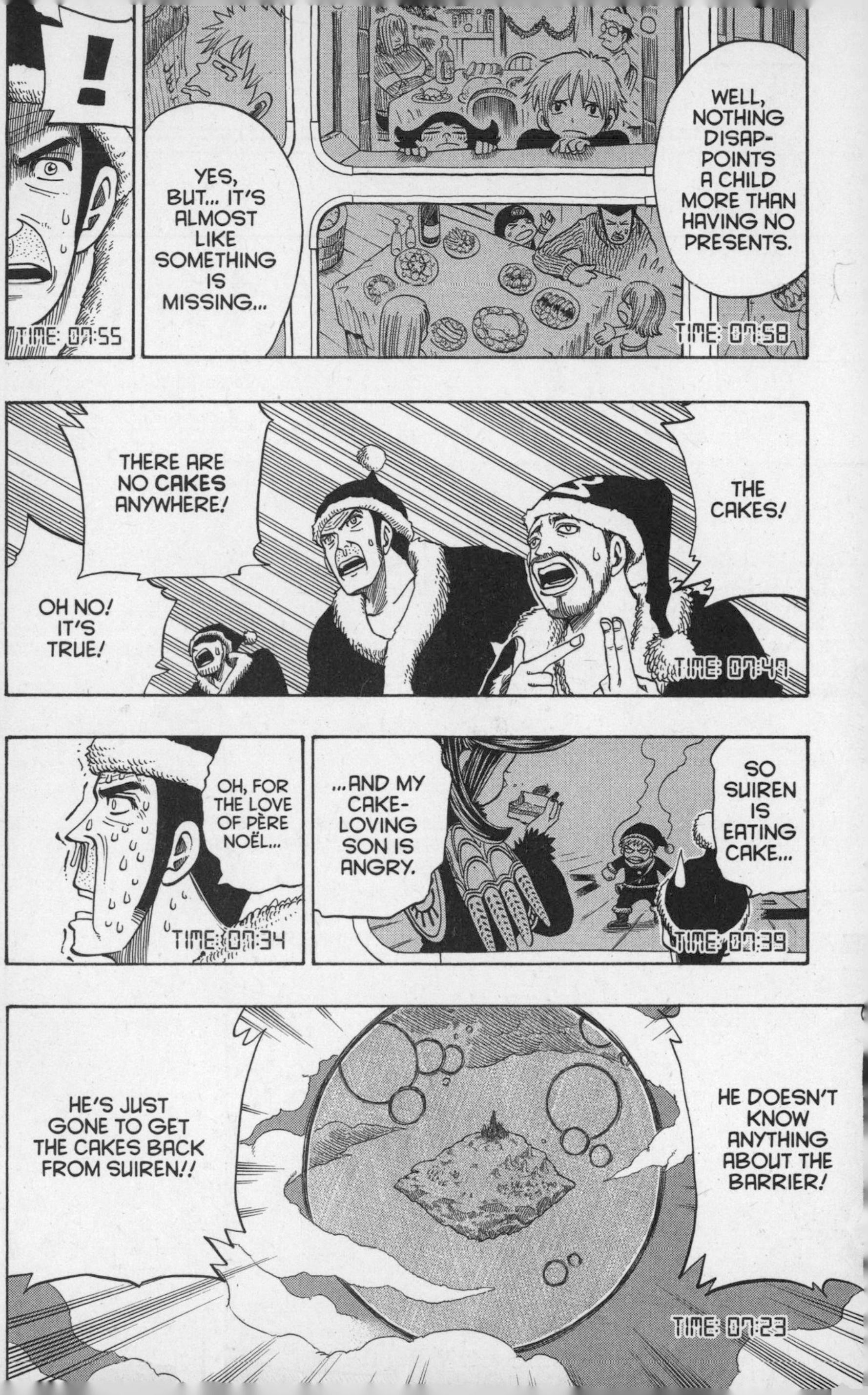
WELL, NOTHING DISAPPOINTS A CHILD MORE THAN HAVING NO PRESENTS.
TIME: 07:58
YES, BUT... IT'S ALMOST LIKE SOMETHING IS MISSING...
!
TIME: 07:55
THE CAKES!
THERE ARE NO CAKES ANYWHERE!
OH NO! IT'S TRUE!
TIME: 07:49
SO SUIREN IS EATING CAKE...
...AND MY CAKE-LOVING SON IS ANGRY.
TIME: 07:39
OH, FOR THE LOVE OF PÈRE NOËL...
TIME: 07:34
HE DOESN'T KNOW ANYTHING ABOUT THE BARRIER!
HE'S JUST GONE TO GET THE CAKES BACK FROM SUIREN!!
TIME: 07:23

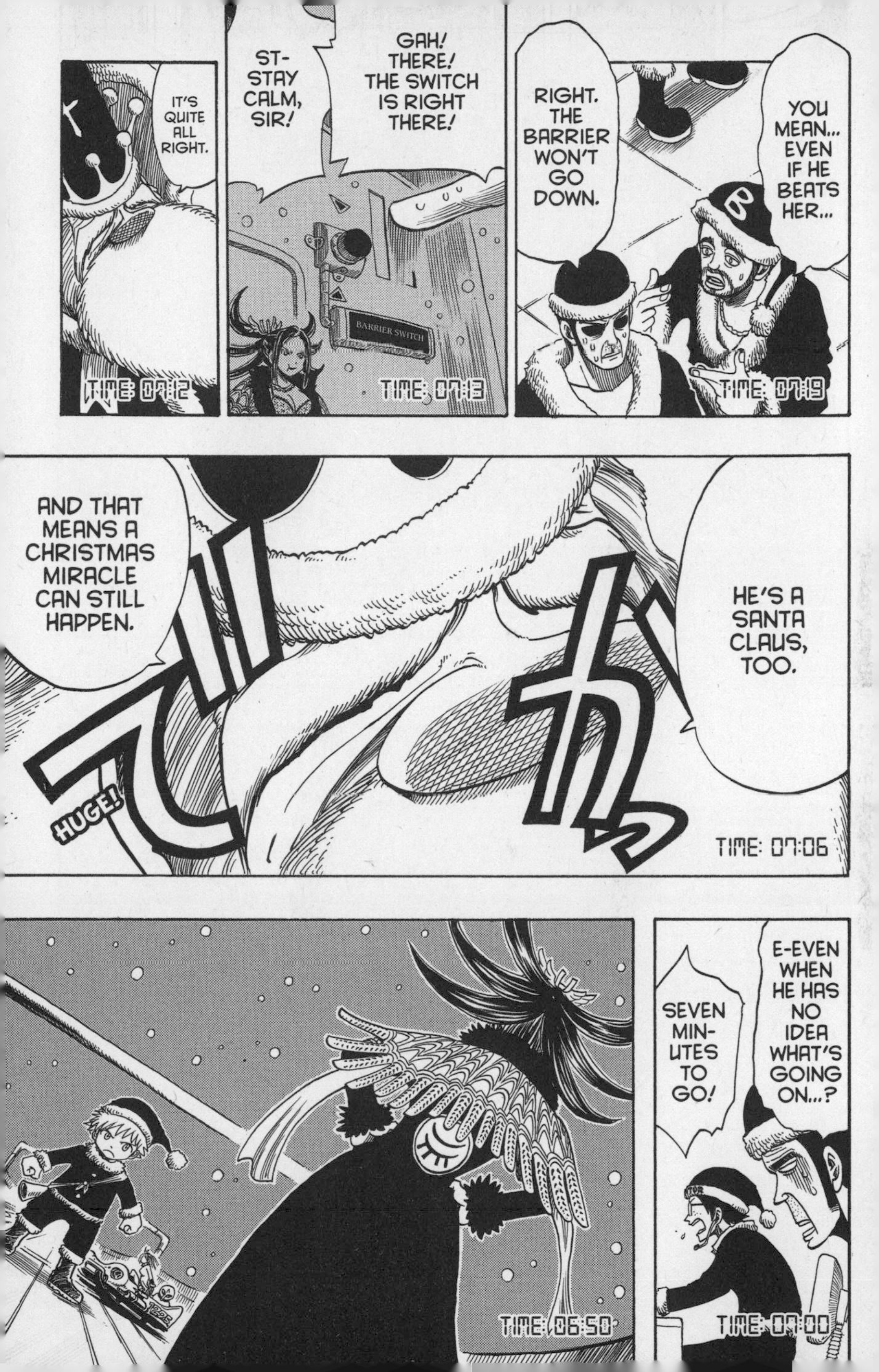
YOU MEAN... EVEN IF HE BEATS HER...
RIGHT. THE BARRIER WON'T GO DOWN.
TIME: 07:19
GAH! THERE! THE SWITCH IS RIGHT THERE!
ST-STAY CALM, SIR!
BARRIER SWITCH
TIME: 07:13
IT'S QUITE ALL RIGHT.
TIME: 07:12
HE'S A SANTA CLAUS, TOO.
AND THAT MEANS A CHRISTMAS MIRACLE CAN STILL HAPPEN.
HUGE!
TIME: 07:06
E-EVEN WHEN HE HAS NO IDEA WHAT'S GOING ON...?
SEVEN MINUTES TO GO!
TIME: 07:00
TIME: 06:50

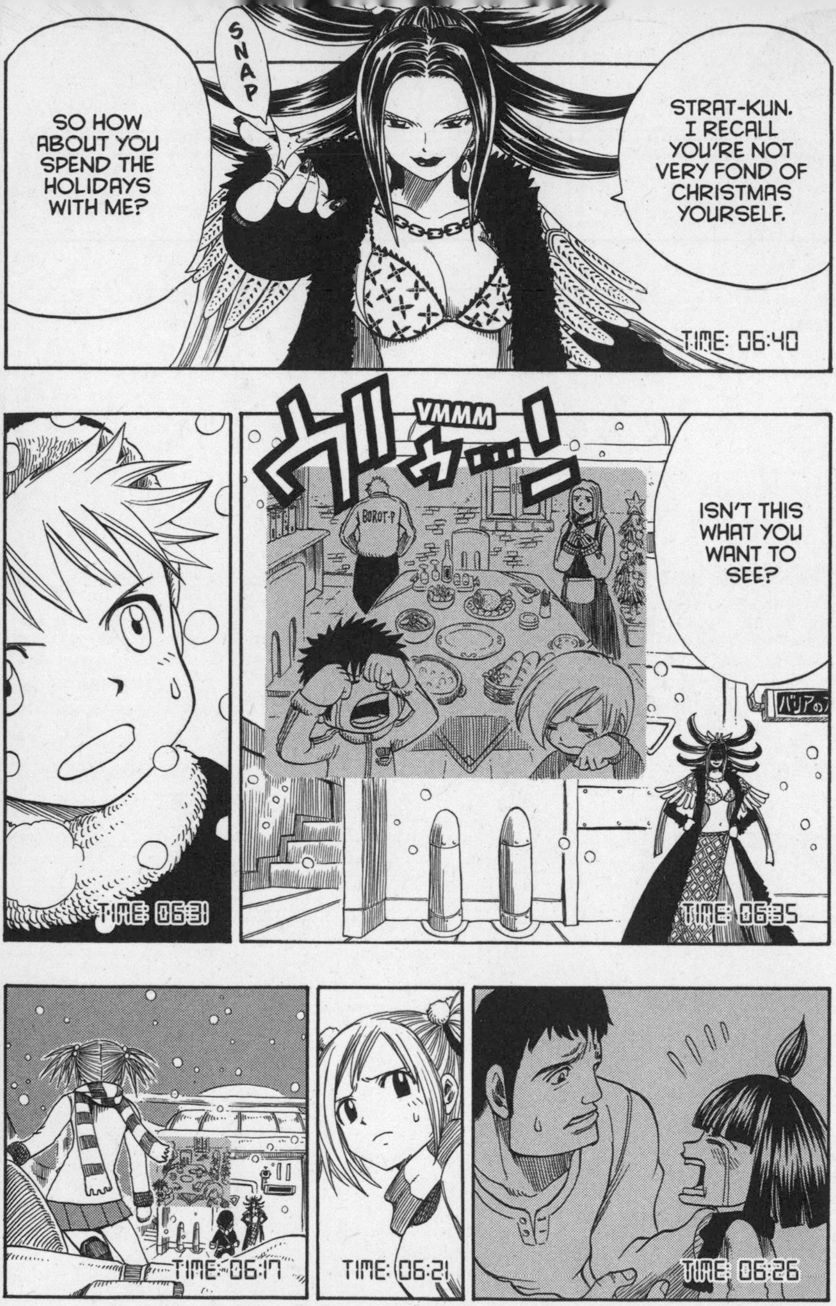
STRAT-KUN. I RECALL YOU'RE NOT VERY FOND OF CHRISTMAS YOURSELF.
SNAP
SO HOW ABOUT YOU SPEND THE HOLIDAYS WITH ME?
TIME: 06:40
VMMM
ISN'T THIS WHAT YOU WANT TO SEE?
BOROT-P
TIME: 06:35
TIME: 06:31
TIME: 06:26
TIME: 06:21
TIME: 06:17

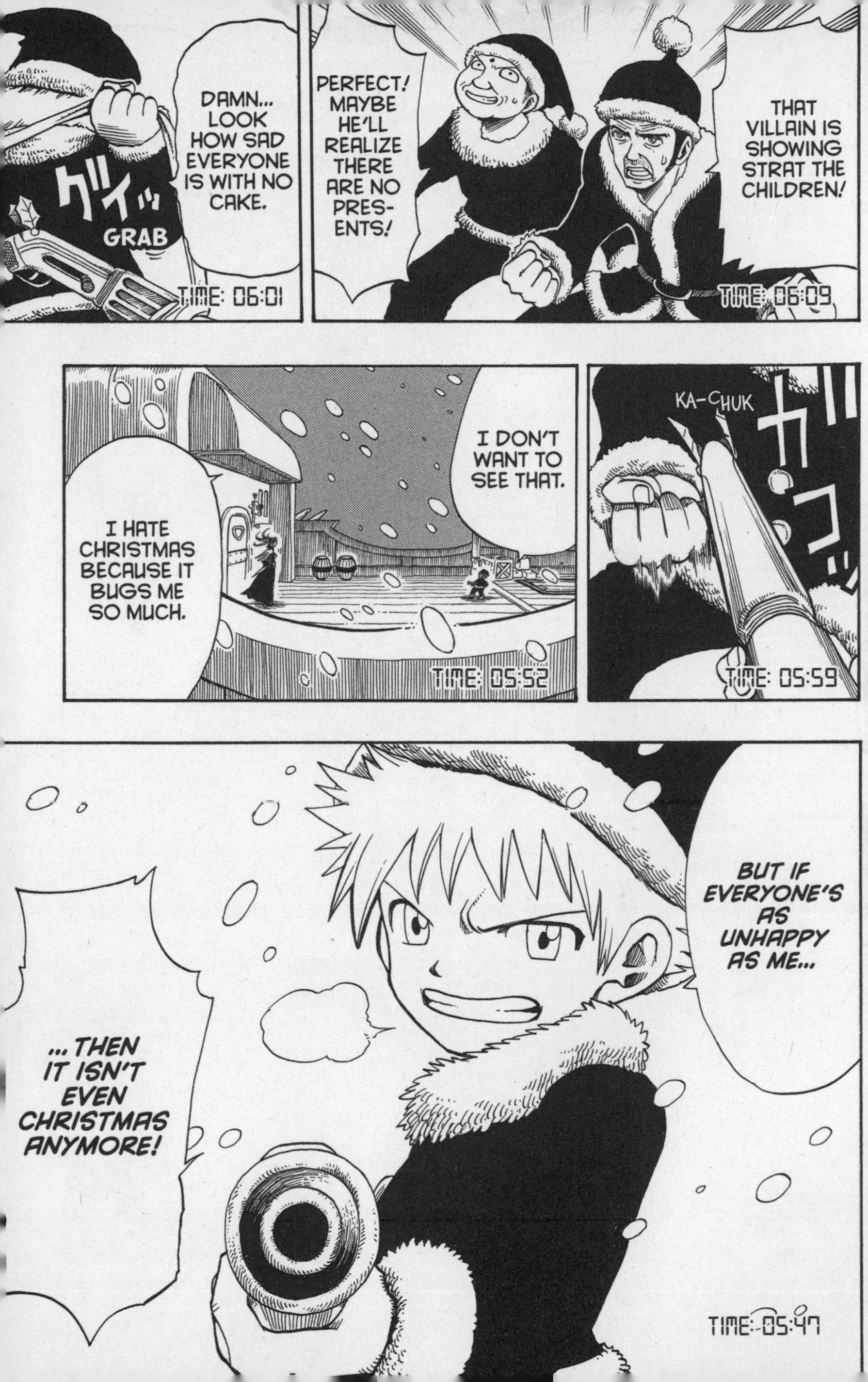
THAT VILLAIN IS SHOWING STRAT THE CHILDREN!
PERFECT! MAYBE HE'LL REALIZE THERE ARE NO PRES-ENTS!
TIME: 06:09
DAMN... LOOK HOW SAD EVERYONE IS WITH NO CAKE.
グイッ
GRAB
TIME: 06:01
ガコッ
KA-CHUK
TIME: 05:59
I DON'T WANT TO SEE THAT.
I HATE CHRISTMAS BECAUSE IT BUGS ME SO MUCH.
TIME: 05:52
BUT IF EVERYONE'S AS UNHAPPY AS ME...
...THEN IT ISN'T EVEN CHRISTMAS ANYMORE!
TIME: 05:47

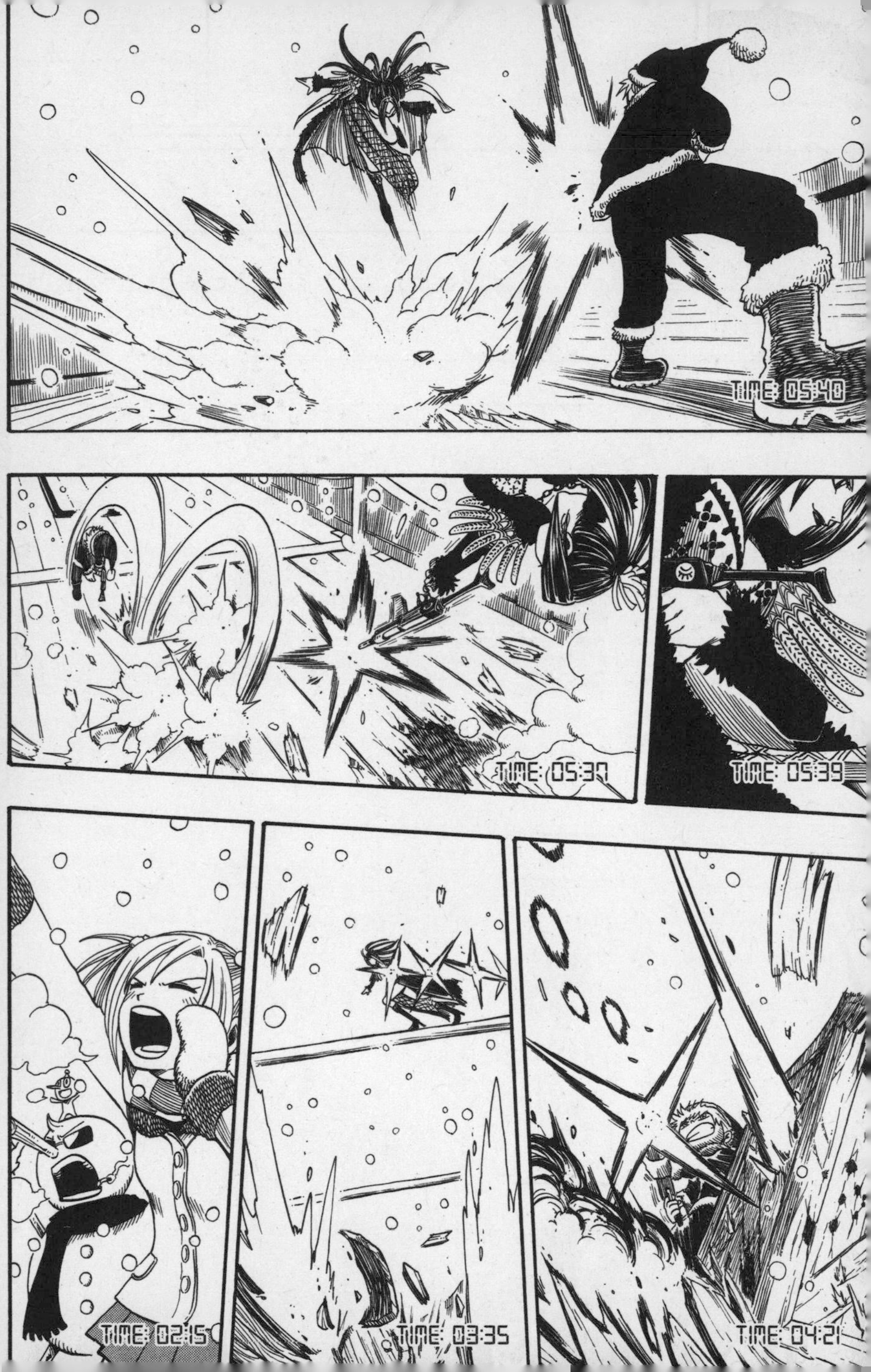
TIME: 05:40
TIME: 05:39
TIME: 05:37
TIME: 04:21
TIME: 03:35
TIME: 02:15

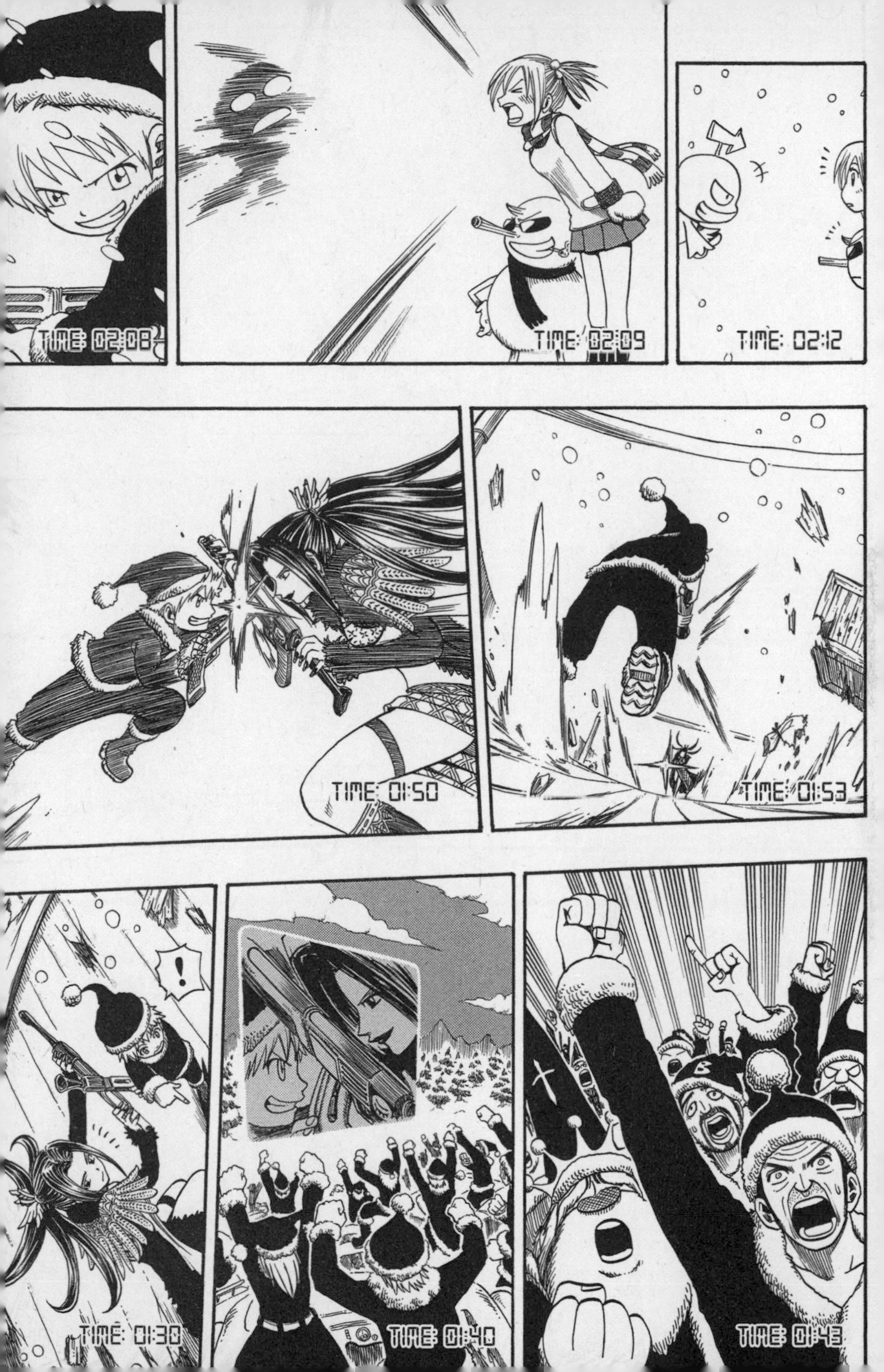
TIME: 02:12
TIME: 02:09
TIME: 02:08
TIME: 01:53
TIME: 01:50
TIME: 01:43
TIME: 01:40
!
TIME: 01:30

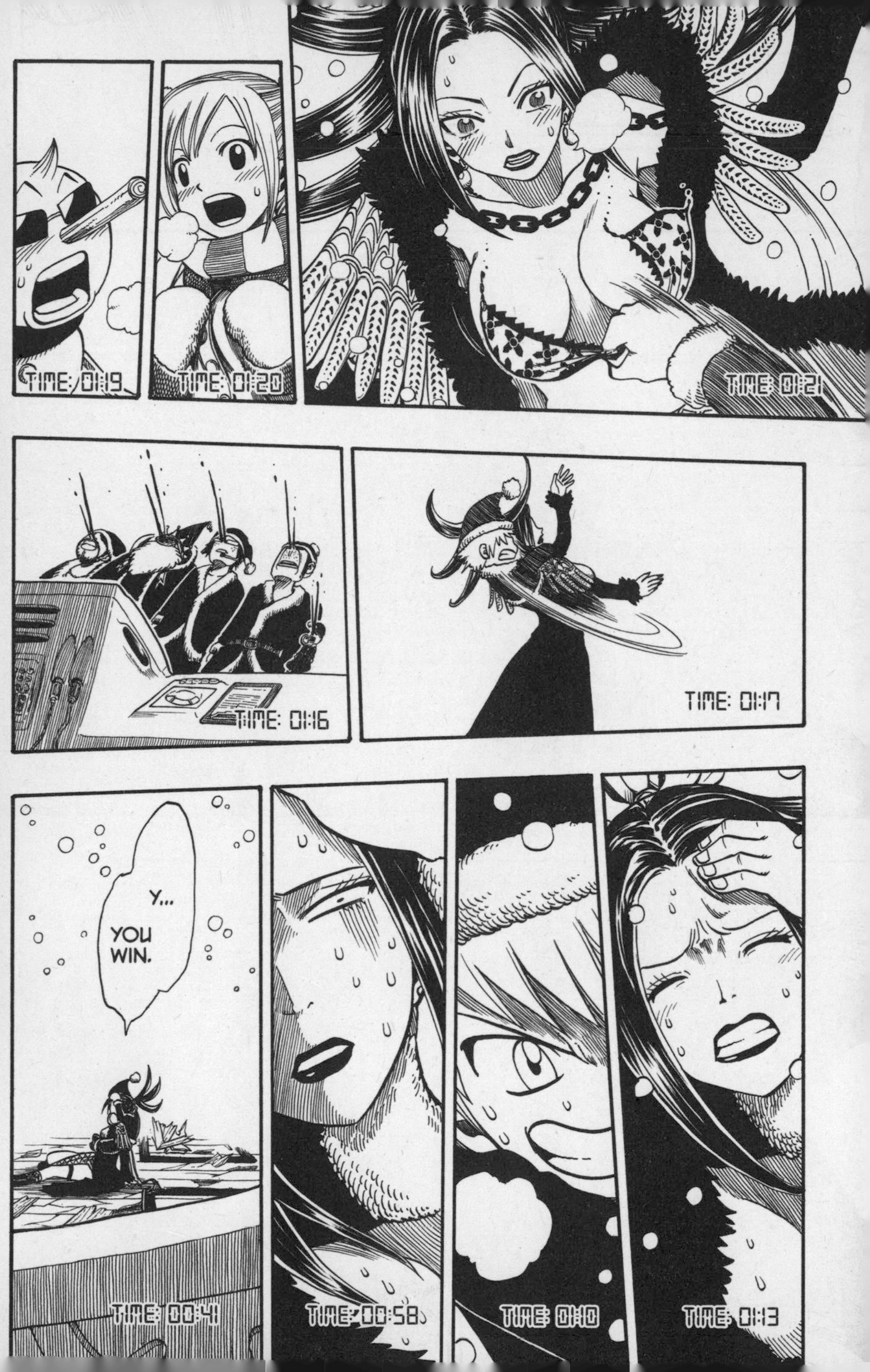
TIME: 01:21
TIME: 01:20
TIME: 01:19
TIME: 01:17
TIME: 01:16
TIME: 01:13
TIME: 01:10
TIME: 00:58
Y... YOU WIN.
TIME: 00:41

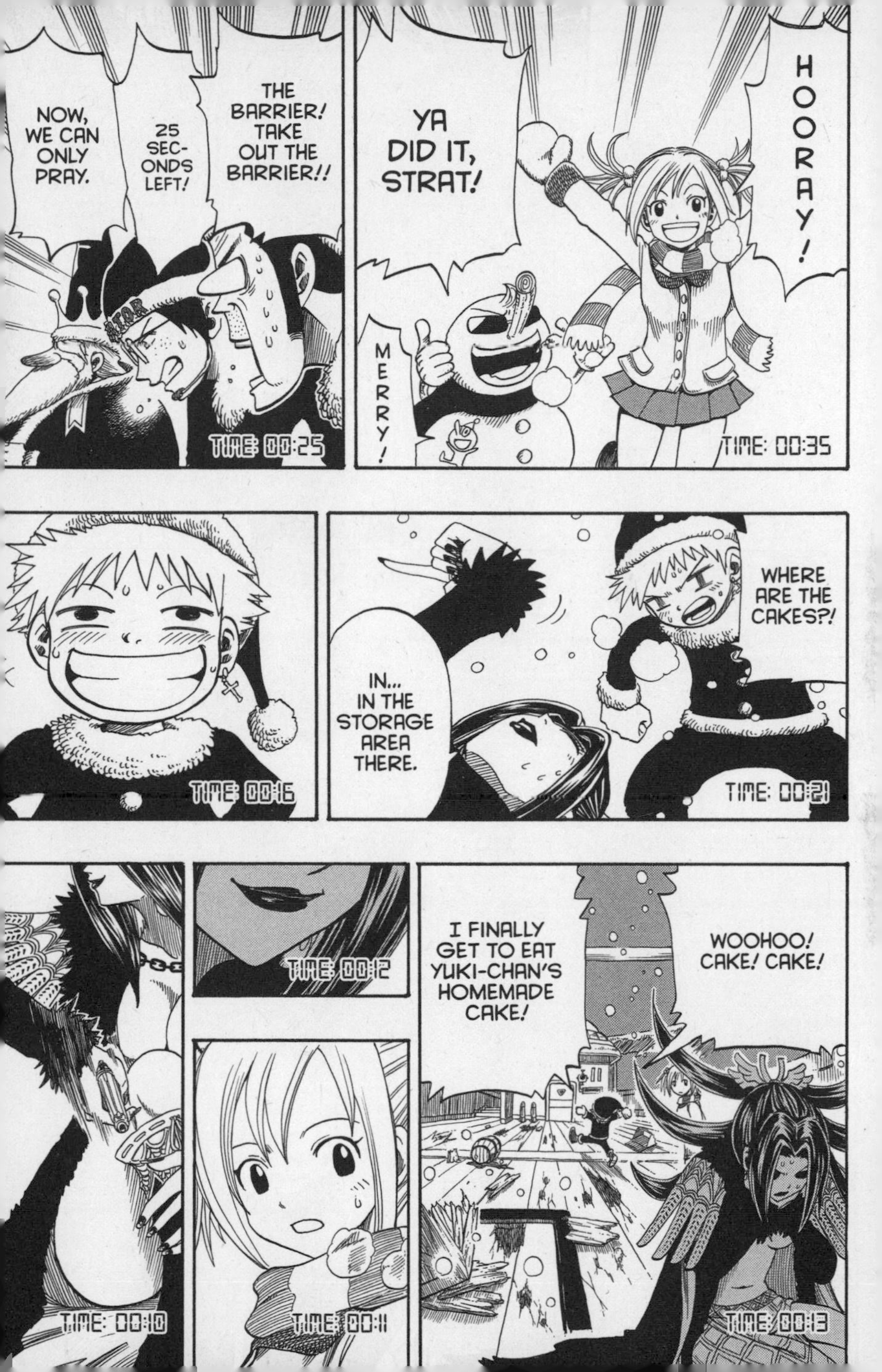
HOORAY!
YA DID IT, STRAT!
MERRY!
TIME: 00:35
THE BARRIER! TAKE OUT THE BARRIER!!
25 SECONDS LEFT!
NOW, WE CAN ONLY PRAY.
TIME: 00:25
WHERE ARE THE CAKES?!
IN... IN THE STORAGE AREA THERE.
TIME: 00:21
TIME: 00:16
WOOHOO! CAKE! CAKE!
I FINALLY GET TO EAT YUKI-CHAN'S HOMEMADE CAKE!
TIME: 00:13
TIME: 00:12
TIME: 00:11
TIME: 00:10

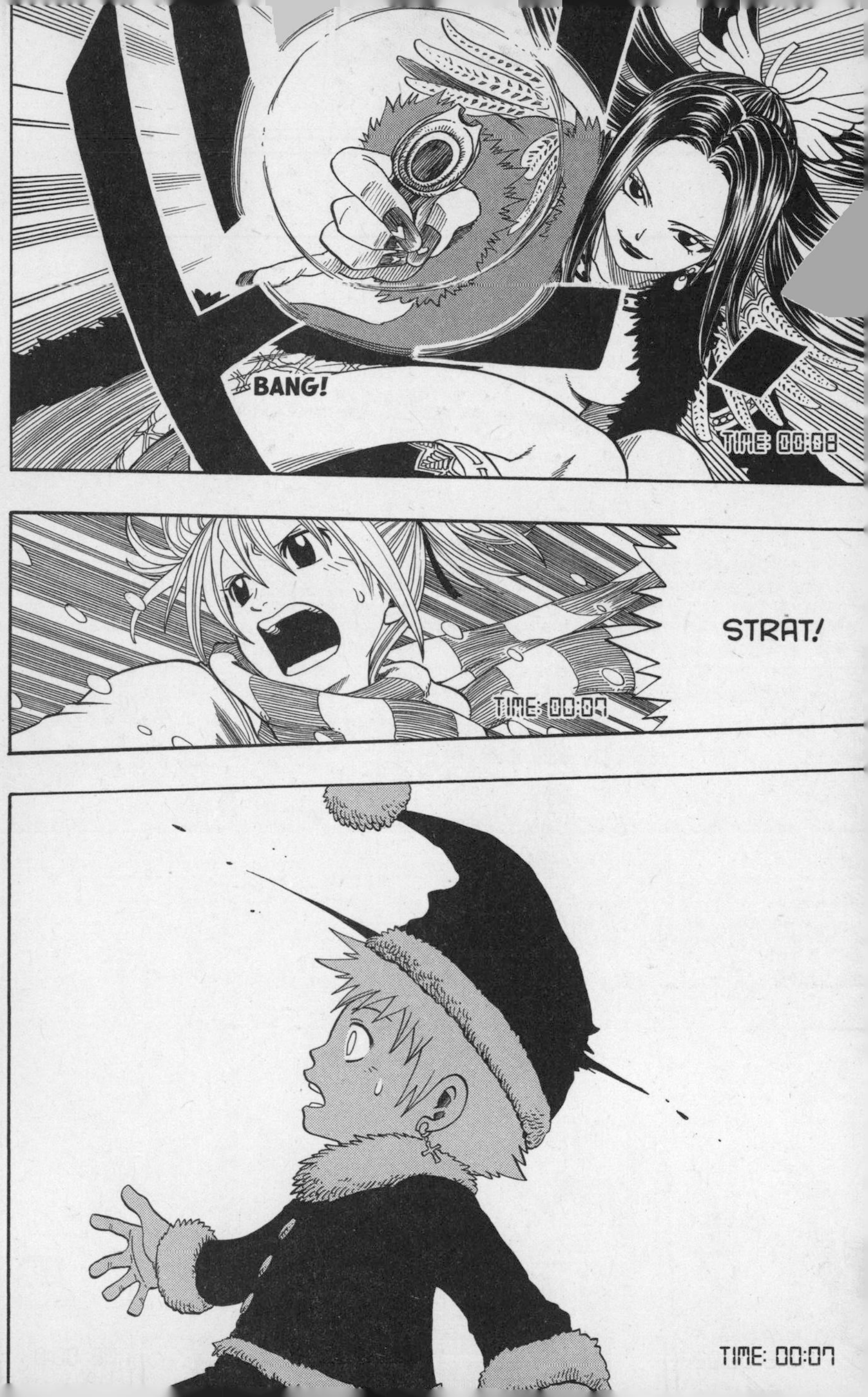
BANG!
TIME: 00:08
STRAT!
TIME: 00:07
TIME: 00:07

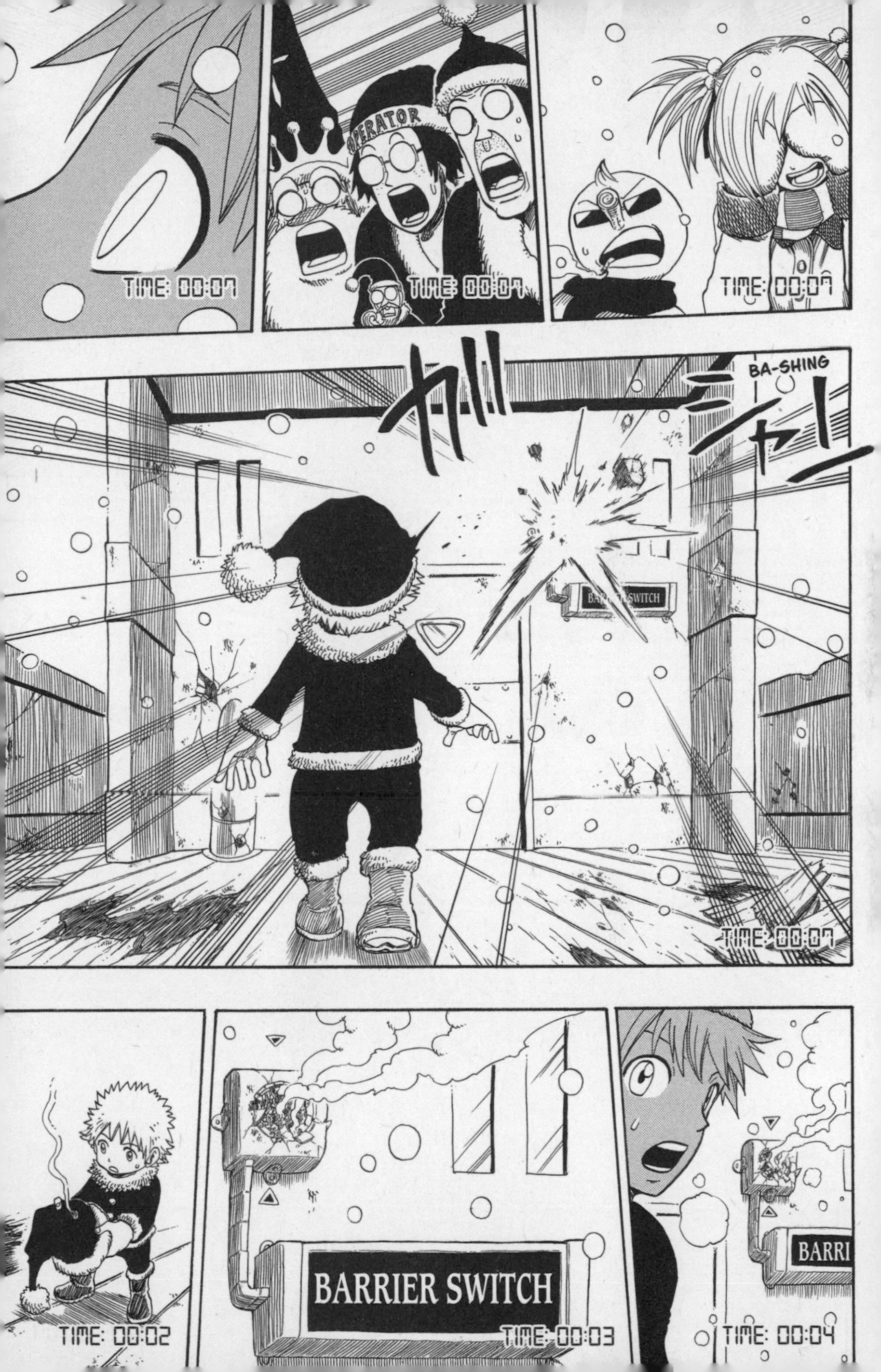
TIME: 00:07
OPERATOR
TIME: 00:07
TIME: 00:07
ガシャーン
BA-SHING
TIME: 00:07
BARRI
TIME: 00:04
BARRIER SWITCH
TIME: 00:03
TIME: 00:02

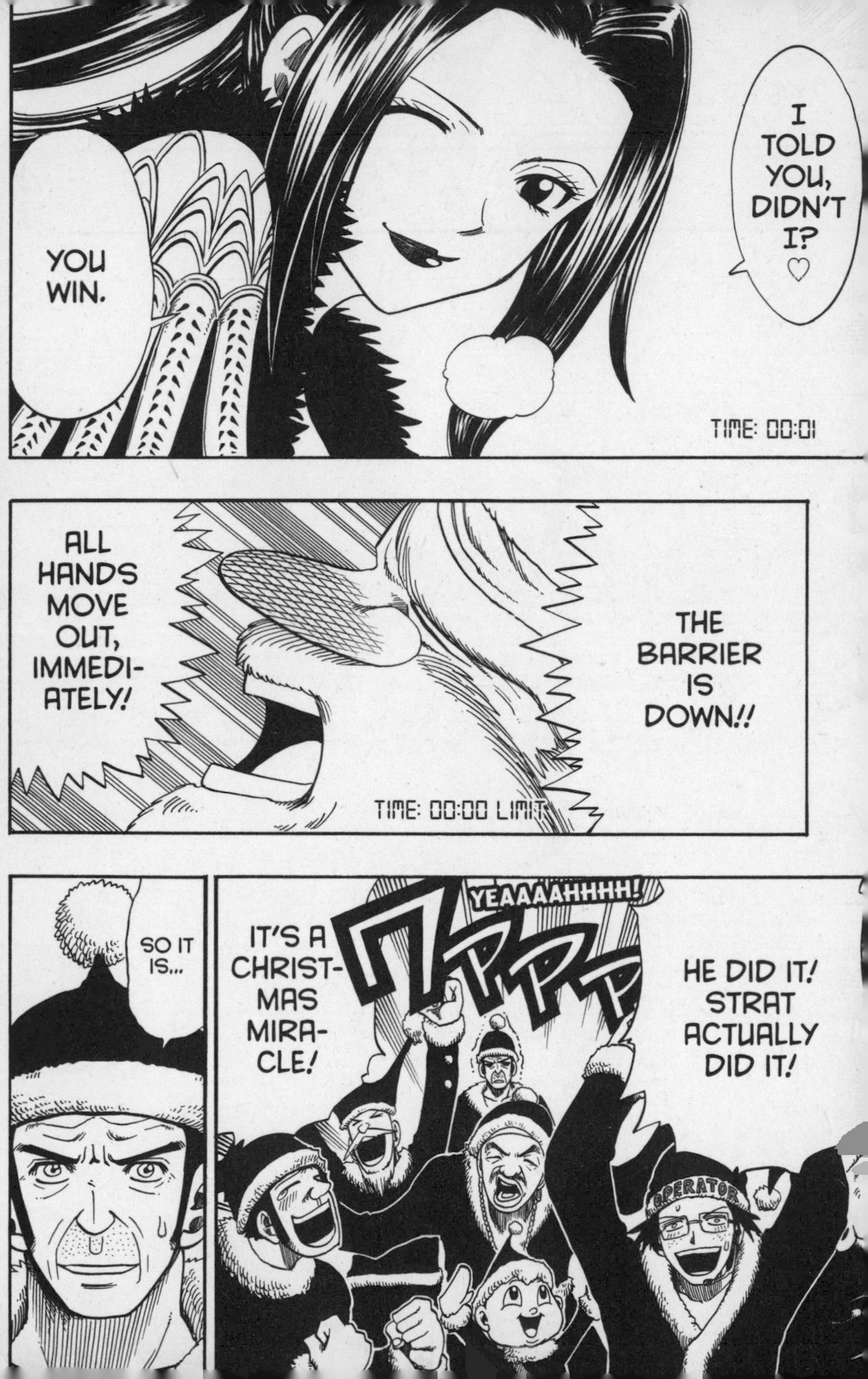
I TOLD YOU, DIDN'T I? ♡
YOU WIN.
TIME: 00:01
THE BARRIER IS DOWN!!
ALL HANDS MOVE OUT, IMMEDIATELY!
TIME: 00:00 LIMIT
HE DID IT! STRAT ACTUALLY DID IT!
YEAAAAHHHH!
IT'S A CHRISTMAS MIRACLE!
OPERATOR
SO IT IS...

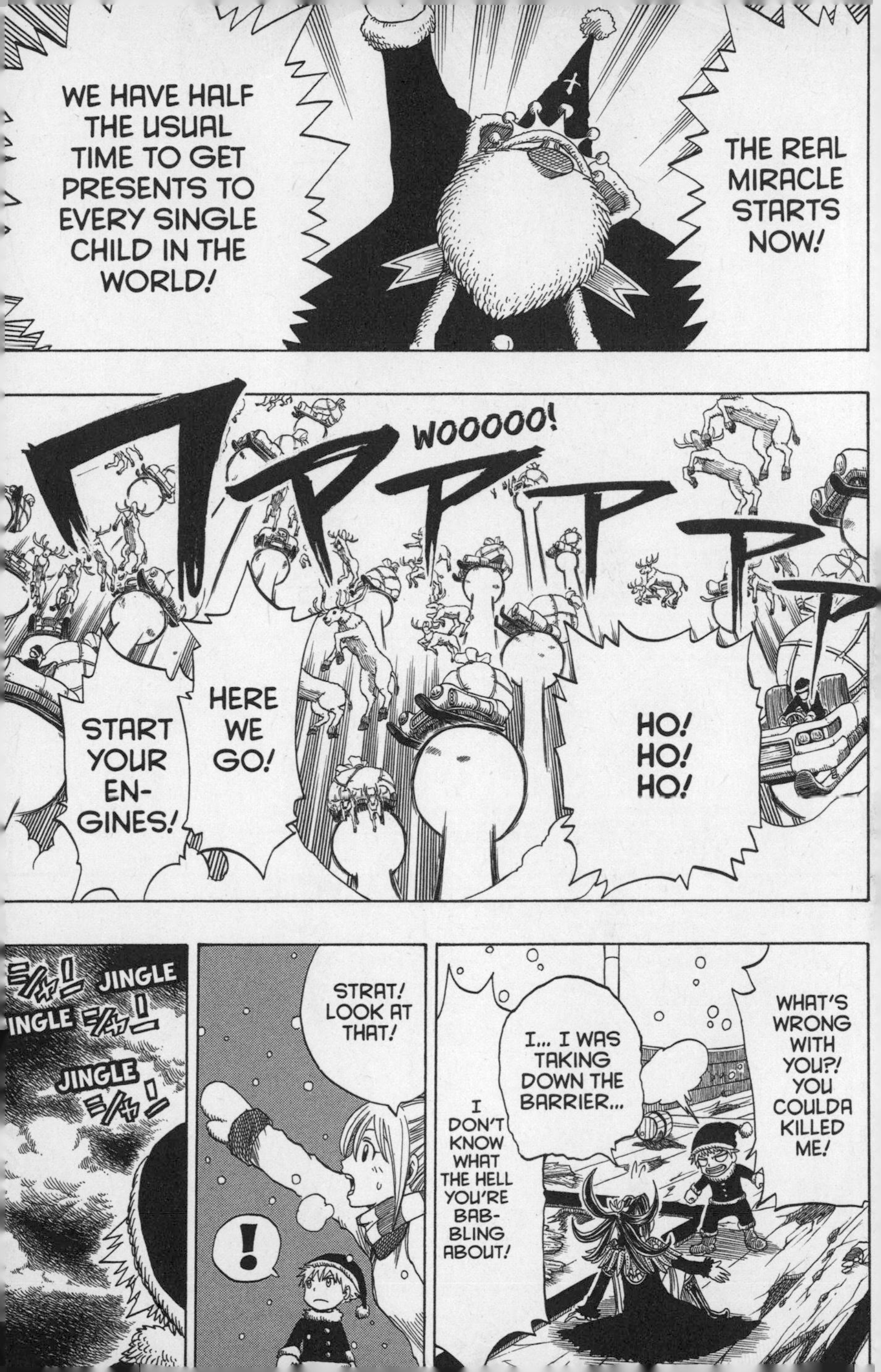
WE HAVE HALF THE USUAL TIME TO GET PRESENTS TO EVERY SINGLE CHILD IN THE WORLD!
THE REAL MIRACLE STARTS NOW!
WOOOOO!
HO! HO! HO!
HERE WE GO!
START YOUR EN-GINES!
WHAT'S WRONG WITH YOU?! YOU COULDA KILLED ME!
I... I WAS TAKING DOWN THE BARRIER...
I DON'T KNOW WHAT THE HELL YOU'RE BAB-BLING ABOUT!
STRAT! LOOK AT THAT!
!
JINGLE
JINGLE
JINGLE

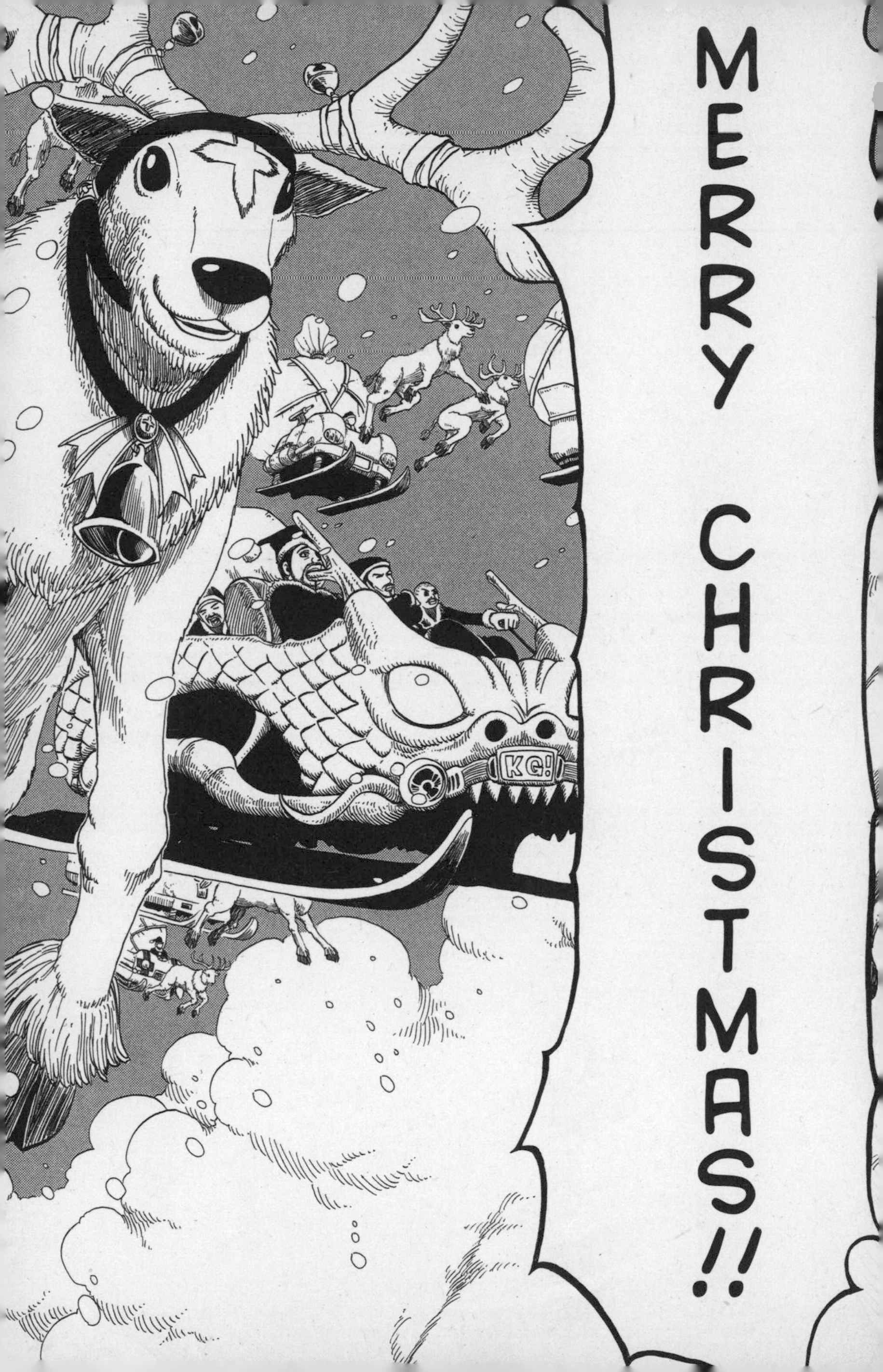
MERRY CHRISTMAS!!
KG!

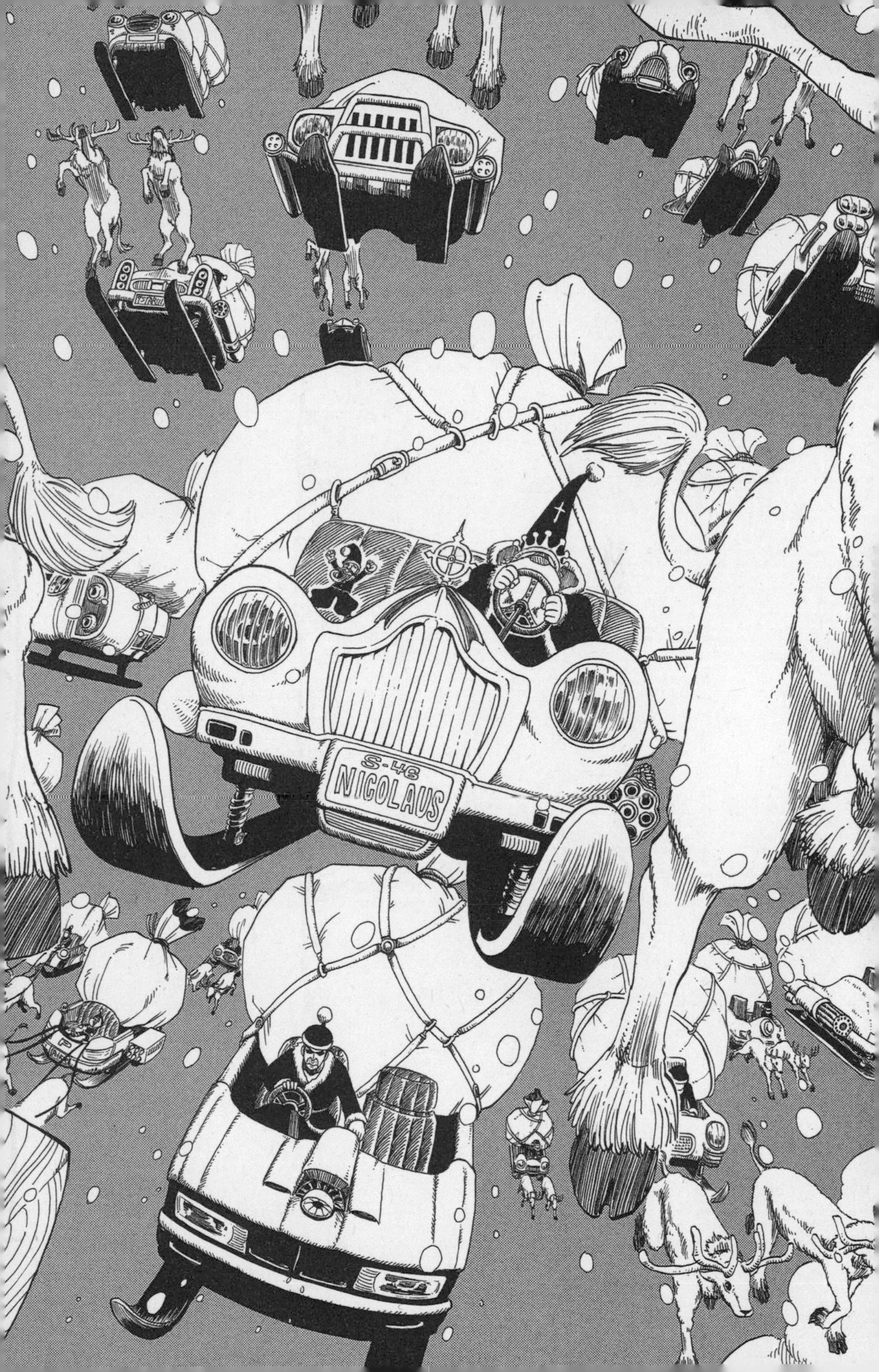
S-46
NICOLAUS

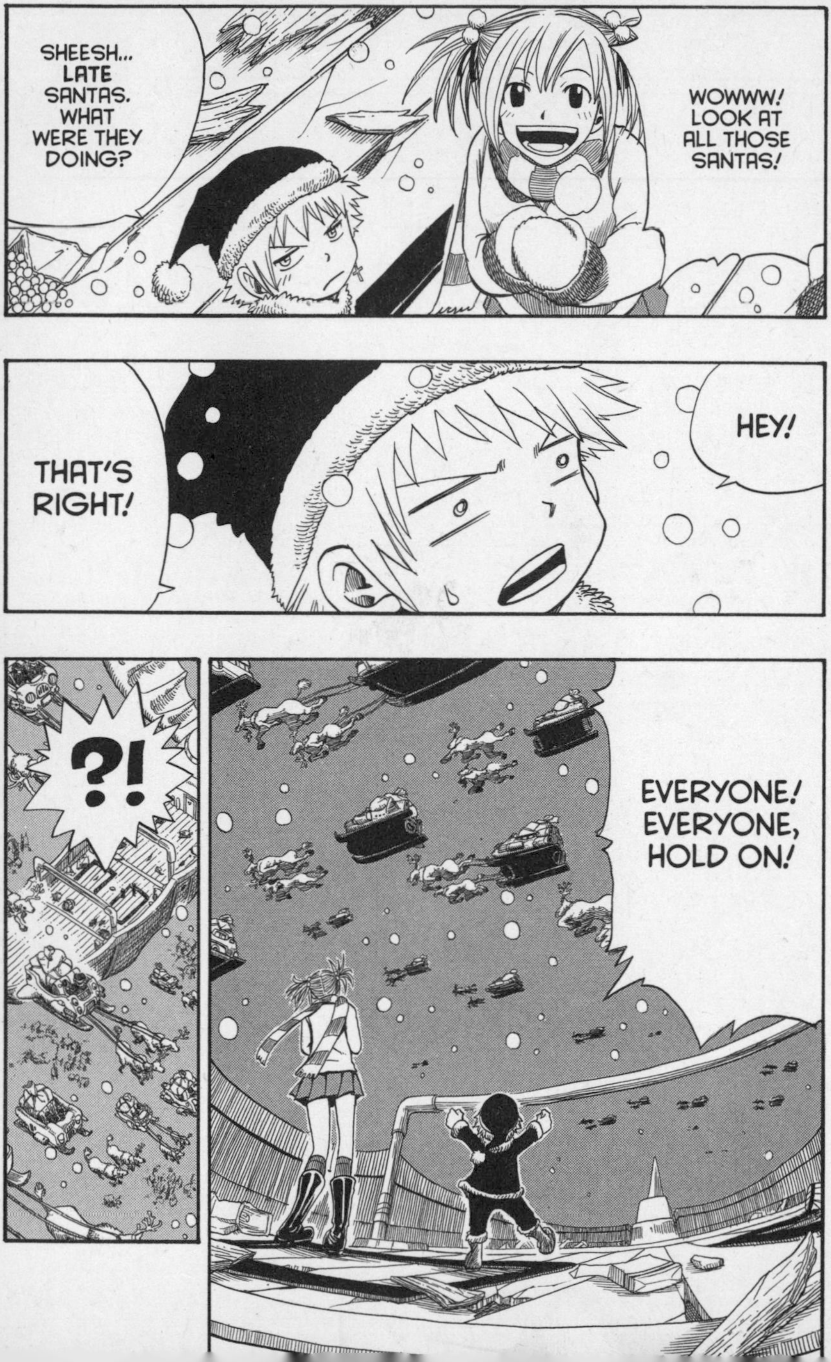
WOWWW! LOOK AT ALL THOSE SANTAS!
SHEESH... LATE SANTAS. WHAT WERE THEY DOING?
HEY!
THAT'S RIGHT!
EVERYONE! EVERYONE, HOLD ON!
?!

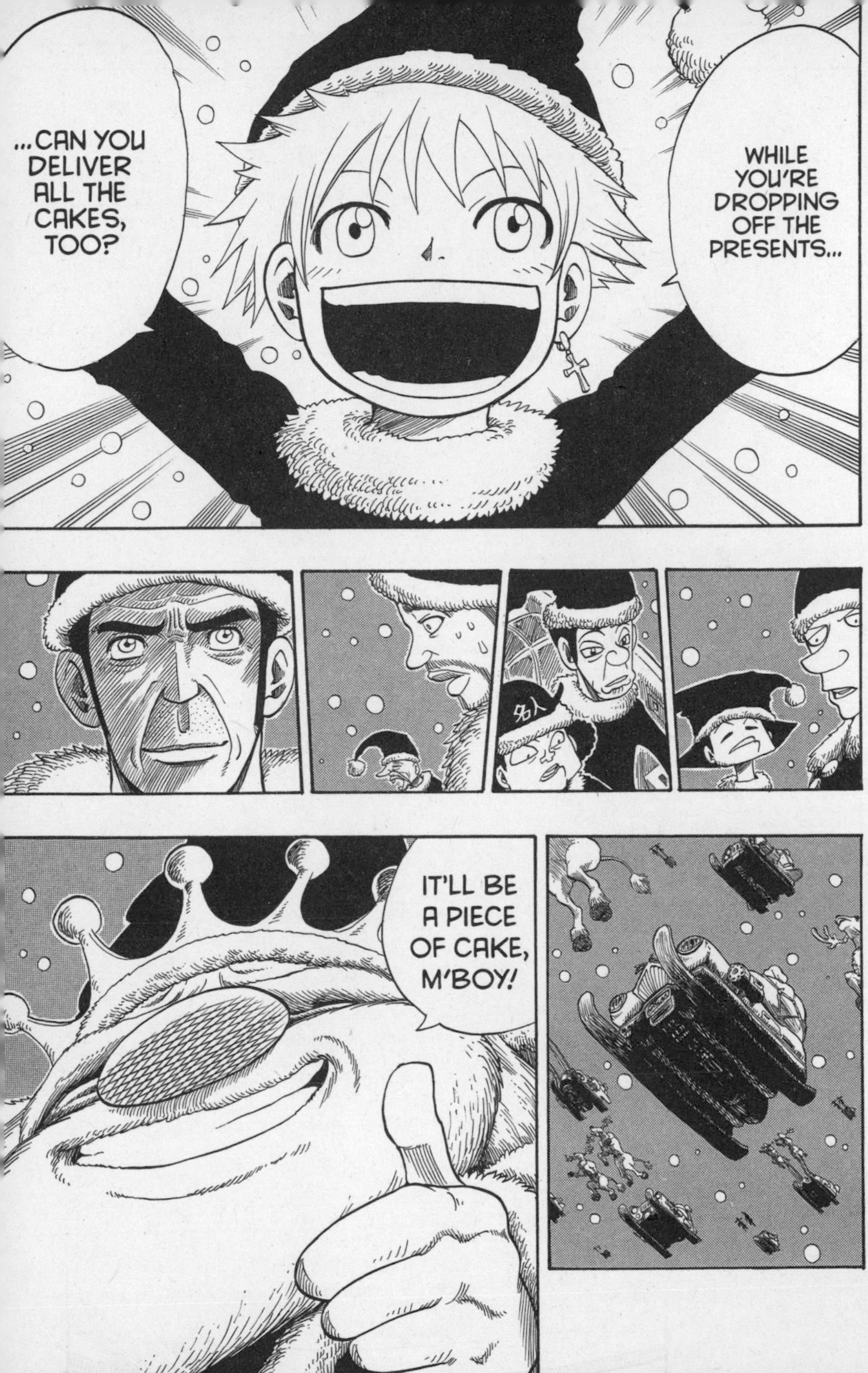
WHILE YOU'RE DROPPING OFF THE PRESENTS...
...CAN YOU DELIVER ALL THE CAKES, TOO?
IT'LL BE A PIECE OF CAKE, M'BOY!

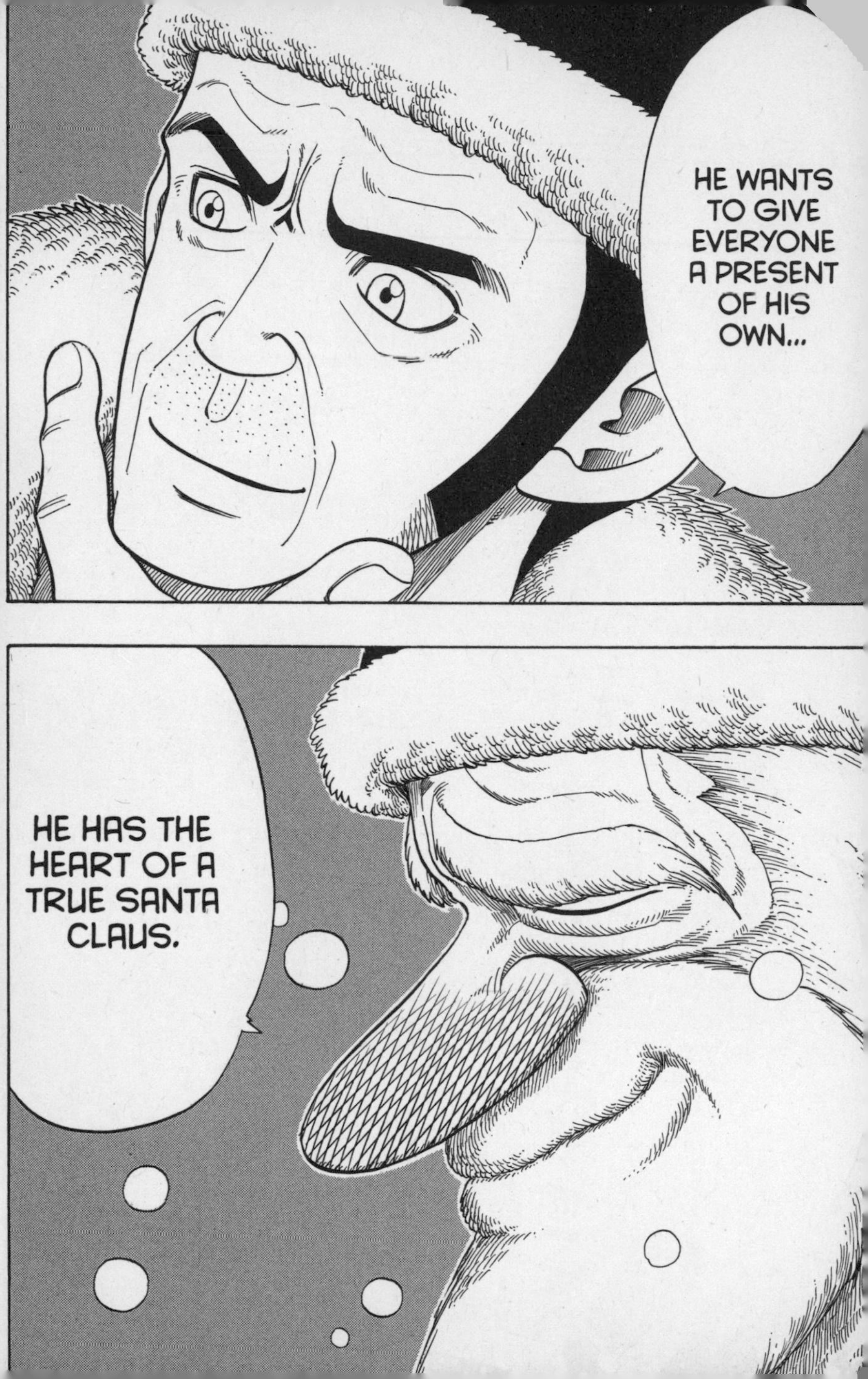
HE WANTS TO GIVE EVERYONE A PRESENT OF HIS OWN...
HE HAS THE HEART OF A TRUE SANTA CLAUS.

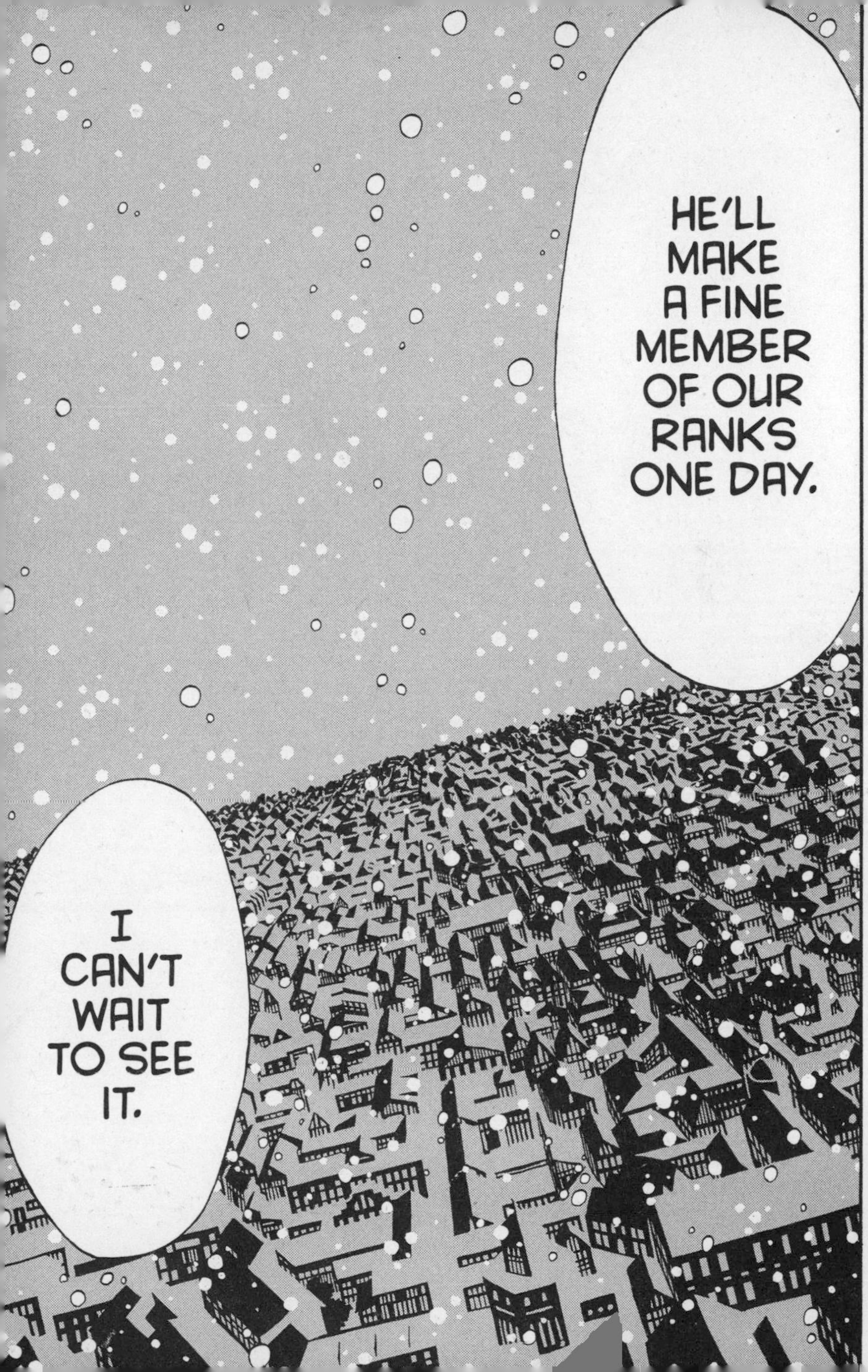
HE'LL MAKE A FINE MEMBER OF OUR RANKS ONE DAY.
I CAN'T WAIT TO SEE IT.

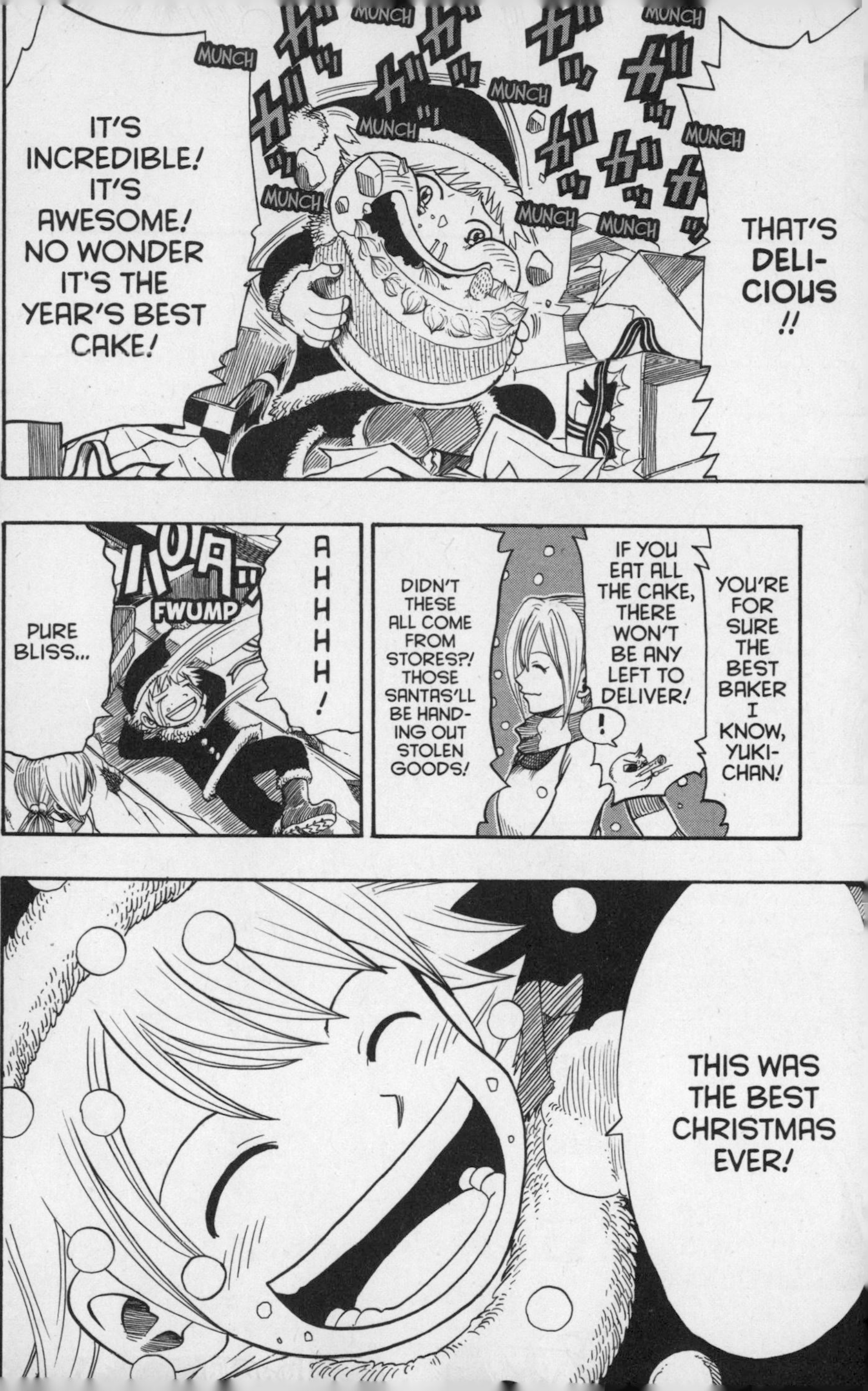
MUNCH
THAT'S DELICIOUS!!
IT'S INCREDIBLE! IT'S AWESOME! NO WONDER IT'S THE YEAR'S BEST CAKE!
YOU'RE FOR SURE THE BEST BAKER I KNOW, YUKI-CHAN!
IF YOU EAT ALL THE CAKE, THERE WON'T BE ANY LEFT TO DELIVER!
!
DIDN'T THESE ALL COME FROM STORES?! THOSE SANTAS'LL BE HANDING OUT STOLEN GOODS!
AHHHHH!
FWUMP
PURE BLISS...
THIS WAS THE BEST CHRISTMAS EVER!

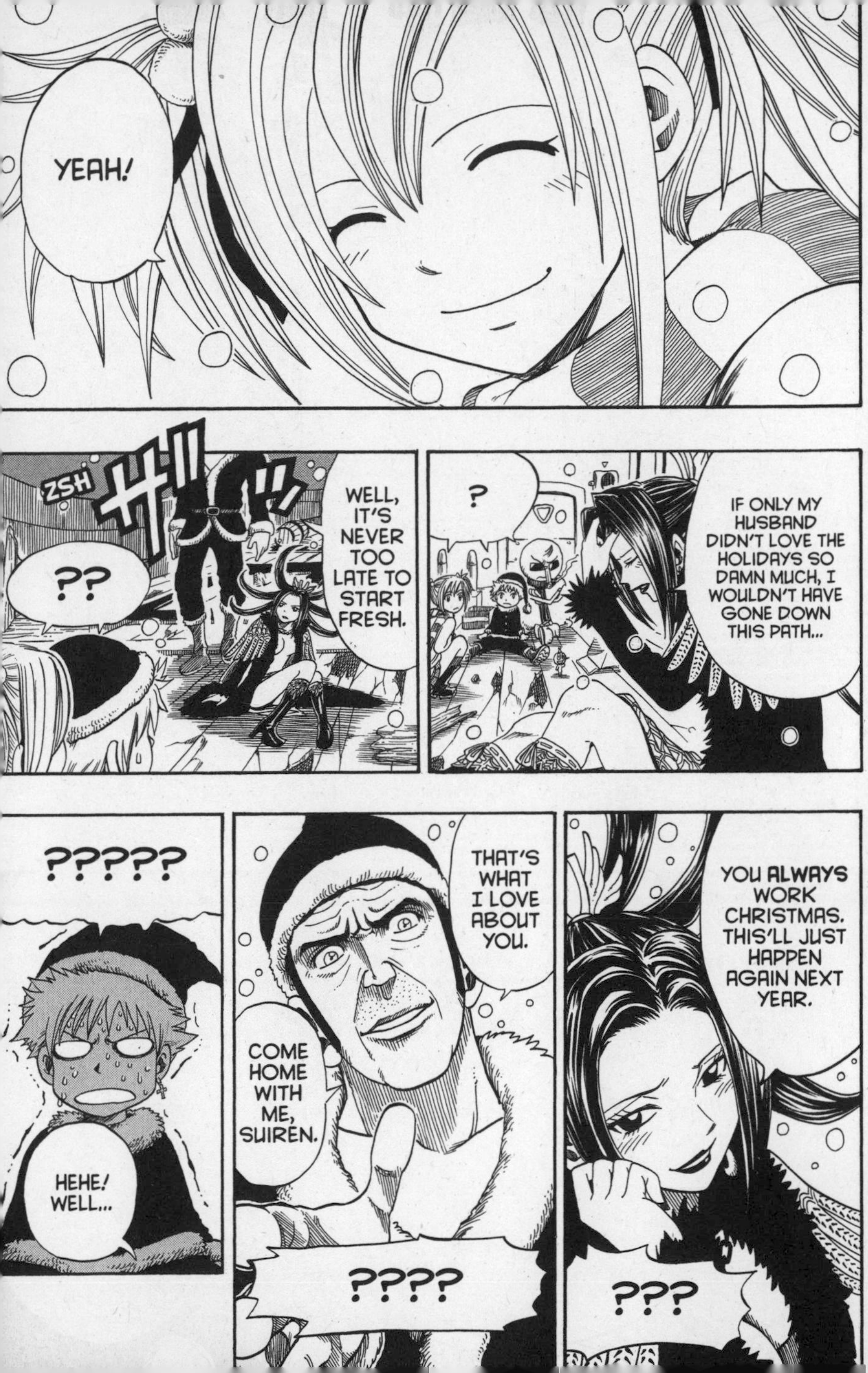
YEAH!
IF ONLY MY HUSBAND DIDN'T LOVE THE HOLIDAYS SO DAMN MUCH, I WOULDN'T HAVE GONE DOWN THIS PATH...
?
WELL, IT'S NEVER TOO LATE TO START FRESH.
ZSH
??
YOU ALWAYS WORK CHRISTMAS. THIS'LL JUST HAPPEN AGAIN NEXT YEAR.
???
THAT'S WHAT I LOVE ABOUT YOU.
COME HOME WITH ME, SUIREN.
????
?????
HEHE! WELL...

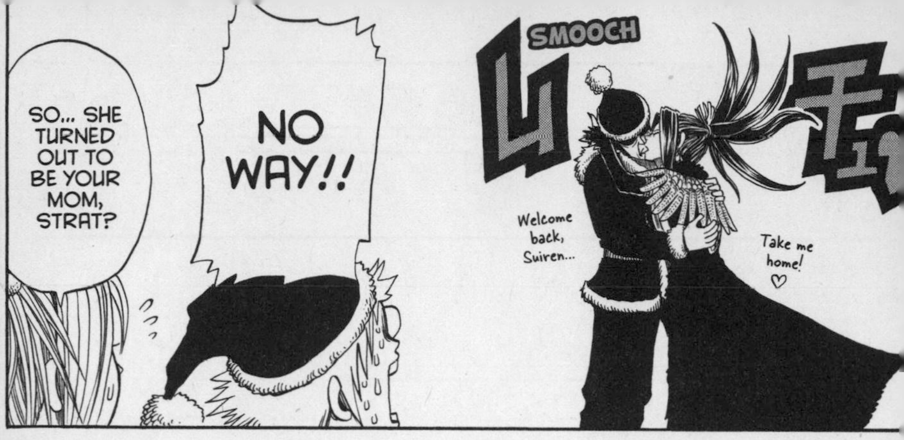
SMOOCH
Take me home! ♡
Welcome back, Suiren...
NO WAY!!
SO... SHE TURNED OUT TO BE YOUR MOM, STRAT?

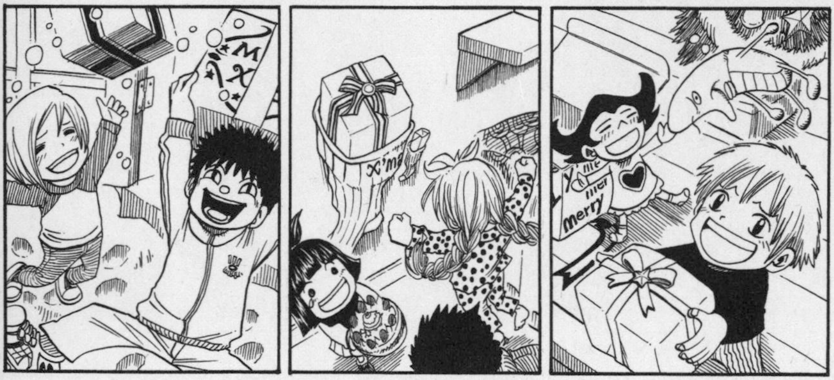

MAY IT BE A HAPPY DAY FOR ALL MY READERS OUT THERE...

MERRY CHRISTMAS!!

FIRST PUBLISHED: *WEEKLY SHONEN MAGAZINE* 2003 (NO. 2/3 DOUBLE-ISSUE)

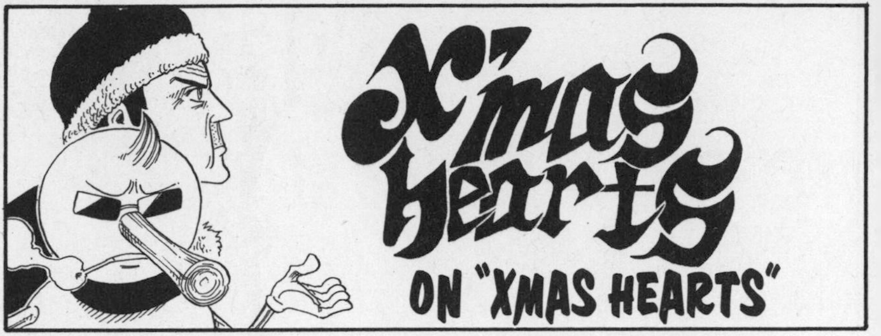

X'mas Hearts on "Xmas Hearts"

They didn't specifically request me to do a holiday piece–I just happened to hear that the magazine would be coming out around Christmas, and thought maybe I'd do something seasonal. Hmmm. I was hoping for something deep and moving, but... Well...this is how it turned out (sweats). Strat is really my least favorite among the protagonists of my own stories (smirk). I do like his dad, Greco, whom I modeled on Mel Gibson (circa *Ransom*). In the original draft, there was a moment when Greco gets really surprised at something, and for about 16 panels he just stands there with his eyes wide going, "Gah... ah... ahhhh..." But because it didn't make much sense (okay, because it made **no** sense), I cut that scene myself. It was based on something Mel Gibson does a lot in his movies (I'm a fanboy; sorry), where he'll get really surprised and just stand there gaping (very sorry). I was hoping to pay homage to that, but I dropped it.

As for the names of the characters, Strat and Greco both come from guitars. Johnny's name is a nod to an old movie, *Johnny Suede.* "Yuki-chan" just sounded wintery.* Saint Nicholas is, of course, the real Santa Claus. Suiren (the water lily) is a flower. As for Snowbits... er, I forget.

*"YUKI" MEANS "SNOW" IN JAPANESE

CHRISTMAS MEMORIES, ET. AL. ♡

Yeah, sure! (LOL) I thought about calling this essay "Heart Christmas," but never mind my love stories. (You don't want to hear those anyway, do you?) I thought we could talk about presents instead! The present I most remember is one I got when I was very small: walkie-talkies! I know it's hard to imagine at a time when everyone carries a cell phone in their pocket, but back then, a short-range wireless device was epoch-making!! (Oh, that means revolutionary.) The day after I got them, my friends and I spent all our time absorbed in playing detectives or spies. Unfortunately, one of the units eventually got dropped in a river and we couldn't play anymore.

Know what? I recently discovered a home video with footage from that Christmas. By total happenstance, it's the only video of my father. If I'm not mistaken, he was gone by the next Christmas. In the video, I'm round and pudgy (haha), so much that I want to ask myself how many times I'm going to ask for "seconds"! (Eight times, if you're wondering.) My little sister, who's now the mother of two children, was a little monkey herself (smiles). And my mom, who was much younger then, is wearing a party hat. The video shows an all-around pretty happy family. There's just one thing in the video I can't quite past. My dad gives me my present (walkie-talkies!!). And fat little Hiro is obviously overjoyed... But he never says thank you! That makes me really angry. Yes, I know it's past-me we're talking about. But I just want to shout at him, "Your dad's not gonna be there next Christmas! You'll never get another chance to thank him!" "Thank you" is such a simple expression, but so important! Dear readers... when somebody gives you a gift... I'm sure you say it, right?

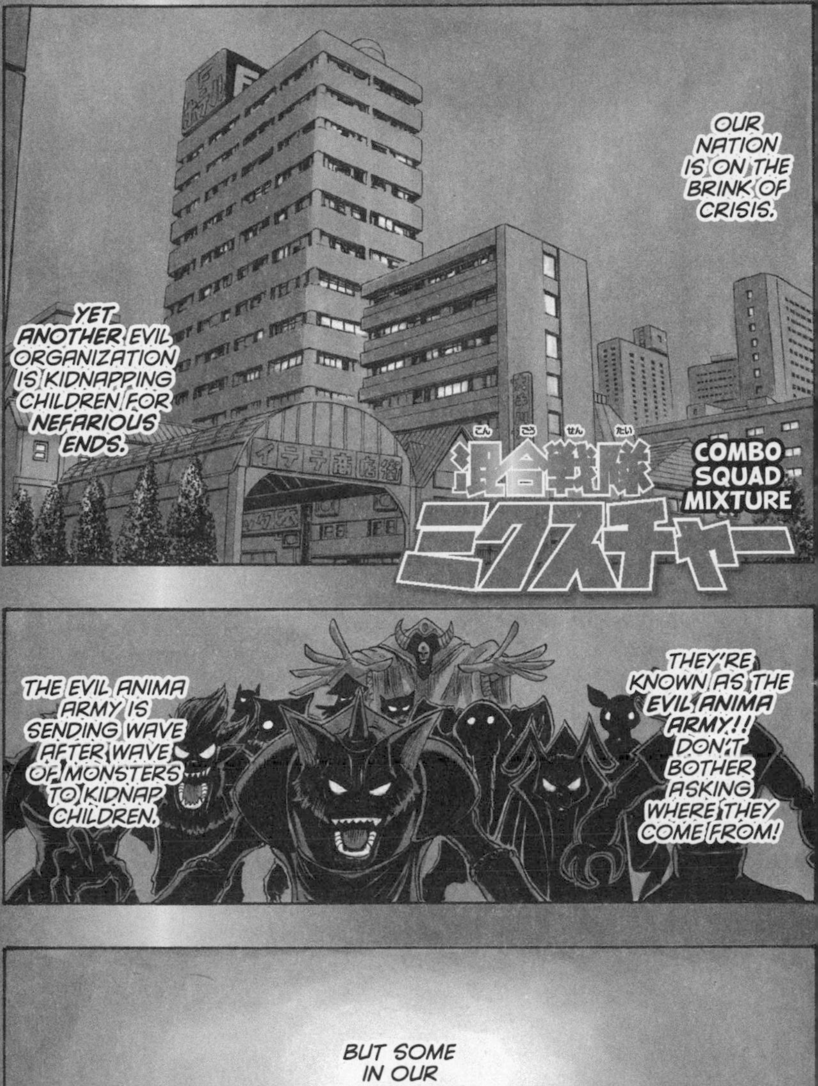
OUR NATION IS ON THE BRINK OF CRISIS.
YET ANOTHER EVIL ORGANIZATION IS KIDNAPPING CHILDREN FOR NEFARIOUS ENDS.
混合戦隊 ミクスチャー
COMBO SQUAD MIXTURE
THEY'RE KNOWN AS THE EVIL ANIMA ARMY!! DON'T BOTHER ASKING WHERE THEY COME FROM!
THE EVIL ANIMA ARMY IS SENDING WAVE AFTER WAVE OF MONSTERS TO KIDNAP CHILDREN.
BUT SOME IN OUR COUNTRY RISE TO OPPOSE THEM!

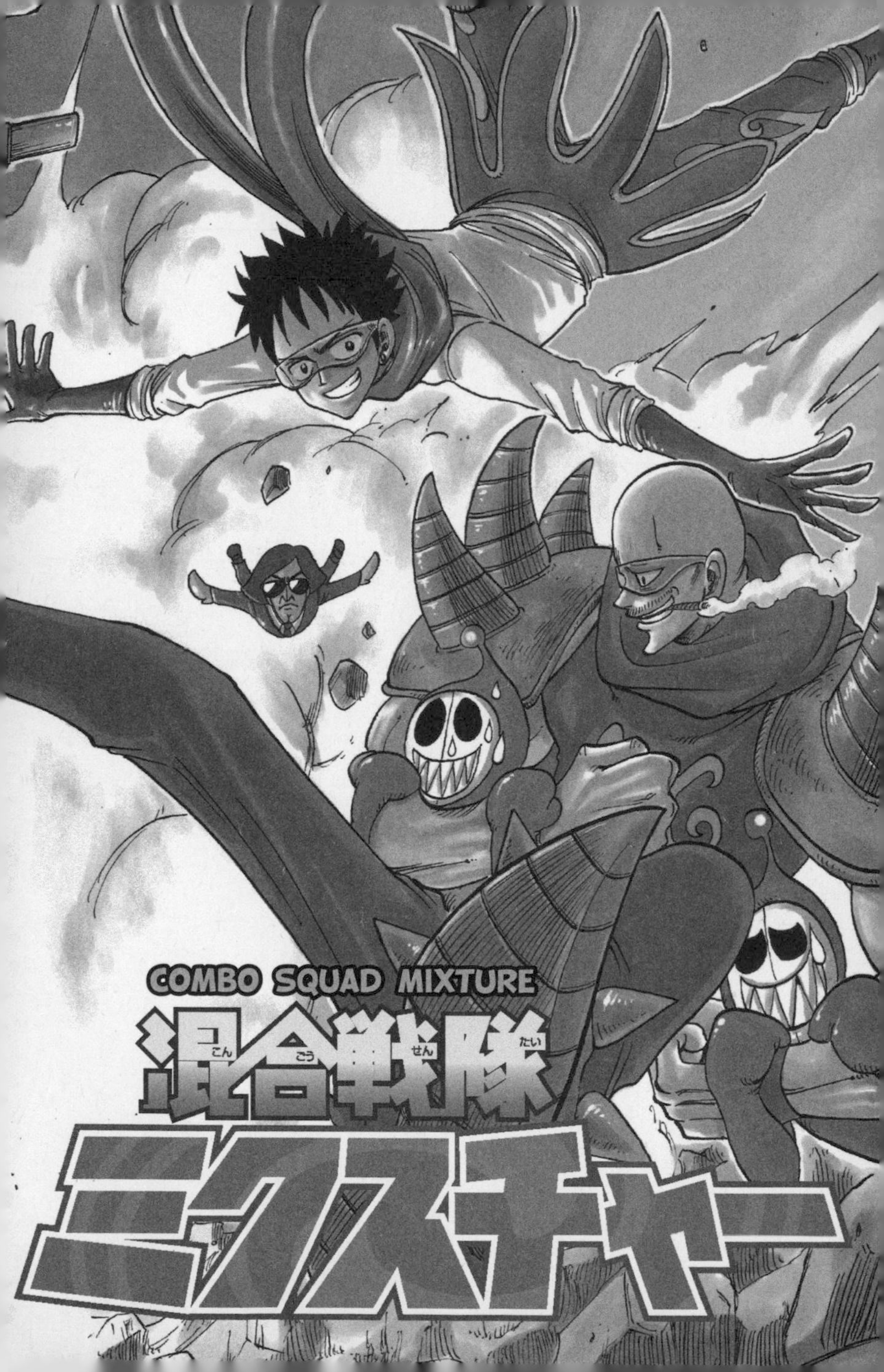
COMBO SQUAD MIXTURE
混合戦隊(こんごうせんたい)
ミクスチャー

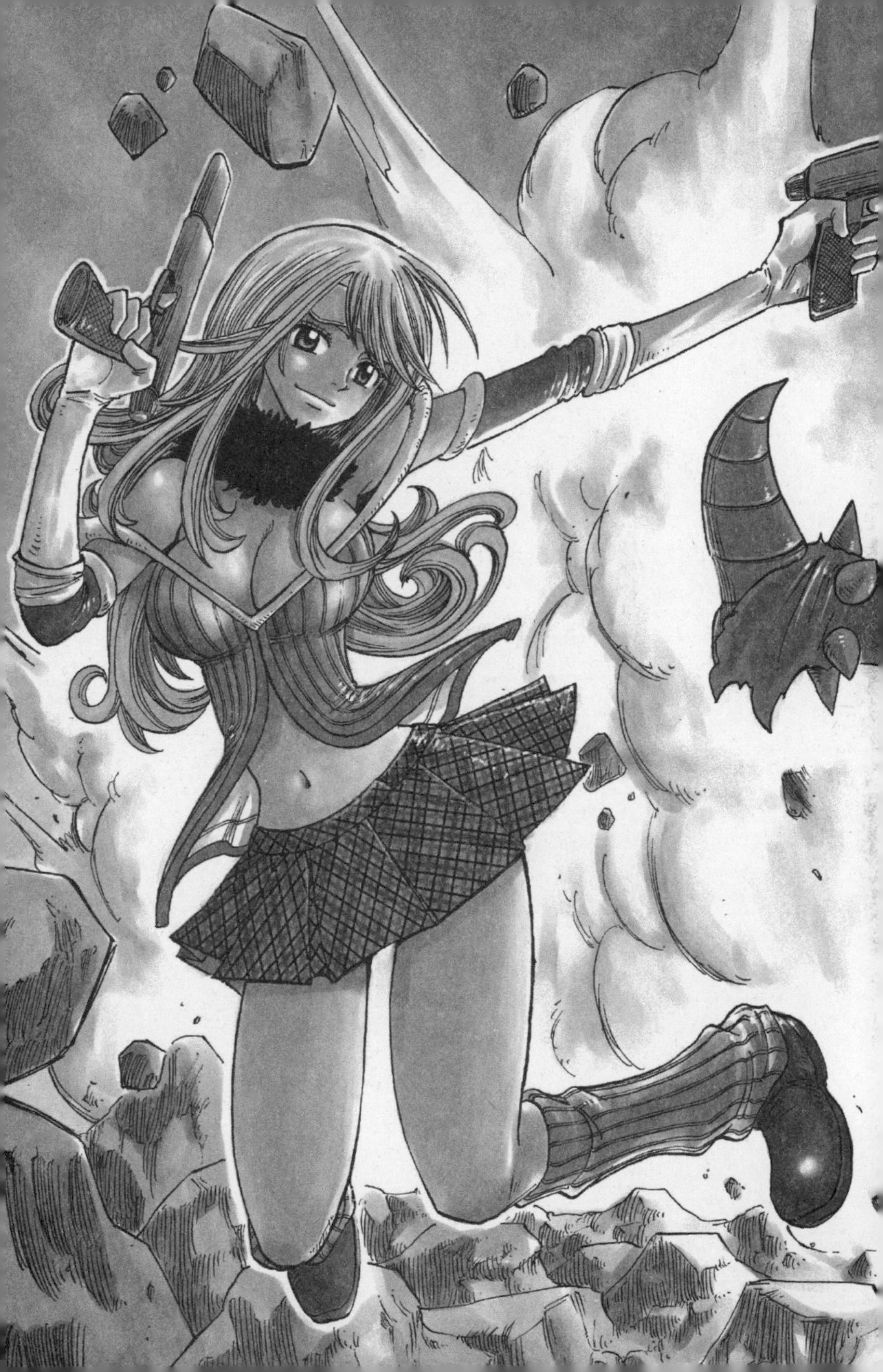

混合戦隊

ミクスチャー

COMBO SQUAD MIXTURE

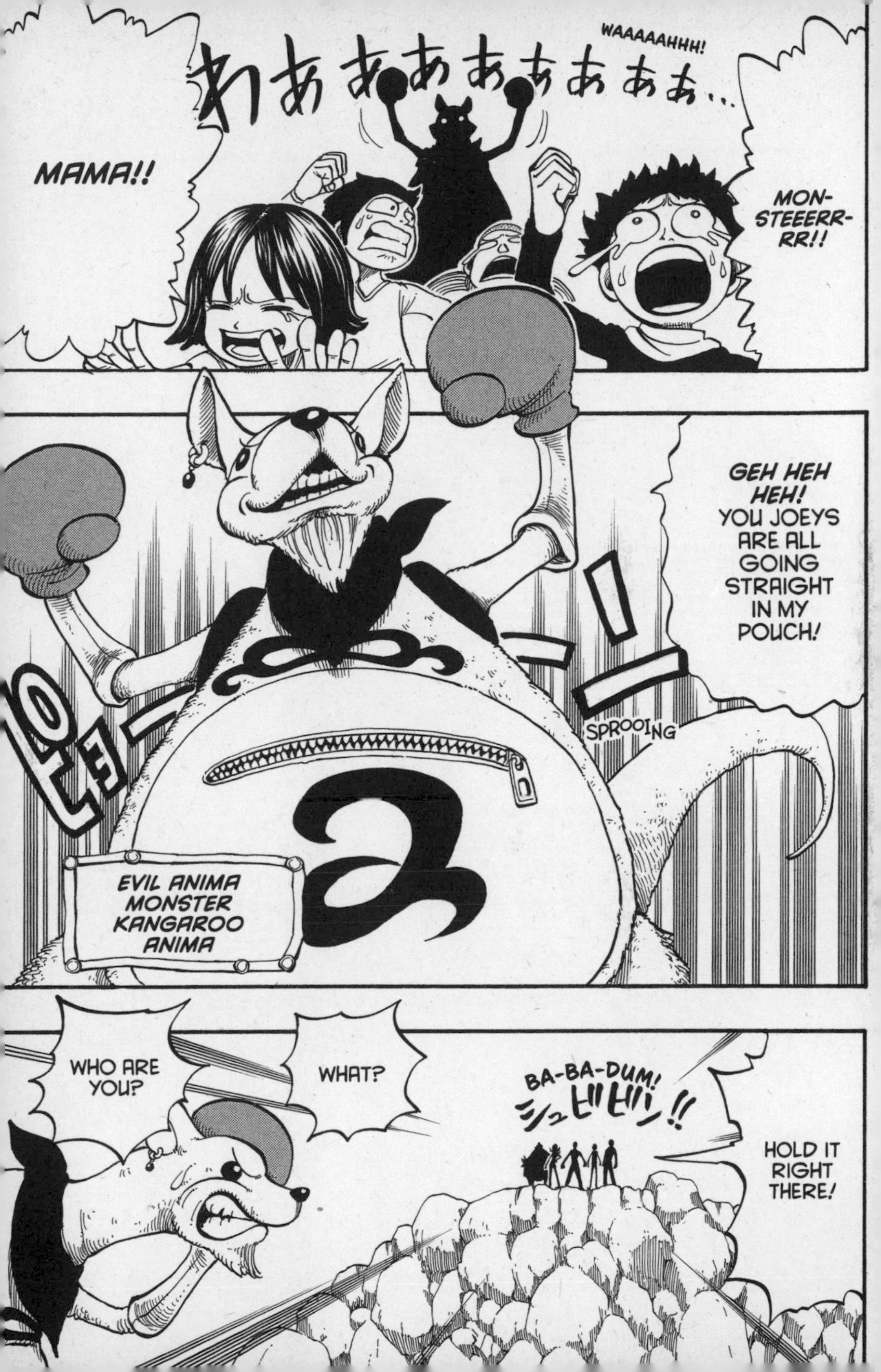
WAAAAAHHH!
わあああああああ…
MON-STEEERR-RR!!
MAMA!!
GEH HEH HEH! YOU JOEYS ARE ALL GOING STRAIGHT IN MY POUCH!
SPROOING
EVIL ANIMA MONSTER KANGAROO ANIMA
HOLD IT RIGHT THERE!
BA-BA-DUM!
シュビビン!!
WHAT?
WHO ARE YOU?

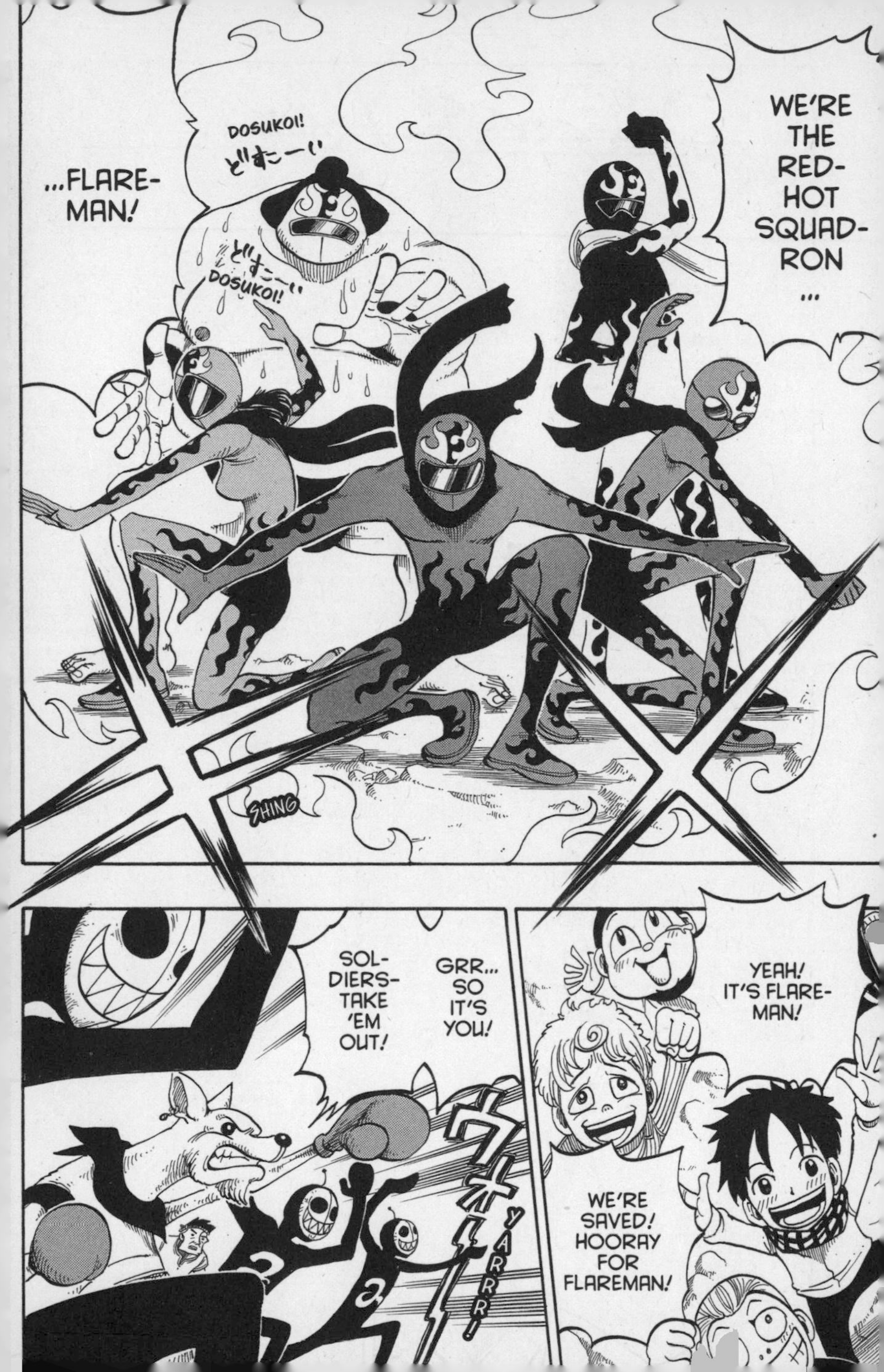
WE'RE THE RED-HOT SQUAD-RON ...
DOSUKOI!
どすこーい
どすこーい
DOSUKOI!!
...FLARE-MAN!
SHING
YEAH! IT'S FLARE-MAN!
WE'RE SAVED! HOORAY FOR FLAREMAN!
GRR... SO IT'S YOU!
SOL-DIERS-TAKE 'EM OUT!
YARRR!

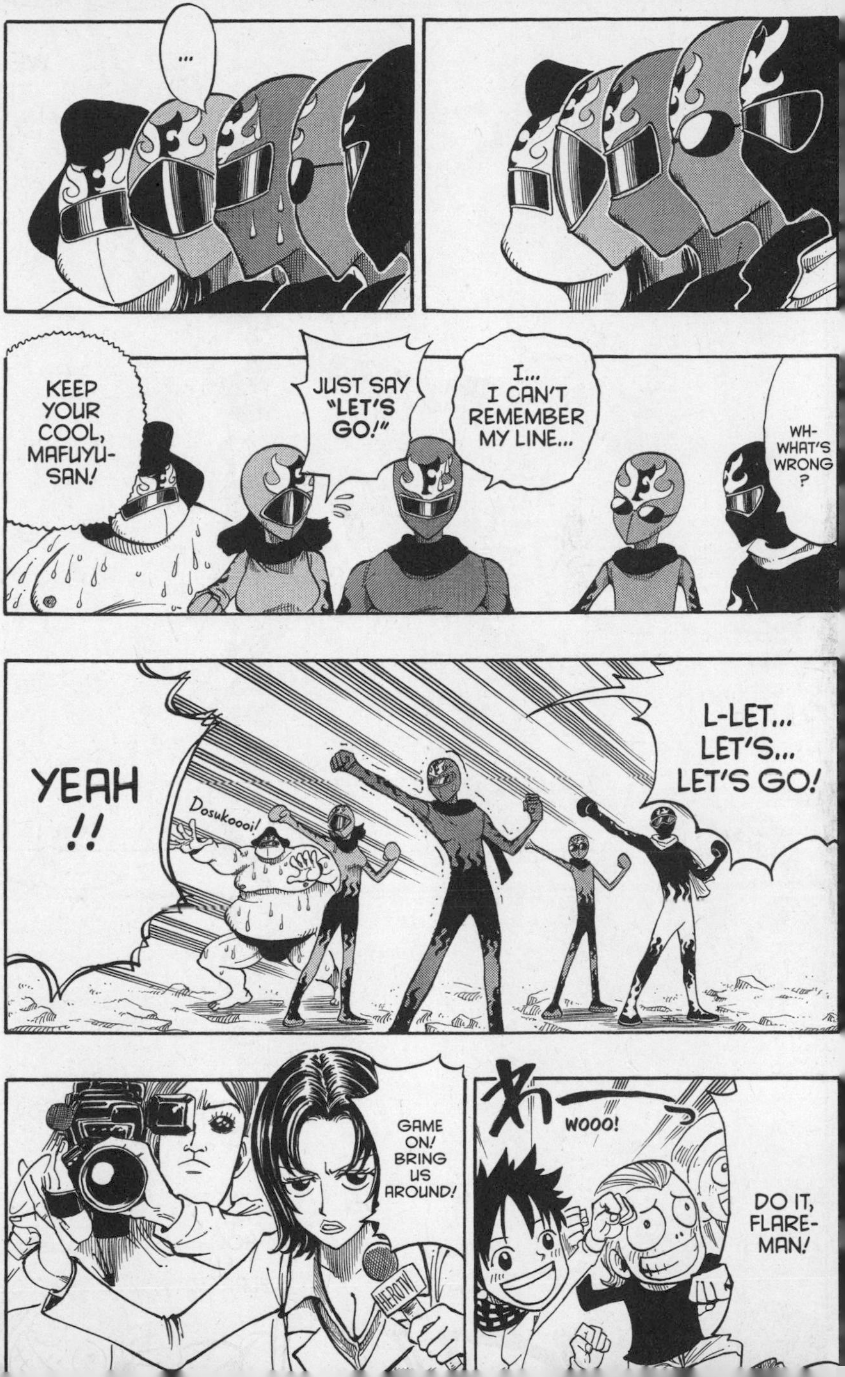
...
WH-WHAT'S WRONG?
I... I CAN'T REMEMBER MY LINE...
JUST SAY "LET'S GO!"
KEEP YOUR COOL, MAFUYU-SAN!
L-LET... LET'S... LET'S GO!
YEAH!!
Dosukoooi!
わー
WOOO!
DO IT, FLARE-MAN!
GAME ON! BRING US AROUND!
HERO TV

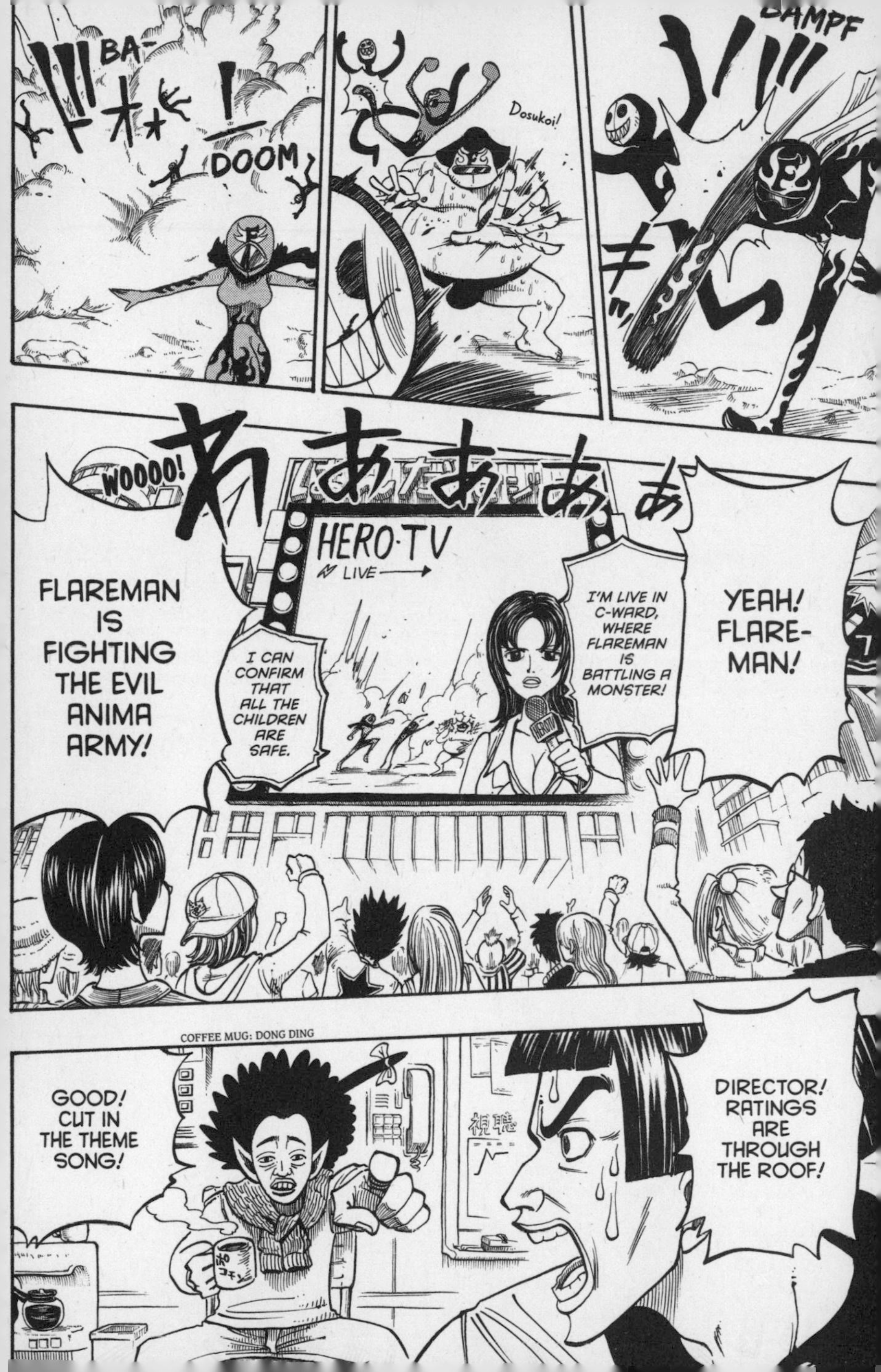
BAMPF
Dosukoi!
BA-
DOOM
YEAH! FLARE-MAN!
HERO·TV
LIVE
I'M LIVE IN C-WARD, WHERE FLAREMAN IS BATTLING A MONSTER!
I CAN CONFIRM THAT ALL THE CHILDREN ARE SAFE.
WOOOO!
FLAREMAN IS FIGHTING THE EVIL ANIMA ARMY!
DIRECTOR! RATINGS ARE THROUGH THE ROOF!
視聴
COFFEE MUG: DONG DING
GOOD! CUT IN THE THEME SONG!

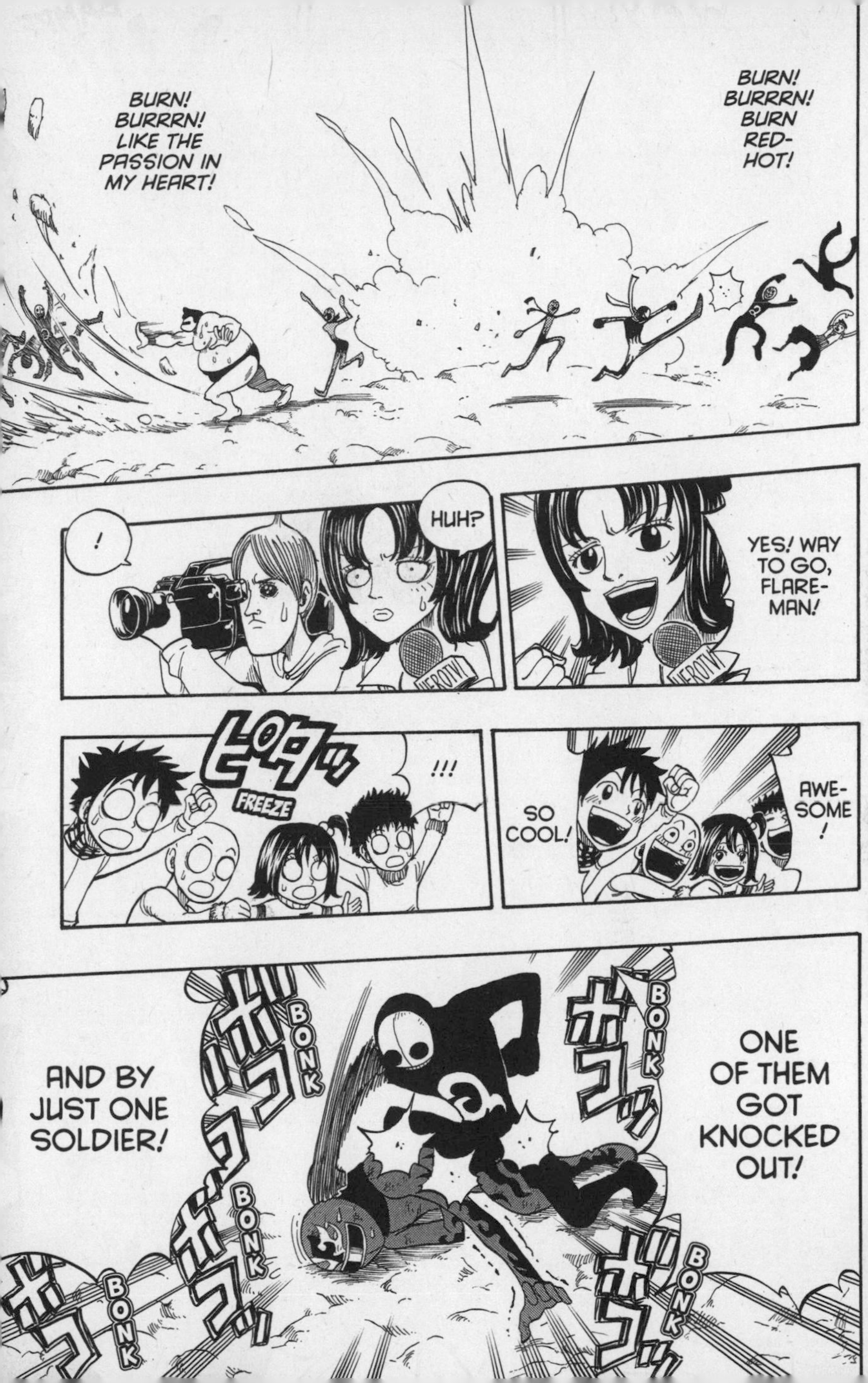
BURN! BURRRN! BURN RED-HOT!
BURN! BURRRN! LIKE THE PASSION IN MY HEART!
YES! WAY TO GO, FLARE-MAN!
HUH?
!
AWESOME!
SO COOL!
!!!
FREEZE
BONK
ONE OF THEM GOT KNOCKED OUT!
AND BY JUST ONE SOLDIER!
BONK
BONK
BONK
BONK

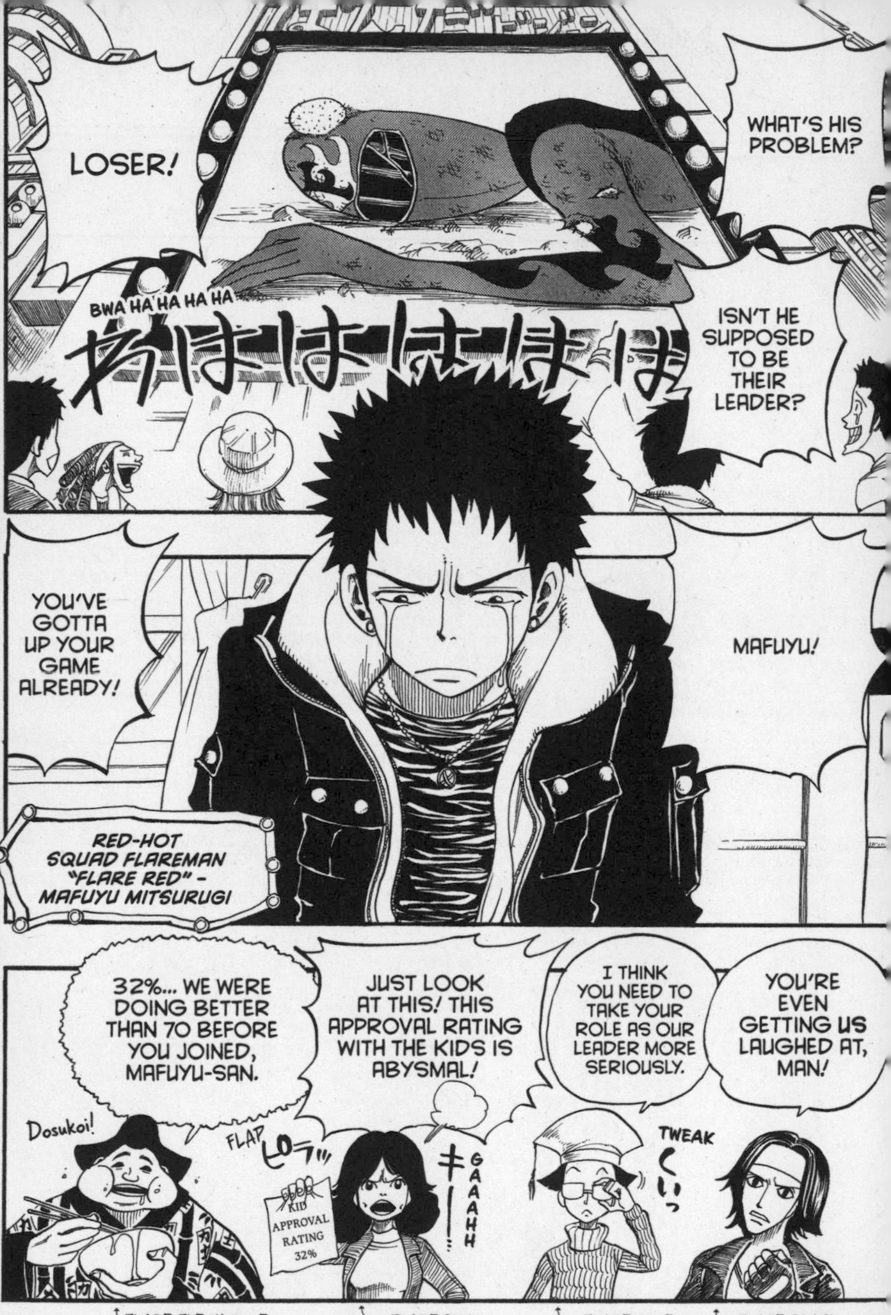
WHAT'S HIS PROBLEM?
ISN'T HE SUPPOSED TO BE THEIR LEADER?
LOSER!
BWA HA HA HA HA
わはははは
MAFUYU!
YOU'VE GOTTA UP YOUR GAME ALREADY!
RED-HOT SQUAD FLAREMAN "FLARE RED" - MAFUYU MITSURUGI
YOU'RE EVEN GETTING US LAUGHED AT, MAN!
TWEAK
くいっ
I THINK YOU NEED TO TAKE YOUR ROLE AS OUR LEADER MORE SERIOUSLY.
JUST LOOK AT THIS! THIS APPROVAL RATING WITH THE KIDS IS ABYSMAL!
GAAAHH
キー!
FLAP
ピラッ
KID APPROVAL RATING 32%
32%... WE WERE DOING BETTER THAN 70 BEFORE YOU JOINED, MAFUYU-SAN.
Dosukoi!

FLARE FLESHTONE FLARE PINK FLARE BLUE FLARE BLACK

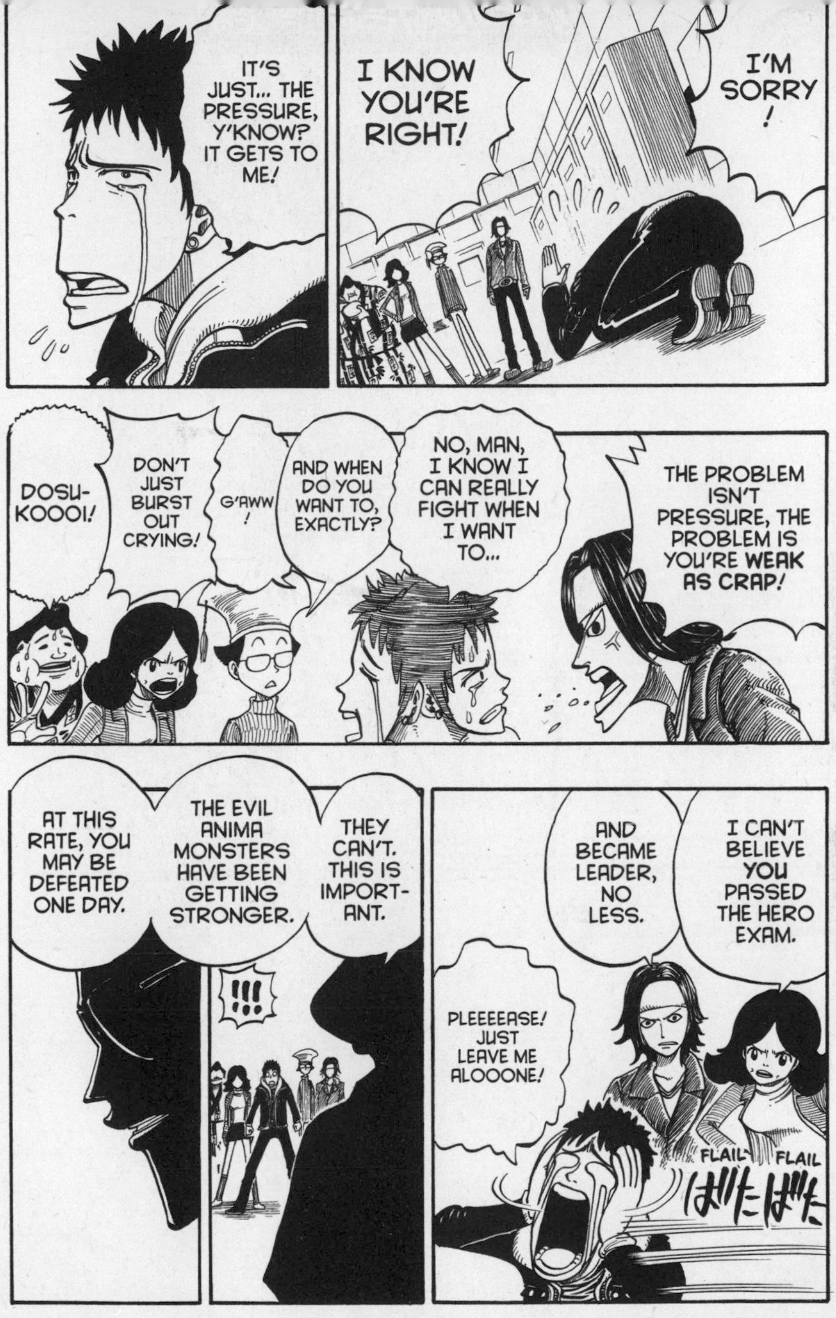
I'M SORRY!
I KNOW YOU'RE RIGHT!
IT'S JUST... THE PRESSURE, Y'KNOW? IT GETS TO ME!
THE PROBLEM ISN'T PRESSURE, THE PROBLEM IS YOU'RE WEAK AS CRAP!
NO, MAN, I KNOW I CAN REALLY FIGHT WHEN I WANT TO...
AND WHEN DO YOU WANT TO, EXACTLY?
G'AWW!
DON'T JUST BURST OUT CRYING!
DOSU-KOOOI!
I CAN'T BELIEVE YOU PASSED THE HERO EXAM.
AND BECAME LEADER, NO LESS.
PLEEEEASE! JUST LEAVE ME ALOOONE!
FLAIL FLAIL
ばたばた
THEY CAN'T. THIS IS IMPORT-ANT.
THE EVIL ANIMA MONSTERS HAVE BEEN GETTING STRONGER.
AT THIS RATE, YOU MAY BE DEFEATED ONE DAY.
!!!

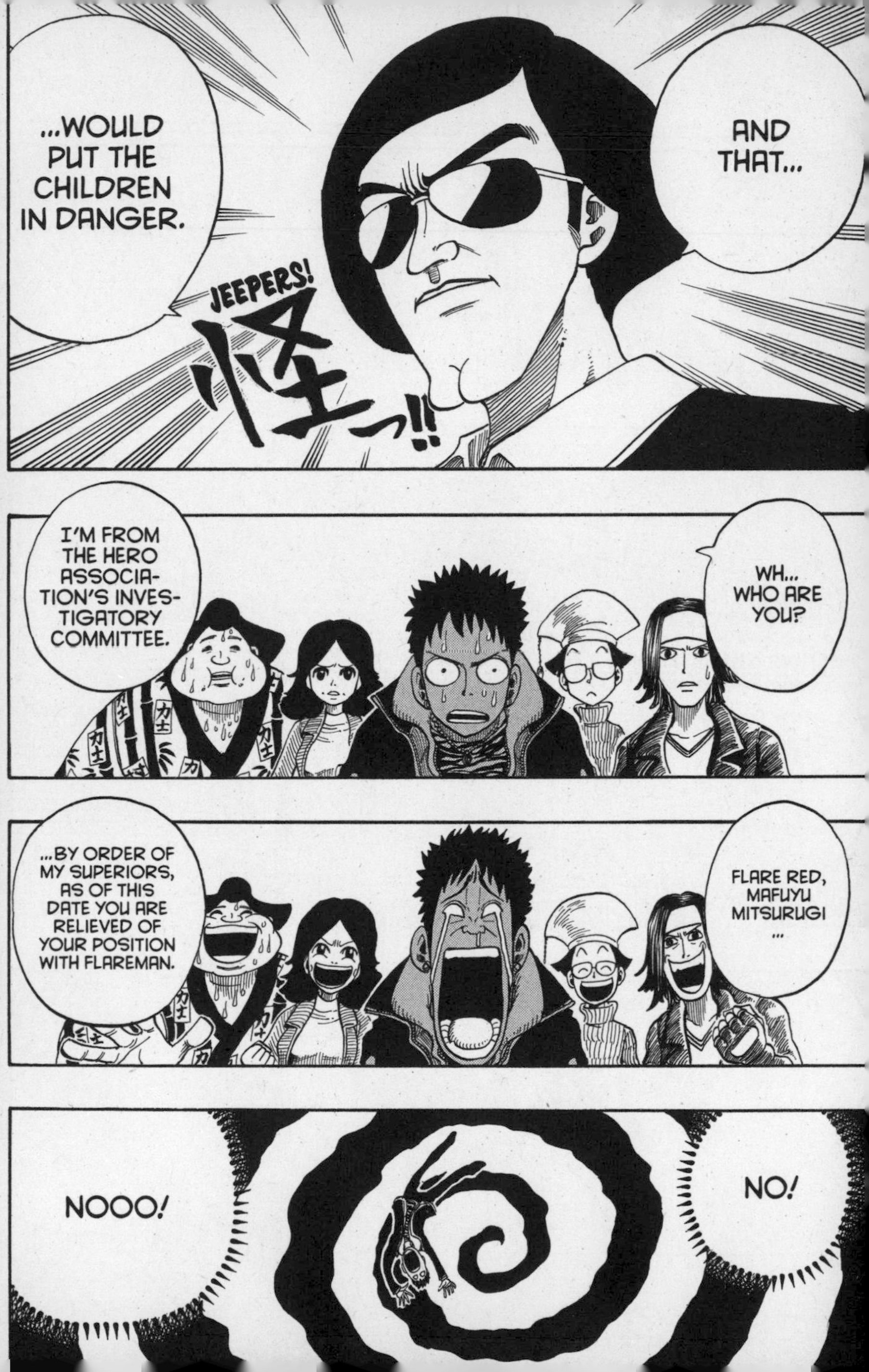
AND THAT...
...WOULD PUT THE CHILDREN IN DANGER.
JEEPERS!
怪っ!!
WH... WHO ARE YOU?
I'M FROM THE HERO ASSOCIATION'S INVESTIGATORY COMMITTEE.
FLARE RED, MAFUYU MITSURUGI ...
...BY ORDER OF MY SUPERIORS, AS OF THIS DATE YOU ARE RELIEVED OF YOUR POSITION WITH FLAREMAN.
NO!
NOOO!

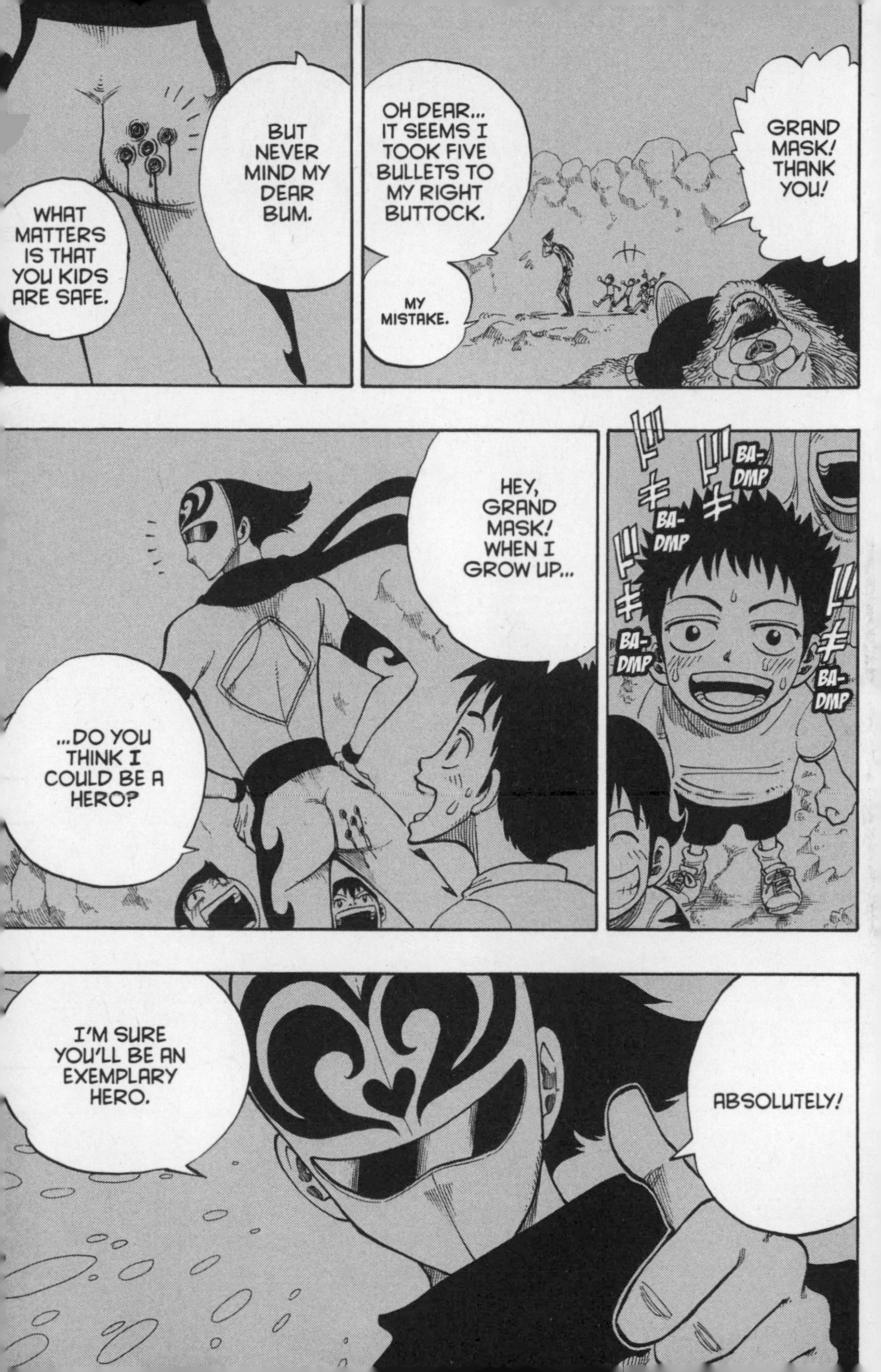
GRAND MASK! THANK YOU!
OH DEAR... IT SEEMS I TOOK FIVE BULLETS TO MY RIGHT BUTTOCK.
MY MISTAKE.
BUT NEVER MIND MY DEAR BUM.
WHAT MATTERS IS THAT YOU KIDS ARE SAFE.
BA-DMP
BA-DMP
BA-DMP
BA-DMP
HEY, GRAND MASK! WHEN I GROW UP...
...DO YOU THINK I COULD BE A HERO?
ABSOLUTELY!
I'M SURE YOU'LL BE AN EXEMPLARY HERO.

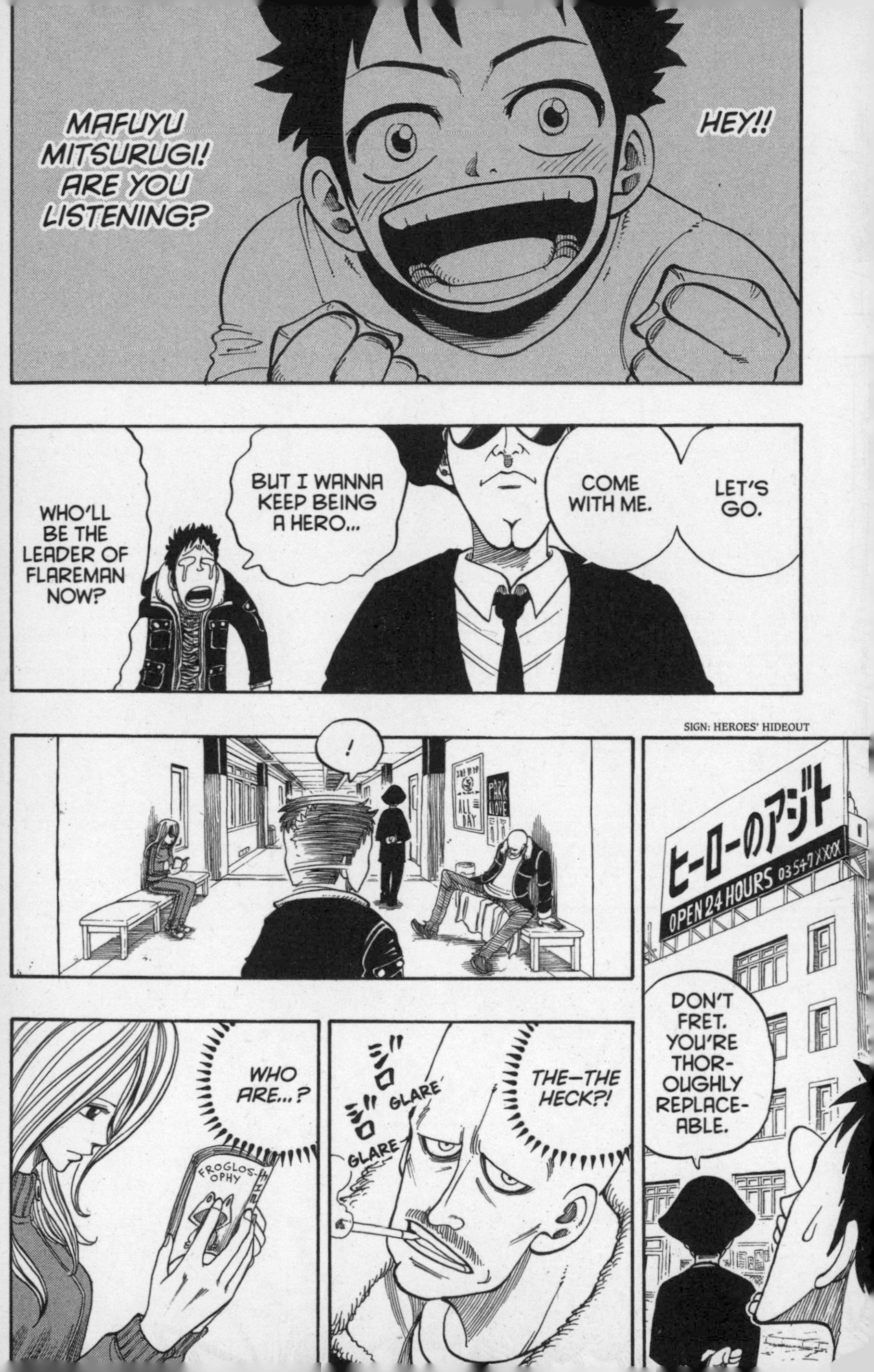
HEY!!
MAFUYU MITSURUGI! ARE YOU LISTENING?
LET'S GO.
COME WITH ME.
BUT I WANNA KEEP BEING A HERO...
WHO'LL BE THE LEADER OF FLAREMAN NOW?
SIGN: HEROES' HIDEOUT
ヒーローのアジト
OPEN 24 HOURS 03547XXXX
DON'T FRET. YOU'RE THOR-OUGHLY REPLACE-ABLE.
!
ALL DAY
PARK LOVE
THE—THE HECK?!
ジロ GLARE
ジロ GLARE
WHO ARE...?
FROGLOS-OPHY

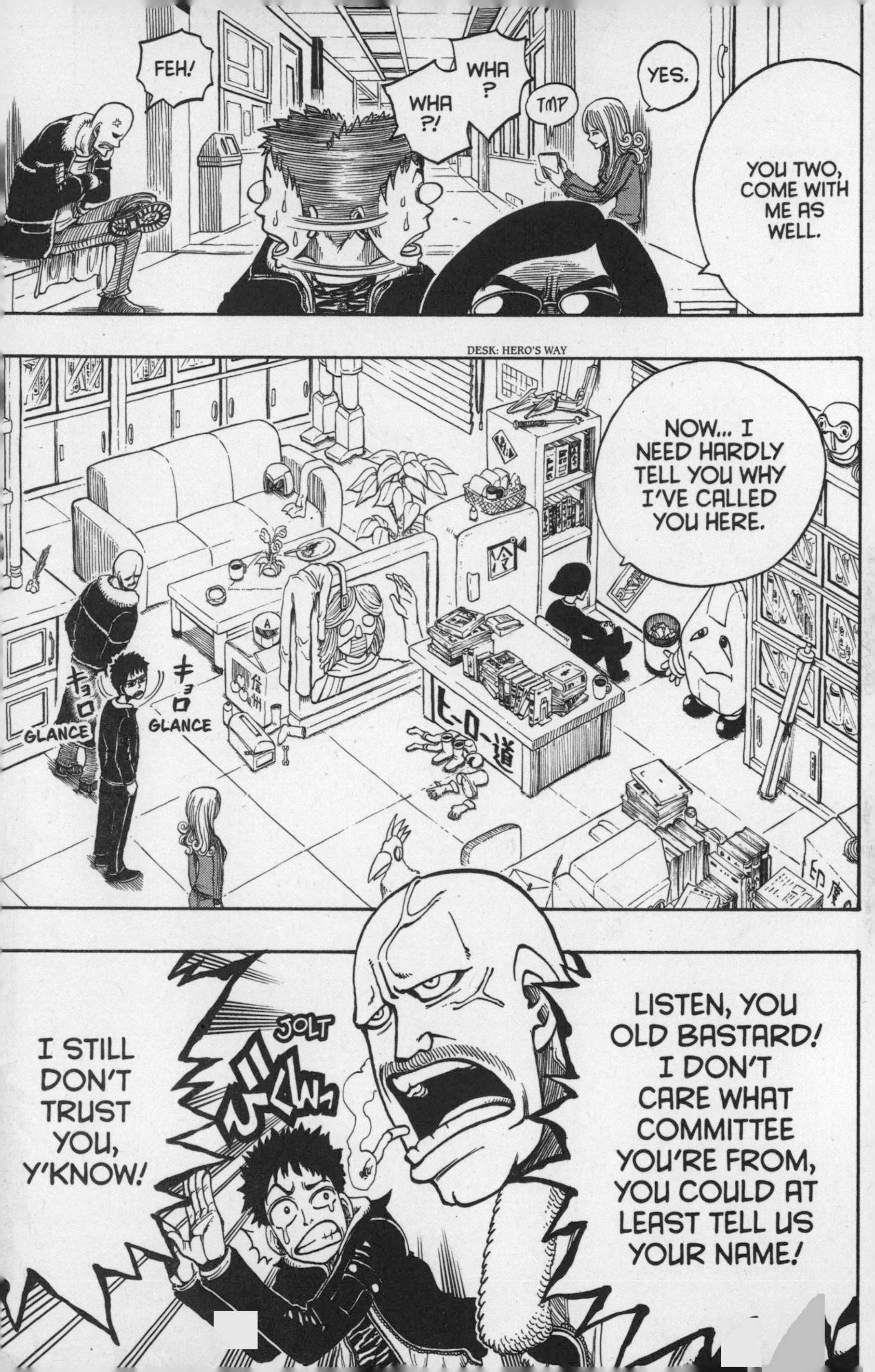
YOU TWO, COME WITH ME AS WELL.
YES.
TMP
WHA ?
WHA ?!
FEH!
DESK: HERO'S WAY
NOW... I NEED HARDLY TELL YOU WHY I'VE CALLED YOU HERE.
GLANCE
GLANCE
LISTEN, YOU OLD BASTARD! I DON'T CARE WHAT COMMITTEE YOU'RE FROM, YOU COULD AT LEAST TELL US YOUR NAME!
JOLT
I STILL DON'T TRUST YOU, Y'KNOW!

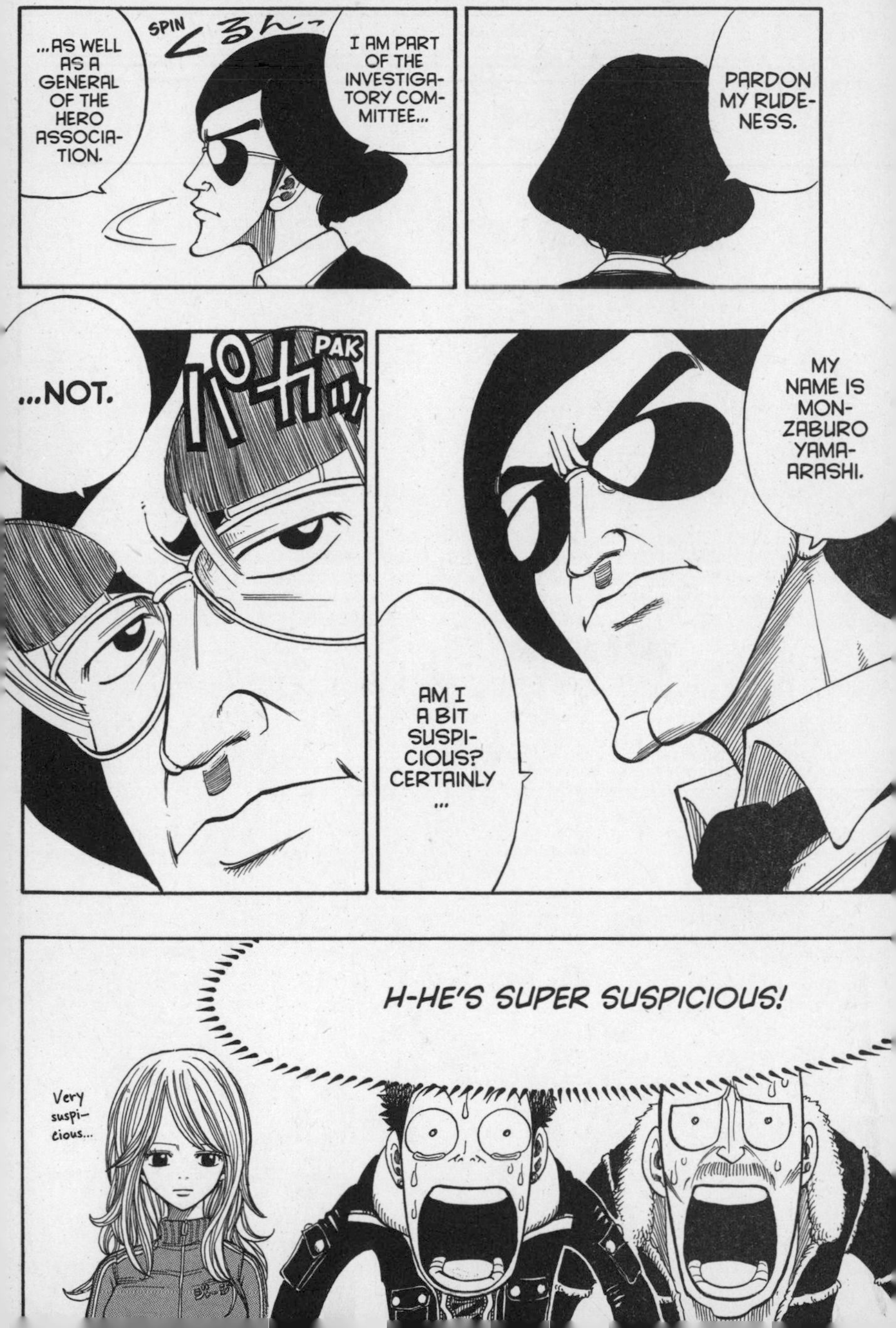
PARDON MY RUDENESS.
I AM PART OF THE INVESTIGATORY COMMITTEE...
SPIN くるん
...AS WELL AS A GENERAL OF THE HERO ASSOCIATION.
MY NAME IS MONZABURO YAMAARASHI.
AM I A BIT SUSPICIOUS? CERTAINLY...
PAK パカッ
...NOT.
H-HE'S SUPER SUSPICIOUS!
Very suspicious...

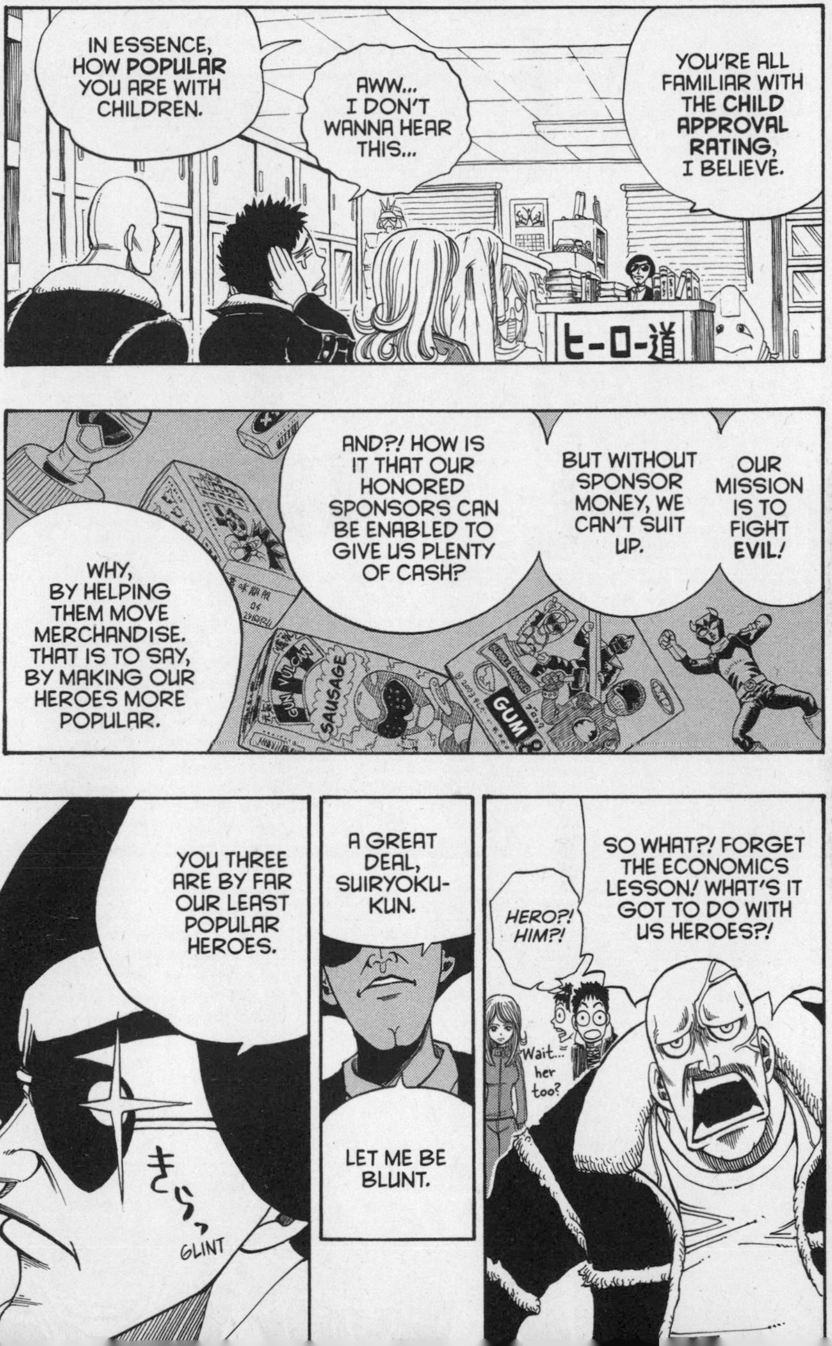
YOU'RE ALL FAMILIAR WITH THE CHILD APPROVAL RATING, I BELIEVE.
AWW... I DON'T WANNA HEAR THIS...
IN ESSENCE, HOW POPULAR YOU ARE WITH CHILDREN.
ヒーロー道
OUR MISSION IS TO FIGHT EVIL!
BUT WITHOUT SPONSOR MONEY, WE CAN'T SUIT UP.
AND?! HOW IS IT THAT OUR HONORED SPONSORS CAN BE ENABLED TO GIVE US PLENTY OF CASH?
WHY, BY HELPING THEM MOVE MERCHANDISE. THAT IS TO SAY, BY MAKING OUR HEROES MORE POPULAR.
SAUSAGE
GUM
SO WHAT?! FORGET THE ECONOMICS LESSON! WHAT'S IT GOT TO DO WITH US HEROES?!
HERO?! HIM?!
Wait... her too?
A GREAT DEAL, SUIRYOKU-KUN.
LET ME BE BLUNT.
YOU THREE ARE BY FAR OUR LEAST POPULAR HEROES.
POPULARITY
きらっ
GLINT

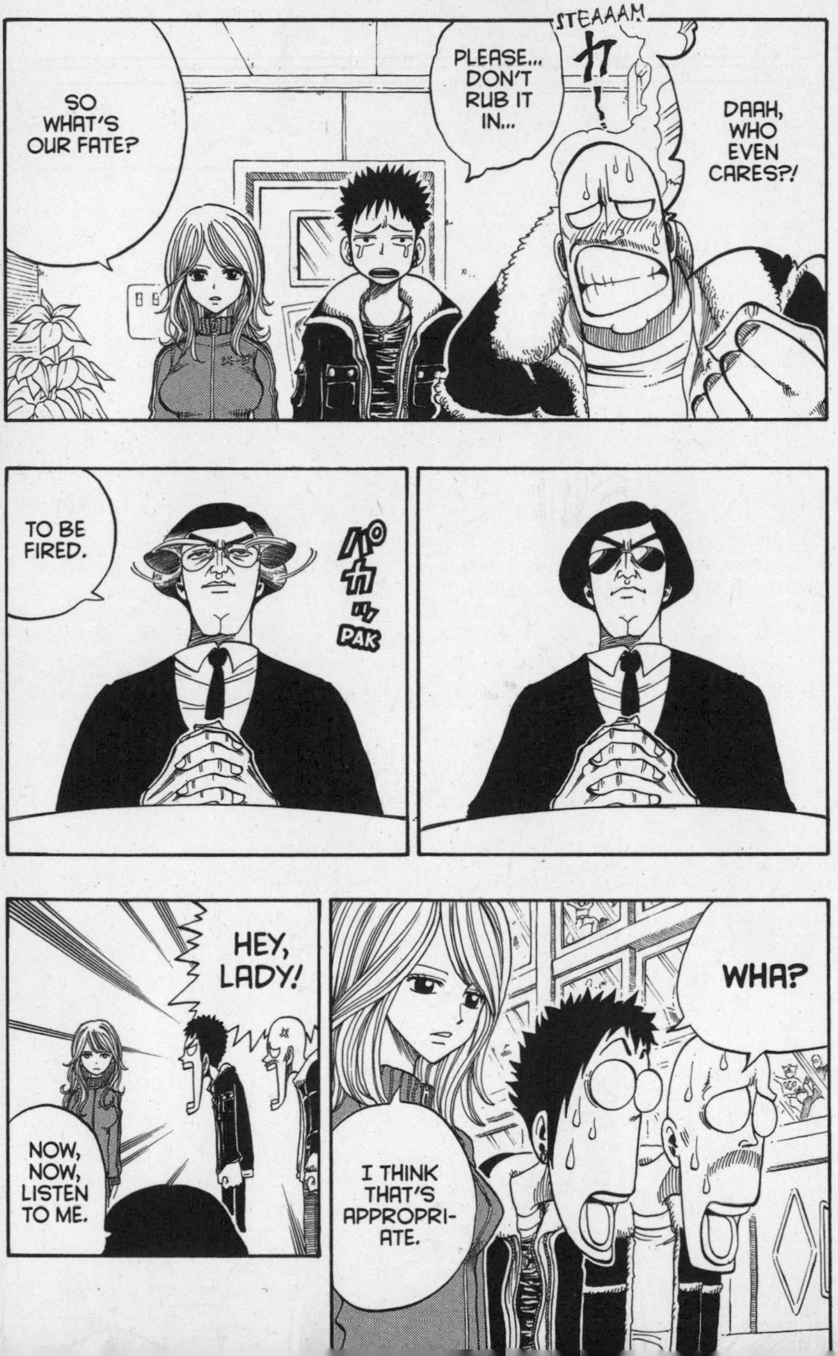
STEAAAM
DAAH, WHO EVEN CARES?!
PLEASE... DON'T RUB IT IN...
SO WHAT'S OUR FATE?
PAK
TO BE FIRED.
WHA?
I THINK THAT'S APPROPRI-ATE.
HEY, LADY!
NOW, NOW, LISTEN TO ME.

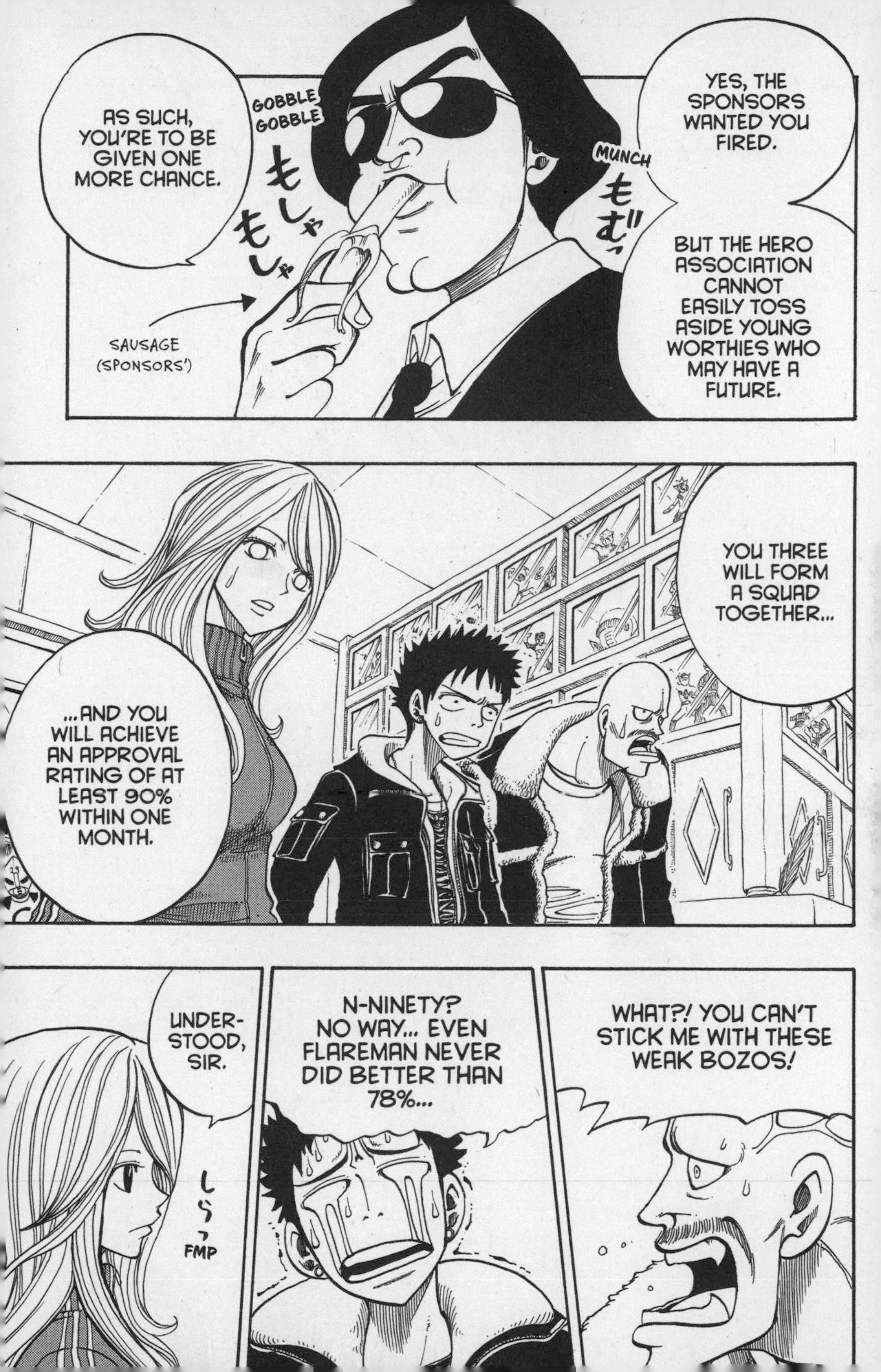

YES, THE SPONSORS WANTED YOU FIRED.
MUNCH
もむ
BUT THE HERO ASSOCIATION CANNOT EASILY TOSS ASIDE YOUNG WORTHIES WHO MAY HAVE A FUTURE.
GOBBLE GOBBLE
もしゃもしゃ
AS SUCH, YOU'RE TO BE GIVEN ONE MORE CHANCE.
SAUSAGE (SPONSORS')
YOU THREE WILL FORM A SQUAD TOGETHER...
...AND YOU WILL ACHIEVE AN APPROVAL RATING OF AT LEAST 90% WITHIN ONE MONTH.
WHAT?! YOU CAN'T STICK ME WITH THESE WEAK BOZOS!
N-NINETY? NO WAY... EVEN FLAREMAN NEVER DID BETTER THAN 78%...
UNDER-STOOD, SIR.
しらっ
FMP

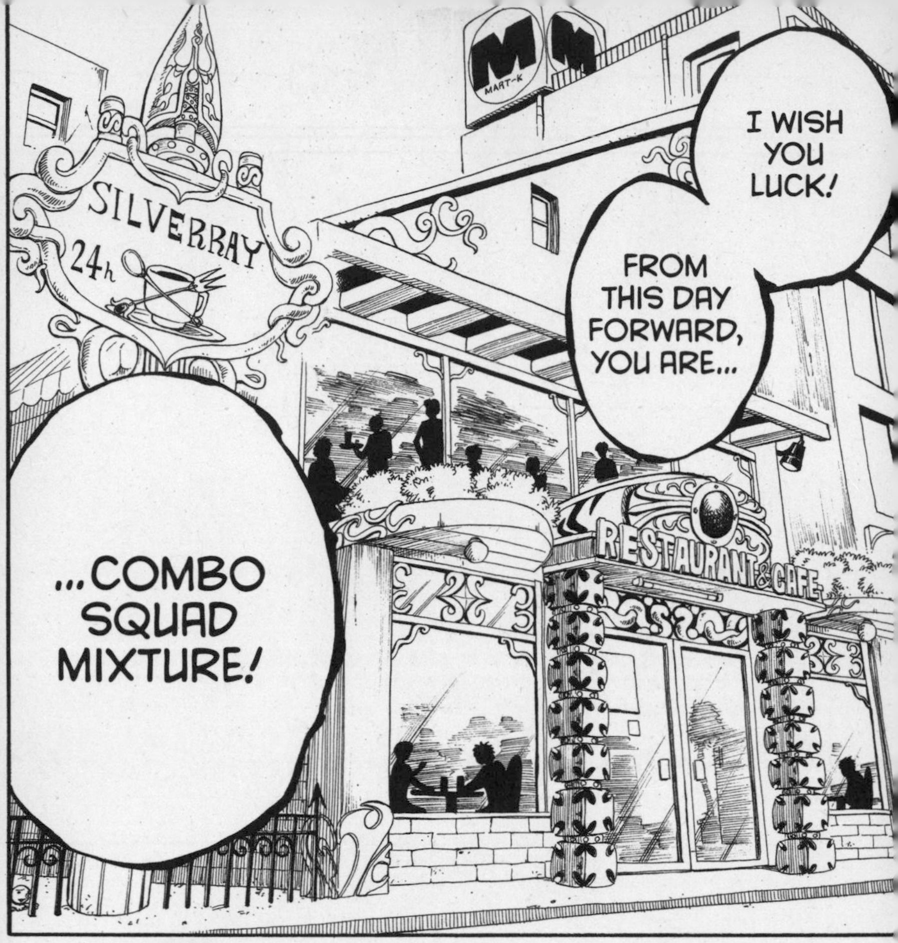
I WISH YOU LUCK!
FROM THIS DAY FORWARD, YOU ARE...
MART-K
SILVERRAY
24h
RESTAURANT & CAFE
...COMBO SQUAD MIXTURE!

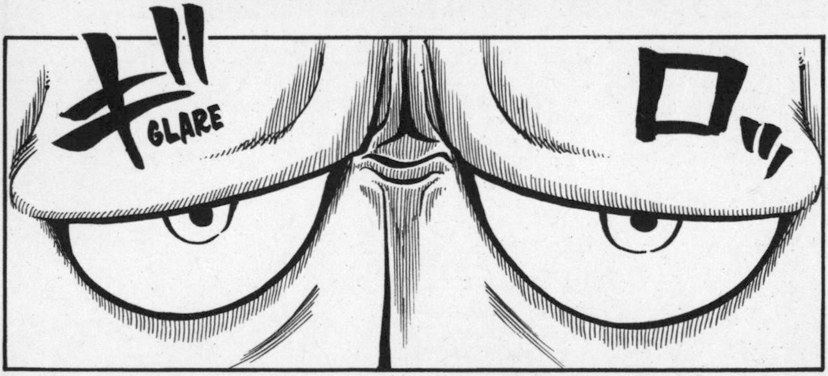
ギロッ
GLARE

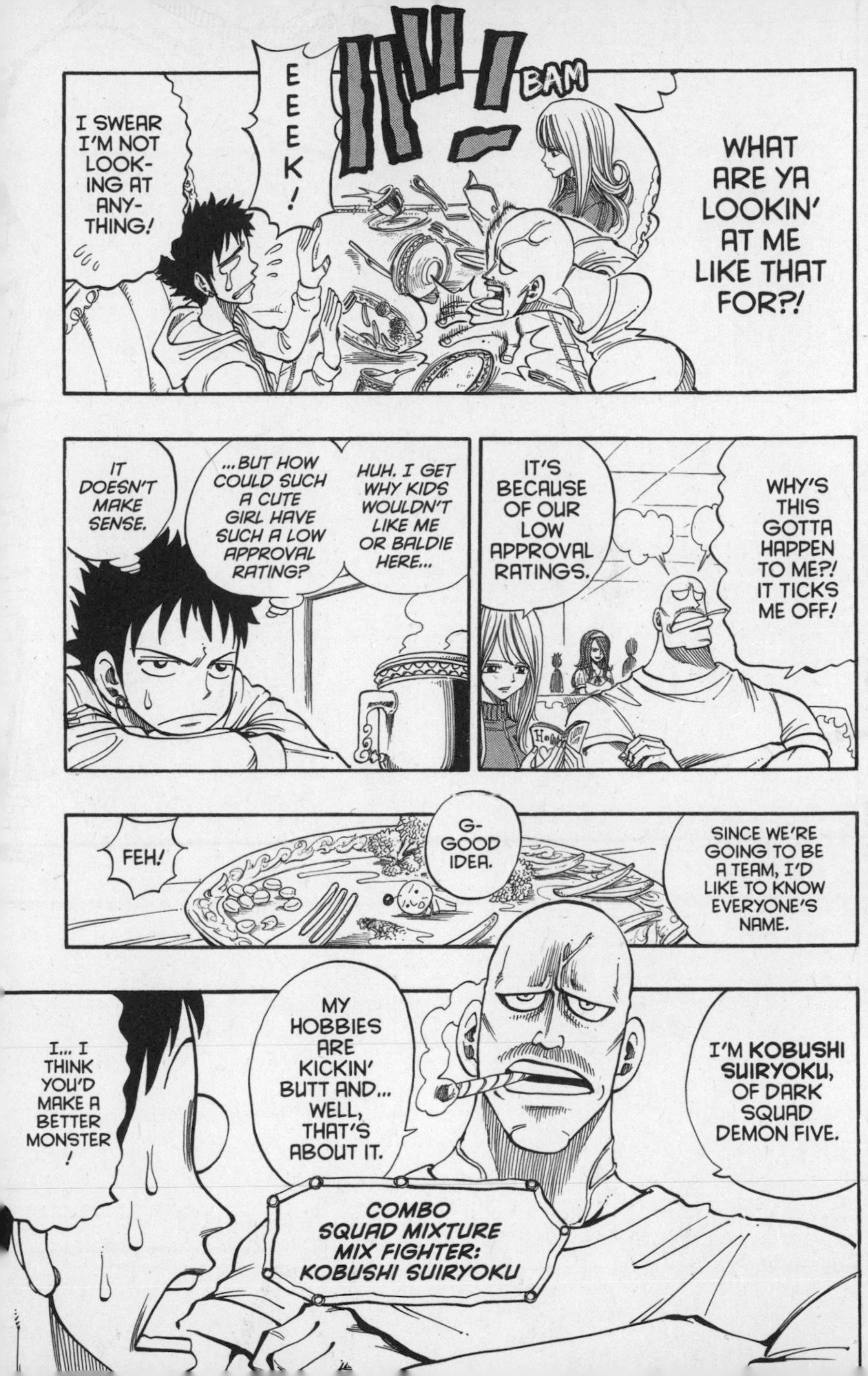
WHAT ARE YA LOOKIN' AT ME LIKE THAT FOR?!
BAM
EEEEK!
I SWEAR I'M NOT LOOKING AT ANYTHING!
WHY'S THIS GOTTA HAPPEN TO ME?! IT TICKS ME OFF!
IT'S BECAUSE OF OUR LOW APPROVAL RATINGS.
HUH. I GET WHY KIDS WOULDN'T LIKE ME OR BALDIE HERE...
...BUT HOW COULD SUCH A CUTE GIRL HAVE SUCH A LOW APPROVAL RATING?
IT DOESN'T MAKE SENSE.
SINCE WE'RE GOING TO BE A TEAM, I'D LIKE TO KNOW EVERYONE'S NAME.
G-GOOD IDEA.
FEH!
I'M KOBUSHI SUIRYOKU, OF DARK SQUAD DEMON FIVE.
MY HOBBIES ARE KICKIN' BUTT AND... WELL, THAT'S ABOUT IT.
COMBO SQUAD MIXTURE MIX FIGHTER: KOBUSHI SUIRYOKU
I... I THINK YOU'D MAKE A BETTER MONSTER!

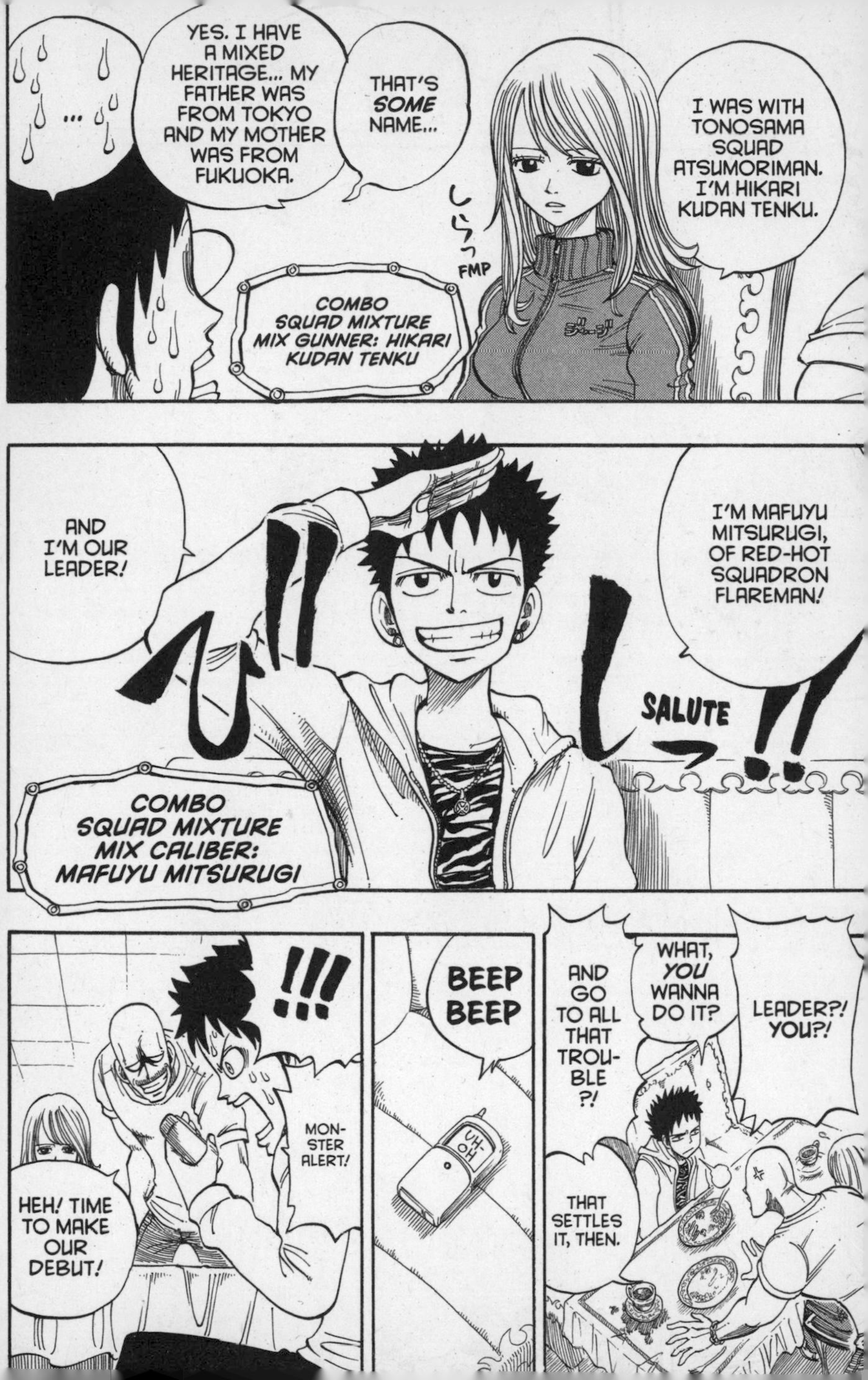
I WAS WITH TONOSAMA SQUAD ATSUMORIMAN. I'M HIKARI KUDAN TENKU.
FMP
THAT'S *SOME* NAME...
YES. I HAVE A MIXED HERITAGE... MY FATHER WAS FROM TOKYO AND MY MOTHER WAS FROM FUKUOKA.
...
COMBO SQUAD MIXTURE MIX GUNNER: HIKARI KUDAN TENKU
I'M MAFUYU MITSURUGI, OF RED-HOT SQUADRON FLAREMAN!
AND I'M OUR LEADER!
SALUTE
COMBO SQUAD MIXTURE MIX CALIBER: MAFUYU MITSURUGI
LEADER?! YOU?!
WHAT, *YOU* WANNA DO IT?
AND GO TO ALL THAT TROUBLE?!
THAT SETTLES IT, THEN.
BEEP BEEP
UH-OH
!!!
MONSTER ALERT!
HEH! TIME TO MAKE OUR DEBUT!

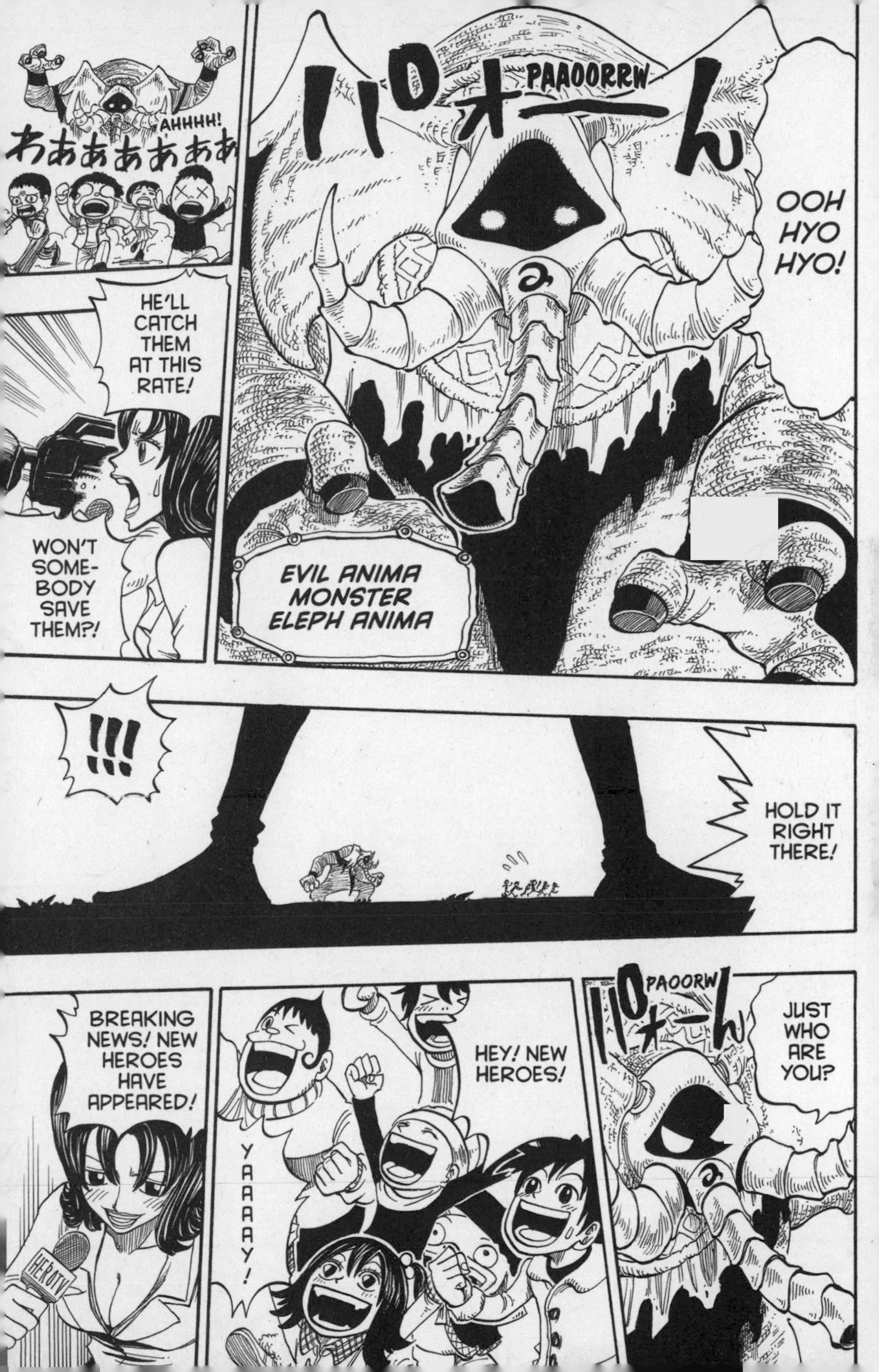
パオーん
PAAOORRW
OOH HYO HYO!
EVIL ANIMA MONSTER ELEPH ANIMA
AHHHH!
わああああああ
HE'LL CATCH THEM AT THIS RATE!
WON'T SOME-BODY SAVE THEM?!
HOLD IT RIGHT THERE!
!!!
パオーん
PAOORW
JUST WHO ARE YOU?
HEY! NEW HEROES!
YAAAAAY!
BREAKING NEWS! NEW HEROES HAVE APPEARED!
HERO TV

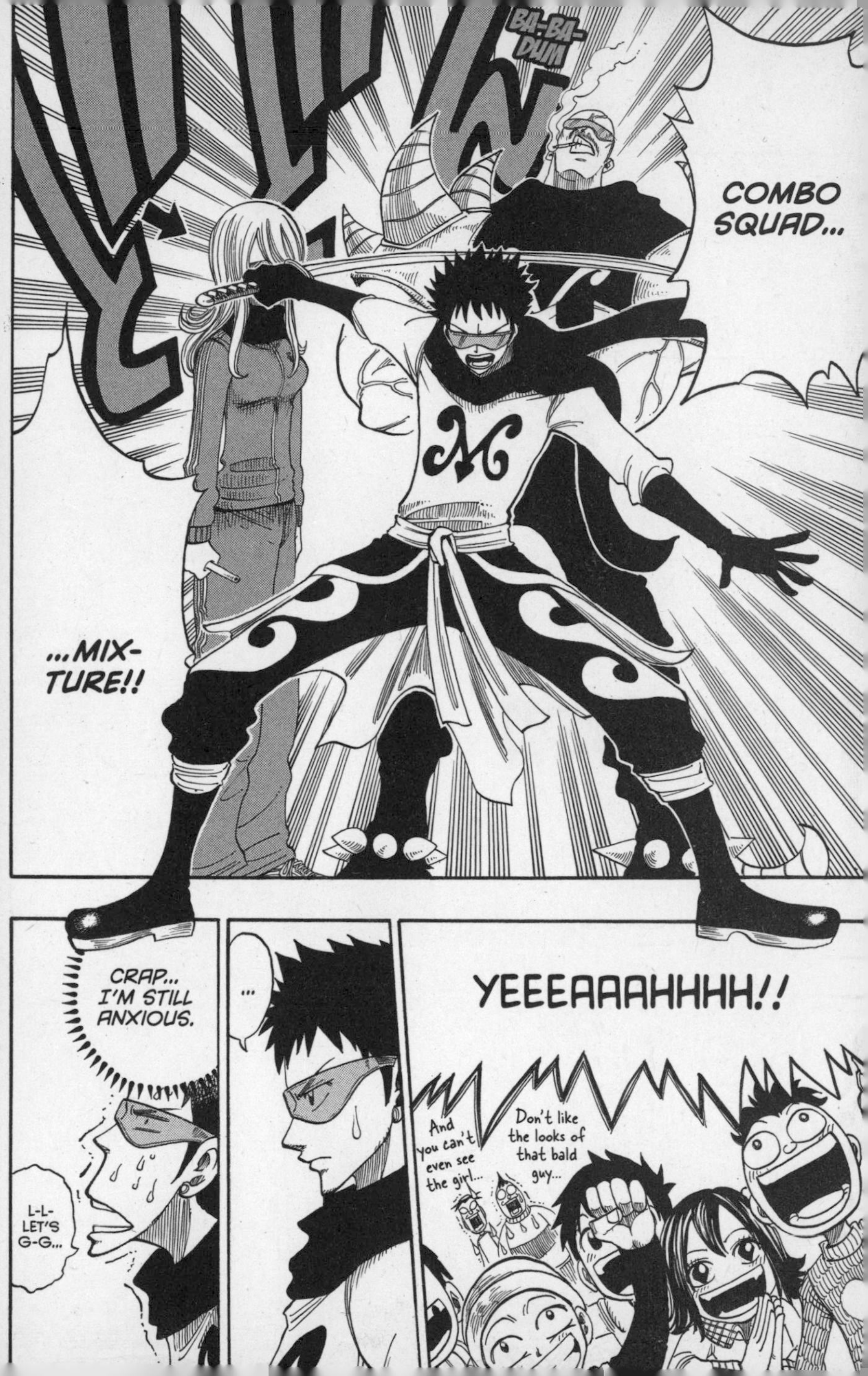
BA-BA-DUM
COMBO SQUAD...
...MIX-TURE!!
YEEEAAAHHHH!!
Don't like the looks of that bald guy...
And you can't even see the girl...
...
CRAP... I'M STILL ANXIOUS.
L-L-LET'S G-G...

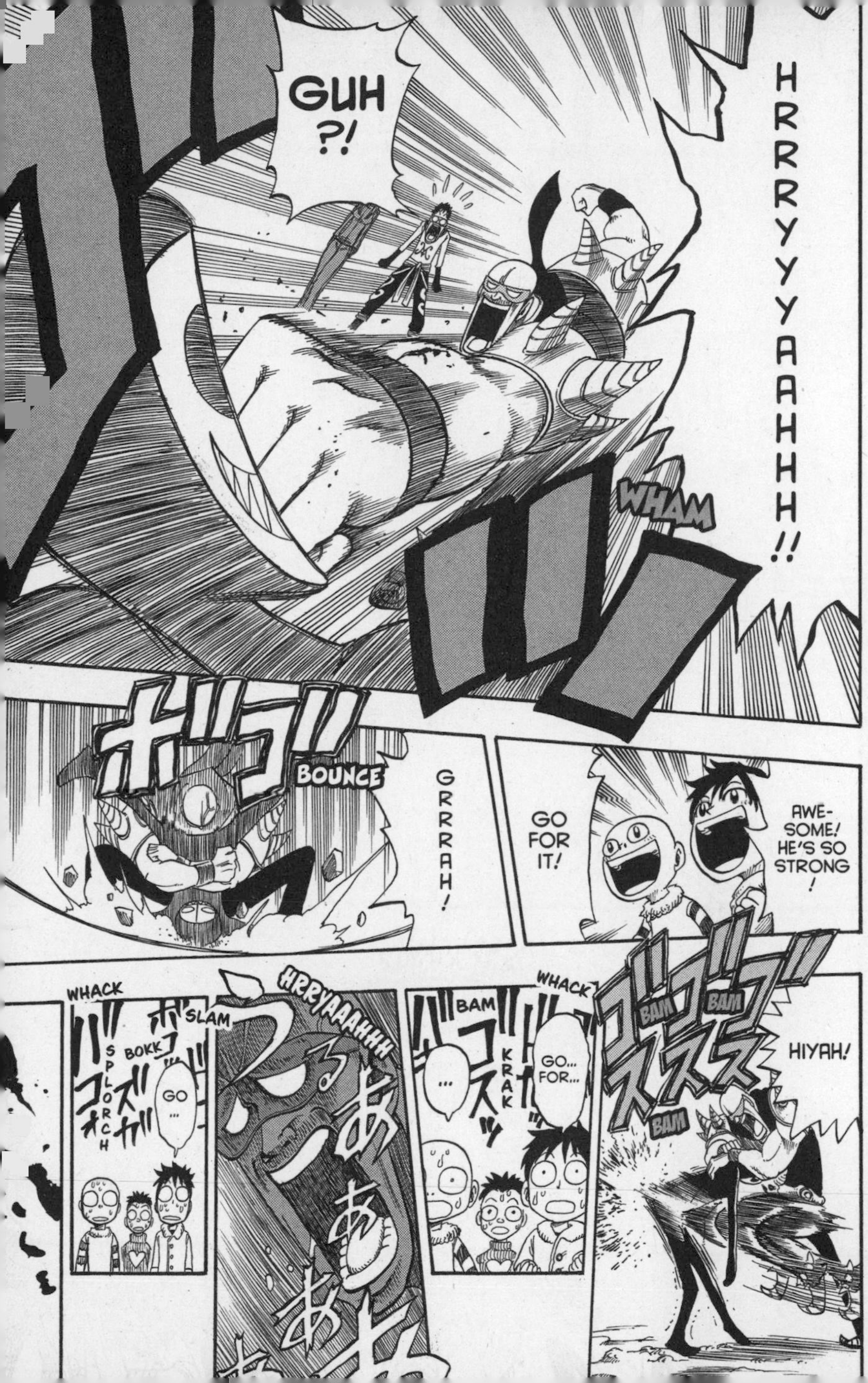
HRRRYYYAAHHHH!!
WHAM
GUH ?!
AWE-SOME! HE'S SO STRONG!
GO FOR IT!
GRRRAH!
BOUNCE
HIYAH!
BAM
BAM
BAM
GO... FOR...
WHACK
KRAK
BAM
...
HRRYAAAHHHH
GO ...
SLAM
BOKK
WHACK
SPLORCH

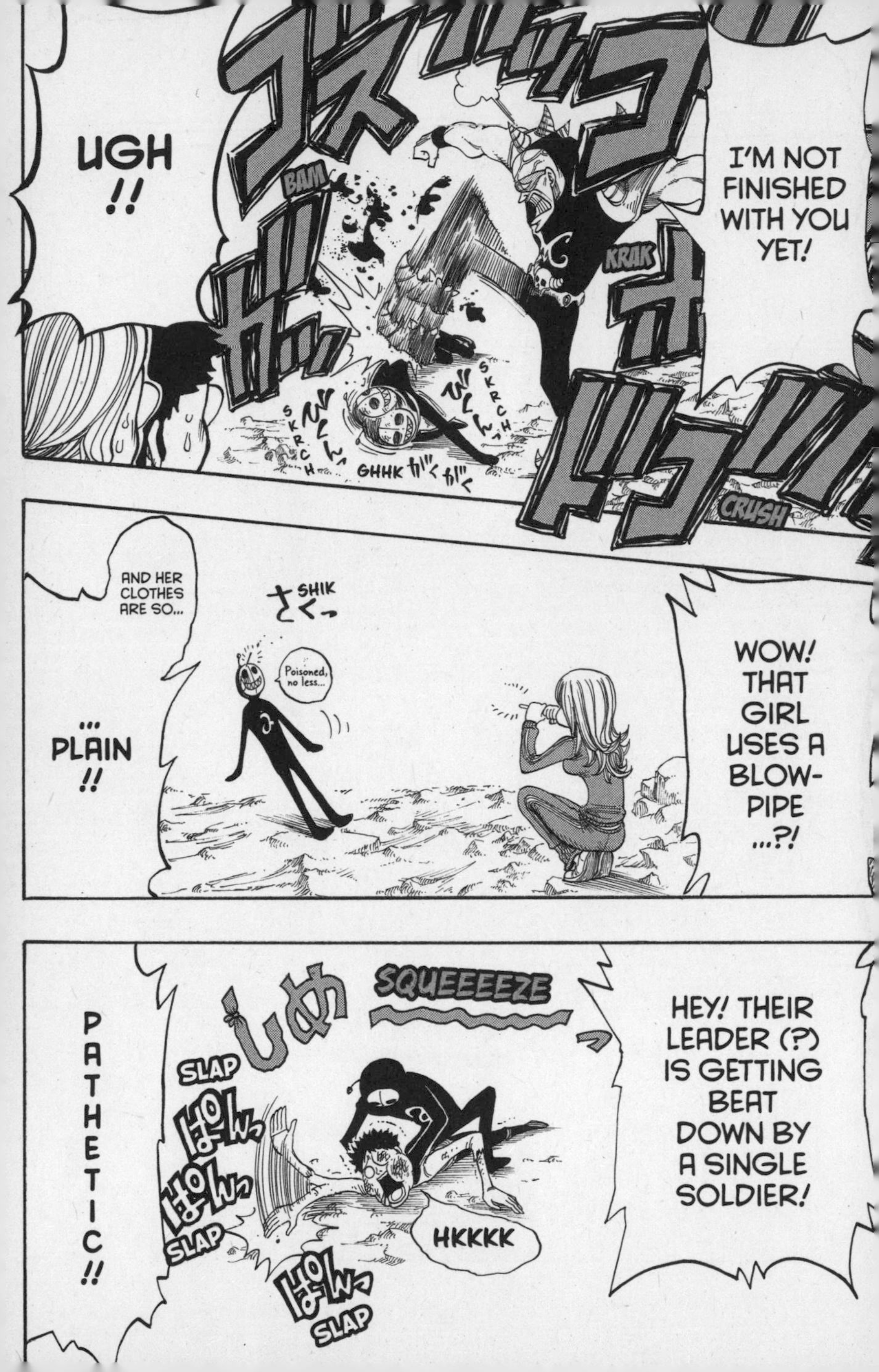
I'M NOT FINISHED WITH YOU YET!
KRAK
BAM
CRUSH
SKRCH
SKRCH
GHHK
UGH!!
WOW! THAT GIRL USES A SINGLE BLOW-PIPE ...?!
SHIK
Poisoned, no less...
AND HER CLOTHES ARE SO...
...PLAIN!!
HEY! THEIR LEADER (?) IS GETTING BEAT DOWN BY A SINGLE SOLDIER!
SQUEEEEEZE
SLAP
SLAP
HKKKK
SLAP
PATHETIC!!

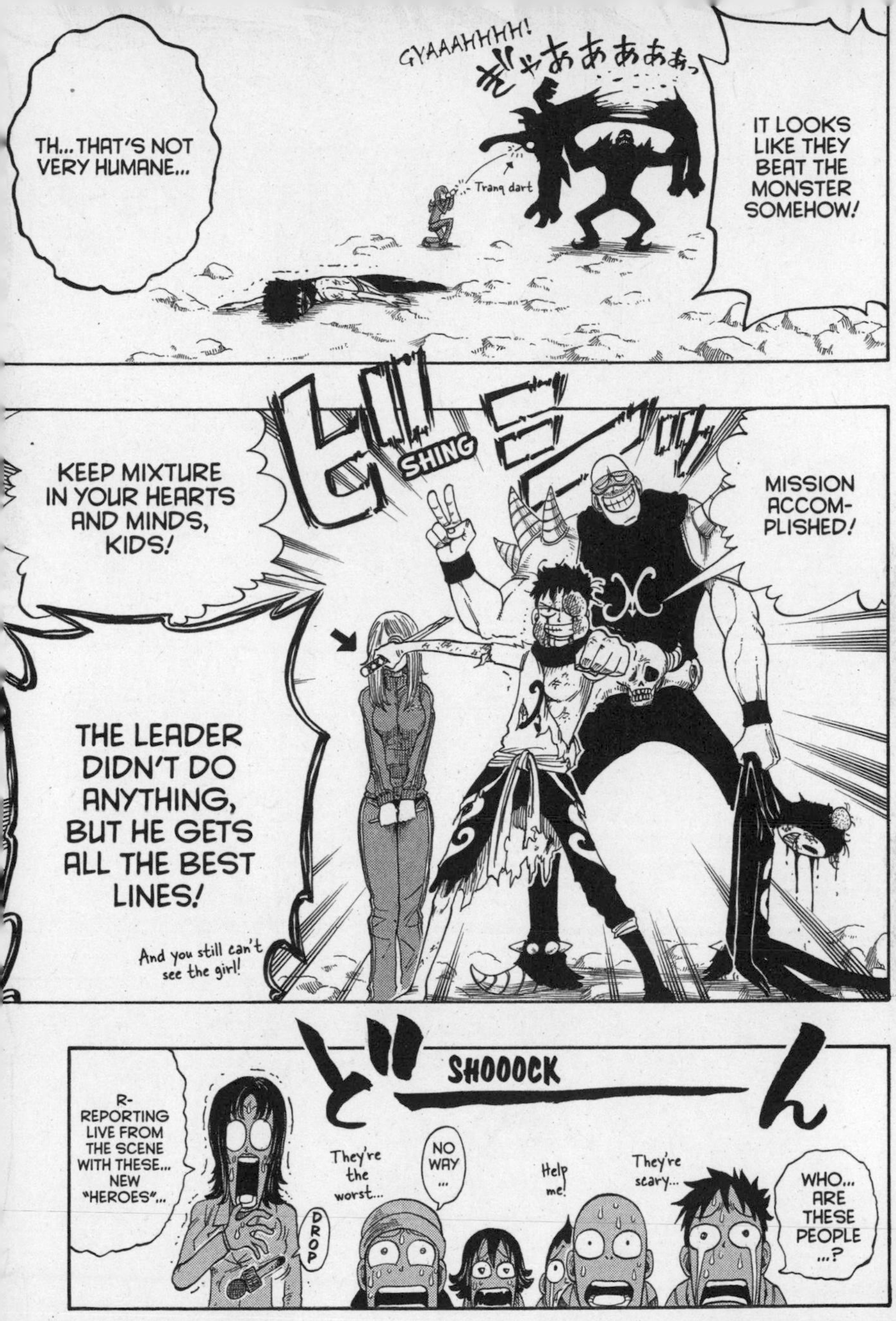
IT LOOKS LIKE THEY BEAT THE MONSTER SOMEHOW!
GYAAAHHHH!
ぎゃあああああっ
Tranq dart
TH...THAT'S NOT VERY HUMANE...
SHING
MISSION ACCOM-PLISHED!
KEEP MIXTURE IN YOUR HEARTS AND MINDS, KIDS!
THE LEADER DIDN'T DO ANYTHING, BUT HE GETS ALL THE BEST LINES!
And you still can't see the girl!
SHOOOCK
WHO... ARE THESE PEOPLE ...?
They're scary...
Help me!
NO WAY ...
They're the worst...
DROP
R-REPORTING LIVE FROM THE SCENE WITH THESE... NEW "HEROES"...

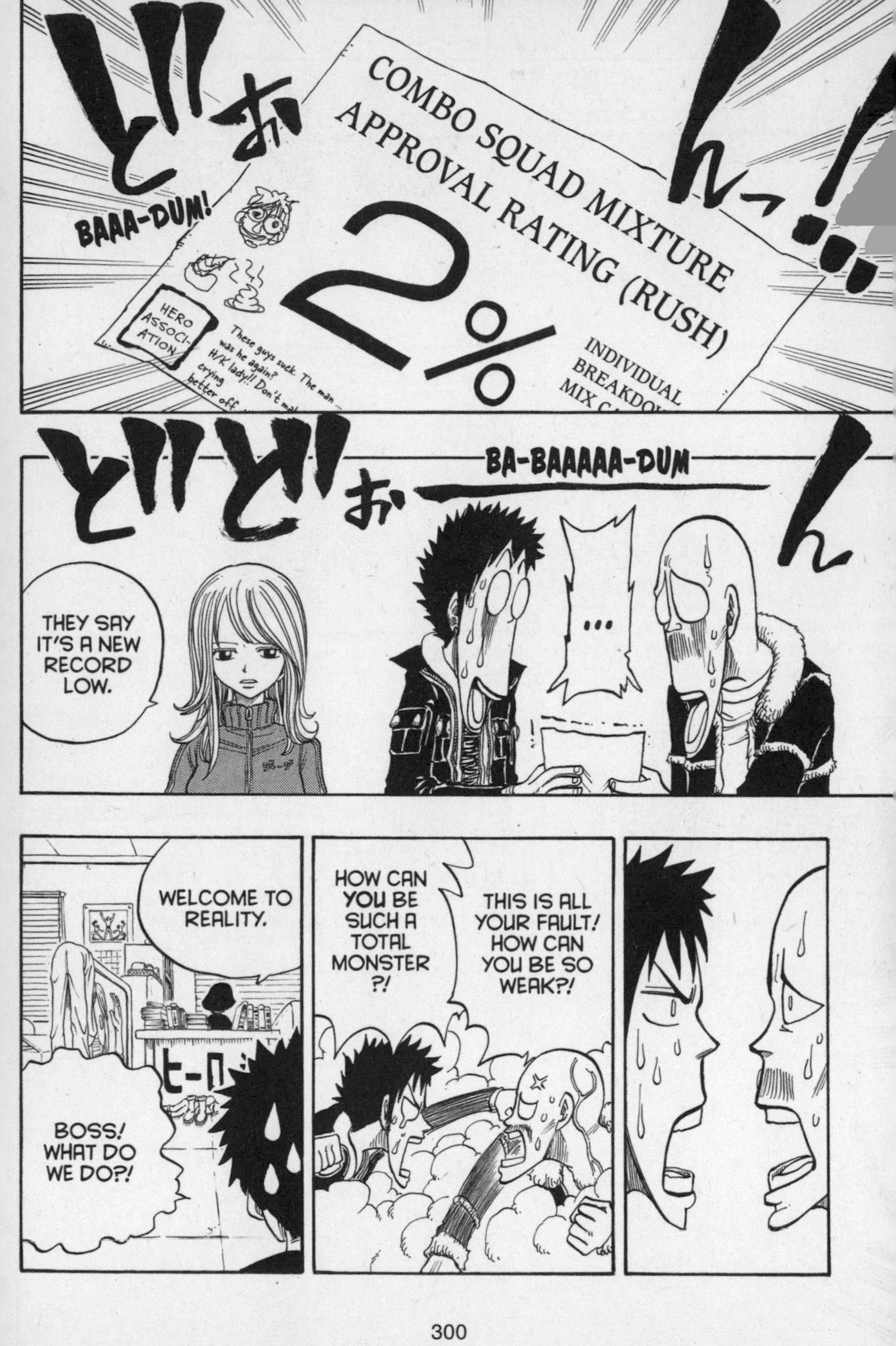
COMBO SQUAD MIXTURE APPROVAL RATING (RUSH)
2%
BAAA-DUM!
HERO ASSOCIATION
These guys suck. The man ... was he again?
H/K lady!! Don't
crying
INDIVIDUAL
BA-BAAAAA-DUM
...
THEY SAY IT'S A NEW RECORD LOW.
THIS IS ALL YOUR FAULT! HOW CAN YOU BE SO WEAK?!
HOW CAN YOU BE SUCH A TOTAL MONSTER?!
WELCOME TO REALITY.
BOSS! WHAT DO WE DO?!

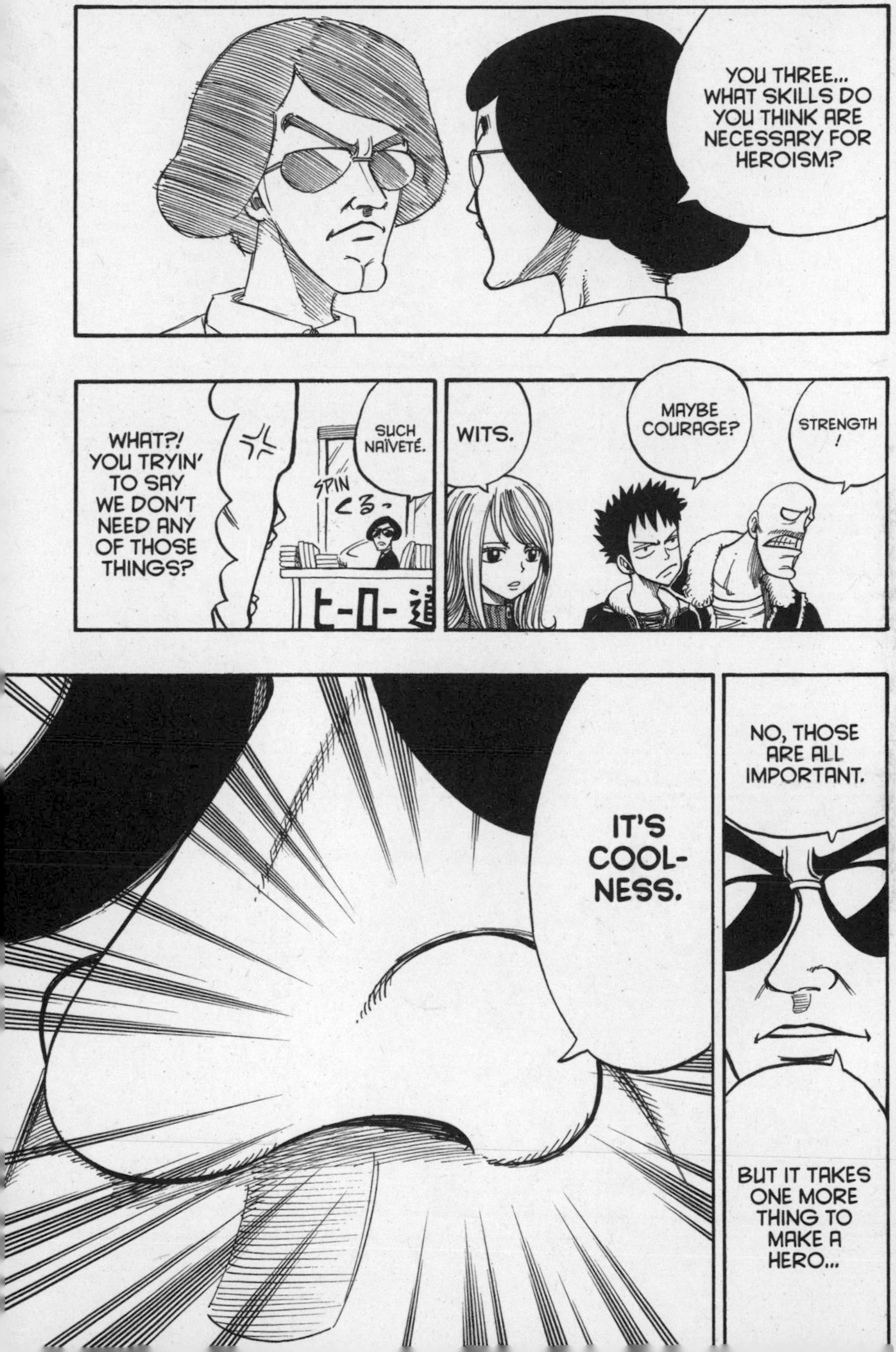
YOU THREE... WHAT SKILLS DO YOU THINK ARE NECESSARY FOR HEROISM?
STRENGTH!
MAYBE COURAGE?
WITS.
SUCH NAÏVETÉ.
SPIN
くるっ
ヒーロー道
WHAT?! YOU TRYIN' TO SAY WE DON'T NEED ANY OF THOSE THINGS?
NO, THOSE ARE ALL IMPORTANT.
BUT IT TAKES ONE MORE THING TO MAKE A HERO...
IT'S COOL-NESS.

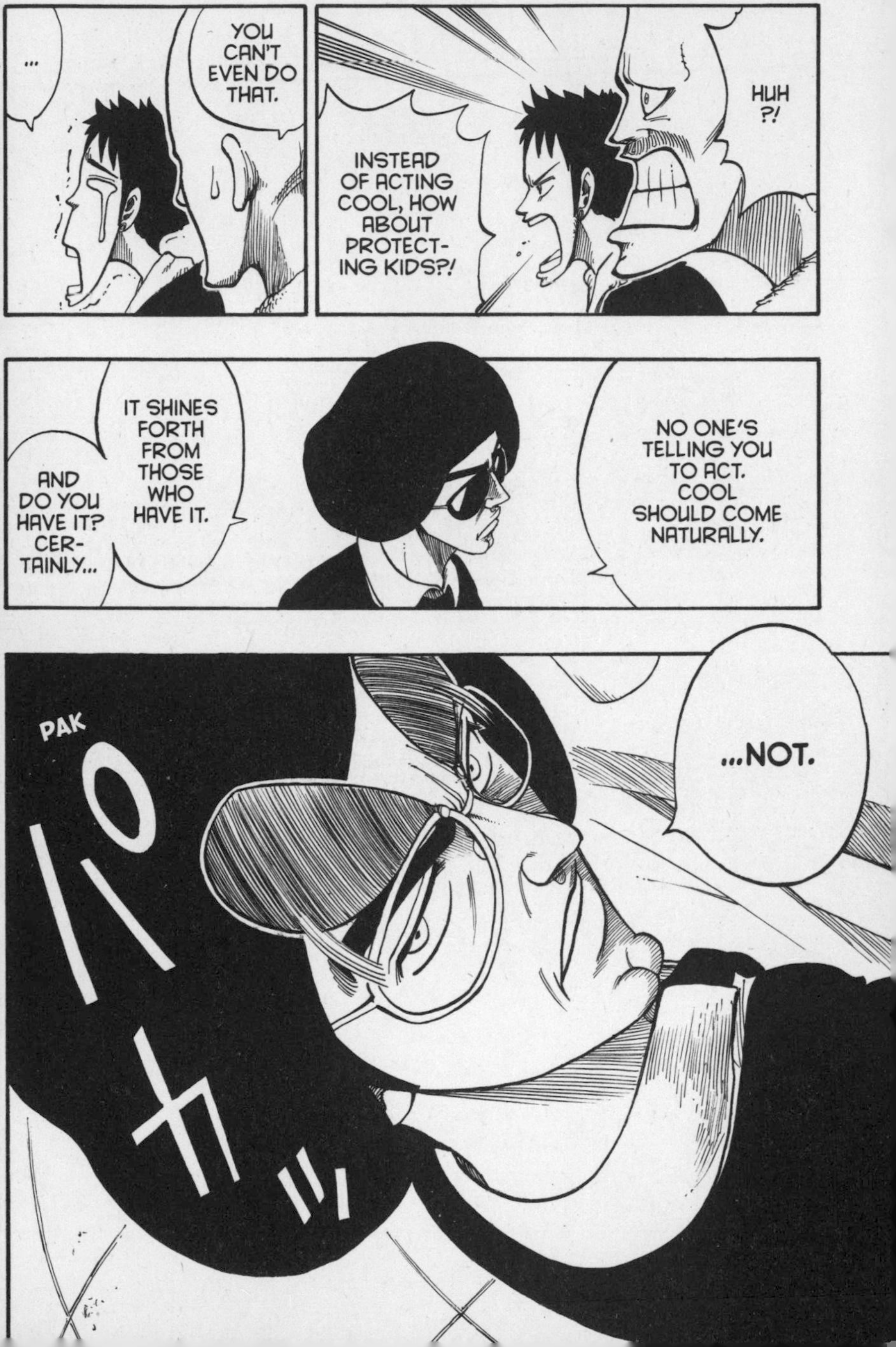
HUH ?!
INSTEAD OF ACTING COOL, HOW ABOUT PROTECTING KIDS?!
YOU CAN'T EVEN DO THAT.
...
NO ONE'S TELLING YOU TO ACT. COOL SHOULD COME NATURALLY.
IT SHINES FORTH FROM THOSE WHO HAVE IT.
AND DO YOU HAVE IT? CERTAINLY...
...NOT.
PAK
パチッ

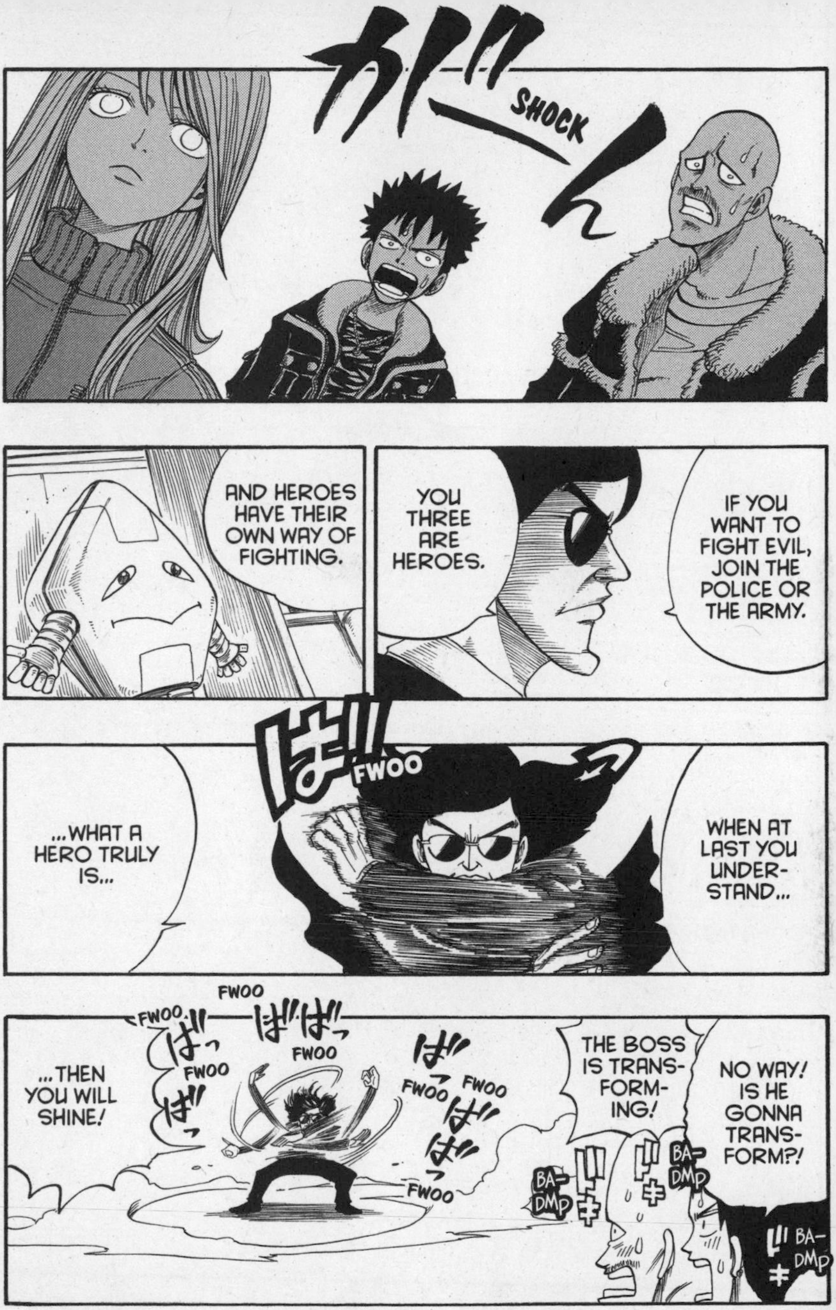
SHOCK
IF YOU WANT TO FIGHT EVIL, JOIN THE POLICE OR THE ARMY.
YOU THREE ARE HEROES.
AND HEROES HAVE THEIR OWN WAY OF FIGHTING.
FWOO
WHEN AT LAST YOU UNDER-STAND...
...WHAT A HERO TRULY IS...
NO WAY! IS HE GONNA TRANS-FORM?!
THE BOSS IS TRANS-FORM-ING!
BA-DMP
BA-DMP
BA-DMP
FWOO
FWOO
FWOO
FWOO
FWOO
FWOO
FWOO
...THEN YOU WILL SHINE!

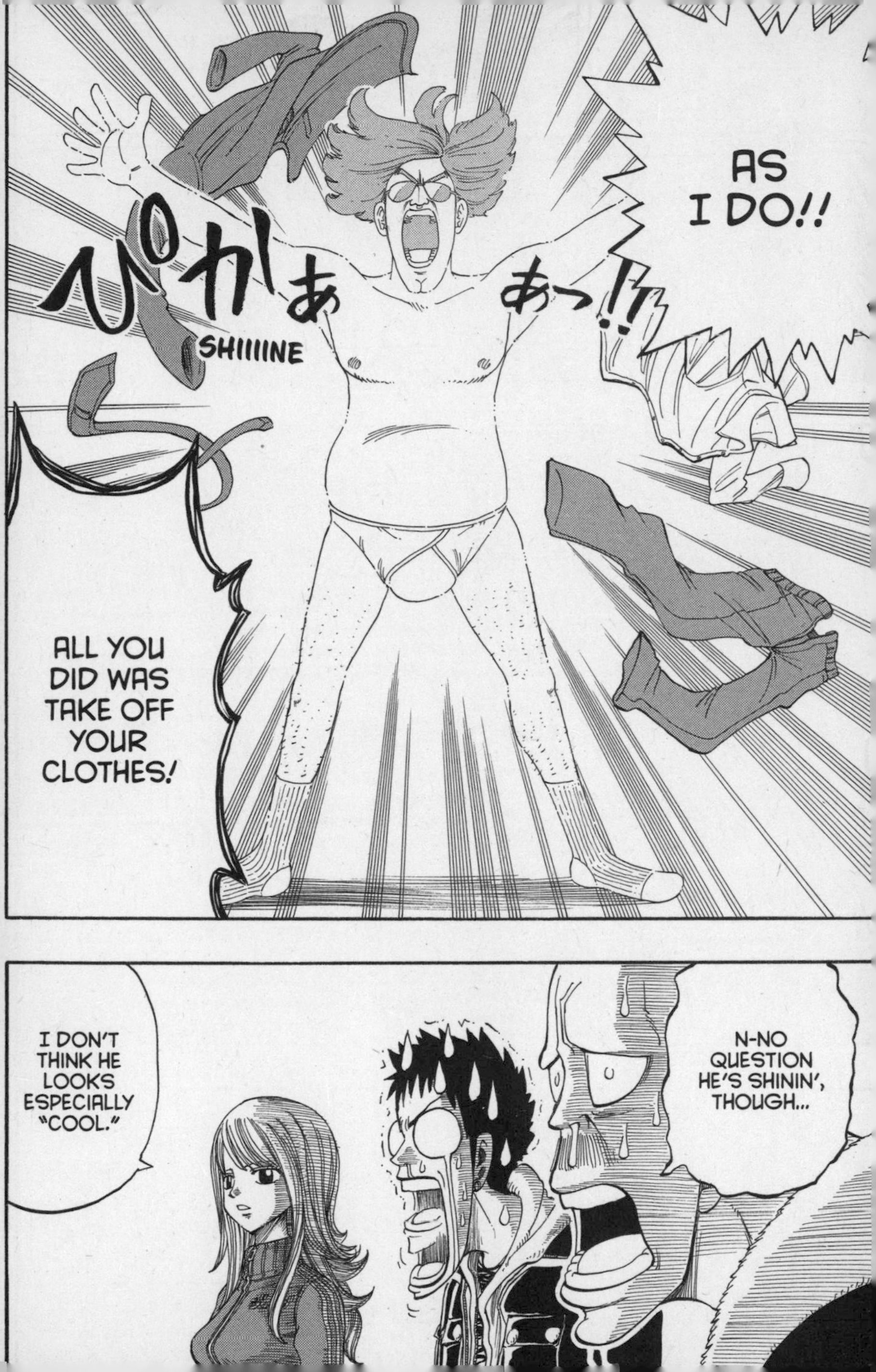
AS I DO!!
ぴかああっ!!
SHIIIINE
ALL YOU DID WAS TAKE OFF YOUR CLOTHES!
N-NO QUESTION HE'S SHININ', THOUGH...
I DON'T THINK HE LOOKS ESPECIALLY "COOL."

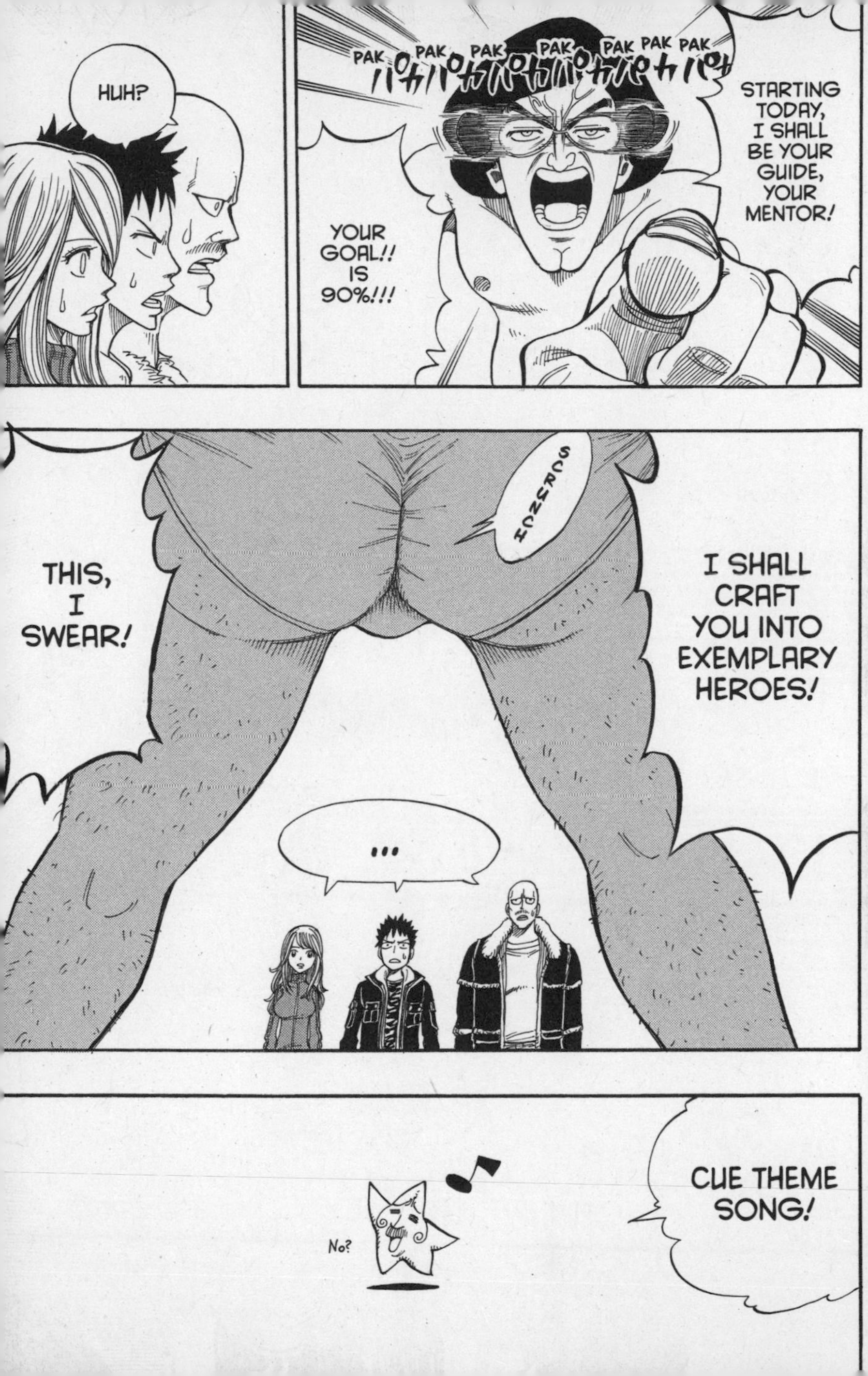
PAK PAK PAK PAK PAK PAK PAK
STARTING TODAY, I SHALL BE YOUR GUIDE, YOUR MENTOR!
YOUR GOAL!! IS 90%!!!
HUH?
I SHALL CRAFT YOU INTO EXEMPLARY HEROES!
SCRUNCH
THIS, I SWEAR!
...
CUE THEME SONG!
No?

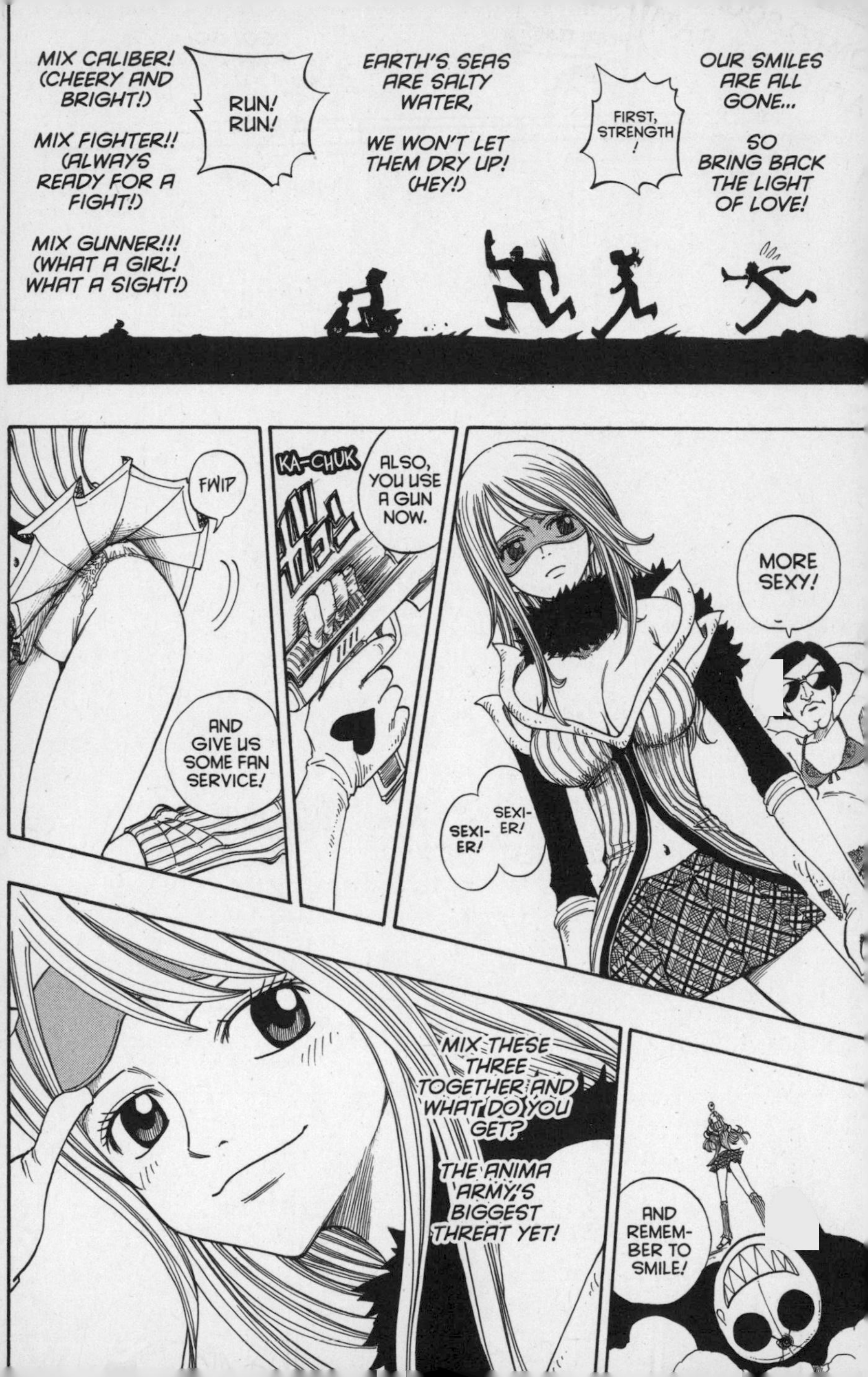
OUR SMILES ARE ALL GONE...
SO BRING BACK THE LIGHT OF LOVE!
FIRST, STRENGTH!
EARTH'S SEAS ARE SALTY WATER,
WE WON'T LET THEM DRY UP! (HEY!)
RUN! RUN!
MIX CALIBER! (CHEERY AND BRIGHT!)
MIX FIGHTER!! (ALWAYS READY FOR A FIGHT!)
MIX GUNNER!!! (WHAT A GIRL! WHAT A SIGHT!)
MORE SEXY!
SEXIER!
SEXIER!
KA-CHUK
ALSO, YOU USE A GUN NOW.
FWIP
AND GIVE US SOME FAN SERVICE!
AND REMEMBER TO SMILE!
MIX THESE THREE TOGETHER AND WHAT DO YOU GET?
THE ANIMA ARMY'S BIGGEST THREAT YET!

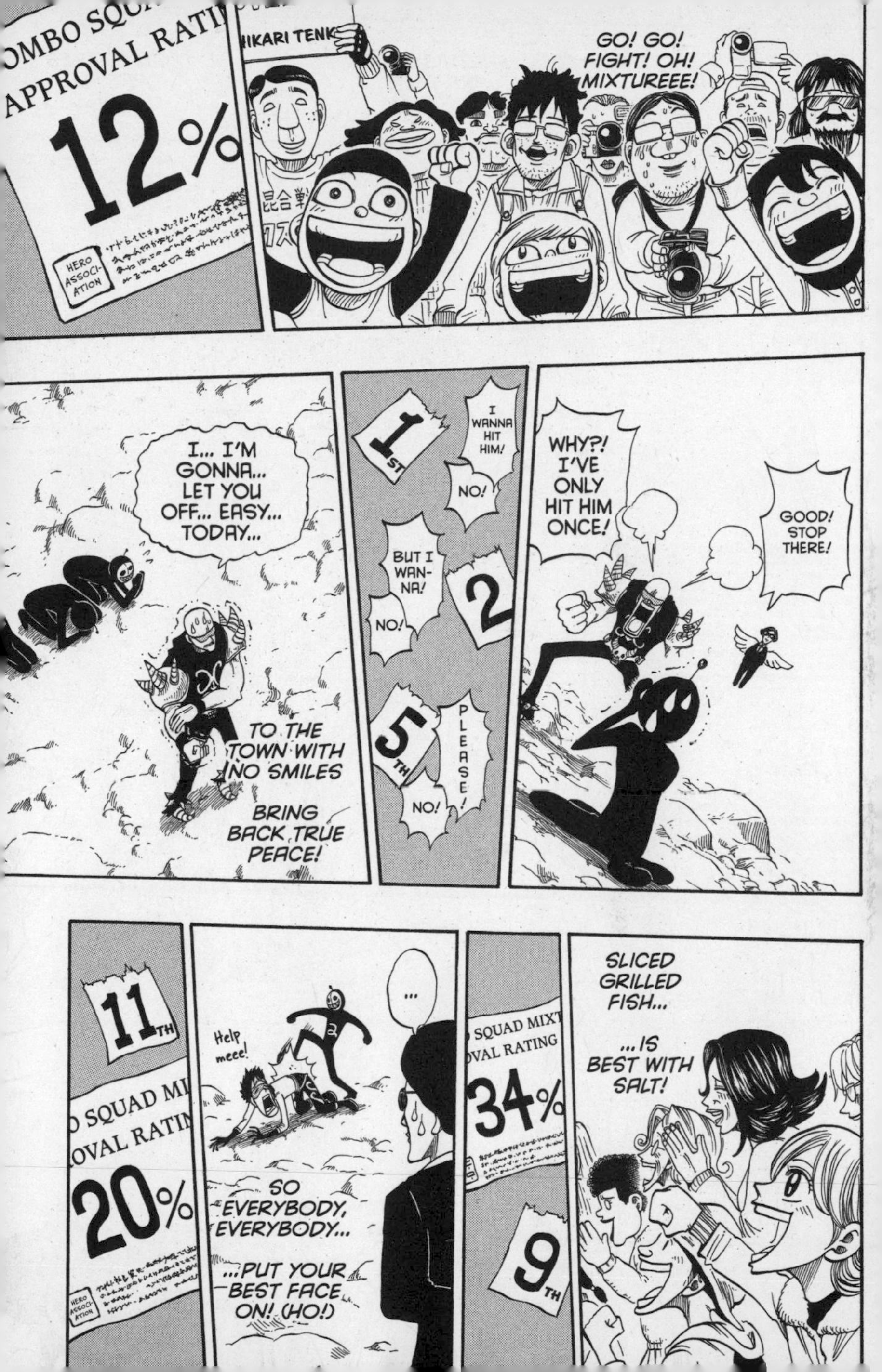
HIKARI TENK
GO! GO! FIGHT! OH! MIXTUREEE!
OMBO SQU
APPROVAL RATI
12%
HERO ASSOCIATION
GOOD! STOP THERE!
WHY?! I'VE ONLY HIT HIM ONCE!
1ST
I WANNA HIT HIM!
NO!
BUT I WANNA!
NO!
2
5TH
PLEASE!
NO!
I... I'M GONNA... LET YOU OFF... EASY... TODAY...
TO THE TOWN WITH NO SMILES
BRING BACK TRUE PEACE!
SLICED GRILLED FISH...
...IS BEST WITH SALT!
O SQUAD MIXT
OVAL RATING
34%
9TH
...
Help meee!
SO EVERYBODY, EVERYBODY...
...PUT YOUR BEST FACE ON! (HO!)
11TH
O SQUAD MI
OVAL RATIN
20%
HERO ASSOCIATION

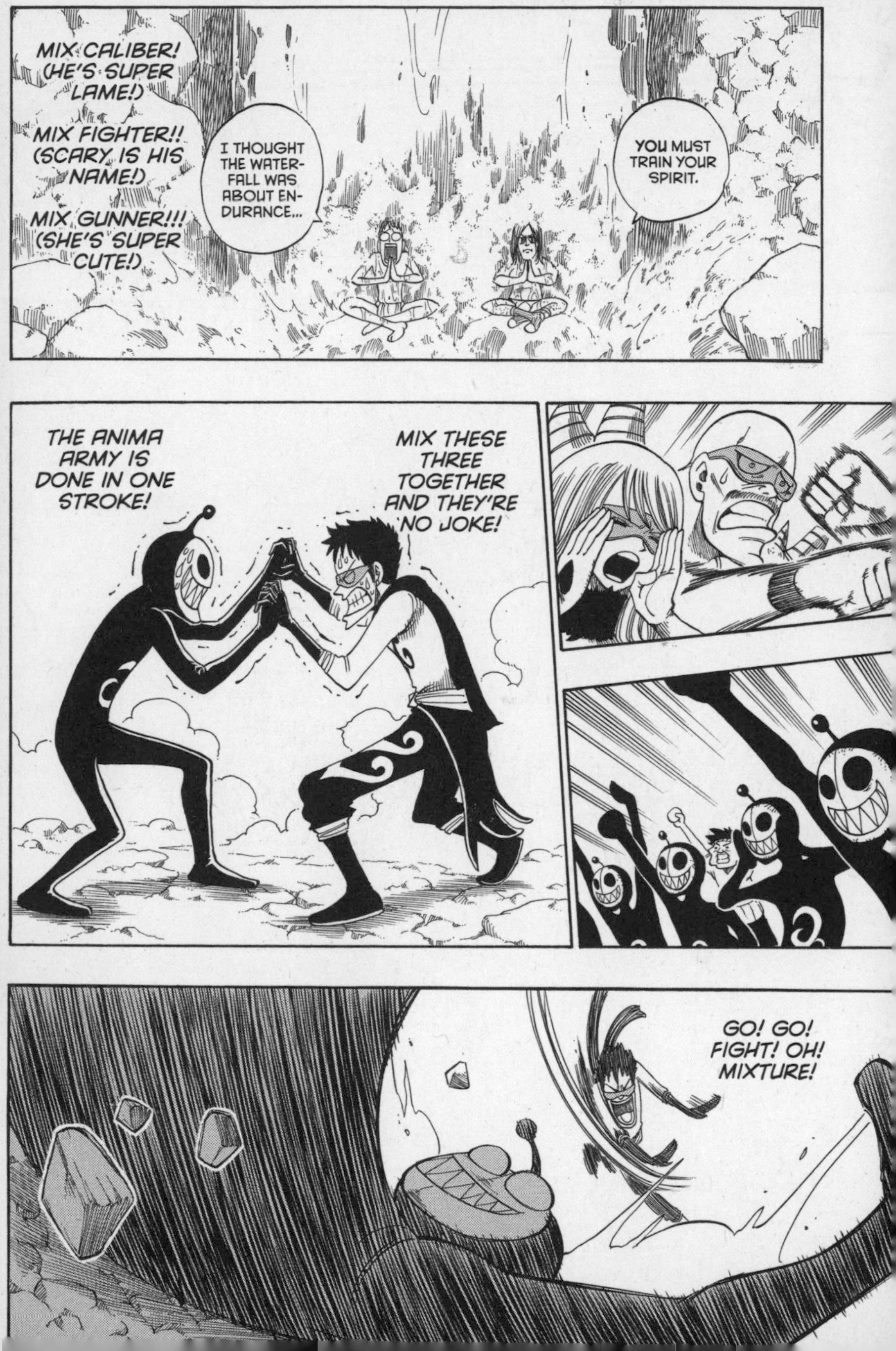
YOU MUST TRAIN YOUR SPIRIT.
I THOUGHT THE WATER-FALL WAS ABOUT EN-DURANCE...
MIX CALIBER! (HE'S SUPER LAME!)
MIX FIGHTER!! (SCARY IS HIS NAME!)
MIX GUNNER!!! (SHE'S SUPER CUTE!)
MIX THESE THREE TOGETHER AND THEY'RE NO JOKE!
THE ANIMA ARMY IS DONE IN ONE STROKE!
GO! GO! FIGHT! OH! MIXTURE!

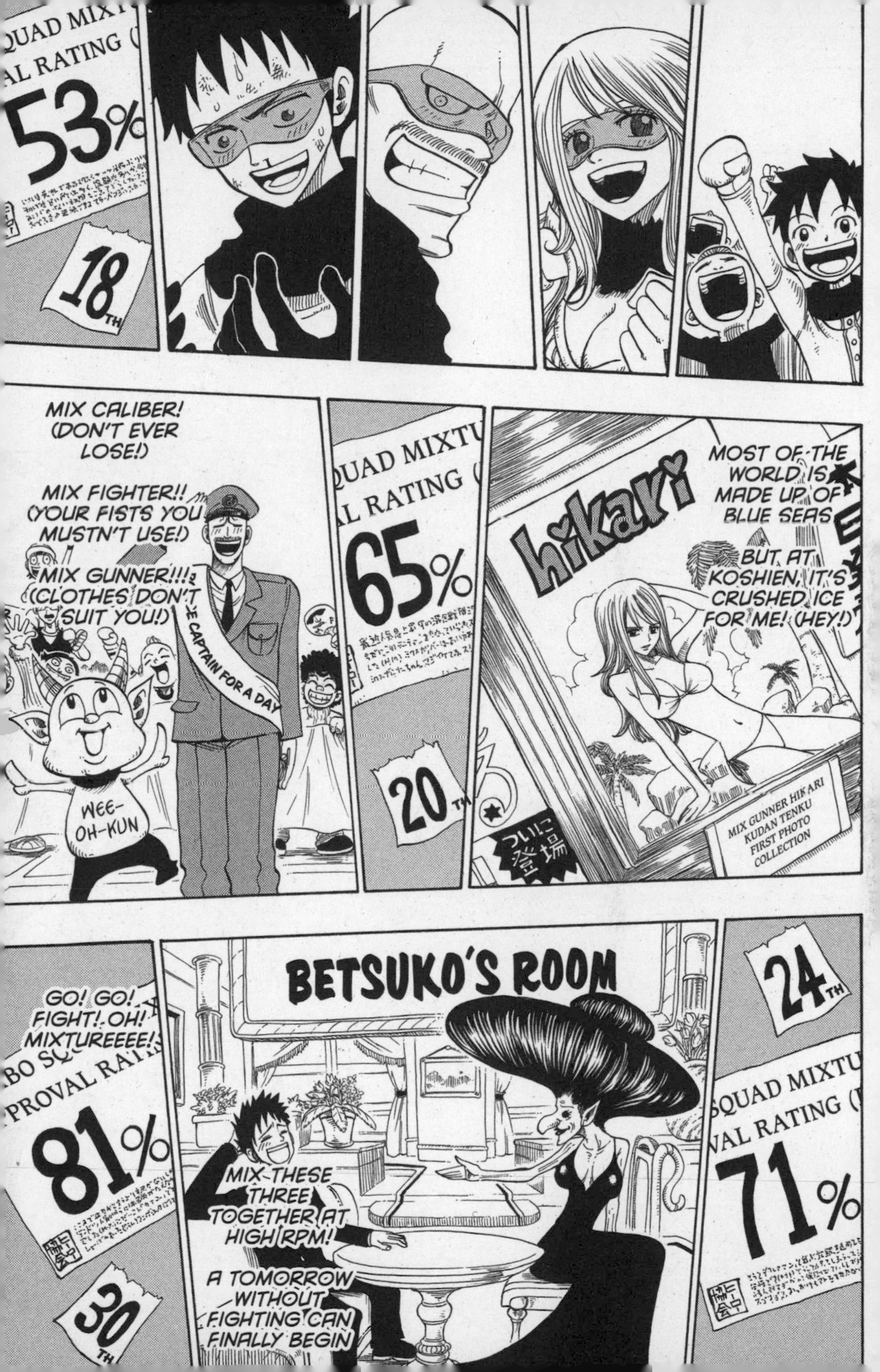
QUAD MIX
AL RATING
53%
18TH
MOST OF THE WORLD IS MADE UP OF BLUE SEAS
BUT AT KOSHIEN, IT'S CRUSHED ICE FOR ME! (HEY!)
hikari
MIX GUNNER HIKARI KUDAN TENKU FIRST PHOTO COLLECTION
ついに登場
QUAD MIXTU
AL RATING
65%
20TH
MIX CALIBER! (DON'T EVER LOSE!)
MIX FIGHTER!! (YOUR FISTS YOU MUSTN'T USE!)
MIX GUNNER!!! (CLOTHES DON'T SUIT YOU!)
CAPTAIN FOR A DAY
WEE-OH-KUN
24TH
SQUAD MIXTU
VAL RATING
71%
BETSUKO'S ROOM
MIX THESE THREE TOGETHER AT HIGH RPM!
A TOMORROW WITHOUT FIGHTING CAN FINALLY BEGIN
GO! GO! FIGHT! OH! MIXTUREEEE!
BO SQ
PROVAL RA
81%
30TH

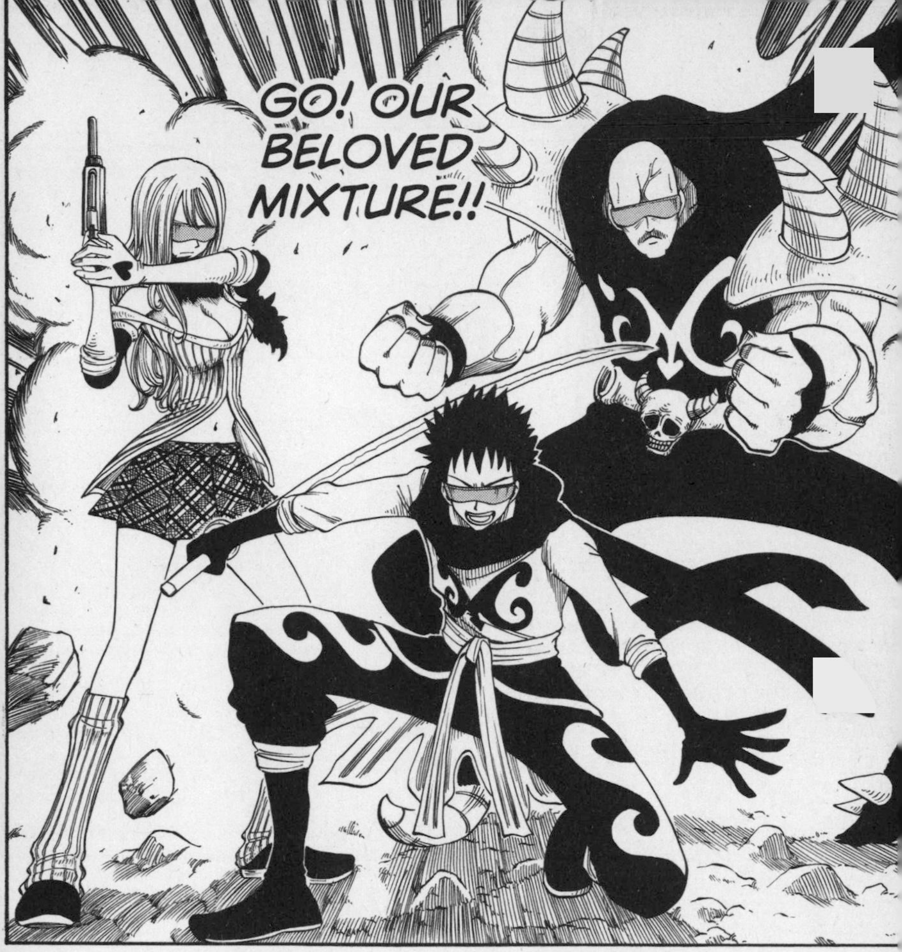
GO! OUR BELOVED MIXTURE!!
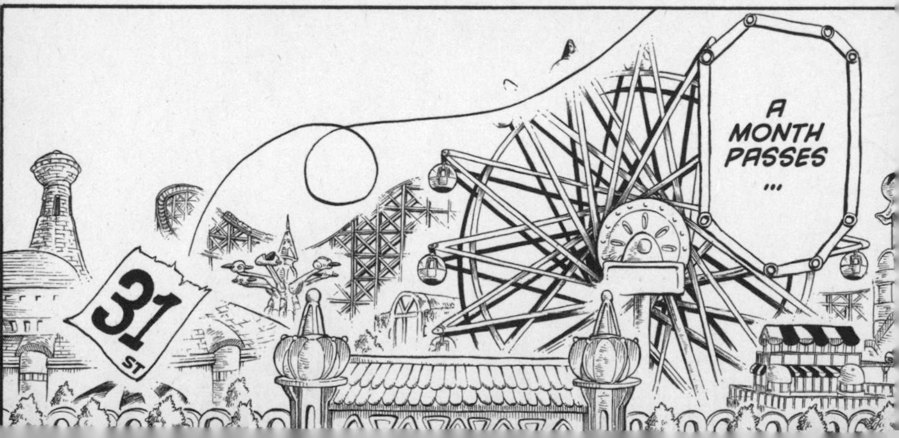
A MONTH PASSES ...
31 ST

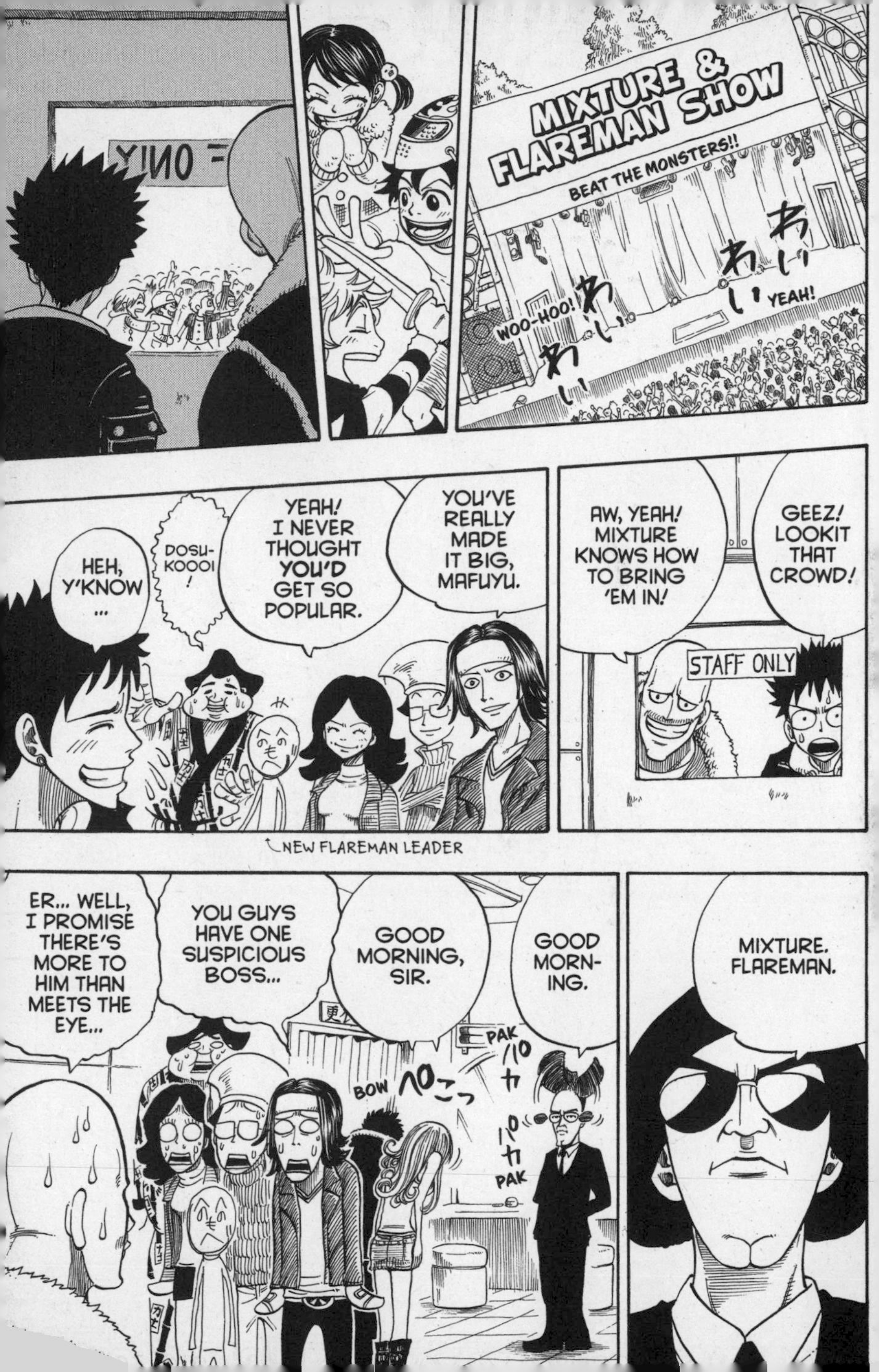
MIXTURE & FLAREMAN SHOW
BEAT THE MONSTERS!!
わい わい
YEAH!
WOO-HOO!
わい わい
GEEZ! LOOKIT THAT CROWD!
AW, YEAH! MIXTURE KNOWS HOW TO BRING 'EM IN!
STAFF ONLY
YOU'VE REALLY MADE IT BIG, MAFUYU.
YEAH! I NEVER THOUGHT YOU'D GET SO POPULAR.
DOSU-KOOOI!
HEH, Y'KNOW ...
NEW FLAREMAN LEADER
MIXTURE. FLAREMAN.
GOOD MORN-ING.
GOOD MORNING, SIR.
PAK パカ
BOW ぺこっ
パカ PAK
YOU GUYS HAVE ONE SUSPICIOUS BOSS...
ER... WELL, I PROMISE THERE'S MORE TO HIM THAN MEETS THE EYE...

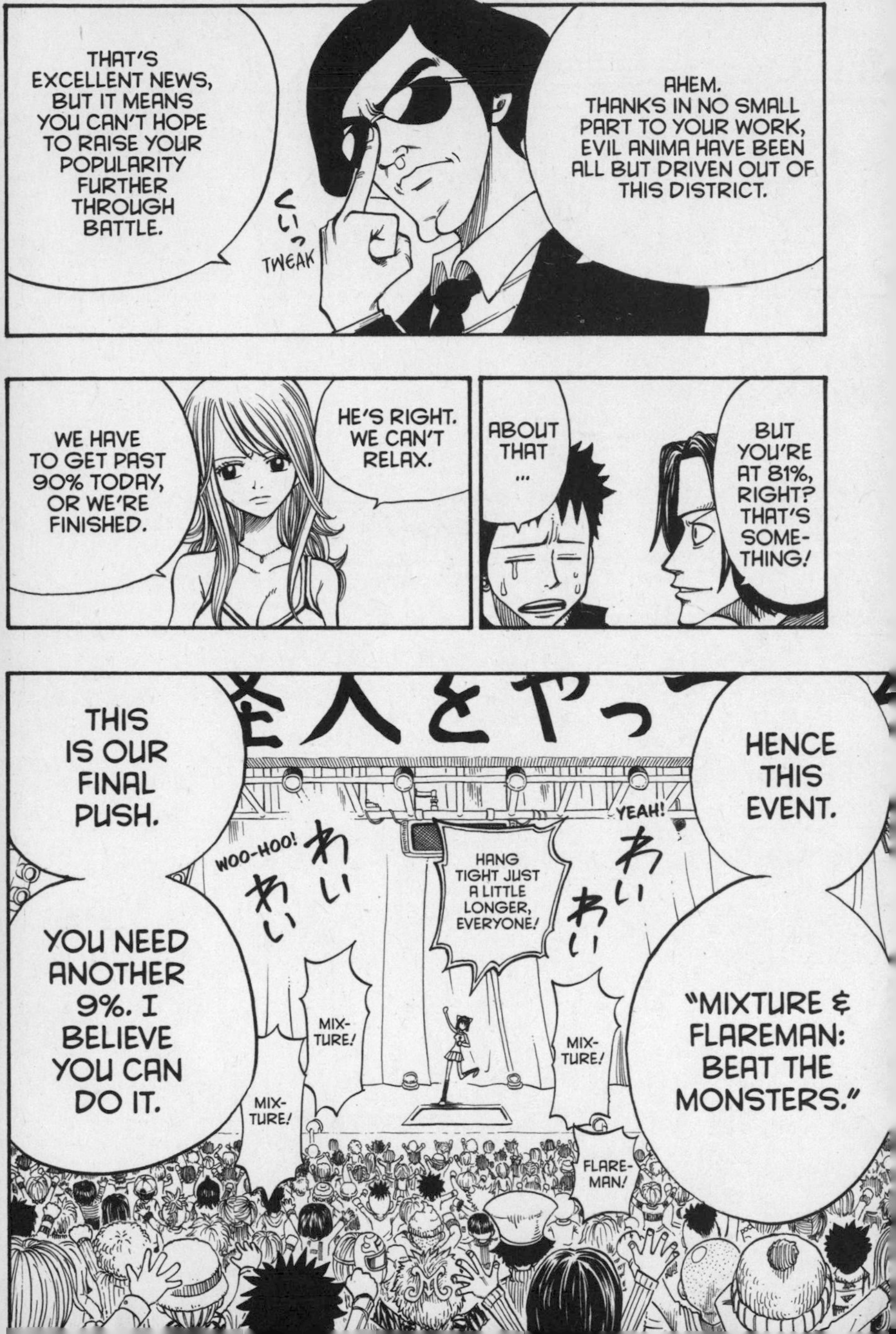
AHEM.
THANKS IN NO SMALL PART TO YOUR WORK, EVIL ANIMA HAVE BEEN ALL BUT DRIVEN OUT OF THIS DISTRICT.
THAT'S EXCELLENT NEWS, BUT IT MEANS YOU CAN'T HOPE TO RAISE YOUR POPULARITY FURTHER THROUGH BATTLE.
くいっ
TWEAK
BUT YOU'RE AT 81%, RIGHT? THAT'S SOME-THING!
ABOUT THAT ...
HE'S RIGHT. WE CAN'T RELAX.
WE HAVE TO GET PAST 90% TODAY, OR WE'RE FINISHED.
HENCE THIS EVENT.
THIS IS OUR FINAL PUSH.
YEAH!
わい
わい
HANG TIGHT JUST A LITTLE LONGER, EVERYONE!
WOO-HOO!
わい
わい
"MIXTURE & FLAREMAN: BEAT THE MONSTERS."
YOU NEED ANOTHER 9%. I BELIEVE YOU CAN DO IT.
MIX-TURE!
MIX-TURE!
MIX-TURE!
FLARE-MAN!

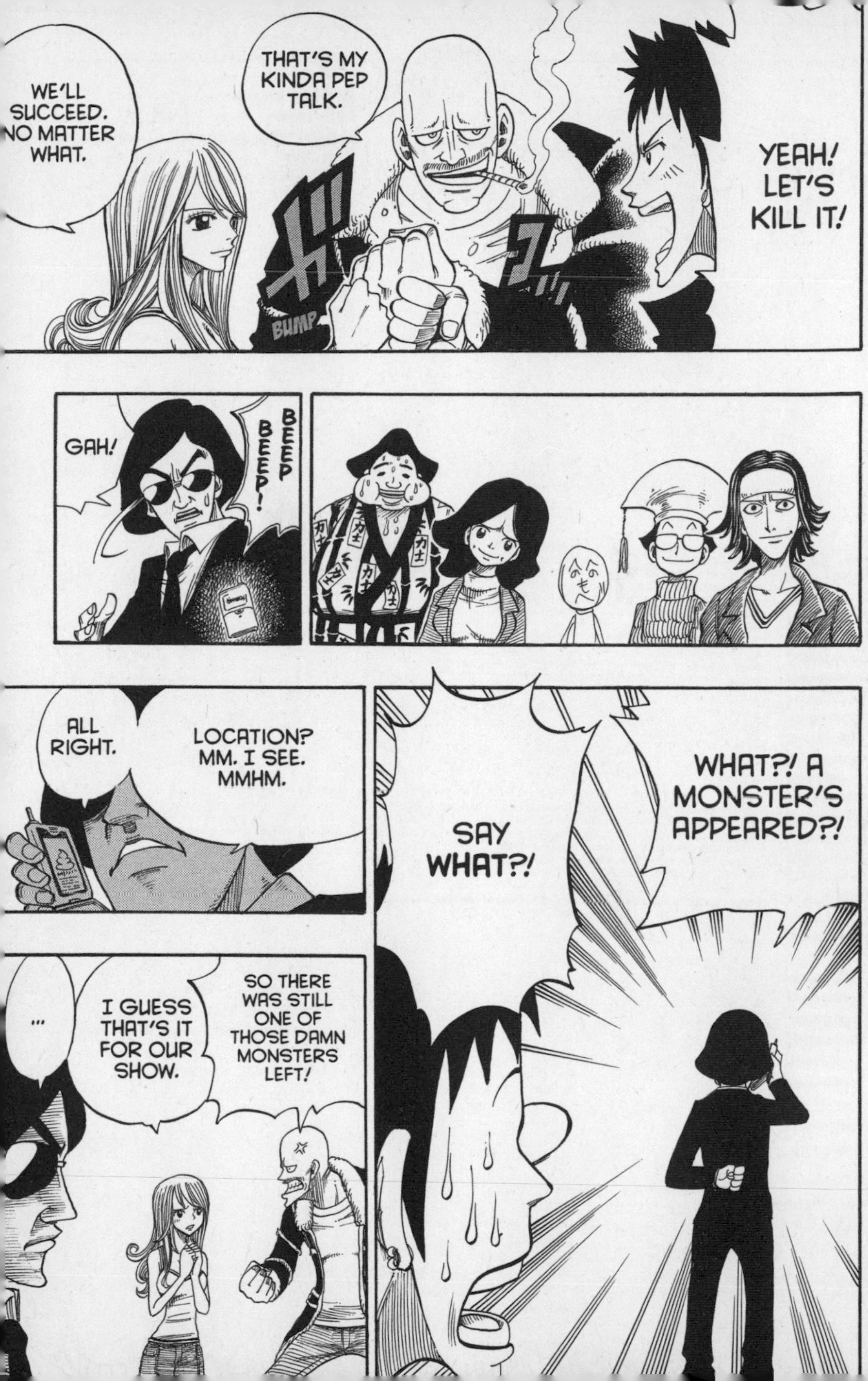
YEAH! LET'S KILL IT!
THAT'S MY KINDA PEP TALK.
WE'LL SUCCEED. NO MATTER WHAT.
BUMP
BEEP BEEP!
GAH!
WHAT?! A MONSTER'S APPEARED?!
SAY WHAT?!
LOCATION? MM. I SEE. MMHM.
ALL RIGHT.
SO THERE WAS STILL ONE OF THOSE DAMN MONSTERS LEFT!
I GUESS THAT'S IT FOR OUR SHOW.
...

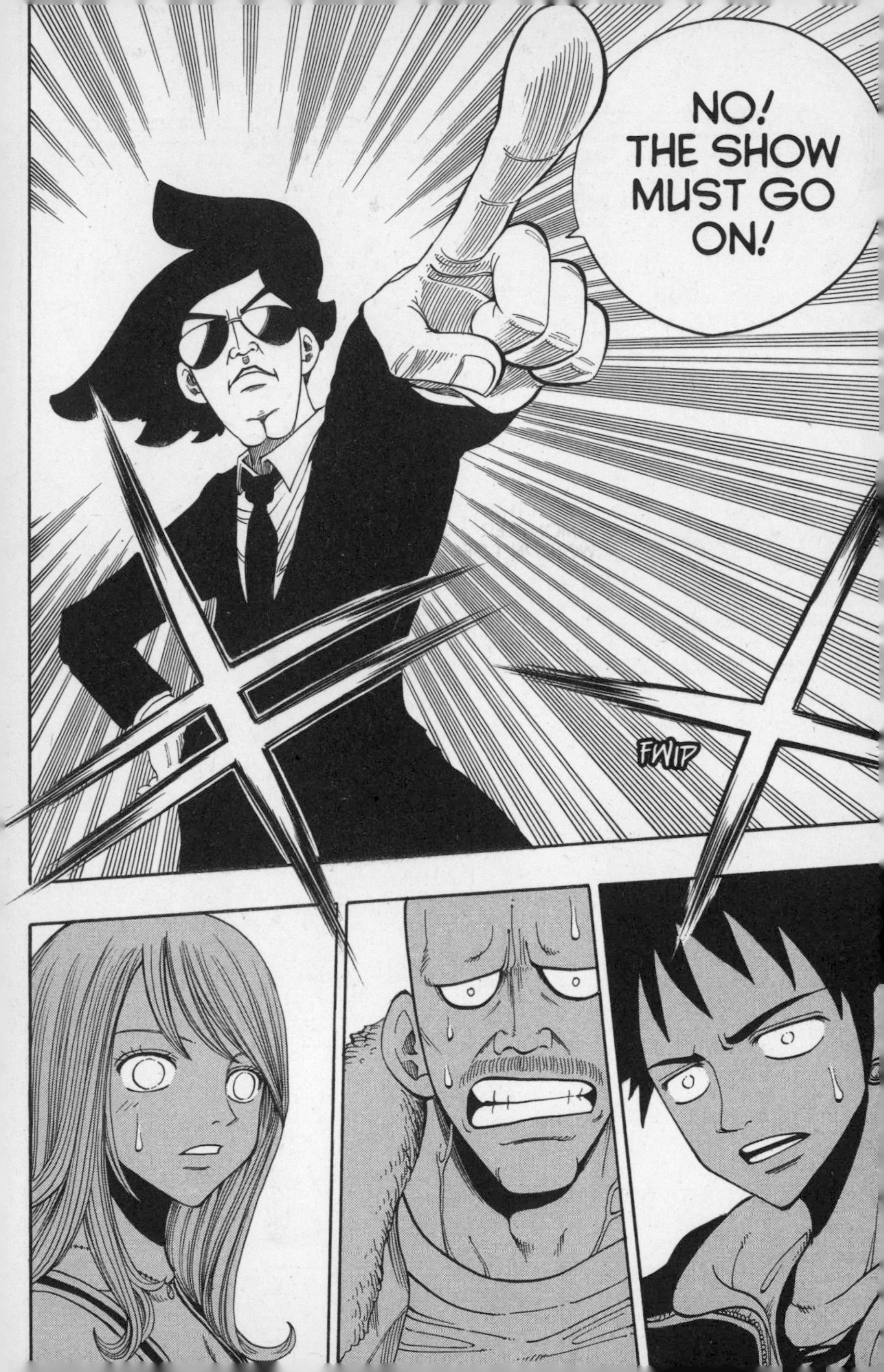
NO! THE SHOW MUST GO ON!
FWIP

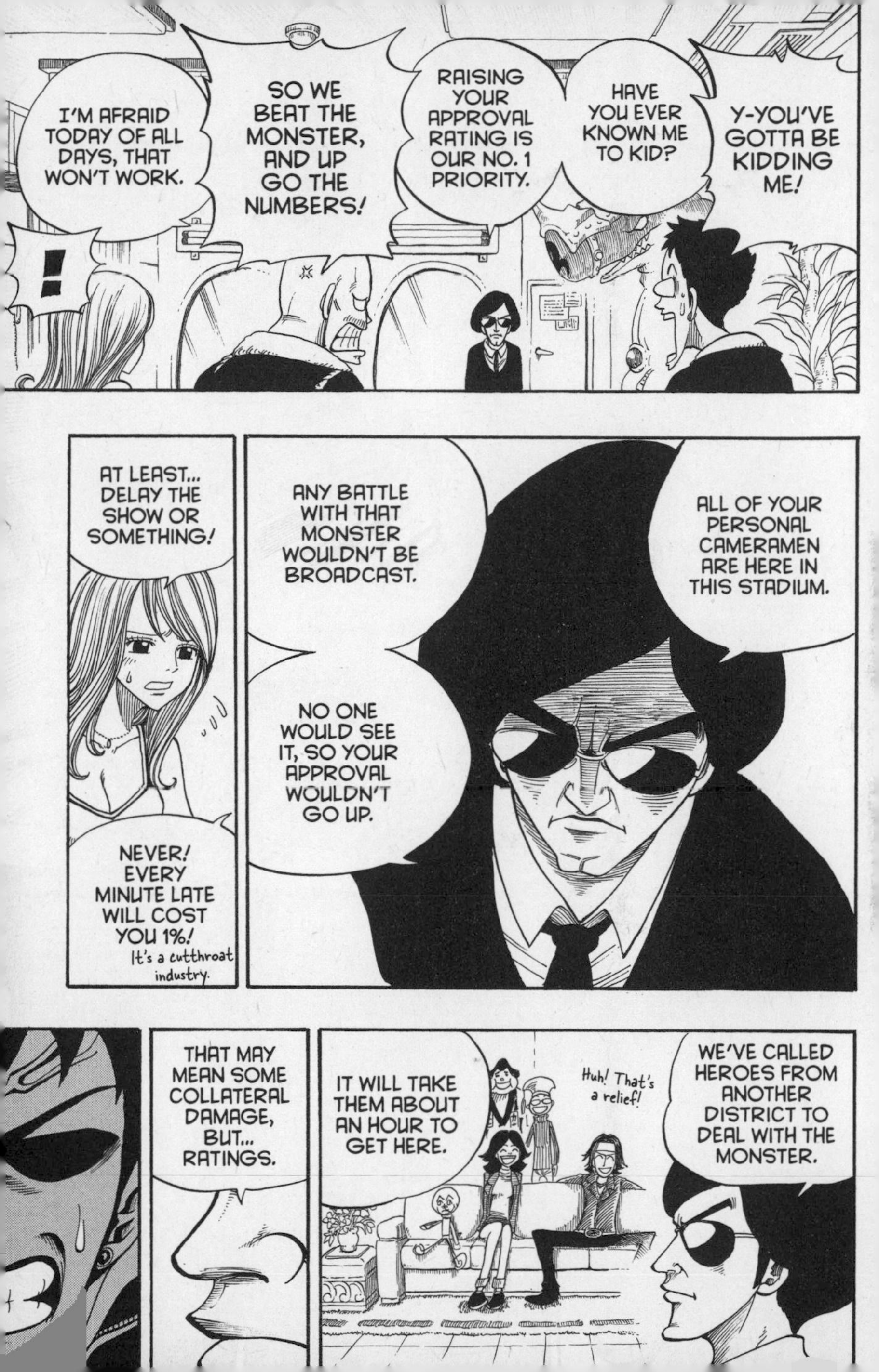
Y-YOU'VE GOTTA BE KIDDING ME!
HAVE YOU EVER KNOWN ME TO KID?
RAISING YOUR APPROVAL RATING IS OUR NO. 1 PRIORITY.
SO WE BEAT THE MONSTER, AND UP GO THE NUMBERS!
I'M AFRAID TODAY OF ALL DAYS, THAT WON'T WORK.
!
ALL OF YOUR PERSONAL CAMERAMEN ARE HERE IN THIS STADIUM.
ANY BATTLE WITH THAT MONSTER WOULDN'T BE BROADCAST.
NO ONE WOULD SEE IT, SO YOUR APPROVAL WOULDN'T GO UP.
AT LEAST... DELAY THE SHOW OR SOMETHING!
NEVER! EVERY MINUTE LATE WILL COST YOU 1%!
It's a cutthroat industry.
WE'VE CALLED HEROES FROM ANOTHER DISTRICT TO DEAL WITH THE MONSTER.
Huh! That's a relief!
IT WILL TAKE THEM ABOUT AN HOUR TO GET HERE.
THAT MAY MEAN SOME COLLATERAL DAMAGE, BUT... RATINGS.

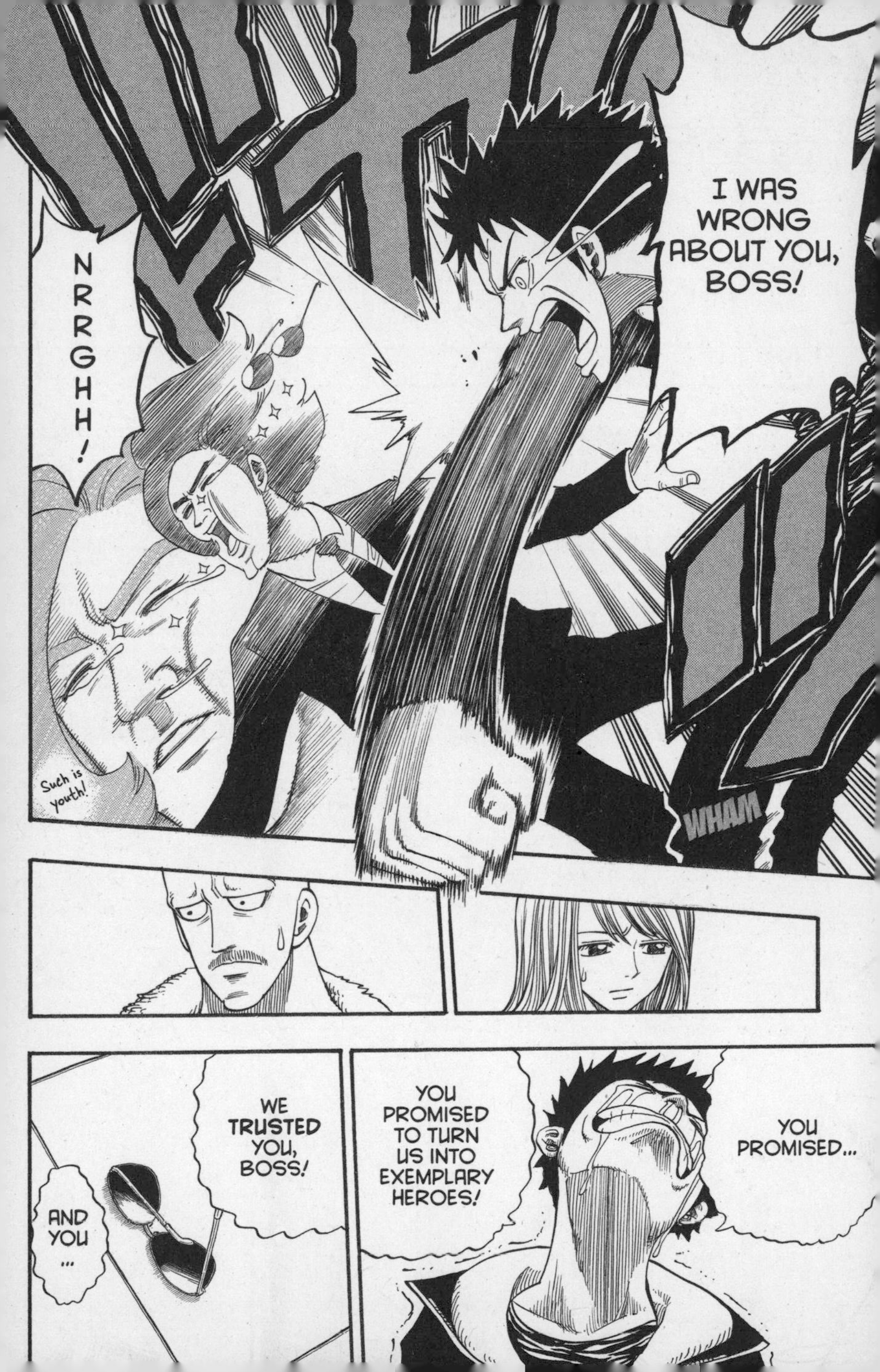
I WAS WRONG ABOUT YOU, BOSS!
NRRGHH!
WHAM
Such is youth!
YOU PROMISED...
YOU PROMISED TO TURN US INTO EXEMPLARY HEROES!
WE TRUSTED YOU, BOSS!
AND YOU ...

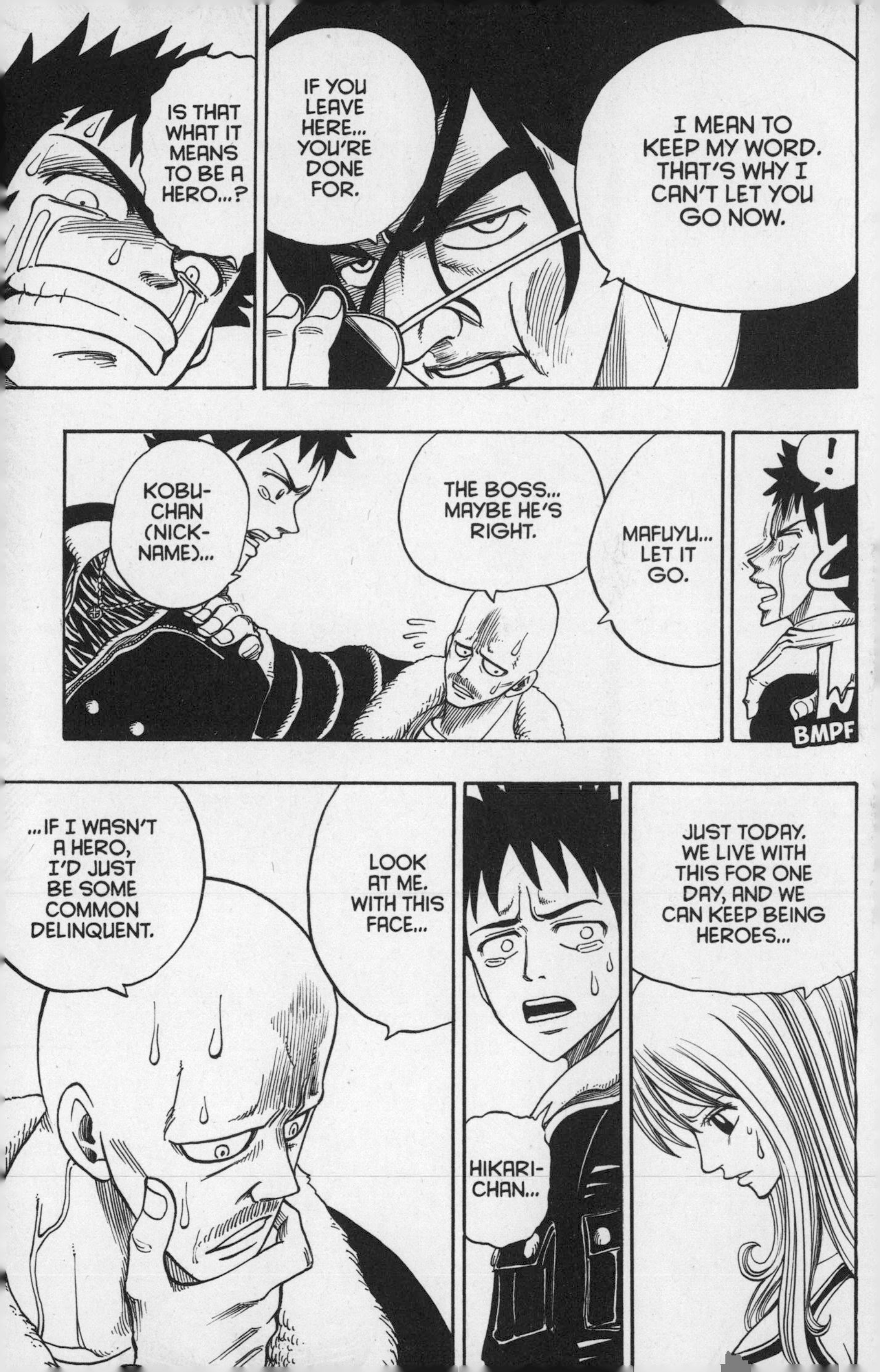
I MEAN TO KEEP MY WORD. THAT'S WHY I CAN'T LET YOU GO NOW.
IF YOU LEAVE HERE... YOU'RE DONE FOR.
IS THAT WHAT IT MEANS TO BE A HERO...?
!
BMPF
MAFUYU... LET IT GO.
THE BOSS... MAYBE HE'S RIGHT.
KOBU-CHAN (NICK-NAME)...
JUST TODAY. WE LIVE WITH THIS FOR ONE DAY, AND WE CAN KEEP BEING HEROES...
HIKARI-CHAN...
LOOK AT ME. WITH THIS FACE...
...IF I WASN'T A HERO, I'D JUST BE SOME COMMON DELINQUENT.

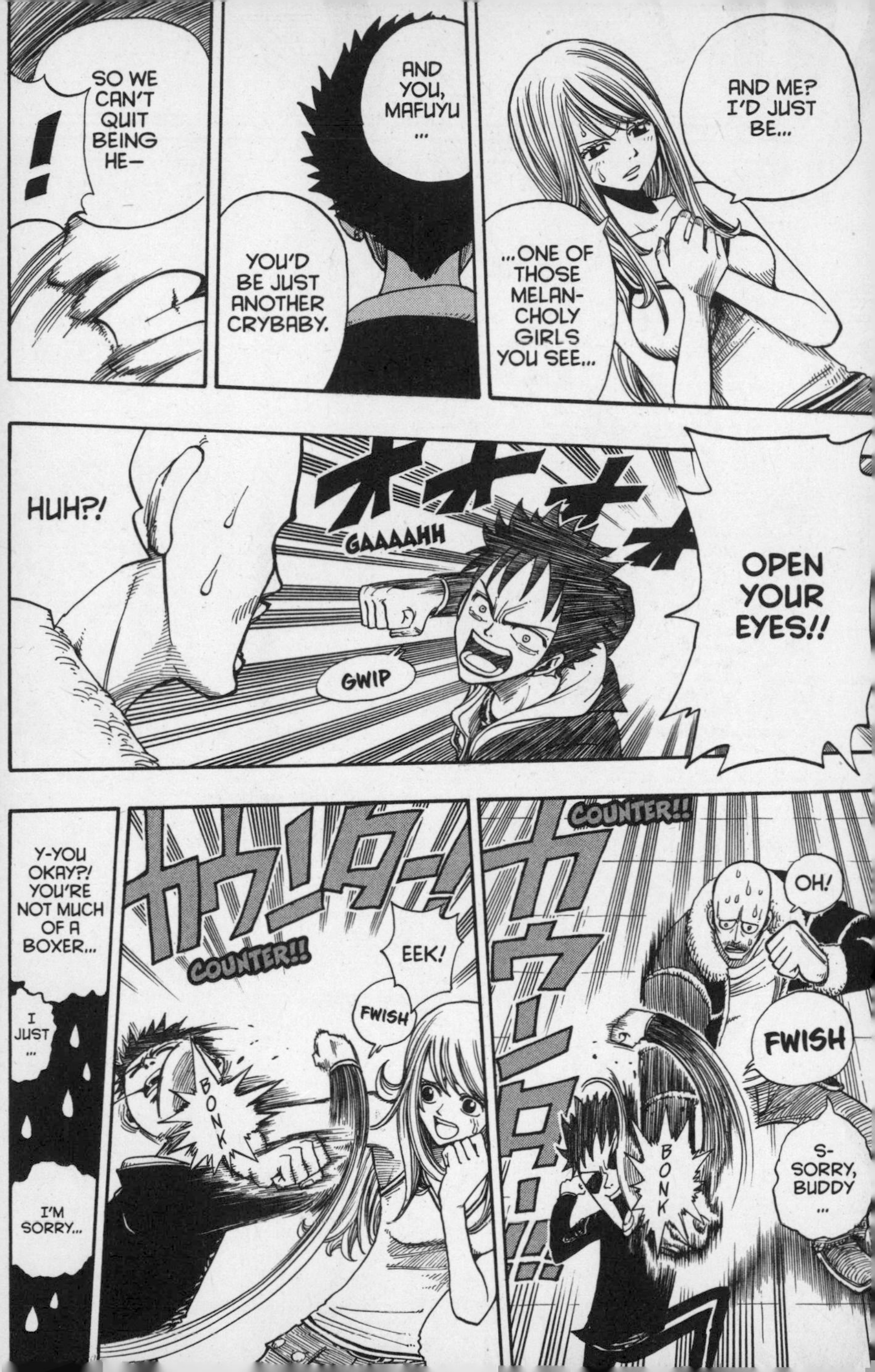
AND ME? I'D JUST BE...
...ONE OF THOSE MELAN-CHOLY GIRLS YOU SEE...
AND YOU, MAFUYU ...
YOU'D BE JUST ANOTHER CRYBABY.
!
SO WE CAN'T QUIT BEING HE—
OPEN YOUR EYES!!
GAAAAHH
HUH?!
GWIP
カウンター!!
COUNTER!!
OH!
FWISH
S-SORRY, BUDDY ...
BONK
カウンター!!
COUNTER!!
EEK!
FWISH
BONK
Y-YOU OKAY?! YOU'RE NOT MUCH OF A BOXER...
I JUST ...
I'M SORRY...

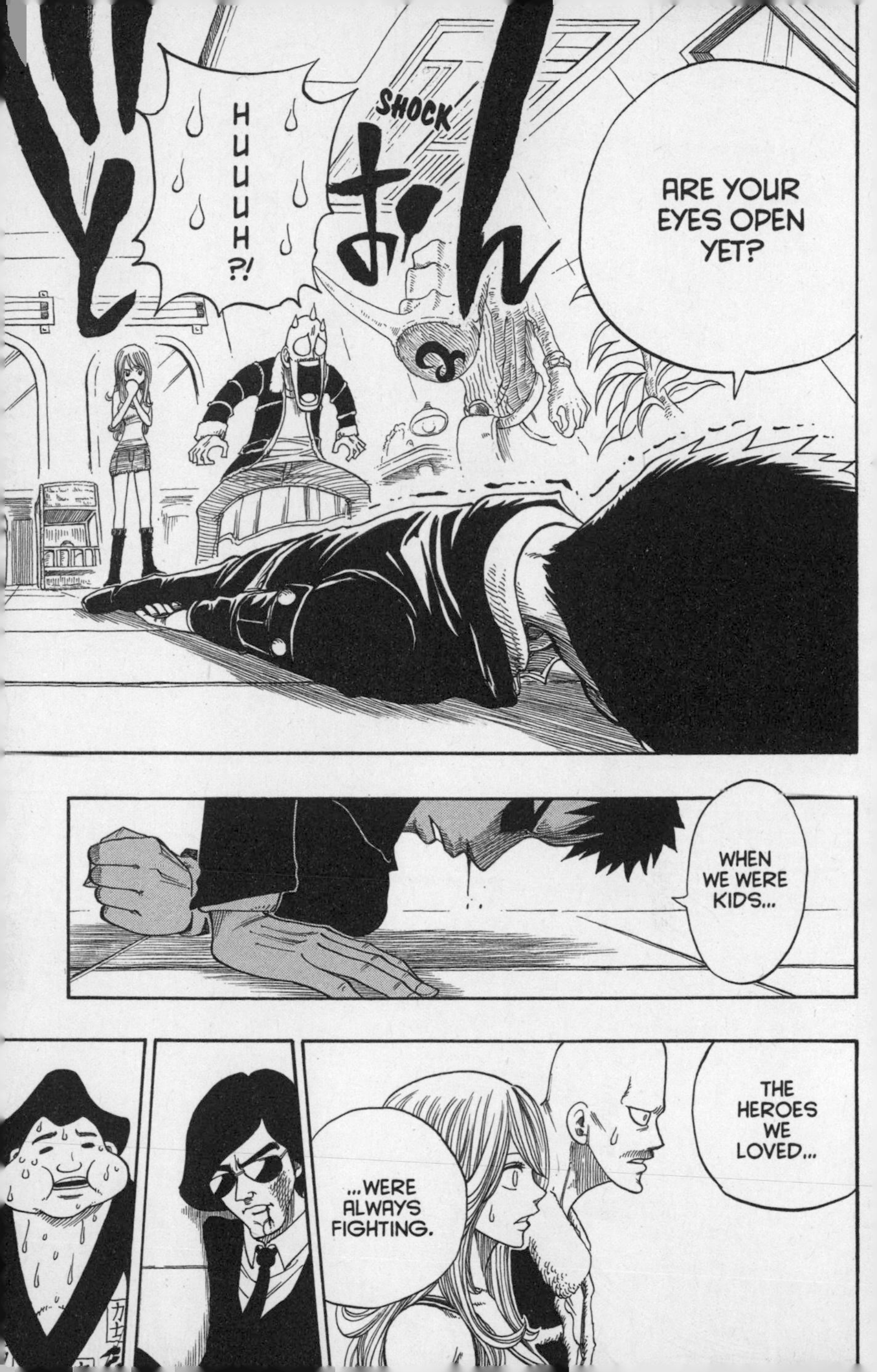
ARE YOUR EYES OPEN YET?
SHOCK
HUUUUH?!
WHEN WE WERE KIDS...
THE HEROES WE LOVED...
...WERE ALWAYS FIGHTING.

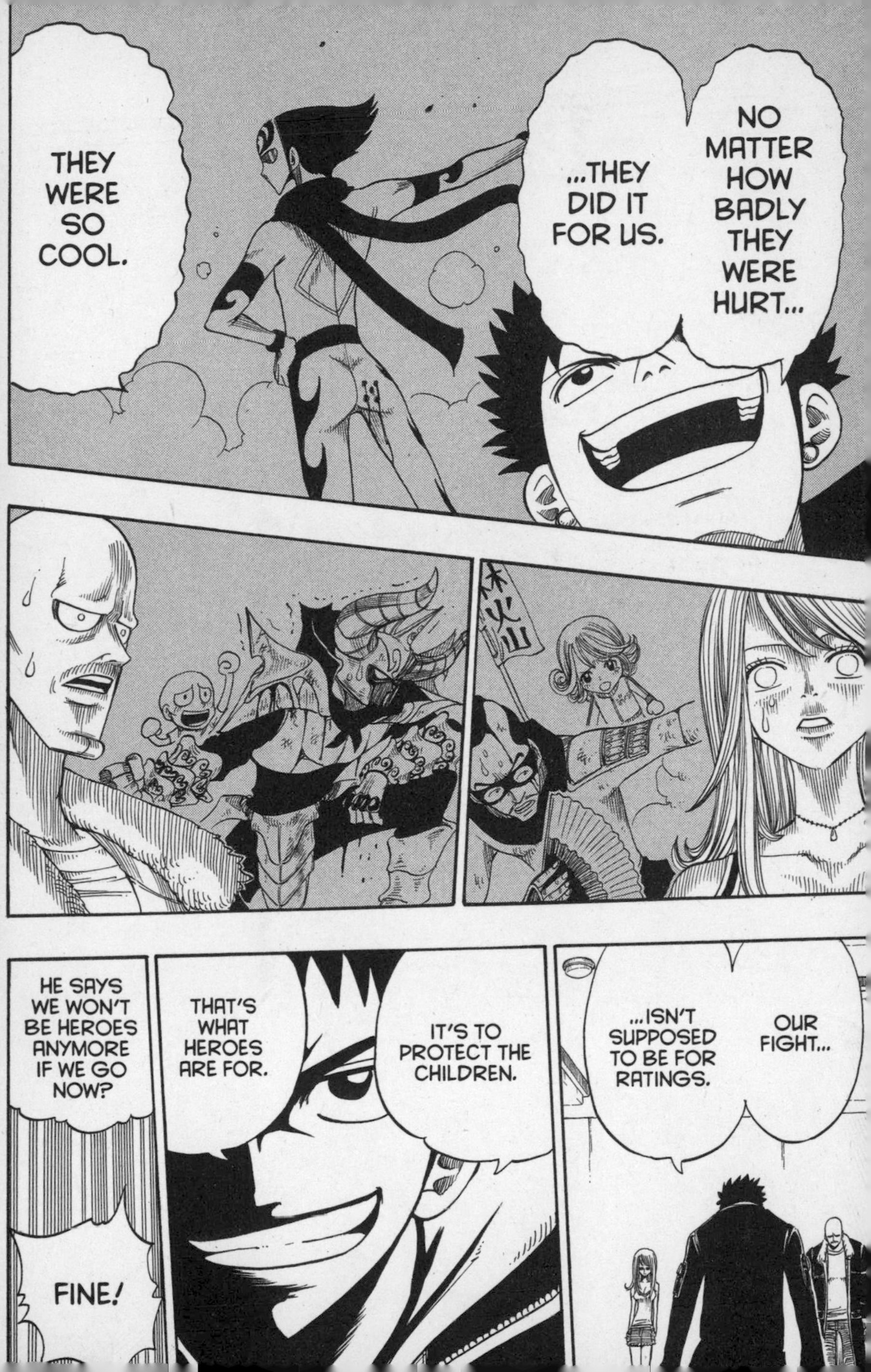
NO MATTER HOW BADLY THEY WERE HURT...
...THEY DID IT FOR US.
THEY WERE SO COOL.
OUR FIGHT...
...ISN'T SUPPOSED TO BE FOR RATINGS.
IT'S TO PROTECT THE CHILDREN.
THAT'S WHAT HEROES ARE FOR.
HE SAYS WE WON'T BE HEROES ANYMORE IF WE GO NOW?
FINE!

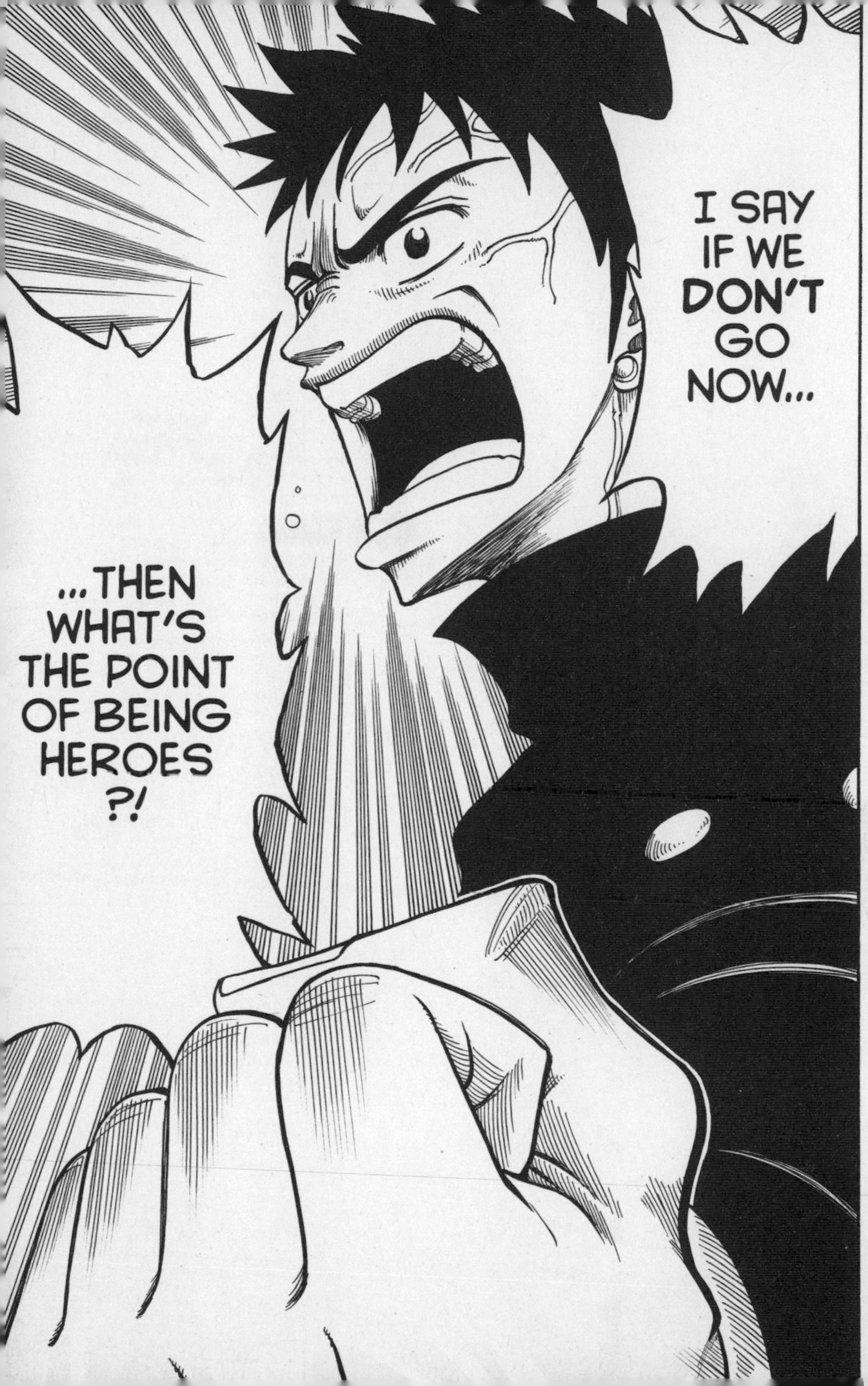
I SAY IF WE DON'T GO NOW...
...THEN WHAT'S THE POINT OF BEING HEROES ?!

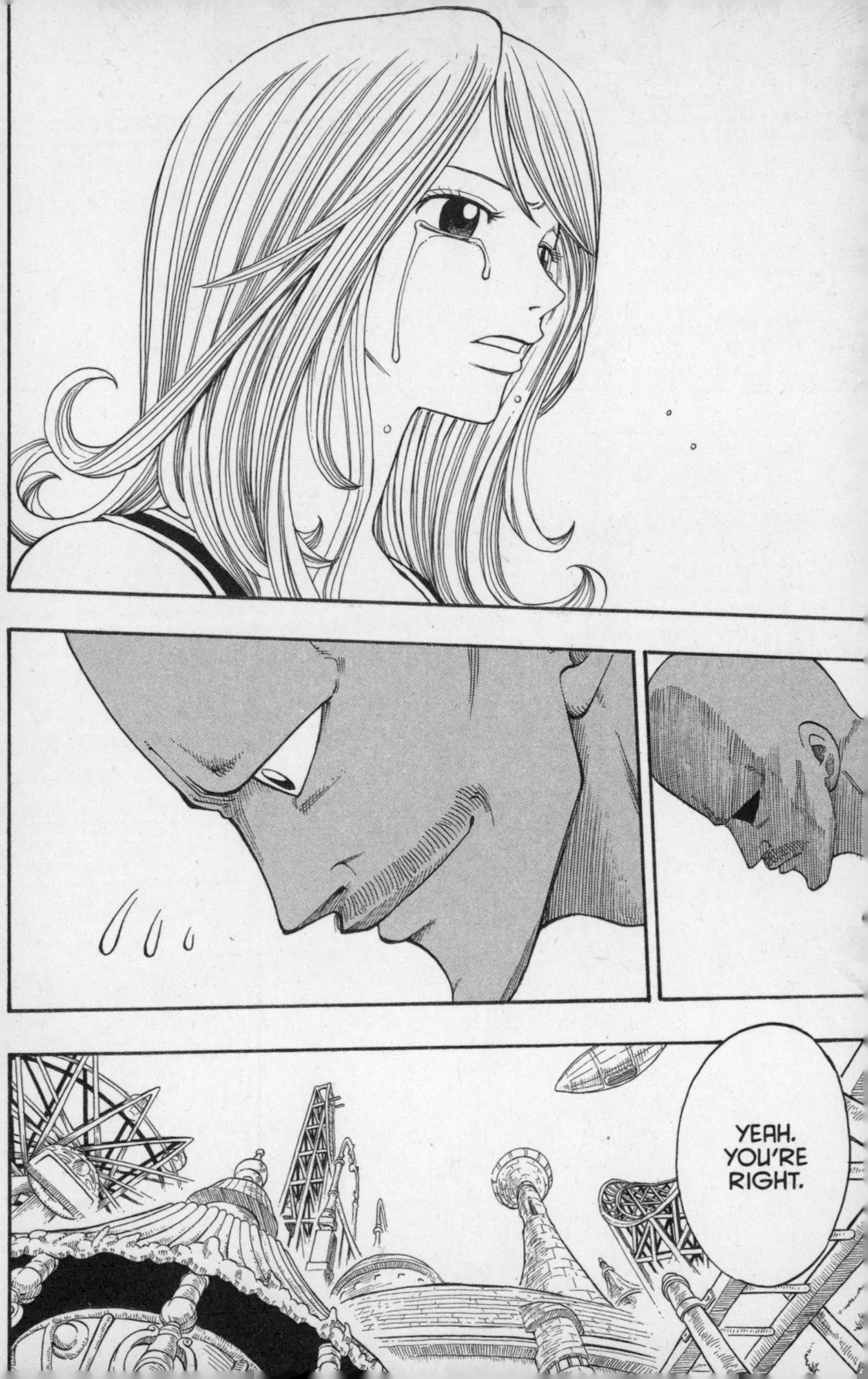
YEAH. YOU'RE RIGHT.

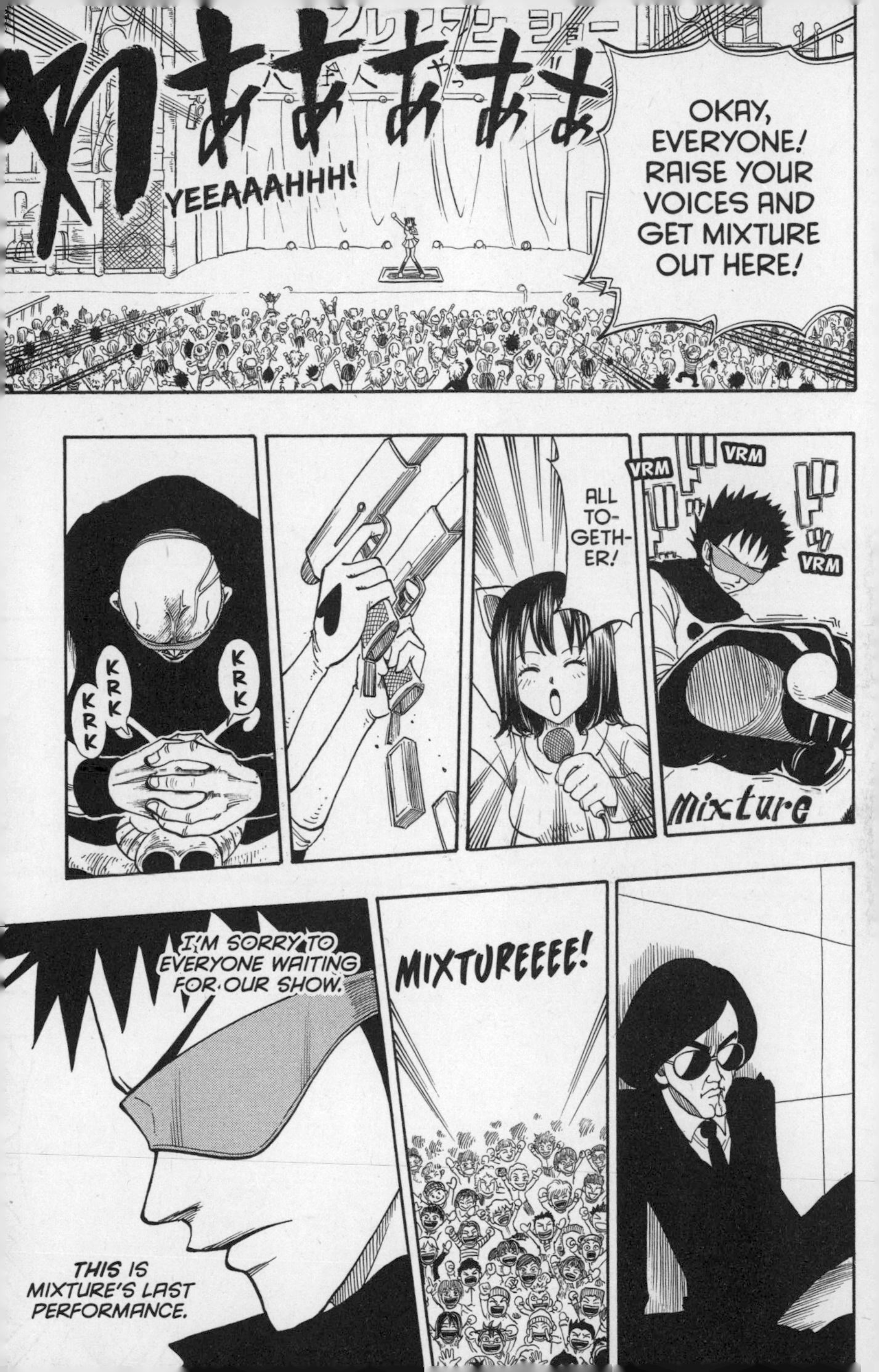
OKAY, EVERYONE! RAISE YOUR VOICES AND GET MIXTURE OUT HERE!
わあああああ
YEEAAAHHH!
VRM
VRM
VRM
VRM
Mixture
ALL TO-GETH-ER!
KRK
KRK
KRK
MIXTUREEEE!
I'M SORRY TO EVERYONE WAITING FOR OUR SHOW.
THIS IS MIXTURE'S LAST PERFORMANCE.

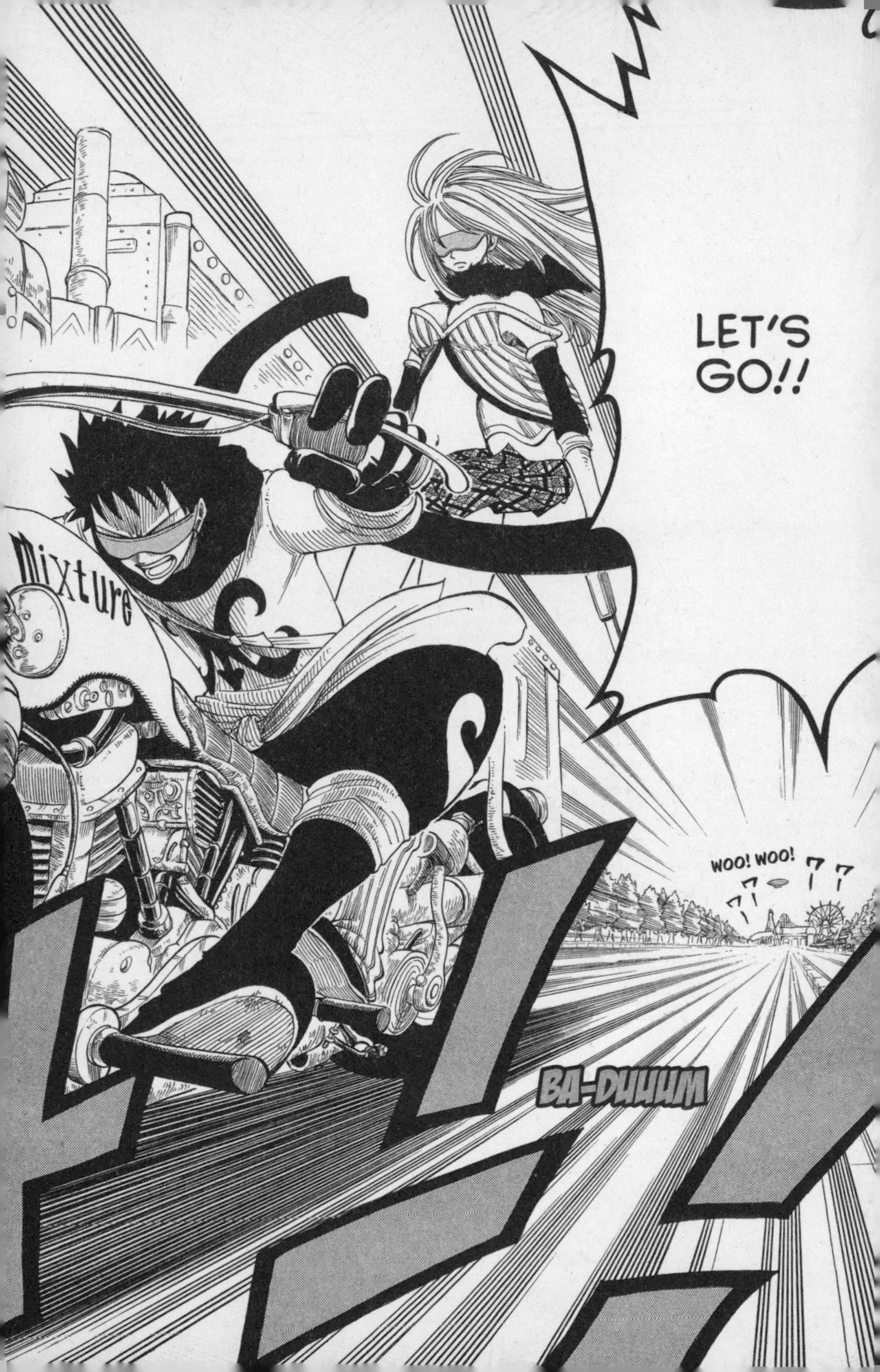
LET'S GO!!
WOO! WOO!
Mixture
BA-DUUUM

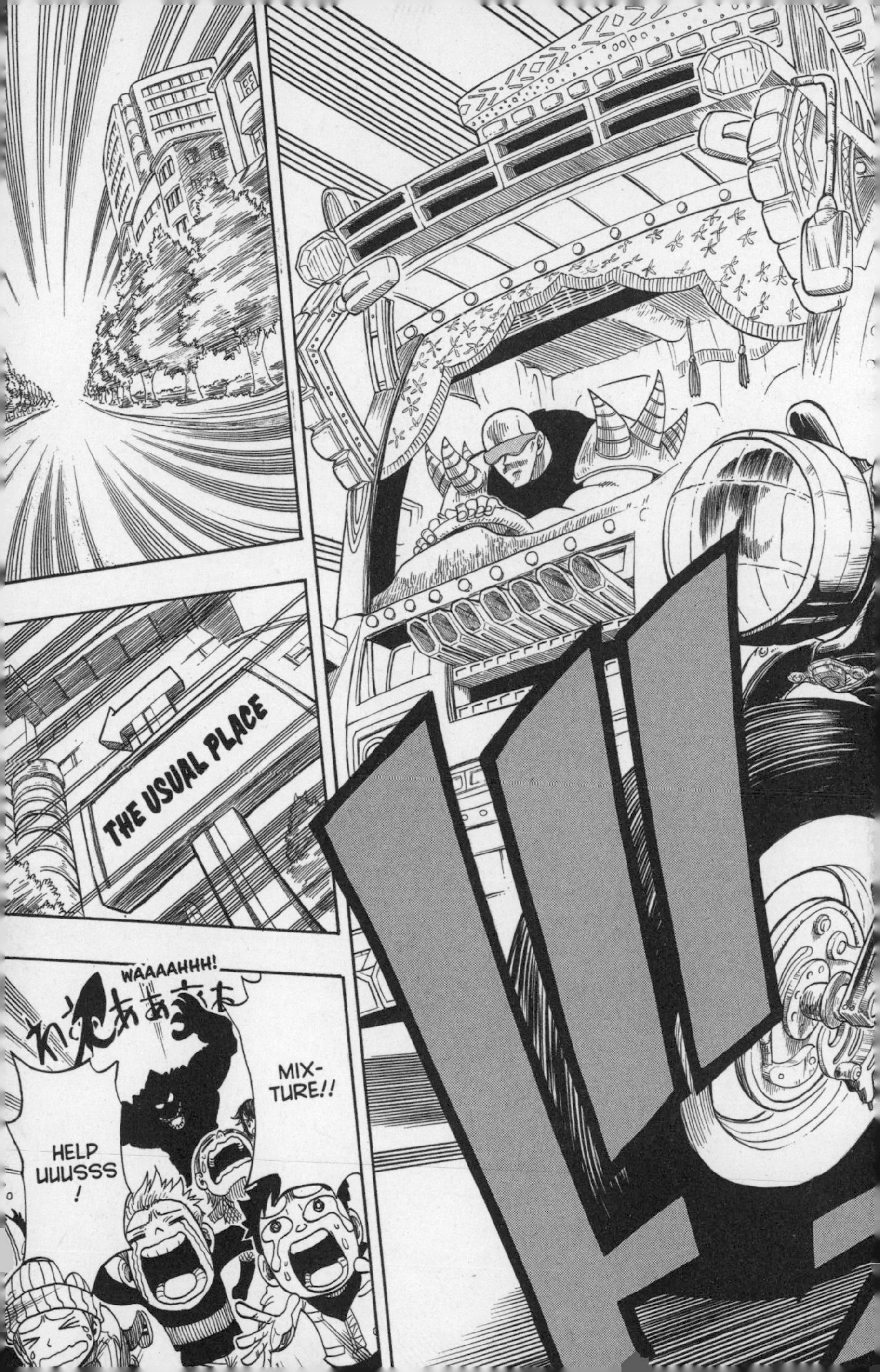
THE USUAL PLACE
WAAAAHHH!
MIX-TURE!!
HELP UUUSSS!

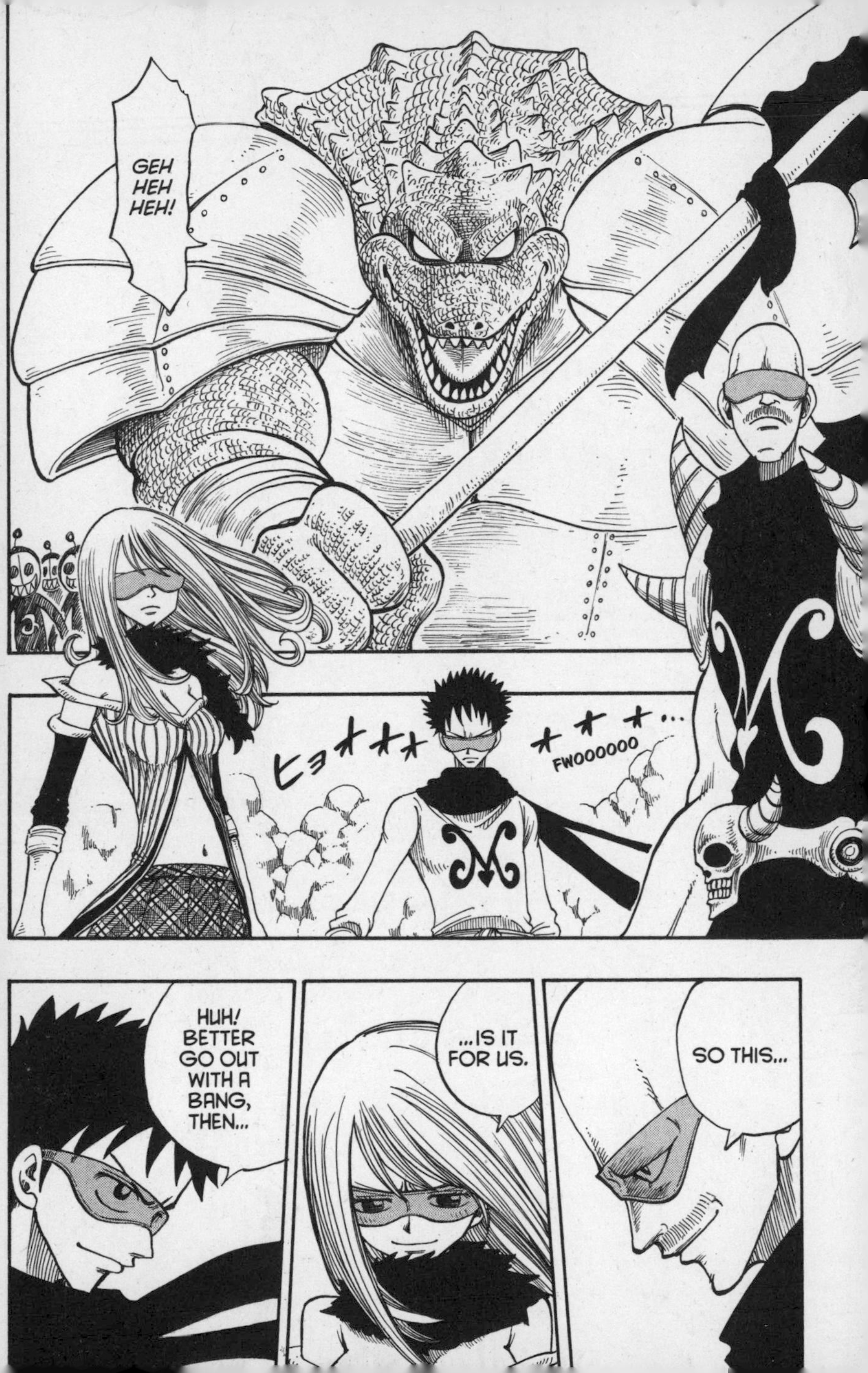
GEH HEH HEH!
ヒョオオオ
オオオ…
FWOOOOOO
SO THIS...
...IS IT FOR US.
HUH! BETTER GO OUT WITH A BANG, THEN...

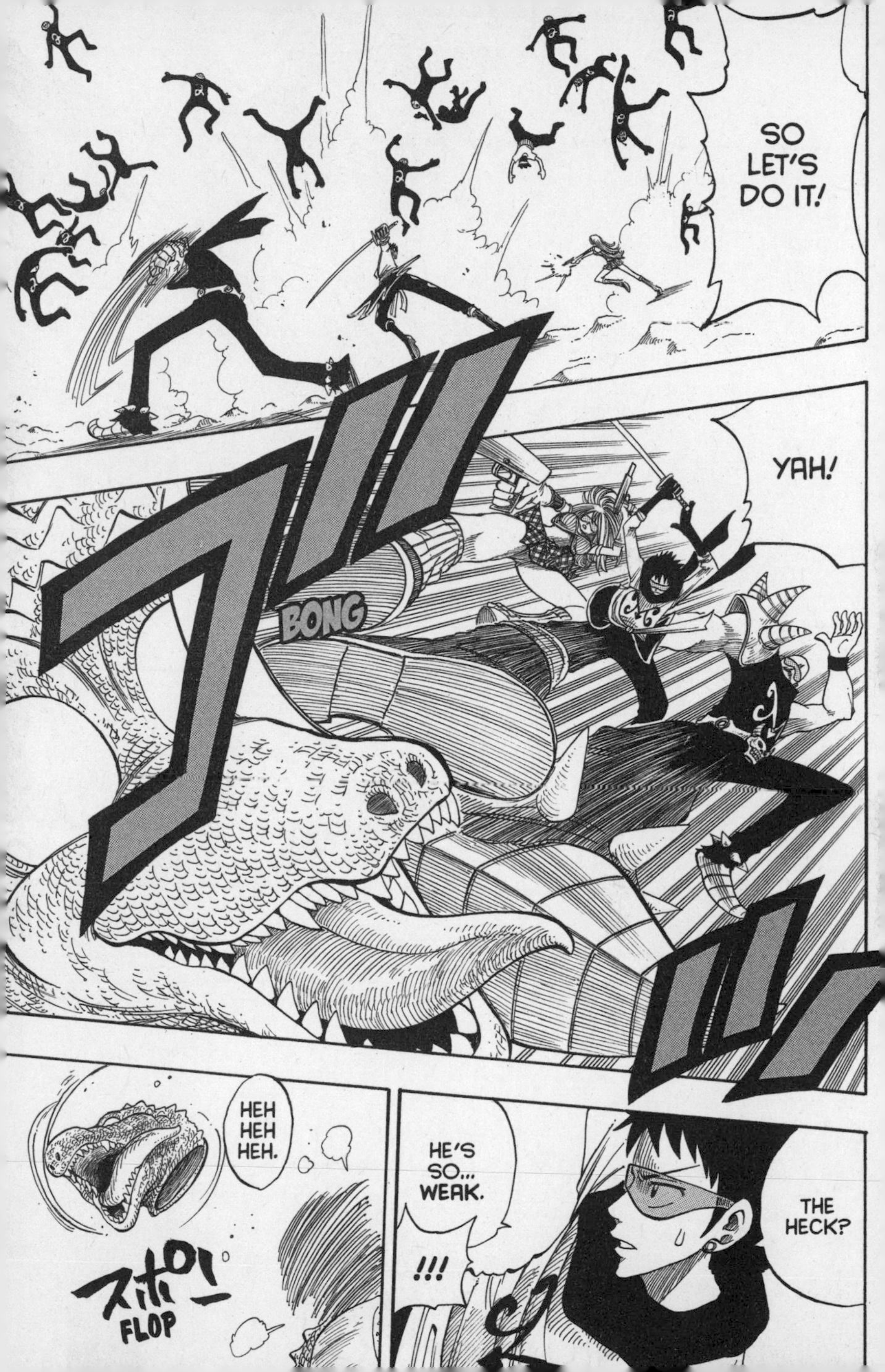
SO LET'S DO IT!
YAH!
BONG
HE'S SO... WEAK.
THE HECK?
!!!
HEH HEH HEH.
スポー
FLOP

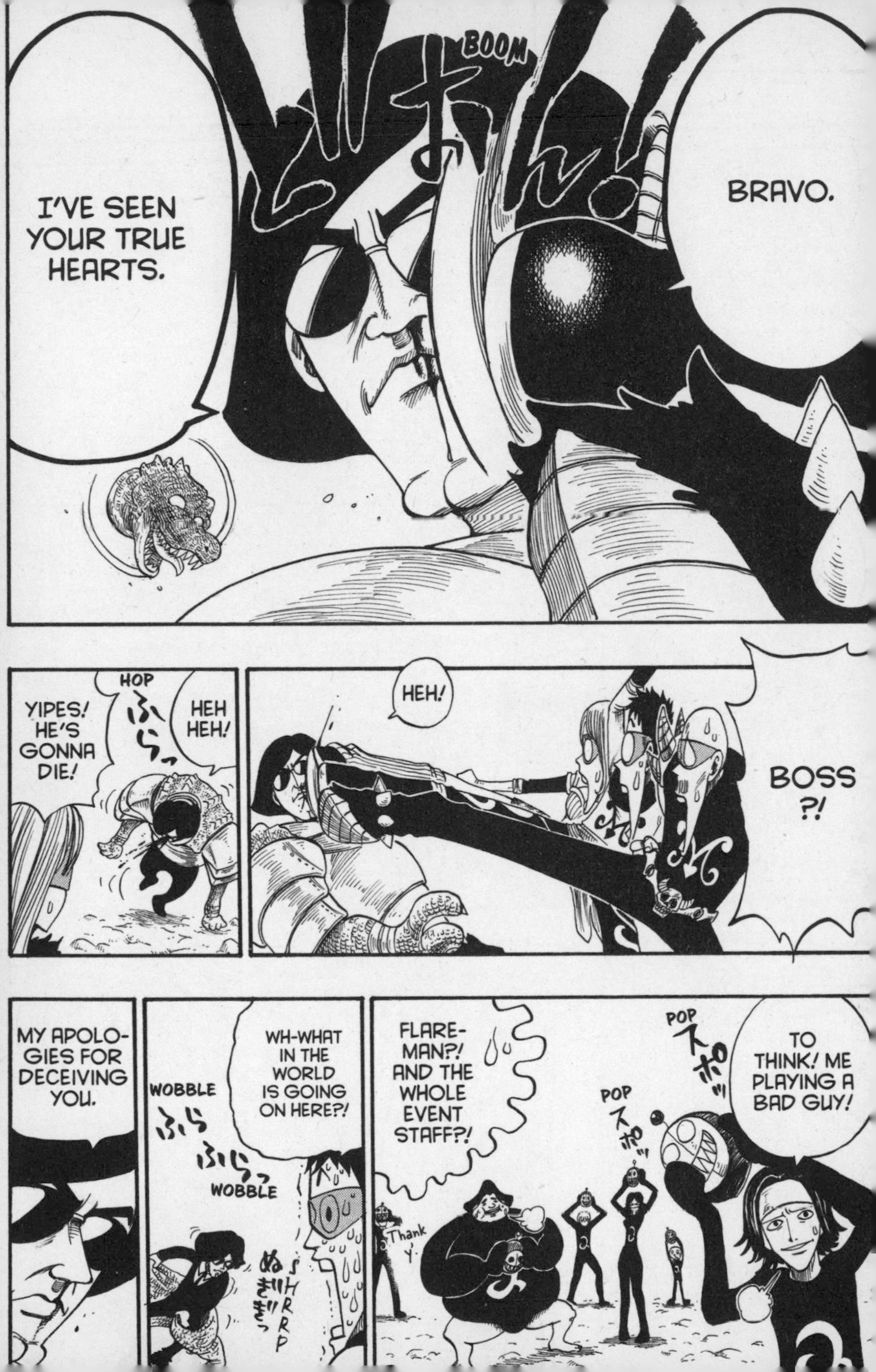

BOOM
どおん!!
BRAVO.
I'VE SEEN YOUR TRUE HEARTS.
BOSS?!
HEH!
HEH HEH!
HOP
ふらっ
YIPES! HE'S GONNA DIE!
TO THINK! ME PLAYING A BAD GUY!
POP
スポッ
POP
スポッ
FLARE-MAN?! AND THE WHOLE EVENT STAFF?!
Thank y
WH-WHAT IN THE WORLD IS GOING ON HERE?!
SHRRP
ぬぎっ
WOBBLE
ふら
ふらっ
WOBBLE
MY APOLOGIES FOR DECEIVING YOU.

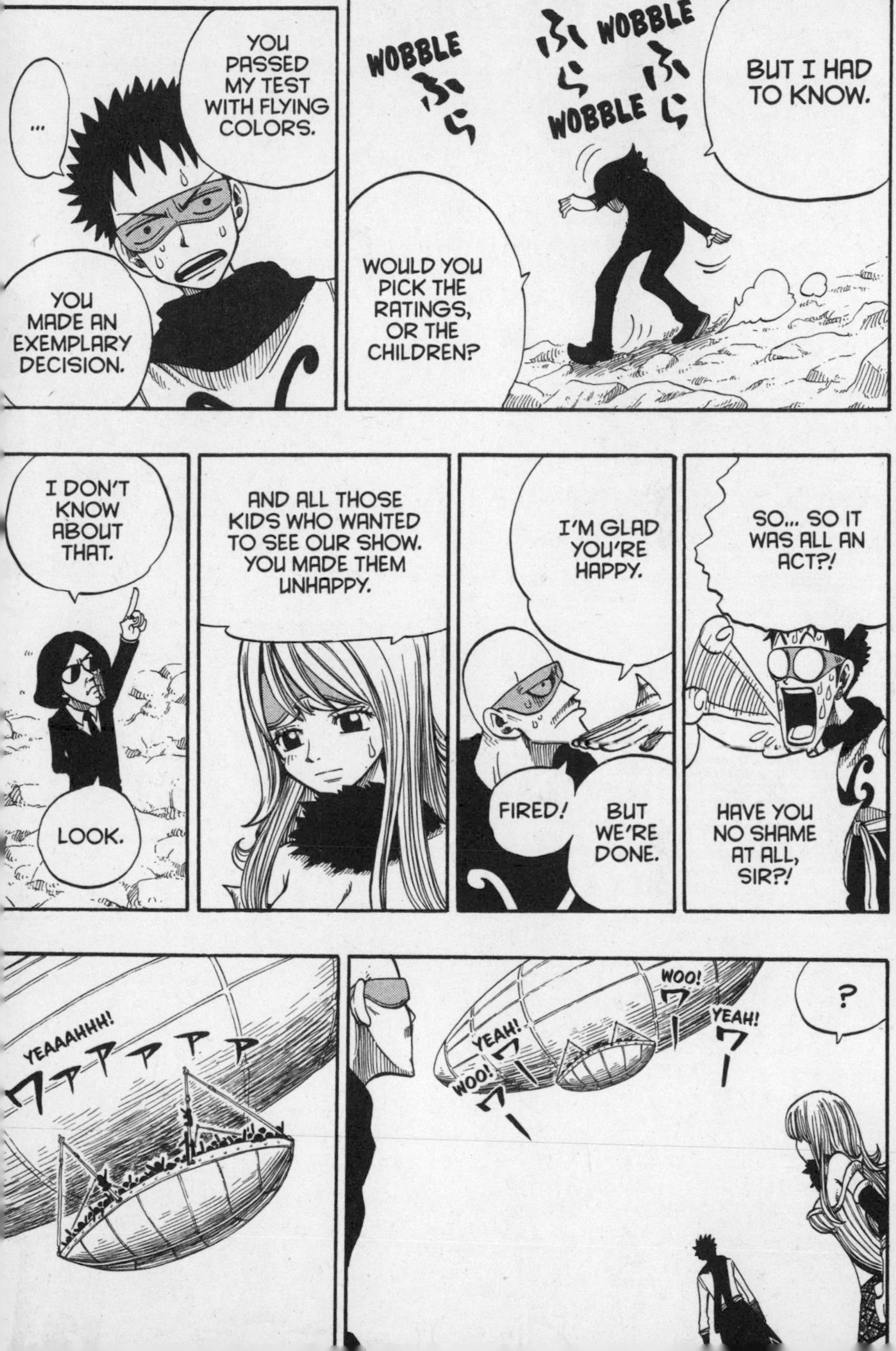
BUT I HAD TO KNOW.
WOBBLE WOBBLE
WOBBLE
WOBBLE
WOULD YOU PICK THE RATINGS, OR THE CHILDREN?
YOU PASSED MY TEST WITH FLYING COLORS.
...
YOU MADE AN EXEMPLARY DECISION.
SO... SO IT WAS ALL AN ACT?!
HAVE YOU NO SHAME AT ALL, SIR?!
I'M GLAD YOU'RE HAPPY.
BUT WE'RE DONE.
FIRED!
AND ALL THOSE KIDS WHO WANTED TO SEE OUR SHOW. YOU MADE THEM UNHAPPY.
I DON'T KNOW ABOUT THAT.
LOOK.
?
YEAH!
WOO!
YEAH!
WOO!
YEAAAHHH!

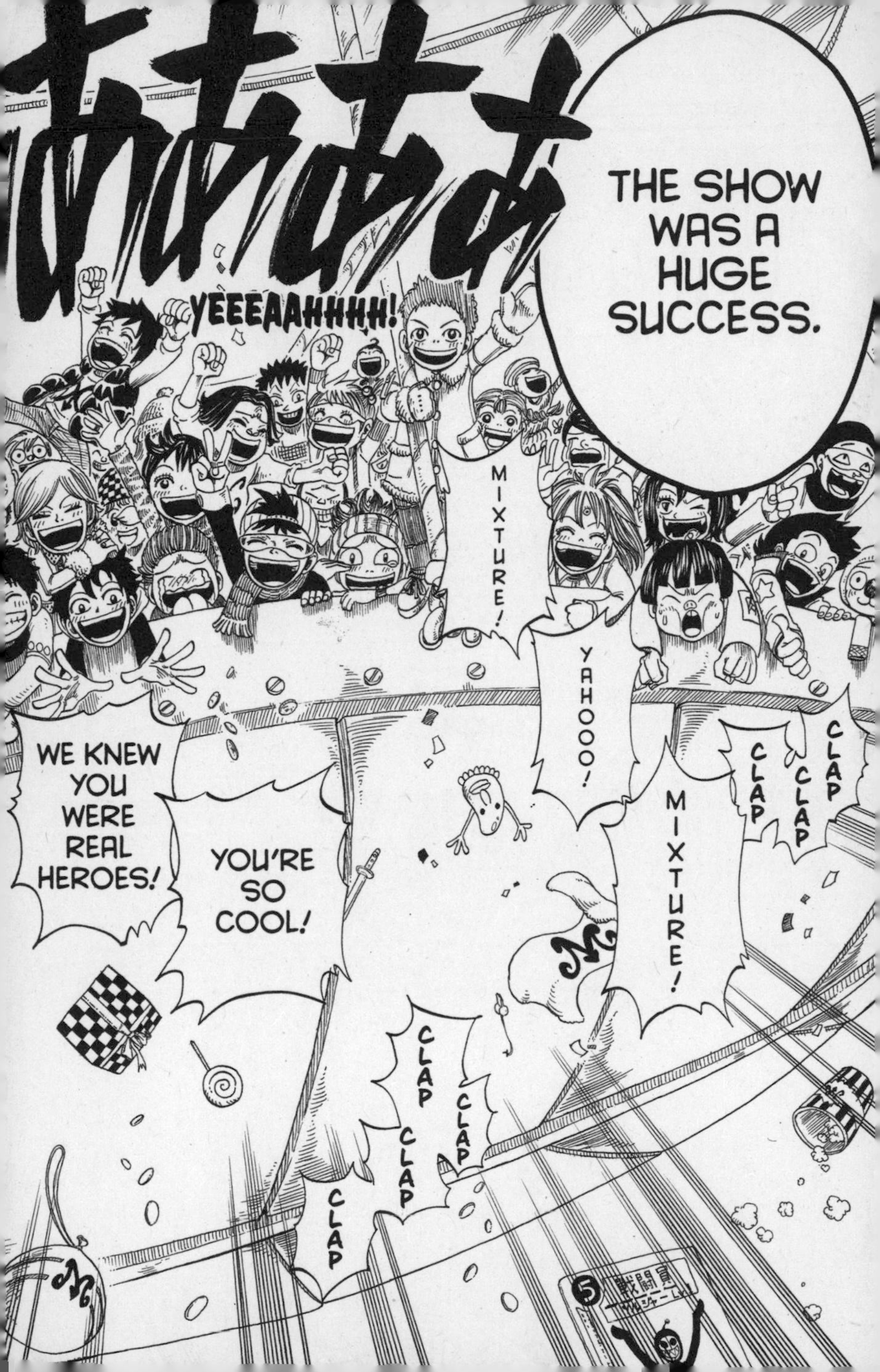
THE SHOW WAS A HUGE SUCCESS.
YEEEAAHHHH!
MIXTURE!
CLAP CLAP CLAP
MIXTURE!
YAHOOO!
YOU'RE SO COOL!
WE KNEW YOU WERE REAL HEROES!
CLAP CLAP CLAP CLAP CLAP

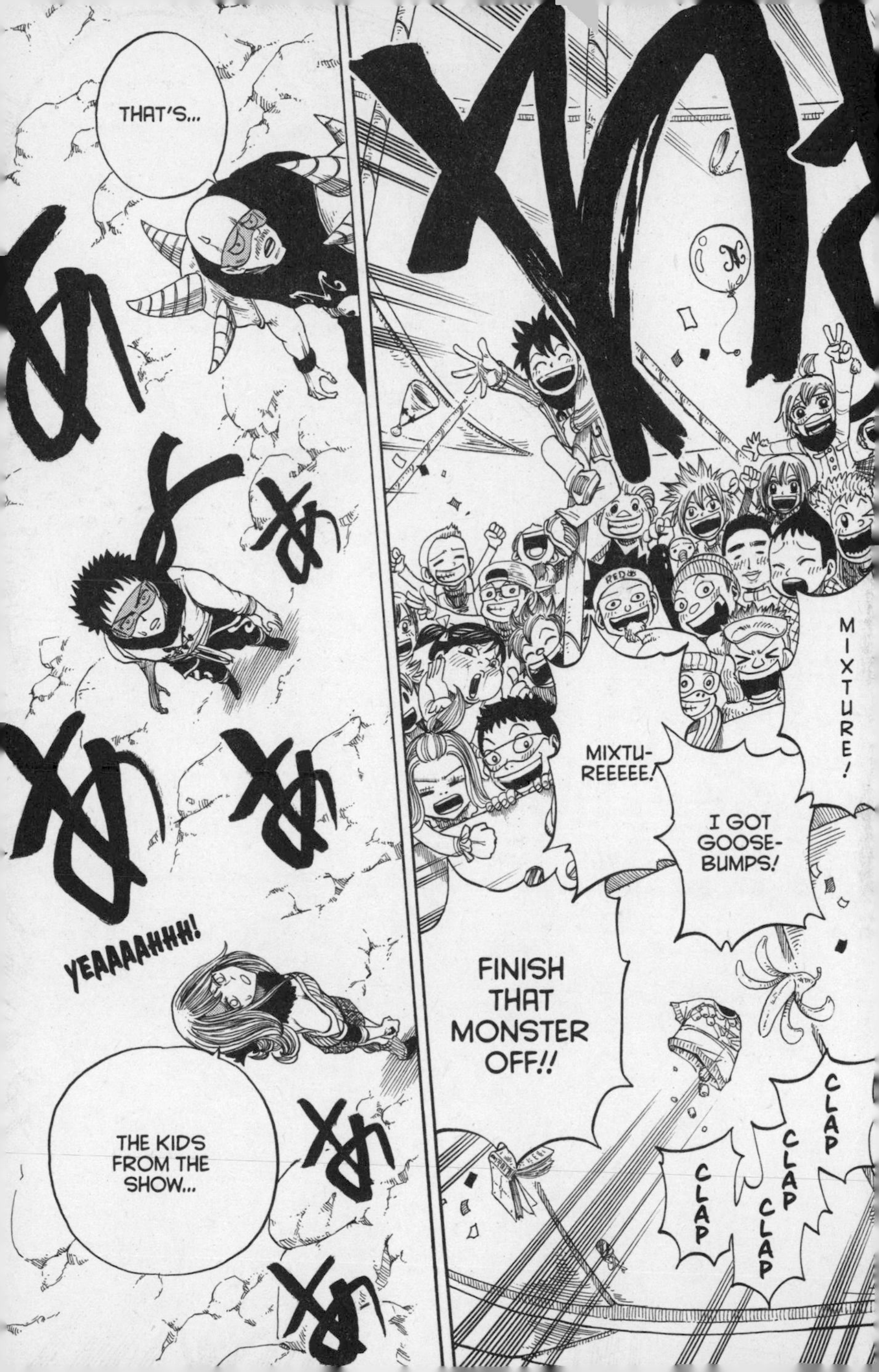
MIXTURE!
MIXTU-REEEEE!
I GOT GOOSE-BUMPS!
FINISH THAT MONSTER OFF!!
CLAP CLAP CLAP CLAP
THAT'S...
YEAAAAHHH!
THE KIDS FROM THE SHOW...

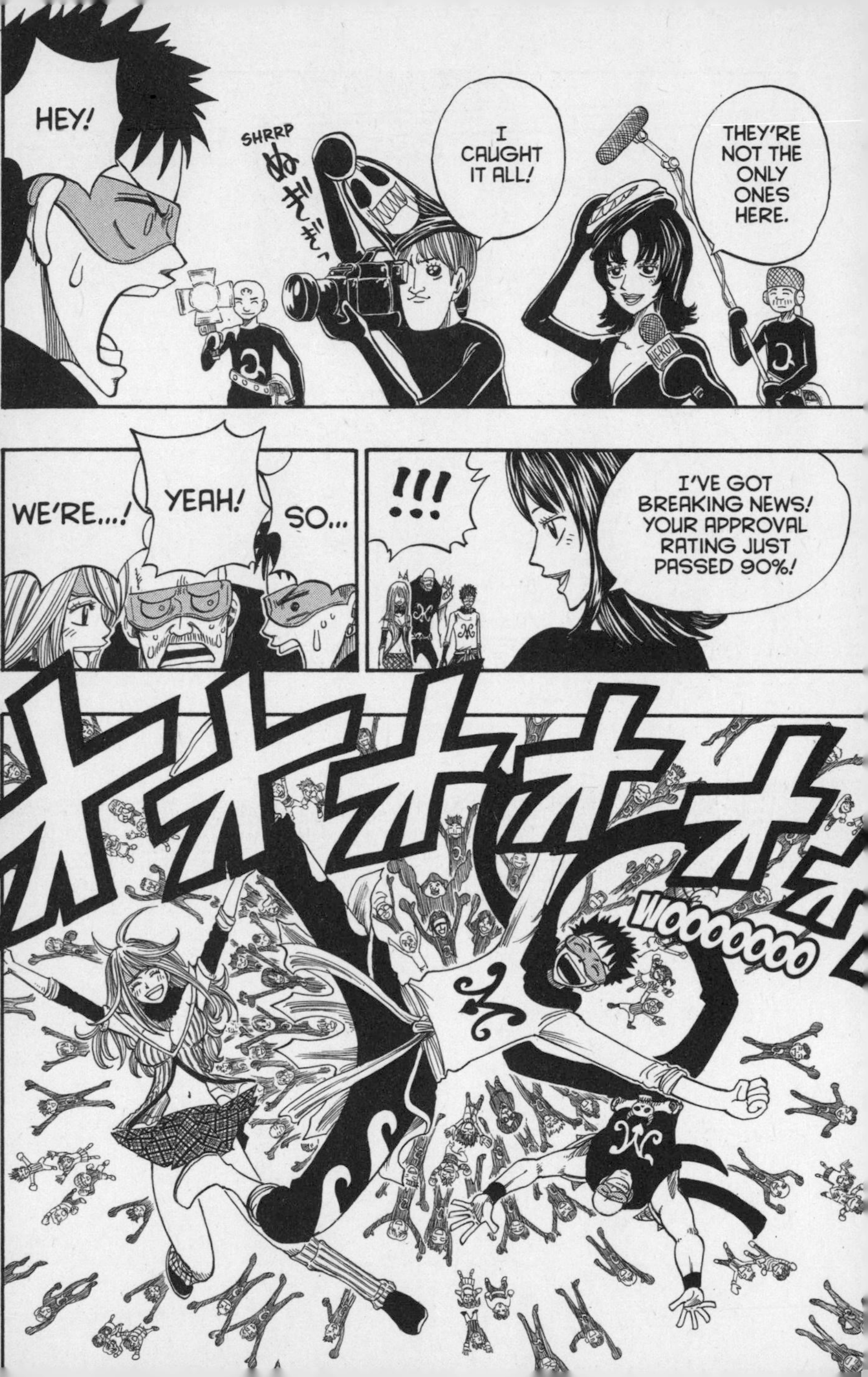
THEY'RE NOT THE ONLY ONES HERE.
I CAUGHT IT ALL!
SHRRP
ぬぎぎぎっ
HEY!
I'VE GOT BREAKING NEWS! YOUR APPROVAL RATING JUST PASSED 90%!
!!!
SO...
YEAH!
WE'RE...!
WOOOOOOO

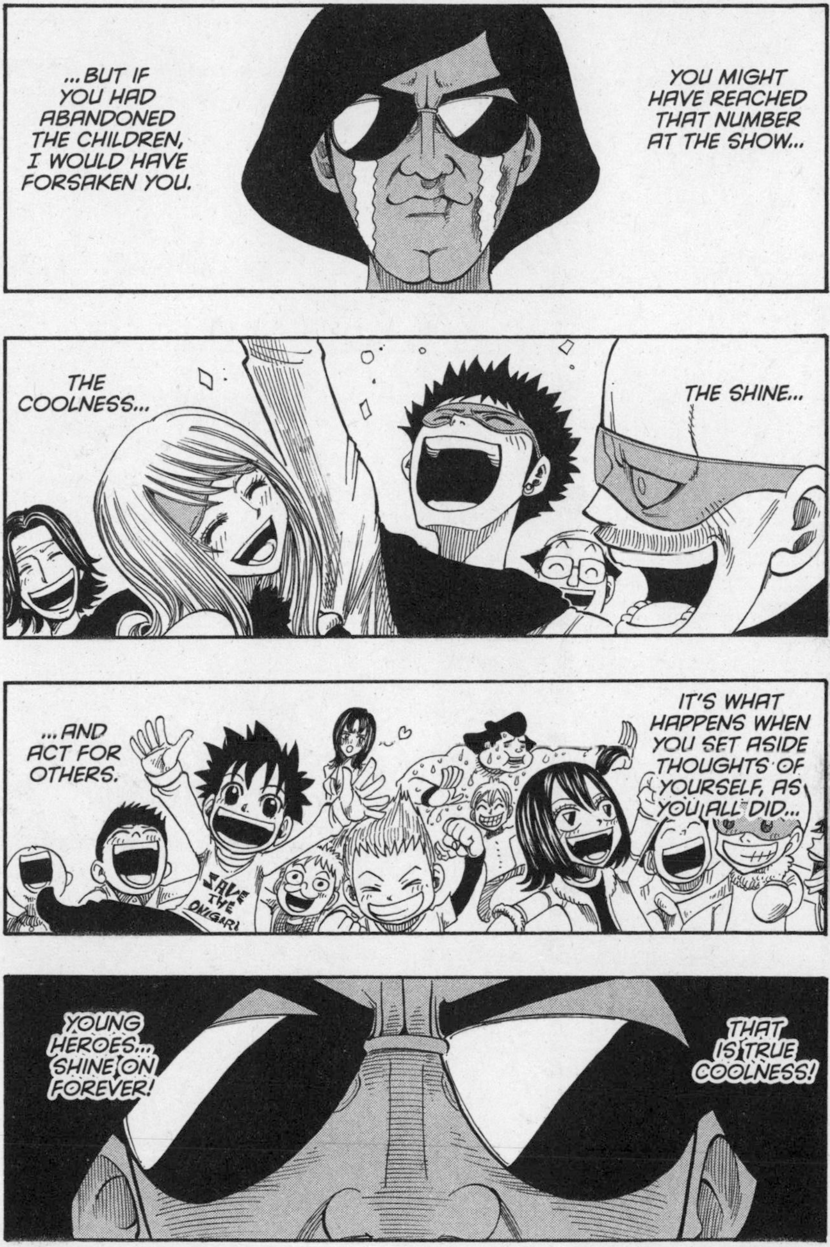
YOU MIGHT HAVE REACHED THAT NUMBER AT THE SHOW...
...BUT IF YOU HAD ABANDONED THE CHILDREN, I WOULD HAVE FORSAKEN YOU.
THE SHINE...
THE COOLNESS...
IT'S WHAT HAPPENS WHEN YOU SET ASIDE THOUGHTS OF YOURSELF, AS YOU ALL DID...
...AND ACT FOR OTHERS.
SAVE THE ONIGARI
THAT IS TRUE COOLNESS!
YOUNG HEROES... SHINE ON FOREVER!

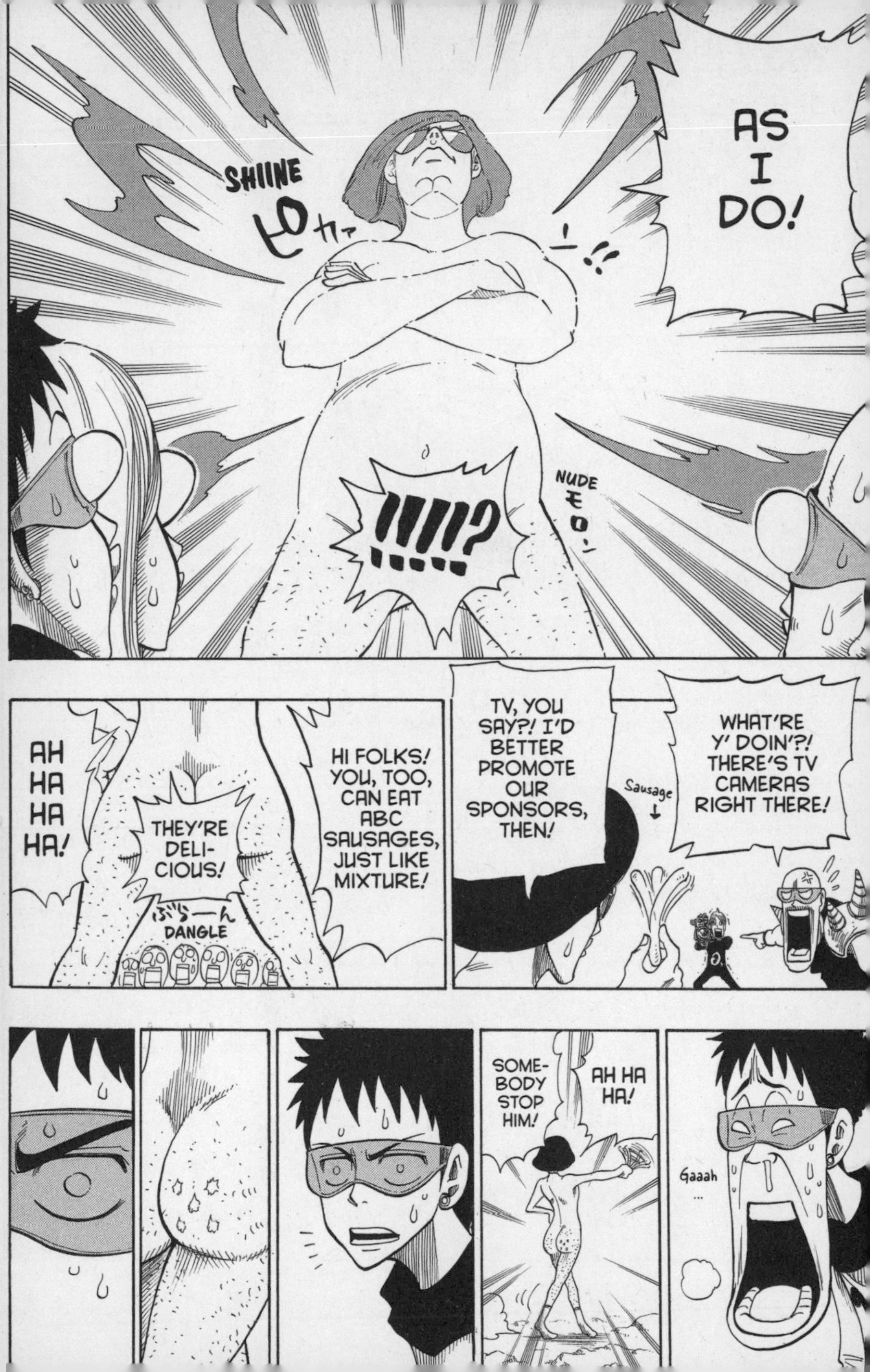

AS I DO!
SHIINE
ピカァ
!!
NUDE
モロッ
!!!!?
!!!!!
WHAT'RE Y' DOIN'?! THERE'S TV CAMERAS RIGHT THERE!
Sausage ↓
TV, YOU SAY?! I'D BETTER PROMOTE OUR SPONSORS, THEN!
HI FOLKS! YOU, TOO, CAN EAT ABC SAUSAGES, JUST LIKE MIXTURE!
THEY'RE DELI-CIOUS!
AH HA HA HA!
ぶらーん
DANGLE
Gaaah ...
AH HA HA!
SOME-BODY STOP HIM!

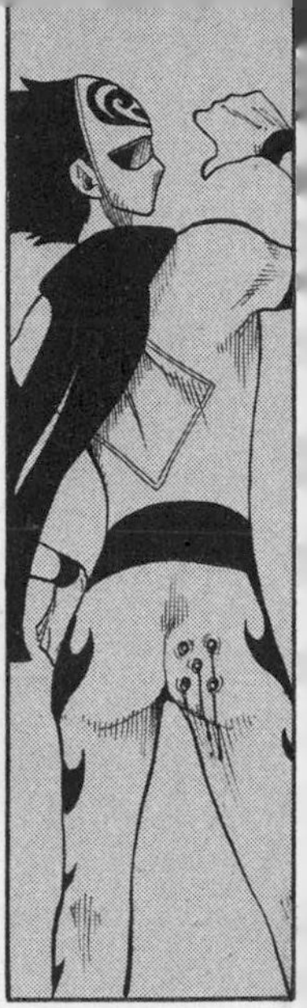

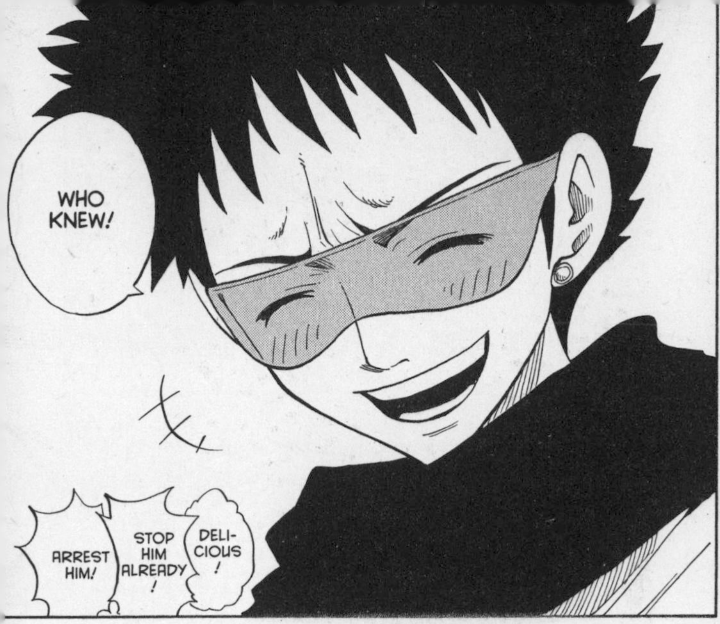
WHO KNEW!
DELI-CIOUS!
STOP HIM ALREADY!
ARREST HIM!

SIGN: HEROS' HIDEOUT

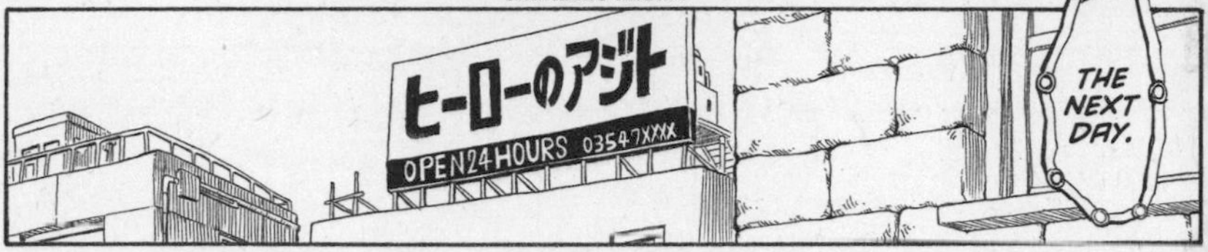
THE NEXT DAY.
ヒーローのアジト
OPEN24HOURS 03547XXXX

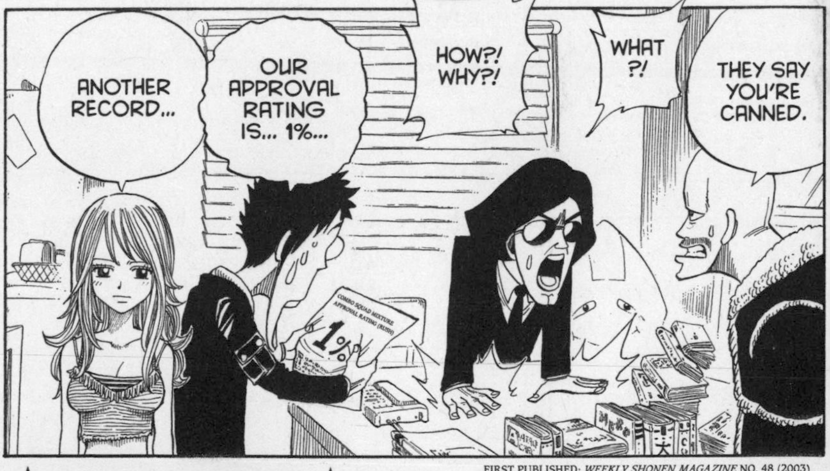
THEY SAY YOU'RE CANNED.
WHAT?!
HOW?! WHY?!
OUR APPROVAL RATING IS... 1%...
ANOTHER RECORD...
COMBO SQUAD MIXTURE APPROVAL RATING (RUSH)
1%

FIRST PUBLISHED: *WEEKLY SHONEN MAGAZINE* NO. 48 (2003)

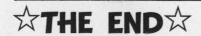

☆THE END☆

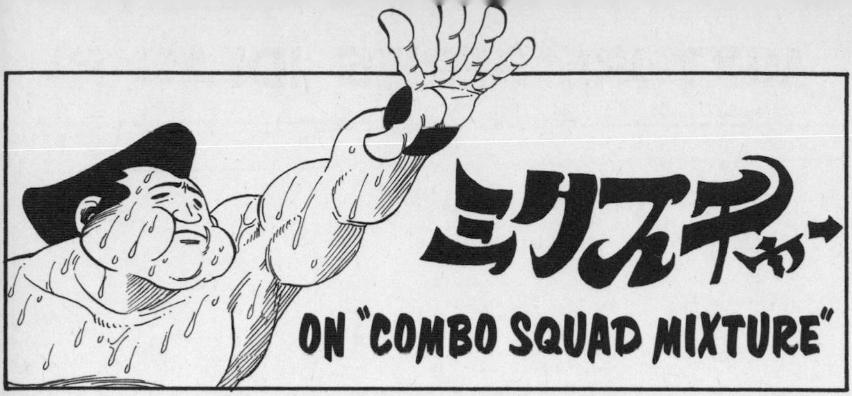
ミクスチャー
ON "COMBO SQUAD MIXTURE"

Dosukoooi! If you've been reading these notes pages throughout Parts 1 and 2, you might have noticed that I have a habit of taking ideas for series and paring them down to short stories. But this is one that I actually designed from the outset to stand on its own as a short piece. It ended up pretty packed, and I actually started to wonder if it might make a good series. So it was the opposite pattern this time. Don't worry... I won't do it (LOL). But since I went to all the trouble of coming up with ideas, I thought I'd share some of them on the next couple pages. Anyway, this piece was obviously inspired by the ranger/hero-squad shows they run on Sunday mornings. (Or is that only in Tokyo?) I was obsessed with heroes as a kid (I even thought maybe I could be one, just like the protagonist of this story), and watched those shows all the time, but as I got older I watched them less and less. That makes sense, as I was no longer the target demographic, but I got to a point where I stopped watching them entirely. Then one day I turned on the television and they happened to be running one of those shows. I watched it, for old time's sake, and just like before, I was totally sucked in! Those transformations still get me even today.

Let me offer a word of explanation before I go. There's a comedic flavor to this story, and some readers might think I'm making fun of these heroes, but that's certainly not the case. I'm not about iconoclasm, here! I'm actually paying homage. I swear, they're really awesome!

Sorry, my enthusiasm slipped through there. If any staff on any of these shows happen to be reading this...how about Mixture for the next big thing? (grins)

MIXTURE SERIES IDEAS (1)

Red-Hot Squad Flareman

Hero Rank 7

Dosukoi

Flare Red

Flare Fleshtone
Daisaku Egawa
(Komusubi)

Flare Pink
Lin Lin
(Is a Chinese hero)

F-no-suke
(that's his
name)

Flare Blue
Mogura Abe
(on a diet)

Flare Black
Yoshio Raido
(Really wanted to
be a bike rider,
not a hero)

Dark Squad Demon Five

Tonosama Squad

Hero Rank 35

Whaddaya say
we go over to
Anima?

Yeah.

Hero Rank 48

We shall regain
Princess Hikari!

Even
so!

Ninpopo!

FWEEE

Since Kobushi left, some weird
stuff has been going on.

They see how popular Hikari is now
and want her back.

MIXTURE SERIES IDEAS (2)

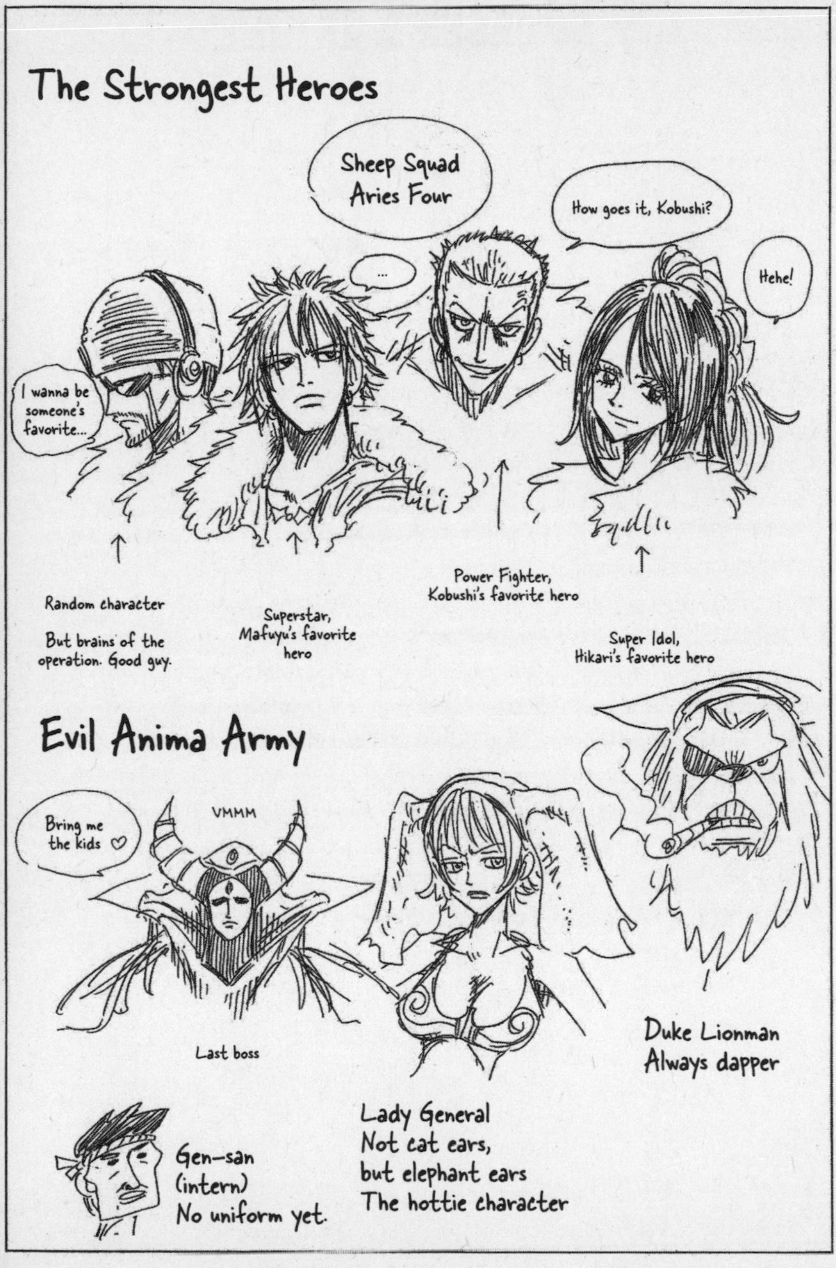
The Strongest Heroes
Sheep Squad Aries Four
How goes it, Kobushi?
Hehe!
...
I wanna be someone's favorite...
Random character
But brains of the operation. Good guy.
Superstar, Mafuyu's favorite hero
Power Fighter, Kobushi's favorite hero
Super Idol, Hikari's favorite hero
Evil Anima Army
Bring me the kids ♡
VMMM
Last boss
Duke Lionman
Always dapper
Lady General
Not cat ears,
but elephant ears
The hottie character
Gen-san
(intern)
No uniform yet.

PARK MANAGER'S AFTERWORD

Ahem. Thank you very kindly for reading all the way to the end. If you also read Part 1, thank you even more. If you've also read *Rave Master*, thank you even more than that. I also want to say thank you to all the people who helped produce this book. I really appreciate it!

I'd like to address what a short story is to me. I think the definition is "trial and relaxation." My résumé as a manga artist is still pretty short; I've only created one full world for *Rave Master* (*Editor's Note: As of the initial release in Japan). When you spend enough time in one world, you start wanting to experience others. Short stories give me that opportunity. You can discover some incredible places, along with some kind of forgettable ones. But I think it's wonderful to at least get to try something new. It's also sort of a relaxing journey for someone like me, who's spent all his time in one particular setting. I'd love to keep doing short pieces any time I have the chance. I mean... *any* time... okay?

A final word to everyone who's read this far. Thank you so much!

All right, then! See you in volume 3 (if there ever is one)!!

Catch ya later!

HIRO MASHIMA

*SHIRT: MANAGER

In the original Japanese title,
the *-en* in *Mashima-en* can also
be found in words like:
Yuuenchi (amusement park)
which means fun!
Doubutsuen (zoo)
which means weird animals?
Koshien (a famous high school
baseball tournament)
which means passion!
Kouen (park)
which means relaxation!
Gakuen (academy)
which means ??
Toshimaen (a popular amusement park)
which means stuffing yourself!

Amazing how many meanings can be
packed into this one little word.
All right!
We hope you enjoyed Part 2.

TRANSLATION NOTES

Group Elephant, page 14
It's normal for students in a given year at a Japanese school to be divided by homeroom. However, usually these groups are known as Group 1, Group 2, etc. "Group Elephant" (*zou-gumi*) is a fictional touch.

2-chome, page 25
Addresses in Japan are usually divided into blocks, or cho. "2-chome" is "Block 2."

Yoshinoya Beef Bowls, page 63
Yoshinoya is a ubiquitous chain in Japan that serves affordable beef bowls and more.

Nagano Prefecture, page 64
Nagano Prefecture is located roughly in the center of the main Japanese island of Honshu, and it's typically seen as rather rural and isolated, especially from a Tokyoite's perspective.

Boys and Bugs, page 64
In this panel, the author depicts himself holding a beetle. Catching bugs (especially beetles), and occasionally making them fight, is something of a traditional pastime for Japanese boys.

Bacterium, page 134
In *Anpanman*, a popular Japanese animated show for children, a villain named Baikin-man (named after bacterium) causes trouble for the heroes. The heroes are different types of bread, and are weak to water and bacteria!

Ura, page 158
Ura is Japanese for "back" or "behind," but has a secondary meaning of "hidden" or "secret."

Equator, page 188
The wizard's original question is, "What's the red stuff that flows through the human body?" One of the possible answers is "equator," or *sekidou*, because the word literally means "red path."

Question 3, page 193
The original question is about the reading of the kanji.

Medaka Senior High, page 208
The school's name plays on the expression *me ga takai* (lit. "high-eyed"), meaning discerning or perceptive.

Third Year, page 209
In Japan, students spend six years in elementary school, three in middle school, and three in high school. Hence, Mikiya's third year is his last in high school.

Magazine, page 211
Nobu can be seen reading something titled *Magazine*, a nod to *Weekly Shonen Magazine*, in which most of these stories first appeared.

Paid to date, page 212
Enjo kousai (or *enkou* for short) means "compensated dating" and is a phenomenon where young women get paid (in gifts or cash) to go out on dates, typically with older men.

Physicals, page 215
School physicals are done at school, usually once a year.

The New Year, page 225
Mikiya means the new calendar year, not the new school year, which starts in April in Japan. (The Japanese school year ends in March, hence why he and his friends have just two months til graduation.)

Stamp, page 227
A *hanko* or *inkan* is a stamp or seal featuring a person's name or, in this case, title. This stamp serves many of the same purposes as a person's signature, and although signing one's name is known in Japan (interestingly, Reiko uses the verb *sain suru* or "affix one's signature" when making her request of the principal), in many cases a seal is preferred.

Level 1 Test, page 277
Japan has standardized examinations (*kentei shiken*) for almost every imaginable subject, from language ability to secretarial skills. These tests are graded, with 1 being the highest level.

絶, page 300
One of the would-be wizards has the character 絶 inscribed on his forehead. This character means "to end" or "to cease," and presumably has something to do with the magic the boy uses.

Crush Gear, page 305
Crush Gear was an anime and manga series from the early 2000s, featuring battling toys of the same name.

Dosukoi, page 368
A word commonly associated with shouting sumo wrestlers, although few actual sumo wrestlers say it.

Kobushi, page 381
Kobushi's name means "fist."

Tonosama Squad Atsumoriman, page 382
The word *tono-sama* means "lord" and is associated with nobles or officials of Japan's medieval era. Atsumori is the name of a famous samurai who appears in the epic poem *The Tale of the Heike* (*Heike Monogatari*).

Koshien, page 397
Koshien is a long-standing and extremely beloved high school baseball tournament. It takes place in the summer, which means it usually takes place in brutal heat, hence the reference to crushed ice.

Wee-oh-kun, page 397
In Japan, almost every organization (especially public ones) has some kind of mascot character. This one is called "Biibo-kun," after the Japanese onomatopoeia for the sound of a police siren.

Komusubi, page 425
That is, a sumo wrestler of the fourth-highest rank.

Hiro Mashima's Playground is a work of fiction.
Names, characters, places, and incidents are the products of the author's imagination or are used fictitiously. Any resemblance to actual events, locales, or persons, living or dead, is entirely coincidental.

A Kodansha Comics Trade Paperback Original.

Published in the United States by Kodansha Comics, an imprint of Kodansha USA Publishing, LLC, New York.

Publication rights for this English edition arranged through Kodansha Ltd., Tokyo.

First published in Japan in 2003 by Kodansha Ltd., Tokyo, as *Mashima-En: Mashima Hiro Tanpenshû*, volumes 1 and 2.

ISBN 978-1-63236-759-4

Translation: Kevin Steinbach
Lettering: AndWorld Design
Editing: Haruko Hashimoto
Kodansha Comics edition cover: Phil Balsman